THE SELECTED WRITINGS OF
RALPH WALDO EMERSON

THE SELECTED WRITINGS OF
RALPH WALDO EMERSON

EDITED BY BROOKS ATKINSON

THE MODERN LIBRARY

NEW YORK

1992 Modern Library Edition

Biographical note copyright © 1992 by Random House, Inc.
Copyright 1940, © 1968 by Random House, Inc.

Jacket portrait courtesy of Culver Pictures

LIBRARY OF CONGRESS CATALOGING-IN-PUBLICATION DATA
Emerson, Ralph Waldo, 1803–1882.
[Selections. 1992]
The selected writings of Ralph Waldo Emerson/edited
by Brooks Atkinson
p. cm.
ISBN 0-679-60018-3 (alk. paper)
I. Atkinson, Brooks, 1894–1984. II. Title
PS1603.A87 1992
814´.3—dc20 92-50234

Modern Library website address: www.modernlibrary.com

Printed in the United States of America on acid-free paper

9

RALPH WALDO EMERSON

Ralph Waldo Emerson was born on May 25, 1803, in Boston, Massachusetts. At Harvard he won prizes for his oratory and essays. He studied briefly at Harvard Divinity School but was forced to interrupt his courses because of eye trouble. In 1826 he began a career as a minister, eventually becoming junior pastor of the Second Church of Boston. He married Ellen Tucker in 1829, despite the fact that she was already ill with tuberculosis; she died two years later at the age of nineteen.

After the death of his wife, Emerson went to Europe, where he met Landor, Mill, Coleridge, Wordsworth, Carlyle, and others. On his return he settled in Concord, Massachusetts, and a year later married Lydia Jackson. What would eventually be called the Transcendental Club had begun to form around him, its members including Margaret Fuller, Bronson Alcott, and Orestes Brownson. The spiritual ferment of the Concord group found expression in Emerson's first significant work, the essay "Nature" (1836), in which he sketched the ideas that his later writings were to elaborate: "The use of natural history is to give us aid in supernatural history: the use of the outer creation, to give us language for the beings and changes of the inward creation. . . . By degrees we may come to know the primitive sense of the permanent objects of nature, so that the world shall be to us an open book, and every form significant of its hidden life and final cause." This was followed by two profoundly influential orations, "The American Scholar," a powerful statement of individualism, and "The Harvard Divinity School Address," whose unorthodox religious views created a scandal: "Historical

Christianity has fallen into the error that corrupts all attempts to communicate religion. . . . It has dwelt, it dwells, with noxious exaggeration about the *person* of Jesus. The soul knows no persons."

Around this time Emerson became closely associated with Henry David Thoreau and with the mystical poet Jones Very. He gave up preaching and collaborated with Margaret Fuller on the journal *The Dial,* in which he began to publish his essays. These appeared in book form as *Essays: First Series* (1841) and *Essays: Second Series* (1844). He became more involved in political issues, launching attacks on the Mexican War and slavery. His essays had made him an internationally known figure, and on a return trip to Europe in 1847 he met with a wide range of writers and thinkers, including Dickens, Tocqueville, and Tennyson. He published further collections of his essays and public addresses—*Nature, Addresses, and Lectures* (1849), *Representative Men* (1850), *English Traits* (1856), *The Conduct of Life* (1860)—while lecturing against slavery throughout the Northeast. Whitman's *Leaves of Grass* elicited an enthusiastic response from him, although he attempted to persuade the poet to tone down the poem's sexual imagery.

Following the Civil War, Emerson continued to lecture energetically, publishing *Society and Solitude* (1870) and the verse collection *May-Day and Other Pieces* (1867). In 1872 his health began to fail, and after a final trip to Europe he settled into a quieter routine as his memory gradually weakened. He died in Concord, of pneumonia, on April 27, 1882.

CONTENTS

Contents

NATURE

[Nature *was Emerson's first book. He had been med-*
itating on it several years before he published it in
1836. Some of it he wrote in the same room where
Hawthorne wrote Mosses from an Old Manse. *Five*
hundred copies of Nature *were published anony-*
mously. Although the book made a few friends in
England, notably Carlyle, Richard Monckton Milnes
and John Sterling, it was not enthusiastically
received as a whole. It was not reissued until 1847.]

A subtle chain of countless rings
The next unto the farthest brings;
The eye reads omens where it goes,
And speaks all languages the rose;
And, striving to be man, the worm ·
Mounts through all the spires of form.

INTRODUCTION

OUR AGE is retrospective. It builds the sepulchres of the fathers. It writes biographies, histories, and criticism. The foregoing generations beheld God and nature face to face; we, through their eyes. Why should not we also enjoy an original relation to the universe? Why should not we have a poetry and philosophy of insight and not of tradition, and a religion by revelation to us, and not the history of theirs? Embosomed for a season in nature, whose floods of life stream around and through us, and invite us, by the powers they supply, to action proportioned to nature, why should we grope among the dry bones of the past, or put the living generation into masquerade out of its faded wardrobe? The sun shines to-day also. There is more wool and flax in the fields. There are new lands, new men, new thoughts. Let us demand our own works and laws and worship.

Undoubtedly we have no questions to ask which are unanswerable. We must trust the perfection of the creation so far as to believe that whatever curiosity the order of things has awakened in our minds, the order of things can satisfy. Every man's condition is a solution in hieroglyphic to those inquiries he would put. He acts it as life, before he apprehends it as truth. In like manner, nature is already, in its forms and tendencies, describing its own design. Let us interrogate the great apparition that shines so peacefully around us. Let us inquire, to what end is nature?

All science has one aim, namely, to find a theory of nature. We have theories of races and of functions, but scarcely yet a remote approach to an idea of creation. We are now so far from the road to truth, that religious teachers dispute and hate each other, and speculative men are esteemed unsound and frivolous. But to a sound judgment, the most abstract truth is the most practical. Whenever a true theory appears, it will be its own evidence. Its test is, that it will explain all phenomena. Now many are thought not only unexplained but inexplicable; as language, sleep, madness, dreams, beasts, sex.

Philosophically considered, the universe is composed of Nature and the Soul. Strictly speaking, therefore, all that is separate from us, all which Philosophy distinguishes as the NOT ME, that is, both nature and art, all other men and my own body, must be ranked under this name, NATURE. In enumerating values of nature and casting up their sum, I shall use the word in both senses—in its common and in its philosophical import. In inquiries so general as our present one, the inaccuracy is not material; no confusion of thought will occur. *Nature*, in the common sense, refers to essences unchanged by man; space, the air, the river, the leaf. *Art* is applied to the mixture of his will with the same things, as in a house, a canal, a statue, a picture. But his operations taken together are so insignificant, a little chipping, baking, patching, and washing, that in an impression so grand as that of the world on the human mind, they do not vary the result.

NATURE

TO GO into solitude, a man needs to retire as much from his chamber as from society. I am not solitary whilst I read and write, though nobody is with me. But if a man would be alone, let him look at the stars. The rays that come from those heavenly worlds will separate between him and what he touches. One might think the atmosphere was made transparent with this design, to give man, in the heavenly bodies, the perpetual presence of the sublime. Seen in the streets of cities, how great they are! If the stars should appear one night in a thousand years, how would men believe and adore; and preserve for many generations the remembrance of the city of God which had been shown! But every night come out these envoys of beauty, and light the universe with their admonishing smile.

The stars awaken a certain reverence, because though always present, they are inaccessible; but all natural objects make a kindred impression, when the mind is open to their influence. Nature never wears a mean appearance. Neither does the wisest man extort her secret, and lose his curiosity by finding out all her perfection. Nature never became a toy to a wise spirit. The flowers, the animals, the mountains, reflected the wisdom of his best hour, as much as they had delighted the simplicity of his childhood.

When we speak of nature in this manner, we have a distinct but most poetical sense in the mind. We mean the integrity of impression made by manifold natural objects. It is this which distinguishes the stick of timber of the wood-cutter from the tree of the poet. The charming landscape which I saw this morning is indubitably made up of some twenty or thirty farms. Miller owns this field, Locke that, and Manning the woodland beyond. But none of them owns the landscape. There is a property in the horizon which no man has but he whose eye can integrate all the parts, that is, the poet. This is the best part of these men's farms, yet to this their warranty-deeds give no title.

To speak truly, few adult persons can see nature. Most persons do not see the sun. At least they have a very superficial seeing. The sun illuminates only the eye of the man, but shines into the eye and the heart of the child. The lover of nature is he whose inward and outward senses are still truly adjusted to each other; who has retained the spirit of infancy even into the era of manhood. His intercourse with heaven and earth becomes part of his daily food. In the presence of nature a wild delight runs through the man, in spite of real sorrows. Nature says—he is my creature, and maugre all his impertinent griefs, he shall be glad with me. Not the sun or the summer alone, but every hour and season yields its tribute of delight; for every hour and change corresponds to and authorizes a different state of the mind, from breathless noon to grimmest midnight. Nature is a setting that fits equally well a comic or a mourning piece. In good health, the air is a cordial of incredible virtue. Crossing a bare common, in snow puddles, at twilight, under a clouded sky, without having in my thoughts any occurrence of special good fortune, I have enjoyed a perfect exhilaration. I am glad to the brink of fear. In the woods, too, a man casts off his years, as the snake his slough, and at what period soever of life is always a child. In the woods is perpetual youth. Within these plantations of God, a decorum and sanctity reign, a perennial festival is dressed, and the guest sees not how he should tire of them in a thousand years. In the woods, we return to reason and faith. There I feel that nothing can befall me in life—no disgrace, no calamity (leaving me my eyes), which nature cannot repair. Standing on the bare ground—my head bathed by the blithe air and uplifted into infinite space—all mean egotism vanishes. I become a transparent eyeball; I am nothing; I see all; the currents of the Universal Being circulate through me; I am part or parcel of God. The name of the nearest friend sounds then foreign and accidental: to be brothers, to be acquaintances, master or servant, is then a trifle and a disturbance. I am the lover of uncontained and immortal beauty. In the wilderness, I find something more dear and connate than in streets or villages. In the tranquil landscape, and especially in the distant line of the horizon, man beholds somewhat as beautiful as his own nature.

The greatest delight which the fields and woods minister is the suggestion of an occult relation between man and the vegetable. I am not alone and unacknowledged. They nod to me, and I to them. The waving of the boughs in the storm is new to me and old. It takes me by surprise, and yet is not unknown. Its effect is like that of a higher thought or a better emotion coming over me, when I deemed I was thinking justly or doing right.

Yet it is certain that the power to produce this delight does not reside in nature, but in man, or in a harmony of both. It is necessary to use these pleasures with great temperance. For nature is not always tricked in holiday attire, but the same scene which yesterday breathed perfume and glittered as for the frolic of the nymphs is overspread with melancholy to-day. Nature always wears the colors of the spirit. To a man laboring under calamity, the heat of his own fire hath sadness in it. Then there is a kind of contempt of the landscape felt by him who has just lost by death a dear friend. The sky is less grand as it shuts down over less worth in the population.

II

COMMODITY

WHOEVER CONSIDERS the final cause of the world will discern a multitude of uses that enter as parts into that result. They all admit of being thrown into one of the following classes: Commodity; Beauty; Language; and Discipline.

Under the general name of commodity, I rank all those advantages which our senses owe to nature. This, of course, is a benefit which is temporary and mediate, not ultimate, like its service to the soul. Yet although low, it is perfect in its kind, and is the only use of nature which all men apprehend. The misery of man appears like childish petulance, when we explore the steady and prodigal provision that has been made for his support and delight on this green ball which floats him through the heavens. What angels invented these splendid ornaments, these rich conveniences, this ocean of air above, this ocean of water beneath, this firmament of earth between? this zodiac of lights, this tent of dropping clouds, this striped coat of climates, this fourfold year? Beasts, fire, water, stones, and corn serve him. The field is at once his floor, his work-yard, his play-ground, his garden, and his bed.

"More servants wait on man
Than he'll take notice of."

Nature, in its ministry to man, is not only the material, but is also the process and the result. All the parts incessantly work into each other's hands for the profit of man. The wind sows the seed; the sun evaporates the sea; the wind blows the vapor to the field; the ice, on the other side of the planet, condenses rain on this; the rain feeds the plant; the plant feeds the animal; and thus the endless circulations of the divine charity nourish man.

The useful arts are reproductions or new combinations by the wit of man, of the same natural benefactors. He no longer waits for favoring gales, but by means of steam, he realizes the fable of Aeolus's bag, and carries the two and thirty winds in the boiler of his boat. To diminish friction, he paves the road with iron bars, and, mounting a coach with a ship-load of men, animals, and merchandise behind him, he darts through the country, from town to town, like an eagle or a swallow through the air. By the aggregate of these aids, how is the face of the world changed, from the era of Noah to that of Napoleon! The private poor man hath cities, ships, canals, bridges, built for him. He goes to the post-office, and the human race run on his errands; to the book-shop, and the human race read and write of all that happens for him; to the court-house, and nations repair his wrongs. He sets his house upon the road, and the human race go forth every morning, and shovel out the snow, and cut a path for him.

But there is no need of specifying particulars in this class of uses. The catalogue is endless, and the examples so obvious, that I shall leave them to the reader's reflection, with the general remark, that this mercenary benefit is one which has respect to a farther good. A man is fed, not that he may be fed, but that he may work.

III

BEAUTY

A NOBLER WANT of man is served by nature, namely, the love of Beauty

The ancient Greeks called the world κόσμος, beauty. Such is the constitution of all things, or such the plastic power of the human eye, that the primary forms, as the sky, the mountain, the tree, the animal, give us a delight *in and for themselves*; a pleasure arising from outline, color, motion, and grouping. This seems partly owing to the eye itself. The eye is the best of artists. By the mutual action of its structure and of the laws of light, perspective is produced, which integrates every mass of objects, of what character soever, into a well colored and shaded globe, so that where the particular objects are mean and unaffecting, the landscape which they compose is round and symmetrical. And as the eye is the best composer, so light is the first of painters. There is no object so foul that intense light will not make beautiful. And the stimulus it affords to the sense, and a sort of infinitude which it hath, like space and time, make all matter gay. Even the corpse has its own beauty. But besides this general grace diffused over nature, almost all the individual forms are agreeable to the eye, as is proved by our endless imitations of some of them, as the acorn, the grape, the pine-cone, the wheat-ear, the egg, the wings and forms of most birds, the lion's claw, the serpent, the butterfly, sea-shells, flames, clouds, buds, leaves, and the forms of many trees, as the palm.

For better consideration, we may distribute the aspects of Beauty in a threefold manner.

1. First, the simple perception of natural forms is a delight. The influence of the forms and actions in nature is so needful to man, that, in its lowest functions, it seems to lie on the confines of commodity and beauty. To the body and mind which have been cramped by noxious work or company, nature is medicinal and restores their tone. The tradesman, the attorney comes out of the din and craft of the street and sees the sky and the woods, and is a man again. In their eternal calm, he finds himself. The health of the eye seems to demand a horizon. We are never tired, so long as we can see far enough.

But in other hours, Nature satisfies by its loveliness, and without any mixture of corporeal benefit. I see the spectacle of morning from the hilltop over against my house, from daybreak to sunrise, with emotions which an angel might share. The long slender bars of cloud float like fishes in the sea of crimson light. From the earth, as a shore, I look out into that silent sea. I seem to partake its rapid transformations; the active enchantment reaches my dust, and I dilate and conspire with the morning wind. How does Nature deify us with a few and cheap elements! Give me health and a day, and I will make the pomp of emperors ridiculous. The dawn is my Assyria, the sunset and moonrise my Paphos, and unimaginable realms of faerie; broad noon shall be my England of the senses and the understanding; the night shall be my Germany of mystic philosophy and dreams.

Not less excellent, except for our less susceptibility in the afternoon, was the charm, last evening, of a January sunset. The western clouds divided and subdivided themselves into pink flakes modulated with tints of unspeakable softness, and the air had so much life and sweetness that it was a pain to come within doors. What was it that nature would say? Was there no meaning in the live repose of the valley behind the mill, and which Homer or Shakspeare could not re-form for me in words? The leafless trees become spires of flame in the sunset, with the blue east for their background, and the stars of the dead calices of flowers, and every withered stem and stubble rimed with frost, contribute something to the mute music.

The inhabitants of cities suppose that the country landscape is pleasant only half the year. I please myself with the graces of the winter scenery, and believe that we are as much touched by it as by the genial influences of summer. To the attentive eye, each moment of the year has its own beauty, and in the same field, it beholds, every hour, a picture which was never seen before and which shall never be seen again. The heavens change every moment, and reflect their glory or gloom on the plains beneath. The state of the crop in the surrounding farms alters the expression of the earth from week to week. The succession of native plants in the pastures and roadsides, which make the silent clock by which time tells the summer hours, will make even the divisions of the day sensible to a keen observer. The tribes of birds and insects, like the plants punctual to their time, follow each other, and the year has room for all. By watercourses, the variety is greater. In July, the blue pontederia or pickerel-weed blooms in large beds in the shallow parts of our pleasant river, and swarms with yellow butterflies in continual motion. Art cannot rival this pomp of purple and gold. Indeed the river is a perpetual gala, and boasts each month a new ornament.

But this beauty of Nature which is seen and felt as beauty, is the least part. The shows of day, the dewy morning, the rainbow, mountains, orchards in blossom, stars, moonlight, shadows in still water, and the like, if too eagerly hunted, become shows merely, and mock us with their unreality. Go out of the house to see the moon, and 't is mere tin-

sel; it will not please as when its light shines upon your necessary journey. The beauty that shimmers in the yellow afternoons of October,
who ever could clutch it? Go forth to find it, and it is gone; 't is only
a mirage as you look from the windows of diligence.

2. The presence of a higher, namely, of the spiritual element is
essential to its perfection. The high and divine beauty which can be
loved without effeminacy, is that which is found in combination with
the human will. Beauty is the mark God sets upon virtue. Every natural action is graceful. Every heroic act is also decent, and causes the
place and the bystanders to shine. We are taught by great actions that
the universe is the property of every individual in it. Every rational
creature has all nature for his dowry and estate. It is his, if he will. He
may divest himself of it; he may creep into a corner, and abdicate his
kingdom, as most men do, but he is entitled to the world by his constitution. In proportion to the energy of his thought and will, he takes
up the world into himself. "All those things for which men plough,
build, or sail, obey virtue;" said Sallust. "The winds and waves," said
Gibbon, "are always on the side of the ablest navigators." So are the
sun and moon and all the stars of heaven. When a noble act is done—
perchance in a scene of great natural beauty; when Leonidas and his
three hundred martyrs consume one day in dying, and the sun and
moon come each and look at them once in the steep defile of
Thermopylae; when Arnold Winkelried, in the high Alps, under the
shadow of the avalanche, gathers in his side a sheaf of Austrian spears
to break the line for his comrades; are not these heroes entitled to add
the beauty of the scene to the beauty of the deed? When the bark of
Columbus nears the shore of America; before it the beach lined with
savages, fleeing out of all their huts of cane; the sea behind; and the
purple mountains of the Indian Archipelago around, can we separate
the man from the living picture? Does not the New World clothe his
form with her palm-groves and savannahs as fit drapery? Ever does
natural beauty steal in like air, and envelop great actions. When Sir
Harry Vane was dragged up the Tower-hill, sitting on a sled, to suffer
death as the champion of the English laws, one of the multitude cried
out to him, "You never sate on so glorious a seat!" Charles II, to intimidate the citizens of London, caused the patriot Lord Russell to be
drawn in an open coach through the principal streets of the city on his
way to the scaffold. "But," his biographer says, "the multitude imag-

· ·

ined they saw liberty and virtue sitting by his side." In private places, among sordid objects, an act of truth or heroism seems at once to draw to itself the sky as its temple, the sun as its candle. Nature stretches out her arms to embrace man, only let his thoughts be of equal greatness. Willingly does she follow his steps with the rose and the violet, and bend her lines of grandeur and grace; to the decoration of her darling child. Only let his thoughts be of equal scope, and the frame will suit the picture. A virtuous man is in unison with her works, and makes the central figure of the visible sphere. Homer, Pindar, Socrates, Phocion, associate themselves fitly in our memory with the geography and climate of Greece. The visible heavens and earth sympathize with Jesus. And in common life whosoever has seen a person of powerful character and happy genius, will have remarked how easily he took all things along with him—the persons, the opinions, and the day, and nature became ancillary to a man.

3. There is still another aspect under which the beauty of the world may be viewed, namely, as it becomes an object of the intellect. Beside the relation of things to virtue, they have a relation to thought. The intellect searches out the absolute order of things as they stand in the mind of God, and without the colors of affection. The intellectual and the active powers seem to succeed each other, and the exclusive activity of the one generates the exclusive activity of the other. There is something unfriendly in each to the other, but they are like the alternate periods of feeding and working in animals; each prepares and will be followed by the other. Therefore does beauty, which, in relation to actions, as we have seen, comes unsought, and comes because it is unsought, remain for the apprehension and pursuit of the intellect; and then again, in its turn, of the active power. Nothing divine dies. All good is eternally reproductive. The beauty of nature re-forms itself in the mind, and not for barren contemplation, but for new creation.

All men are in some degree impressed by the face of the world; same men even to delight. This love of beauty is Taste. Others have the same love in such excess, that, not content with admiring, they seek to embody it in new forms. The creation of beauty is Art.

The production of a work of art throws a light upon the mystery of humanity. A work of art is an abstract or epitome of the world. It is the result or expression of nature, in miniature. For although the works of nature are innumerable and all different, the result or the expression of them all is similar and single. Nature is a sea of forms radically alike and even unique. A leaf, a sunbeam, a landscape, the ocean, make an analogous impression on the mind. What is common to them all—that perfectness and harmony, is beauty. The standard of beauty is the entire circuit of natural forms—the totality of nature; which the Italians expressed by defining beauty "il più nell' uno." Nothing is quite beautiful alone; nothing but is beautiful in the whole. A single object is only so far beautiful as it suggests this universal grace. The poet, the painter, the sculptor, the musician, the architect, seek each to concentrate this radiance of the world on one point, and each in his several work to satisfy the love of beauty which stimulates him to produce. Thus is Art a nature passed through the alembic of man. Thus in art does Nature work through the will of a man filled with the beauty of her first works.

The world thus exists to the soul to satisfy the desire of beauty. This element I call an ultimate end. No reason can be asked or given why the soul seeks beauty. Beauty, in its largest and profoundest sense, is one expression for the universe. God is the all-fair. Truth, and goodness, and beauty, are but different faces of the same All. But beauty in nature is not ultimate. It is the herald of inward and eternal beauty, and is not alone a solid and satisfactory good. It must stand as a part, and not as yet the last or highest expression of the final cause of Nature.

IV

LANGUAGE

LANGUAGE IS a third use which Nature subserves to man. Nature is the vehicle of thought, and in a simple, double, and three-fold degree.

1. Words are signs of natural facts.

2. Particular natural facts are symbols of particular spiritual facts.

3. Nature is the symbol of spirit.

1. Words are signs of natural facts. The use of natural history is to give us aid in supernatural history; the use of the outer creation, to give us language for the beings and changes of the inward creation. Every word which is used to express a moral or intellectual fact, if traced to its root, is found to be borrowed from some material appearance. *Right* means *straight*; *wrong* means *twisted*; *Spirit* primarily means

wind; transgression, the crossing of a line; supercilious, the raising of the eyebrow. We say the heart to express emotion, the head to denote thought; and thought and emotion are words borrowed from sensible things, and now appropriated to spiritual nature. Most of the process by which this transformation is made, is hidden from us in the remote time when language was framed; but the same tendency may be daily observed in children. Children and savages use only nouns or names of things, which they convert into verbs, and apply to analogous mental acts.

2. But this origin of all words that convey a spiritual import—so conspicuous a fact in the history of language—is our least debt to nature. It is not words only that are emblematic; it is things which are emblematic. Every natural fact is a symbol of some spiritual fact. Every appearance in nature corresponds to some state of the mind, and that state of the mind can only be described by presenting that natural appearance as its picture. An enraged man is a lion, a cunning man is a fox, a firm man is a rock, a learned man is a torch. A lamb is innocence; a snake is subtle spite; flowers express to us the delicate affections. Light and darkness are our familiar expression for knowledge and ignorance; and heat for love. Visible distance behind and before us, is respectively our image of memory and hope.

Who looks upon a river in a meditative hour and is not reminded of the flux of all things? Throw a stone into the stream, and the circles that propagate themselves are the beautiful type of all influence. Man is conscious of a universal soul within or behind his individual life, wherein, as in a firmament, the natures of Justice, Truth, Love, Freedom, arise and shine. This universal soul he calls Reason: it is not mine, or thine, or his, but we are its; we are its property and men. And the blue sky in which the private earth is buried, the sky with its eternal calm, and full of everlasting orbs, is the type of Reason. That which intellectually considered we call Reason, considered in relation to nature, we call Spirit. Spirit is the Creator. Spirit hath life in itself. And man in all ages and countries embodies it in his language as the FATHER.

It is easily seen that there is nothing lucky or capricious in these analogies, but that they are constant, and pervade nature. These are not the dreams of a few poets, here and there, but man is an analogist, and studies relations in all objects. He is placed in the centre of beings, and a ray of relation passes from every other being to him. And neither can man be understood without these objects, nor these objects without man. All the facts in natural history taken by themselves, have no value, but are barren, like a single sex. But marry it to human history, and it is full of life. Whole floras, all Linnæus', and Buffon's volumes, are dry catalogues of facts; but the most trivial of these facts, the habit of a plant, the organs, or work, or noise of an insect, applied to the illustration of a fact in intellectual philosophy, or in any way associated to human nature, affects us in the most lively and agreeable manner. The seed of a plant—to what affecting analogies in the nature of man is that little fruit made use of, in all discourse, up to the voice of Paul, who calls the human corpse a seed—"It is sown a natural body; it is raised a spiritual body." The motion of the earth round its axis and round the sun, makes the day and the year. These are certain amounts of brute light and heat. But is there no intent of an analogy between man's life and the seasons? And do the seasons gain no grandeur or pathos from that analogy? The instincts of the ant are very unimportant considered as the ant's; but the moment a ray of relation is seen to extend from it to man, and the little drudge is seen to be a monitor, a little body with a mighty heart, then all its habits, even that said to be recently observed, that it never sleeps, become sublime.

Because of this radical correspondence between visible things and human thoughts, savages, who have only what is necessary, converse in figures. As we go back in history, language becomes more picturesque, until its infancy, when it is all poetry; or all spiritual facts are represented by natural symbols. The same symbols are found to make the original elements of all languages. It has moreover been observed, that the idioms of all languages approach each other in passages of the greatest eloquence and power. And as this is the first language, so is it the last. This immediate dependence of language upon nature, this conversion of an outward phenomenon into a type of somewhat in human life, never loses its power to affect us. It is this which gives that piquancy to the conversation of a strong-natured farmer or backwoodsman, which all men relish.

A man's power to connect his thought with its proper symbol, and so to utter it, depends on the simplicity of his character, that is, upon his love of truth and his desire to communicate it without loss. The corruption of man is followed by the corruption of language. When simplicity of character and the sovereignty of ideas is broken up by the prevalence of secondary desires—the desire of riches, of pleasure, of power, and of praise—and duplicity and falsehood take place of simplicity and truth, the power over nature as an interpreter of the will is in a degree lost; new imagery ceases to be created, and old words are perverted to stand for things which are not; a paper currency is employed, when there is no bullion in the vaults. In due time the fraud is manifest, and words lose all power to stimulate the understanding or the affections. Hundreds of writers may be found in every long-civilized nation who for a short time believe and make others believe that they see and utter truths, who do not of themselves clothe one thought in its natural garment, but who feed unconsciously on the language created by the primary writers of the country, those, namely, who hold primarily on nature.

But wise men pierce this rotten diction and fasten words again to visible things; so that picturesque language is at once a commanding certificate that he who employs it is a man in alliance with truth and God. The moment our discourse rises above the ground line of familiar facts and is inflamed with passion or exalted by thought, it clothes itself in images. A man conversing in earnest, if he watch his intellectual processes, will find that a material image more or less luminous arises in his mind, contemporaneous with every thought, which furnishes the vestment of the thought. Hence, good writing and brilliant discourse are perpetual allegories. This imagery is spontaneous. It is the blending of experience with the present action of the mind. It is proper creation. It is the working of the Original Cause through the instruments he has already made.

These facts may suggest the advantage which the country-life possesses, for a powerful mind, over the artificial and curtailed life of cities. We know more from nature than we can at will communicate. Its light flows into the mind evermore, and we forget its presence. The poet, the orator, bred in the woods, whose senses have been nourished by their fair and appeasing changes, year after year, without design and without heed—shall not lose their lesson altogether, in the roar of cities or the broil of politics. Long hereafter, amidst agitation and terror in national councils—in the hour of revolution—these solemn images shall reappear in their morning lustre, as fit symbols and words of the thoughts which the passing events shall awaken. At the call of a noble sentiment, again the woods wave, the pines murmur, the river rolls and shines, and the cattle low upon the mountains, as he saw and heard them in his infancy. And with these forms, the spells of persuasion, the keys of power are put into his hands.

3. We are thus assisted by natural objects in the expression of particular meanings. But how great a language to convey such pepper-corn informations! Did it need such noble races of creatures, this profusion of forms, this host of orbs in heaven, to furnish man with the dictionary and grammar of his municipal speech? Whilst we use this grand cipher to expedite the affairs of our pot and kettle, we feel that we have not yet put it to its use, neither are able. We are like travellers using the cinders of a volcano to roast their eggs. Whilst we see that it always stands ready to clothe what we would say, we cannot avoid the question whether the characters are not significant of themselves. Have mountains, and waves, and skies, no significance but what we consciously give them when we employ them as emblems of our thoughts? The world is emblematic. Parts of speech are metaphors, because the whole of nature is a metaphor of the human mind. The laws of moral nature answer to those of matter as face to face in a glass. "The visible world and the relation of its parts, is the dial plate of the invisible." The axioms of physics translate the laws of ethics. Thus, "the whole is greater than its part;" "reaction is equal to action;" "the smallest weight may be made to lift the greatest, the difference of weight being compensated by time;" and many the like propositions, which have an ethical as well as physical sense. These propositions have a much more extensive and universal sense when applied to human life, than when confined to technical use.

In like manner, the memorable words of history and the proverbs of nations consist usually of a natural fact, selected as a picture or parable of a moral truth. Thus: A rolling stone gathers no moss; A bird in the hand is worth two in the bush; A cripple in the right way will beat a racer in the wrong; Make hay while the sun shines; 'T is hard to carry a full cup even; Vinegar is the son of wine; The last ounce broke the camel's back; Long-lived trees make roots first—and the like. In their primary sense these are trivial facts, but we repeat them for the value of their analogical import. What is true of proverbs, is true of all fables, parables, and allegories.

This relation between the mind and matter is not fancied by some poet, but stands in the will of God, and so is free to be known by all men. It appears to men, or it does not appear. When in fortunate hours we ponder this miracle, the wise man doubts if at all other times he is not blind and deaf;

> "Can such things be,
> And overcome us like a summer's cloud,
> Without our special wonder?"

for the universe becomes transparent, and the light of higher laws than its own shines through it. It is the standing problem which has exercised the wonder and the study of every fine genius since the world began; from the era of the Egyptians and the Brahmins to that of Pythagoras, of Plato, of Bacon, of Leibnitz, of Swedenborg. There sits the Sphinx at the road-side, and from age to age, as each prophet comes by, he tries his fortune at reading her riddle. There seems to be a necessity in spirit to manifest itself in material forms; and day and night, river and storm, beast and bird, acid and alkali, preëxist in necessary Ideas in the mind of God, and are what they are by virtue of preceding affections in the world of spirit. A Fact is the end or last issue of spirit. The visible creation is the terminus or the circumference of the invisible world. "Material objects," said a French philosopher, "are necessarily kinds of *scoriæ* of the substantial thoughts of the Creator, which must always preserve an exact relation to their first origin; in other words, visible nature must have a spiritual and moral side."

This doctrine is abstruse, and though the images of "garment," "scoriæ," "mirror," etc., may stimulate the fancy, we must summon the aid of subtler and more vital expositors to make it plain. "Every scripture is to be interpreted by the same spirit which gave it forth," is the fundamental law of criticism. A life in harmony with Nature, the love of truth and of virtue, will purge the eyes to understand her text. By degrees we may come to know the primitive sense of the permanent objects of nature, so that the world shall be to us an open book, and every form significant of its hidden life and final cause.

A new interest surprises us, whilst, under the view now suggested, we contemplate the fearful extent and multitude of objects; since "every object rightly seen, unlocks a new faculty of the soul." That which was unconscious truth, becomes, when interpreted and defined in an object, a part of the domain of knowledge—a new weapon in the magazine of power.

V

DISCIPLINE

IN VIEW of the significance of nature, we arrive at once at a new fact, that nature is a discipline. This use of the world includes the preceding uses, as parts of itself.

Space, time, society, labor, climate, food, locomotion, the animals, the mechanical forces, give us sincerest lessons, day by day, whose meaning is unlimited. They educate both the Understanding and the Reason. Every property of matter is a school for the understanding—its solidity or resistance, its inertia, its extension, its figure, its divisibility. The understanding adds, divides, combines, measures, and finds nutriment and room for its activity in this worthy scene. Meantime, Reason transfers all these lessons into its own world of thought, by perceiving the analogy that marries Matter and Mind.

1. Nature is a discipline of the understanding in intellectual truths. Our dealing with sensible objects is a constant exercise in the necessary lessons of difference, of likeness, of order, of being and seeming, of progressive arrangement; of ascent from particular to general; of combination to one end of manifold forces. Proportioned to the importance of the organ to be formed, is the extreme care with which its tuition is provided—a care pretermitted in no single case. What tedious training, day after day, year after year, never ending, to form the common sense; what continual reproduction of annoyances, inconveniences, dilemmas; what rejoicing over us of little men; what disputing of prices, what reckonings of interest—and all to form the Hand of the mind— to instruct us that "good thoughts are no better than good dreams, unless they be executed!"

The same good office is performed by Property and its filial systems of debt and credit. Debt, grinding debt, whose iron face the widow, the orphan, and the sons of genius fear and hate—debt, which consumes so much time, which so cripples and disheartens a great spirit with cares that seem so base, is a preceptor whose lessons cannot be foregone, and is needed most by those who suffer from it most.

Moreover, property, which has been well compared to snow—"if it fall level to-day, it will be blown into drifts to-morrow," is the surface action of internal machinery, like the index on the face of a clock. Whilst now it is the gymnastics of the understanding, it is hiving, in the foresight of the spirit, experience in profounder laws.

The whole character and fortune of the individual are affected by the least inequalities in the culture of the understanding; for example, in the perception of differences. Therefore is Space, and therefore Time, that man may know that things are not huddled and lumped, but sundered and individual. A bell and a plough have each their use, and neither can do the office of the other. Water is good to drink, coal to burn, wool to wear; but wool cannot be drunk, nor water spun, nor coal eaten. The wise man shows his wisdom in separation, in gradation, and his scale of creatures and of merits is as wide as nature. The foolish have no range in their scale, but suppose every man is as every other man. What is not good they call the worst, and what is not hateful, they call the best.

In like manner, what good heed Nature forms in us! She pardons no mistakes. Her yea is yea, and her nay, nay.

The first steps in Agriculture, Astronomy, Zoölogy (those first steps which the farmer, the hunter, and the sailor take), teach that Nature's dice are always loaded; that in her heaps and rubbish are concealed sure and useful results.

How calmly and genially the mind apprehends one after another the laws of physics! What noble emotions dilate the mortal as he enters into the councils of the creation, and feels by knowledge the privilege to BE! His insight refines him. The beauty of nature shines in his own breast. Man is greater that he can see this, and the universe less, because Time and Space relations vanish as laws are known.

Here again we are impressed and even daunted by the immense Universe to be explored. "What we know is a point to what we do not know." Open any recent journal of science, and weigh the problems suggested concerning Light, Heat, Electricity, Magnetism, Physiology, Geology, and judge whether the interest of natural science is likely to be soon exhausted.

Passing by many particulars of the discipline of nature, we must not omit to specify two.

The exercise of the Will, or the lesson of power, is taught in every event. From the child's successive possession of his several senses up to the hour when he saith, "Thy will be done!" he is learning the secret that he can reduce under his will not only particular events but great classes, nay, the whole series of events, and so conform all facts to his character. Nature is thoroughly mediate. It is made to serve. It receives the dominion of man as meekly as the ass on which the Saviour rode. It offers all its kingdoms to man as the raw material which he may mould into what is useful. Man is never weary of working it up. He forges the subtile and delicate air into wise and melodious words, and gives them wing as angels of persuasion and command. One after another his victorious thought comes up with and reduces all things, until the world becomes at last only a realized will—the double of the man.

2. Sensible objects conform to the premonitions of Reason and reflect the conscience. All things are moral; and in their boundless changes have an unceasing reference to spiritual nature. Therefore is nature glorious with form, color, and motion; that every globe in the remotest heaven, every chemical change from the rudest crystal up to the laws of life, every change of vegetation from the first principle of growth in the eye of a leaf, to the tropical forest and antediluvian coalmine, every animal function from the sponge up to Hercules, shall hint or thunder to man the laws of right and wrong, and echo the Ten Commandments. Therefore is Nature ever the ally of Religion: lends all her pomp and riches to the religious sentiment. Prophet and priest, David, Isaiah, Jesus, have drawn deeply from this source. This ethical character so penetrates the bone and marrow of nature, as to seem the end for which it was made. Whatever private purpose is answered by any member or part, this is its public and universal function, and is never omitted. Nothing in nature is exhausted in its first use. When a thing has served an end to the uttermost, it is wholly new for an ulterior service. In God, every end is converted into a new means. Thus the use of commodity, regarded by itself, is mean and squalid. But it is to the mind an education in the doctrine of Use, namely, that a thing is good only so far as it serves; that a conspiring of parts and efforts to the production of an end is essential to any being. The first and gross manifestation of this truth is our inevitable and hated training in values and wants, in corn and meat.

It has already been illustrated, that every natural process is a version of a moral sentence. The moral law lies at the centre of nature and radiates to the circumference. It is the pith and marrow of every substance, every relation, and every process. All things with which we deal, preach to us. What is a farm but a mute gospel? The chaff and the wheat, weeds and plants, blight, rain, insects, sun—it is a sacred emblem from the first furrow of spring to the last stack which the snow of winter overtakes in the fields. But the sailor, the shepherd, the miner, the merchant, in their several resorts, have each an experience precisely parallel, and leading to the same conclusion: because all organizations are radically alike. Nor can it be doubted that this moral sentiment which thus scents the air, grows in the grain, and impregnates the waters of the world, is caught by man and sinks into his soul. The moral influence of nature upon every individual is that amount of truth which it illustrates to him. Who can estimate this? Who can guess how much firmness the sea-beaten rock has taught the fisherman? How much tranquillity has been reflected to man from the azure sky, over whose unspotted deeps the winds forevermore drive flocks of stormy clouds, and leave no wrinkle or stain? How much industry and providence and affection we have caught from the pantomime of brutes? What a searching preacher of self-command is the varying phenomenon of Health!

Herein is especially apprehended the unity of Nature—the unity in variety—which meets us everywhere. All the endless variety of things make an identical impression. Xenophanes complained in his old age, that, look where he would, all things hastened back to Unity. He was weary of seeing the same entity in the tedious variety of forms. The fable of Proteus has a cordial truth. A leaf, a drop, a crystal, a moment of time, is related to the whole, and partakes of the perfection of the whole. Each particle is a microcosm, and faithfully renders the likeness of the world.

Not only resemblances exist in things whose analogy is obvious, as when we detect the type of the human hand in the flipper of the fossil saurus, but also in objects wherein there is great superficial unlikeness. Thus architecture is called "frozen music," be De Staël and Goethe. Vitruvius thought an architect should be a musician. "A Gothic church," said Coleridge, "is a petrified religion." Michael Angelo maintained, that, to an architect, a knowledge of anatomy is essential. In Haydn's oratorios, the notes present to the imagination not only motions, as of the snake, the stag, and the elephant, but colors also; as the green grass. The law of harmonic sounds reappears in the harmonic colors. The granite is differenced in its laws only by the more or less of heat from the river that wears it away. The river, as it flows, resembles the air that flows over it; the air resembles the light which traverses it with more subtile currents; the light resembles the heat which rides with it through Space. Each creature is only a modification of the other; the likeness in them is more than the difference, and their radical law is one and the same. A rule of one art, or a law of one organization, holds true throughout nature. So intimate is this Unity, that, it is easily seen, it lies under the undermost garment of Nature, and betrays its source in Universal Spirit. For it pervades Thought also. Every universal truth which we express in words, implies or supposes every other truth. *Omne verum vero consonat.* It is like a great circle on a sphere, comprising all possible circles; which, however, may be drawn and comprise it in like manner. Every such truth is the absolute Ens seen from one side. But it has innumerable sides.

The central Unity is still more conspicuous in actions. Words are finite organs of the infinite mind. They cannot cover the dimensions of what is in truth. They break, chop, and impoverish it. An action is the perfection and publication of thought. A right action seems to fill the eye, and to be related to all nature. "The wise man, in doing one thing, does all; or, in the one thing he does rightly, he sees the likeness of all which is done rightly."

Words and actions are not the attributes of brute nature. They introduce us to the human form, of which all other organizations appear to be degradations. When this appears among so many that surround it, the spirit prefers it to all others. It says, "From such as this have I drawn joy and knowledge; in such as this have I found and beheld myself; I will speak to it; it can speak again; it can yield me thought already formed and alive." In fact, the eye—the mind—is always accompanied by these forms, male and female; and these are incomparably the richest informations of the power and order that lie at the heart of things. Unfortunately every one of them bears the marks as of some injury; is marred and superficially defective. Nevertheless, far different from the deaf and dumb nature around them, these all rest like fountain-pipes on the unfathomed sea of thought and virtue whereto they alone, of all organizations, are the entrances.

It were a pleasant inquiry to follow into detail their ministry to our education, but where would it stop? We are associated in adolescent and adult life with some friends, who, like skies and waters, are coextensive with our idea; who, answering each to a certain affection of the soul, satisfy our desire on that side; whom we lack power to put at such focal distance from us, that we can mend or even analyze them. We cannot choose but love them. When much intercourse with a friend has supplied us with a standard of excellence, and has increased our respect for the resources of God who thus sends a real person to outgo our ideal; when he has, moreover, become an object of thought, and, whilst his character retains all its unconscious effect, is converted in the mind into solid and sweet wisdom—it is a sign to us that his office is closing, and he is commonly withdrawn from our sight in a short time.

VI

IDEALISM

THUS is the unspeakable but intelligible and practicable meaning of the world conveyed to man, the immortal pupil, in every object of sense. To this one end of Discipline, all parts of nature conspire.

A noble doubt perpetually suggests itself—whether this end be not the Final Cause of the Universe; and whether nature outwardly exists. It is a sufficient account of that Appearance we call the World, that God will teach a human mind, and so makes it the receiver of a certain number of congruent sensations, which we call sun and moon, man and woman, house and trade. In my utter impotence to test the authenticity of the report of my senses, to know whether the impressions they make on me correspond with outlying objects, what difference does it make, whether Orion is up there in heaven, or some god paints the image in the firmament of the soul? The relations of parts and the end of the whole remaining the same, what is the difference, whether land and sea interact, and worlds revolve and intermingle without number or end—deep yawning under deep, and galaxy balancing galaxy, throughout absolute space—or whether, without relations of time and space, the same appearances are inscribed in the constant faith of man? Whether nature enjoy a substantial existence without, or is only in the apocalypse of the mind, it is alike useful and alike venerable to me. Be

. . . .

it what it may, it is ideal to me so long as I cannot try the accuracy of my senses.

The frivolous make themselves merry with the Ideal theory, as if its consequences were burlesque; as if it affected the stability of nature. It surely does not. God never jests with us, and will not compromise the end of nature by permitting any inconsequence in its procession. Any distrust of the permanence of laws would paralyze the faculties of man. Their permanence is sacredly respected, and his faith therein is perfect. The wheels and springs of man are all set to the hypothesis of the permanence of nature. We are not built like a ship to be tossed, but like a house to stand. It is a natural consequence of this structure, that so long as the active powers predominate over the reflective, we resist with indignation any hint that nature is more short-lived or mutable than spirit. The broker, the wheelwright, the carpenter, the tollman, are much displeased at the intimation.

But whilst we acquiesce entirely in the permanence of natural laws, the question of the absolute existence of nature still remains open. It is the uniform effect of culture on the human mind, not to shake our faith in the stability of particular phenomena, as of heat, water, azote; but to lead us to regard nature as phenomenon, not a substance; to attribute necessary existence to spirit; to esteem nature as an accident and an effect.

To the senses and the unrenewed understanding, belongs a sort of instinctive belief in the absolute existence of nature. In their view man and nature are indissolubly joined. Things are ultimates, and they never look beyond their sphere. The presence of Reason mars this faith. The first effort of thought tends to relax this despotism of the senses which binds us to nature as if we were a part of it, and shows us nature aloof, and, as it were, afloat. Until this higher agency intervened, the animal eye sees, with wonderful accuracy, sharp outlines and colored surfaces. When the eye of Reason opens, to outline and surface are at once added grace and expression. These proceed from imagination and affection, and abate somewhat of the angular distinctness of objects. If the Reason be stimulated to more earnest vision, outlines and surfaces become transparent, and are no longer seen; causes and spirits are seen through them. The best moments of life are these delicious awakenings of the higher powers, and the reverential withdrawing of nature before its God.

Let us proceed to indicate the effects of culture.

1. Our first institution in the Ideal philosophy is a hint from Nature herself.

Nature is made to conspire with spirit to emancipate us. Certain mechanical changes, a small alteration in our local position, apprizes us of a dualism. We are strangely affected by seeing the shore from a moving ship, from a balloon, or through the tints of an unusual sky. The least change in our point of view gives the whole world a pictorial air. A man who seldom rides, needs only to get into a coach and traverse his own town, to turn the street into a puppet-show. The men, the women—talking, running, bartering, fighting—the earnest mechanic, the lounger, the beggar, the boys, the dogs, are unrealized at once, or, at least, wholly detached from all relation to the observer, and seen as apparent, not substantial beings. What new thoughts are suggested by seeing a face of country quite familiar, in the rapid movement of the railroad car! Nay, the most wonted objects (make a very slight change in the point of vision), please us most. In a camera obscura, the butcher's cart, and the figure of one of our own family amuse us. So a portrait of a well-known face gratifies us. Turn the eyes upside down, by looking at the landscape through your legs, and how agreeable is the picture, though you have seen it any time these twenty years!

In these cases, by mechanical means, is suggested the difference between the observer and the spectacle—between man and nature. Hence arises a pleasure mixed with awe; I may say, a low degree of the sublime is felt, from the fact, probably, that man is hereby apprized that whilst the world is a spectacle, something in himself is stable.

2. In a higher manner the poet communicates the same pleasure. By a few strokes he delineates, as on air, the sun, the mountain, the camp, the city, the hero, the maiden, not different from what we know them, but only lifted from the ground and afloat before the eye. He unfixes the land and the sea, makes them revolve around the axis of his primary thought, and disposes them anew. Possessed himself by a heroic passion, he uses matter as symbols of it. The sensual man conforms thoughts to things; the poet conforms things to his thoughts. The one esteems nature as rooted and fast; the other, as fluid, and impresses his being thereon. To him, the refractory world is ductile and flexible; he invests dust and stones with humanity, and makes them the words

of the Reason. The Imagination may be defined to be the use which the Reason makes of the material world. Shakspeare possesses the power of subordinating nature for the purposes of expression, beyond all poets. His imperial muse tosses the creation like a bauble from hand to hand, and uses it to embody any caprice of thought that is uppermost in his mind. The remotest spaces of nature are visited, and the farthest sundered things are brought together, by a subtile spiritual connection. We are made aware that magnitude of material things is relative, and all objects shrink and expand to serve the passion of the poet. Thus in his sonnets, the lays of birds, the scents and dyes of flowers he finds to be the *shadow* of his beloved; time, which keeps her from him, is his *chest*; the suspicion she has awakened, is her *ornament*;

> The ornament of beauty is Suspect
> A crow which flies in heaven's sweetest air.

His passion is not the fruit of chance; it swells, as he speaks, to a city, or a state.

> No, it was builded far from accident;
> It suffers not in smiling pomp, nor falls
> Under the brow of thralling discontent;
> It fears not policy, that heretic,
> That works on leases of short numbered hours,
> But all alone stands hugely politic.

In the strength of his constancy, the Pyramids seem to him recent and transitory. The freshness of youth and love dazzles him with its resemblance to morning;

> Take those lips away
> Which so sweetly were forsworn;
> And those eyes,—the break of day,
> Lights that do mislead the morn.

The wild beauty of this hyperbole, I may say in passing, it would not be easy to match in literature.

This transfiguration which all material objects undergo through the passion of the poet—this power which he exerts to dwarf the great, to magnify the small—might be illustrated by a thousand examples from his Plays. I have before me the Tempest, and will cite only these few lines.

> ARIEL. The strong based promontory
> Have I made shake, and by the spurs plucked up
> The pine and cedar.

Prospero calls for music to soothe the frantic Alonzo, and his companions;

> A solemn air, and the best comforter
> To an unsettled fancy, cure thy brains
> Now useless, boiled within thy skull.

Again;

> The charm dissolves apace,
> And, as the morning steals upon the night,
> Melting the darkness, so their rising senses
> Begin to chase the ignorant fumes that mantle
> Their clearer reason.
> Their understanding
> Begins to swell: and the approaching tide
> Will shortly fill the reasonable shores
> That now lie foul and muddy.

The perception of real affinities between events (that is to say, of *ideal* affinities, for those only are real), enables the poet thus to make free with the most imposing forms and phenomena of the world, and to assert the predominance of the soul.

3. Whilst thus the poet animates nature with his own thoughts, he differs from the philosopher only herein, that the one proposes Beauty as his main end; the other Truth. But the philosopher, not less than the poet, postpones the apparent order and relations of things to the empire of thought. "The problem of philosophy," according to Plato, "is, for all that exists conditionally, to find a ground unconditioned and absolute." It proceeds on the faith that a law determines all phenomena, which being known, the phenomena can be predicted. That law, when

in the mind, is an idea. Its beauty is infinite. The true philosopher and the true poet are one, and a beauty, which is truth, and a truth, which is beauty, is the aim of both. Is not the charm of one of Plato's or Aristotle's definitions strictly like that of the Antigone of Sophocles? It is, in both cases, that a spiritual life has been imparted to nature; that the solid seeming block of matter has been pervaded and dissolved by a thought; that this feeble human being has penetrated the vast masses of nature with an informing soul, and recognized itself in their harmony, that is, seized their law. In physics, when this is attained, the memory disburthens itself of its cumbrous catalogues of particulars, and carries centuries of observation in a single formula.

Thus even in physics, the material is degraded before the spiritual. The astronomer, the geometer, rely on their irrefragable analysis, and disdain the results of observation. The sublime remark of Euler on his law of arches, "This will be found contrary to all experience, yet is true;" had already transferred nature into the mind, and left matter like an outcast corpse.

4. Intellectual science has been observed to beget invariably a doubt of the existence of matter. Turgot said, "He that has never doubted the existence of matter, may be assured he has no aptitude for metaphysical inquiries." It fastens the attention upon immortal necessary uncreated natures, that is, upon Ideas; and in their presence we feel that the outward circumstance is a dream and a shade. Whilst we wait in this Olympus of gods, we think of nature as an appendix to the soul. We ascend into their region, and know that these are the thoughts of the Supreme Being. "These are they who were set up from everlasting, from the beginning, or ever the earth was. When he prepared the heavens, they were there; when he established the clouds above, when he strengthened the fountains of the deep. Then they were by him, as one brought up with him. Of them took he counsel."

Their influence is proportionate. As objects of science they are accessible to few men. Yet all men are capable of being raised by piety or by passion, into their region. And no man touches these divine natures, without becoming, in some degree, himself divine. Like a new soul, they renew the body. We become physically nimble and lightsome; we tread on air; life is no longer irksome, and we think it will never be so. No man fears age or misfortune or death in their serene company, for he is transported out of the district of change. Whilst we behold unveiled the nature of Justice and Truth, we learn the difference between the absolute and the conditional or relative. We apprehend the absolute. As it were, for the first time, *we exist*. We become immortal, for we learn that time and space are relations of matter; that with a perception of truth or a virtuous will they have no affinity.

5. Finally, religion and ethics, which may be fitly called the practice of ideas, or the introduction of ideas into life, have an analogous effect with all lower culture, in degrading nature and suggesting its dependence on spirit. Ethics and religion differ herein; that the one is the system of human duties commencing from man; the other, from God. Religion includes the personality of God; Ethics does not. They are one to our present design. They both put nature under foot. The first and last lesson of religion is, "The things that are seen, are temporal; the things that are unseen, are eternal." It puts an affront upon nature. It does that for the unschooled, which philosophy does for Berkeley and Viasa. The uniform language that may be heard in the churches of the most ignorant sects is—"Contemn the unsubstantial shows of the world; they are vanities, dreams, shadows, unrealities; seek the realities of religion." The devotee flouts nature. Some theosophists have arrived at a certain hostility and indignation towards matter, as the Manichean and Plotinus. They distrusted in themselves any looking back to these flesh-pots of Egypt. Plotinus was ashamed of his body. In short, they might all say of matter, what Michael Angelo said of external beauty, "It is the frail and weary weed, in which God dresses the soul which he has called into time."

It appears that motion, poetry, physical and intellectual science, and religion, all tend to affect our convictions of the reality of the external world. But I own there is something ungrateful in expanding too curiously the particulars of the general proposition, that all culture tends to imbue us with idealism. I have no hostility to nature, but a child's love to it. I expand and live in the warm day like corn and melons. Let us speak her fair. I do not wish to fling stones at my beautiful mother, nor soil my gentle nest. I only wish to indicate the true position of nature in regard to man, wherein to establish man all right education tends; as the ground which to attain is the object of human life, that is, of man's connection with nature. Culture inverts the vulgar view of nature, and brings the mind to call that apparent which it uses to call real, and that real which it uses to call visionary. Children, it is true, believe in the external world. The belief that it appears only, is an afterthought, but with culture this faith will as surely arise on the mind as did the first.

The advantage of the ideal theory over the popular faith is this, that it presents the world in precisely that view which is most desirable to the mind. It is, in fact, the view which Reason, both speculative and practical, that is, philosophy and virtue, take. For seen in the light of thought, the world always is phenomenal; and virtue subordinates it to the mind. Idealism sees the world in God. It beholds the whole circle of persons and things, of actions and events, of country and religion, not as painfully accumulated, atom after atom, act after act, in an aged creeping Past, but as one vast picture which God paints on the instant eternity for the contemplation of the soul. Therefore the soul holds itself off from a too trivial and microscopic study of the universal tablet. It respects the end too much to immerse itself in the means. It sees something more important in Christianity than the scandals of ecclesiastical history or the niceties of criticism; and, very incurious concerning persons or miracles, and not at all disturbed by chasms of historical evidence, it accepts from God the phenomenon, as it finds it, as the pure and awful form of religion in the world. It is not hot and passionate at the appearance of what it calls its own good or bad fortune, at the union or opposition of other persons. No man is its enemy. It accepts whatsoever befalls, as part of its lesson. It is a watcher more than a doer, and it is a doer, only that it may the better watch.

VII

SPIRIT

IT IS essential to a true theory of nature and of man, that it should contain somewhat progressive. Uses that are exhausted or that may be, and facts that end in the statement, cannot be all that is true of this brave lodging wherein man is harbored, and wherein all his faculties find appropriate and endless exercise. And all the uses of nature admit of being summed in one, which yields the activity of man an infinite scope. Through all its kingdoms, to the suburbs and outskirts of things, it is faithful to the cause whence it had its origin. It always speaks of Spirit. It suggests the absolute. It is a perpetual effect. It is a great shadow pointing always to the sun behind us.

The aspect of Nature is devout. Like the figure of Jesus, she stands with bended head, and hands folded upon the breast. The happiest man is he who learns from nature the lesson of worship.

Of that ineffable essence which we call Spirit, he that thinks most, will say least. We can foresee God in the coarse, and, as it were, distant phenomena of matter; but when we try to define and describe himself, both language and thought desert us, and we are as helpless as fools and savages. That essence refuses to be recorded in propositions, but when man has worshipped him intellectually, the noblest ministry of nature is to stand as the apparition of God. It is the organ through which the universal spirit speaks to the individual, and strives to lead back the individual to it.

When we consider Spirit, we see that the views already presented do not include the whole circumference of man. We must add some related thoughts.

Three problems are put by nature to the mind: What is matter? Whence is it? and Whereto? The first of these questions only, the ideal theory answers. Idealism saith: matter is a phenomenon, not a substance. Idealism acquaints us with the total disparity between the evidence of our own being and the evidence of the world's being. The one is perfect; the other, incapable of any assurance; the mind is a part of the nature of things; the world is a divine dream, from which we may presently awake to the glories and certainties of day. Idealism is a hypothesis to account for nature by other principles than those of carpentry and chemistry. Yet, if it only deny the existence of matter, it does not satisfy the demands of the spirit. It leaves God out of me. It leaves me in the splendid labyrinth of my perceptions, to wander without end. Then the heart resists it, because it balks the affections in denying substantive being to men and women. Nature is so pervaded with human life that there is something of humanity in all and in every particular. But this theory makes nature foreign to me, and does not account for that consanguinity which we acknowledge to it.

Let it stand then, in the present state of our knowledge, merely as a useful introductory hypothesis, serving to apprize us of the eternal distinction between the soul and the world.

But when, following the invisible steps of thoughts, we come to inquire, Whence is matter? and Whereto? many truths arise to us out of the recesses of consciousness. We learn that the highest is present to the soul of man; that the dread universal essence, which is not wisdom, or love, or beauty, or power, but all in one, and each entirely, is that for which all things exist, and that by which they are; that spirit creates; that behind nature, throughout nature, spirit is present; one and not compound it does not act upon us from without, that is, in space and time, but spiritually, or through ourselves: therefore, that spirit, that is, the Supreme Being, does not build up nature around us, but puts it forth through us, as the life of the tree puts forth new branches and leaves through the pores of the old. As a plant upon the earth, so a man rests upon the bosom of God; he is nourished by unfailing fountains, and draws at his need inexhaustible power. Who can set bounds to the possibilities of man? Once inhale the upper air, being admitted to behold the absolute natures of justice and truth, and we learn that man has access to the entire mind of the Creator, is himself the creator in the finite. This view, which admonishes me where the sources of wisdom and power lie, and points to virtue as to

> "The golden key
> Which opes the palace of eternity,"

carries upon its face the highest certificate of truth, because it animates me to create my own world through the purification of my soul.

The world proceeds from the same spirit as the body of man. It is a remoter and inferior incarnation of God, a projection of God in the unconscious. But it differs from the body in one important respect. It is not, like that, now subjected to the human will. Its serene order is inviolable by us. It is, therefore, to us, the present expositor of the divine mind. It is a fixed point whereby we may measure our departure. As we degenerate, the contrast between us and our house is more evident. We are as much strangers in nature as we are aliens from God. We do not understand the notes of birds. The fox and the deer run away from us; the bear and tiger rend us. We do not know the uses of more than a few plants, as corn and the apple, the potato and the vine. Is not the landscape, every glimpse of which hath a grandeur, a face of him? Yet this may show us what discord is between man and nature, for you cannot freely admire a noble landscape if laborers are digging in the field hard by. The poet finds something ridiculous in his delight until he is out of the sight of men.

VIII

PROSPECTS

IN INQUIRIES respecting the laws of the world and the frame of things, the highest reason is always the truest. That which seems faintly possible, it is so refined, is often faint and dim because it is deepest seated in the mind among the eternal verities. Empirical science is apt to cloud the sight, and by the very knowledge of functions and processes to bereave the student of the manly contemplation of the whole. The savant becomes unpoetic. But the best read naturalist who lends an entire and devout attention to truth, will see that there remains much to learn of his relation to the world, and that it is not to be learned by any addition or subtraction or other comparison of known quantities, but is arrived at by untaught sallies of the spirit, by a continual self-recovery, and by entire humility. He will perceive that there are far more excellent qualities in the student than preciseness and infallibility; that a guess is often more fruitful than an indisputable affirmation, and that a dream may let us deeper into the secret of nature than a hundred concerted experiments.

For the problems to be solved are precisely those which the physiologist and the naturalist omit to state. It is not so pertinent to man to know all the individuals of the animal kingdom, as it is to know whence and whereto is this tyrannizing unity in his constitution, which evermore separates and classifies things, endeavoring to reduce the most diverse to one form. When I behold a rich landscape, it is less to my purpose to recite correctly the order and superposition of the strata, than to know why all thought of multitude is lost in a tranquil sense of unity. I cannot greatly honor minuteness in details, so long as there is no hint to explain the relation between things and thoughts; no ray upon the *metaphysics* of conchology, of botany, of the arts, to show the relation of the forms of flowers, shells, animals, architecture, to the mind, and build science upon ideas. In a cabinet of natural history, we become sensible of a certain occult recognition and sympathy in regard to the most unwieldy and eccentric form of beast, fish, and insect. The American who has been confined, in his own country, to the sight of buildings designed after foreign models, is surprised on entering York Minster or St. Peter's at Rome, by the feeling that these structures are imitations also—faint copies of an invisible archetype. Nor has science sufficient humanity, so long as the naturalist overlooks that wonderful congruity which subsists between man and the world; of which he is lord, not because he is the most subtile inhabitant, but because he is its head and heart, and finds something of himself in every great and small thing, in every mountain stratum, in every new law of color, fact of astronomy, or atmospheric influence which observation or analysis lays open. A perception of this mystery inspires the muse of George Herbert, the beautiful psalmist of the seventeenth century. The following lines are part of his little poem on Man.

> Man is all symmetry,
> Full of proportions, one limb to another,
> And all to all the world besides.
> Each part may call the farthest, brother;
> For head with foot hath private amity,
> And both with moons and tides.
>
> Nothing hath got so far
> But man hath caught and kept it as his prey;
> His eyes dismount the highest star:
> He is in little all the sphere.
> Herbs gladly cure our flesh, because that they
> Find their acquaintance there.
>
> For us, the winds do blow,
> The earth doth rest, heaven move, and fountains flow;
> Nothing we see, but means our good,
> As our delight, or as our treasure;
> The whole is either our cupboard of food,
> Or cabinet of pleasure.
>
> The stars have us to bed:
> Night draws the curtain; which the sun withdraws.

Music and light attend our head.
All things unto our flesh are kind,
In their descent and being; to our mind,
In their ascent and cause.

More servants wait on man
Than he'll take notice of. In every path,
He treads down that which doth befriend him
When sickness makes him pale and wan.
Oh mighty love! Man is one world, and hath
Another to attend him.

The perception of this class of truths makes the attraction which draws men to science, but the end is lost sight of in attention to the means. In view of this half-sight of science, we accept the sentence of Plato, that "poetry comes nearer to vital truth than history." Every surmise and vatication of the mind is entitled to a certain respect, and we learn to prefer imperfect theories, and sentences which contain glimpses of truth, to digested systems which have no one valuable suggestion. A wise writer will feel that the ends of study and composition are best answered by announcing undiscovered regions of thought, and so communicating, through hope, new activity to the torpid spirit.

I shall therefore conclude this essay with some traditions of man and nature, which a certain poet sang to me; and which, as they have always been in the world, and perhaps reappear to every bard, may be both history and prophecy.

'The foundations of man are not in matter, but in spirit. But the element of spirit is eternity. To it, therefore, the longest series of events, the oldest chronologies are young and recent. In the cycle of the universal man, from whom the known individuals proceed, centuries are points, and all history is but the epoch of one degradation.

'We distrust and deny inwardly our sympathy with nature. We own and disown our relation to it, by turns. We are like Nebuchadnezzar, dethroned, bereft of reason, and eating grass like an ox. But who can set limits to the remedial force of spirit?

'A man is a god in ruin. When men are innocent, life shall be longer, and shall pass into the immortal as gently as we awake from dreams. Now, the world would be insane and rabid, if these disorganizations should last for hundreds of years. It is kept in check by death and infancy. Infancy is the perpetual Messiah, which comes into the arms of fallen men, and pleads with them to return to paradise.

'Man is the dwarf of himself. Once he was permeated and dissolved by spirit. He filled nature with his overflowing currents. Out from him sprang the sun and moon; from man the sun, from woman the moon. The laws of his mind, the periods of his actions externized themselves into day and night, into the year and the seasons. But, having made for himself this huge shell, his waters retired; he no longer fills the veins and veinlets; he is shrunk to a drop. He sees that the structure still fits him, but fits him colossally. Say, rather, once it fitted him, now it corresponds to him from far and on high. He adores timidly his own work. Now is man the follower of the sun, and woman the follower of the moon. Yet sometimes he starts in his slumber, and wonders at himself and his house, and muses strangely at the resemblance betwixt him and it. He perceives that if his law is still paramount, if still he have elemental power, if his word is sterling yet in nature, it is not conscious power, it is not inferior but superior to his will. It is instinct.' Thus my Orphic poet sang.

At present, man applies to nature but half his force. He works on the world with his understanding alone. He lives in it and masters it by a penny-wisdom; and he that works most in it is but a half-man, and whilst his arms are strong and his digestion good, his mind is imbruted, and he is a selfish savage. His relation to nature, his power over it, is through the understanding, as by manure; the economic use of fire, wind, water, and the mariner's needle; steam, coal, chemical agriculture; the repairs of the human body by the dentist and the surgeon. This is such a resumption of power as if a banished king should buy his territories inch by inch, instead of vaulting at once into his throne. Meantime, in the thick darkness, there are not wanting gleams of a better light—occasional examples of the action of man upon nature with his entire force—with reason as well as understanding. Such examples are, the traditions of miracles in the earliest antiquity of all nations; the history of Jesus Christ; the achievements of a principle, as in religious and political revolutions, and in the abolition of the slave-trade; the miracles of enthusiasm, as those reported of Swedenborg, Hohenlohe, and the Shakers; many obscure and yet contested facts, now arranged under the name of Animal Magnetism; prayer; eloquence; self-healing;

and the wisdom of children. These are examples of Reason's momentary grasp of the sceptre; the exertions of a power which exists not in time or space, but an instantaneous in-streaming causing power. The difference between the actual and the ideal force of man is happily figured by the schoolmen, in saying, that the knowledge of man is an evening knowledge, *vespertina cognitio*, but that of God is a morning knowledge, *matutina cognitio*.

The problem of restoring to the world original and eternal beauty is solved by the redemption of the soul. The ruin or the blank that we see when we look at nature, is in our own eye, The axis of vision is not coincident with the axis of things, and so they appear not transparent but opaque. The reason why the world lacks unity, and lies broken and in heaps, is because man is disunited with himself. He cannot be a naturalist until he satisfies all the demands of the spirit. Love is as much its demand as perception. Indeed, neither can be perfect without the other. In the uttermost meaning of the words, thought is devout, and devotion is thought. Deep calls unto deep. But in actual life, the marriage is not celebrated. There are innocent men who worship God after the tradition of their fathers, but their sense of duty has not yet extended to the use of all their faculties. And there are patient naturalists, but they freeze their subject under the wintry light of the understanding. Is not prayer also a study of truth—a sally of the soul into the unfound infinite? No man ever prayed heartily without learning something. But when a faithful thinker, resolute to detach every object from personal relations and see it in the light of thought, shall, at the same time, kindle science with the fire of the holiest affections, then will God go forth anew into the creation.

It will not need, when the mind is prepared for study, to search for objects. The invariable mark of wisdom is to see the miraculous in the common. What is a day? What is a year? What is summer? What is woman? What is a child? What is sleep? To our blindness, these things seem unaffecting. We make fables to hide the baldness of the fact and conform it, as we say, to the higher law of the mind. But when the fact is seen under the light of an idea, the gaudy fable fades and shrivels. We behold the real higher law. To the wise, therefore, a fact is true poetry, and the most beautiful of fables. These wonders are brought to our own door. You also are a man. Man and woman and their social life, poverty, labor, sleep, fear, fortune, are known to you.

Learn that none of these things is superficial, but that each phenomenon has its roots in the faculties and affections of the mind. Whilst the abstract question occupies your intellect, nature brings it in the concrete to be solved by your hands. It were a wise inquiry for the closet, to compare, point by point, especially at remarkable crises in life, our daily history with the rise and progress of ideas in the mind.

So shall we come to look at the world with new eyes. It shall answer the endless inquiry of the intellect—What is truth? and of the affections—What is good? by yielding itself passive to the educated Will. Then shall come to pass what my poet said: 'Nature is not fixed but fluid. Spirit alters, moulds, makes it. The immobility or bruteness of nature is the absence of spirit; to pure spirit it is fluid, it is volatile, it is obedient. Every spirit builds itself a house, and beyond its house a world, and beyond its world a heaven. Know then that the world exists for you. For you is the phenomenon perfect. What we are, that only can we see. All that Adam had, all that Cæsar could, you have and can do. Adam called his house, heaven and earth; Cæsar called his house, Rome; you perhaps call yours, a cobbler's trade; a hundred acres of ploughed land; or a scholar's garret. Yet line for line and point for point your dominion is as great as theirs, though without fine names. Build therefore your own world. As fast as you conform your life to the pure idea in your mind, that will unfold its great proportions. A correspondent revolution in things will attend the influx of the spirit. So fast will disagreeable appearances, swine, spiders, snakes, pests, madhouses, prisons, enemies, vanish; they are temporary and shall be no more seen. The sordor and filths of nature, the sun shall dry up and the wind exhale. As when the summer comes from the south the snowbanks melt and the face of the earth becomes green before it, so shall the advancing spirit create its ornaments along its path, and carry with it the beauty it visits and the song which enchants it; it shall draw beautiful faces, warm hearts, wise discourse, and heroic acts, around its way, until evil is no more seen. The kingdom of man over nature, which cometh not with observation—a dominion such as now is beyond his dream of God—he shall enter without more wonder than the blind man feels who is gradually restored to sight.'

THE AMERICAN
SCHOLAR

[This is the Phi Beta Kappa address that Emerson delivered at Harvard in 1837. It was received with great enthusiasm.]

THE AMERICAN SCHOLAR

Mr. President and Gentlemen:

I greet you on the recommencement of our literary year. Our anniversary is one of hope, and, perhaps, not enough of labor. We do not meet for games of strength or skill, for the recitation of histories, tragedies, and odes, like the ancient Greeks; for parliaments of love and poesy, like the Troubadours; nor for the advancement of science, like our contemporaries in the British and European capitals. Thus far, our holiday has been simply a friendly sign of the survival of the love of letters amongst a people too busy to give to letters any more. As such it is precious as the sign of an indestructible instinct. Perhaps the time is already come when it ought to be, and will be, something else; when the sluggard intellect of this continent will look from under its iron lids and fill the postponed expectation of the world with something better than the exertions of mechanical skill. Our day of dependence, our long apprenticeship to the learning of other lands, draws to a close. The millions that around us are rushing into life, cannot always be fed on the sere remains of foreign harvests. Events, actions arise, that must be sung, that will sing themselves. Who can doubt that poetry will revive and lead in a new age, as the star in the constellation Harp, which now flames in our zenith, astronomers announce, shall one day be the polestar for a thousand years?

In this hope I accept the topic which not only usage but the nature of our association seem to prescribe to this day—the American Scholar. Year by year we come up hither to read one more chapter of his biography. Let us inquire what light new days and events have thrown on his character and his hopes.

It is one of those fables which out of an unknown antiquity convey an unlooked-for wisdom, that the gods, in the beginning, divided Man into men, that he might be more helpful to himself; just as the hand was divided into fingers, the better to answer its end.

The old fable covers a doctrine ever new and sublime; that there is One Man—present to all particular men only partially, or through one faculty; and that you must take the whole society to find the whole man. Man is not a farmer, or a professor, or an engineer, but he is all. Man is priest, and scholar, and statesman, and producer, and soldier. In the divided or social state these functions are parcelled out to individuals, each of whom aims to do his stint of the joint work, whilst each other performs his. The fable implies that the individual, to possess himself, must sometimes return from his own labor to embrace all the other laborers. But, unfortunately, this original unit, this fountain of power, has been so distributed to multitudes, has been so minutely subdivided and peddled out, that it is spilled into drops, and cannot be gathered. The state of society is one in which the members have suffered amputation from the trunk, and strut about so many walking monsters—a good finger, a neck, a stomach, an elbow, but never a man.

Man is thus metamorphosed into a thing, into many things. The planter, who is Man sent out into the field to gather food, is seldom cheered by any idea of the true dignity of his ministry. He sees his bushel and his cart, and nothing beyond, and sinks into the farmer, instead of Man on the farm. The tradesman scarcely ever gives an ideal worth to his work, but is ridden by the routine of his craft, and the soul is subject to dollars. The priest becomes a form; the attorney a statute-book; the mechanic a machine; the sailor a rope of the ship.

In this distribution of functions the scholar is the delegated intellect. In the right state he is *Man Thinking*. In the degenerate state, when the victim of society, he tends to become a mere thinker, or still worse, the parrot of other men's thinking.

In this view of him, as Man Thinking, the theory of his office is contained. Him Nature solicits with all her placid, all her monitory pictures; him the past instructs; him the future invites. Is not indeed every man a student, and do not all things exist for the student's behoof? And, finally, is not the true scholar the only true master? But the old oracle said, "All things have two handles: beware of the wrong one." In life, too often, the scholar errs with mankind and forfeits his privilege. Let us see him in his school, and consider him in reference to the main influences he receives.

I. The first in time and the first in importance of the influences upon the mind is that of nature. Every day, the sun; and, after sunset, Night and her stars. Ever the winds blow; ever the grass grows. Every day, men and women, conversing—beholding and beholden. The scholar is he of all men whom this spectacle most engages. He must settle its value in his mind. What is nature to him? There is never a beginning, there is never an end, to the inexplicable continuity of this web of God, but always circular power returning into itself. Therein it resembles his own spirit, whose beginning, whose ending, he never can find—so entire, so boundless. Far too as her splendors shine, system on system shooting like rays, upward, downward, without centre, without circumference—in the mass and in the particle, Nature hastens to render account of herself to the mind. Classification begins. To the young mind every thing is individual, stands by itself. By and by, it finds how to join two things and see in them one nature; then three, then three thousand; and so, tyrannized over by its own unifying instinct, it goes on tying things together, diminishing anomalies, discovering roots running under ground whereby contrary and remote things cohere and flower out from one stem. It presently learns that since the dawn of history there has been a constant accumulation and classifying of facts. But what is classification but the perceiving that these objects are not chaotic, and are not foreign, but have a law which is also a law of the human mind? The astronomer discovers that geometry, a pure abstraction of the human mind, is the measure of planetary motion. The chemist finds proportions and intelligible method throughout matter; and science is nothing but the finding of analogy, identity, in the most remote parts. The ambitious soul sits down before each refractory fact; one after another reduces all strange constitutions, all new powers, to their class and their law, and goes on forever to animate the last fibre of organization, the outskirts of nature, by insight.

Thus to him, to this schoolboy under the bending dome of day, is suggested that he and it proceed from one root; one is leaf and one is flower; relation, sympathy, stirring in every vein. And what is that root? Is not that the soul of his soul? A thought too bold; a dream too wild. Yet when this spiritual light shall have revealed the law of more earthly natures—when he has learned to worship the soul, and to see that the natural philosophy that now is, is only the first gropings of its gigantic hand, he shall look forward to an ever expanding knowledge as to a becoming creator. He shall see that nature is the opposite of the soul, answering to it part for part. One is seal and one is print. Its beauty is the beauty of his own mind. Its laws are the laws of his own mind. Nature then becomes to him the measure of his attainments. So much of nature as he is ignorant of, so much of his own mind does he not yet possess. And, in fine, the ancient precept, "Know thyself," and the modern precept, "Study nature," become at last one maxim.

II. The next great influence into the spirit of the scholar is the mind of the Past—in whatever form, whether of literature, of art, of institutions, that mind is inscribed. Books are the best type of the influence of the past, and perhaps we shall get at the truth—learn the amount of this influence more conveniently—by considering their value alone.

The theory of books is noble. The scholar of the first age received into him the world around; brooded thereon; gave it the new arrangement of his own mind, and uttered it again. It came into him life; it went out from him truth. It came to him short-lived actions; it went out from him immortal thoughts. It came to him business; it went from him poetry. It was dead fact; now, it is quick thought. It can stand, and it can go. It now endures, it now flies, it now inspires. Precisely in proportion to the depth of mind from which it issued, so high does it soar, so long does it sing.

Or, I might say, it depends on how far the process had gone, of transmuting life into truth. In proportion to the completeness of the distillation, so will the purity and imperishableness of the product be. But none is quite perfect. As no air-pump can by any means make a perfect vacuum, so neither can any artist entirely exclude the conventional, the local, the perishable from his book, or write a book of pure thought, that shall be as efficient, in all respects, to a remote posterity, as to contemporaries, or rather to the second age. Each age, it is found, must write its own books; or rather, each generation for the next succeeding. The books of an older period will not fit this.

Yet hence arises a grave mischief. The sacredness which attaches to the act of creation, the act of thought, is transferred to the record. The poet chanting was felt to be a divine man: henceforth the chant is divine also. The writer was a just and wise spirit: henceforward it is settled the book is perfect; as love of the hero corrupts into worship of his statue. Instantly the book becomes noxious: the guide is a tyrant. The sluggish and perverted mind of the multitude, slow to open to the incursions of Reason, having once so opened, having once received this book, stands upon it, and makes an outcry if it is disparaged. Colleges are built on it. Books are written on it by thinkers, not by Man Thinking; by men of talent, that is, who start wrong, who set out from accepted dogmas, not from their own sight of principles. Meek young men grow up in libraries, believing it their duty to accept the views which Cicero, which Locke, which Bacon, have given; forgetful that Cicero, Locke, and Bacon were only young men in libraries when they wrote these books.

Hence, instead of Man Thinking, we have the bookworm. Hence the book-learned class, who value books, as such; not as related to nature and the human constitution, but as making a sort of Third Estate with the world and the soul. Hence the restorers of readings, the emendators, the bibliomaniacs of all degrees.

Books are the best of things, well used; abused, among the worst. What is the right use? What is the one end which all means go to effect? They are for nothing but to inspire. I had better never see a book than to be warped by its attraction clean out of my own orbit, and made a satellite instead of a system. The one thing in the world, of value, is the active soul. This every man is entitled to; this every man contains within him, although in almost all men obstructed and as yet unborn. The soul active sees absolute truth and utters truth, or creates. In this action it is genius; not the privilege of here and there a favorite, but the sound estate of every man. In its essence it is progressive. The book, the college, the school of art, the institution of any kind, stop with some past utterance of genius. This is good, say they—let us hold by this. They pin me down. They look backward and not forward. But genius looks forward: the eyes of man are set in his forehead, not in his hindhead: man hopes: genius creates. Whatever talents may be, if the man create not, the pure efflux of the Deity is not his; cinders and smoke there may be, but not yet flame. There are creative manners, there are creative actions, and creative words; manners, actions, words, that is, indicative of no custom or authority, but springing spontaneous from the mind's own sense of good and fair.

On the other part, instead of being its own seer, let it receive from another mind its truth, though it were in torrents of light, without periods of solitude, inquest, and self-recovery, and a fatal disservice is done. Genius is always sufficiently the enemy of genius by over-influence. The literature of every nation bears me witness. The English dramatic poets have Shakspearized now for two hundred years.

Undoubtedly there is a right way of reading, so it be sternly subordinated. Man Thinking must not be subdued by his instruments. Books are for the scholar's idle times. When he can read God directly, the hour is too precious to be wasted in other men's transcripts of their readings. But when the intervals of darkness come, as come they must—when the sun is hid and the stars withdraw their shining—we repair to the lamps which were kindled by their ray, to guide our steps to the East again, where the dawn is. We hear, that we may speak. The Arabian proverb says, "A fig tree, looking on a fig tree, becometh fruitful."

It is remarkable, the character of the pleasure we derive from the best books. They impress us with the conviction that one nature wrote and the same reads. We read the verses of one of the great English poets, of Chaucer, of Marvell, of Dryden, with the most modern joy—with a pleasure, I mean, which is in great part caused by the abstraction of all *time* from their verses. There is some awe mixed with the joy of our surprise, when this poet, who lived in some past world, two or three hundred years ago, says that which lies close to my own soul, that which I also had well-nigh thought and said. But for the evidence thence afforded to the philosophical doctrine of the identity of all minds, we should suppose some preëstablished harmony, some foresight of souls that were to be, and some preparation of stores for their future wants, like the fact observed in insects, who lay up food before death for the young grub they shall never see.

I would not be hurried by any love of system, by any exaggeration of instincts, to underrate the Book. We all know, that as the human body can be nourished on any food, though it were boiled grass and the broth of shoes, so the human mind can be fed by any knowledge. And great and heroic men have existed who had almost no other information than by the printed page. I only would say that it needs a strong head to bear that diet. One must be an inventor to read well. As the proverb says, "He that would bring home the wealth of the Indies, must carry out the wealth of the Indies." There is then creative reading as well as creative writing. When the mind is braced by labor and invention, the page of whatever book we read becomes luminous with manifold allusion. Every sentence is doubly significant, and the sense of our author is as broad as the world. We then see, what is always true, that as the seer's hour of vision is short and rare among heavy days and months, so is its record, perchance, the least part of his volume. The discerning will read, in his Plato or Shakspeare, only that least part— only the authentic utterances of the oracles; all the rest he rejects, were it never so many times Plato's and Shakspeare's.

Of course there is a portion of reading quite indispensable to a wise man. History and exact science he must learn by laborious reading. Colleges, in like manner, have their indispensable office—to teach elements. But they can only highly serve us when they aim not to drill, but to create; when they gather from far every ray of various genius to their hospitable halls, and by the concentrated fires, set the hearts of their youth on flame. Thought and knowledge are natures in which apparatus and pretension avail nothing. Gowns and pecuniary foundations, though of towns of gold, can never countervail the least sentence or syllable of wit. Forget this, and our American colleges will recede in their public importance, whilst they grow richer every year.

III. There goes in the world a notion that the scholar should be a recluse, a valetudinarian—as unfit for any handiwork or public labor as a penknife for an axe. The so-called "practical men" sneer at speculative men, as if, because they speculate or *see*, they could do nothing. I have heard it said that the clergy—who are always, more universally than any other class, the scholars of their day—are addressed as women; that the rough, spontaneous conversation of men they do not hear, but only a mincing and diluted speech. They are often virtually disfranchised; and indeed there are advocates for their celibacy. As far as this is true of the studious classes, it is not just and wise. Action is with the scholar subordinate, but it is essential. Without it he is not yet man. Without it thought can never ripen into truth. Whilst the world hangs before the eye as a cloud of beauty, we cannot even see its beauty. Inaction is cowardice, but there can be no scholar without the heroic mind. The preamble of thought, the transition through which it passes from the unconscious to the conscious, is action. Only so much do I know, as I have lived. Instantly we know whose words are loaded with life, and whose not.

The world—this shadow of the soul, or *other me*—lies wide around. Its attractions are the keys which unlock my thoughts and make me acquainted with myself. I run eagerly into this resounding tumult. I grasp the hands of those next me, and take my place in the ring to suffer and to work, taught by an instinct that so shall the dumb abyss be vocal with speech. I pierce its order; I dissipate its fear; I dispose of it within the circuit of my expanding life. So much only of life as I know by experience, so much of the wilderness have I vanquished and planted, or so far have I extended my being, my dominion. I do not see how any man can afford, for the sake of his nerves and his nap, to spare any action in which he can partake. It is pearls and rubies to his discourse. Drudgery, calamity, exasperation, want, are instructors in eloquence and wisdom. The true scholar grudges every opportunity of action past by, as a loss of power. It is the raw material out of which the intellect moulds her splendid products. A strange process too, this by which experience is converted into thought, as a mulberry leaf is converted into satin. The manufacture goes forward at all hours.

The actions and events of our childhood and youth are now matters of calmest observation. They lie like fair pictures in the air. Not so with our recent actions—with the business which we now have in hand. On this we are quite unable to speculate. Our affections as yet circulate through it. We no more feel or know it than we feel the feet, or the hand, or the brain of our body. The new deed is yet a part of life—remains for a time immersed in our unconscious life. In some contemplative hour it detaches itself from the life like a ripe fruit, to become a thought of the mind. Instantly it is raised, transfigured; the corruptible has put on incorruption. Henceforth it is an object of beauty, however base its origin and neighborhood. Observe too the impossibility of antedating this act. In its grub state, it cannot fly, it cannot shine, it is a dull grub. But suddenly, without observation, the selfsame thing unfurls beautiful wings, and is an angel of wisdom. So is there no fact, no event, in our private history, which shall not, sooner or later, lose its adhesive, inert form, and astonish us by soaring from our body into the empyrean. Cradle and infancy, school and playground, the fear of boys, and dogs, and ferrules, the love of little maids and berries, and many another fact that once filled the whole sky, are gone already; friend and relative, profession and party, town and country, nation and world, must also soar and sing.

Of course, he who has put forth his total strength in fit actions has the richest return of wisdom. I will not shut myself out of this globe of action, and transplant an oak into a flowerpot, there to hunger and pine; nor trust the revenue of some single faculty, and exhaust one vein of thought, much like those Savoyards, who, getting their livelihood by carving shepherds, shepherdesses, and smoking Dutchmen, for all Europe, went out one day to the mountain to find stock, and discovered that they had whittled up the last of their pine trees. Authors we have, in numbers, who have written out their vein, and who, moved by a commendable prudence, sail for Greece or Palestine, follow the trapper into the prairie, or ramble round Algiers, to replenish their merchantable stock.

If it were only for a vocabulary, the scholar would be covetous of action. Life is our dictionary. Years are well spent in country labors; in town; in the insight into trades and manufactures; in frank intercourse with many men and women; in science; in art; to the one end of mastering in all their facts a language by which to illustrate and embody our perceptions. I learn immediately from any speaker how much he has already lived, through the poverty or the splendor of his speech. Life lies behind us as the quarry from whence we get tiles and copestones for the masonry of to-day. This is the way to learn grammar. Colleges and books only copy the language which the field and the work-yard made.

But the final value of action, like that of books, and better than books, is that it is a resource. That great principle of Undulation in nature, that shows itself in the inspiring and expiring of the breath; in desire and satiety; in the ebb and flow of the sea; in day and night; in heat and cold; and, as yet more deeply ingrained in every atom and every fluid, is known to us under the name of Polarity—these "fits of easy transmission and reflection," as Newton called them, are the law of nature because they are the law of spirit.

The mind now thinks, now acts, and each fit reproduces the other. When the artist has exhausted his materials, when the fancy no longer paints, when thoughts are no longer apprehended and books are a weariness—he has always the resources to live. Character is higher than intellect. Thinking is the function. Living is the functionary. The stream retreats to its source. A great soul will be strong to live, as well as strong to think. Does he lack organ or medium to impart his truths? He can still fall back on this elemental force of living them. This is a total act. Thinking is a partial act. Let the grandeur of justice shine in his affairs. Let the beauty of affection cheer his lowly roof. Those "far from fame", who dwell and act with him, will feel the force of his constitution in the doings and passages of the day better than it can be measured by any public and designed display. Time shall teach him that the scholar loses no hour which the man lives. Herein he unfolds the sacred germ of his instinct, screened from influence. What is lost in seemliness is gained in strength. Not out of those on whom systems of education have exhausted their culture, comes the helpful giant to destroy the old or to build the new, but out of unhandselled savage nature; out of terrible Druids and Berserkers come at last Alfred and Shakspeare.

I hear therefore with joy whatever is beginning to be said of the dignity and necessity of labor to every citizen. There is virtue yet in the hoe and the spade, for learned as well as for unlearned hands. And labor is everywhere welcome; always we are invited to work; only be this limitation observed, that a man shall not for the sake of wider activity sacrifice any opinion to the popular judgments and modes of action.

I have now spoken of the education of the scholar by nature, by books, and by action. It remains to say somewhat of his duties.

They are such as become Man Thinking. They may all be comprised in self-trust. The office of the scholar is to cheer, to raise, and to guide men by showing them facts amidst appearances. He plies the slow, unhonored, and unpaid task of observation. Flamsteed and Herschel, in their glazed observatories, may catalogue the stars with the praise of all men, and the results being splendid and useful, honor is sure. But he, in his private observatory, cataloguing obscure and nebulous stars of the human mind, which as yet no man has thought of as such—watching days and months sometimes for a few facts; correcting still his old records; must relinquish display and immediate fame. In the long period of his preparation he must betray often an ignorance and shiftlessness in popular arts, incurring the disdain of the able who shoulder him aside. Long he must stammer in his speech; often forego the living for the dead. Worse yet, he must accept—how often!—poverty and solitude. For the ease and pleasure of treading the old road, accepting the fashions, the education, the religion of society, he takes the cross of making his own, and, of course, the self-accusation, the faint heart, the frequent uncertainty and loss of time, which are the nettles and tangling vines in the way of the self-relying and self-directed; and the state of virtual hostility in which he seems to stand to society, and especially to educated society. For all this loss and scorn, what off-set? He is to find consolation in exercising the highest functions of human nature. He is one who raises himself from private considerations and breathes and lives on public and illustrious thoughts. He is the world's eye. He is the world's heart. He is to resist the vulgar prosperity that retrogrades ever to barbarism, by preserving and communicating heroic sentiments, noble biographies, melodious verse, and the conclusions of history. Whatsoever oracles the human heart, in all emergencies, in all solemn hours, has uttered as its commentary on the world of actions—these he shall receive and impart. And whatsoever new verdict Reason from her inviolable seat pronounces on the passing men and events of to-day—this he shall hear and promulgate.

These being his functions, it becomes him to feel all confidence in himself, and to defer never to the popular cry. He and he only knows the world. The world of any moment is the merest appearance. Some great decorum, some fetish of a government, some ephemeral trade, or war, or man, is cried up by half mankind and cried down by the other half, as if all depended on this particular up or down. The odds are that the whole question is not worth the poorest thought which the scholar has lost in listening to the controversy. Let him not quit his belief that a popgun is a popgun, though the ancient and honorable of the earth affirm it to be the crack of doom. In silence, in steadiness, in severe abstraction, let him hold by himself; add observation to observation, patient of neglect, patient of reproach, and bide his own time—happy enough if he can satisfy himself alone that this day he has seen something truly. Success treads on every right step. For the instinct is sure, that prompts him to tell his brother what he thinks. He then learns that in going down into the secrets of his own mind he has descended into the secrets of all minds. He learns that he who has mastered any law in his private thoughts, is master to that extent of all men whose language he speaks, and of all into whose language his own can be translated. The poet, in utter solitude remembering his spontaneous thoughts and recording them, is found to have recorded that which men in crowded cities find true for them also. The orator distrusts at first the fitness of his frank confessions, his want of knowledge of the persons he addresses, until he finds that he is the complement of his hearers; that they drink his words because he fulfils for them their own nature; the deeper he dives into his privatest, secretest presentiment, to his wonder he finds this is the most acceptable, most public, and universally true. The people delight in it; the better part of every man feels, This is my music; this is myself.

In self-trust all the virtues are comprehended. Free should the scholar be—free and brave. Free even to the definition of freedom, "without any hindrance that does not arise out of his own constitution." Brave; for fear is a thing which a scholar by his very function puts behind him. Fear always springs from ignorance. It is a shame to him if his tranquillity, amid dangerous times, arise from the presumption that like children and women his is a protected class; or if he seek a temporary peace by the diversion of his thoughts from politics or vexed questions, hiding his head like an ostrich in the flowering bushes, peeping into microscopes, and turning rhymes, as a boy whistles to keep his courage up. So is the danger a danger still; so is the fear worse. Manlike let him turn and face it. Let him look into its eye and search its nature, inspect its origin—see the whelping of this lion—which lies no great way back; he will then find in himself a perfect comprehension of its nature and extent; he will have made his hands meet on the other side, and can henceforth defy it and pass on superior. The world is his who can see through its pretension. What deafness, what stone-blind custom, what overgrown error you behold is there only by sufferance—by your sufferance. See it to be a lie, and you have already dealt it its mortal blow.

Yes, we are the cowed—we the trustless. It is a mischievous notion that we are come late into nature; that the world was finished a long time ago. As the world was plastic and fluid in the hands of God, so it is ever to so much of his attributes as we bring to it. To ignorance and sin, it is flint. They adapt themselves to it as they may; but in proportion as a man has any thing in him divine, the firmament flows before him and takes his signet and form. Not he is great who can alter matter, but he who can alter my state of mind. They are the kings of the world who give the color of their present thought to all nature and all art, and persuade men by the cheerful serenity of their carrying the matter, that this thing which they do is the apple which the ages have desired to pluck, now at last ripe, and inviting nations to the harvest. The great man makes the great thing. Wherever Macdonald sits, there is the head of the table. Linnæus makes botany the most alluring of studies, and wins it from the farmer and the herb-woman; Davy, chem-

istry; and Cuvier, fossils. The day is always his who works in it with
serenity and great aims. The unstable estimates of men crowd to him
whose mind is filled with a truth, as the heaped waves of the Atlantic
follow the moon.

For this self-trust, the reason is deeper than can be fathomed—
darker than can be enlightened. I might not carry with me the feeling of
my audience in stating my own belief. But I have already shown the
ground of my hope, in adverting to the doctrine that man is one. I
believe man has been wronged; he has wronged himself. He has almost
lost the light that can lead him back to his prerogatives. Men are
become of no account. Men in history, men in the world of to-day, are
bugs, are spawn, and are called "the mass" and "the herd." In a century, in a millennium, one or two men; that is to say, one or two
approximations to the right state of every man. All the rest behold in
the hero or the poet their own green and crude being—ripened; yes,
and are content to be less, so that may attain to its full stature. What
a testimony, full of grandeur, full of pity, is borne to the demands of
his own nature, by the poor clansman, the poor partisan, who rejoices
in the glory of his chief. The poor and the low find some amends to
their immense moral capacity, for their acquiescence in a political and
social inferiority. They are content to be brushed like flies from the
path of a great person, so that justice shall be done by him to that common nature which it is the dearest desire of all to see enlarged and
glorified. They sun themselves in the great man's light, and feel it to be
their own element. They cast the dignity of man from their downtrod
selves upon the shoulders of a hero, and will perish to add one drop of
blood to make that great heart beat, those giant sinews combat and conquer. He lives for us, and we live in him.

Men, such as they are, very naturally seek money or power; and
power because it is as good as money—the "spoils," so called "of
office." And why not? for they aspire to the highest, and this, in their
sleep-walking, they dream is highest. Wake them and they shall quit
the false good and leap to the true, and leave governments to clerks and
desks. This revolution is to be wrought by the gradual domestication of
the idea of Culture. The main enterprise of the world for splendor, for
extent, is the upbuilding of a man. Here are the materials strewn along
the ground. The private life of one man shall be a more illustrious
monarchy, more formidable to its enemy, more sweet and serene in its

influence to its friend, than any kingdom in history. For a man, rightly viewed, comprehendeth the particular natures of all men. Each philosopher, each bard, each actor has only done for me, as by a delegate, what one day I can do for myself. The books which once we valued more than the apple of the eye, we have quite exhausted. What is that but saying that we have come up with the point of view which the universal mind took through the eyes of one scribe; we have been that man, and have passed on. First, one, then another, we drain all cisterns, and waxing greater by all these supplies, we crave a better and more abundant food. The man has never lived that can feed us ever. The human mind cannot be enshrined in a person who shall set a barrier on any one side to this unbounded, unboundable empire. It is one central fire, which, flaming now out of the lips of Etna, lightens the capes of Sicily, and now out of the throat of Vesuvius, illuminates the towers and vineyards of Naples. It is one light which beams out of a thousand stars. It is one soul which animates all men.

But I have dwelt perhaps tediously upon this abstraction of the Scholar. I ought not to delay longer to add what I have to say of nearer reference to the time and to this country.

Historically, there is thought to be a difference in the ideas which predominate over successive epochs, and there are data for marking the genius of the Classic, of the Romantic, and now of the Reflective or Philosophical age. With the views I have intimated of the oneness or the identity of the mind through all individuals, I do not much dwell on these differences. In fact, I believe each individual passes through all three. The boy is a Greek; the youth, romantic; the adult, reflective. I deny not, however, that a revolution in the leading idea may be distinctly enough traced.

Our age is bewailed as the age of Introversion. Must that needs be evil? We, it seems, are critical; we are embarrassed with second thoughts; we cannot enjoy any thing for hankering to know whereof the pleasure consists; we are lined with eyes; we see with our feet; the time is infected with Hamlet's unhappiness—

"Sicklied o'er with the pale cast of thought."

It is so bad then? Sight is the last thing to be pitied. Would we be

· ·

blind? Do we fear lest we should outsee nature and God, and drink
truth dry? I look upon the discontent of the literary class as a mere
announcement of the fact that they find themselves not in the state of
mind of their fathers, and regret the coming state as untried; as a boy
dreads the water before he has learned that he can swim. If there is any
period one would desire to be born in, is it not the age of Revolution;
when the old and the new stand side by side and admit of being compared; when the energies of all men are searched by fear and by hope;
when the historic glories of the old can be compensated by the rich possibilities of the new era? This time, like all times, is a very good one,
if we but know what to do with it.

I read with some joy of the auspicious signs of the coming days,
as they glimmer already through poetry and art, through philosophy
and science, through church and state.

One of these signs is the fact that the same movement which
effected the elevation of what was called the lowest class in the state,
assumed in literature a very marked and as benign an aspect. Instead of
the sublime and beautiful, the near, the low, the common, was explored
and poetized. That which had been negligently trodden under foot by
those who were harnessing and provisioning themselves for long journeys into far countries, is suddenly found to be richer than all foreign
parts. The literature of the poor, the feelings of the child, the philosophy of the street, the meaning of household life, are the topics of the
time. It is a great stride. It is a sign—is it not?—of new vigor when the
extremities are made active, when currents of warm life run into the
hands and the feet. I ask not for the great, the remote, the romantic;
what is doing in Italy or Arabia; what is Greek art, or Provencal min-
strelsy; I embrace the common, I explore and sit at the feet of the
familiar, the low. Give me insight into to-day, and you may have the
antique and future worlds. What would we really know the meaning of?
The meal in the firkin; the milk in the pan; the ballad in the street; the
news of the boat; the glance of the eye; the form and the gait of the
body; show me the ultimate reason of these matters; show me the sublime presence of the highest spiritual cause lurking, as always it does
lurk, in these suburbs and extremities of nature; let me see every trifle
bristling with the polarity that ranges it instantly on an eternal law; and
the shop, the plough, and the ledger referred to the like cause by which

light undulates and poets sing; and the world lies no longer a dull miscellany and lumber-room, but has form and order; there is no trifle,
there is no puzzle, but one design unites and animates the farthest pinnacle and the lowest trench.

This idea has inspired the genius of Goldsmith, Burns, Cowper,
and, in a newer time, of Goethe, Wordsworth, and Carlyle. This idea
they have differently followed and with various success. In contrast
with their writing, the style of Pope, of Johnson, of Gibbon, looks cold
and pedantic. This writing is blood-warm. Man is surprised to find that
things near are not less beautiful and wondrous than things remote.
The near explains the far. The drop is a small ocean. A man is related
to all nature. This perception of the worth of the vulgar is fruitful in
discoveries. Goethe, in this very thing the most modern of the moderns, has shown us, as none ever did, the genius of the ancients.

There is one man of genius who has done much for this philosophy
of life, whose literary value has never yet been rightly estimated; I mean
Emanuel Swedenborg. The most imaginative of men, yet writing with
the precision of a mathematician, he endeavored to engraft a purely
philosophical Ethics on the popular Christianity of his time. Such an
attempt of course must have difficulty which no genius could sur-
mount. But he saw and showed the connection between nature and the
affections of the soul. He pierced the emblematic or spiritual character
of the visible, audible, tangible word. Especially did his shade-loving
muse hover over and interpret the lower parts of nature; he showed the
mysterious bond that allies moral evil to the foul material forms, and
has given in epical parables a theory of insanity, of beasts, of unclean
and fearful things.

Another sign of our times, also marked by an analogous political
movement, is the new importance given to the single person. Every
thing that tends to insulate the individual—to surround him with barriers of natural respect, so that each man shall feel the world is his, and
man shall treat with man as a sovereign state with a sovereign state—
tends to true union as well as greatness. "I learned," said the
melancholy Pestalozzi, "that no man in God's wide earth is either willing or able to help any other man." Help must come from the bosom
alone. The scholar is that man who must take up into himself all the
ability of the time, all the contributions of the past, all the hopes of the
future. He must be an university of knowledges. If there be one lesson

more than another which should pierce his ear, it is, The world is nothing, the man is all; in yourself is the law of all nature, and you know
not yet how a globule of sap ascends; in yourself slumbers the whole
of Reason; it is for you to know all; it is for you to dare all. Mr.
President and Gentlemen, this confidence in the unsearched might of
man belongs, by all motives, by all prophecy, by all preparation, to the
American Scholar. We have listened too long to the courtly muses of
Europe. The spirit of the American free-man is already suspected to
be timid, imitative, tame. Public and private avarice make the air we
breathe thick and fat. The scholar is decent, indolent, complaisant. See
already the tragic consequence. The mind of this country, taught to aim
at low objects, eats upon itself. There is no work for any but the decorous and the complaisant. Young men of the fairest promise, who begin
life upon our shores, inflated by the mountain winds, shined upon by
all the stars of God, find the earth below not in unison with these, but
are hindered from action by the disgust which the principles on which
business is managed inspire, and turn drudges, or die of disgust, some
of them suicides. What is the remedy? They did not yet see, and thousands of young men as hopeful now crowding to the barriers for the
career do not yet see, that if the single man plant himself indomitably
on his instincts, and there abide, the huge world will come round to
him. Patience—patience; with the shades of all the good and great for
company; and for solace the perspective of your own infinite life; and
for work the study and the communication of principles, the making
those instincts prevalent, the conversion of the world. Is it not the chief
disgrace in the world, not to be an unit; not to be reckoned one character; not to yield that peculiar fruit which each man was created to
bear, but to be reckoned in the gross, in the hundred, or the thousand,
of the party, the section, to which we belong; and our opinion predicted
geographically, as the north, or the south? Not so, brothers and
friends—please God, ours shall not be so. We will walk on our own
feet; we will work with our own hands; we will speak our own minds.
The study of letters shall be no longer a name for pity, for doubt, and
for sensual indulgence. The dread of man and the love of man shall be
a wall of defence and a wreath of joy around all. A nation of men will
for the first time exist, because each believes himself inspired by the
Divine Soul which also inspires all men.

AN ADDRESS

[*This address was delivered before the senior class of the Harvard Divinity School on Sunday evening, July 15, 1838. Emerson had been invited to give it, not by the officers of the school, but by the senior class. What Emerson said was so objectionable to many clergymen that the officers of the school publicly disclaimed responsibility for it. Nearly thirty years passed before Emerson was invited again to speak at Harvard.*]

AN ADDRESS

IN THIS refulgent summer, it has been a luxury to draw the breath of life. The grass grows, the buds burst, the meadow is spotted with fire and gold in the tint of flowers. The air is full of birds, and sweet with the breath of the pine, the balm-of-Gilead, and the new hay. Night brings no gloom to the heart with its welcome shade. Through the transparent darkness the stars pour their almost spiritual rays. Man under them seems a young child, and his huge globe a toy. The cool night bathes the world as with a river, and prepares his eyes again for the crimson dawn. The mystery of nature was never displayed more happily. The corn and the wine have been freely dealt to all creatures, and the never-broken silence with which the old bounty goes forward has not yielded yet one word of explanation. One is constrained to respect the perfection of this world in which our senses converse. How wide; how rich; what invitation from every property it gives to every faculty of man! In its fruitful soils; in its navigable sea; in its mountains of metal and stone; in its forests of all woods; in its animals; in its chemical ingredients; in the powers and path of light, heat, attraction and life, it is well worth the pith and heart of great men to subdue and enjoy it. The planters, the mechanics, the inventors, the astronomers, the builders of cities, and the captains, history delights to honor.

But when the mind opens and reveals the laws which traverse the universe and make things what they are, then shrinks the great world at once into a mere illustration and fable of this mind. What am I? and What is? asks the human spirit with a curiosity new-kindled, but never to be quenched. Behold these outrunning laws, which our imperfect apprehension can see tend this way and that, but not come full circle. Behold these infinite relations, so like, so unlike; many, yet one. I would study, I would know, I would admire forever. These works of thought have been the entertainments of the human spirit in all ages.

A more secret, sweet, and overpowering beauty appears to man when his heart and mind open to the sentiment of virtue. Then he is instructed in what is above him. He learns that his being is without

63

. . . .

bound; that to the good, to the perfect, he is born, low as he now lies in evil and weakness. That which he venerates is still his own, though he has not realized it yet. *He ought.* He knows the sense of that grand word, though his analysis fails to render account of it. When in innocency or when by intellectual perception he attains to say—"I love the Right; Truth is beautiful within and without for evermore. Virtue, I am thine; save me; use me; thee will I serve, day and night, in great, in small, that I may be not virtuous, but virtue;" then is the end of the creation answered, and God is well pleased.

The sentiment of virtue is a reverence and delight in the presence of certain divine laws. It perceives that this homely game of life we play, covers, under what seem foolish details, principles that astonish. The child amidst his baubles is learning the action of light, motion, gravity, muscular force; and in the game of human life, love, fear, justice, appetite, man, and God, interact. These laws refuse to be adequately stated. They will not be written out on paper, or spoken by the tongue. They elude our persevering thought; yet we read them hourly in each other's faces, in each other's actions, in our own remorse. The moral traits which are all globed into every virtuous act and thought—in speech we must sever, and describe or suggest by painful enumeration of many particulars. Yet, as this sentiment is the essence of all religion, let me guide your eye to the precise objects of the sentiment, by an enumeration of some of those classes of facts in which this element is conspicuous.

The intuition of the moral sentiment is an insight of the perfection of the laws of the soul. These laws execute themselves. They are out of time, out of space, and not subject to circumstance. Thus in the soul of man there is a justice whose retributions are instant and entire. He who does a good deed is instantly ennobled. He who does a mean deed is by the action itself contracted. He who puts off impurity, thereby puts on purity. If a man is at heart just, then in so far is he God; the safety of God, the immortality of God, the majesty of God do enter into that man with justice. If a man dissemble, deceive, he deceives himself, and goes out of acquaintance with his own being. A man in the view of absolute goodness, adores, with total humility. Every step so downward, is a step upward. The man who renounces himself, comes to himself.

See how this rapid intrinsic energy worketh everywhere, righting wrongs, correcting appearances, and bringing up facts to a harmony with thoughts. Its operation in life, though slow to the senses, is at last as sure as in the soul. By it a man is made the Providence to himself, dispensing good to his goodness, and evil to his sin. Character is always known. Thefts never enrich; alms never impoverish; murder will speak out of stone walls. The least admixture of a lie—for example, the taint of vanity, any attempt to make a good impression, a favorable appearance—will instantly vitiate the effect. But speak the truth, and all nature and all spirits help you with unexpected furtherance. Speak the truth, and all things alive or brute are vouchers, and the very roots of the grass underground there do seem to stir and move to bear you witness. See again the perfection of the Law as it applies itself to the affections, and becomes the law of society. As we are, so we associate. The good, by affinity, seek the good; the vile, by affinity, the vile. Thus of their own volition, souls proceed into heaven, into hell.

These facts have always suggested to man the sublime creed that the world is not the product of manifold power, but of one will, of one mind; and that one mind is everywhere active, in each ray of the star, in each wavelet of the pool; and whatever opposes that will is everywhere balked and baffled, because things are made so, and not otherwise. Good is positive. Evil is merely privative, not absolute: it is like cold, which is the privation of heat. All evil is so much death or nonentity. Benevolence is absolute and real. So much benevolence as a man hath, so much life hath he. For all things proceed out of this same spirit, which is differently named love, justice, temperance, in its different applications, just as the ocean receives different names on the several shores which it washes. All things proceed out of the same spirit, and all things conspire with it. Whilst a man seeks good ends, he is strong by the whole strength of nature. In so far as he roves from these ends, he bereaves himself of power, or auxiliaries; his being shrinks out of all remote channels, he becomes less and less, a mote, a point, until absolute badness is absolute death.

The perception of this law of laws awakens in the mind a sentiment which we call the religious sentiment, and which makes our highest happiness. Wonderful is its power to charm and to command. It is a mountain air. It is the embalmer of the world. It is myrrh and storax, and chlorine and rosemary. It makes the sky and the hills sublime, and the silent song of the stars is it. By it is the universe made safe and habitable, not by science or power. Thought may work cold and intransitive in things, and find no end or unity; but the dawn of the sentiment of virtue on the heart, gives and is the assurance that Law is sovereign over all natures; and the worlds, time, space, eternity, do seem to break out into joy.

This sentiment is divine and deifying. It is the beatitude of man. It makes him illimitable. Through it, the soul first knows itself. It corrects the capital mistake of the infant man, who seeks to be great by following the great, and hopes to derive advantages *from another*—by showing the fountain of all good to be in himself, and that he, equally with every man, is an inlet into the deeps of Reason. When he says, "I ought;" when love warms him; when he chooses, warned from on high, the good and great deed; then, deep melodies wander through his soul from Supreme Wisdom. Then he can worship, and be enlarged by his worship; for he can never go behind this sentiment. In the sublimest flights of the soul, rectitude is never surmounted, love is never outgrown.

This sentiment lies at the foundation of society, and successively creates all forms of worship. The principle of veneration never dies out. Man fallen into superstition, into sensuality, is never quite without the visions of the moral sentiment. In like manner, all the expressions of this sentiment are sacred and permanent in proportion to their purity. The expressions of this sentiment affect us more than all other compositions. The sentences of the oldest time, which ejaculate this piety, are still fresh and fragrant. This thought dwelled always deepest in the minds of men in the devout and contemplative East; not alone in Palestine, where it reached its purest expression, but in Egypt, in Persia, in India, in China. Europe has always owed to oriental genius its divine impulses. What these holy bards said, all sane men found agreeable and true. And the unique impression of Jesus upon mankind, whose name is not so much written as ploughed into the history of this world, is proof of the subtle virtue of this infusion.

Meantime, whilst the doors of the temple stand open, night and day, before every man, and the oracles of this truth cease never, it is guarded by one stern condition; this, namely, it is an intuition. It cannot be received at second hand. Truly speaking, it is not instruction, but provocation, that I can receive from another soul. What he announces, I must find true in me, or reject; and on his word, or as his second, be he who he may, I can accept nothing. On the contrary, the absence of this primary faith is the presence of degradation. As is the flood, so is the ebb. Let this faith depart, and the very words it spake and the things it made become false and hurtful. Then falls the church, the state, art, letters, life. The doctrine of the divine nature being forgotten, a sickness infects and dwarfs the constitution. Once man was all; now he is an appendage, a nuisance. And because the indwelling Supreme Spirit cannot wholly be got rid of, the doctrine of it suffers this perversion, that the divine nature is attributed to one or two persons, and denied to all the rest, and denied with fury. The doctrine of inspiration is lost; the base doctrine of the majority of voices usurps the place of the doctrine of the soul. Miracles, prophecy, poetry, the ideal life, the holy life, exist as ancient history merely; they are not in the belief, nor in the aspiration of society; but, when suggested, seem ridiculous. Life is comic or pitiful as soon as the high ends of being fade out of sight, and man becomes near-sighted, and can only attend to what addresses the senses.

These general views, which, whilst they are general, none will contest, find abundant illustration in the history of religion, and especially in the history of the Christian church. In that, all of us have had our birth and nurture. The truth contained in that, you, my young friends, are now setting forth to teach. As the Cultus, or established worship of the civilized world, it has great historical interest for us. Of its blessed words, which have been the consolation of humanity, you need not that I should speak. I shall endeavor to discharge my duty to you on this occasion, by pointing out two errors in its administration, which daily appear more gross from the point of view we have just now taken.

Jesus Christ belonged to the true race of prophets. He saw with open eye the mystery of the soul. Drawn by its severe harmony, ravished with its beauty, he lived in it, and had his being there. Alone in all history he estimated the greatness of man. One man was true to what is in you and me. He saw that God incarnates himself in man, and evermore goes forth anew to take possession of his World. He said, in this jubilee of sublime emotion, 'I am divine. Through me, God acts; through me, speaks. Would you see God, see me; or see thee, when thou also thinkest as I now think.' But what a distortion did his doctrine and memory suffer in the same, in the next, and the following ages! There is no doctrine of the Reason which will bear to be taught by the Understanding. The understanding caught this high chant from the poet's lips, and said, in the next age, 'This was Jehovah come down out of heaven. I will kill you, if you say he was a man.' The idioms of his language and the figures of his rhetoric have usurped the place of his truth; and churches are not built on his principles, but on his tropes. Christianity became a Mythus, as the poetic teaching of Greece and of Egypt, before. He spoke of miracles; for he felt that man's life was a miracle, and all that man doth, and he knew that this daily miracle shines as the character ascends. But the word Miracle, as pronounced by Christian churches, gives a false impression; it is Monster. It is not one with the blowing clover and the falling rain.

He felt respect for Moses and the prophets, but no unfit tenderness at postponing their initial revelations to the hour and the man that now is; to the eternal revelation in the heart. Thus was he a true man. Having seen that the law in us is commanding, he would not suffer it to be commanded. Boldly, with hand, and heart, and life, he declared it was God. Thus is he, as I think, the only soul in history who has appreciated the worth of man.

1. In this point of view we become sensible of the first defect of historical Christianity. Historical Christianity has fallen into the error that corrupts all attempts to communicate religion. As it appears to us, and as it has appeared for ages, it is not the doctrine of the soul, but an exaggeration of the personal, the positive, the ritual. It has dwelt, it dwells, with noxious exaggeration about the person of Jesus. The soul knows no persons. It invites every man to expand to the full circle of the universe, and will have no preferences but those of spontaneous love. But by this eastern monarchy of a Christianity, which indolence and fear have built, the friend of man is made the injurer of man. The manner in which his name is surrounded with expressions which were once sallies of admiration and love, but are now petrified into official titles, kills all generous sympathy and liking. All who hear me, feel that the language that describes Christ to Europe and America is not the style of friendship and enthusiasm to a good and noble heart, but is appropriated and formal—paints a demigod, as the Orientals or the Greeks would describe Osiris or Apollo. Accept the injurious impositions of our early catechetical instruction, and even honesty and self-denial were but splendid sins, if they did not wear the Christian name. One would rather be

"A pagan, suckled in a creed outworn,"

than to be defrauded of his manly right in coming into nature and finding not names and places, not land and professions, but even virtue and truth foreclosed and monopolized. You shall not be a man even. You shall not own the world; you shall not dare and live after the infinite Law that is in you, and in company with the infinite Beauty which heaven and earth reflect to you in all lovely forms; but you must subordinate your nature to Christ's nature; you must accept our interpretations, and take his portrait as the vulgar draw it.

That is always best which gives me to myself. The sublime is excited in me by the great stoical doctrine, Obey thyself. That which shows God in me, fortifies me. That which shows God out of me, makes me a wart and a wen. There is no longer a necessary reason for my being. Already the long shadows of untimely oblivion creep over me, and I shall decease forever.

The divine bards are the friends of my virtue, of my intellect, of my strength. They admonish me that the gleams which flash across my mind are not mine, but God's; that they had the like, and were not disobedient to the heavenly vision. So I love them. Noble provocations go out from them, inviting me to resist evil; to subdue the world; and to Be. And thus, by his holy thoughts, Jesus serves us, and thus only. To aim to convert a man by miracles is a profanation of the soul. A true conversion, a true Christ, is now, as always, to be made by the reception of beautiful sentiments. It is true that a great and rich soul, like his, falling among the simple, does so preponderate, that, as his did, it names the world. The world seems to them to exist for him, and they have not yet drunk so deeply of his sense as to see that only by coming again to themselves, or to God in themselves, can they grow forevermore. It is a low benefit to give me something; it is a high benefit to enable me to do somewhat of myself. The time is coming when all men will see that the gift of God to the soul is not a vaunting, overpowering, excluding sanctity, but a sweet, natural goodness, a goodness like thine and mine, and that so invites thine and mine to be and to grow.

The injustice of the vulgar tone of preaching is not less flagrant to Jesus than to the souls which it profanes. The preachers do not see that they make his gospel not glad, and shear him of the locks of beauty and the attributes of heaven. When I see a majestic Epaminondas, or Washington; when I see among my contemporaries a true orator, an upright judge, a dear friend; when I vibrate to the melody and fancy of a poem; I see beauty that is to be desired. And so lovely, and with yet more entire consent of my human being, sounds in my ear the severe music of the bards that have sung of the true God in all ages. Now do not degrade the life and dialogues of Christ out of the circle of this charm, by insulation and peculiarity. Let them lie as they befell, alive and warm, part of human life and the landscape and the cheerful day.

2. The second defect of the traditionary and limited way of using the mind of Christ is a consequence of the first; this, namely; that the Moral Nature, that Law of laws whose revelations introduce greatness—yea, God himself—into the open soul, is not explored as the fountain of the established teaching in society. Men have come to speak of the revelation as somewhat long ago given and done, as if God were dead. The injury to faith throttles the preacher; and the goodliest of institutions becomes an uncertain and inarticulate voice.

It is very certain that it is the effect of conversation with the beauty of the soul, to beget a desire and need to impart to others the same knowledge and love. If utterance is denied, the thought lies like a burden on the man. Always the seer is a sayer. Somehow his dream is told; somehow he publishes it with solemn joy: sometimes with pencil on canvas, sometimes with chisel on stone, sometimes in towers and aisles of granite, his soul's worship is builded; sometimes in anthems of indefinite music; but clearest and most permanent, in words.

The man enamored of this excellency becomes its priest or poet. The office is coeval with the world. But observe the condition, the spiritual limitation of the office. The spirit only can teach. Not any profane man, not any sensual, not any liar, not any slave can teach, but only he can give, who has; he only can create, who is. The man on whom the soul descends, through whom the soul speaks, alone can teach. Courage, piety, love, wisdom, can teach; and every man can open his door to these angels, and they shall bring him the gift of tongues. But the man who aims to speak as books enable, as synods use, as the fashion guides, and as interest commands, babbles. Let him hush.

To this holy office you propose to devote yourselves. I wish you may feel your call in throbs of desire and hope. The office is the first in the world. It is of that reality that it cannot suffer the deduction of any falsehood. And it is my duty to say to you that the need was never greater of new revelation than now. From the views I have already expressed, you will infer the sad conviction, which I share, I believe, with numbers, of the universal decay and now almost death of faith in society. The soul is not preached. The Church seems to totter to its fall, almost all life extinct. On this occasion, any complaisance would be criminal which told you, whose hope and commission it is to preach the faith of Christ, that the faith of Christ is preached.

It is time that this ill-suppressed murmur of all thoughtful men against the famine of our churches; this moaning of the heart because it is bereaved of the consolation, the hope, the grandeur that come alone out of the culture of the moral nature—should be heard through the sleep of indolence, and over the din of routine. This great and perpetual office of the preacher is not discharged. Preaching is the expression of the moral sentiment in application to the duties of life. In how many churches, by how many prophets, tell me, is man made sensible that he is an infinite Soul; that the earth and heavens are passing into his mind; that he is drinking forever the soul of God? Where now sounds the persuasion, that by its very melody imparadises my heart, and so affirms its own origin in heaven? Where shall I hear words such as in elder ages drew men to leave all and follow—father and mother, house and land, wife and child? Where shall I hear these august laws of moral being so pronounced as to fill my ear, and I feel ennobled by the offer of my uttermost action and passion? The test of the true faith, certainly, should be its power to charm and command the soul, as the laws of nature control the activity of the hands—so commanding that we find pleasure and honor in obeying. The faith should blend with the light of rising and of setting suns, with the flying cloud, the singing bird, and the breath of flowers. But now the priest's Sabbath has lost the splendor of nature; it is unlovely; we are glad when it is done; we can make, we do make, even sitting in our pews, a far better, holier, sweeter, for ourselves.

Whenever the pulpit is usurped by a formalist, then is the worshipper defrauded and disconsolate. We shrink as soon as the prayers begin, which do not uplift, but smite and offend us. We are fain to wrap our cloaks about us, and secure, as best we can, a solitude that hears not. I once heard a preacher who sorely tempted me to say I would go to church no more. Men go, thought I, where they are wont to go, else had no soul entered the temple in the afternoon. A snow-storm was falling around us. The snow-storm was real, the preacher merely spectral, and the eye felt the sad contrast in looking at him, and then out of the window behind him into the beautiful meteor of the snow. He had lived in vain. He had no one word intimating that he had laughed or wept, was married or in love, had been commended, or cheated, or chagrined. If he had ever lived and acted, we were none the wiser for it. The capital secret of his profession, namely, to convert life into truth, he had not learned. Not one fact in all his experience had he yet imported into his doctrine. This man had ploughed and planted and talked and bought and sold; he had read books; he had eaten and drunken; his head aches, his heart throbs; he smiles and suffers; yet was there not a surmise, a hint, in all the discourse, that he had ever lived at all. Not a line did he draw out of real history. The true preacher can be known by this, that he deals out to the people his life—life passed through the fire of thought. But of the bad preacher, it could not be told from his sermon what age of the world he fell in; whether he had a father or a child; whether he was a freeholder or a pauper; whether he was a citizen or a countryman; or any other fact of his biography. It seemed strange that the people should come to church. It seemed as if their houses were very unentertaining, that they should prefer this thoughtless clamor. It shows that there is a commanding attraction in the moral sentiment, that can lend a faint tint of light to dulness and ignorance coming in its name and place. The good hearer is sure he has been touched sometimes; is sure there is somewhat to be reached, and some word that can reach it. When he listens to these vain words, he comforts himself by their relation to his remembrance of better hours, and so they clatter and echo unchallenged.

I am not ignorant that when we preach unworthily, it is not always quite in vain. There is a good ear, in some men, that draws supplies to virtue out of very indifferent nutriment. There is poetic truth concealed in all the commonplaces of prayer and of sermons, and though fool-ishly spoken, they may be wisely heard; for each is some select expression that broke out in a moment of piety from some stricken or jubilant soul, and its excellency made it remembered. The prayers and even the dogmas of our church are like the zodiac of Denderah and the astronomical monuments of the Hindoos, wholly insulated from anything now extant in the life and business of the people. They mark the height to which the waters once rose. But this docility is a check upon the mischief from the good and devout. In a large portion of the community, the religious service gives rise to quite other thoughts and emotions. We need not chide the negligent servant. We are struck with pity, rather, at the swift retribution of his sloth. Alas for the unhappy man that is called to stand in the pulpit, and not give bread of life. Everything that befalls, accuses him. Would he ask contributions for the missions, foreign or domestic? Instantly his face is suffused with shame, to propose to his parish that they should send money a hundred or a thousand miles, to furnish such poor fare as they have at home and would do well to go the hundred or the thousand miles to escape. Would he urge people to a godly way of living; and can he ask a fellow-creature to come to Sabbath meetings, when he and they all know what is the poor uttermost they can hope for therein? Will he invite them privately to the Lord's Supper? He dares not. If no heart warm this rite, the hollow, dry, creaking formality is too plain, than that he can face a man of wit and energy and put the invitation without terror. In the street, what has he to say to the bold village blasphemer? The village blasphemer sees fear in the face, form, and gait of the minister.

Let me not taint the sincerity of this plea by any oversight of the claims of good men. I know and honor the purity and strict conscience of numbers of the clergy. What life the public worship retains, it owes to the scattered company of pious men, who minister here and there in the churches, and who, sometimes accepting with too great tenderness the tenet of the elders, have not accepted from others, but from their own heart, the genuine impulses of virtue, and so still command our love and awe, to the sanctity of character. Moreover, the exceptions are not so much to be found in a few eminent preachers, as in the better hours, the truer inspirations of all—nay, in the sincere moments of every man. But, with whatever exception, it is still true that tradition characterizes the preaching of this country; that it comes out of the memory, and not out of the soul; that it aims at what is usual, and not at what is necessary and eternal; that thus historical Christianity destroys the power of preaching, by withdrawing it from the exploration of the moral nature of man; where the sublime is, where are the resources of astonishment and power. What a cruel injustice it is to that

Law, the joy of the whole earth, which alone can make thought dear and rich; that Law whose fatal sureness the astronomical orbits poorly emulate; that it is travestied and depreciated, that it is behooted and behowled, and not a trait, not a word of it articulated. The pulpit in losing sight of this Law, loses its reason, and gropes after it knows not what. And for want of this culture the soul of the community is sick and faithless. It wants nothing so much as a stern, high, stoical, Christian discipline, to make it know itself and the divinity that speaks through it. Now man is ashamed of himself; he skulks and sneaks through the world, to be tolerated, to be pitied, and scarcely in a thousand years does any man dare to be wise and good, and so draw after him the tears and blessings of his kind.

Certainly there have been periods when, from the inactivity of the intellect on certain truths, a greater faith was possible in names and persons. The Puritans in England and America found in the Christ of the Catholic Church and in the dogmas inherited from Rome, scope for their austere piety and their longings for civil freedom. But their creed is passing away, and none arises in its room. I think no man can go with his thoughts about him into one of our churches, without feeling that what hold the public worship had on men is gone, or going. It has lost its grasp on the affection of the good and the fear of the bad. In the country, neighborhoods, half parishes are *signing off*, to use the local term. It is already beginning to indicate character and religion to withdraw from the religious meetings. I have heard a devout person, who prized the Sabbath, say in bitterness of heart, "On Sundays, it seems wicked to go to church." And the motive that holds the best there is now only a hope and a waiting. What was once a mere circumstance, that the best and the worst men in the parish, the poor and the rich, the learned and the ignorant, young and old, should meet one day as fellows in one house, in sign of an equal right in the soul, has come to be a paramount motive for going thither.

My friends, in these two errors, I think, I find the causes of a decaying church and a wasting unbelief. And what greater calamity can fall upon a nation than the loss of worship? Then all things go to decay. Genius leaves the temple to haunt the senate or the market. Literature becomes frivolous. Science is cold. The eye of youth is not lighted by the hope of other worlds, and age is without honor. Society lives to trifles, and when men die we do not mention them.

And now, my brothers, you will ask, What in these desponding days can be done by us? The remedy is already declared in the ground of our complaint of the Church. We have contrasted the Church with the Soul. In the soul then let the redemption be sought. Wherever a man comes, there comes revolution. The old is for slaves. When a man comes, all books are legible, all things transparent, all religions are forms. He is religious. Man is the wonderworker. He is seen amid miracles. All men bless and curse. He saith yea and nay, only. The stationariness of religion; the assumption that the age of inspiration is past, that the Bible is closed; the fear of degrading the character of Jesus by representing him as a man; indicate with sufficient clearness the falsehood of our theology. It is the office of a true teacher to show us that God is, not was; that He speaketh, not spake. The true Christianity—a faith like Christ's in the infinitude of men—is lost. None believeth in the soul of man, but only in some man or person old and departed. Ah me! no man goeth alone. All men go in flocks to this saint or that poet, avoiding the God who seeth in secret. They cannot see in secret; they love to be blind in public. They think society wiser than their soul, and know not that one soul, and their soul, is wiser than the whole world. See how nations and races flit by on the sea of time and leave no ripple to tell where they floated or sunk, and one good soul shall make the name of Moses, or of Zeno, or of Zoroaster, reverend forever. None assayeth the stern ambition to be the Self of the nation and of nature, but each would be an easy secondary to some Christian scheme, or sectarian connection, or some eminent man. Once leave your own knowledge of God, your own sentiment, and take secondary knowledge, as St. Paul's, or George Fox's, or Swedenborg's, and you get wide from God with every year this secondary form lasts, and if, as now, for centuries—the chasm yawns to that breadth, that men can scarcely be convinced there is in them anything divine.

Let me admonish you, first of all, to go alone; to refuse the good models, even those which are sacred in the imagination of men, and dare to love God without mediator or veil. Friends enough you shall find who will hold up to your emulation Wesleys and Oberlins, Saints and Prophets. Thank God for these good men, but say, 'I also am a man.' Imitation cannot go above its model. The imitator dooms himself to hopeless mediocrity. The inventor did it because it was natural to him, and so in him it has a charm. In the imitator something else is natural, and he bereaves himself of his own beauty, to come short of another man's.

Yourself a newborn bard of the Holy Ghost, cast behind you all conformity, and acquaint men at first hand with Deity. Look to it first and only, that fashion, custom, authority, pleasure, and money, are nothing to you—are not bandages over your eyes, that you cannot see— but live with the privilege of the immeasurable mind. Not too anxious to visit periodically all families and each family in your parish connection—when you meet one of these men or women, be to them a divine man; be to them thought and virtue; let their timid aspirations find in you a friend; let their trampled instincts be genially tempted out in your atmosphere; let their doubts know that you have doubted, and their wonder feel that you have wondered. By trusting your own heart, you shall gain more confidence in other men. For all our penny-wisdom, for all our soul-destroying slavery to habit, it is not to be doubted that all men have sublime thoughts; that all men value the few real hours of life; they love to be heard; they love to be caught up into the vision of principles. We mark with light in the memory the few interviews we have had, in the dreary years of routine and of sin, with souls that made our souls wiser; that spoke what we thought; that told us what we knew; that gave us leave to be what we inly were. Discharge to men the priestly office, and, present or absent, you shall be followed with their love as by an angel.

And, to this end, let us not aim at common degrees of merit. Can we not leave, to such as love it, the virtue that glitters for the commendation of society, and ourselves pierce the deep solitudes of absolute ability and worth? We easily come up to the standard of goodness in society. Society's praise can be cheaply secured, and almost all men are content with those easy merits; but the instant effect of conversing with God will be to put them away. There are persons who are not actors, not speakers, but influences; persons too great for fame, for display; who disdain eloquence; to whom all we call art and artist, seems too nearly allied to show and by-ends, to the exaggeration of the finite and selfish, and loss of the universal. The orators, the poets, the commanders encroach on us only as fair women do, by our allowance and homage. Slight them by preoccupation of mind, slight them, as you can well afford to do, by high and universal aims, and they instantly feel that you have right, and that it is in lower places that they must shine.

They also feel your right; for they with you are open to the influx of the all-knowing Spirit, which annihilates before its broad noon the little shades and gradations of intelligence in the compositions we call wiser and wisest.

In such high communion let us study the grand strokes of rectitude: a bold benevolence, an independence of friends, so that not the unjust wishes of those who love us shall impair our freedom, but we shall resist for truth's sake the freest flow of kindness, and appeal to sympathies far in advance; and—what is the highest form in which we know this beautiful element—a certain solidity of merit, that has nothing to do with opinion, and which is so essentially and manifestly virtue, that it is taken for granted that the right, the brave, the generous step will be taken by it, and nobody thinks of commending it. You would compliment a coxcomb doing a good act, but you would not praise an angel. The silence that accepts merit as the most natural thing in the world, is the highest applause. Such souls, when they appear, are the Imperial Guard of Virtue, the perpetual reserve, the dictators of fortune. One needs not praise their courage—they are the heart and soul of nature. O my friends, there are resources in us on which we have not drawn. There are men who rise refreshed on hearing a threat; men to whom a crisis which intimidates and paralyzes the majority—demanding not the faculties of prudence and thrift, but comprehension, immovableness, the readiness of sacrifice—comes graceful and beloved as a bride. Napoleon said of Massena, that he was not himself until the battle began to go against him; then, when the dead began to fall in ranks around him, awoke his powers of combination, and he put on terror and victory as a robe. So it is in rugged crises, in unweariable endurance, and in aims which put sympathy out of question, that the angel is shown. But these are heights that we can scarce remember and look up to without contrition and shame. Let us thank God that such things exist.

And now let us do what we can to rekindle the smouldering, nigh quenched fire on the altar. The evils of the church that now is are manifest. The question returns, What shall we do? I confess, all attempts to project and establish a Cultus with new rites and forms, seem to me vain. Faith makes us, and not we it, and faith makes its own forms. All attempts to contrive a system are as cold as the new worship introduced by the French to the goddess of Reason—to-day, pasteboard and filigree, and ending to-morrow in madness and murder. Rather let the breath of new life be breathed by you through the forms already existing. For if once you are alive, you shall find they shall become plastic and new. The remedy to their deformity is first, soul, and second, soul, and evermore, soul. A whole popedom of forms one pulsation of virtue can uplift and vivify. Two inestimable advantages Christianity has given us; first the Sabbath, the jubilee of the whole world, whose light dawns welcome alike into the closet of the philosopher, into the garret of toil, and into prison-cells, and everywhere suggests, even to the vile, the dignity of spiritual being. Let it stand forevermore, a temple, which new love, new faith, new sight shall restore to more than its first splendor to mankind. And secondly, the institution of preaching—the speech of man to men—essentially the most flexible of all organs, of all forms. What hinders that now, everywhere, in pulpits, in lecture-rooms, in houses, in fields, wherever the invitation of men or your own occasions lead you, you speak the very truth, as your life and conscience teach it, and cheer the waiting, fainting hearts of men with new hope and new revelation?

I look for the hour when that supreme Beauty which ravished the souls of those Eastern men, and chiefly of those Hebrews, and through their lips spoke oracles to all time, shall speak in the West also. The Hebrew and Greek Scriptures contain immortal sentences, that have been bread of life to millions. But they have no epical integrity; are fragmentary; are not shown in their order to the intellect. I look for the new Teacher that shall follow so far those shining laws that he shall see them come full circle; shall see their rounding complete grace; shall see the world to be the mirror of the soul; shall see the identity of the law of gravitation with purity of heart; and shall show that the Ought, that Duty, is one thing with Science, with Beauty, and with Joy.

THE
TRANSCENDENTALIST

[*This was the fourth of a series of eight lectures on "The Times" which Emerson delivered at the Masonic Temple in Boston in the winter of 1841-42. It was printed in* The Dial *for January, 1843.*]

THE TRANSCENDENTALIST

THE FIRST THING we have to say respecting what are called new views here in New England, at the present time, is, that they are not new, but the very oldest of thoughts cast into the mould of these new times. The light is always identical in its composition, but it falls on a great variety of objects, and by so falling is first revealed to us, not in its own form, for it is formless, but in theirs; in like manner, thought only appears in the objects it classifies. What is popularly called Transcendentalism among us, is Idealism; Idealism as it appears in 1842. As thinkers, mankind have ever divided into two sects, Materialists and Idealists; the first class founding on experience, the second on consciousness; the first class beginning to think from the data of the senses, the second class perceive that the senses are not final, and say, The senses give us representations of things, but what are the things themselves, they cannot tell. The materialist insists on facts, on history, on the force of circumstances and the animal wants of man; the idealist on the power of Thought and of Will, on inspiration, on miracle, on individual culture. These two modes of thinking are both natural, but the idealist contends that his way of thinking is in higher nature. He concedes all that the other affirms, admits the impressions of sense, admits their coherency, their use and beauty, and then asks the materialist for his grounds of assurance that things are as his senses represent them. But I, he says, affirm facts not affected by the illusions of sense, facts which are of the same nature as the faculty which reports them, and not liable to doubt; facts which in their first appearance to us assume a native superiority to material facts, degrading these into a language by which the first are to be spoken; facts which it only needs a retirement from the senses to discern. Every materialist will be an idealist; but an idealist can never go backward to be a materialist.

The idealist, in speaking of events, sees them as spirits. He does not deny the sensuous fact: by no means; but he will not see that alone. He does not deny the presence of this table, this chair, and the walls of this room, but he looks at these things as the reverse side of the tapestry, as the *other end*, each being a sequel or completion of a spiritual fact which nearly concerns him. This manner of looking at things transfers every object in nature from an independent and anomalous position without there, into the consciousness. Even the materialist Condillac, perhaps the most logical expounder of materialism, was constrained to say, "Though we should soar into the heavens, though we should sink into the abyss, we never go out of ourselves; it is always our own thoughts that we perceive." What more could an idealist say?

The materialist, secure in the certainty of sensation, mocks at fine-spun theories, at star-gazers and dreams, and believes that his life is solid, that he at least takes nothing for granted, but knows where he stands, and what he does. Yet how easy it is to show him that he also is a phantom walking and working amid phantoms, and that he need only ask a question or two beyond his daily questions to find his solid universe growing dim and impalpable before his sense. The sturdy capitalist, no matter how deep and square on blocks of Quincy granite he lays the foundations of his banking-house or Exchange, must set it, at last, not on a cube corresponding to the angles of his structure, but on a mass of unknown materials and solidity, red-hot or white-hot perhaps at the core, which rounds off to an almost perfect sphericity, and lies floating in soft air, and goes spinning away, dragging bank and banker with it at a rate of thousands of miles the hour, he knows not whither—a bit of bullet, now glimmering, now darkling through a small cubic space on the edge of an unimaginable pit of emptiness. And this wild balloon, in which his whole venture is embarked, is a just symbol of his whole state and faculty. One thing at least, he says, is certain, and does not give me the headache, that figures do not lie; the multiplication table has been hitherto found unimpeachable truth; and, moreover, if I put a gold eagle in my safe, I find it again to-morrow; but for these thoughts, I know not whence they are. They change and pass away. But ask him why he believes that an uniform experience will continue uniform, or on what grounds he founds his faith in his figures, and he will perceive that his mental fabric is built up on just as strange and quaking foundations as his proud edifice of stone.

In the order of thought, the materialist takes his departure from the external world, and esteems a man as one product of that. The idealist takes his departure from his consciousness, and reckons the world an appearance. The materialist respects sensible masses, Society, Government, social art and luxury, every establishment, every mass, whether majority of numbers, or extent of space, or amount of objects, every social action. The idealist has another measure, which is metaphysical, namely the *rank* which things themselves take in his consciousness; not at all the size or appearance. Mind is the only reality, of which men and all other natures are better or worse reflectors. Nature, literature, history, are only subjective phenomena. Although in his action overpowered by the laws of action, and so, warmly cooperating with men, even preferring them to himself, yet when he speaks scientifically, or after the order of thought, he is constrained to degrade persons into representatives of truths. He does not respect labor, or the products of labor, namely property, otherwise than as a manifold symbol, illustrating with wonderful fidelity of details the laws of being; he does not respect government, except as far as it reiterates the law of his mind; nor the church, nor charities, nor arts, for themselves; but hears, as at a vast distance, what they say, as if his consciousness would speak to him through a pantomimic scene. His thought—that is the Universe. His experience inclines him to behold the procession of facts you call the world, as flowing perpetually outward from an invisible, unsounded centre in himself, centre alike of him and of them, and necessitating him to regard all things as having a subjective or relative existence, relative to that aforesaid Unknown Centre of him.

From this transfer of the world into the consciousness, this beholding of all things in the mind, follow easily his whole ethics. It is simpler to be self-dependent. The height, the deity of man is to be self-sustained, to need no gift, no foreign force. Society is good when it does not violate me, but best when it is likest to solitude. Everything real is self-existent. Everything divine shares the self-existence of Deity. All that you call the world is the shadow of that substance which you are, the perpetual creation of the powers of thought, of those that are dependent and of those that are independent of your will. Do not cumber yourself with fruitless pains to mend and remedy remote effects; let the soul be erect, and all things will go well. You think me the child of my circumstances: I make my circumstances. Let any thought or motive of mine be different from that they are, the difference will transform my condition and economy. I—this thought which is called I—is the mould into which the world is poured like melted wax. The mould is invisible, but the world betrays the shape of the mould. You call it the power of circumstance, but it is the power of me. Am I in harmony with myself? my position will seem to you just and commanding. Am I vicious and insane? my fortunes will seem to you obscure and descending. As I am, so shall I associate, and so shall I act; Cæsar's history will paint out Cæsar. Jesus acted so, because he thought so. I do not wish to overlook or to gainsay any reality; I say I make my circumstance; but if you ask me, Whence am I? I feel like other men my relation to that Fact which cannot be spoken, or defined, nor even thought, but which exists, and will exist.

The Transcendentalist adopts the whole connection of spiritual doctrine. He believes in miracle, in the perpetual openness of the human mind to new influx of light and power; he believes in inspiration, and in ecstasy. He wishes that the spiritual principle should be suffered to demonstrate itself to the end, in all possible applications to the state of man, without the admission of anything unspiritual; that is, anything positive, dogmatic, personal. Thus the spiritual measure of inspiration is the depth of the thought, and never, who said it? And so he resists all attempts to palm other rules and measures on the spirit than its own.

In action he easily incurs the charge of anti-nomianism by his avowal that he, who has the Law-giver, may with safety not only neglect, but even contravene every written commandment. In the play of Othello, the expiring Desdemona absolves her husband of the murder, to her attendant Emilia. Afterwards, when Emilia charges him with the crime, Othello exclaims,

"You heard her say herself it was not I."

Emilia replies,

"The more angel she, and thou the blacker devil."

Of this fine incident, Jacobi, the Transcendental moralist, makes use, with other parallel instances, in his reply to Fichte. Jacobi, refusing all measure of right and wrong except the determinations of the private spirit, remarks that there is no crime but has sometimes been a

virtue. "I," he says, "am that atheist, that godless person who, in opposition to an imaginary doctrine of calculation, would lie as the dying
Desdemona lied; would lie and deceive, as Pylades when he personated
Orestes; would assassinate like Timoleon; would perjure myself like
Epaminondas and John de Witt; I would resolve on suicide like Cato;
I would commit sacrilege with David; yea, and pluck ears of corn on
the Sabbath, for no other reason than that I was fainting for lack of
food. For I have assurance in myself that in pardoning these faults
according to the letter, man exerts the sovereign right which the
majesty of his being confers on him; he sets the seal of his divine nature
to the grace he accords."

In like manner, if there is anything grand and daring in human
thought or virtue, any reliance on the vast, the unknown; any presentiment, any extravagance of faith, the spiritualist adopts it as most in
nature. The oriental mind has always tended to this largeness.
Buddhism is an expression of it. The Buddhist, who thanks no man,
who says, "Do not flatter your benefactors," but who, in his conviction that every good deed can by no possibility escape its reward, will
not deceive the benefactor by pretending that he has done more than he
should, is a Transcendentalist.

You will see by this sketch that there is no such thing as a
Transcendental *party*; that there is no pure Transcendentalist; that we
know of none but prophets and heralds of such a philosophy; that all
who by strong bias of nature have leaned to the spiritual side in doctrine, have stopped short of their goal. We have had many harbingers
and forerunners; but of a purely spiritual life, history has afforded no
example. I mean we have yet no man who has leaned entirely on his
character, and eaten angels' food; who, trusting to his sentiments, found
life made of miracles; who, working for universal aims, found himself
fed, he knew not how; clothed, sheltered, and weaponed, he knew not
how, and yet it was done by his own hands. Only in the instinct of the
lower animals we find the suggestion of the methods of it, and something higher than our understanding. The squirrel hoards nuts and the
bee gathers honey, without knowing what they do, and they are thus
provided for without selfishness or disgrace.

Shall we say then that Transcendentalism is the Saturnalia or
excess of Faith; the presentiment of a faith proper to man in his
integrity, excessive only when his imperfect obedience hinders the sat-

isfaction of his wish? Nature is transcendental, exists primarily, necessarily, ever works and advances, yet takes no thought for the morrow. Man owns the dignity of the life which throbs around him, in chemistry, and tree, and animal, and in the involuntary functions of his own body; yet he is balked when he tries to fling himself into this enchanted circle, where all is done without degradation. Yet genius and virtue predict in man the same absence of private ends and of condescension to circumstances, united with every trait and talent of beauty and power.

This way of thinking, falling on Roman times, made Stoic philosophers; falling on despotic times, made patriot Catos and Brutuses; falling on superstitious times, made prophets and apostles; on popish times, made protestants and ascetic monks, preachers of Faith against the preachers of Works; on prelatical times, made Puritans and Quakers; and falling on Unitarian and commercial times, makes the peculiar shades of Idealism which we know.

It is well known to most of my audience that the Idealism of the present day acquired the name of Transcendental from the use of that term by Immanuel Kant, of Königsberg, who replied to the skeptical philosophy of Locke, which insisted that there was nothing in the intellect which was not previously in the experience of the senses, by showing that there was a very important class of ideas or imperative forms, which did not come by experience, but through which experience was acquired; that these were intuitions of the mind itself; and he denominated them *Transcendental* forms. The extraordinary profoundness and precision of that man's thinking have given vogue to his nomenclature, in Europe and America, to that extent that whatever belongs to the class of intuitive thought is popularly called at the present day *Transcendental*.

Although, as we have said, there is no pure Transcendentalist, yet the tendency to respect the intuitions and to give them, at least in our creed, all authority over our experience, has deeply colored the conversation and poetry of the present day; and the history of genius and of religion in these times, though impure, and as yet not incarnated in any powerful individual, will be the history of this tendency.

It is a sign of our times, conspicuous to the coarsest observer, that many intelligent and religious persons withdraw themselves from the common labors and competitions of the market and the caucus, and

. . . .

betake themselves to a certain solitary and critical way of living, from which no solid fruit has yet appeared to justify their separation. They hold themselves aloof: they feel the disproportion between their faculties and the work offered them, and they prefer to ramble in the country and perish of ennui, to the degradation of such charities and such ambitions as the city can propose to them. They are striking work, and crying out for somewhat worthy to do! What they do is done only because they are overpowered by the humanities that speak on all sides; and they consent to such labor as is open to them, though to their lofty dream the writing of Iliads or Hamlets, or the building of cities or empires seems drudgery.

Now every one must do after his kind, be he asp or angel, and these must. The question which a wise man and a student of modern history will ask, is, what that kind is? And truly, as in ecclesiastical history we take so much pains to know what the Gnostics, what the Essenes, what the Manichees, and what the Reformers believed, it would not misbecome us to inquire nearer home, what these companions and contemporaries of ours think and do, at least so far as these thoughts and actions appear to be not accidental and personal, but common to many, and the inevitable flower of the Tree of Time. Our American literature and spiritual history are, we confess, in the optative mood; but whoso knows these seething brains, these admirable radicals, these unsocial worshippers, these talkers who talk the sun and moon away, will believe that this heresy cannot pass away without leaving its mark.

They are lonely; the spirit of their writing and conversation is lonely; they repel influences; they shun general society; they incline to shut themselves in their chamber in the house, to live in the country rather than in the town, and to find their tasks and amusements in solitude. Society, to be sure, does not like this very well; it saith, Whoso goes to walk alone, accuses the whole world; he declares all to be unfit to be his companions; it is very uncivil, nay, insulting; Society will retaliate. Meantime, this retirement does not proceed from any whim on the part of these separators; but if any one will take pains to talk with them, he will find that this part is chosen both from temperament and from principle; with some unwillingness too, and as a choice of the less of two evils; for these persons are not by nature melancholy, sour, and unsocial—they are not stockish or brute—but joyous, susceptible, affectionate; they have even more than others a great wish to be loved. Like the young Mozart, they are rather ready to cry ten times a day, "But are you sure you love me?" Nay, if they tell you their whole thought, they will own that love seems to them the last and highest gift of nature; that there are persons whom in their hearts they daily thank for existing—persons whose faces are perhaps unknown to them, but whose fame and spirit have penetrated their solitude—and for whose sake they wish to exist. To behold the beauty of another character, which inspires a new interest in our own; to behold the beauty lodged in a human being, with such vivacity of apprehension that I am instantly forced home to inquire if I am not deformity itself; to behold in another the expression of a love so high that it assures itself—assures itself also to me against every possible casualty except my unworthiness; these are degrees on the scale of human happiness to which they have ascended; and it is a fidelity to this sentiment which has made common association distasteful to them. They wish a just and even fellowship, or none. They cannot gossip with you, and they do not wish, as they are sincere and religious, to gratify any mere curiosity which you may entertain. Like fairies, they do not wish to be spoken of. Love me, they say, but do not ask who is my cousin and my uncle. If you do not need to hear my thought, because you can read it in my face and behavior, then I will tell it you from sunrise to sunset. If you cannot divine it, you would not understand what I say. I will not molest myself for you. I do not wish to be profaned.

And yet, it seems as if this loneliness, and not this love, would prevail in their circumstances, because of the extravagant demand they make on human nature. That, indeed, constitutes a new feature in their portrait, that they are the most exacting and extortionate critics. Their quarrel with every man they meet is not with his kind, but with his degree. There is not enough of him—that is the only fault. They prolong their privilege of childhood in this wise; of doing nothing, but making immense demands on all the gladiators in the lists of action and fame. They make us feel the strange disappointment which overcasts every human youth. So many promising youths, and never a finished man! The profound nature will have a savage rudeness; the delicate one will be shallow, or the victim of sensibility; the richly accomplished will have some capital absurdity; and so every piece has a crack. 'T is strange, but this masterpiece is the result of such an extreme delicacy that the most unobserved flaw in the boy will neutralize the most aspiring genius, and spoil the work. Talk with a seaman of the hazards to life in his profession and he will ask you, 'Where are the old sailors? Do you not see that all are young men?' And we, on this sea of human thought, in like manner inquire, Where are the old idealists? where are they who represented to the last generation that extravagant hope which a few happy aspirants suggest to ours? In looking at the class of counsel, and power, and wealth, and at the matronage of the land, amidst all the prudence and all the triviality, one asks, Where are they who represented genius, virtue, the invisible and heavenly world, to these? Are they dead—taken in early ripeness to the gods—as ancient wisdom foretold their fate? Or did the high idea die out of them, and leave their unperfumed body as its tomb and tablet, announcing to all that the celestial inhabitant, who once gave them beauty, had departed? Will it be better with the new generation? We easily predict a fair future to each new candidate who enters the lists, but we are frivolous and volatile, and by low aims and ill example do what we can to defeat this hope. Then these youths bring us a rough but effectual aid. By their unconcealed dissatisfaction they expose our poverty and the insignificance of man to man. A man is a poor limitary benefactor. He ought to be a shower of benefits—a great influence, which should never let his brother go, but should refresh old merits continually with new ones; so that though absent he should never be out of my mind, his name never far from my lips; but if the earth should open at my side, or my last hour were come, his name should be the prayer I should utter to the Universe. But in our experience, man is cheap and friendship wants its deep sense. We affect to dwell with our friends in their absence, but we do not; when deed, word, or letter comes not, they let us go. These exacting children advertise us of our wants. There is no compliment, no smooth speech with them; they pay you only this one compliment, of insatiable expectation; they aspire, they severely exact, and if they only stand fast in this watchtower, and persist in demanding unto the end, and without end, then are they terrible friends, whereof poet and priest cannot choose but stand in awe; and what if they eat clouds, and drink wind, they have not been without service to the race of man.

   With this passion for what is great and extraordinary, it cannot be wondered at that they are repelled by vulgarity and frivolity in people.

They say to themselves, It is better to be alone than in bad company. And it is really a wish to be met—the wish to find society for their hope and religion—which prompts them to shun what is called society. They feel that they are never so fit for friendship as when they have quitted mankind and taken themselves to friend. A picture, a book, a favorite spot in the hills or the woods which they can people with the fair and worthy creation of the fancy, can give them often forms so vivid that these for the time shall seem real, and society the illusion.

But their solitary and fastidious manners not only withdraw them from the conversation, but from the labors of the world; they are not good citizens, not good members of society; unwillingly they bear their part of the public and private burdens; they do not willingly share in the public charities, in the public religious rites, in the enterprises of education, of missions foreign and domestic, in the abolition of the slave-trade, or in the temperance society. They do not even like to vote. The philanthropists inquire whether Transcendentalism does not mean sloth: they had as lief hear that their friend is dead, as that he is a Transcendentalist; for then is he paralyzed, and can never do anything for humanity. What right, cries the good world, has the man of genius to retreat from work, and indulge himself? The popular literary creed seems to be, 'I am a sublime genius; I ought not therefore to labor.' But genius is the power to labor better and more availably. Deserve thy genius: exalt it. The good, the illuminated, sit apart from the rest, censuring their dulness and vices, as if they thought that by sitting very grand in their chairs, the very brokers, attorneys, and congressmen would see the error of their ways, and flock to them. But the good and wise must learn to act, and carry salvation to the combatants and demagogues in the dusty arena below.

On the part of these children it is replied that life and their faculty seem to them gifts too rich to be squandered on such trifles as you propose to them. What you call your fundamental institutions, your great and holy causes, seem to them great abuses, and, when nearly seen, paltry matters. Each 'cause' as it is called—say Abolition, Temperance, say Calvinism, or Unitarianism—becomes speedily a little shop, where the article, let it have been at first never so subtle and ethereal, is now made up into portable and convenient cakes, and retailed in small quantities to suit purchasers. You make very free use of these words 'great' and 'holy,' but few things appear to them such. Few persons have any magnificence of nature to inspire enthusiasm, and the philanthropies and charities have a certain air of quackery. As to the general course of living, and the daily employments of men, they cannot see much virtue in these, since they are parts of this vicious circle; and as no great ends are answered by the men, there is nothing noble in the arts by which they are maintained. Nay, they have made the experiment and found that from the liberal professions to the coarsest manual labor, and from the courtesies of the academy and the college to the conventions of the cotillon-room and the morning call, there is a spirit of cowardly compromise and seeming which intimates a frightful skepticism, a life without love, and an activity without an aim.

Unless the action is necessary, unless it is adequate, I do not wish to perform it. I do not wish to do one thing but once. I do not love routine. Once possessed of the principle, it is equally easy to make four or forty thousand applications of it. A great man will be content to have indicated in any the slightest manner his perception of the reigning Idea of his time, and will leave to those who like it the multiplication of examples. When he has hit the white, the rest may shatter the target. Every thing admonishes us how needlessly long life is. Every moment of a hero so raises and cheers us that a twelvemonth is an age. All that the brave Xanthus brings home from his wars is the recollection that at the storming of Samos, "in the heat of the battle, Pericles smiled on me, and passed on to another detachment." It is the quality of the moment, not the number of days, of events, or of actors, but imports.

New, we confess, and by no means happy, is our condition: if you want the aid of our labor, we ourselves stand in greater want of the labor. We are miserable with inaction. We perish of rest and rust: but we do not like your work.

'Then,' says the world, 'show me your own.'

'We have none.'

'What will you do, then?' cries the world.

'We will wait.'

'How long?'

'Until the Universe beckons and calls us to work.'

'But whilst you wait, you grow old and useless.'

'Be it so: I can sit in a corner and *perish* (as you call it), but I will not move until I have the highest command. If no call should come for

. . . .

years, for centuries, then I know that the want of the Universe is the attestation of faith by my abstinence. Your virtuous projects, so called, do not cheer me. I know that which shall come will cheer me. If I cannot work, at least I need not lie. All that is clearly due today is not to lie. In other places other men have encountered sharp trials, and have behaved themselves well. The martyrs were sawn asunder, or hung alive on meat-hooks. Cannot we screw our courage to patience and truth, and without complaint, or even with good-humor, await our turn of action in the Infinite Counsels?'

But to come a little closer to the secret of these persons, we must say that to them it seems a very easy matter to answer the objections of the man of the world, but not so easy to dispose of the doubts and objections that occur to themselves. They are exercised in their own spirit with queries which acquaint them with all adversity, and with the trials of the bravest heroes. When I asked them concerning their private experience, they answered somewhat in this wise: It is not to be denied that there must be some wide difference between my faith and other faith; and mine is a certain brief experience, which surprised me in the highway or in the market, in some place, at some time—whether in the body or out of the body. God knoweth—and made me aware that I had played the fool with fools all this time, but that law existed for me and for all; that to me belonged trust, a child's trust and obedience, and the worship of ideas, and I should never be fool more. Well, in the space of an hour probably, I was let down from this height; I was at my old tricks, the selfish member of a selfish society. My life is superficial, takes no root in the deep world; I ask, When shall I die and be relieved of the responsibility of seeing a Universe I do not use? I wish to exchange this flash-of-lightning faith for continuous daylight, this fever-glow for a benign climate.

These two states of thought diverge every moment, and stand in wild contrast. To him who looks at his life from these moments of illumination, it will seem that he skulks and plays a mean, shiftless and subaltern part in the world. That is to be done which he has not skill to do, or to be said which others can say better, and he lies by, or occupies his hands with some plaything, until his hour comes again. Much of our reading, much of our labor, seems mere waiting; it was not that we were born for. Any other could do it as well or better. So little skill enters into these works, so little do they mix with the divine life, that it really signifies little what we do, whether we turn a grindstone, or ride, or run, or make fortunes, or govern the state. The worst feature of this double consciousness is, that the two lives, of the understanding and of the soul, which we lead, really show very little relation to each other; never meet and measure each other: one prevails now, all buzz and din; and the other prevails then, all infinitude and paradise; and, with the progress of life, the two discover no greater disposition to reconcile themselves. Yet, what is my faith? What am I? What but a thought of serenity and independence, an abode in the deep blue sky? Presently the clouds shut down again; yet we retain the belief that this pretty web we weave will at last be overshot and reticulated with veins of the blue, and that the moments will characterize the days. Patience, then, is for us, is it not? Patience, and still patience. When we pass, as presently we shall, into some new infinitude, out of this Iceland of negations, it will please us to reflect that though we had few virtues or consolations, we bore with our indigence, nor once strove to repair it with hypocrisy or false heat of any kind.

But this class are not sufficiently characterized if we omit to add that they are lovers and worshippers of Beauty. In the eternal trinity of Truth, Goodness, and Beauty, each in its perfection including the three, they prefer to make Beauty the sign and head. Something of the same taste is observable in all the moral movements of the time, in the religious and benevolent enterprises. They have a liberal, even an æsthetic spirit. A reference to Beauty in action sounds, to be sure, a little hollow and ridiculous in the ears of the old church. In politics, it has often sufficed, when they treated of justice, if they kept the bounds of selfish calculation. If they granted restitution, it was prudence which granted it. But the justice which is now claimed for the black, and the pauper, and the drunkard, is for Beauty—is for a necessity to the soul of the agent, not of the beneficiary. I say this is the tendency, not yet the realization. Our virtue totters and trips, does not yet walk firmly. Its representatives are austere; they preach and denounce; their rectitude is not yet a grace. They are still liable to that slight taint of burlesque which in our strange world attaches to the zealot. A saint should be as dear as the apple of the eye. Yet we are tempted to smile, and we flee from the working to the speculative reformer, to escape that same slight ridicule. Alas for these days of derision and criticism! We call the Beautiful the highest, because it appears to us the golden mean, escaping the dowdiness of the good and the heartlessness of the true. They are lovers of nature also, and find an indemnity in the inviolable order of the world for the violated order and grace of man.

There is, no doubt, a great deal of well-founded objection to be spoken or felt against the sayings and doings of this class, some of whose traits we have selected; no doubt they will lay themselves open to criticism and to lampoons, and as ridiculous stories will be to be told of them as of any. There will be cant and pretension; there will be subtilty and moonshine. These persons are of unequal strength, and do not all prosper. They complain that everything around them must be denied; and if feeble, it takes all their strength to deny, before they can begin to lead their own life. Grave seniors insist on their respect to this institution and that usage; to an obsolete history; to some vocation, or college, or etiquette, or beneficiary, or charity, or morning or evening call, which they resist as what does not concern them. But it costs such sleepless nights, alienations and misgivings—they have so many moods about it; these old guardians never change their minds; they have but one mood on the subject, namely, that Antony is very perverse—that it is quite as much as Antony can do to assert his rights, abstain from what he thinks foolish, and keep his temper. He cannot help the reaction of this injustice in his own mind. He is braced-up and stilted; all freedom and flowing genius, all sallies of wit and frolic nature are quite out of the question; it is well if he can keep from lying, injustice, and suicide. This is no time for gaiety and grace. His strength and spirits are wasted in rejection. But the strong spirits overpower those around them without effort. Their thought and emotion comes in like a flood, quite withdraws them from all notice of these carping critics; they surrender themselves with glad heart to the heavenly guide, and only by implication reject the clamorous nonsense of the hour. Grave seniors talk to the deaf—church and old book mumble and ritualize to an unheeding, preoccupied and advancing mind, and thus they by happiness of greater momentum lose no time, but take the right road at first.

But all these of whom I speak are not proficients; they are novices; they only show the road in which man should travel, when the soul has greater health and prowess. Yet let them feel the dignity of their charge, and deserve a larger power. Their heart is the ark in which the fire is concealed which shall burn in the broader and universal flame. Let them obey the Genius then most when his impulse is wildest; then most when he seems to lead to uninhabitable deserts of thought and life; for the path which the hero travels alone is the highway of health and benefit to mankind. What is the privilege and nobility of our nature but its persistency, through its power to attach itself to what is permanent?

Society also has its duties in reference to this class, and must behold them with what charity it can. Possibly some benefit may yet accrue from them to the state. In our Mechanics' Fair, there must be not only bridges, ploughs, carpenters' planes, and baking troughs, but also some few finer instruments—rain-gauges, thermometers, and telescopes; and in society, besides farmers, sailors, and weavers, there must be a few persons of purer fire kept specially as gauges and meters of character; persons of a fine, detecting instinct, who note the smallest accumulations of wit and feeling in the bystander. Perhaps too there might be room for the exciters and monitors; collectors of the heavenly spark, with power to convey the electricity to others. Or, as the storm-tossed vessel at sea speaks the frigate or 'line packet' to learn its longitude, so it may not be without its advantage that we should now and then encounter rare and gifted men, to compare the points of our spiritual compass, and verify our bearings from superior chronometers.

Amidst the downward tendency and proneness of things, when every voice is raised for a new road or another statute or a subscription of stock; for an improvement in dress, or in dentistry; for a new house or a larger business; for a political party, or the division of an estate; will you not tolerate one or two solitary voices in the land, speaking for thoughts and principles not marketable or perishable? Soon these improvements and mechanical inventions will be superseded; these modes of living lost out of memory; these cities rotted, ruined by war, by new inventions, by new seats of trade, or the geologic changes: all gone, like the shells which sprinkle the sea-beach with a white colony to-day, forever renewed to be forever destroyed. But the thoughts which these few hermits strove to proclaim by silence as well as by speech, not only by what they did, but by what they forbore to do, shall abide in beauty and strength, to reorganize themselves in nature, to invest themselves anew in other, perhaps higher endowed and happier mixed clay than ours, in fuller union with the surrounding system.

THE LORD'S SUPPER

[*This is a sermon that Emerson preached before the Second Church of which he was pastor in Boston, September 9, 1832. In the preceding June he had asked the Church for permission to discontinue administering the sacrament according to existing ritual, since he did not believe that Jesus had intended men to observe it century after century. In this sermon, which was the result of much scholarship and meditating on Emerson's part, he set forth the reasons why he could not conscientiously observe the Communion. After considerable discussion in committees the Church regretfully was unable to accede to Emerson's request. His resignation was accepted with affectionate regret. Although Emerson filled pulpit engagements many times afterward, he never again accepted a permanent appointment.*]

I like a church; I like a cowl,
I love a prophet of the soul;
And on my heart monastic aisles
Fall like sweet strains, or pensive smiles:
Yet not for all his faith can see
Would I that cowlèd churchman be.
Why should the vest on him allure,
Which I could not on me endure?

The word unto the prophet spoken
Was writ on tables yet unbroken;
The word by seers or sibyls told,
In groves of oak, or fanes of gold,
Still floats upon the morning wind,
Still whispers to the willing mind.

THE LORD'S SUPPER

The Kingdom of God is not meat and drink; but righteousness, and peace and joy in the Holy Ghost.—ROMANS xiv. 17.

IN THE history of the Church no subject has been more fruitful of controversy than the Lord's Supper. There never has been any unanimity in the understanding of its nature, nor any uniformity in the mode of celebrating it. Without considering the frivolous questions which have been lately debated as to the posture in which men should partake of it; whether mixed or unmixed wine should be served; whether leavened or unleavened bread should be broken; the questions have been settled differently in every church, who should be admitted to the feast, and how often it should be prepared. In the Catholic Church, infants were at one time permitted and then forbidden to partake; and since the ninth century the laity receive the bread only, the cup being reserved to the priesthood. So, as to the time of the solemnity. In the Fourth Lateran Council, it was decreed that any believer should communicate at least once in a year—at Easter. Afterwards it was determined that this Sacrament should be received three times in the year—at Easter, Whitsuntide and Christmas. But more important controversies have arisen respecting its nature. The famous question of the Real Presence was the main controversy between the Church of England and the Church of Rome. The doctrine of the Consubstantiation taught by Luther was denied by Calvin. In the Church of England, Archbishops Laud and Wake maintained that the elements were an Eucharist, or sacrifice of Thanksgiving to God; Cudworth and Warburton, that this was not a sacrifice, but a sacrificial feast; and Bishop Hoadley, that it was neither a sacrifice nor a feast after sacrifice, but a simple commemoration. And finally, it is now near two hundred years since the Society of Quakers denied the authority of the rite altogether, and gave good reasons for disusing it.

I allude to these facts only to show that, so far from the Supper being a tradition in which men are fully agreed, there has always been

. . . .

the widest room for difference of opinion upon this particular. Having recently given particular attention to this subject, I was led to the conclusion that Jesus did not intend to establish an institution for perpetual observance when he ate the Passover with his disciples; and further, to the opinion that it is not expedient to celebrate it as we do. I shall now endeavor to state distinctly my reasons for these two opinions.

I. The authority of the rite.

An account of the Last Supper of Christ with his disciples is given by the four Evangelists, Matthew, Mark, Luke and John.

In St. Matthew's Gospel (Matt. xxvi. 26-30) are recorded the words of Jesus in giving bread and wine on that occasion to his disciples, but no expression occurs intimating that this feast was hereafter to be commemorated. In St. Mark (Mark xiv. 22-25) the same words are recorded, and still with no intimation that the occasion was to be remembered. St. Luke (Luke xxii. I9), after relating the breaking of the bread, has these words: "This do in remembrance of me." In St. John, although other occurrences of the same evening are related, this whole transaction is passed over without notice.

Now observe the facts. Two of the Evangelists, namely, Matthew and John, were of the twelve disciples, and were present on that occasion. Neither of them drops the slightest intimation of any intention on the part of Jesus to set up anything permanent. John especially, the beloved disciple, who has recorded with minuteness the conversation and the transactions of that memorable evening, has quite omitted such a notice. Neither does it appear to have come to the knowledge of Mark, who, though not an eye-witness, relates the other facts. This material fact, that the occasion was to be remembered, is found in Luke alone, who was not present. There is no reason, however, that we know, for rejecting the account of Luke. I doubt not, the expression was used by Jesus. I shall presently consider its meaning. I have only brought these accounts together, that you may judge whether it is likely that a solemn institution, to be continued to the end of time by all mankind, as they should come, nation after nation, within the influence of the Christian religion, would have been established in this slight manner— in a manner so slight, that the intention of commemorating it should not appear, from their narrative, to have caught the ear or dwelt in the mind of the only two among the twelve who wrote down what happened.

Still we must suppose that the expression, "This do in remembrance of me," had come to the ear of Luke from some disciple who was present. What did it really signify? It is a prophetic and an affectionate expression. Jesus is a Jew, sitting with his countrymen, celebrating their national feast. He thinks of his own impending death, and wishes the minds of his disciples to be prepared for it. "When hereafter," he says to them, "you shall keep the Passover, it will have an altered aspect to your eyes. It is now a historical covenant of God with the Jewish nation. Hereafter it will remind you of a new covenant sealed with my blood. In years to come, as long as your people shall come up to Jerusalem to keep this feast, the connection which has subsisted between us will give a new meaning in your eyes to the national festival, as the anniversary of my death." I see natural feeling and beauty in the use of such language from Jesus, a friend to his friends; I can readily imagine that he was willing and desirous, when his disciples met, his memory should hallow their intercourse; but I cannot bring myself to believe that in the use of such an expression he looked beyond the living generation, beyond the abolition of the festival he was celebrating, and the scattering of the nation, and meant to impose a memorial feast upon the whole world.

Without presuming to fix precisely the purpose in the mind of Jesus, you will see that many opinions may be entertained of his intention, all consistent with the opinion that he did not design a perpetual ordinance. He may have foreseen that his disciples would meet to remember him, and that with good effect. It may have crossed his mind that this would be easily continued a hundred or a thousand years—as men more easily transmit a form than a virtue—and yet have been altogether out of his purpose to fasten it upon men in all times and all countries.

But though the words, "Do this in remembrance of me," do not occur in Matthew, Mark or John, and although it should be granted us that, taken alone, they do not necessarily import so much as is usually thought, yet many persons are apt to imagine that the very striking and personal manner in which the eating and drinking is described, indicates a striking and formal purpose to found a festival. And I admit that this impression might probably be left upon the mind of one who read only the passages under consideration in the New Testament. But this impression is removed by reading any narrative of the mode in which the ancient or the modern Jews have kept the Passover. It is then perceived that the leading circumstances in the Gospels are only a faithful account of that ceremony. Jesus did not celebrate the Passover, and afterwards the Supper, but the Supper was the Passover. He did with his disciples exactly what every master of a family in Jerusalem was doing at the same hour with his household. It appears that the Jews ate the lamb and the unleavened bread and drank wine after a prescribed manner. It was the custom for the master of the feast to break the bread and to bless it, using this formula, which the Talmudists have preserved to us, "Blessed be Thou, O Lord, our God, who givest us the fruit of the vine"—and then to give the cup to all. Among the modern Jews, who in their dispersion retain the Passover, a hymn is also sung after this ceremony, specifying the twelve great works done by God for the deliverance of their fathers out of Egypt.

But still it may be asked, Why did Jesus make expressions so extraordinary and emphatic as these—"This is my body which is broken for you. Take; eat. This is my blood which is shed for you. Drink it"?—I reply they are not extraordinary expressions from him. They were familiar in his mouth. He always taught by parables and symbols. It was the national way of teaching, and was largely used by him. Remember the readiness which he always showed to spiritualize every occurrence. He stopped and wrote on the sand. He admonished his disciples respecting the leaven of the Pharisees. He instructed the woman of Samaria respecting living water. He permitted himself to be anointed, declaring that it was for his interment. He washed the feet of his disciples. These are admitted to be symbolical actions and expressions. Here, in like manner, he calls the bread his body, and bids the disciples eat. He had used the same expression repeatedly before. The reason why St. John does not repeat his words on this occasion seems to be that he had reported a similar discourse of Jesus to the people of Capernaum more at length already (John vi. 27-60). He there tells the Jews, "Except ye eat the flesh of the Son of Man and drink his blood, ye have no life in you." And when the Jews on that occasion complained that they did not comprehend what he meant, he added for their better understanding, and as if for our understanding, that we might not think his body was to be actually eaten, that he only meant we should live by his commandment. He closed his discourse with these explanatory expressions: "The flesh profiteth nothing; the words that I speak to you, they are spirit and they are life."

Whilst I am upon this topic, I cannot help remarking that it is not a little singular that we should have preserved this rite and insisted upon perpetuating one symbolical act of Christ whilst we have totally neglected all others—particularly one other which had at least an equal claim to our observance. Jesus washed the feet of his disciples and told them that, as he had washed their feet, they ought to wash one another's feet; for he had given them an example, that they should do as he had done to them. I ask any person who believes the Supper to have been designed by Jesus to be commemorated forever, to go and read the account of it in the other Gospels, and then compare with it the account of this transaction in St. John, and tell me if this be not much more explicitly authorized than the Supper. It only differs in this, that we have found the Supper used in New England and the washing of the feet not. But if we had found it an established rite in our churches, on grounds of mere authority, it would have been impossible to have argued against it. That rite is used by the Church of Rome, and by the Sandemanians. It has been very properly dropped by other Christians. Why? For two reasons: (1) because it was a local custom, and unsuitable in western countries; and (2) because it was typical, and all understood that humility is the thing signified. But the Passover was local too, and does not concern us, and its bread and wine were typical, and do not help us to understand the redemption which they signified. These views of the original account of the Lord's Supper lead me to esteem it an occasion full of solemn and prophetic interest, but never intended by Jesus to be the foundation of a perpetual institution.

It appears, however, in Christian history that the disciples had very early taken advantage of these impressive words of Christ to hold religious meetings, where they broke bread and drank wine as symbols. I look upon this fact as very natural in the circumstances of the Church. The disciples lived together; they threw all their property into a common stock; they were bound together by the memory of Christ, and nothing could be more natural than that this eventful evening should be affectionately remembered by them; that they, Jews like Jesus, should adopt his expressions and his types, and furthermore, that what was done with peculiar propriety by them, his personal friends, with less propriety should come to be extended to their companions also. In this way religious feasts grew up among the early Christians. They were readily adopted by the Jewish converts, who were familiar with religious feasts, and also by the Pagan converts, whose idolatrous worship had been made up of sacred festivals, and who very readily abused these to gross riot, as appears from the censures of St. Paul. Many persons consider this fact, the observance of such a memorial feast by the early disciples, decisive of the question whether it ought to be observed by us. There was good reason for his personal friends to remember their friend and repeat his words. It was only too probable that among the half-converted Pagans and Jews, any rite, any form, would find favor, whilst yet unable to comprehend the spiritual character of Christianity.

The circumstance, however, that St. Paul adopts these views, has seemed to many persons conclusive in favor of the institution. I am of opinion that it is wholly upon the Epistle to the Corinthians, and not upon the Gospels, that the ordinance stands. Upon this matter of St. Paul's view of the Supper, a few important considerations must be stated.

The end which he has in view, in the eleventh chapter of the first Epistle, is not to enjoin upon his friends to observe the Supper, but to censure their abuse of it. We quote the passage nowadays as if it enjoined attendance upon the Supper; but he wrote it merely to chide them for drunkenness. To make their enormity plainer, he goes back to the origin of this religious feast to show what sort of feast that was, out of which this riot of theirs came, and so relates the transactions of the Last Supper. "I have received of the Lord," he says, "that which I delivered to you." By this expression it is often thought that a miraculous communication is implied; but certainly without good reason, if it is remembered that St. Paul was living in the lifetime of all the apostles who could give him an account of the transaction; and it is contrary to all reason to suppose that God should work a miracle to convey information that could so easily be got by natural means. So that the import of the expression is that he had received the story of an eyewitness such as we also possess.

But there is a material circumstance which diminishes our confidence in the correctness of the Apostle's view; and that is, the observation that his mind had not escaped the prevalent error of the

primitive Church, the belief, namely, that the second coming of Christ
would shortly occur, until which time, he tells them, this feast was to
be kept. Elsewhere he tells them that at that time the world would be
burnt up with fire, and a new government established, in which the
Saints would sit on thrones; so slow were the disciples, during the life
and after the ascension of Christ, to receive the idea which we receive,
that his second coming was a spiritual kingdom, the dominion of his
religion in the hearts of men, to be extended gradually over the whole
world. In this manner we may see clearly enough how this ancient ordinance got its footing among the early Christians, and this single
expectation of a speedy reappearance of a temporal Messiah, which kept
its influence even over so spiritual a man as St. Paul, would naturally
tend to preserve the use of the rite when once established.

We arrive, then, at this conclusion: first, that it does not appear,
from a careful examination of the account of the Last Supper in the
Evangelists, that it was designed by Jesus to be perpetual; secondly,
that it does not appear that the opinion of St. Paul, all things considered, ought to alter our opinion derived from the Evangelists.

One general remark before quitting this branch of this subject. We
ought to be cautious in taking even the best ascertained opinions and
practices of the primitive Church for our own. If it could be satisfac-
torily shown that they esteemed it authorized and to be transmitted
forever, that does not settle the question for us. We know how invet-
erately they were attached to their Jewish prejudices, and how often
even the influence of Christ failed to enlarge their views. On every
other subject succeeding times have learned to form a judgment more
in accordance with the spirit of Christianity than was the practice of
the early ages.

II. But it is said: "Admit that the rite was not designed to be perpetual. What harm doth it? Here it stands, generally accepted, under
some form, by the Christian world, the undoubted occasion of much
good; is it not better it should remain?" This is the question of expediency.

I proceed to state a few objections that in my judgment lie against
its use in its present form.

1. If the view which I have taken of the history of the institution be
correct, then the claim of authority should be dropped in administering it. You say, every time you celebrate the rite, that Jesus enjoined

it; and the whole language you use conveys that impression. But if you read the New Testament as I do, you do not believe he did.

2. It has seemed to me that the use of this ordinance tends to produce confusion in our views of the relation of the soul to God. It is the old objection to the doctrine of the Trinity—that the true worship was transferred from God to Christ, or that such confusion was introduced into the soul that an undivided worship was given nowhere. Is not that the effect of the Lord's Supper? I appeal now to the convictions of communicants, and ask such persons whether they have not been occasionally conscious of a painful confusion of thought between the worship due to God and the commemoration due to Christ. For the service does not stand upon the basis of a voluntary act, but is imposed by authority. It is an expression of gratitude to Christ, enjoined by Christ. There is an endeavor to keep Jesus in mind, whilst yet the prayers are addressed to God. I fear it is the effect of this ordinance to clothe Jesus with an authority which he never claimed and which distracts the mind of the worshipper. I know our opinions differ much respecting the nature and offices of Christ, and the degree of veneration to which he is entitled. I am so much a Unitarian as this: that I believe the human mind can admit but one God, and that every effort to pay religious homage to more than one being goes to take away all right ideas. I appeal, brethren, to your individual experience. In the moment when you make the least petition to God, though it be but a silent wish that he may approve you, or add one moment to your life—do you not, in the very act, necessarily exclude all other beings from your thought? In that act, the soul stands alone with God, and Jesus is no more present to your mind than your brother or your child.

But is not Jesus called in Scripture the Mediator? He is the mediator in that only sense in which possibly any being can mediate between God and man—that is, an instructor of man. He teaches us how to become like God. And a true disciple of Jesus will receive the light he gives most thankfully; but the thanks he offers, and which an exalted being will accept, are not compliments, commemorations, but the use of that instruction.

3. Passing other objections, I come to this, that the use of the elements, however suitable to the people and the modes of thought in the East, where it originated, is foreign and unsuited to affect us. Whatever long usage and strong association may have done in some individuals to

deaden this repulsion, I apprehend that their use is rather tolerated than loved by any of us. We are not accustomed to express our thoughts or emotions by symbolical actions. Most men find the bread and wine no aid to devotion, and to some it is a painful impediment. To eat bread is one thing; to love the precepts of Christ and resolve to obey them is quite another.

The statement of this objection leads me to say that I think this difficulty, wherever it is felt, to be entitled to the greatest weight. It is alone a sufficient objection to the ordinance. It is my own objection. This mode of commemorating Christ is not suitable to me. That is reason enough why I should abandon it. If I believed it was enjoined by Jesus on his disciples, and that he even contemplated making permanent this mode of commemoration, every way agreeable to an Eastern mind, and yet on trial it was disagreeable to my own feelings, I should not adopt it. I should choose other ways which, as more effectual upon me, he would approve more. For I choose that my remembrances of him should be pleasing, affecting, religious. I will love him as a glorified friend, after the free way of friendship, and not pay him a stiff sign of respect, as men do those whom they fear. A passage read from his discourses, a moving provocation to works like his, any act or meeting which tends to awaken a pure thought, a flow of love, an original design of virtue, I call a worthy, a true commemoration.

4. The importance ascribed to this particular ordinance is not consistent with the spirit of Christianity. The general object and effect of the ordinance is unexceptionable. It has been, and is, I doubt not, the occasion of indefinite good; but an importance is given by Christians to it which never can belong to any form. My friends, the Apostle well assures us that "the kingdom of God is not meat and drink, but righteousness, and peace, and joy in the Holy Ghost." I am not so foolish as to declaim against forms. Forms are as essential as bodies; but to exalt particular forms, to adhere to one form a moment after it is outgrown, is unreasonable, and it is alien to the spirit of Christ. If I understand the distinction of Christianity, the reason why it is to be preferred over all other systems and is divine is this, that it is a moral system; that it presents men with truths which are their own reason, and enjoins practices that are their own justification; that if miracles may be said to have been its evidence to the first Christians they are not its evidence to us, but the doctrines themselves; that every practice

is Christian which praises itself, and every practice unchristian which condemns itself. I am not engaged to Christianity by decent forms, or saving ordinances; it is not usage, it is not what I do not understand, that binds me to it—let these be the sandy foundations of falsehoods. What I revere and obey in it is its reality, its boundless charity, its deep interior life, the rest it gives to mind, the echo it returns to my thoughts, the perfect accord it makes with my reason through all its representation of God and His Providence; and the persuasion and courage that come out thence to lead me upward and onward. Freedom is the essence of this faith. It has for its object simply to make men good and wise. Its institutions then should be as flexible as the wants of men. That form out of which the life and suitableness have departed should be as worthless in its eyes as the dead leaves that are falling around us.

And therefore, although for the satisfaction of others I have labored to show by the history that this rite was not intended to be perpetual; although I have gone back to weigh the expressions of Paul, I feel that here is the true point of view. In the midst of considerations as to what Paul thought, and why he so thought, I cannot help feeling that it is time misspent to argue to or from his convictions, or those of Luke and John, respecting any form. I seem to lose the substance in seeking the shadow. That for which Paul lived and died so gloriously; that for which Jesus gave himself to be crucified; the end that animated the thousand martyrs and heroes who have followed his steps, was to redeem us from a formal religion, and teach us to seek our well-being in the formation of the soul. The whole world was full of idols and ordinances. The Jewish was a religion of forms; it was all body, it had no life, and the Almighty God was pleased to qualify and send forth a man to teach men that they must serve him with the heart; that only that life was religious which was thoroughly good; that sacrifice was smoke, and forms were shadows. This man lived and died true to this purpose; and now, with his blessed word and life before us, Christians must contend that it is a matter of vital importance—really a duty, to commemorate him by a certain form, whether that form be agreeable to their understandings or not. Is not this to make vain the gift of God? Is not this to turn back the hand on the dial? Is not this to make men—to make ourselves—forget that not forms, but duties; not names, but righteousness and love are enjoined; and that in the eye of God there is no other measure of the value of any one form than the measure of its use?

There remain some practical objections to the ordinance, into which I shall not now enter. There is one on which I had intended to say a few words; I mean the unfavorable relation in which it places that numerous class of persons who abstain from it merely from disinclination to the rite.

Influenced by these considerations, I have proposed to the brethren of the Church to drop the use of the elements and the claim of authority in the administration of this ordinance, and have suggested a mode in which a meeting for the same purpose might be held, free of objection.

My brethren have considered my views with patience and candor, and have recommended, unanimously, an adherence to the present form. I have therefore been compelled to consider whether it becomes me to administer it. I am clearly of opinion I ought not. This discourse has already been so far extended that I can only say that the reason of my determination is shortly this: It is my desire, in the office of a Christian minister, to do nothing which I cannot do with my whole heart. Having said this, I have said all. I have no hostility to this institution; I am only stating my want of sympathy with it. Neither should I ever have obtruded this opinion upon other people, had I not been called by my office to administer it. That is the end of my opposition, that I am not interested in it. I am content that it stands to the end of the world, if it please men and please Heaven, and I shall rejoice in all the good it produces.

As it is the prevailing opinion and feeling in our religious community that it is an indispensable part of the pastoral office to administer this ordinance, I am about to resign into your hands that office which you have confided to me. It has many duties for which I am feebly qualified. It has some which it will always be my delight to discharge according to my ability, wherever I exist. And whilst the recollection of its claims oppresses me with a sense of my unworthiness, I am consoled by the hope that no time and no change can deprive me of the satisfaction of pursuing and exercising its highest functions.

ESSAYS
FIRST SERIES

[Emerson's second book was published in 1841. It was almost immediately issued in England with a preface by Carlyle. Most of the essays were composed from lectures that Emerson had been giving in various places during the preceding years.]

HISTORY

There is no great and no small
To the Soul that maketh all:
And where it cometh, all things are;
And it cometh everywhere.

I am owner of the sphere
Of the seven stars and the solar year,
Of Cæsar's hand, and Plato's brain,
Of Lord Christ's heart, and Shakspeare's strain.

THERE is one mind common to all individual men. Every man is an
inlet to the same and to all of the same. He that is once admitted to
the right of reason is made a freeman of the whole estate. What Plato
has thought, he may think; what a saint has felt, he may feel; what at
any time has befallen any man, he can understand. Who hath access
to this universal mind is a party to all that is or can be done, for this
is the only and sovereign agent.

Of the works of this mind history is the record. Its genius is illustrated by the entire series of days. Man is explicable by nothing less
than all his history. Without hurry, without rest, the human spirit goes
forth from the beginning to embody every faculty, every thought, every
emotion which belongs to it, in appropriate events. But the thought is
always prior to the fact; all the facts of history preëxist in the mind as
laws. Each law in turn is made by circumstances predominant, and the
limits of nature give power to but one at a time. A man is the whole
encyclopædia of facts. The creation of a thousand forests is in one
acorn, and Egypt, Greece, Rome, Gaul, Britain, America, lie folded
already in the first man. Epoch after epoch, camp, kingdom, empire,
republic, democracy, are merely the application of his manifold spirit to
the manifold world.

This human mind wrote history, and this must read it. The Sphinx
must solve her own riddle. If the whole of history is in one man, it is all
to be explained from individual experience. There is a relation between
the hours of our life and the centuries of time. As the air I breathe is

113

drawn from the great repositories of nature, as the light on my book is yielded by a star a hundred millions of miles distant, as the poise of my body depends on the equilibrium of centrifugal and centripetal forces, so the hours should be instructed by the ages and the ages explained by the hours. Of the universal mind each individual man is one more incarnation. All its properties consist in him. Each new fact in his private experience flashes a light on what great bodies of men have done, and the crises of his life refer to national crises. Every revolution was first a thought in one man's mind, and when the same thought occurs to another man, it is the key to that era. Every reform was once a private opinion, and when it shall be a private opinion again it will solve the problem of the age. The fact narrated must correspond to something in me to be credible or intelligible. We, as we read, must become Greeks, Romans, Turks, priest and king, martyr and executioner; must fasten these images to some reality in our secret experience, or we shall learn nothing rightly. What befell Asdrubal or Cæsar Borgia is as much an illustration of the mind's powers and depravations as what has befallen us. Each new law and political movement has a meaning for you. Stand before each of its tablets and say, 'Under this mask did my Proteus nature hide itself.' This remedies the defect of our too great nearness to ourselves. This throws our actions into perspective—and as crabs, goats, scorpions, the balance and the waterpot lose their meanness when hung as signs in the zodiac, so I can see my own vices without heat in the distant persons of Solomon, Alcibiades, and Catiline.

It is the universal nature which gives worth to particular men and things. Human life, as containing this, is mysterious and inviolable, and we hedge it round with penalties and laws. All laws derive hence their ultimate reason; all express more or less distinctly some command of this supreme, illimitable essence. Property also holds of the soul, covers great spiritual facts, and instinctively we at first hold to it with swords and laws and wide and complex combinations. The obscure consciousness of this fact is the light of all our day, the claim of claims; the plea for education, for justice, for charity; the foundation of friendship and love and of the heroism and grandeur which belong to acts of self-reliance. It is remarkable that involuntarily we always read as superior beings. Universal history, the poets, the romancers, do not in their stateliest pictures—in the sacerdotal, the imperial palaces, in the triumphs of will or of genius—anywhere lose our ear, anywhere make us feel that we intrude, that this is for better men; but rather is it true that in their grandest strokes we feel most at home. All that Shakspeare says of the king, yonder slip of a boy that reads in the corner feels to be true of himself. We sympathize in the great moments of history, in the great discoveries, the great resistances, the great prosperities of men; because there law was enacted, the sea was searched, the land was found, or the blow was struck, *for us*, as we ourselves in that place would have done or applauded.

We have the same interest in condition and character. We honor the rich because they have externally the freedom, power, and grace which we feel to be proper to man, proper to us. So all that is said of the wise man by Stoic or Oriental or modern essayist, describes to each reader his own idea, describes his unattained but attainable self. All literature writes the character of the wise man. Books, monuments, pictures, conversation, are portraits in which he finds the lineaments he is forming. The silent and the eloquent praise him and accost him, and he is stimulated wherever he moves, as by personal allusions. A true aspirant therefore never needs look for allusions personal and laudatory in discourse. He hears the commendation, not of himself, but, more sweet, of that character he seeks, in every word that is said concerning character, yea further in every fact and circumstance—in the running river and the rustling corn. Praise is looked, homage tendered, love flows, from mute nature, from the mountains and the lights of the firmament.

These hints, dropped as it were from sleep and night, let us use in broad day. The student is to read history actively and not passively; to esteem his own life the text, and books the commentary. Thus compelled, the Muse of history will utter oracles, as never to those who do not respect themselves. I have no expectation that any man will read history aright who thinks that what was done in a remote age, by men whose names have resounded far, has any deeper sense than what he is doing to-day.

The world exists for the education of each man. There is no age or state of society or mode of action in history to which there is not somewhat corresponding in his life. Every thing tends in a wonderful manner to abbreviate itself and yield its own virtue to him. He should see that he can live all history in his own person. He must sit solidly

at home, and not suffer himself to be bullied by kings or empires, but
know that he is greater than all the geography and all the government
of the world; he must transfer the point of view from which history is
commonly read; from Rome and Athens and London, to himself, and
not deny his conviction that he is the court, and if England or Egypt
have anything to say to him he will try the case; if not, let them forever
be silent. He must attain and maintain that lofty sight where facts yield
their secret sense, and poetry and annals are alike. The instinct of the
mind, the purpose of nature, betrays itself in the use we make of the
signal narrations of history. Time dissipates to shining ether the solid
angularity of facts. No anchor, no cable, no fences avail to keep a fact
a fact. Babylon, Troy, Tyre, Palestine, and even early Rome are passing already into fiction. The Garden of Eden, the sun standing still in
Gibeon, is poetry thenceforward to all nations. Who cares what the fact
was, when we have made a constellation of it to hang in heaven an
immortal sign? London and Paris and New York must go the same
way. "What is history," said Napoleon, "but a fable agreed upon?"
This life of ours is stuck round with Egypt, Greece, Gaul, England,
War, Colonization, Church, Court and Commerce, as with so many
flowers and wild ornaments grave and gay. I will not make more
account of them. I believe in Eternity. I can find Greece, Asia, Italy,
Spain and the Islands—the genius and creative principle of each and
of all eras, in my own mind.

We are always coming up with the emphatic facts of history in our
private experience and verifying them here. All history becomes subjective; in other words there is properly no history, only biography.
Every mind must know the whole lesson for itself—must go over the
whole ground. What it does not see, what it does not live, it will not
know. What the former age has epitomized into a formula or rule for
manipular convenience, it will lose all the good of verifying for itself, by
means of the wall of that rule. Somewhere, sometime, it will demand
and find compensation for that loss, by doing the work itself. Fergu-
son discovered many things in astronomy which had long been known.
The better for him.

History must be this or it is nothing. Every law which the state
enacts indicates a fact in human nature; that is all. We must in ourselves see the necessary reason of every fact—see how it could and must
be. So stand before every public and private work; before an oration of

Burke, before a victory of Napoleon, before a martyrdom of Sir Thomas More, of Sidney, of Marmaduke Robinson; before a French Reign of Terror, and a Salem hanging of witches; before a fanatic Revival and the Animal Magnetism in Paris, or in Providence. We assume that we under like influence should be alike affected, and should achieve the like; and we aim to master intellectually the steps and reach the same height or the same degradation that our fellow, our proxy has done.

All inquiry into antiquity, all curiosity respecting the Pyramids, the excavated cities, Stonehenge, the Ohio Circles, Mexico, Memphis—is the desire to do away with this wild, savage, and preposterous There or Then, and introduce in its place the Here and the Now. Belzoni digs and measures in the mummy-pits and pyramids of Thebes until he can see the end of the difference between the monstrous work and himself. When he has satisfied himself, in general and in detail, that it was made by such a person as he, so armed and so motived, and to ends to which he himself should also have worked, the problem is solved; his thought lives along the whole line of temples and sphinxes and catacombs, passes through them all with satisfaction, and they live again to the mind, or are *now*.

A Gothic cathedral affirms that it was done by us and not done by us. Surely it was by man, but we find it not in our man. But we apply ourselves to the history of its production. We put ourselves into the place and state of the builder. We remember the forest-dwellers, the first temples, the adherence to the first type and the decoration of it as the wealth of the nation increased; the value which is given to wood by carving led to the carving over the whole mountain of stone of a cathedral. When we have gone through this process, and added thereto the Catholic Church, its cross, its music, its processions, its Saints' days and image-worship, we have as it were been the man that made the minster; we have seen how it could and must be. We have the sufficient reason.

The difference between men is in their principle of association. Some men classify objects by color and size and other accidents of appearance; others by intrinsic likeness, or by the relation of cause and effect. The progress of the intellect is to the clearer vision of pauses, which neglects surface differences. To the poet, to the philosopher, to the saint, all things are friendly and sacred, all events profitable, all days holy, all men divine. For the eye is fastened on the life, and slights the circumstance. Every chemical substance, every plant, every animal in its growth, teaches the unity of cause, the variety of appearance.

Upborne and surrounded as we are by this all-creating nature, soft and fluid as a cloud or the air, why should we be such hard pedants, and magnify a few forms? Why should we make account of time, or of magnitude, or of figure? The soul knows them not, and genius, obeying its law, knows how to play with them as a young child plays with gray-beards and in churches. Genius studies the causal thought, and far back in the womb of things sees the rays parting from one orb, that diverge, ere they fall, by infinite diameters. Genius watches the monad through all his masks as he performs the metempsychosis of nature. Genius detects through the fly, through the caterpillar, through the grub, through the egg, the constant individual; through countless individuals the fixed species; through many species the genus; through all genera the steadfast type; through all the kingdoms of organized life the eternal unity. Nature is a mutable cloud which is always and never the same. She casts the same thought into troops of forms, as a poet makes twenty fables with one moral. Through the bruteness and toughness of matter, a subtle spirit bends all things to its own will. The adamant streams into soft but precise form before it, and whilst I look at it its outline and texture are changed again. Nothing is so fleeting as form; yet never does it quite deny itself. In man we still trace the remains or hints of all that we esteem badges of servitude in the lower races; yet in him they enhance his nobleness and grace; as Io, in Aeschylus, transformed to a cow, offends the imagination; but how changed when as Isis in Egypt she meets Osiris-Jove, a beautiful woman with nothing of the metamorphosis left but the lunar horns as the splendid ornament of her brows!

The identity of history is equally intrinsic, the diversity equally obvious. There is, at the surface, infinite variety of things; at the centre there is simplicity of cause. How many are the acts of one man in which we recognize the same character! Observe the sources of our information in respect to the Greek genius. We have the *civil history* of that people, as Herodotus, Thucydides, Xenophon, and Plutarch have given it; a very sufficient account of what manner of persons they were and what they did. We have the same national mind expressed for us again in their *literature*, in epic and lyric poems, drama, and philosophy; a very complete form. Then we have it once more in their *architecture*, a beauty as of temperance itself, limited to the straight line and the square—a builded geometry. Then we have it once again in sculpture, the "tongue on the balance of expression," a multitude of forms in the utmost freedom of action and never transgressing the ideal serenity; like votaries performing some religious dance before the gods, and, though in convulsive pain or mortal combat, never daring to break the figure and decorum of their dance. Thus of the genius of one remarkable people we have a fourfold representation: and to the senses what more unlike than an ode of Pindar, a marble centaur, the peristyle of the Parthenon, and the last actions of Phocion?

Every one must have observed faces and forms which, without any resembling feature, make a like impression on the beholder. A particular picture or copy of verses, if it do not awaken the same train of images, will yet superinduce the same sentiment as some wild mountain walk, although the resemblance is nowise obvious to the senses, but is occult and out of the reach of the understanding. Nature is an endless combination and repetition of a very few laws. She hums the old well-known air through innumerable variations.

Nature is full of a sublime family likeness throughout her works, and delights in startling us with resemblances in the most unexpected quarters. I have seen the head of an old sachem of the forest which at once reminded the eye of a bald mountain summit, and the furrows of the brow suggested the strata of the rock. There are men whose manners have the same essential splendor as the simple and awful sculpture on the friezes of the Parthenon and the remains of the earliest Greek art. And there are compositions of the same strain to be found in the books of all ages. What is Guido's Rospigliosi Aurora but a morning thought, as the horses in it are only a morning cloud? If any one will but take pains to observe the variety of actions to which he is equally inclined in certain moods of mind, and those to which he is averse, he will see how deep is the chain of affinity.

A painter told me that nobody could draw a tree without in some sort becoming a tree; or draw a child by studying the outlines of its form merely—but by watching for a time his motions and plays, the painter enters into his nature and can then draw him at will in every attitude. So Roos "entered into the inmost nature of a sheep." I knew a draughtsman employed in a public survey who found that he could not sketch the rocks until their geological structure was first explained to him. In a certain state of thought is the common origin of very diverse works. It is the spirit and not the fact that is identical. By a deeper apprehension, and not primarily by a painful acquisition of many manual skills, the artist attains the power of awakening other souls to a given activity.

It has been said that "common souls pay with what they do, nobler souls with that which they are." And why? Because a profound nature awakens in us by its actions and words, by its very looks and manners, the same power and beauty that a gallery of sculpture or of pictures addresses.

Civil and natural history, the history of art and of literature, must be explained from individual history, or must remain words. There is nothing but is related to us, nothing that. does not interest us—kingdom, college, tree, horse, or iron shoe—the roots of all things are in man. Santa Croce and the Dome of St. Peter's are lame copies after a divine model. Strasburg Cathedral is a material counterpart of the soul of Erwin of Steinbach. The true poem is the poet's mind; the true ship is the shipbuilder. In the man, could we lay him open, we should see the reason for the last flourish and tendril of his work; as every spine and tint in the sea-shell preëxists in the secreting organs of the fish. The whole of heraldry and of chivalry is in courtesy. A man of fine manners shall pronounce your name with all the ornament that titles of nobility could ever add.

The trivial experience of every day is always verifying some old prediction to us and converting into things the words and signs which we had heard and seen without heed. A lady with whom I was riding in the forest said to me that the woods always seemed to her to wait, as if the genii who inhabit them suspended their deeds until the wayfarer had passed onward; a thought which poetry has celebrated in the dance of the fairies, which breaks off on the approach of human feet. The man who has seen the rising moon break out of the clouds at midnight, has been present like an archangel at the creation of light and of the world. I remember one summer day in the fields my companion pointed out to me a broad cloud, which might extend a quarter of a mile parallel to the horizon, quite accurately in the form of a cherub as painted over churches—a round block in the centre, which it was easy to animate with eyes and mouth, supported on either side by wide-stretched symmetrical wings. What appears once in the atmosphere

. . . .

may appear often, and it was undoubtedly the archetype of that familiar ornament. I have seen in the sky a chain of summer lightning which
at once showed to me that the Greeks drew from nature when they
painted the thunderbolt in the hand of Jove. I have seen a snow-drift
along the sides of the stone wall which obviously gave the idea of the
common architectural scroll to abut a tower.

By surrounding ourselves with the original circumstances we invent
anew the orders and the ornaments of architecture, as we see how each
people merely decorated its primitive abodes. The Doric temple preserves the semblance of the wooden cabin in which the Dorian dwelt.
The Chinese pagoda is plainly a Tartar tent. The Indian and Egyptian
temples still betray the mounds and subterranean houses of their forefathers. "The custom of making houses and tombs in the living rock,"
says Heeren in his Researches on the Ethiopians, "determined very naturally the principal character of the Nubian Egyptian architecture to
the colossal form which it assumed. In these caverns, already prepared
by nature, the eye was accustomed to dwell on huge shapes and masses,
so that when art came to the assistance of nature it could not move on
a small scale without degrading itself. What would statues of the usual
size, or neat porches and wings have been, associated with those gigantic halls before which only Colossi could sit as watchmen or lean on
the pillars of the interior?"

The Gothic church plainly originated in a rude adaptation of the
forest trees, with all their boughs, to a festal or solemn arcade; as the
bands about the cleft pillars still indicate the green withes that tied
them. No one can walk in a road cut through pine woods, without
being struck with the architectural appearance of the grove, especially in
winter, when the barrenness of all other trees shows the low arch of the
Saxons. In the woods in a winter afternoon one will see as readily the
origin of the stained glass window, with which the Gothic cathedrals
are adorned, in the colors of the western sky seen through the bare and
crossing branches of the forest. Nor can any lover of nature enter the
old piles of Oxford and the English cathedrals, without feeling that the
forest overpowered the mind of the builder, and that his chisel, his saw
and plane still reproduced its ferns, its spikes of flowers, its locust, elm,
oak, pine, fir and spruce.

The Gothic cathedral is a blossoming in stone subdued by the
insatiable demand of harmony in man. The mountain of granite blooms

into an eternal flower, with the lightness and delicate finish as well as the aerial proportions and perspective of vegetable beauty.

In like manner all public facts are to be individualized, all private facts are to be generalized. Then at once History becomes fluid and true, and Biography deep and sublime. As the Persian imitated in the slender shafts and capitals of his architecture the stem and flower of the lotus and palm, so the Persian court in its magnificent era never gave over the nomadism of its barbarous tribes, but travelled from Ecbatana, where the spring was spent, to Susa in summer and to Babylon for the winter.

In the early history of Asia and Africa, Nomadism and Agriculture are the two antagonist facts. The geography of Asia and of Africa necessitated a nomadic life. But the nomads were the terror of all those whom the soil or the advantages of a market had induced to build towns. Agriculture therefore was a religious injunction, because of the perils of the state from nomadism. And in these late and civil countries of England and America these propensities still fight out the old battle, in the nation and in the individual. The nomads of Africa were constrained to wander, by the attacks of the gad-fly, which drives the cattle mad, and so compels the tribe to emigrate in the rainy season and to drive off the cattle to the higher sandy regions. The nomads of Asia follow the pasturage from month to month. In America and Europe the nomadism is of trade and curiosity; a progress, certainly, from the gad-fly of Astaboras to the Anglo and Italomania of Boston Bay. Sacred cities, to which a periodical religious pilgrimage was enjoined, or stringent laws and customs tending to invigorate the national bond, were the check on the old rovers; and the cumulative values of long residence are the restraints on the itinerancy of the present day. The antagonism of the two tendencies is not less active in individuals, as the love of adventure or the love of repose happens to predominate. A man of rude health and flowing spirits has the faculty of rapid domestication, lives in his wagon and roams through all latitudes as easily as a Calmuc. At sea, or in the forest, or in the snow, he sleeps as warm, dines with as good appetite, and associates as happily as beside his own chimneys. Or perhaps his facility is deeper seated, in the increased range of his faculties of observation, which yield him points of interest wherever fresh objects meet his eyes. The pastoral nations were needy and hungry to desperation; and this intellectual nomadism, in its excess, bankrupts the mind through the dissipation of power on a miscellany of objects. The home-keeping wit, on the other hand, is that continence or content which finds all the elements of life in its own soil; and which has its own perils of monotony and deterioration, if not stimulated by foreign infusions.

Every thing the individual sees without him corresponds to his states of mind, and every thing is in turn intelligible to him, as his onward thinking leads him into the truth to which that fact or series belongs.

The primeval world—the Fore-World, as the Germans say—I can dive to it in myself as well as grope for it with researching fingers in catacombs, libraries, and the broken reliefs and torsos of ruined villas.

What is the foundation of that interest all men feel in Greek history, letters, art and poetry, in all its periods from the Heroic or Homeric age down to the domestic life of the Athenians and Spartans, four or five centuries later? What but this, that every man passes personally through a Grecian period. The Grecian state is the era of the bodily nature, the perfection of the senses—of the spiritual nature unfolded in strict unity with the body. In it existed those human forms which supplied the sculptor with his models of Hercules, Phœbus, and Jove; not like the forms abounding in the streets of modern cities, wherein the face is a confused blur of features, but composed of incorrupt, sharply defined and symmetrical features, whose eye-sockets are so formed that it would be impossible for such eyes to squint and take furtive glances on this side and on that, but they must turn the whole head. The manners of that period are plain and fierce. The reverence exhibited is for personal qualities; courage, address, self-command, justice, strength, swiftness, a loud voice, a broad chest. Luxury and elegance are not known. A sparse population and want make every man his own valet, cook, butcher and soldier, and the habit of supplying his own needs educates the body to wonderful performances. Such are the Agamemnon and Diomed of Homer, and not far different is the picture Xenophon gives of himself and his compatriots in the Retreat of the Ten Thousand. "After the army had crossed the river Teleboas in Armenia, there fell much snow, and the troops lay miserably on the ground covered with it. But Xenophon arose naked, and taking an axe, began to split wood; whereupon others rose and did the like." Throughout his army exists a boundless liberty of speech. They quar-

rel for plunder, they wrangle with the generals on each new order, and
Xenophon is as sharp-tongued as any and sharper-tongued than most,
and so gives as good as he gets. Who does not see that this is a gang
of great boys, with such a code of honor and such lax discipline as great
boys have?

The costly charm of the ancient tragedy, and indeed of all the old
literature, is that the persons speak simply—speak as persons who have
great good sense without knowing it, before yet the reflective habit has
become the predominant habit of the mind. Our admiration of the
antique is not admiration of the old, but of the natural. The Greeks are
not reflective, but perfect in their senses and in their health, with the
finest physical organization in the world. Adults acted with the simplicity and grace of children. They made vases, tragedies and statues,
such as healthy senses should—that is, in good taste. Such things have
continued to be made in all ages, and are now, wherever a healthy
physique exists; but, as a class, from their superior organization, they
have surpassed all. They combine the energy of manhood with the
engaging unconciousness of childhood. The attraction of these manners is that they belong to man, and are known to every man in virtue
of his being once a child; besides that there are always individuals who
retain these characteristics. A person of child-like genius and inborn
energy is still a Greek, and revives our love of the Muse of Hellas. I
admire the love of nature in the Philoctetes. In reading those fine apos-
trophes to sleep, to the stars, rocks, mountains and waves, I feel time
passing away as an ebbing sea. I feel the eternity of man, the identity of
his thought. The Greek had, it seems, the same fellow-beings as I. The
sun and moon, water and fire, met his heart precisely as they meet
mine. Then the vaunted distinction between Greek and English,
between Classic and Romantic schools, seems superficial and pedantic.
When a thought of Plato becomes a thought to me—when a truth that
fired the soul of Pindar fires mine, time is no more. When I feel that
we two meet in a perception, that our two souls are tinged with the
same hue, and do as it were run into one, why should I measure
degrees of latitude, why should I count Egyptian years?

The student interprets the age of chivalry by his own age of
chivalry, and the days of maritime adventure and circumnavigation by
quite parallel miniature experiences of his own. To the sacred history of
the world he has the same key. When the voice of a prophet out of the

deeps of antiquity merely echoes to him a sentiment of his infancy, a prayer of his youth, he then pierces to the truth through all the confusion of tradition and the caricature of institutions.

Rare, extravagant spirits come by us at intervals, who disclose to us new facts in nature. I see that men of God have from time to time walked among men and made their commission felt in the heart and soul of the commonest hearer. Hence evidently the tripod, the priest, the priestess inspired by the divine afflatus.

Jesus astonishes and overpowers sensual people. They cannot unite him to history, or reconcile him with themselves. As they come to revere their intuitions and aspire to live holily, their own piety explains every fact, every word.

How easily these old worships of Moses, of Zoroaster, of Menu, of Socrates, domesticate themselves in the mind. I cannot find any antiquity in them. They are mine as much as theirs.

I have seen the first monks and anchorets, without crossing seas or centuries. More than once some individual has appeared to me with such negligence of labor and such commanding contemplation, a haughty beneficiary begging in the name of God, as made good to the nineteenth century Simeon the Stylite, the Thebais, and the first Capuchins.

The priestcraft of the East and West, of the Magian, Brahmin, Druid, and Inca, is expounded in the individual's private life. The cramping influence of a hard formalist on a young child, in repressing his spirits and courage, paralyzing the understanding, and that without producing indignation, but only fear and obedience, and even much sympathy with the tyranny—is a familiar fact, explained to the child when he becomes a man, only by seeing that the oppressor of his youth is himself a child tyrannized over by those names and words and forms of whose influence he was merely the organ to the youth. The fact teaches him how Belus was worshipped and how the Pyramids were built, better than the discovery by Champollion of the names of all the workmen and the cost of every tile. He finds Assyria and the Mounds of Cholula at his door, and himself has laid the courses.

Again, in that protest which each considerate person makes against the superstition of his times, he repeats step for step the part of old reformers, and in the search after truth finds, like them, new perils to virtue. He learns again what moral vigor is needed to supply the girdle

. . . .

of a superstition. A great licentiousness treads on the heels of a reformation. How many times in the history of the world has the Luther of
the day had to lament the decay of piety in his own household! "Doctor," said his wife to Martin Luther, one day, "how is it that whilst
subject to papacy we prayed so often and with such fervor, whilst now
we pray with the utmost coldness and very seldom?"

The advancing man discovers how deep a property he has in literature—in all fable as well as in all history. He finds that the poet was
no odd fellow who described strange and impossible situations, but that
universal man wrote by his pen a confession true for one and true for
all. His own secret biography he finds in lines wonderfully intelligible
to him, dotted down before he was born. One after another he comes
up in his private adventures with every fable of Aesop, of Homer, of
Hafiz, of Ariosto, of Chaucer, of Scott, and verifies them with his own
head and hands.

The beautiful fables of the Greeks, being proper creations of the
imagination and not of the fancy, are universal verities. What a range of
meanings and what perpetual pertinence has the story of Prometheus!
Beside its primary value as the first chapter of the history of Europe
(the mythology thinly veiling authentic facts, the invention of the
mechanic arts and the migration of colonies) it gives the history of religion, with some closeness to the faith of later ages. Prometheus is the
Jesus of the old mythology. He is the friend of man; stands between
the unjust "justice" of the Eternal Father and the race of mortals, and
readily suffers all things on their account. But where it departs from
the Calvinistic Christianity and exhibits him as the defier of Jove, it
represents a state of mind which readily appears wherever the doctrine
of Theism is taught in a crude, objective form, and which seems the
self-defence of man against this untruth, namely a discontent with the
believed fact that a God exists, and a feeling that the obligation of reverence is onerous. It would steal if it could the fire of the Creator, and
live apart from him and independent of him. The Prometheus Vinctus
is the romance of skepticism. Not less true to all time are the details of
that stately apologue. Apollo kept the flocks of Admetus, said the poets.
When the gods come among men, they are not known. Jesus was not;
Socrates and Shakspeare were not. Antæus was suffocated by the gripe
of Hercules, but every time he touched his mother-earth his strength
was renewed. Man is the broken giant, and in all his weakness both his

body and his mind are invigorated by habits of conversation with nature. The power of music, the power of poetry, to unfix and as it were clap wings to solid nature, interprets the riddle of Orpheus. The philosophical perception of identity through endless mutations of form makes him know the Proteus. What else am I who laughed or wept yesterday, who slept last night like a corpse, and this morning stood and ran? And what see I on any side but the transmigrations of Proteus? I can symbolize my thought by using the name of any creature, of any fact, because every creature is man agent or patient. Tantalus is but a name for you and me. Tantalus means the impossibility of drinking the waters of thought which are always gleaming and waving within sight of the soul. The transmigration of souls is no fable. I would it were; but men and women are only half human. Every animal of the barn-yard, the field and the forest, of the earth and of the waters that are under the earth, has contrived to get a footing and to leave the print of its features and form in some one or other of these upright, heaven-facing speakers. Ah! brother, stop the ebb of thy soul—ebbing downward into the forms into whose habits thou hast now for many years slid. As near and proper to us is also that old fable of the Sphinx, who was said to sit in the road-side and put riddles to every passenger. If the man could not answer, she swallowed him alive. If he could solve the riddle, the Sphinx was slain. What is our life but an endless flight of winged facts or events? In splendid variety these changes come, all putting questions to the human spirit. Those men who cannot answer by a superior wisdom these facts or questions of time, serve them. Facts encumber them, tyrannize over them, and make the men of routine, the men of sense, in whom a literal obedience to facts has extinguished every spark of that light by which man is truly man. But if the man is true to his better instincts or sentiments, and refuses the dominion of facts, as one that comes of a higher race; remains fast by the soul and sees the principle, then the facts fall aptly and supple into their places; they know their master, and the meanest of them glorifies him.

See in Goethe's Helena the same desire that every word should be a thing. These figures, he would say, these Chirons, Griffins, Phorkyas, Helen and Leda, are somewhat, and do exert a specific influence on the mind. So far then are they eternal entities, as real to-day as in the first Olympiad. Much revolving them he writes out freely his humor, and

. . . .

gives them body to his own imagination. And although that poem be as vague and fantastic as a dream, yet is it much more attractive than the more regular dramatic pieces of the same author, for the reason that it operates a wonderful relief to the mind from the routine of customary images—awakens the reader's invention and fancy by the wild freedom of the design, and by the unceasing succession of brisk shocks of surprise.

The universal nature, too strong for the petty nature of the bard, sits on his neck and writes through his hand; so that when he seems to vent a mere caprice and wild romance, the issue is an exact allegory. Hence Plato said that "poets utter great and wise things which they do not themselves understand." All the fictions of the Middle Age explain themselves as a masked or frolic expression of that which in grave earnest the mind of that period toiled to achieve. Magic and all that is ascribed to it is a deep presentiment of the powers of science. The shoes of swiftness, the sword of sharpness, the power of subduing the elements, of using the secret virtues of minerals, of understanding the voices of birds, are the obscure efforts of the mind in a right direction. The preternatural prowess of the hero, the gift of perpetual youth, and the like, are alike the endeavor of the human spirit "to bend the shows of things to the desires of the mind."

In Perceforest and Amadis de Gaul a garland and a rose bloom on the head of her who is faithful, and fade on the brow of the inconstant. In the story of the Boy and the Mantle even a mature reader may be surprised with a glow of virtuous pleasure at the triumph of the gentle Venelas; and indeed all the postulates of elfin annals—that the fairies do not like to be named; that their gifts are capricious and not to be trusted; that who seeks a treasure must not speak; and the like—I find true in Concord, however they might be in Cornwall or Bretagne.

Is it otherwise in the newest romance? I read the Bride of Lammermoor. Sir William Ashton is a mask for a vulgar temptation, Ravenswood Castle a fine name for proud poverty, and the foreign mission of state only a Bunyan disguise for honest industry. We may all shoot a wild bull that would toss the good and beautiful, by fighting down the unjust and sensual. Lucy Ashton is another name for fidelity, which is always beautiful and always liable to calamity in this world.

But along with the civil and metaphysical history of man, another history goes daily forward—that of the external world—in which he is not less strictly implicated. He is the compend of time; he is also the correlative of nature. His power consists in the multitude of his affinities, in the fact that his life is intertwined with the whole chain of organic and inorganic being. In old Rome the public roads beginning at the Forum proceeded north, south, east, west, to the centre of every province of the empire, making each market-town of Persia, Spain and Britain pervious to the soldiers of the capital: so out of the human heart go as it were highways to the heart of every object in nature, to reduce it under the dominion of man. A man is a bundle of relations, a knot of roots, whose flower and fruitage is the world. His faculties refer to natures out of him and predict the world he is to inhabit, as the fins of the fish foreshow that water exists, or the wings of an eagle in the egg presuppose air. He cannot live without a world. Put Napoleon in an island prison, let his faculties find no men to act on, no Alps to climb, no stake to play for, and he would beat the air, and appear stupid. Transport him to large countries, dense population, complex interests and antagonist power, and you shall see that the man Napoleon, bounded that is by such a profile and outline, is not the virtual Napoleon. This is but Talbot's shadow—

> "His substance is not here.
> For what you see is but the smallest part
> And least proportion of humanity;
> But were the whole frame here,
> It is of such a spacious, lofty pitch,
> Your roof were not sufficient to contain it."

Columbus needs a planet to shape his course upon. Newton and Laplace need myriads of age and thick-strewn celestial areas. One may say a gravitating solar system is already prophesied in the nature of Newton's mind. Not less does the brain of Davy or of Gay-Lussac, from childhood exploring the affinities and repulsions of particles, anticipate the laws of organization. Does not the eye of the human embryo predict the light? the ear of Handel predict the witchcraft of harmonic sound? Do not the constructive fingers of Watt, Fulton, Whittemore, Arkwright, predict the fusible, hard, and temperable texture of metals, the properties of stone, water, and wood? Do not the

lovely attributes of the maiden child predict the refinements and decorations of civil society? Here also we are reminded of the action of man
on man. A mind might ponder its thoughts for ages and not gain so
much self-knowledge as the passion of love shall teach it in a day. Who
knows himself before he has been thrilled with indignation at an outrage, or has heard an eloquent tongue, or has shared the throb of
thousands in a national exultation or alarm? No man can antedate his
experience, or guess what faculty or feeling a new object shall unlock,
any more than he can draw to-day the face of a person whom he shall
see tomorrow for the first time.

I will not now go behind the general statement to explore the reason of this correspondency. Let it suffice that in the light of these two
facts, namely, that the mind is One, and that nature is its correlative,
history is to be read and written.

Thus in all ways does the soul concentrate and reproduce its treasures for each pupil. He too shall pass through the whole cycle of
experience. He shall collect into a focus the rays of nature. History no
longer shall be a dull book. It shall walk incarnate in every just and
wise man. You shall not tell me by languages and titles a catalogue of
the volumes you have read. You shall make me feel what periods you
have lived. A man shall be the Temple of Fame. He shall walk, as the
poets have described that goddess, in a robe painted all over with wonderful events and experiences; his own form and features by their
exalted intelligence shall be that variegated vest. I shall find in him the
Foreworld; in his childhood the Age of Gold, the Apples of Knowledge,
the Argonautic Expedition, the calling of Abraham, the building of the
Temple, the Advent of Christ, the Dark Ages, the Revival of Letters,
the Reformation, the discovery of new lands, the opening of new sciences and new regions in man. He shall be the priest of Pan, and bring
with him into humble cottages the blessing of the morning stars, and all
the recorded benefits of heaven and earth.

Is there somewhat overweening in this claim? Then I reject all I
have written, for what is the use of pretending to know what we know
not? But it is the fault of our rhetoric that we cannot strongly state one
fact without seeming to belie some other. I hold our actual knowledge
very cheap. Hear the rats in the wall, see the lizard on the fence, the
fungus under foot, the lichen on the log. What do I know sympatheti-
cally, morally, of either of these worlds of life? As old as the Caucasian

man—perhaps older—these creatures have kept their counsel beside him, and there is no record of any word or sign that has passed from one to the other. What connection do the books show between the fifty or sixty chemical elements and the historical eras? Nay, what does history yet record of the metaphysical annals of man? What light does it shed on those mysteries which we hide under the names Death and Immortality? Yet every history should be written in a wisdom which divined the range of our affinities and looked at facts as symbols. I am ashamed to see what a shallow village tale our so-called History is. How many times we must say Rome, and Paris, and Constantinople! What does Rome know of rat and lizard? What are Olympiads and Consulates to these neighboring systems of being? Nay, what food or experience or succor have they for the Esquimaux seal-hunter, for the Kanàka in his canoe, for the fisherman, the stevedore, the porter?

Broader and deeper we must write our annals—from an ethical reformation, from an influx of the ever new, ever sanative conscience— if we would trulier express our central and wide-related nature, instead of this old chronology of selfishness and pride to which we have too long lent our eyes. Already that day exists for us, shines in on us at unawares, but the path of science and of letters is not the way into nature. The idiot, the Indian, the child and unschooled farmer's boy stand nearer to the light by which nature is to be read, than the dissector or the antiquary.

SELF-RELIANCE

"Ne te quæsiveris extra."

Man is his own star; and the soul that can
Render an honest and a perfect man,
Commands all light, all influence, all fate;
Nothing to him falls early or too late.
Our acts our angels are, or good or ill,
Our fatal shadows that walk by us still.

Epilogue to Beaumont and Fletcher's Honest Man's Fortune.

Cast the bantling on the rocks,
Suckle him with the she-wolf's teat,
Wintered with the hawk and fox,
Power and speed be hands and feet.

I READ the other day some verses written by an eminent painter which were original and not conventional. The soul always hears an admonition in such lines, let the subject be what it may. The sentiment they instil is of more value than any thought they may contain. To believe your own thought, to believe that what is true for you in your private heart is true for all men—that is genius. Speak your latent conviction, and it shall be the universal sense; for the inmost in due time becomes the outmost, and our first thought is rendered back to us by the trumpets of the Last Judgment. Familiar as the voice of the mind is to each, the highest merit we ascribe to Moses, Plato and Milton is that they set at naught books and traditions, and spoke not what men, but what *they* thought. A man should learn to detect and watch that gleam of light which flashes across his mind from within, more than the lustre of the firmament of bards and sages. Yet he dismisses without notice his thought, because it is his. In every work of genius we recognize our own rejected thoughts; they come back to us with a certain alienated majesty. Great works of art have no more affecting lesson for us than this. They teach us to abide by our spontaneous impression with good-humored inflexibility then most when the whole cry of voices is on the

gather immortal palms must not be hindered by the name of goodness, but must explore if it be goodness. Nothing is at last sacred but the integrity of your own mind. Absolve you to yourself, and you shall have the suffrage of the world. I remember an answer which when quite young I was prompted to make to a valued adviser who was wont to importune me with the dear old doctrines of the church. On my saying, "What have I to do with the sacredness of traditions, if I live wholly from within?" my friend suggested—"But these impulses may be from below, not from above." I replied, "They do not seem to me to be such; but if I am the Devil's child, I will live then from the Devil." No law can be sacred to me but that of my nature. Good and bad are but names very readily transferable to that or this; the only right is what is after my constitution; the only wrong what is against it. A man is to carry himself in the presence of all opposition as if every thing were titular and ephemeral but he. I am ashamed to think how easily we capitulate to badges and names, to large societies and dead institutions. Every decent and well-spoken individual affects and sways me more than is right. I ought to go upright and vital, and speak the rude truth in all ways. If malice and vanity wear the coat of philanthropy, shall that pass? If an angry bigot assumes this bountiful cause of Abolition, and comes to me with his last news from Barbadoes, why should I not say to him, 'Go love thy infant; love thy wood-chopper; be good-natured and modest; have that grace; and never varnish your hard, uncharitable ambition with this incredible tenderness for black folk a thousand miles off. Thy love afar is spite at home.' Rough and grace-less would be such greeting, but truth is handsomer than the affectation of love. Your goodness must have some edge to it—else it is none. The doctrine of hatred must be preached, as the counteraction of the doctrine of love, when that pules and whines. I shun father and mother and wife and brother when my genius calls me. I would write on the lintels of the door-post, Whim. I hope it is somewhat better than whim at last, but we cannot spend the day in explanation. Expect me not to show cause why I seek or why I exclude company. Then again, do not tell me, as a good man did to-day, of my obligation to put all poor men in good situations. Are they my poor? I tell thee, thou foolish philanthropist, that I grudge the dollar, the dime, the cent I give to such men as do not belong to me and to whom I do not belong. There is a class of persons to whom by all spiritual affinity I am bought and sold; for them I will go to prison if need be; but your miscellaneous popular charities; the education at college of fools; the building of meeting-houses to the vain end to which many now stand; alms to sots, and the thousand-fold Relief Societies; though I confess with shame I some-times succumb and give the dollar, it is a wicked dollar, which by and by I shall have the manhood to withhold.

Virtues are, in the popular estimate, rather the exception than the rule. There is the man and his virtues. Men do what is called a good action, as some piece of courage or charity, much as they would pay a fine in expiation of daily non-appearance on parade. Their works are done as an apology or extenuation of their living in the world—as invalids and the insane pay a high board. Their virtues are penances. I do not wish to expiate, but to live. My life is for itself and not for a spectacle. I much prefer that it should be of a lower strain, so it be gen-uine and equal, than that it should be glittering and unsteady. I wish it to be sound and sweet, and not to need diet and bleeding. I ask pri-mary evidence that you are a man, and refuse this appeal from the man to his actions. I know that for myself it makes no difference whether I do or forbear those actions which are reckoned excellent. I cannot con-sent to pay for a privilege where I have intrinsic right. Few and mean as my gifts may be, I actually am, and do not need for my own assur-ance or the assurance of my fellows any secondary testimony.

What I must do is all that concerns me, not what the people think. This rule, equally arduous in actual and in intellectual life, may serve for the whole distinction between greatness and meanness. It is the harder because you will always find those who think they know what is your duty better than you know it. It is easy in the world to live after the world's opinion; it is easy in solitude to live after our own; but the great man is he who in the midst of the crowd keeps with perfect sweetness the independence of solitude.

The objection to conforming to usages that have become dead to you is that it scatters your force. It loses your time and blurs the impression of your character. If you maintain a dead church, contribute to a dead Bible-society, vote with a great party either for the govern-ment or against it, spread your table like base housekeepers—under all these screens I have difficulty to detect the precise man you are: and of course so much force is withdrawn from your proper life. But do your work, and I shall know you. Do your work, and you shall reinforce yourself. A man must consider what a blind-man's-buff is this game of conformity. If I know your sect I anticipate your argument. I hear a preacher announce for his text and topic the expediency of one of the institutions of his church. Do I not know beforehand that not possibly can he say a new and spontaneous word? Do I not know that with all this ostentation of examining the grounds of the institution he will do no such thing? Do I not know that he is pledged to himself not to look but at one side, the permitted side, not as a man, but as a parish minister? He is a retained attorney, and these airs of the bench are the emptiest affectation. Well, most men have bound their eyes with one or another handkerchief, and attached themselves to some one of these communities of opinion. This conformity makes them not false in a few particulars, authors of a few lies, but false in all particulars. Their every truth is not quite true. Their two is not the real two, their four not the real four; so that every word they say chagrins us and we know not where to begin to set them right. Meantime nature is not slow to equip us in the prison-uniform of the party to which we adhere. We come to wear one cut of face and figure, and acquire by degrees the gentlest asinine expression. There is a mortifying experience in particular, which does not fail to wreak itself also in the general history; I mean "the foolish face of praise," the forced smile which we put on in company where we do not feel at ease, in answer to conversation which does not interest us. The muscles, not spontaneously moved but moved by a low usurping wilfulness, grow tight about the outline of the face, with the most disagreeable sensation.

For nonconformity the world whips you with its displeasure. And therefore a man must know how to estimate a sour face. The bystanders look askance on him in the public street or in the friend's parlor. If this aversion had its origin in contempt and resistance like his own he might well go home with a sad countenance; but the sour faces of the multitude, like their sweet faces, have no deep cause, but are put on and off as the wind blows and a newspaper directs. Yet is the discontent of the multitude more formidable than that of the senate and the college. It is easy enough for a firm man who knows the world to brook the rage of the cultivated classes. Their rage is decorous and prudent, for they are timid, as being very vulnerable themselves. But when to their feminine rage the indignation of the people is added, when the ignorant and the poor are aroused, when the unintelligent brute force that lies at the bottom of society is made to growl and mow, it needs the habit of magnanimity and religion to treat it godlike as a trifle of no concernment.

The other terror that scares us from self-trust is our consistency; a reverence for our past act or word because the eyes of others have no other data for computing our orbit than our past acts, and we are loth to disappoint them.

But why should you keep your head over your shoulder? Why drag about this corpse of your memory, lest you contradict some what you have stated in this or that public place? Suppose you should contradict yourself; what then? It seems to be a rule of wisdom never to rely on your memory alone, scarcely even in acts of pure memory, but to bring the past for judgment into the thousand-eyed present, and live ever in a new day. In your metaphysics you have denied personality to the Deity, yet when the devout motions of the soul come, yield to them heart and life, though they should clothe God with shape and color. Leave your theory, as Joseph his coat in the hand of the harlot, and flee.

A foolish consistency is the hobgoblin of little minds, adored by little statesmen and philosophers and divines. With consistency a great soul has simply nothing to do. He may as well concern himself with his shadow on the wall. Speak what you think now in hard words and to-morrow speak what to-morrow thinks in hard words again, though it contradict every thing you said to-day.—'Ah, so you shall be sure to be misunderstood.'—Is it so bad then to be misunderstood? Pythagoras was misunderstood, and Socrates, and Jesus, and Luther, and Copernicus, and Galileo, and Newton, and every pure and wise spirit that ever took flesh. To be great is to be misunderstood.

I suppose no man can violate his nature. All the sallies of his will are rounded in by the law of his being, as the inequalities of Andes and Himmaleh are insignificant in the curve of the sphere. Nor does it matter how you gauge and try him. A character is like an acrostic or Alexandrian stanza; read it forward, backward, or across, it still spells the same thing. In this pleasing contrite wood-life which God allows me, let me record day by day my honest thought without prospect or retrospect, and, I cannot doubt, it will be found symmetrical, though I mean it not and see it not. My book should smell of pines and resound with the hum of insects. The swallow over my window should inter-

sum total of both is the same. Why all this deference to Alfred and Scanderbeg and Gustavus? Suppose they were virtuous; did they wear out virtue? As great a stake depends on your private act to-day as followed their public and renowned steps. When private men shall act with original views, the lustre will be transferred from the actions of kings to those of gentlemen.

The world has been instructed by its kings, who have so magnetized the eyes of nations. It has been taught by this colossal symbol the mutual reverence that is due from man to man. The joyful loyalty with which men have everywhere suffered the king, the noble, or the great proprietor to walk among them by a law of his own, make his own scale of men and things and reverse theirs, pay for benefits not with money but with honor, and represent the law in his person, was the hieroglyphic by which they obscurely signified their consciousness of their own right and comeliness, the right of every man.

The magnetism which all original action exerts is explained when we inquire the reason of self-trust. Who is the Trustee? What is the aboriginal Self, on which a universal reliance may be grounded? What is the nature and power of that science-baffling star, without parallax, without calculable elements, which shoots a ray of beauty even into trivial and impure actions, if the least mark of independence appear? The inquiry leads us to that source, at once the essence of genius, of virtue, and of life, which we call Spontaneity or Instinct. We denote this primary wisdom as Intuition, whilst all later teachings are tuitions. In that deep force, the last fact behind which analysis cannot go, all things find their common origin. For the sense of being which in calm hours rises, we know not how, in the soul, is not diverse from things, from space, from light, from time, from man, but one with them and proceeds obviously from the same source whence their life and being also proceed. We first share the life by which things exist and afterwards see them as appearances in nature and forget that we have shared their cause. Here is the fountain of action and of thought. Here are the lungs of that inspiration which giveth man wisdom and which cannot be denied without impiety and atheism. We lie in the lap of immense intelligence, which makes us receivers of its truth and organs of its activity. When we discern justice, when we discern truth, we do nothing of ourselves, but allow a passage to its beams. If we ask whence this comes, if we seek to pry into the soul that causes, all philosophy is at fault. Its presence or its absence is all we can affirm. Every man discriminates between the voluntary acts of his mind and his involuntary perceptions, and knows that to his involuntary perceptions a perfect faith is due. He may err in the expression of them, but he knows that these things are so, like day and night, not to be disputed. My wilful actions and acquisitions are but roving; the idlest reverie, the faintest native emotion, command my curiosity and respect. Thoughtless people contradict as readily the statement of perceptions as of opinions, or rather much more readily; for they do not distinguish between perception and notion. They fancy that I choose to see this or that thing. But perception is not whimsical, but fatal. If I see a trait, my children will see it after me, and in course of time all mankind—although it may chance that no one has seen it before me. For my perception of it is as much a fact as the sun.

The relations of the soul to the divine spirit are so pure that it is profane to seek to interpose helps. It must be that when God speaketh he should communicate, not one thing, but all things; should fill the world with his voice; should scatter forth light, nature, time, souls, from the centre of the present thought; and new date and new create the whole. Whenever a mind is simple and receives a divine wisdom, old things pass away—means, teachers, texts, temples fall; it lives now, and absorbs past and future into the present hour. All things are made sacred by relation to it—one as much as another. All things are dissolved to their centre by their cause, and in the universal miracle petty and particular miracles disappear. If therefore a man claims to know and speak of God and carries you backward to the phraseology of some old mouldered nation in another country, in another world, believe him not. Is the acorn better than the oak which is its fulness and completion? Is the parent better than the child into whom he has cast his ripened being? Whence then this worship of the past? The centuries are conspirators against the sanity and authority of the soul. Time and space are but physiological colors which the eye makes, but the soul is light: where it is, is day; where it was, is night; and history is an impertinence and an injury if it be any thing more than a cheerful apologue or parable of my being and becoming.

Man is timid and apologetic; he is no longer upright; he dares not say 'I think,' 'I am,' but quotes some saint or sage. He is ashamed before the blade of grass or the blowing rose. These roses under my window make no reference to former roses or to better ones; they are for what they are; they exist with God to-day. There is no time to them. There is simply the rose; it is perfect in every moment of its existence. Before a leaf-bud has burst, its whole life acts; in the full-blown flower there is no more; in the leafless root there is no less. Its nature is satisfied and it satisfies nature in all moments alike. But man postpones or remembers; he does not live in the present, but with reverted eye laments the past, or, heedless of the riches that surround him, stands on tiptoe to foresee the future. He cannot be happy and strong until he too lives with nature in the present, above time.

This should be plain enough. Yet see what strong intellects dare not yet hear God himself unless he speak the phraseology of I know not what David, or Jeremiah, or Paul. We shall not always set so great a price on a few texts, on a few lives. We are like children who repeat by rote the sentences of grandames and tutors, and, as they grow older, of the men of talents and character they chance to see—painfully recollecting the exact words they spoke; afterwards, when they come into the point of view which those had who uttered these sayings, they understand them and are willing to let the words go; for at any time they can use words as good when occasion comes. If we live truly, we shall see truly. It is as easy for the strong man to be strong, as it is for the weak to be weak. When we have new perception, we shall gladly disburden the memory of its hoarded treasures as old rubbish. When a man lives with God, his voice shall be as sweet as the murmur of the brook and the rustle of the corn.

And now at last the highest truth on this subject remains unsaid; probably cannot be said; for all that we say is the far-off remembering of the intuition. That thought by what I can now nearest approach to say it, is this. When good is near you, when you have life in yourself, it is not by any known or accustomed way; you shall not discern the footprints of any other; you shall not see the face of man; you shall not hear any name; the way, the thought, the good, shall be wholly strange and new. It shall exclude example and experience. You take the way from man, not to man. All persons that ever existed are its forgotten ministers. Fear and hope are alike beneath it. There is somewhat low even in hope. In the hour of vision there is nothing that can be called gratitude, nor properly joy. The soul raised over passion beholds identity and eternal causation, perceives the self-existence of Truth and Right, and calms itself with knowing that all things go well. Vast spaces of nature, the Atlantic Ocean, the South Sea; long intervals of time, years, centuries, are of no account. This which I think and feel underlay every former state of life and circumstances, as it does underlie my present, and what is called life and what is called death.

Life only avails, not the having lived. Power ceases in the instant of repose; it resides in the moment of transition from a past to a new state, in the shooting of the gulf, in the darting to an aim. This one fact the world hates; that the soul *becomes*; for that forever degrades the past, turns all riches to poverty, all reputation to a shame, confounds the saint with the rogue, shoves Jesus and Judas equally aside. Why then do we prate of self-reliance? Inasmuch as the soul is present there will be power not confident but agent. To talk of reliance is a poor external way of speaking. Speak rather of that which relies because it works and is. Who has more obedience than I masters me, though he should not raise his finger. Round him I must revolve by the gravitation of spirits. We fancy it rhetoric when we speak of eminent virtue. We do not yet see that virtue is Height, and that a man or a company of men, plastic and permeable to principles, by the law of nature must overpower and ride all cities, nations, kings, rich men, poets, who are not.

This is the ultimate fact which we so quickly reach on this, as on every topic, the resolution of all into the ever-blessed ONE. Self-existence is the attribute of the Supreme Cause, and it constitutes the measure of good by the degree in which it enters into all lower forms. All things real are so by so much virtue as they contain. Commerce, husbandry, hunting, whaling, war, eloquence, personal weight, are somewhat, and engage my respect as examples of its presence and impure action. I see the same law working in nature for conservation and growth. Power is, in nature, the essential measure of right. Nature suffers nothing to remain in her kingdoms which cannot help itself. The genesis and maturation of a planet, its poise and orbit, the bended tree recovering itself from the strong wind, the vital resources of every animal and vegetable, are demonstrations of the self-sufficing and therefore self-relying soul.

Thus all concentrates: let us not rove; let us sit at home with the cause. Let us stun and astonish the intruding rabble of men and books and institutions by a simple declaration of the divine fact. Bid the invaders take the shoes from off their feet, for God is here within. Let our simplicity judge them, and our docility to our own law demonstrate the poverty of nature and fortune beside our native riches.

But now we are a mob. Man does not stand in awe of man, nor is his genius admonished to stay at home, to put itself in communication with the internal ocean, but it goes abroad to beg a cup of water of the urns of other men. We must go alone. I like the silent church before the service begins, better than any preaching. How far off, how cool, how chaste the persons look, begirt each one with a precinct or sanctuary! So let us always sit. Why should we assume the faults of our friend, or wife, or father, or child, because they sit around our hearth, or are said to have the same blood? All men have my blood and I all men's. Not for that will I adopt their petulance or folly, even to the extent of being ashamed of it. But your isolation must not be mechanical, but spiritual, that is, must be elevation. At times the whole world seems to be in conspiracy to importune you with emphatic trifles. Friend, client, child, sickness, fear, want, charity, all knock at once at thy closet door and say—'Come out unto us.' But keep thy state; come not into their confusion. The power men possess to annoy me I give them by a weak curiosity. No man can come near me but through my act. "What we love that we have, but by desire we bereave ourselves of the love."

If we cannot at once rise to the sanctities of obedience and faith, let us at least resist our temptations; let us enter into the state of war and wake Thor and Woden, courage and constancy, in our Saxon breasts. This is to be done in our smooth times by speaking the truth. Check this lying hospitality and lying affection. Live no longer to the expectation of these deceived and deceiving people with whom we converse. Say to them, 'O father, O mother, O wife, O brother, O friend, I have lived with you after appearances hitherto. Henceforward I am the truth's. Be it known unto you that henceforward I obey no law less than the eternal law. I will have no covenants but proximities. I shall endeavor to nourish my parents, to support my family, to be the chaste husband of one wife—but these relations I must fill after a new and unprecedented way. I appeal from your customs. I must be myself. I cannot break myself any longer for you, or you. If you can love me for what I am, we shall be the happier. If you cannot, I will still seek to deserve that you should. I will not hide my tastes or aversions. I will so trust that what is deep is holy, that I will do strongly before the sun

and moon whatever inly rejoices me and the heart appoints. If you are
noble, I will love you; if you are not, I will not hurt you and myself by
hypocritical attentions. If you are true, but not in the same truth with
me, cleave to your companions; I will seek my own. I do this not selfishly but humbly and truly. It is alike your interest, and mine, and all
men's, however long we have dwelt in lies, to live in truth. Does this
sound harsh to-day? You will soon love what is dictated by your nature
as well as mine, and if we follow the truth it will bring us out safe at
last.'—But so may you give these friends pain. Yes, but I cannot sell
my liberty and my power, to save their sensibility. Besides, all persons
have their moments of reason, when they look out into the region of
absolute truth; then will they justify me and do the same thing.

The populace think that your rejection of popular standards is a
rejection of all standard, and mere antinomianism; and the bold sensualist will use the name of philosophy to gild his crimes. But the law of
consciousness abides. There are two confessionals, in one or the other
of which we must be shriven. You may fulfil your round of duties by
clearing yourself in the *direct*, or in the *reflex* way. Consider whether
you have satisfied your relations to father, mother, cousin, neighbor,
town, cat and dog—whether any of these can upbraid you. But I may
also neglect this reflex standard and absolve me to myself. I have my
own stern claims and perfect circle. It denies the name of duty to many
offices that are called duties. But if I can discharge its debts it enables
me to dispense with the popular code. If any one imagines that this law
is lax, let him keep its commandment one day.

And truly it demands something godlike in him who has cast off
the common motives of humanity and has ventured to trust himself for
a taskmaster. High be his heart, faithful his will, clear his sight, that
he may in good earnest be doctrine, society, law, to himself, that a simple purpose may be to him as strong as iron necessity is to others!

If any man consider the present aspects of what is called by distinction *society*, he will see the need of these ethics. The sinew and
heart of man seem to be drawn out, and we are become timorous,
desponding whimperers. We are afraid of truth, afraid of fortune, afraid
of death, and afraid of each other. Our age yields no great and perfect
persons. We want men and women who shall renovate life and our
social state, but we see that most natures are insolvent, cannot satisfy
their own wants, have an ambition out of all proportion to their prac-

tical force and do lean and beg day and night continually. Our housekeeping is mendicant, our arts, our occupations, our marriages, our religion we have not chosen, but society has chosen for us. We are parlor soldiers. We shun the rugged battle of fate, where strength is born.

If our young men miscarry in their first enterprises they lose all heart. If the young merchant fails, men say he is ruined. If the finest genius studies at one of our colleges and is not installed in an office within one year afterwards in the cities or suburbs of Boston or New York, it seems to his friends and to himself that he is right in being disheartened and in complaining the rest of his life. A sturdy lad from New Hampshire or Vermont, who in turn tries all the professions, who *teams it, farms it, peddles*, keeps a school, preaches, edits a newspaper, goes to Congress, buys a township, and so forth, in successive years, and always like a cat falls on his feet, is worth a hundred of these city dolls. He walks abreast with his days and feels no shame in not 'studying a profession,' for he does not postpone his life, but lives already. He has not one chance, but a hundred chances. Let a Stoic open the resources of man and tell men they are not leaning willows, but can and must detach themselves; that with the exercise of self-trust, new powers shall appear; that a man is the word made flesh, born to shed healing to the nations; that he should be ashamed of our compassion, and that the moment he acts from himself, tossing the laws, the books, idolatries and customs out of the window, we pity him no more but thank and revere him; and that teacher shall restore the life of man to splendor and make his name dear to all history.

It is easy to see that a greater self-reliance must work a revolution in all the offices and relations of men; in their religion; in their education; in their pursuits; their modes of living; their association; in their property; in their speculative views.

1. In what prayers do men allow themselves! That which they call a holy office is not so much as brave and manly. Prayer looks abroad and asks for some foreign addition to come through some foreign virtue, and loses itself in endless mazes of natural and supernatural, and mediatorial and miraculous. Prayer that craves a particular commodity, anything less than all good, is vicious. Prayer is the contemplation of the facts of life from the highest point of view. It is the soliloquy of a beholding and jubilant soul. It is the spirit of God pronouncing his works good. But prayer as a means to effect a private end is meanness

and theft. It supposes dualism and not unity in nature and consciousness. As soon as the man is at one with God, he will not beg. He will then see prayer in all action. The prayer of the farmer kneeling in his field to weed it, the prayer of the rower kneeling with the stroke of his oar, are true prayers heard throughout nature, though for cheap ends. Caratach, in Fletcher's "Bonduca," when admonished to inquire the mind of the god Audate, replies—

> His hidden meaning lies in our endeavors;
> Our valors are our best gods.

Another sort of false prayers are our regrets. Discontent is the want of self-reliance: it is infirmity of will. Regret calamities if you can thereby help the sufferer; if not, attend your own work and already the evil begins to be repaired. Our sympathy is just as base. We come to them who weep foolishly and sit down and cry for company, instead of imparting to them truth and health in rough electric shocks, putting them once more in communication with their own reason. The secret of fortune is joy in our hands. Welcome evermore to gods and men is the self-helping man. For him all doors are flung wide; him all tongues greet, all honors crown, all eyes follow with desire. Our love goes out to him and embraces him because he did not need it. We solicitously and apologetically caress and celebrate him because he held on his way and scorned our disapprobation. The gods love him because men hated him. "To the persevering mortal," said Zoroaster, "the blessed Immortals are swift."

As men's prayers are a disease of the will, so are their creeds a disease of the intellect. They say with those foolish Israelites, 'Let not God speak to us, lest we die. Speak thou, speak any man with us, and we will obey.' Everywhere I am hindered of meeting God in my brother, because he has shut his own temple doors and recites fables merely of his brother's, or his brother's brother's God. Every new mind is a new classification. If it prove a mind of uncommon activity and power, a Locke, a Lavoisier, a Hutton, a Bentham, a Fourier, it imposes its classification on other men, and lo! a new system. In proportion to the depth of the thought, and so to the number of the objects it touches and brings within reach of the pupil, is his complacency. But chiefly is this apparent in creeds and churches, which are also classifications of some powerful mind acting on the elemental thought of duty and man's relation to the Highest. Such is Calvinism, Quakerism, Swedenborgism. The pupil takes the same delight in subordinating every thing to the new terminology as a girl who has just learned botany in seeing a new earth and new seasons thereby. It will happen for a time that the pupil will find his intellectual power has grown by the study of his master's mind. But in all unbalanced minds the classification is idolized, passes for the end and not for a speedily exhaustible means, so that the walls of the system blend to their eye in the remote horizon with the walls of the universe; the luminaries of heaven seem to them hung on the arch their master built. They cannot imagine how you aliens have any right to see—how you can see; 'It must be somehow that you stole the light from us.' They do not yet perceive that light, unsystematic, indomitable, will break into any cabin, even into theirs. Let them chirp awhile and call it their own. If they are honest and do well, presently their neat new pinfold will be too strait and low, will crack, will lean, will rot and vanish, and the immortal light, all young and joyful, million-orbed, million-colored, will beam over the universe as on the first morning.

2. It is for want of self-culture that the superstition of Travelling, whose idols are Italy, England, Egypt, retains its fascination for all educated Americans. They who made England, Italy, or Greece venerable in the imagination, did so by sticking fast where they were, like an axis of the earth. In manly hours we feel that duty is our place. The soul is no traveller; the wise man stays at home, and when his necessities, his duties, on any occasion call him from his house, or into foreign lands, he is at home still and shall make men sensible by the expression of his countenance that he goes, the missionary of wisdom and virtue, and visits cities and men like a sovereign and not like an interloper or a valet.

I have no churlish objection to the circumnavigation of the globe for the purposes of art, of study, and benevolence, so that the man is first domesticated, or does not go abroad with the hope of finding somewhat greater than he knows. He who travels to be amused, or to get somewhat which he does not carry, travels away from himself, and grows old even in youth among old things. In Thebes, in Palmyra, his will and mind have become old and dilapidated as they. He carries ruins to ruins.

Travelling is a fool's paradise. Our first journeys discover to us the indifference of places. At home I dream that at Naples, at Rome, I can be intoxicated with beauty and lose my sadness. I pack my trunk, embrace my friends, embark on the sea and at last wake up in Naples, and there beside me is the stern fact, the sad self, unrelenting, identical, that I fled from. I seek the Vatican and the palaces. I affect to be intoxicated with sights and suggestions, but I am not intoxicated. My giant goes with me wherever I go.

3. But the rage of travelling is a symptom of a deeper unsoundness affecting the whole intellectual action. The intellect is vagabond, and our system of education fosters restlessness. Our minds travel when our bodies are forced to stay at home. We imitate; and what is imitation but the travelling of the mind? Our houses are built with foreign taste; our shelves are garnished with foreign ornaments; our opinions, our tastes, our faculties, lean, and follow the Past and the Distant. The soul created the arts wherever they have flourished. It was in his own mind that the artist sought his model. It was an application of his own thought to the thing to be done and the conditions to be observed. And why need we copy the Doric or the Gothic model? Beauty, convenience, grandeur of thought and quaint expression are as near to us as to any, and if the American artist will study with hope and love the precise thing to be done by him, considering the climate, the soil, the length of the day, the wants of the people, the habit and form of the government, he will create a house in which all these will find themselves fitted, and taste and sentiment will be satisfied also.

Insist on yourself; never imitate. Your own gift you can present every moment with the cumulative force of a whole life's cultivation; but of the adopted talent of another you have only an extemporaneous half possession. That which each can do best, none but his Maker can teach him. No man yet knows what it is, nor can, till that person has exhibited it. Where is the master who could have taught Shakspeare? Where is the master who could have instructed Franklin, or Washington, or Bacon, or Newton? Every great man is a unique. The Scipionism of Scipio is precisely that part he could not borrow. Shakspeare will never be made by the study of Shakspeare. Do that which is assigned you, and you cannot hope too much or dare too much. There is at this moment for you an utterance brave and grand as that of the colossal chisel of Phidias, or trowel of the Egyptians, or the pen of

Moses or Dante, but different from all these. Not possibly will the soul, all rich, all eloquent, with thousand-cloven tongue, deign to repeat itself; but if you can hear what these patriarchs say, surely you can reply to them in the same pitch of voice; for the ear and the tongue are two organs of one nature. Abide in the simple and noble regions of thy life, obey thy heart, and thou shalt reproduce the Foreworld again.

4. As our Religion, our Education, our Art look abroad, so does our spirit of society. All men plume themselves on the improvement of society, and no man improves.

Society never advances. It recedes as fast on one side as it gains on the other. It undergoes continual changes; it is barbarous, it is civilized, it is christianized, it is rich, it is scientific; but this change is not amelioration. For every thing that is given, something is taken. Society acquires new arts and loses old instincts. What a contrast between the well-clad, reading, writing, thinking American, with a watch, a pencil and a bill of exchange in his pocket, and the naked New Zealander, whose property is a club, a spear, a mat and an undivided twentieth of a shed to sleep under! But compare the health of the two men and you shall see that the white man has lost his aboriginal strength. If the traveller tell us truly, strike the savage with a broad-axe and in a day or two the flesh shall unite and heal as if you struck the blow into soft pitch, and the same blow shall send the white to his grave.

The civilized man has built a coach, but has lost the use of his feet. He is supported on crutches, but lacks so much support of muscle. He has a fine Geneva watch, but he fails of the skill to tell the hour by the sun. A Greenwich nautical almanac he has, and so being sure of the information when he wants it, the man in the street does not know a star in the sky. The solstice he does not observe; the equinox he knows as little; and the whole bright calendar of the year is without a dial in his mind. His note-books impair his memory; his libraries overload his wit; the insurance-office increases the number of accidents; and it may be a question whether machinery does not encumber; whether we have not lost by refinement some energy, by a Christianity, entrenched in establishments and forms, some vigor of wild virtue. For every Stoic was a Stoic; but in Christendom where is the Christian?

There is no more deviation in the moral standard than in the standard of height or bulk. No greater men are now than ever were. A singular equality may be observed between the great men of the first and of the last ages; nor can all the science, art, religion, and philosophy of the nineteenth century avail to educate greater men than Plutarch's heroes, three or four and twenty centuries ago. Not in time is the race progressive. Phocion, Socrates, Anaxagoras, Diogenes, are great men, but they leave no class. He who is really of their class will not be called by their name, but will be his own man, and in his turn the founder of a sect. The arts and inventions of each period are only its costume and do not invigorate men. The harm of the improved machinery may compensate its good. Hudson and Behring accomplished so much in their fishing-boats as to astonish Parry and Franklin, whose equipment exhausted the resources of science and art. Galileo, with an opera-glass, discovered a more splendid series of celestial phenomena than any one since. Columbus found the New World in an undecked boat. It is curious to see the periodical disuse and perishing of means and machinery which were introduced with loud laudation a few years or centuries before. The great genius returns to essential man. We reckoned the improvements of the art of war among the triumphs of science, and yet Napoleon conquered Europe by the bivouac, which consisted of falling back on naked valor and disencumbering it of all aids. The Emperor held it impossible to make a perfect army, says Las Cases, "without abolishing our arms, magazines, commissaries and carriages, until, in imitation of the Roman custom, the soldier should receive his supply of corn, grind it in his hand-mill and bake his bread himself."

Society is a wave. The wave moves onward, but the water of which it is composed does not. The same particle does not rise from the valley to the ridge. Its unity is only phenomenal. The persons who make up a nation to-day, next year die, and their experience dies with them.

And so the reliance on Property, including the reliance on governments which protect it, is the want of self-reliance. Men have looked away from themselves and at things so long that they have come to esteem the religious, learned and civil institutions as guards of property, and they deprecate assaults on these, because they feel them to be assaults on property. They measure their esteem of each other by what each has, and not by what each is. But a cultivated man becomes ashamed of his property, out of new respect for his nature. Especially he hates what he has if he see that it is accidental—came to him by inheritance, or gift, or crime; then he feels that it is not having; it does not belong to him, has no root in him and merely lies there because no revolution or no robber takes it away. But that which a man is, does always by necessity acquire; and what the man acquires, is living property, which does not wait the beck of rulers, or mobs, or revolutions, or fire, or storm, or bankruptcies, but perpetually renews itself wherever the man breathes. "Thy lot or portion of life," said the Caliph Ali, "is seeking after thee; therefore be at rest from seeking after it." Our dependence on these foreign goods leads us to our slavish respect for numbers. The political parties meet in numerous conventions; the greater the concourse and with each new uproar of announcement, The delegation from Essex! The Democrats from New Hampshire! The Whigs of Maine! the young patriot feels himself stronger than before by a new thousand of eyes and arms. In like manner the reformers summon conventions and vote and resolve in multitude. Not so, O friends! will the God deign to enter and inhabit you, but by a method precisely the reverse. It is only as a man puts off all foreign support and stands alone that I see him to be strong and to prevail. He is weaker by every recruit to his banner. Is not a man better than a town? Ask nothing of men, and, in the endless mutation, thou only firm column must presently appear the upholder of all that surrounds thee. He who knows that power is inborn, that he is weak because he has looked for good out of him and elsewhere, and, so perceiving, throws himself unhesitatingly on his thought, instantly rights himself, stands in the erect position, commands his limbs, works miracles; just as a man who stands on his feet is stronger than a man who stands on his head.

So use all that is called Fortune. Most men gamble with her, and gain all, and lose all, as her wheel rolls. But do thou leave as unlawful these winnings, and deal with Cause and Effect, the chancellors of God. In the Will work and acquire, and thou hast chained the wheel of Chance, and shall sit hereafter out of fear from her rotations. A political victory, a rise of rents, the recovery of your sick or the return of your absent friend, or some other favorable event raises your spirits, and you think good days are preparing for you. Do not believe it. Nothing can bring you peace but yourself. Nothing can bring you peace but the triumph of principles.

COMPENSATION

The wings of Time are black and
    white,
Pied with morning and with night.
Mountain tall and ocean deep
Trembling balance duly keep.
In changing moon, in tidal wave,
Glows the feud of Want and Have.
Gauge of more and less through
    space
Electric star and pencil plays.
The lonely Earth amid the balls
That hurry through the eternal halls,
A makeweight flying to the void,
Supplemental asteroid,
Or compensatory spark,
Shoots across the neutral Dark.
Man's the elm, and Wealth the vine,

Stanch and strong the tendrils
    twine:
Though the frail ringlets thee
    deceive,
None from its stock that vine can
    reave.
Fear not, then, thou child infirm,
There's no god dare wrong a worm.
Laurel crowns cleave to deserts
And power to him who power
    exerts;
Hast not thy share? On wingèd feet,
Lo! it rushes thee to meet;
And all that Nature made thy own,
Floating in air or pent in stone,
Will rive the hills and swim the sea
And, like thy shadow, follow thee.

EVER SINCE I was a boy I have wished to write a discourse on Compensation; for it seemed to me when very young that on this subject life was ahead of theology and the people knew more than the preachers taught. The documents too from which the doctrine is to be drawn, charmed my fancy by their endless variety, and lay always before me, even in sleep; for they are the tools in our hands, the bread in our basket, the transactions of the street, the farm and the dwelling-house; greetings, relations, debts and credits, the influence of character, the nature and endowment of all men. It seemed to me also that in it might be shown men a ray of divinity, the present action of the soul of this world, clean from all vestige of tradition; and so the heart of man might be bathed by an inundation of eternal love, conversing with that which he knows was always and always must be, because it really is now. It appeared moreover that if this doctrine could be stated in terms with any resemblance to those bright intuitions in which this truth is sometimes revealed to us, it would be a star in many dark hours and crooked passages in our journey, that would not suffer us to lose our way.

I was lately confirmed in these desires by hearing a sermon at church. The preacher, a man esteemed for his orthodoxy, unfolded in the ordinary manner the doctrine of the Last Judgment. He assumed that judgment is not executed in this world; that the wicked are successful; that the good are miserable; and then urged from reason and from Scripture a compensation to be made to both parties in the next life. No offence appeared to be taken by the congregation at this doctrine. As far as I could observe when the meeting broke up they separated without remark on the sermon.

Yet what was the import of this teaching? What did the preacher mean by saying that the good are miserable in the present life? Was it that houses and lands, offices, wine, horses, dress, luxury, are had by unprincipled men, whilst the saints are poor and despised; and that a compensation is to be made to these last hereafter, by giving them the like gratifications another day—bank-stock and doubloons, venison and champagne? This must be the compensation intended; for what else? Is it that they are to have leave to pray and praise? to love and serve men? Why, that they can do now. The legitimate inference the disciple would draw was—'We are to have *such* a good time as the sinners have now'; or, to push it to its extreme import—'You sin now, we shall sin by and by; we would sin now, if we could; not being successful we expect our revenge to-morrow.'

The fallacy lay in the immense concession that the bad are successful; that justice is not done now. The blindness of the preacher consisted in deferring to the base estimate of the market of what constitutes a manly success, instead of confronting and convicting the world from the truth; announcing the presence of the soul; the omnipotence of the will; and so establishing the standard of good and ill, of success and falsehood.

I find a similar base tone in the popular religious works of the day and the same doctrines assumed by the literary men when occasionally they treat the related topics. I think that our popular theology has gained in decorum, and not in principle, over the superstitions it has displaced. But men are better than their theology. Their daily life gives it the lie. Every ingenuous and aspiring soul leaves the doctrine behind him in his own experience, and all men feel sometimes the falsehood which they cannot demonstrate. For men are wiser than they know. That which they hear in schools and pulpits without afterthought, if said in conversation would probably be questioned in silence. If a man dogmatize in a mixed company on Providence and the divine laws, he is answered by a silence which conveys well enough to an observer the dissatisfaction of the hearer, but his incapacity to make his own statement.

I shall attempt in this and the following chapter to record some facts that indicate the path of the law of Compensation; happy beyond my expectation if I shall truly draw the smallest arc of this circle.

Polarity, or action and reaction, we meet in every part of nature; in darkness and light; in heat and cold; in the ebb and flow of waters; in male and female; in the inspiration and expiration of plants and animals; in the equation of quantity and quality in the fluids of the animal body; in the systole and diastole of the heart; in the undulations of fluids and of sound; in the centrifugal and centripetal gravity; in electricity, galvanism, and chemical affinity. Superinduce magnetism at one end of a needle, the opposite magnetism takes place at the other end. If the south attracts, the north repels. To empty here, you must condense there. An inevitable dualism bisects nature, so that each thing is a half, and suggests another thing to make it whole; as, spirit, matter; man, woman; odd, even; subjective, objective; in, out; upper, under; motion, rest; yea, nay.

Whilst the world is thus dual, so is every one of its parts. The entire system of things gets represented in every particle. There is somewhat that resembles the ebb and flow of the sea, day and night, man and woman, in a single needle of the pine, in a kernel of corn, in each individual of every animal tribe. The reaction, so grand in the elements, is repeated within these small boundaries. For example, in the animal kingdom the physiologist has observed that no creatures are favorites, but a certain compensation balances every gift and every defect. A surplusage given to one part is paid out of a reduction from another part of the same creature. If the head and neck are enlarged, the trunk and extremities are cut short.

The theory of the mechanic forces is another example. What we gain in power is lost in time, and the converse. The periodic or compensating errors of the planets is another instance. The influences of climate and soil in political history is another. The cold climate invigorates. The barren soil does not breed fevers, crocodiles, tigers or scorpions.

The same dualism underlies the nature and condition of man. Every excess causes a defect; every defect an excess. Every sweet hath its sour; every evil its good. Every faculty which is a receiver of pleasure has an equal penalty put on its abuse. It is to answer for its moderation with its life. For every grain of wit there is a grain of folly. For every thing you have missed, you have gained something else; and for every thing you gain, you lose something. If riches increase, they are increased that use them. If the gatherer gathers too much, Nature takes out of the man what she puts into his chest; swells the estate, but kills the owner. Nature hates monopolies and exceptions. The waves of the sea do not more speedily seek a level from their loftiest tossing than the varieties of condition tend to equalize themselves. There is always some levelling circumstance that puts down the overbearing, the strong, the rich, the fortunate, substantially on the same ground with all others. Is a man too strong and fierce for society and by temper and position a bad citizen—a morose ruffian, with a dash of the pirate in him?— Nature sends him a troop of pretty sons and daughters who are getting along in the dame's classes at the village school, and love and fear for them smooths his grim scowl to courtesy. Thus she contrives to intenerate the granite and felspar, takes the boar out and puts the lamb in and keeps her balance true.

The farmer imagines power and place are fine things. But the President has paid dear for his White House. It has commonly cost him all his peace, and the best of his manly attributes. To preserve for a short time so conspicuous an appearance before the world, he is content to eat dust before the real masters who stand erect behind the throne. Or do men desire the more substantial and permanent grandeur of genius? Neither has this an immunity. He who by force of will or of thought is great and overlooks thousands, has the charges of that eminence. With every influx of light comes new danger. Has he light? he must bear witness to the light, and always outrun that sympathy which gives him such keen satisfaction, by his fidelity to new revelations of the incessant soul. He must hate father and mother, wife and child. Has he all that the world loves and admires and covets?—he must cast behind him their admiration and afflict them by faithfulness to his truth and become a byword and a hissing.

This law writes the laws of cities and nations. It is in vain to build or plot or combine against it. Things refuse to be mismanaged long. *Res nolunt diu male administrari.* Though no checks to a new evil appear, the checks exist, and will appear. If the government is cruel, the governor's life is not safe. If you tax too high, the revenue will yield nothing. If you make the criminal code sanguinary, juries will not convict. If the law is too mild, private vengeance comes in. If the government is a terrific democracy, the pressure is resisted by an over-charge of energy in the citizen, and life glows with a fiercer flame. The true life and satisfactions of man seem to elude the utmost rigors or felicities of condition and to establish themselves with great indiffer-ency under all varieties of circumstances. Under all governments the influence of character remains the same—in Turkey and in New Eng-land about alike. Under the primeval despots of Egypt, history honestly confesses that man must have been as free as culture could make him.

These appearances indicate the fact that the universe is represented in every one of its particles. Every thing in nature contains all the pow-ers of nature. Every thing is made of one hidden stuff; as the naturalist sees one type under every metamorphosis, and regards a horse as a run-ning man, a fish as a swimming man, a bird as a flying man, a tree as a rooted man. Each new form repeats not only the main character of the type, but part for part all the details, all the aims, furtherances, hin-drances, energies and whole system of every other. Every occupation, trade, art, transaction, is a compend of the world and a correlative of every other. Each one is an entire emblem of human life; of its good and ill, its trials, its enemies, its course and its end. And each one must somehow accommodate the whole man and recite all his destiny.

The world globes itself in a drop of dew. The microscope cannot find the animalcule which is less perfect for being little. Eyes, ears, taste, smell, motion, resistance, appetite, and organs of reproduction that take hold on eternity—all find room to consist in the small crea-ture. So do we put our life into every act. The true doctrine of omnipresence is that God reappears with all his parts in every moss and cobweb. The value of the universe contrives to throw itself into every point. If the good is there, so is the evil; if the affinity, so the repulsion; if the force, so the limitation.

Thus is the universe alive. All things are moral. That soul which within us is a sentiment, outside of us is a law. We feel its inspiration; but there in history we can see its fatal strength. "It is in the world, and the world was made by it." Justice is not postponed. A perfect equity adjusts its balance in all parts of life. Ἀεὶ Γὰρ εὖ πίπτουσιν οἱ Διὸζ χύδοι—The dice of God are always loaded. The world looks like a multiplication-table, or a mathematical equation, which, turn it how you will, balances itself. Take what figure you will, its exact value, nor more nor less, still returns to you. Every secret is told, every crime is punished, every virtue rewarded, every wrong redressed, in silence and certainty. What we call retribution is the universal necessity by which the whole appears wherever a part appears. If you see smoke, there must be fire. If you see a hand or a limb, you know that the trunk to which it belongs is there behind.

Every act rewards itself, or in other words integrates itself, in a twofold manner; first in the thing, or in real nature; and secondly in the circumstance, or in apparent nature. Men call the circumstance the retribution. The causal retribution is in the thing and is seen by the soul. The retribution in the circumstance is seen by the understanding; it is inseparable from the thing, but is often spread over a long time and so does not become distinct until after many years. The specific stripes may follow late after the offence, but they follow because they accompany it. Crime and punishment grow out of one stem. Punishment is a fruit that unsuspected ripens within the flower of the pleasure which concealed it. Cause and effect, means and ends, seed and fruit, cannot be severed; for the effect already blooms in the cause, the end preëxists in the means, the fruit in the seed.

Whilst thus the world will be whole and refuses to be disparted, we seek to act partially, to sunder, to appropriate; for example—to gratify the senses we sever the pleasure of the senses from the needs of the character. The ingenuity of man has always been dedicated to the solution of one problem—how to detach the sensual sweet, the sensual strong, the sensual bright, etc., from the moral sweet, the moral deep, the moral fair; that is, again, to contrive to cut clean off this upper surface so thin as to leave it bottomless; to get a *one end*, without an *other end*. The soul says, 'Eat;' the body would feast. The soul says, 'The man and woman shall be one flesh and one soul;' the body would join the flesh only. The soul says, 'Have dominion over all things to the ends of virtue'; the body would have the power over things to its own ends.

The soul strives amain to live and work through all things. It would be the only fact. All things shall be added unto it—power, pleasure, knowledge, beauty. The particular man aims to be somebody; to set up for himself; to truck and higgle for a private good; and, in particulars, to ride that he may ride; to dress that he may be dressed; to eat that he may eat; and to govern, that he may be seen. Men seek to be great; they would have offices, wealth, power and fame. They think that to be great is to possess one side of nature—the sweet, without the other side, the bitter.

This dividing and detaching is steadily counteracted. Up to this day it must be owned no projector has had the smallest success. The parted water reunites behind our hand. Pleasure is taken out of pleasant things, profit out of profitable things, power out of strong things, as soon as we seek to separate them from the whole. We can no more halve things and get the sensual good, by itself, than we can get an inside that shall have no outside, or a light without a shadow. "Drive out Nature with a fork, she comes running back."

Life invests itself with inevitable conditions, which the unwise seek to dodge, which one and another brags that he does not know, that they do not touch him; but the brag is on his lips, the conditions are in his soul. If he escapes them in one part they attack him in another more vital part. If he has escaped them in form and in the appearance, it is because he has resisted his life and fled from himself, and the retribution is so much death. So signal is the failure of all attempts to make this separation of the good from the tax, that the experiment would not be tried—since to try it is to be mad—but for the circumstance that when the disease began in the will, of rebellion and separation, the intellect is at once infected, so that the man ceases to see God whole in each object, but is able to see the sensual allurement of an object and not see the sensual hurt; he sees the mermaid's head but not the dragon's tail, and thinks he can cut off that which he would have from that which he would not have. "How secret art thou who dwellest in the highest heavens in silence, O thou only great God, sprinkling with an unwearied providence certain penal blindness upon such as have unbridled desires!"

The human soul is true to these facts in the painting of fable, of history, of law, of proverbs, of conversation. It finds a tongue in literature unawares. Thus the Greeks called Jupiter, Supreme Mind; but having traditionally ascribed to him many base actions, they involuntarily made amends to reason by tying up the hands of so bad a god. He is made as helpless as a king of England. Prometheus knows one secret which Jove must bargain for; Minerva, another. He cannot get his own thunders; Minerva keeps the key of them:—

> "Of all the gods, I only know the keys
> That ope the solid doors within whose vaults
> His thunders sleep."

A plain confession of the in-working of the All and of its moral aim. The Indian mythology ends in the same ethics; and it would seem impossible for any fable to be invented and get any currency which was not moral. Aurora forgot to ask youth for her lover, and though Tithonus is immortal, he is old. Achilles is not quite invulnerable; the sacred waters did not wash the heel by which Thetis held him. Siegfried, in the Nibelungen, is not quite immortal, for a leaf fell on his back whilst he was bathing in the dragon's blood, and that spot which it covered is mortal. And so it must be. There is a crack in every thing God has made. It would seem there is always this vindictive circumstance stealing in at unawares even into the wild poesy in which the human fancy attempted to make bold holiday and to shake itself free of the old laws—this back-stroke, this kick of the gun, certifying that the law is fatal; that in nature nothing can be given, all things are sold.

This is that ancient doctrine of Nemesis, who keeps watch in the universe and lets no offence go unchastised. The Furies, they said, are attendants on justice, and if the sun in heaven should transgress his path they would punish him. The poets related that stone walls and iron swords and leathern thongs had an occult sympathy with the wrongs of their owners; that the belt which Ajax gave Hector dragged the Trojan hero over the field at the wheels of the car of Achilles, and the sword which Hector gave Ajax was that on whose point Ajax fell. They recorded that when the Thasians erected a statue to Theagenes, a victor in the games, one of his rivals went to it by night and endeavored to throw it down by repeated blows, until at last he moved it from its pedestal and was crushed to death beneath its fall.

This voice of fable has in it somewhat divine. It came from thought above the will of the writer. That is the best part of each writer which has nothing private in it; that which he does not know; that which flowed out of his constitution and not from his too active invention; that which in the study of a single artist you might not easily find, but in the study of many you would abstract as the spirit of them all. Phidias it is not, but the work of man in that early Hellenic world that I would know. The name and circumstance of Phidias, however convenient for history, embarrass when we come to the highest criticism. We are to see that which man was tending to do in a given period, and was hindered, or, if you will, modified in doing, by the interfering volitions of Phidias, of Dante, of Shakspeare, the organ whereby man at the moment wrought.

Still more striking is the expression of this fact in the proverbs of all nations, which are always the literature of reason, or the statements of an absolute truth without qualification. Proverbs, like the sacred books of each nation, are the sanctuary of the intuitions. That which the droning world, chained to appearances, will not allow the realist to say in his own words, it will suffer him to say in proverbs without contradiction. And this law of laws, which the pulpit, the senate and the college deny, is hourly preached in all markets and workshops by flights of proverbs, whose teaching is as true and as omnipresent as that of birds and flies.

All things are double, one against another.—Tit for tat; an eye for an eye; a tooth for a tooth; blood for blood; measure for measure; love for love.—Give, and it shall be given you.—He that watereth shall be watered himself.—What will you have? quoth God; pay for it and take it.—Nothing venture, nothing have.—Thou shalt be paid exactly for what thou hast done, no more, no less.—Who doth not work shall not eat.—Harm watch, harm catch.—Curses always recoil on the head of him who imprecates them.—If you put a chain around the neck of a slave, the other end fastens itself around your own.—Bad counsel confounds the adviser.—The Devil is an ass.

It is thus written, because it is thus in life. Our action is overmastered and characterized above our will by the law of nature. We aim at a petty end quite aside from the public good, but our act arranges itself by irresistible magnetism in a line with the poles of the world.

A man cannot speak but he judges himself. With his will or against his will he draws his portrait to the eye of his companions by every word. Every opinion reacts on him who utters it. It is a thread-ball thrown at a mark, but the other end remains in the thrower's bag. Or rather it is a harpoon hurled at the whale, unwinding, as it flies, a coil of cord in the boat, and, if the harpoon is not good, or not well thrown, it will go nigh to cut the steersman in twain or to sink the boat.

You cannot do wrong without suffering wrong. "No man had ever a point of pride that was not injurious to him," said Burke. The exclusive in fashionable life does not see that he excludes himself from enjoyment, in the attempt to appropriate it. The exclusionist in religion does not see that he shuts the door of heaven on himself, in striving to shut out others. Treat men as pawns and ninepins and you shall suffer as well as they. If you leave out their heart, you shall lose your own. The senses would make things of all persons; of women, of children, of the poor. The vulgar proverb, "I will get it from his purse or get it from his skin," is sound philosophy.

All infractions of love and equity in our social relations are speedily punished. They are punished by fear. Whilst I stand in simple relations to my fellow-man, I have no displeasure in meeting him. We meet as water meets water, or as two currents of air mix, with perfect diffusion and interpenetration of nature. But as soon as there is any departure from simplicity and attempt at halfness, or good for me that is not good for him, my neighbor feels the wrong; he shrinks from me as far as I have shrunk from him; his eyes no longer seek mine; there is war between us; there is hate in him and fear in me.

All the old abuses in society, universal and particular, all unjust accumulations of property and power, are avenged in the same manner. Fear is an instructor of great sagacity and the herald of all revolutions. One thing he teaches, that there is rottenness where he appears. He is a carrion crow, and though you see not well what he hovers for, there is death somewhere. Our property is timid, our laws are timid, our cultivated classes are timid. Fear for ages has boded and mowed and gibbered over government and property. That obscene bird is not there for nothing. He indicates great wrongs which must be revised.

Of the like nature is that expectation of change which instantly follows the suspension of our voluntary activity. The terror of cloudless noon, the emerald of Polycrates, the awe of prosperity, the instinct which leads every generous soul to impose on itself tasks of a noble asceticism and vicarious virtue, are the tremblings of the balance of justice through the heart and mind of man.

Experienced men of the world know very well that it is best to pay scot and lot as they go along, and that a man often pays dear for a small frugality. The borrower runs in his own debt. Has a man gained any thing who has received a hundred favors and rendered none? Has he gained by borrowing, through indolence or cunning, his neighbor's wares, or horses, or money? There arises on the deed the instant acknowledgment of benefit on the one part and of debt on the other; that is, of superiority and inferiority. The transaction remains in the memory of himself and his neighbor; and every new transaction alters according to its nature their relation to each other. He may soon come to see that he had better have broken his own bones than to have ridden in his neighbor's coach, and that "the highest price he can pay for a thing is to ask for it."

A wise man will extend this lesson to all parts of life, and know that it is the part of prudence to face every claimant and pay every just demand on your time, your talents, or your heart. Always pay; for first or last you must pay your entire debt. Persons and events may stand for a time between you and justice, but it is only a postponement. You must pay at last your own debt. If you are wise you will dread a prosperity which only loads you with more. Benefit is the end of nature. But for every benefit which you receive, a tax is levied. He is great who confers the most benefits. He is base—and that is the one base thing in the universe—to receive favors and render none. In the order of nature we cannot render benefits to those from whom we receive them, or only seldom. But the benefit we receive must be rendered again, line for line, deed for deed, cent for cent, to somebody. Beware of too much good staying in your hand. It will fast corrupt and worm worms. Pay it away quickly in some sort.

Labor is watched over by the same pitiless laws. Cheapest, say the prudent, is the dearest labor. What we buy in a broom, a mat, a wagon, a knife, is some application of good sense to a common want. It is best to pay in your land a skilful gardener, or to buy good sense applied to gardening; in your sailor, good sense applied to navigation; in the house, good sense applied to cooking, sewing, serving; in your agent, good sense applied to accounts and affairs. So do you multiply your presence, or spread yourself throughout your estate. But because of the dual constitution of things, in labor as in life there can be no cheating. The thief steals from himself. The swindler swindles himself. For the real price of labor is knowledge and virtue, whereof wealth and credit are signs. These signs, like paper money, may be counterfeited or stolen, but that which they represent, namely, knowledge and virtue, cannot be counterfeited or stolen. These ends of labor cannot be answered but by real exertions of the mind, and in obedience to pure motives. The cheat, the defaulter, the gambler, cannot extort the knowledge of material and moral nature which his honest care and pains yield to the operative. The law of nature is, Do the thing, and you shall have the power; but they who do not the thing have not the power.

Human labor, through all its forms, from the sharpening of a stake to the construction of a city or an epic, is one immense illustration of the perfect compensation of the universe. The absolute balance of Give and Take, the doctrine that every thing has its price—and if that price is not paid, not that thing but something else is obtained, and that it is impossible to get anything without its price—is not less sublime in the columns of a leger than in the budgets of states, in the laws of light and darkness, in all the action and reaction of nature. I cannot doubt that the high laws which each man sees implicated in those processes with which he is conversant, the stern ethics which sparkle on his chisel-edge, which are measured out by his plumb and foot-rule, which stand as manifest in the footing of the shop-bill as in the history of a state—do recommend to him his trade, and though seldom named, exalt his business to his imagination.

The league between virtue and nature engages all things to assume a hostile front to vice. The beautiful laws and substances of the world persecute and whip the traitor. He finds that things are arranged for truth and benefit, but there is no den in the wide world to hide a rogue. Commit a crime, and the earth is made of glass. Commit a crime, and it seems as if a coat of snow fell on the ground, such as reveals in the woods the track of every partridge and fox and squirrel and mole. You cannot recall the spoken word, you cannot wipe out the foot-track, you cannot draw up the ladder, so as to leave no inlet or clew. Some damning circumstance always transpires. The laws and substances of nature—water, snow, wind, gravitation—become penalties to the thief.

On the other hand the law holds with equal sureness for all right action. Love, and you shall be loved. All love is mathematically just, as much as the two sides of an algebraic equation. The good man has absolute good, which like fire turns every thing to its own nature, so that you cannot do him any harm; but as the royal armies sent against Napoleon, when he approached cast down their colors and from enemies became friends, so disasters of all kinds, as sickness, offence, poverty, prove benefactors:—

> "Winds blow and waters roll
> Strength to the brave and power and deity,
> Yet in themselves are nothing."

The good are befriended even by weakness and defect. As no man had ever a point of pride that was not injurious to him, so no man had ever a defect that was not somewhere made useful to him. The stag in the fable admired his horns and blamed his feet, but when the hunter came, his feet saved him, and afterwards, caught in the thicket, his horns destroyed him. Every man in his lifetime needs to thank his faults. As no man thoroughly understands a truth until he has contended against it, so no man has a thorough acquaintance with the hindrances or talents of men until he has suffered from the one and seen the triumph of the other over his own want of the same. Has he a defect of temper that unfits him to live in society? Thereby he is driven to entertain himself alone and acquire habits of self-help; and thus, like the wounded oyster, he mends his shell with pearl.

Our strength grows out of our weakness. The indignation which arms itself with secret forces does not awaken until we are pricked and stung and sorely assailed. A great man is always willing to be little. Whilst he sits on the cushion of advantages, he goes to sleep. When he is pushed, tormented, defeated, he has a chance to learn something; he has been put on his wits, on his manhood; he has gained facts; learns his ignorance; is cured of the insanity of conceit; has got moderation and real skill. The wise man throws himself on the side of his assailants. It is more his interest than it is theirs to find his weak point. The wound cicatrizes and falls off from him like a dead skin, and when they would triumph, lo! he has passed on invulnerable. Blame is safer than praise. I hate to be defended in a newspaper. As long as all that is said is said against me, I feel a certain assurance of success. But as soon as honeyed words of praise are spoken for me, I feel as one that lies unprotected before his enemies. In general, every evil to which we do not succumb is a benefactor. As the Sandwich Islander believes that the strength and valor of the enemy he kills passes into himself, so we gain the strength of the temptation we resist.

The same guards which protect us from disaster, defect and enmity, defend us, if we will, from selfishness and fraud. Bolts and bars are not the best of our institutions, nor is shrewdness in trade a mark of wisdom. Men suffer all their life long under the foolish superstition that they can be cheated. But it is as impossible for a man to be cheated by any one but himself, as for a thing to be and not to be at the same time. There is a third silent party to all our bargains. The nature and soul of things takes on itself the guaranty of the fulfilment of every contract, so that honest service cannot come to loss. If you serve an ungrateful master, serve him the more: Put God in your debt. Every stroke shall be repaid. The longer the payment is withholden, the better for you; for compound interest on compound interest is the rate and usage of this exchequer.

The history of persecution is a history of endeavors to cheat nature, to make water run up hill, to twist a rope of sand. It makes no difference whether the actors be many or one, a tyrant or a mob. A mob is a society of bodies voluntarily bereaving themselves of reason and traversing its work. The mob is man voluntarily descending to the nature of the beast. Its fit hour of activity is night. Its actions are insane, like its whole constitution. It persecutes a principle; it would whip a right; it would tar and feather justice, by inflicting fire and outrage upon the houses and persons of those who have these. It resembles the prank of boys, who run with fire-engines to put out the ruddy aurora streaming to the stars. The inviolate spirit turns their spite against the wrongdoers. The martyr cannot be dishonored. Every lash inflicted is a tongue of fame; every prison a more illustrious abode; every burned book or house enlightens the world; every suppressed or expunged word reverberates through the earth from side to side. Hours of sanity and consideration are always arriving to communities, as to individuals, when the truth is seen and the martyrs are justified.

Thus do all things preach the indifferency of circumstances. The man is all. Every thing has two sides, a good and an evil. Every advantage has its tax. I learn to be content. But the doctrine of compensation is not the doctrine of indifferency. The thoughtless say, on hearing these representations—What boots it to do well? there is one event to good and evil; if I gain any good I must pay for it; if I lose any good I gain some other; all actions are indifferent.

There is a deeper fact in the soul than compensation, to wit, its own nature. The soul is not a compensation, but a life. The soul *is*. Under all this running sea of circumstance, whose waters ebb and flow with perfect balance, lies the aboriginal abyss of real Being. Essence, or God, is not a relation or a part, but the whole. Being is the vast affirmative, excluding negation, self-balanced, and swallowing up all relations, parts and times within itself. Nature, truth, virtue, are the influx from thence. Vice is the absence or departure of the same. Nothing, Falsehood, may indeed stand as the great Night or shade on which as a background the living universe paints itself forth, but no fact is begotten by it; it cannot work, for it is not. It cannot work any good; it cannot work any harm. It is harm inasmuch as it is worse not to be than to be.

We feel defrauded of the retribution due to evil acts, because the criminal adheres to his vice and contumacy and does not come to a crisis or judgment anywhere in visible nature. There is no stunning confutation of his nonsense before men and angels. Has he therefore outwitted the law? Inasmuch as he carries the malignity and the lie with him he so far deceases from nature. In some manner there will be a demonstration of the wrong to the understanding also; but, should we not see it, this deadly deduction makes square the eternal account.

Neither can it be said, on the other hand, that the gain of rectitude must be bought by any loss. There is no penalty to virtue; no penalty to wisdom; they are proper additions of being. In a virtuous action I properly *am*; in a virtuous act I add to the world; I plant into deserts conquered from Chaos and Nothing and see the darkness receding on the limits of the horizon. There can be no excess to love, none to knowledge, none to beauty, when these attributes are considered in the purest sense. The soul refuses limits, and always affirms an Optimism, never a Pessimism.

Man's life is a progress, and not a station. His instinct is trust. Our instinct uses "more" and "less" in application to man, of the *presence of the soul*, and not of its absence; the brave man is greater than the coward; the true, the benevolent, the wise, is more a man and not less, than the fool and knave. There is no tax on the good of virtue, for that is the incoming of God himself, or absolute existence, without any comparative. Material good has its tax, and if it came without desert or sweat, has no root in me, and the next wind will blow it away. But all the good of nature is the soul's, and may be had if paid for in nature's lawful coin, that is, by labor which the heart and the head allow. I no longer wish to meet a good I do not earn, for example to find a pot of buried gold, knowing that it brings with it new burdens. I do not wish more external goods—neither possessions, nor honors, nor powers, nor persons. The gain is apparent; the tax is certain. But there is no tax on the knowledge that the compensation exists and that it is not desirable to dig up treasure. Herein I rejoice with a serene eternal peace. I contract the boundaries of possible mischief. I learn the wisdom of St. Bernard—"Nothing can work me damage except myself; the harm that I sustain I carry about with me, and never am a real sufferer but by my own fault."

In the nature of the soul is the compensation for the inequalities of condition. The radical tragedy of nature seems to be the distinction of More and Less. How can Less not feel the pain; how not feel indignation or malevolence towards More? Look at those who have less faculty, and one feels sad and knows not well what to make of it. He almost shuns their eye; he fears they will upbraid God. What should they do? It seems a great injustice. But see the facts nearly and these mountainous inequalities vanish. Love reduces them as the sun melts the iceberg in the sea. The heart and soul of all men being one, this bitterness of *His* and *Mine* ceases. His is mine. I am my brother and my brother is me. If I feel over-shadowed and outdone by great neighbors, I can yet love; I can still receive; and he that loveth maketh his own the grandeur he loves. Thereby I make the discovery that my brother is my guardian, acting for me with the friendliest designs, and the estate I so admired and envied is my own. It is the nature of the soul to appropriate all things. Jesus and Shakspeare are fragments of the soul, and by love I conquer and incorporate them in my own conscious domain. His virtue—is not that mine? His wit—if it cannot be made mine, it is not wit.

Such also is the natural history of calamity. The changes which break up at short intervals the prosperity of men are advertisements of a nature whose law is growth. Every soul is by this intrinsic necessity quitting its whole system of things, its friends and home and laws and faith, as the shell-fish crawls out of its beautiful but stony case, because it no longer admits of its growth, and slowly forms a new house. In proportion to the vigor of the individual these revolutions are frequent, until in some happier mind they are incessant and all worldly relations hang very loosely about him, becoming as it were a transparent fluid membrane through which the living form is seen, and not, as in most men, an indurated heterogeneous fabric of many dates and of no settled character, in which the man is imprisoned. Then there can be enlargement, and the man of to-day scarcely recognizes the man of yesterday. And such should be the outward biography of man in time, a putting off of dead circumstances day by day, as he renews his raiment day by day. But to us, in our lapsed estate, resting, not advancing, resisting, not cooperating with the divine expansion, this growth comes by shocks.

We cannot part with our friends. We cannot let our angels go. We do not see that they only go out that archangels may come in. We are idolaters of the old. We do not believe in the riches of the soul, in its proper eternity and omnipresence. We do not believe there is any force in to-day to rival or recreate that beautiful yesterday. We linger in the ruins of the old tent where once we had bread and shelter and organs, nor believe that the spirit can feed, cover, and nerve us again. We cannot again find aught so dear, so sweet, so graceful. But we sit and weep in vain. The voice of the Almighty saith, 'Up and onward for evermore!' We cannot stay amid the ruins. Neither will we rely on the new; and so we walk ever with reverted eyes, like those monsters who look backwards.

And yet the compensations of calamity are made apparent to the understanding also, after long intervals of time. A fever, a mutilation, a cruel disappointment, a loss of wealth, a loss of friends, seems at the moment unpaid loss, and unpayable. But the sure years reveal the deep remedial force that underlies all facts. The death of a dear friend, wife, brother, lover, which seemed nothing but privation, somewhat later assumes the aspect of a guide or genius; for it commonly operates revolutions in our way of life, terminates an epoch of infancy or of youth which was waiting to be closed, breaks up a wonted occupation, or a household, or style of living, and allows the formation of new ones more friendly to the growth of character. It permits or constrains the formation of new acquaintances and the reception of new influences that prove of the first importance to the next years; and the man or woman who would have remained a sunny garden-flower, with no room for its roots and too much sunshine for its head, by the falling of the walls and the neglect of the gardener is made the banian of the forest, yielding shade and fruit to wide neighborhoods of men.

SPIRITUAL LAWS

The living Heaven thy prayers respect,
House at once and architect,
Quarrying man's rejected hours,
Builds therewith eternal towers;
Sole and self-commanded works,
Fears not undermining days,
Grows by decays,
And, by the famous might that lurks
In reaction and recoil,
Makes flame to freeze and ice to boil;
Forging, through swart arms of Offence,
The silver seat of Innocence.

WHEN THE ACT of reflection takes place in the mind, when we look at ourselves in the light of thought, we discover that our life is embosomed in beauty. Behind us, as we go, all things assume pleasing forms, as clouds do far off. Not only things familiar and stale, but even the tragic and terrible are comely as they take their place in the pictures of memory. The river-bank, the weed at the water-side, the old house, the foolish person, however neglected in the passing, have a grace in the past. Even the corpse that has lain in the chambers has added a solemn ornament to the house. The soul will not know either deformity or pain. If in the hours of clear reason we should speak the severest truth, we should say that we had never made a sacrifice. In these hours the mind seems so great that nothing can be taken from us that seems much. All loss, all pain, is particular; the universe remains to the heart unhurt. Neither vexations nor calamities abate our trust. No man ever stated his griefs as lightly as he might. Allow for exaggeration in the most patient and sorely ridden hack that ever was driven. For it is only the finite that has wrought and suffered; the infinite lies stretched in smiling repose.

The intellectual life may be kept clean and healthful if man will live the life of nature and not import into his mind difficulties which are none of his. No man need be perplexed in his speculations. Let him do and say what strictly belongs to him, and though very ignorant of books, his nature shall not yield him any intellectual obstructions and doubts. Our young people are diseased with the theological problems of original sin, origin of evil, predestination and the like. These never presented a practical difficulty to any man—never darkened across any man's road who did not go out of his way to seek them. These are the soul's mumps and measles and whooping-coughs, and those who have not caught them cannot describe their health or prescribe the cure. A simple mind will not know these enemies. It is quite another thing that he should be able to give account of his faith and expound to another the theory of his self-union and freedom. This requires rare gifts. Yet without this self-knowledge there may be a sylvan strength and integrity in that which he is. "A few strong instincts and a few plain rules" suffice us.

My will never gave the images in my mind the rank they now take. The regular course of studies, the years of academical and professional education have not yielded me better facts than some idle books under the bench at the Latin School. What we do not call education is more precious than that which we call so. We form no guess, at the time of receiving a thought, of its comparative value. And education often wastes its effort in attempts to thwart and balk this natural magnetism, which is sure to select what belongs to it.

In like manner our moral nature is vitiated by any interference of our will. People represent virtue as a struggle, and take to themselves great airs upon their attainments, and the question is everywhere vexed when a noble nature is commended, whether the man is not better who strives with temptation. But there is no merit in the matter. Either God is there or he is not there. We love characters in proportion as they are impulsive and spontaneous. The less a man thinks or knows about his virtues the better we like him. Timoleon's victories are the best victories, which ran and flowed like Homer's verses, Plutarch said. When we see a soul whose acts are all regal, graceful and pleasant as roses, we must thank God that such things can be and are, and not turn sourly on the angel and say 'Crump is a better man with his grunting resistance to all his native devils.'

Not less conspicuous is the preponderance of nature over will in all practical life. There is less intention in history than we ascribe to it. We impute deep-laid far-sighted plans to Cæsar and Napoleon; but the best of their power was in nature, not in them. Men of an extraordinary success, in their honest moments, have always sung 'Not unto us, not unto us.' According to the faith of their times they have built altars to Fortune, or to Destiny, or to St. Julian. Their success lay in their parallelism to the course of thought, which found in them an unobstructed channel; and the wonders of which they were the visible conductors seemed to the eye their deed. Did the wires generate the galvanism? It is even true that there was less in them on which they could reflect than in another; as the virtue of a pipe is to be smooth and hollow. That which externally seemed will and immovableness was willingness and self-annihilation. Could Shakspeare give a theory of Shakspeare? Could ever a man of prodigious mathematical genius convey to others any insight into his methods? If he could communicate that secret it would instantly lose its exaggerated value, blending with the daylight and the vital energy the power to stand and to go.

The lesson is forcibly taught by these observations that our life might be much easier and simpler than we make it; that the world might be a happier place than it is; that there is no need of struggles, convulsions, and despairs, of the wringing of the hands and the gnashing of the teeth; that we miscreate our own evils. We interfere with the optimism of nature; for whenever we get this vantage-ground of the past, or of a wiser mind in the present, we are able to discern that we are begirt with laws which execute themselves.

The face of external nature teaches the same lesson. Nature will not have us fret and fume. She does not like our benevolence or our learning much better than she likes our frauds and wars. When we come out of the caucus, or the bank, or the Abolition-convention, or the Temperance-meeting, or the Transcendental club into the fields and woods, she says to us, 'So hot? my little Sir.'

We are full of mechanical actions. We must needs intermeddle and have things in our own way, until the sacrifices and virtues of society are odious. Love should make joy; but our benevolence is unhappy. Our Sunday-schools and churches and pauper-societies are yokes to the neck. We pain ourselves to please nobody. There are natural ways of arriving at the same ends at which these aim, but do not arrive. Why should all virtue work in one and the same way? Why should all give dollars? It is very inconvenient to us country folk, and we do not think any good will come of it. We have not dollars, merchants have; let them give them. Farmers will give corn; poets will sing; women will sew; laborers will lend a hand; the children will bring flowers. And why drag this dead weight of a Sunday-school over the whole Christendom? It is natural and beautiful that childhood should inquire and maturity should teach; but it is time enough to answer questions when they are asked. Do not shut up the young people against their will in a pew and force the children to ask them questions for an hour against their will.

If we look wider, things are all alike; laws and letters and creeds and modes of living seem a travesty of truth. Our society is encumbered by ponderous machinery, which resembles the endless aqueducts which the Romans built over hill and dale and which are superseded by the discovery of the law that water rises to the level of its source. It is a Chinese wall which any nimble Tartar can leap over. It is a standing army, not so good as a peace. It is a graduated, titled, richly appointed empire, quite superfluous when town-meetings are found to answer just as well.

Let us draw a lesson from nature, which always works by short ways. When the fruit is ripe, it falls. When the fruit is despatched, the leaf falls. The circuit of the waters is mere falling. The walking of man and all animals is a falling forward. All our manual labor and works of strength, as prying, splitting, digging, rowing and so forth, are done by dint of continual falling, and the globe, earth, moon, comet, sun, star, fall for ever and ever.

The simplicity of the universe is very different from the simplicity of a machine. He who sees moral nature out and out and thoroughly knows how knowledge is acquired and character formed, is a pedant. The simplicity of nature is not that which may easily be read, but is inexhaustible. The last analysis can no wise be made. We judge of a man's wisdom by his hope, knowing that the perception of the inexhaustibleness of nature is an immortal youth. The wild fertility of nature is felt in comparing our rigid names and reputations with our fluid consciousness. We pass in the world for sects and schools, for erudition and piety, and we are all the time jejune babes. One sees very well how Pyrrhonism grew up. Every man sees that he is that middle point whereof every thing may be affirmed and denied with equal reason. He is old, he is young, he is very wise, he is altogether ignorant. He hears and feels what you say of the seraphim, and of the tin-peddler. There is no permanent wise man except in the figment of the

. . . .

Stoics. We side with the hero, as we read or paint, against the coward and the robber; but we have been ourselves that coward and robber, and shall be again—not in the low circumstance, but in comparison with the grandeurs possible to the soul.

A little consideration of what takes place around us every day would show us that a higher law than that of our will regulates events; that our painful labors are unnecessary and fruitless; that only in our easy, simple, spontaneous action are we strong, and by contenting ourselves with obedience we become divine. Belief and love—a believing love will relieve us of a vast load of care. O my brothers, God exists. There is a soul at the centre of nature and over the will of every man, so that none of us can wrong the universe. It has so infused its strong enchantment into nature that we prosper when we accept its advice, and when we struggle to wound its creatures our hands are glued to our sides, or they beat our own breasts. The whole course of things goes to teach us faith. We need only obey. There is guidance for each of us, and by lowly listening we shall hear the right word. Why need you choose so painfully your place and occupation and associates and modes of action and of entertainment? Certainly there is a possible right for you that precludes the need of balance and wilful election. For you there is a reality, a fit place and congenial duties. Place yourself in the middle of the stream of power and wisdom which animates all whom it floats, and you are without effort impelled to truth, to right and a perfect contentment. Then you put all gainsayers in the wrong. Then you are the world, the measure of right, of truth, of beauty. If we would not be mar-plots with our miserable interferences, the work, the society, letters, arts, science, religion of men would go on far better than now, and the heaven predicted from the beginning of the world, and still predicted from the bottom of the heart, would organize itself, as do now the rose and the air and the sun.

I say, *do not choose*; but that is a figure of speech by which I would distinguish what is commonly called choice among men, and which is a partial act, the choice of the hands, of the eyes, of the appetites, and not a whole act of the man. But that which I call right or goodness, is the choice of my constitution; and that which I call heaven, and inwardly aspire after, is the state or circumstance desirable to my constitution; and the action which I in all my years tend to do, is the work for my faculties. We must hold a man amenable to reason for the choice of his daily craft or profession. It is not an excuse any longer for his deeds that they are the custom of his trade. What business has he with an evil trade? Has he not a calling in his character?

Each man has his own vocation. The talent is the call. There is one direction in which all space is open to him. He has faculties silently inviting him thither to endless exertion. He is like a ship in a river; he runs against obstructions on every side but one, on that side all obstruction is taken away and he sweeps serenely over a deepening channel into an infinite sea. This talent and this call depend on his organization, or the mode in which the general soul incarnates itself in him. He inclines to do something which is easy to him and good when it is done, but which no other man can do. He has no rival. For the more truly he consults his own powers, the more difference will his work exhibit from the work of any other. His ambition is exactly pro-portioned to his powers. The height of the pinnacle is determined by the breadth of the base. Every man has this call of the power to do somewhat unique, and no man has any other call. The pretence that he has another call, a summons by name and personal election and out-ward "signs that mark him extraordinary and not in the roll of common men," is fanaticism, and betrays obtuseness to perceive that there is one mind in all the individuals, and no respect of persons therein.

By doing his work he makes the need felt which he can supply, and creates the taste by which he is enjoyed. By doing his own work he unfolds himself. It is the vice of our public speaking that it has not abandonment. Somewhere, not only every orator but every man should let out all the length of all the reins; should find or make a frank and hearty expression of what force and meaning is in him. The common experience is that the man fits himself as well as he can to the custom-ary details of that work or trade he falls into, and tends it as a dog turns a spit. Then is he a part of the machine he moves; the man is lost. Until he can manage to communicate himself to others in his full stature and proportion, he does not yet find his vocation. He must find in that an outlet for his character, so that he may justify his work to their eyes. If the labor is mean, let him by his thinking and character make it liberal. Whatever he knows and thinks, whatever in his appre-hension is worth doing, that let him communicate, or men will never know and honor him aright. Foolish, whenever you take the meanness and formality of that thing you do, instead of converting it into the obedient spiracle of your character and aims.

We like only such actions as have already long had the praise of men, and do not perceive that any thing man can do may be divinely done. We think greatness entailed or organized in some places or duties, in certain offices or occasions, and do not see that Paganini can extract rapture from a catgut, and Eulenstein from a jews-harp, and a nimble-fingered lad out of shreds of paper with his scissors, and Landseer out of swine, and the hero out of the pitiful habitation and company in which he was hidden. What we call obscure condition or vulgar society is that condition and society whose poetry is not yet written, but which you shall presently make as enviable and renowned as any. In our estimates let us take a lesson from kings. The parts of hospitality, the connection of families, the impressiveness of death, and a thousand other things, royalty makes its own estimate of, and a royal mind will. To make habitually a new estimate—that is elevation.

What a man does, that he has. What has he to do with hope or fear? In himself is his might. Let him regard no good as solid but that which is in his nature and which must grow out of him as long as he exists. The goods of fortune may come and go like summer leaves; let him scatter them on every wind as the momentary signs of his infinite productiveness.

He may have his own. A man's genius, the quality that differences him from every other, the susceptibility to one class of influences, the selection of what is fit for him, the rejection of what is unfit, determines for him the character of the universe. A man is a method, a progressive arrangement; a selecting principle, gathering his like to him wherever he goes. He takes only his own out of the multiplicity that sweeps and circles round him. He is like one of those booms which are set out from the shore on rivers to catch drift-wood, or like the loadstone amongst splinters of steel.

Those facts, words, persons, which dwell in his memory without his being able to say why, remain because they have a relation to him not less real for being as yet unapprehended. They are symbols of value to him as they can interpret parts of his consciousness which he would vainly seek words for in the conventional images of books and other minds. What attracts my attention shall have it, as I will go to the man who knocks at my door, whilst a thousand persons as worthy go by it, to whom I give no regard. It is enough that these particulars speak to me. A few anecdotes, a few traits of character, manners, face, a few incidents, have an emphasis in your memory out of all proportion to their apparent significance if you measure them by the ordinary standards. They relate to your gift. Let them have their weight, and do not reject them and cast about for illustration and facts more usual in literature. What your heart thinks great, is great. The soul's emphasis is always right.

Over all things that are agreeable to his nature and genius the man has the highest right. Everywhere he may take what belongs to his spiritual estate, nor can he take anything else though all doors were open, nor can all the force of men hinder him from taking so much. It is vain to attempt to keep a secret from one who has a right to know it. It will tell itself. That mood into which a friend can bring us is his dominion over us. To the thoughts of that state of mind he has a right. All the secrets of that state of mind he can compel. This is a law which statesmen use in practice. All the terrors of the French Republic, which held Austria in awe, were unable to command her diplomacy. But Napoleon sent to Vienna M. de Narbonne, one of the old noblesse, with the morals, manners and name of that interest, saying that it was indispensable to send to the old aristocracy of Europe men of the same connection, which in fact constitutes a sort of free-masonry. M. de Narbonne in less than a fortnight penetrated all the secrets of the imperial cabinet.

Nothing seems so easy as to speak and to be understood. Yet a man may come to find that the strongest of defences and of ties—that he has been understood; and he who has received an opinion may come to find it the most inconvenient of bonds.

If a teacher have any opinion which he wishes to conceal, his pupils will become as fully indoctrinated into that as into any which he publishes. If you pour water into a vessel twisted into coils and angles, it is vain to say, I will pour it only into this or that; it will find its level in all. Men feel and act the consequences of your doctrine without being able to show how they follow. Show us an arc of the curve, and a good mathematician will find out the whole figure. We are always reasoning from the seen to the unseen. Hence the perfect intelligence that subsists between wise men of remote ages. A man cannot bury his meanings so deep in his book but time and like-minded men will find them. Plato had a secret doctrine, had he? What secret can he conceal from the eyes of Bacon? of Montaigne? of Kant? Therefore Aristotle said of his works, "They are published and not published."

No man can learn what he has not preparation for learning, however near to his eyes is the object. A chemist may tell his most precious secrets to a carpenter, and he shall be never the wiser—the secrets he would not utter to a chemist for an estate. God screens us evermore from premature ideas. Our eyes are holden that we cannot see things that stare us in the face, until the hour arrives when the mind is ripened; then we behold them, and the time when we saw them not is like a dream.

Not in nature but in man is all the beauty and worth he sees. The world is very empty, and is indebted to this gilding, exalting soul for all its pride. "Earth fills her lap with splendors" *not* her own. The vale of Tempe, Tivoli and Rome are earth and water, rocks and sky. There are as good earth and water in a thousand places, yet how unaffecting!

People are not the better for the sun and moon, the horizon and the trees; as it is not observed that the keepers of Roman galleries, or the valets of painters have any elevation of thought, or that librarians are wiser men than others. There are graces in the demeanor of a polished and noble person which are lost upon the eye of a churl. These are like the stars whose light has not yet reached us.

He may see what he maketh. Our dreams are the sequel of our waking knowledge. The visions of the night bear some proportion to the visions of the day. Hideous dreams are exaggerations of the sins of the day. We see our evil affections embodied in bad physiognomies. On the Alps the traveller sometimes beholds his own shadow magnified to a giant, so that every gesture of his hand is terrific. "My children," said an old man to his boys scared by a figure in the dark entry, "my children, you will never see anything worse than yourselves." As in dreams, so in the scarcely less fluid events of the world every man sees himself in colossal, without knowing that it is himself. The good, compared to the evil which he sees, is as his own good to his own evil. Every quality of his mind is magnified in some one acquaintance, and every emotion of his heart in some one. He is like a quincunx of trees, which counts five—east, west, north, or south; or an initial, medial, and terminal acrostic. And why not? He cleaves to one person and avoids another, according to their likeness or unlikeness to himself, truly seeking himself in his associates and moreover in his trade and habits and gestures and meats and drinks, and comes at last to be faithfully represented by every view you take of his circumstances.

He may read what he writes. What can we see or acquire but what we are? You have observed a skilful man reading Virgil. Well, that author is a thousand books to a thousand persons. Take the book into your two hands and read your eyes out, you will never find what I find. If any ingenious reader would have a monopoly of the wisdom or delight he gets, he is as secure now the book is Englished, as if it were imprisoned in the Pelews' tongue. It is with a good book as it is with good company. Introduce a base person among gentlemen, it is all to no purpose; he is not their fellow. Every society protects itself. The company is perfectly safe, and he is not one of them, though his body is in the room.

What avails it to fight with the eternal laws of mind, which adjust the relation of all persons to each other by the mathematical measure of their havings and beings? Gertrude is enamored of Guy; how high, how aristocratic, how Roman his mien and manners! to live with him were life indeed, and no purchase is too great; and heaven and earth are moved to that end. Well, Gertrude has Guy; but what now avails how high, how aristocratic, how Roman his mien and manners, if his heart and aims are in the senate, in the theatre and in the billiard-room, and she has no aims, no conversation that can enchant her graceful lord?

He shall have his own society. We can love nothing but nature. The most wonderful talents, the most meritorious exertions really avail very little with us; but nearness or likeness of nature—how beautiful is the ease of its victory! Persons approach us, famous for their beauty, for their accomplishments, worthy of all wonder for their charms and gifts; they dedicate their whole skill to the hour and the company—with very imperfect result. To be sure it would be ungrateful in us not to praise them loudly. Then, when all is done, a person of related mind, a brother or sister by nature, comes to us so softly and easily, so nearly and intimately, as if it were the blood in our proper veins, that we feel as if some one was gone, instead of another having come; we are utterly relieved and refreshed; it is a sort of joyful solitude. We foolishly think in our days of sin that we must court friends by compliance to the customs of society, to its dress, its breeding, and its estimates. But only that soul can be my friend which I encounter on the line of my own march, that soul to which I do not decline and which does not decline to me, but, native of the same celestial latitude, repeats in its own all my experience. The scholar forgets himself and apes the customs of the man of the world to deserve the smile of beauty, and follows some giddy girl, not yet taught by religious passion to know the noble woman with all that is serene, oracular and beautiful in her soul. Let him be great, and love shall follow him. Nothing is more deeply punished than the neglect of the affinities by which alone society should be formed, and the insane levity of choosing associates by others' eyes.

He may set his own rate. It is a maxim worthy of all acceptation that a man may have that allowance he takes. Take the place and attitude which belong to you, and all men acquiesce. The world must be just. It leaves every man, with profound unconcern, to set his own rate. Hero or driveller, it meddles not in the matter. It will certainly accept your own measure of your doing and being, whether you sneak about and deny your own name, or whether you see your work produced to the concave sphere of the heavens, one with the revolution of the stars.

The same reality pervades all teaching. The man may teach by doing, and not otherwise. If he can communicate himself he can teach, but not by words. He teaches who gives, and he learns who receives. There is no teaching until the pupil is brought into the same state or principle in which you are; a transfusion takes place; he is you and you are he; then is a teaching, and by no unfriendly chance or bad company can he ever quite lose the benefit. But your propositions run out of one ear as they ran in at the other. We see it advertised that Mr. Grand will deliver an oration on the Fourth of July, and Mr. Hand before the Mechanics' Association, and we do not go thither, because we know that these gentlemen will not communicate their own character and experience to the company. If we had reason to expect such a confidence we should go through all inconvenience and opposition. The sick would be carried in litters. But a public oration is an escapade, a non-committal, an apology, a gag, and not a communication, not a speech, not a man.

A like Nemesis presides over all intellectual works. We have yet to learn that the thing uttered in words is not therefore affirmed. It must affirm itself, or no forms of logic or of oath can give it evidence. The sentence must also contain its own apology for being spoken.

The effect of any writing on the public mind is mathematically measurable by its depth of thought. How much water does it draw? If it awaken you to think, if it lift you from your feet with the great voice of eloquence, then the effect is to be wide, slow, permanent, over the minds of men; if the pages instruct you not, they will die like flies in the hour. The way to speak and write what shall not go out of fashion is to speak and write sincerely. The argument which has not power to reach my own practice, I may well doubt will fail to reach yours. But take Sidney's maxim:—"Look in thy heart, and write." He that writes to himself writes to an eternal public. That statement only is fit to be made public which you have come at in attempting to satisfy your own curiosity. The writer who takes his subject from his ear and not from his heart, should know that he has lost as much as he seems to have gained, and when the empty book has gathered all its praise, and half the people say, 'What poetry! what genius!' it still needs fuel to make fire. That only profits which is profitable. Life alone can impart life; and though we should burst we can only be valued as we make ourselves valuable. There is no luck in literary reputation. They who make up the final verdict upon every book are not the partial and noisy readers of the hour when it appears, but a court as of angels, a public not to be bribed, not to be entreated and not to be overawed, decides upon every man's title to fame. Only those books come down which deserve to last. Gilt edges, vellum and morocco, and presentation-copies to all the libraries will not preserve a book in circulation beyond its intrinsic date. It must go with all Walpole's Noble and Royal Authors to its fate. Blackmore, Kotzebue or Pollok may endure for a night, but Moses and Homer stand for ever. There are not in the world at any one time more than a dozen persons who read and understand Plato—never enough to pay for an edition of his works; yet to every generation these come duly down, for the sake of those few persons, as if God brought them in his hand. "No book," said Bentley, "was ever written down by any but itself." The permanence of all books is fixed by no effort, friendly or hostile, but by their own specific gravity, or the intrinsic importance of their contents to the constant mind of man. "Do not trouble yourself too much about the light on your statue," said Michael Angelo to the young sculptor; "the light of the public square will test its value."

In like manner the effect of every action is measured by the depth of the sentiment from which it proceeds. The great man knew not that he was great. It took a century or two for that fact to appear. What he did, he did because he must; it was the most natural thing in the world, and grew out of the circumstances of the moment. But now, every thing he did, even to the lifting of his finger or the eating of bread, looks large, all-related, and is called an institution.

These are the demonstrations in a few particulars of the genius of nature; they show the direction of the stream. But the stream is blood; every drop is alive. Truth has not single victories; all things are its organs—not only dust and stones, but errors and lies. The laws of disease, physicians say, are as beautiful as the laws of health. Our philosophy is affirmative and readily accepts the testimony of negative facts, as every shadow points to the sun. By a divine necessity every fact in nature is constrained to offer its testimony.

Human character evermore publishes itself. The most fugitive deed and word, the mere air of doing a thing, the intimated purpose, expresses character. If you act you show character; if you sit still, if you sleep, you show it. You think because you have spoken nothing when others spoke, and have given no opinion on the times, on the church, on slavery, on marriage, on socialism, on secret societies, on the college, on parties and persons, that your verdict is still expected with curiosity as a reserved wisdom. Far otherwise; your silence answers very loud. You have no oracle to utter, and your fellow-men have learned that you cannot help them; for oracles speak. Doth not Wisdom cry and Understanding put forth her voice?

Dreadful limits are set in nature to the powers of dissimulation. Truth tyrannizes over the unwilling members of the body. Faces never lie, it is said. No man need be deceived who will study the changes of expression. When a man speaks the truth in the spirit of truth, his eye is as clear as the heavens. When he has base ends and speaks falsely, the eye is muddy and sometimes asquint.

I have heard an experienced counsellor say that he never feared the effect upon a jury of a lawyer who does not believe in his heart that his client ought to have a verdict. If he does not believe it his unbelief will appear to the jury, despite all his protestations, and will become their unbelief. This is that law whereby a work of art, of whatever kind, sets us in the same state of mind wherein the artist was when he made it.

That which we do not believe we cannot adequately say, though we may repeat the words never so often. It was this conviction which Swedenborg expressed when he described a group of persons in the spiritual world endeavoring in vain to articulate a proposition which they did not believe; but they could not, though they twisted and folded their lips even to indignation.

A man passes for what he is worth. Very idle is all curiosity concerning other people's estimate of us, and all fear of remaining unknown is not less so. If a man know that he can do any thing—that he can do it better than any one else—he has a pledge of the acknowledgment of that fact by all persons. The world is full of judgment-days, and into every assembly that a man enters, in every action he attempts, he is gauged and stamped. In every troop of boys that whoop and run in each yard and square, a new-comer is as well and accurately weighed in the course of a few days and stamped with his right number, as if he had undergone a formal trial of his strength, speed and temper. A stranger comes from a distant school, with better dress, with trinkets in his pockets, with airs and pretentions; an older boy says to himself, 'It's of no use; we shall find him out tomorrow.' 'What has he done?' is the divine question which searches men and transpierces every false reputation. A fop may sit in any chair of the world nor be distinguished for his hour from Homer and Washington; but there need never be any doubt concerning the respective ability of human beings. Pretension may sit still, but cannot act. Pretension never feigned an act of real greatness. Pretension never wrote an Iliad, nor drove back Xerxes, nor christianized the world, nor abolished slavery.

As much virtue as there is, so much appears; as much goodness as there is, so much reverence it commands. All the devils respect virtue. The high, the generous, the self-devoted sect will always instruct and command mankind. Never was a sincere word utterly lost. Never a magnanimity fell to the ground, but there is some heart to greet and accept it unexpectedly. A man passes for that he is worth. What he is engraves itself on his face, on his form, on his fortunes, in letters of light. Concealment avails him nothing, boasting nothing. There is confession in the glances of our eyes, in our smiles, in salutations, and the grasp of hands. His sin bedaubs him, mars all his good impression. Men know not why they do not trust him, but they do not trust him.

· ·

His vice glasses his eye, cuts lines of mean expression in his cheek, pinches the nose, sets the mark of the beast on the back of the head, and writes O fool! fool! on the forehead of a king.

If you would not be known to do any thing, never do it. A man may play the fool in the drifts of a desert, but every grain of sand shall seem to see. He may be a solitary eater, but he cannot keep his foolish counsel. A broken complexion, a swinish look, ungenerous acts and the want of due knowledge—all blab. Can a cook, a Chiffinch, an Iachimo be mistaken for Zeno or Paul? Confucius exclaimed—"How can a man be concealed? How can a man be concealed?"

On the other hand, the hero fears not that if he withhold the avowal of a just and brave act it will go unwitnessed and unloved. One knows it—himself—and is pledged by it to sweetness of peace and to nobleness of aim which will prove in the end a better proclamation of it than the relating of the incident. Virtue is the adherence in action to the nature of things and the nature of things makes it prevalent. It consists in a perpetual substitution of being for seeming, and with sublime propriety God is described as saying, I AM.

The lesson which these observations convey is, Be, and not seem. Let us acquiesce. Let us take our bloated nothingness out of the path of the divine circuits. Let us unlearn our wisdom of the world. Let us lie low in the Lord's power and learn that truth alone makes rich and great.

If you visit your friend, why need you apologize for not having visited him, and waste his time and deface your own act? Visit him now. Let him feel that the highest love has come to see him, in thee its lowest organ. Or why need you torment yourself and friend by secret self-reproaches that you have not assisted him or complimented him with gifts and salutations heretofore? Be a gift and a benediction. Shine with real light and not with the borrowed reflection of gifts. Common men are apologies for men; they bow the head, excuse themselves with prolix reasons, and accumulate appearances because the substance is not.

We are full of these superstitions of sense, the worship of magnitude. We call the poet inactive, because he is not a president, a merchant, or a porter. We adore an institution, and do not see that it is founded on a thought which we have. But real action is in silent moments. The epochs of our life are not in the visible facts of our choice of a calling, our marriage, our acquisition of an office, and the like, but in a silent thought by the wayside as we walk; in a thought which revises our entire manner of life and says—'Thus hast thou done, but it were better thus.' And all our after years, like menials, serve and wait on this, and according to their ability execute its will. This revisal or correction is a constant force, which, as a tendency, reaches through our lifetime. The object of the man, the aim of these moments, is to make daylight shine through him, to suffer the law to traverse his whole being without obstruction, so that on what point soever of his doing your eye falls it shall report truly of his character, whether it be his diet, his house, his religious forms, his society, his mirth, his vote, his opposition. Now he is not homogeneous, but heterogeneous, and the ray does not traverse; there are no thorough lights, but the eye of the beholder is puzzled, detecting many unlike tendencies and a life not yet at one.

Why should we make it a point with our false modesty to disparage that man we are and that form of being assigned to us? A good man is contented. I love and honor Epaminondas, but I do not wish to be Epaminondas. I hold it more just to love the world of this hour than the world of his hour. Nor can you, if I am true, excite me to the least uneasiness by saying, 'He acted and thou sittest still.' I see action to be good, when the need is, and sitting still to be also good. Epaminondas, if he was the man I take him for, would have sat still with joy and peace, if his lot had been mine. Heaven is large, and affords space for all modes of love and fortitude. Why should we be busy-bodies and superserviceable? Action and inaction are alike to the true. One piece of the tree is cut for a weathercock and one for the sleeper of a bridge; the virtue of the wood is apparent in both.

I desire not to disgrace the soul. The fact that I am here certainly shows me that the soul had need of an organ here. Shall I not assume the post? Shall I skulk and dodge and duck with my unseasonable apologies and vain modesty and imagine my being here impertinent? less pertinent than Epaminondas or Homer being there? and that the soul did not know its own needs? Besides, without any reasoning on the matter, I have no discontent. The good soul nourishes me and unlocks new magazines of power and enjoyment to me every day. I will not meanly decline the immensity of good, because I have heard that it has come to others in another shape.

Besides, why should we be cowed by the name of Action? 'T is a trick of the senses—no more. We know that the ancestor of every action is a thought. The poor mind does not seem to itself to be any thing unless it have an outside badge—some Gentoo diet, or Quaker coat, or Calvinistic prayer-meeting, or philanthropic society, or a great donation, or a high office, or, any how, some wild contrasting action to testify that it is somewhat. The rich mind lies in the sun and sleeps, and is Nature. To think is to act.

Let us, if we must have great actions, make our own so. All action is of an infinite elasticity, and the least admits of being inflated with the celestial air until it eclipses the sun and moon. Let us seek one peace by fidelity. Let me heed my duties. Why need I go gadding into the scenes and philosophy of Greek and Italian history before I have justified myself to my benefactors? How dare I read Washington's campaigns when I have not answered the letters of my own correspondents? Is not that a just objection to much of our reading? It is a pusillanimous desertion of our work to gaze after our neighbors. It is peeping. Byron says of Jack Bunting—

He knew not what to say, and so he swore.

I may say it of our preposterous use of books—He knew not what to do, and so *he read*. I can think of nothing to fill my time with, and I find the Life of Brant. It is a very extravagant compliment to pay to Brant, or to General Schuyler, or to General Washington. My time should be as good as their time—my facts, my net of relations, as good as theirs, or either of theirs. Rather let me do my work so well that other idlers if they choose may compare my texture with the texture of these and find it identical with the best.

This over-estimate of the possibilities of Paul and Pericles, this under-estimate of our own, comes from a neglect of the fact of an identical nature. Bonaparte knew but one merit, and rewarded in one and the same way the good soldier, the good astronomer, the good poet, the good player. The poet uses the names of Cæsar, of Tamerlane, of Bonduca, of Belisarius; the painter uses the conventional story of the Virgin Mary, of Paul, of Peter. He does not therefore defer to the nature of these accidental men, of these stock heroes. If the poet write a true drama, then he is Cæsar, and not the player of Cæsar; then the selfsame strain of thought, emotion as pure, wit as subtle, motions as swift, mounting, extravagant, and a heart as great, self-sufficing, dauntless, which on the waves of its love and hope can uplift all that is reckoned solid and precious in the world—palaces, gardens, money, navies, king-doms—marking its own incomparable worth by the slight it casts on these gauds of men; these all are his, and by the power of these he rouses the nations. Let a man believe in God, and not in names and places and persons. Let the great soul incarnated in some woman's form, poor and sad and single, in some Dolly or Joan, go out to ser-vice and sweep chambers and scour floors, and its effulgent daybeams cannot be muffled or hid, but to sweep and scour will instantly appear supreme and beautiful actions, the top and radiance of human life, and all people will get mops and brooms; until, lo! suddenly the great soul has enshrined itself in some other form and done some other deed, and that is now the flower and head of all living nature.

We are the photometers, we the irritable goldleaf and tinfoil that measure the accumulations of the subtle element. We know the authen-tic effects of the true fire through every one of its million disguises.

LOVE

"I was as a gem concealed;
Me my burning ray revealed."

Koran

EVERY PROMISE of the soul has innumerable fulfilments; each of its joys ripens into a new want. Nature, uncontainable, flowing, forelooking, in the first sentiment of kindness anticipates already a benevolence which shall lose all particular regards in its general light. The introduction to this felicity is in a private and tender relation of one to one, which is the enchantment of human life; which, like a certain divine rage and enthusiasm, seizes on man at one period and works a revolution in his mind and body; unites him to his race, pledges him to the domestic and civic relations, carries him with new sympathy into nature, enhances the power of the senses, opens the imagination, adds to his character heroic and sacred attributes, establishes marriage and gives permanence to human society.

The natural association of the sentiment of love with the heyday of the blood seems to require that in order to portray it in vivid tints, which every youth and maid should confess to be true to their throbbing experience, one must not be too old. The delicious fancies of youth reject the least favor of a mature philosophy, as chilling with age and pedantry their purple bloom. And therefore I know I incur the imputation of unnecessary hardness and stoicism from those who compose the Court and Parliament of Love. But from these formidable censors I shall appeal to my seniors. For it is to be considered that this passion of which we speak, though it begin with the young, yet forsakes not the old, or rather suffers no one who is its servant to grow old, but makes the aged participators of it not less than the tender maiden, though in a different and nobler sort. For it is a fire that kindling its first embers in the narrow nook of a private bosom, caught from a wandering spark out of another private heart, glows and enlarges until it warms and beams upon multitudes of men and women, upon the universal heart of all, and so lights up the whole world and all

190

nature with its generous flames. It matters not therefore whether we attempt to describe the passion at twenty, thirty, or at eighty years. He who paints it at the first period will lose some of its later, he who paints it at the last, some of its earlier traits. Only it is to be hoped that by patience and the Muses' aid we may attain to that inward view of the law which shall describe a truth ever young and beautiful, so central that it shall commend itself to the eye at whatever angle beholden.

And the first condition is that we must leave a too close and lingering adherence to facts, and study the sentiment as it appeared in hope, and not in history. For each man sees his own life defaced and disfigured, as the life of man is not to his imagination. Each man sees over his own experience a certain stain of error, whilst that of other men looks fair and ideal. Let any man go back to those delicious relations which make the beauty of his life, which have given him sincerest instruction and nourishment, he will shrink and moan. Alas! I know not why, but infinite compunctions embitter in mature life the remembrances of budding joy, and cover every beloved name. Every thing is beautiful seen from the point of the intellect, or as truth. But all is sour if seen as experience. Details are melancholy; the plan is seemly and noble. In the actual world—the painful kingdom of time and place—dwell care and canker and fear. With thought, with the ideal, is immortal hilarity, the rose of joy. Round it all the Muses sing. But grief cleaves to names and persons and the partial interests of to-day and yesterday.

The strong bent of nature is seen in the proportion which this topic of personal relations usurps in the conversation of society. What do we wish to know of any worthy person so much as how he has sped in the history of this sentiment? What books in the circulating library circulate? How we glow over these novels of passion, when the story is told with any spark of truth and nature! And what fastens attention, in the intercourse of life, like any passage betraying affection between two parties? Perhaps we never saw them before and never shall meet them again. But we see them exchange a glance or betray a deep emotion, and we are no longer strangers. We understand them and take the warmest interest in the development of the romance. All mankind love a lover. The earliest demonstrations of complacency and kindness are nature's most winning pictures. It is the dawn of civility and grace in the coarse and rustic. The rude village boy teases the girls about the school-house door; but to-day he comes running into the entry and meets one fair child disposing her satchel; he holds her books to help her, and instantly it seems to him as if she removed herself from him infinitely, and was a sacred precinct. Among the throng of girls he runs rudely enough, but one alone distances him; and these two little neighbors, that were so close just now, have learned to respect each other's personality. Or who can avert his eyes from the engaging, half-artful, half-artless ways of school-girls who go into the country shops to buy a skein of silk or a sheet of paper, and talk half an hour about nothing with the broad-faced, good-natured shop-boy. In the village they are on a perfect equality, which love delights in, and without any coquetry the happy, affectionate nature of woman flows out in this pretty gossip. The girls may have little beauty, yet plainly do they establish between them and the good boy the most agreeable, confiding relations; what with their fun and their earnest, about Edgar and Jonas and Almira, and who was invited to the party, and who danced at the dancing-school, and when the singing-school would begin, and other nothings concerning which the parties cooed. By and by that boy wants a wife, and very truly and heartily will he know where to find a sincere and sweet mate, without any risk such as Milton deplores as incident to scholars and great men.

I have been told that in some public discourses of mine my reverence for the intellect has made me unjustly cold to the personal relations. But now I almost shrink at the remembrance of such disparaging words. For persons are love's world, and the coldest philosopher cannot recount the debt of the young soul wandering here in nature to the power of love, without being tempted to unsay, as treasonable to nature, aught derogatory to the social instincts. For though the celestial rapture falling out of heaven seizes only upon those of tender age, and although a beauty overpowering all analysis or comparison and putting us quite beside ourselves we can seldom see after thirty years, yet the remembrance of these visions outlasts all other remembrances, and is a wreath of flowers on the oldest brows. But here is a strange fact; it may seem to many men, in revising their experience, that they have no fairer page in their life's book than the delicious memory of some passages wherein affection contrived to give a witchcraft, surpassing the deep attraction of its own truth, to a parcel of accidental and trivial circumstances. In looking backward they may find that several things which were not the charm have more reality to this groping memory than the charm itself which embalmed them. But be our experience in particulars what it may, no man ever forgot the visitations of that power to his heart and brain, which created all things anew; which was the dawn in him of music, poetry and art; which made the face of nature radiant with purple light, the morning and the night varied enchantments; when a single tone of one voice could make the heart bound, and the most trivial circumstance associated with one form is put in the amber of memory; when he became all eye when one was present, and all memory when one was gone; when the youth becomes a watcher of windows and studious of a glove, a veil, a ribbon, or the wheels of a carriage; when no place is too solitary and none too silent for him who has richer company and sweeter conversation in his new thoughts than any old friends, though best and purest, can give him; for the figures, the motions, the words of the beloved object are not, like other images, written in water, but, as Plutarch said, "enamelled in fire," and make the study of midnight:—

"Thou art not gone being gone, where'er thou art,
    Thou leav'st in him thy watchful eyes, in him thy loving heart."

In the noon and the afternoon of life we still throb at the recollection of days when happiness was not happy enough, but must be drugged with the relish of pain and fear; for he touched the secret of the matter who said of love—

"All other pleasures are not worth its pains:"

and when the day was not long enough, but the night too must be consumed in keen recollections; when the head boiled all night on the pillow with the generous deed it resolved on; when the moonlight was a pleasing fever and the stars were letters and the flowers ciphers and the air was coined into song; when all business seemed an impertinence, and all the men and women running to and fro in the streets, mere pictures.

The passion rebuilds the world for the youth. It makes all things alive and significant. Nature grows conscious. Every bird on the boughs of the tree sings now to his heart and soul. The notes are almost artic-

ulate. The clouds have faces as he looks on them. The trees of the forest, the waving grass and the peeping flowers have grown intelligent;
and he almost fears to trust them with the secret which they seem to
invite. Yet nature soothes and sympathizes. In the green solitude he
finds a dearer home than with men:—

> "Fountain-heads and pathless groves,
>   Places which pale passion loves,
>   Moonlight walks, when all the fowls
>   Are safely housed, save bats and owls,
>   A midnight bell, a passing groan—
>   These are the sounds we feed upon."

Behold there in the wood the fine madman! He is a palace of sweet
sounds and sights; he dilates; he is twice a man; he walks with arms
akimbo; he soliloquizes; he accosts the grass and the trees; he feels the
blood of the violet, the clover and the lily in his veins; and he talks with
the brook that wets his foot.

The heats that have opened his perceptions of natural beauty have
made him love music and verse. It is a fact often observed, that men
have written good verses under the inspiration of passion who cannot
write well under any other circumstances.

The like force has the passion over all his nature. It expands the
sentiment; it makes the clown gentle and gives the coward heart. Into
the most pitiful and abject it will infuse a heart and courage to defy the
world, so only it have the countenance of the beloved object. In giving
him to another it still more gives him to himself. He is a new man, with
new perceptions, new and keener purposes, and a religious solemnity of
character and aims. He does not longer appertain to his family and
society; *he* is somewhat; *he* is a person; *he* is a soul.

And here let us examine a little nearer the nature of that influence
which is thus potent over the human youth. Beauty, whose revelation to
man we now celebrate, welcome as the sun wherever it pleases to shine,
which pleases everybody with it and with themselves, seems sufficient
to itself. The lover cannot paint his maiden to his fancy poor and solitary. Like a tree in flower, so much soft, budding, informing loveliness
is society for itself; and she teaches his eye why Beauty was pictured
with Loves and Graces attending her steps. Her existence makes the

world rich. Though she extrudes all other persons from his attention as cheap and unworthy, she indemnifies him by carrying out her own being into somewhat impersonal, large, mundane, so that the maiden stands to him for a representative of all select things and virtues. For that reason the lover never sees personal resemblances in his mistress to her kindred or to others. His friends find in her a likeness to her mother, or her sisters, or to persons not of her blood. The lover sees no resemblance except to summer evenings and diamond mornings, to rainbows and the song of birds.

The ancients called beauty the flowering of virtue. Who can analyze the nameless charm which glances from one and another face and form? We are touched with emotions of tenderness and complacency, but we cannot find whereat this dainty emotion, this wandering gleam, points. It is destroyed for the imagination by any attempt to refer it to organization. Nor does it point to any relations of friendship or love known and described in society, but, as it seems to me, to a quite other and unattainable sphere, to relations of transcendent delicacy and sweetness, to what roses and violets hint and foreshow. We cannot approach beauty. Its nature is like opaline doves'-neck lustres, hovering and evanescent. Herein it resembles the most excellent things, which all have this rainbow character, defying all attempts at appropriation and use. What else did Jean Paul Richter signify, when he said to music, "Away! away! thou speakest to me of things which in all my endless life I have not found and shall not find." The same fluency may be observed in every work of the plastic arts. The statue is then beautiful when it begins to be incomprehensible, when it is passing out of criticism and can no longer be defined by compass and measuring-wand, but demands an active imagination to go with it and to say what it is in the act of doing. The god or hero of the sculptor is always represented in a transition *from* that which is representable to the senses, *to* that which is not. Then first it ceases to be a stone. The same remark holds of painting. And of poetry the success is not attained when it lulls and satisfies, but when it astonishes and fires us with new endeavors after the unattainable. Concerning it Landor inquires "whether it is not to be referred to some purer state of sensation and existence."

In like manner, personal beauty is then first charming and itself when it dissatisfies us with any end; when it becomes a story without an end; when it suggests gleams and visions and not earthly satisfactions; when it makes the beholder feel his unworthiness; when he cannot feel his right to it, though he were Cæsar; he cannot feel more right to it than to the firmament and the splendors of a sunset.

Hence arose the saying, "If I love you, what is that to you?" We say so because we feel that what we love is not in your will, but above it. It is not you, but your radiance. It is that which you know not in yourself and can never know.

This agrees well with that high philosophy of Beauty which the ancient writers delighted in; for they said that the soul of man, embodied here on earth, went roaming up and down in quest of that other world of its own out of which it came into this, but was soon stupefied by the light of the natural sun, and unable to see any other objects than those of this world, which are but shadows of real things. Therefore the Deity sends the glory of youth before the soul, that it may avail itself of beautiful bodies as aids to its recollection of the celestial good and fair; and the man beholding such a person in the female sex runs to her and finds the highest joy in contemplating the form, movement and intelligence of this person, because it suggests to him the presence of that which indeed is within the beauty, and the cause of the beauty.

If however, from too much conversing with material objects, the soul was gross, and misplaced its satisfaction in the body, it reaped nothing but sorrow; body being unable to fulfil the promise which beauty holds out; but if, accepting the hint of these visions and suggestions which beauty makes to his mind, the soul passes through the body and falls to admire strokes of character, and the lovers contemplate one another in their discourses and their actions, then they pass to the true palace of beauty, more and more inflame their love of it, and by this love extinguishing the base affection, as the sun puts out fire by shining on the hearth, they become pure and hallowed. By conversation with that which is in itself excellent, magnanimous, lowly, and just, the lover comes to a warmer love of these nobilities, and a quicker apprehension of them. Then he passes from loving them in one to loving them in all, and so is the one beautiful soul only the door through which he enters to the society of all true and pure souls. In the particular society of his mate he attains a clearer sight of any spot, any taint which her beauty has contracted from this world, and is able to point it out, and this with mutual joy that they are now able, without offence, to indicate blemishes and hindrances in each other, and give to each all help and comfort in curing the same. And beholding in many souls the traits of the divine beauty, and separating in each soul that which is divine from the taint which it has contracted in the world, the lover ascends to the highest beauty, to love and knowledge of Divinity, by steps on this ladder of created souls.

Somewhat like this have the truly wise told us of love in all ages. The doctrine is not old, nor is it new. If Plato, Plutarch and Apuleius taught it, so have Petrarch, Angelo and Milton. It awaits a truer unfolding in opposition and rebuke to that subterranean prudence which presides at marriages with words that take hold of the upper world, whilst one eye is prowling in the cellar; so that its gravest discourse has a savor of hams and powdering-tubs. Worst, when this sensualism intrudes into the education of young women, and withers the hope and affection of human nature by teaching that marriage signifies nothing but a housewife's thrift, and that woman's life has no other aim.

But this dream of love, though beautiful, is only one scene in our play. In the procession of the soul from within outward, it enlarges its circles ever, like the pebble thrown into the pond, or the light proceeding from an orb. The rays of the soul alight first on things nearest, on every utensil and toy, on nurses and domestics, on the house and yard and passengers, on the circle of household acquaintance, on politics and geography and history. But things are ever grouping themselves according to higher or more interior laws. Neighborhood, size, numbers, habits, persons, lose by degrees their power over us. Cause and effect, real affinities, the longing for harmony between the soul and the circumstances, the progressive, idealizing instinct, predominate later, and the step backward from the higher to the lower relations is impossible. Thus even love, which is the deification of persons, must become more impersonal every day. Of this at first it gives no hint. Little think the youth and maiden who are glancing at each other across crowded rooms with eyes so full of mutual intelligence, of the precious fruit long hereafter to proceed from this new, quite external stimulus. The work of vegetation begins first in the irritability of the bark and leaf-buds. From exchanging glances, they advance to acts of courtesy, of gallantry, then to fiery passion, to plighting troth and marriage. Passion beholds its object as a perfect unit. The soul is wholly embodied, and the body is wholly ensouled:—

> "Her pure and eloquent blood
> Spoke in her cheeks, and so distinctly wrought,
> That one might almost say her body thought."

Romeo, if dead, should be cut up into little stars to make the heav-ens fine. Life, with this pair, has no other aim, asks no more, than Juliet—than Romeo. Night, day, studies, talents, kingdoms, religion, are all contained in this form full of soul, in this soul which is all form. The lovers delight in endearments, in avowals of love, in comparisons of their regards. When alone, they solace themselves with the remem-bered image of the other. Does that other see the same star, the same melting cloud, read the same book, feel the same emotion, that now delights me? They try and weigh their affection, and adding up costly advantages, friends, opportunities, properties, exult in discovering that willingly, joyfully, they would give all as a ransom for the beautiful, the beloved head, not one hair of which shall be harmed. But the lot of humanity is on these children. Danger, sorrow and pain arrive to them as to all. Love prays. It makes covenants with Eternal Power in behalf of this dear mate. The union which is thus effected and which adds a new value to every atom in nature—for it transmutes every thread throughout the whole web of relation into a golden ray, and bathes the soul in a new and sweeter element—is yet a temporary state. Not always can flowers, pearls, poetry, protestations, nor even home in another heart, content the awful soul that dwells in clay. It arouses itself at last from these endearments, as toys, and puts on the harness and aspires to vast and universal aims. The soul which is in the soul of each, craving a perfect beatitude, detects incongruities, defects and dis-proportion in the behavior of the other. Hence arise surprise, expostulation and pain. Yet that which drew them to each other was signs of loveliness, signs of virtue; and these virtues are there, however eclipsed. They appear and reappear and continue to attract; but the regard changes, quits the sign and attaches to the substance. This repairs the wounded affection. Meantime, as life wears on, it proves a game of permutation and combination of all possible positions of the parties, to employ all the resources of each and acquaint each with the strength and weakness of the other. For it is the nature and end of this relation, that they should represent the human race to each other. All that is in the world, which is or ought to be known, is cunningly wrought into the texture of man, of woman:—

> "The person love does to us fit,
> Like manna, has the taste of all in it."

The world rolls; the circumstances vary every hour. The angels that inhabit this temple of the body appear at the windows, and the gnomes and vices also. By all the virtues they are united. If there be virtue, all the vices are known as such; they confess and flee. Their once flaming regard is sobered by time in either breast, and losing in violence what it gains in extent, it becomes a thorough good understanding. They resign each other without complaint to the good offices which man and woman are severally appointed to discharge in time, and exchange the passion which once could not lose sight of its object, for a cheerful disengaged furtherance, whether present or absent, of each other's designs. At last they discover that all which at first drew them together—those once sacred features, that magical play of charms—was deciduous, had a prospective end, like the scaffolding by which the house was built; and the purification of the intellect and the heart from year to year is the real marriage, foreseen and prepared from the first, and wholly above their consciousness. Looking at these aims with which two persons, a man and a woman, so variously and correlatively gifted, are shut up in one house to spend in the nuptial society forty or fifty years, I do not wonder at the emphasis with which the heart prophesies this crisis from early infancy, at the profuse beauty with which the instincts deck the nuptial bower, and nature and intellect and art emulate each other in the gifts and the melody they bring to the epithalamium.

Thus are we put in training for a love which knows not sex, nor person, nor partiality, but which seeks virtue and wisdom everywhere, to the end of increasing virtue and wisdom. We are by nature observers, and thereby learners. That is our permanent state. But we are often made to feel that our affections are but tents of a night. Though slowly and with pain, the objects of the affections change, as the objects of thought do. There are moments when the affections rule and absorb the man and make his happiness dependent on a person or persons. But in health the mind is presently seen again—its overarching vault, bright with galaxies of immutable lights, and the warm loves and fears, that swept over us as clouds, must lose their finite character and blend with God, to attain their own perfection. But we need not fear that we can lose any thing by the progress of the soul. The soul may be trusted to the end. That which is so beautiful and attractive as these relations, must be succeeded and supplanted only by what is more beautiful, and so on for ever.

FRIENDSHIP

A ruddy drop of manly blood
The surging sea outweighs;
The world uncertain comes and goes,
The lover rooted stays.
I fancied he was fled,
And, after many a year,
Glowed unexhausted kindliness
Like daily sunrise there.
My careful heart was free again—
O friend, my bosom said,
Through thee alone the sky is arched,
Through thee the rose is red,
All things through thee take nobler form
And look beyond the earth,
The mill-round of our fate appears
A sun-path in thy worth.
Me too thy nobleness has taught
To master my despair;
The fountains of my hidden life
Are through thy friendship fair.

WE HAVE a great deal more kindness than is ever spoken. Maugre all the selfishness that chills like east winds the world, the whole human family is bathed with an element of love like a fine ether. How many persons we meet in houses, whom we scarcely speak to, whom yet we honor, and who honor us! How many we see in the street, or sit with in church, whom, though silently, we warmly rejoice to be with! Read the language of these wandering eye-beams. The heart knoweth.

The effect of the indulgence of this human affection is a certain cordial exhilaration. In poetry and in common speech the emotions of benevolence and complacency which are felt towards others are likened to the material effects of fire; so swift, or much more swift, more active, more cheering, are these fine inward irradiations. From the highest degree of passionate love to the lowest degree of good-will, they make the sweetness of life.

Our intellectual and active powers increase with our affection. The scholar sits down to write, and all his years of meditation do not furnish him with one good thought or happy expression; but it is necessary to write a letter to a friend—and forthwith troops of gentle thoughts invest themselves, on every hand, with chosen words. See, in any house where virtue and self-respect abide, the palpitation which the approach of a stranger causes. A commended stranger is expected and announced, and an uneasiness betwixt pleasure and pain invades all the hearts of a household. His arrival almost brings fear to the good hearts that would welcome him. The house is dusted, all things fly into their places, the old coat is exchanged for the new, and they must get up a dinner if they can. Of a commended stranger, only the good report is told by others, only the good and new is heard by us. He stands to us for humanity. He is what we wish. Having imagined and invested him, we ask how we should stand related in conversation and action with such a man, and are uneasy with fear. The same idea exalts conversation with him. We talk better than we are wont. We have the nimblest fancy, a richer memory, and our dumb devil has taken leave for the time. For long hours we can continue a series of sincere, graceful, rich communications, drawn from the oldest, secretest experience, so that they who sit by, of our own kinsfolk and acquaintance, shall feel a lively surprise at our unusual powers. But as soon as the stranger begins to intrude his partialities, his definitions, his defects into the conversation, it is all over. He has heard the first, the last and best he will ever hear from us. He is no stranger now. Vulgarity, ignorance, misapprehension are old acquaintances. Now, when he comes, he may get the order, the dress and the dinner—but the throbbing of the heart and the communications of the soul, no more.

What is so pleasant as these jets of affection which make a young world for me again? What so delicious as a just and firm encounter of two, in a thought, in a feeling? How beautiful, on their approach to this beating heart, the steps and forms of the gifted and the true! The moment we indulge our affections, the earth is metamorphosed; there is no winter and no night; all tragedies, all ennuis vanish—all duties even; nothing fills the proceeding eternity but the forms all radiant of beloved persons. Let the soul be assured that somewhere in the universe it should rejoin its friend, and it would be content and cheerful alone for a thousand years.

I awoke this morning with devout thanksgiving for my friends, the old and the new. Shall I not call God the Beautiful, who daily showeth himself so to me in his gifts? I chide society, I embrace solitude, and yet I am not so ungrateful as not to see the wise, the lovely and the noble-minded, as from time to time they pass my gate. Who hears me, who understands me, becomes mine—a possession for all time. Nor is Nature so poor but she gives me this joy several times, and thus we weave social threads of our own, a new web of relations; and, as many thoughts in succession substantiate themselves, we shall by and by stand in a new world of our own creation, and no longer strangers and pilgrims in a traditionary globe. My friends have come to me unsought. The great God gave them to me. By oldest right, by the divine affinity of virtue with itself, I find them, or rather not I, but the Deity in me and in them derides and cancels the thick walls of individual character, relation, age, sex, circumstance, at which he usually connives, and now makes many one. High thanks I owe you, excellent lovers, who carry out the world for me to new and noble depths, and enlarge the meaning of all my thoughts. These are new poetry of the first Bard—poetry without stop—hymn, ode and epic, poetry still flowing, Apollo and the Muses chanting still. Will these too separate themselves from me again, or some of them? I know not, but I fear it not; for my relation to them is so pure that we hold by simple affinity, and the Genius of my life being thus social, the same affinity will exert its energy on whomsoever is as noble as these men and women, wherever I may be.

I confess to an extreme tenderness of nature on this point. It is almost dangerous to me to "crush the sweet poison of misused wine" of the affections. A new person is to me a great event and hinders me from sleep. I have often had fine fancies about persons which have given me delicious hours; but the joy ends in the day; it yields no fruit. Thought is not born of it; my action is very little modified. I must feel pride in my friend's accomplishments as if they were mine, and a property in his virtues. I feel as warmly when he is praised, as the lover when he hears applause of his engaged maiden. We over-estimate the conscience of our friend. His goodness seems better than our goodness, his nature finer, his temptations less. Every thing that is his—his name, his form, his dress, books and instruments—fancy enhances. Our own thought sounds new and larger from his mouth.

Yet the systole and diastole of the heart are not without their analogy in the ebb and flow of love. Friendship, like the immortality of the soul, is too good to be believed. The lover, beholding his maiden, half knows that she is not verily that which he worships; and in the golden hour of friendship we are surprised with shades of suspicion and unbelief. We doubt that we bestow on our hero the virtues in which he shines, and afterwards worship the form to which we have ascribed this divine inhabitation. In strictness, the soul does not respect men as it respects itself. In strict science all persons underlie the same condition of an infinite remoteness. Shall we fear to cool our love by mining for the metaphysical foundation of this Elysian temple? Shall I not be as real as the things I see? If I am, I shall not fear to know them for what they are. Their essence is not less beautiful than their appearance, though it needs finer organs for its apprehension. The root of the plant is not unsightly to science, though for chaplets and festoons we cut the stem short. And I must hazard the production of the bald fact amidst these pleasing reveries, though it should prove an Egyptian skull at our banquet. A man who stands united with his thought conceives magnificently of himself. He is conscious of a universal success, even though bought by uniform particular failures. No advantages, no powers, no gold or force, can be any match for him. I cannot choose but rely on my own poverty more than on your wealth. I cannot make your consciousness tantamount to mine. Only the star dazzles; the planet has a faint, moonlike ray. I hear what you say of the admirable parts and tried temper of the party you praise, but I see well that, for all his purple cloaks, I shall not like him, unless he is at least a poor Greek like me. I cannot deny it, O friend, that the vast shadow of the Phenomenal includes thee also in its pied and painted immensity—thee also, compared with whom all else is shadow. Thou art not Being, as Truth is, as Justice is—thou art not my soul, but a picture and effigy of that. Thou hast come to me lately, and already thou art seizing thy hat and cloak. Is it not that the soul puts forth friends as the tree puts forth leaves, and presently, by the germination of new buds, extrudes the old leaf? The law of nature is alternation for evermore. Each electrical state superinduces the opposite. The soul environs itself with friends that it may enter into a grander self-acquaintance or solitude; and it goes alone for a season that it may exalt its conversation or society. This method betrays itself along the whole history of our personal relations. The instinct of affection revives the hope of union with our mates, and the returning sense of insulation recalls us from the chase. Thus every man passes his life in the search after friendship, and if he should record his true sentiment, he might write a letter like this to each new candidate for his love:—

DEAR FRIEND,

If I was sure of thee, sure of thy capacity, sure to match my mood with thine, I should never think again of trifles in relation to thy comings and goings. I am not very wise; my moods are quite attainable, and I respect thy genius; it is to me as yet unfathomed; yet dare I not presume in thee a perfect intelligence of me, and so thou art to me a delicious torment. Thine ever, or never.

Yet these uneasy pleasures and fine pains are for curiosity and not for life. They are not to be indulged. This is to weave cobweb, and not cloth. Our friendships hurry to short and poor conclusions, because we have made them a texture of wine and dreams, instead of the tough fibre of the human heart. The laws of friendship are austere and eternal, of one web with the laws of nature and of morals. But we have aimed at a swift and petty benefit, to suck a sudden sweetness. We snatch at the slowest fruit in the whole garden of God, which many summers and many winters must ripen. We seek our friend not sacredly, but with an adulterate passion which would appropriate him to ourselves. In vain. We are armed all over with subtle antagonisms, which, as soon as we meet, begin to play, and translate all poetry into stale prose. Almost all people descend to meet. All association must be a compromise, and, what is worst, the very flower and aroma of the flower of each of the beautiful natures disappears as they approach each other. What a perpetual disappointment is actual society, even of the virtuous and gifted! After interviews have been compassed with long foresight we must be tormented presently by baffled blows, by sudden, unseasonable apathies, by epilepsies of wit and of animal spirits, in the heyday of friendship and thought. Our faculties do not play us true, and both parties are relieved by solitude.

I ought to be equal to every relation. It makes no difference how many friends I have and what content I can find in conversing with each, if there be one to whom I am not equal. If I have shrunk unequal from one contest, the joy I find in all the rest becomes mean and cowardly. I should hate myself, if then I made my other friends my asylum:—

> "The valiant warrior famousèd for fight,
> After a hundred victories, once foiled,
> Is from the book of honor razèd quite
> And all the rest forgot for which he toiled."

Our impatience is thus sharply rebuked. Bashfulness and apathy are a tough husk in which a delicate organization is protected from premature ripening. It would be lost if it knew itself before any of the best souls were yet ripe enough to know and own it. Respect the naturlangsamkeit which hardens the ruby in a million years, and works in duration in which Alps and Andes come and go as rainbows. The good spirit of our life has no heaven which is the price of rashness. Love, which is the essence of God, is not for levity, but for the total worth of man. Let us not have this childish luxury in our regards, but the austerest worth; let us approach our friend with an audacious trust in the truth of his heart, in the breadth, impossible to be overturned, of his foundations.

The attractions of this subject are not to be resisted, and I leave, for the time, all account of subordinate social benefit, to speak of that select and sacred relation which is a kind of absolute, and which even leaves the language of love suspicious and common, so much is this purer, and nothing is so much divine.

I do not wish to treat friendships daintily, but with roughest courage. When they are real, they are not glass threads or frostwork, but the solidest thing we know. For now, after so many ages of experience, what do we know of nature or of ourselves? Not one step has man taken toward the solution of the problem of his destiny. In one condemnation of folly stand the whole universe of men. But the sweet sincerity of joy and peace which I draw from this alliance with my brother's soul is the nut itself whereof all nature and all thought is but the husk and shell. Happy is the house that shelters a friend! It might well be built, like a festal bower or arch, to entertain him a single day.

Happier, if he know the solemnity of that relation and honor its law! He who offers himself a candidate for that covenant comes up, like an Olympian, to the great games where the first-born of the world are the competitors. He proposes himself for contests where Time, Want, Danger, are in the lists, and he alone is victor who has truth enough in his constitution to preserve the delicacy of his beauty from the wear and tear of all these. The gifts of fortune may be present or absent, but all the speed in that contest depends on intrinsic nobleness and the contempt of trifles. There are two elements that go to the composition of friendship, each so sovereign that I can detect no superiority in either, no reason why either should be first named. One is truth. A friend is a person with whom I may be sincere. Before him I may think aloud. I am arrived at last in the presence of a man so real and equal that I may drop even those undermost garments of dissimulation, courtesy, and second thought, which men never put off, and may deal with him with the simplicity and wholeness with which one chemical atom meets another. Sincerity is the luxury allowed, like diadems and authority, only to the highest rank; that being permitted to speak truth, as having none above it to court or conform unto. Every man alone is sincere. At the entrance of a second person, hypocrisy begins. We parry and fend the approach of our fellow-man by compliments, by gossip, by amusements, by affairs. We cover up our thought from him under a hundred folds. I knew a man who under a certain religious frenzy cast off this drapery, and omitting all compliment and commonplace, spoke to the conscience of every person he encountered, and that with great insight and beauty. At first he was resisted, and all men agreed he was mad. But persisting—as indeed he could not help doing—for some time in this course, he attained to the advantage of bringing every man of his acquaintance into true relations with him. No man would think of speaking falsely with him, or of putting him off with any chat of markets or reading-rooms. But every man was constrained by so much sincerity to the like plain-dealing, and what love of nature, what poetry, what symbol of truth he had, he did certainly show him. But to most of us society shows not its face and eye, but its side and its back. To stand in true relations with men in a false age is worth a fit of insanity, is it not? We can seldom go erect. Almost every man we meet requires some civility—requires to be humored; he has some fame, some talent, some whim of religion or philanthropy in his head that is not to be questioned, and which spoils all conversation with him. But a friend is a sane man who exercises not my ingenuity, but me. My friend gives me entertainment without requiring any stipulation on my part. A friend therefore is a sort of paradox in nature. I who alone am, I who see nothing in nature whose existence I can affirm with equal evidence to my own, behold now the semblance of my being, in all its height, variety and curiosity, reiterated in a foreign form; so that a friend may well be reckoned the masterpiece of nature.

The other element of friendship is tenderness. We are holden to men by every sort of tie, by blood, by pride, by fear, by hope, by lucre, by lust, by hate, by admiration, by every circumstance and badge and trifle—but we can scarce believe that so much character can subsist in another as to draw us by love. Can another be so blessed and we so pure that we can offer him tenderness? When a man becomes dear to me I have touched the goal of fortune. I find very little written directly to the heart of this matter in books. And yet I have one text which I cannot choose but remember. My author says—"I offer myself faintly and bluntly to those whose I effectually am, and tender myself least to him to whom I am the most devoted." I wish that friendship should have feet, as well as eyes and eloquence. It must plant itself on the ground, before it vaults over the moon. I wish it to be a little of a citizen, before it is quite a cherub. We chide the citizen because he makes love a commodity. It is an exchange of gifts, of useful loans; it is good neighborhood; it watches with the sick; it holds the pall at the funeral; and quite loses sight of the delicacies and nobility of the relation. But though we cannot find the god under this disguise of a sutler, yet on the other hand we cannot forgive the poet if he spins his thread too fine and does not substantiate his romance by the municipal virtues of justice, punctuality, fidelity and pity. I hate the prostitution of the name of friendship to signify modish and worldly alliances. I much prefer the company of ploughboys and tin-peddlers to the silken and perfumed amity which celebrates its days of encounter by a frivolous display, by rides in a curricle and dinners at the best taverns. The end of friendship is a commerce the most strict and homely that can be joined; more strict than any of which we have experience. It is for aid and comfort through all the relations and passages of life and death. It is fit for serene days and graceful gifts and country rambles, but also for rough roads and hard fare, shipwreck, poverty and persecution. It keeps company with the sallies of the wit and the trances of religion. We are to dignify to each other the daily needs and offices of man's life, and embellish it by courage, wisdom and unity. It should never fall into something usual and settled, but should be alert and inventive and add rhyme and reason to what was drudgery.

Friendship may be said to require natures so rare and costly, each so well tempered and so happily adapted, and withal so circumstanced (for even in that particular, a poet says, love demands that the parties be altogether paired), that its satisfaction can very seldom be assured. It cannot subsist in its perfection, say some of those who are learned in this warm lore of the heart, betwixt more than two. I am not quite so strict in my terms, perhaps because I have never known so high a fellowship as others. I please my imagination more with a circle of god-like men and women variously related to each other and between whom subsists a lofty intelligence. But I find this law of *one to one* peremptory for conversation, which is the practice and consummation of friendship. Do not mix waters too much. The best mix as ill as good and bad. You shall have very useful and cheering discourse at several times with two several men, but let all three of you come together and you shall not have one new and hearty word. Two may talk and one may hear, but three cannot take part in a conversation of the most sincere and searching sort. In good company there is never such discourse between two, across the table, as takes place when you leave them alone. In good company the individuals merge their egotism into a social soul exactly co-extensive with the several consciousnesses there present. No partialities of friend to friend, no fondnesses of brother to sister, of wife to husband, are there pertinent, but quite otherwise. Only he may then speak who can sail on the common thought of the party, and not poorly limited to his own. Now this convention, which good sense demands, destroys the high freedom of great conversation, which requires an absolute running of two souls into one.

No two men but being left alone with each other enter into simpler relations. Yet it is affinity that determines *which* two shall converse. Unrelated men give little joy to each other, will never suspect the latent powers of each. We talk sometimes of a great talent for conversation, as if it were a permanent property in some individuals. Conversation is an evanescent relation—no more. A man is reputed to have thought and eloquence; he cannot, for all that, say a word to his cousin or his uncle. They accuse his silence with as much reason as they would blame the insignificance of a dial in the shade. In the sun it will mark the hour. Among those who enjoy his thought he will regain his tongue.

Friendship requires that rare mean betwixt likeness and unlikeness that piques each with the presence of power and of consent in the other party. Let me be alone to the end of the world, rather than that my friend should overstep, by a word or a look, his real sympathy. I am equally balked by antagonism and by compliance. Let him not cease an instant to be himself. The only joy I have in his being mine, is that the *not mine* is *mine*. I hate, where I looked for a manly furtherance or at least a manly resistance, to find a mush of concession. Better be a nettle in the side of your friend than his echo. The condition which high friendship demands is ability to do without it. That high office requires great and sublime parts. There must be very two, before there can be very one. Let it be an alliance of two large, formidable natures, mutually beheld, mutually feared, before yet they recognize the deep identity which, beneath these disparities, unites them.

He only is fit for this society who is magnanimous; who is sure that greatness and goodness are always economy; who is not swift to inter-meddle with his fortunes. Let him not intermeddle with this. Leave to the diamond its ages to grow, nor expect to accelerate the births of the eternal. Friendship demands a religious treatment. We talk of choosing our friends, but friends are self-elected. Reverence is a great part of it. Treat your friend as a spectacle. Of course he has merits that are not yours, and that you cannot honor if you must needs hold him close to your person. Stand aside; give those merits room; let them mount and expand. Are you the friend of your friend's buttons, or of his thought? To a great heart he will be a stranger in a thousand particulars, that he may come near in the holiest ground. Leave it to girls and boys to regard a friend as property, and to suck a short and all-confounding pleasure, instead of the noblest benefit.

Let us buy our entrance to this guild by a long probation. Why should we desecrate noble and beautiful souls by intruding on them? Why insist on rash personal relations with your friend? Why go to his house, or know his mother and brother and sisters? Why be visited by him at your own? Are these things material to our covenant? Leave this touching and clawing. Let him be to me a spirit. A message, a thought, a sincerity, a glance from him, I want, but not news, nor pottage. I can get politics and chat and neighborly conveniences from cheaper companions. Should not the society of my friend be to me poetic, pure, universal and great as nature itself? Ought I to feel that our tie is profane in comparison with yonder bar of cloud that sleeps on the horizon, or that clump of waving grass that divides the brook? Let us not vilify, but raise it to that standard. That great defying eye, that scornful beauty of his mien and action, do not pique yourself on reducing, but rather fortify and enhance. Worship his superiorities; wish him not less by a thought, but hoard and tell them all. Guard him as thy counterpart. Let him be to thee for ever a sort of beautiful enemy, untamable, devoutly revered, and not a trivial conveniency to be soon outgrown and cast aside. The hues of the opal, the light of the diamond, are not to be seen if the eye is too near. To my friend I write a letter and from him I receive a letter. That seems to you a little. It suffices me. It is a spiritual gift, worthy of him to give and of me to receive. It profanes nobody. In these warm lines the heart will trust itself, as it will not to the tongue, and pour out the prophecy of a godlier existence than all the annals of heroism have yet made good.

Respect so far the holy laws of this fellowship as not to prejudice its perfect flower by your impatience for its opening. We must be our own before we can be another's. There is at least this satisfaction in crime, according to the Latin proverb—you can speak to your accomplice on even terms. *Crimen quos inquinat, æquat.* To those whom we admire and love, at first we cannot. Yet the least defect of self-possession vitiates, in my judgment, the entire relation. There can never be deep peace between two spirits, never mutual respect, until in their dialogue each stands for the whole world.

What is so great as friendship, let us carry with what grandeur of spirit we can. Let us be silent—so we may hear the whisper of the gods. Let us not interfere. Who set you to cast about what you should say to the select souls, or how to say any thing to such? No matter how ingenious, no matter how graceful and bland. There are innumerable degrees of folly and wisdom, and for you to say aught is to be frivolous. Wait, and thy heart shall speak. Wait until the necessary and everlasting overpowers you, until day and night avail themselves of your lips. The only reward of virtue is virtue; the only way to have a friend is to be one. You shall not come nearer a man by getting into his house. If unlike, his soul only flees the faster from you, and you shall never catch a true glance of his eye. We see the noble afar off and they repel us; why should we intrude? Late—very late—we perceive that no arrangements, no introductions, no consuetudes or habits of society would be of any avail to establish us in such relations with them as we desire—but solely the uprise of nature in us to the same degree it is in them; then shall we meet as water with water; and if we should not meet them then, we shall not want them, for we are already they. In the last analysis, love is only the reflection of a man's own worthiness from other men. Men have sometimes exchanged names with their friends, as if they would signify that in their friend each loved his own soul.

The higher the style we demand of friendship, of course the less easy to establish it with flesh and blood. We walk alone in the world. Friends such as we desire are dreams and fables. But a sublime hope cheers ever the faithful heart, that elsewhere, in other regions of the universal power, souls are now acting, enduring and daring, which can love us and which we can love. We may congratulate ourselves that the period of nonage, of follies, of blunders and of shame, is passed in solitude, and when we are finished men we shall grasp heroic hands in heroic hands. Only be admonished by what you already see, not to strike leagues of friendship with cheap persons, where no friendship can be. Our impatience betrays us into rash and foolish alliances which no god attends. By persisting in your path, though you forfeit the little you gain the great. You demonstrate yourself, so as to put yourself out of the reach of false relations, and you draw to you the first-born of the world—those rare pilgrims whereof only one or two wander in nature at once, and before whom the vulgar great show as spectres and shadows merely.

It is foolish to be afraid of making our ties too spiritual, as if so we could lose any genuine love. Whatever correction of our popular views we make from insight, nature will be sure to bear us out in, and though it seem to rob us of some joy, will repay us with a greater. Let us feel if we will the absolute insulation of man. We are sure that we have all in us. We go to Europe, or we pursue persons, or we read books, in the instinctive faith that these will call it out and reveal us to ourselves. Beggars all. The persons are such as we; the Europe, an old faded garment of dead persons; the books, their ghosts. Let us drop this idolatry. Let us give over this mendicancy. Let us even bid our dearest friends farewell, and defy them, saying 'Who are you? Unhand me: I will be dependent no more.' Ah! seest thou not, O brother, that thus we part only to meet again on a higher platform, and only be more each other's because we are more our own? A friend is Janus-faced; he looks to the past and the future. He is the child of all my foregoing hours, the prophet of those to come, and the harbinger of a greater friend.

I do then with my friends as I do with my books. I would have them where I can find them, but I seldom use them. We must have society on our own terms, and admit or exclude it on the slightest cause. I cannot afford to speak much with my friend. If he is great he makes me so great that I cannot descend to converse. In the great days, presentiments hover before me in the firmament. I ought then to dedicate myself to them. I go in that I may seize them, I go out that I may seize them. I fear only that I may lose them receding into the sky in which now they are only a patch of brighter light. Then, though I prize my friends, I cannot afford to talk with them and study their visions, lest I lose my own. It would indeed give me a certain household joy to quit this lofty seeking, this spiritual astronomy or search of stars, and come down to warm sympathies with you; but then I know well I shall mourn always the vanishing of my mighty gods. It is true, next week I shall have languid moods, when I can well afford to occupy myself with foreign objects; then I shall regret the lost literature of your mind, and wish you were by my side again. But if you come perhaps you will fill my mind only with new visions; not with yourself but with your lustres, and I shall not be able any more than now to converse with you. So I will owe to my friends this evanescent intercourse. I will receive from them not what they have but what they are. They shall give me that which properly they cannot give, but which emanates from them. But they shall not hold me by any relations less subtile and pure. We will meet as though we met not, and part as though we parted not.

It has seemed to me lately more possible than I knew, to carry a friendship greatly, on one side, without due correspondence on the other. Why should I cumber myself with regrets that the receiver is not capacious? It never troubles the sun that some of his rays fall wide and vain into ungrateful space, and only a small part on the reflecting planet. Let your greatness educate the crude and cold companion. If he is unequal, he will presently pass away; but thou art enlarged by thy own shining, and no longer a mate for frogs and worms, dost soar and burn with the gods of the empyrean. It is thought a disgrace to love unrequited. But the great will see that true love cannot be unrequited. True love transcends the unworthy object and dwells and broods on the eternal, and when the poor interposed mask crumbles, it is not sad, but feels rid of so much earth and feels its independency the surer. Yet these things may hardly be said without a sort of treachery to the relation. The essence of friendship is entireness, a total magnanimity and trust. It must not surmise or provide for infirmity. It treats its object as a god, that it may defy both.

PRUDENCE

Theme no poet gladly sung,
Fair to old and foul to young;
Scorn not thou the love of parts,
And the articles of arts.
Grandeur of the perfect sphere
Thanks the atoms that cohere.

WHAT RIGHT have I to write on Prudence, whereof I have little, and that of the negative sort? My prudence consists in avoiding and going without, not in the inventing of means and methods, not in adroit steering, not in gentle repairing. I have no skill to make money spend well, no genius in my economy, and whoever sees my garden discovers that I must have some other garden. Yet I love facts, and hate lubricity and people without perception. Then I have the same title to write on prudence that I have to write on poetry or holiness. We write from aspiration and antagonism, as well as from experience. We paint those qualities which we do not possess. The poet admires the man of energy and tactics; the merchant breeds his son for the church or the bar; and where a man is not vain and egotistic you shall find what he has not by his praise. Moreover it would be hardly honest in me not to balance these fine lyric words of Love and Friendship with words of coarser sound, and whilst my debt to my senses is real and constant, not to own it in passing.

Prudence is the virtue of the senses. It is the science of appearances. It is the outmost action of the inward life. It is God taking thought for oxen. It moves matter after the laws of matter. It is content to seek health of body by complying with physical conditions, and health of mind by the laws of the intellect.

The world of the senses is a world of shows; it does not exist for itself, but has a symbolic character; and a true prudence or law of shows recognizes the co-presence of other laws and knows that its own office is subaltern; knows that it is surface and not centre where it works. Prudence is false when detached. It is legitimate when it is the

Natural History of the soul incarnate, when it unfolds the beauty of laws within the narrow scope of the senses.

There are all degrees of proficiency in knowledge of the world. It is sufficient to our present purpose to indicate three. One class live to the utility of the symbol, esteeming health and wealth a final good. Another class live above this mark to the beauty of the symbol, as the poet and artist and the naturalist and man of science. A third class live above the beauty of the symbol to the beauty of the thing signified; these are wise men. The first class have common sense; the second, taste; and the third, spiritual perception. Once in a long time, a man traverses the whole scale, and sees and enjoys the symbol solidly, then also has a clear eye for its beauty, and lastly, whilst he pitches his tent on this sacred volcanic isle of nature, does not offer to build houses and barns thereon—reverencing the splendor of the God which he sees bursting through each chink and cranny.

The world is filled with the proverbs and acts and winkings of of a base prudence, which is a devotion to matter, as if we possessed no other faculties than the palate, the nose, the touch, the eye and ear; a prudence which adores the Rule of Three, which never subscribes, which never gives, which seldom lends, and asks but one question of any project—Will it bake bread? This is a disease like a thickening of the skin until the vital organs are destroyed. But culture, revealing the high origin of the apparent world and aiming at the perfection of the man at the end, degrades every thing else, as health and bodily life, into means. It sees prudence not to be a several faculty, but a name for wisdom and virtue conversing with the body and its wants. Cultivated men always feel and speak so, as if a great fortune, the achievement of a civil or social measure, great personal influence, a graceful and commanding address, had their value as proofs of the energy of the spirit. If a man lose his balance and immerse himself in any trades or pleasures for their own sake, he may be a good wheel or pin, but he is not a cultivated man.

The spurious prudence, making the senses final, is the god of sots and cowards, and is the subject of all comedy. It is nature's joke, and therefore literature's. The true prudence limits this sensualism by admitting the knowledge of an internal and real world. This recognition once made, the order of the world and the distribution of affairs and times, being studied with the co-perception of their subordinate place, will reward any degree of attention. For our existence, thus apparently attached in nature to the sun and the returning moon and the periods which they mark—so susceptible to climate and to country, so alive to social good and evil, so fond of splendor and so tender to hunger and cold and debt—reads all its primary lessons out of these books.

Prudence does not go behind nature and ask whence it is. It takes the laws of the world whereby man's being is conditioned, as they are, and keeps these laws that it may enjoy their proper good. It respects space and time, climate, want, sleep, the law of polarity, growth and death. There revolve, to give bound and period to his being on all sides, the sun and moon, the great formalists in the sky: here lies stubborn matter, and will not swerve from its chemical routine. Here is a planted globe, pierced and belted with natural laws and fenced and distributed externally with civil partitions and properties which impose new restraints on the young inhabitant.

We eat of the bread which grows in the field. We live by the air which blows around us and we are poisoned by the air that is too cold or too hot, too dry or too wet. Time, which shows so vacant, indivisible and divine in its coming, is slit and peddled into trifles and tatters. A door is to be painted, a lock to be repaired. I want wood or oil, or meal or salt; the house smokes, or I have a headache; then the tax, and an affair to be transacted with a man without heart or brains, and the stinging recollection of an injurious or very awkward word—these eat up the hours. Do what we can, summer will have its flies; if we walk in the woods we must feed mosquitos; if we go a-fishing we must expect a wet coat. Then climate is a great impediment to idle persons; we often resolve to give up the care of the weather, but still we regard the clouds and the rain.

We are instructed by these petty experiences which usurp the hours and years. The hard soil and four months of snow make the inhabitant of the northern temperate zone wiser and abler than his fellow who enjoys the fixed smile of the tropics. The islander may ramble all day at will. At night he may sleep on a mat under the moon, and wherever a wild date-tree grows, nature has, without a prayer even, spread a table for his morning meal. The northerner is perforce a householder. He must brew, bake, salt and preserve his food, and pile wood and coal. But as it happens that not one stroke can labor lay to without some new acquaintance with nature, and as nature is inexhaustibly significant, the inhabitants of these climates have always excelled the southerner in force. Such is the value of these matters that a man who knows other things can never know too much of these. Let him have accurate perceptions. Let him, if he have hands, handle; if eyes, measure and discriminate; let him accept and hive every fact of chemistry, natural history and economics; the more he has, the less is he willing to spare any one. Time is always bringing the occasions that disclose their value. Some wisdom comes out of every natural and innocent action. The domestic man, who loves no music so well as his kitchen clock and the airs which the logs sing to him as they burn on the hearth, has solaces which others never dream of. The application of means to ends insures victory and the songs of victory not less in a farm or a shop than in the tactics of party or of war. The good husband finds method as efficient in the packing of fire-wood in a shed or in the harvesting of fruits in the cellar, as in Peninsular campaigns or the files of the Department of State. In the rainy day he builds a workbench, or gets his tool-box set in the corner of the barn-chamber, and stored with nails, gimlet, pincers, screwdriver and chisel. Herein he tastes an old joy of youth and childhood, the cat-like love of garrets, presses and corn-chambers, and of the conveniences of long housekeeping. His garden or his poultry-yard tells him many pleasant anecdotes. One might find argument for optimism in the abundant flow of this saccharine element of pleasure in every suburb and extremity of the good world. Let a man keep the law—any law—and his way will be strown with satisfactions. There is more difference in the quality of our pleasures than in the amount.

On the other hand, nature punishes any neglect of prudence. If you think the senses final, obey their law. If you believe in the soul, do not clutch at sensual sweetness before it is ripe on the slow tree of cause and effect. It is vinegar to the eyes to deal with men of loose and imperfect perception. Dr. Johnson is reported to have said—"If the child says he looked out of this window, when he looked out of that— whip him." Our American character is marked by a more than average delight in accurate perception, which is shown by the currency of the byword, "No mistake." But the discomfort of unpunctuality, of confusion of thought about facts, inattention to the wants of to-morrow, is of no nation. The beautiful laws of time and space, once dislocated by our inaptitude, are holes and dens. If the hive be disturbed by rash and stupid hands, instead of honey it will yield us bees. Our words and actions to be fair must be timely. A gay and pleasant sound is the whetting of the scythe in the mornings of June, yet what is more lonesome and sad than the sound of a whetstone or mower's rifle when it is too late in the season to make hay? Scatter-brained and "afternoon" men spoil much more than their own affair in spoiling the temper of those who deal with them. I have seen a criticism on some paintings, of which I am reminded when I see the shiftless and unhappy men who are not true to their senses. The last Grand Duke of Weimar, a man of superior understanding, said—"I have sometimes remarked in the presence of great works of art, and just now especially in Dresden, how much a certain property contributes to the effect which gives life to the figures, and to the life an irresistible truth. This property is the hitting, in all the figures we draw, the right centre of gravity. I mean the placing the figures firm upon their feet, making the hands grasp, and fastening the eyes on the spot where they should look. Even lifeless figures, as vessels and stools—let them be drawn ever so correctly—lose all effect so soon as they lack the resting upon their centre of gravity, and have a certain swimming and oscillating appearance. The Raphael in the Dresden gallery (the only great affecting picture which I have seen) is the quietest and most passionless piece you can imagine; a couple of saints who worship the Virgin and Child. Nevertheless it awakens a deeper impression than the contortions of ten crucified martyrs. For beside all the resistless beauty of form, it possesses in the highest degree the property of the perpendicularity of all the figures." This perpendicularity we demand of all the figures in this picture of life. Let them stand on their feet, and not float and swing. Let us know where to find them. Let them discriminate between what they remember and what they dreamed, call a spade a spade, give us facts, and honor their own senses with trust.

But what man shall dare task another with imprudence? Who is prudent? The men we call greatest are least in this kingdom. There is a certain fatal dislocation in our relation to nature, distorting our modes of living and making every law our enemy, which seems at last to have aroused all the wit and virtue in the world to ponder the question of Reform. We must call the highest prudence to counsel, and ask why health and beauty and genius should now be the exception rather than the rule of human nature? We do not know the properties of plants and animals and the laws of nature, through our sympathy with the same; but this remains the dream of poets. Poetry and prudence should be coincident. Poets should be lawgivers; that is, the boldest lyric inspiration should not chide and insult, but should announce and lead the civil code and the day's work. But now the two things seem irreconcilably parted. We have violated law upon law until we stand amidst ruins, and when by chance we espy a coincidence between reason and the phenomena, we are surprised. Beauty should be the dowry of every man and woman, as invariably as sensation; but it is rare. Health or sound organization should be universal. Genius should be the child of genius and every child should be inspired; but now it is not to be predicted of any child, and nowhere is it pure. We call partial half-lights, by courtesy, genius; talent which converts itself to money; talent which glitters today that it may dine and sleep well to-morrow; and society is officered by *men of parts*, as they are properly called, and not by divine men. These use their gift to refine luxury, not to abolish it. Genius is always ascetic, and piety, and love. Appetite shows to the finer souls as a disease, and they find beauty in rites and bounds that resist it.

We have found out fine names to cover our sensuality withal, but no gifts can raise intemperance. The man of talent affects to call his transgressions of the laws of the senses trivial and to count them nothing considered with his devotion to his art. His art never taught him lewdness, nor the love of wine, nor the wish to reap where he had not sowed. His art is less for every deduction from his holiness, and less for every defect of common sense. On him who scorned the world, as he said, the scorned world wreaks its revenge. He that despiseth small things will perish by little and little. Goethe's Tasso is very likely to be a pretty fair historic portrait, and that is true tragedy. It does not seem to me so genuine grief when some tyrannous Richard the Third oppresses and slays a score of innocent persons, as when Antonio and Tasso, both apparently right, wrong each other. One living after the maxims of this world and consistent and true to them, the other fired with all divine sentiments, yet grasping also at the pleasures of sense, without submitting to their law. That is a grief we all feel, a knot we cannot untie. Tasso's is no unfrequent case in modern biography. A man of genius, of an ardent temperament, reckless of physical laws, self-indulgent, becomes presently unfortunate, querulous, a "discomfortable cousin," a thorn to himself and to others.

The scholar shames us by his bifold life. Whilst something higher than prudence is active, he is admirable; when common sense is wanted, he is an encumbrance. Yesterday, Cæsar was not so great; to-day, the felon at the gallows' foot is not more miserable. Yesterday, radiant with the light of an ideal world in which he lives, the first of men; and now oppressed by wants and by sickness, for which he must thank himself. He resembles the pitiful drivellers whom travellers describe as frequenting the bazaars of Constantinople, who skulk about all day, yellow, emaciated, ragged, sneaking; and at evening, when the bazaars are open, slink to the opium-shop, swallow their morsel and become tranquil and glorified seers. And who has not seen the tragedy of imprudent genius struggling for years with paltry pecuniary difficulties, at last sinking, chilled, exhausted and fruitless, like a giant slaughtered by pins?

Is it not better that a man should accept the first pains and mortifications of this sort, which nature is not slack in sending him, as hints that he must expect no other good than the just fruit of his own labor and self-denial? Health, bread, climate, social position, have their importance, and he will give them their due. Let him esteem Nature a perpetual counsellor, and her perfections the exact measure of our deviations. Let him make the night night, and the day day. Let him control the habit of expense. Let him see that as much wisdom may be expended on a private economy as on an empire, and as much wisdom may be drawn from it. The laws of the world are written out for him on every piece of money in his hand. There is nothing he will not be the better for knowing, were it only the wisdom of Poor Richard, or the State-Street prudence of buying by the acre to sell by the foot; or the thrift of the agriculturist, to stick a tree between whiles, because it will grow whilst he sleeps; or the prudence which consists in husbanding little strokes of the tool, little portions of time, particles of stock and small gains. The eye of prudence may never shut. Iron, if kept at the ironmonger's, will rust; beer, if not brewed in the right state of the atmosphere, will sour; timber of ships will rot at sea, or if laid up high and dry, will strain, warp and dry-rot; money, if kept by us, yields no rent and is liable to loss; if invested, is liable to depreciation of the particular kind of stock. Strike, says the smith, the iron is white; keep the rake, says the haymaker, as nigh the scythe as you can, and the cart as nigh the rake. Our Yankee trade is reputed to be very much on the extreme of this prudence. It takes bank-notes, good, bad, clean, ragged, and saves itself by the speed with which it passes them off. Iron cannot rust, nor beer sour, nor timber rot, nor calicos go out of fashion, nor money stocks depreciate, in the few swift moments in which the Yankee suffers any one of them to remain in his possession. In skating over thin ice our safety is in our speed.

Let him learn a prudence of a higher strain. Let him learn that every thing in nature, even motes and feathers, go by law and not by luck, and that what he sows he reaps. By diligence and self-command let him put the bread he eats at his own disposal, that he may not stand in bitter and false relations to other men; for the best good of wealth is freedom. Let him practice the minor virtues. How much of human life is lost in waiting! Let him not make his fellow-creatures wait. How many words and promises are promises of conversation! Let his be words of fate. When he sees a folded and sealed scrap of paper float round the globe in a pine ship and come safe to the eye for which it was written, amidst a swarming population, let him likewise feel the admonition to integrate his being across all these distracting forces, and keep a slender human word among the storms, distances and accidents that drive us hither and thither, and, by persistency, make the paltry force of one man reappear to redeem its pledge after months and years in the most distant climates.

We must not try to write the laws of any one virtue, looking at that only. Human nature loves no contradictions, but is symmetrical. The prudence which secures an outward well-being is not to be studied by one set of men, whilst heroism and holiness are studied by another, but they are reconcilable. Prudence concerns the present time, persons, property and existing forms. But as every fact hath its roots in the soul, and if the soul were changed would cease to be, or would become some other thing—the proper administration of outward things will always rest on a just apprehension of their cause and origin; that is, the good man will be the wise man, and the single-hearted the politic man. Every violation of truth is not only a sort of suicide in the liar, but is a stab at the health of human society. On the most profitable lie the course of events presently lays a destructive tax; whilst frankness invites frankness, puts the parties on a convenient footing and makes their business a friendship. Trust men and they will be true to you; treat them greatly

. . . .

and they will show themselves great, though they make an exception in your favor to all their rules of trade.

So, in regard to disagreeable and formidable things, prudence does not consist in evasion or in flight, but in courage. He who wishes to walk in the most peaceful parts of life with any serenity must screw himself up to resolution. Let him front the object of his worst apprehension, and his stoutness will commonly make his fear groundless. The Latin proverb says, "In battles the eye is first overcome." Entire self-possession may make a battle very little more dangerous to life than a match at foils or at football. Examples are cited by soldiers of men who have seen the cannon pointed and the fire given to it, and who have stepped aside from the path of the ball. The terrors of the storm are chiefly confined to the parlor and the cabin. The drover, the sailor, buffets it all day, and his health renews itself at as vigorous a pulse under the sleet as under the sun of June.

In the occurrence of unpleasant things among neighbors, fear comes readily to heart and magnifies the consequence of the other party; but it is a bad counsellor. Every man is actually weak and apparently strong. To himself he seems weak; to others, formidable. You are afraid of Grim; but Grim also is afraid of you. You are solicitous of the good-will of the meanest person, uneasy at his ill-will. But the sturdiest offender of your peace and of the neighborhood, if you rip up his claims, is as thin and timid as any, and the peace of society is often kept, because, as children say, one is afraid and the other dares not. Far off, men swell, bully and threaten; bring them hand to hand, and they are a feeble folk.

It is a proverb that 'courtesy costs nothing;' but calculation might come to value love for its profit. Love is fabled to be blind, but kindness is necessary to perception; love is not a hood, but an eye-water. If you meet a sectary or a hostile partisan, never recognize the dividing lines, but meet on what common ground remains—if only that the sun shines and the rain rains for both; the area will widen very fast, and ere you know it, the boundary mountains on which the eye had fastened have melted into air. If they set out to contend, Saint Paul will lie and Saint John will hate. What low, poor, paltry, hypocritical people an argument on religion will make of the pure and chosen souls! They will shuffle and crow, crook and hide, feign to confess here, only that they may brag and conquer there, and not a thought has enriched either party, and not an emotion of bravery, modesty, or hope. So neither should you put yourself in a false position with your contemporaries by indulging a vein of hostility and bitterness. Though your views are in straight antagonism to theirs, assume an identity of sentiment, assume that you are saying precisely that which all think, and in the flow of wit and love roll out your paradoxes in solid column, with not the infirmity of a doubt. So at least shall you get an adequate deliverance. The natural motions of the soul are so much better than the voluntary ones that you will never do yourself justice in dispute. The thought is not then taken hold of by the right handle, does not show itself proportioned and in its true bearings, but bears extorted, hoarse, and half witness. But assume a consent and it shall presently be granted, since really and underneath their external diversities, all men are of one heart and mind.

Wisdom will never let us stand with any man or men on an unfriendly footing. We refuse sympathy and intimacy with people, as if we waited for some better sympathy and intimacy to come. But whence and when? To-morrow will be like to-day. Life wastes itself whilst we are preparing to live. Our friends and fellow-workers die off from us. Scarcely can we say we see new men, new women, approaching us. We are too old to regard fashion, too old to expect patronage of any greater or more powerful. Let us suck the sweetness of those affections and consuetudes that grow near us. These old shoes are easy to the feet. Undoubtedly we can easily pick faults in our company, can easily whisper names prouder, and that tickle the fancy more. Every man's imagination hath its friends; and life would be dearer with such companions. But if you cannot have them on good mutual terms, you cannot have them. If not the Deity but our ambition hews and shapes the new relations, their virtue escapes, as strawberries lose their flavor in garden-beds.

Thus truth, frankness, courage, love, humility and all the virtues range themselves on the side of prudence, or the art of securing a present well-being. I do not know if all matter will be found to be made of one element, as oxygen or hydrogen, at last, but the world of manners and actions is wrought of one stuff, and begin where we will, we are pretty sure in a short space to be mumbling our ten commandments.

HEROISM

"Paradise is under the shadow of swords."

Mahomet.

Ruby wine is drunk by knaves
Sugar spends to fatten slaves,
Rose and vine-leaf deck buffoons;
Thunderclouds are Jove's festoons,
Drooping oft in wreaths of dread
Lightning-knotted round his head:
The hero is not fed on sweets
Daily his own heart he eats;
Chambers of the great are jails,
And head-winds right for royal sails.

IN THE ELDER ENGLISH DRAMATISTS, and mainly in the plays of Beaumont and Fletcher, there is a constant recognition of gentility, as if a noble behavior were as easily marked in the society of their age as color is in our American population. When any Rodrigo, Pedro or Valerio enters, though he be a stranger, the duke or governor exclaims, 'This is a gentleman'—and proffers civilities without end; but all the rest are slag and refuse. In harmony with this delight in personal advantages there is in their plays a certain heroic cast of character and dialogue—as in Bonduca, Sophocles, the Mad Lover, the Double Marriage—wherein the speaker is so earnest and cordial and on such deep grounds of character, that the dialogue, on the slightest additional incident in the plot, rises naturally into poetry. Among many texts take the following. The Roman Martius has conquered Athens—all but the invincible spirits of Sophocles, the duke of Athens, and Dorigen, his wife. The beauty of the latter inflames Martius, and he seeks to save her husband; but Sophocles will not ask his life, although assured that a word will save him, and the execution of both proceeds:—

Valerius.   Bid thy wife farewell.

Soph. No, I will take no leave. My Dorigen,
Yonder, above, 'bout Ariadne's crown,
My spirit shall hover for thee. Prithee, haste.

Dor. Stay, Sophocles—with this tie up my sight;
Let not soft nature so transformèd be,
And lose her gentler sexed humanity,
To make me see my lord bleed. So, 't is well;
Never one object underneath the sun
Will I behold before my Sophocles:
Farewell; now teach the Romans how to die.

Mar. Dost know what 't is to die?

Soph.   Thou dost not, Martius,
And, therefore, not what 't is to live; to die
Is to begin to live. It is to end
An old, stale, weary work and to commence
A newer and a better. 'T is to leave
Deceitful knaves for the society
Of gods and goodness. Thou thyself must part
At last from all thy garlands, pleasures, triumphs,
And prove thy fortitude what then 't will do.

Val. But art not grieved nor vexed to leave thy life thus?

Soph. Why should I grieve or vex for being sent
To them I ever loved best? Now I'll kneel,
But with my back toward thee: 't is the last duty
This trunk can do the gods.

Mar.   Strike, strike, Valerius,
Or Martius' heart will leap out at his mouth.
This is a man, a woman. Kiss thy lord,
And live with all the freedom you were wont.

O love! thou doubly hast afflicted me
With virtue and with beauty. Treacherous heart,
My hand shall cast thee quick into my urn,
Ere thou transgress this knot of piety.

Val. What ails my brother?

Soph.   Martius, O Martius,
Thou now hast found a way to conquer me.

Dor. O star of Rome! what gratitude can speak
Fit words to follow such a deed as this?

Mar. This admirable duke, Valerius,
With his disdain of fortune and of death,
Captived himself, has captivated me,
And though my arm hath ta'en his body here,
His soul hath subjugated Martius' soul.
By Romulus, he is all soul, I think;
He hath no flesh, and spirit cannot be gyved,
Then we have vanquished nothing; he is free,
And Martius walks now in captivity.

I do not readily remember any poem, play, sermon, novel or oration that our press vents in the last few years, which goes to the same tune. We have a great many flutes and flageolets, but not often the sound of any fife. Yet Wordsworth's "Laodamia," and the ode of "Dion," and some sonnets, have a certain noble music; and Scott will sometimes draw a stroke like the portrait of Lord Evandale given by Balfour of Burley. Thomas Carlyle, with his natural taste for what is manly and daring in character, has suffered no heroic trait in his favorites to drop from his biographical and historical pictures. Earlier, Robert Burns has given us a song or two. In the Harleian Miscellanies there is an account of the battle of Lutzen which deserves to be read. And Simon Ockley's History of the Saracens recounts the prodigies of individual valor, with admiration all the more evident on the part of the narrator that he seems to think that his place in Christian Oxford requires of him some proper protestations of abhorrence. But if we explore the literature of Heroism we shall quickly come to Plutarch, who is its Doctor and historian. To him we owe the Brasidas, the Dion, the Epaminondas, the Scipio of old, and I must think we are more deeply indebted to him than to all the ancient writers. Each of his "Lives" is a refutation to the despondency and cowardice of our religious and political theorists. A wild courage, a Stoicism not of the schools but of the blood, shines in every anecdote, and has given that book its immense fame.

We need books of this tart cathartic virtue more than books of political science or of private economy. Life is a festival only to the wise. Seen from the nook and chimney-side of prudence, it wears a ragged and dangerous front. The violations of the laws of nature by our predecessors and our contemporaries are punished in us also. The disease and deformity around us certify the infraction of natural, intellectual and moral laws, and often violation on violation to breed such compound misery. A lockjaw that bends a man's head back to his heels; hydrophobia that makes him bark at his wife and babes; insanity that makes him eat grass; war, plague, cholera, famine, indicate a certain ferocity in nature, which, as it had its inlet by human crime, must have its outlet by human suffering. Unhappily no man exists who has not in his own person become to some amount a stockholder in the sin, and so made himself liable to a share in the expiation.

Our culture therefore must not omit the arming of the man. Let him hear in season that he is born into the state of war, and that the commonwealth and his own well-being require that he should not go dancing in the weeds of peace, but warned, self-collected and neither defying nor dreading the thunder, let him take both reputation and life in his hand, and with perfect urbanity dare the gibbet and the mob by the absolute truth of his speech and the rectitude of his behavior.

Towards all this external evil the man within the breast assumes a warlike attitude, and affirms his ability to cope single-handed with the infinite army of enemies. To this military attitude of the soul we give the name of Heroism. Its rudest form is the contempt for safety and ease, which makes the attractiveness of war. It is a self-trust which slights the restraints of prudence, in the plenitude of its energy and power to repair the harms it may suffer. The hero is a mind of such balance that no disturbances can shake his will, but pleasantly and as it were merrily he advances to his own music, alike in frightful alarms and in the tipsy mirth of universal dissoluteness. There is somewhat not philosophical in heroism; there is somewhat not holy in it; it seems not to know that other souls are of one texture with it; it has pride; it is the extreme of individual nature. Nevertheless we must profoundly revere it. There is somewhat in great actions which does not allow us to go behind them. Heroism feels and never reasons, and therefore is always right; and although a different breeding, different religion and greater intellectual activity would have modified or even reversed the particular action, yet for the hero that thing he does is the highest deed, and is not open to the censure of philosophers or divines. It is the avowal of the unschooled man that he finds a quality in him that is negligent of expense, of health, of life, of danger, of hatred, of reproach, and knows that his will is higher and more excellent than all actual and all possible antagonists.

Heroism works in contradiction to the voice of mankind and in contradiction, for a time, to the voice of the great and good. Heroism is an obedience to a secret impulse of an individual's character. Now to no other man can its wisdom appear as it does to him, for every man must be supposed to see a little farther on his own proper path than any one else. Therefore just and wise men take umbrage at his act, until after some little time be past; then they see it to be in unison with their acts. All prudent men see that the action is clean contrary to a sensual prosperity; for every heroic act measures itself by its contempt of some external good. But it finds its own success at last, and then the prudent also extol.

Self-trust is the essence of heroism. It is the state of the soul at war, and its ultimate objects are the last defiance of falsehood and wrong, and the power to bear all that can be inflicted by evil agents. It speaks the truth and it is just, generous, hospitable, temperate, scornful of petty calculations and scornful of being scorned. It persists; it is of an undaunted boldness and of a fortitude not to be wearied out. Its jest is the littleness of common life. That false prudence which dotes on health and wealth is the butt and merriment of heroism. Heroism, like Plotinus, is almost ashamed of its body. What shall it say then to the sugar-plums and cats'-cradles, to the toilet, compliments, quarrels, cards and custard, which rack the wit of all society? What joys has kind nature provided for us dear creatures! There seems to be no interval between greatness and meanness. When the spirit is not master of the world, then it is its dupe. Yet the little man takes the great hoax so innocently, works in it so headlong and believing, is born red, and dies gray, arranging his toilet, attending on his own health, laying traps for sweet food and strong wine, setting his heart on a horse or a rifle, made happy with a little gossip or a little praise, that the great soul cannot choose but laugh at such earnest nonsense. "Indeed, these humble considerations make me out of love with greatness. What a disgrace is it to me to take note how many pairs of silk stockings thou hast, namely, these and those that were the peach-colored ones; or to bear the inventory of thy shirts, as one for superfluity, and one other for use!"

Citizens, thinking after the laws of arithmetic, consider the inconvenience of receiving strangers at their fireside, reckon narrowly the loss of time and the unusual display; the soul of a better quality thrusts back the unseasonable economy into the vaults of life, and says, I will obey the God, and the sacrifice and the fire he will provide. Ibn Haukal, the Arabian geographer, describes a heroic extreme in the hospitality of Sogd, in Bukharia. "When I was in Sogd I saw a great building, like a palace, the gates of which were open and fixed back to the wall with large nails. I asked the reason, and was told that the house had not been shut, night or day, for a hundred years. Strangers may present themselves at any hour and in whatever number; the master has amply provided for the reception of the men and their animals, and is never happier than when they tarry for some time. Nothing of the kind have I seen in any other country." The magnanimous know very well that they who give time, or money, or shelter, to the stranger—so it be done for love and not for ostentation—do, as it were, put God under obligation to them, so perfect are the compensations of the universe. In some way the time they seem to lose is redeemed and the pains they seem to take remunerate themselves. These men fan the flame of human love and raise the standard of civil virtue among mankind. But hospitality must be for service and not for show, or it pulls down the host. The brave soul rates itself too high to value itself by the splendor of its table and draperies. It gives what it hath, and all it hath, but its own majesty can lend a better grace to bannocks and fair water than belong to city feasts.

The temperance of the hero proceeds from the same wish to do no dishonor to the worthiness he has. But he loves it for its elegancy, not for its austerity. It seems not worth his while to be solemn and denounce with bitterness flesh-eating or wine-drinking, the use of tobacco, or opium, or tea, or silk, or gold. A great man scarcely knows how he dines, how he dresses but without railing or precision his living is natural and poetic. John Eliot, the Indian Apostle, drank water, and said of wine—"It is a noble, generous liquor and we should be humbly thankful for it, but, as I remember, water was made before it." Better still is the temperance of King David, who poured out on the ground unto the Lord the water which three of his warriors had brought him to drink at the peril of their lives.

It is told of Brutus, that when he fell on his sword after the battle of Philippi, he quoted a line of Euripides—"O Virtue! I have followed thee through life, and I find thee at last but a shade." I doubt not the hero is slandered by this report. The heroic soul does not sell its justice and its nobleness. It does not ask to dine nicely and to sleep warm. The essence of greatness is the perception that virtue is enough. Poverty is its ornament. It does not need plenty, and can very well abide its loss.

But that which takes my fancy most in the heroic class, is the good-humor and hilarity they exhibit. It is a height to which common duty can very well attain, to suffer and to dare with solemnity. But these rare souls set opinion, success, and life at so cheap a rate that they will not soothe their enemies by petitions, or the show of sorrow, but wear their own habitual greatness. Scipio, charged with peculation, refuses to do himself so great a disgrace as to wait for justification, though he had the scroll of his accounts in his hands, but tears it to pieces before the tribunes. Socrates's condemnation of himself to be maintained in all honor in the Prytaneum, during his life, and Sir Thomas More's playfulness at the scaffold, are of the same strain. In Beaumont and Fletcher's "Sea Voyage," Juletta tells the stout captain and his company—

> *Jul.* Why, slaves, 't is in our power to hang ye.
> *Master.*   Very likely,
> 'T is in our powers, then, to be hanged, and scorn ye.

These replies are sound and whole. Sport is the bloom and glow of a perfect health. The great will not condescend to take any thing seriously; all must be as gay as the song of a canary, though it were the

· ·

building of cities or the eradication of old and foolish churches and nations which have cumbered the earth long thousands of years. Simple hearts put all the history and customs of this world behind them, and play their own game in innocent defiance of the Blue-Laws of the world; and such would appear, could we see the human race assembled in vision, like little children frolicking together, though to the eyes of mankind at large they wear a stately and solemn garb of works and influences.

The interest these fine stories have for us, the power of a romance over the boy who grasps the forbidden book under his bench at school, our delight in the hero, is the main fact to our purpose. All these great and transcendent properties are ours. If we dilate in beholding the Greek energy, the Roman pride, it is that we are already domesticating the same sentiment. Let us find room for this great guest in our small houses. The first step of worthiness will be to disabuse us of our super-stitious associations with places and times, with number and size. Why should these words, Athenian, Roman, Asia and England, so tingle in the ear? Where the heart is, there the muses, there the gods sojourn, and not in any geography of fame. Massachusetts, Connecticut River and Boston Bay you think paltry places, and the ear loves names of for-eign and classic topography. But here we are; and, if we will tarry a little, we may come to learn that here is best. See to it only that thy-self is here, and art and nature, hope and fate, friends, angels and the Supreme Being shall not be absent from the chamber where thou sittest. Epaminondas, brave and affectionate, does not seem to us to need Olympus to die upon, nor the Syrian sunshine. He lies very well where he is. The Jerseys were handsome ground enough for Washing-ton to tread, and London streets for the feet of Milton. A great man makes his climate genial in the imagination of men, and its air the beloved element of all delicate spirits. That country is the fairest which is inhabited by the noblest minds. The pictures which fill the imagi-nation in reading the actions of Pericles, Xenophon, Columbus, Bayard, Sidney, Hampden, teach us how needlessly mean our life is; that we, by the depth of our living, should deck it with more than regal or national splendor, and act on principles that should interest man and nature in the length of our days.

We have seen or heard of many extraordinary young men who never ripened, or whose performance in actual life was not extraordinary. When we see their air and mien, when we hear them speak of society, of books, of religion, we admire their superiority; they seem to throw contempt on our entire polity and social state; theirs is the tone of a youthful giant who is sent to work revolutions. But they enter an active profession and the forming Colossus shrinks to the common size of man. The magic they used was the ideal tendencies, which always make the Actual ridiculous; but the tough world had its revenge the moment they put their horses of the sun to plough in its furrow. They found no example and no companion, and their heart fainted. What then? The lesson they gave in their first aspirations is yet true; and a better valor and a purer truth shall one day organize their belief. Or why should a woman liken herself to any historical woman, and think, because Sappho, or Sévigné, or De Staël, or the cloistered souls who have had genius and cultivation do not satisfy the imagination and the serene Themis, none can—certainly not she? Why not? She has a new and unattempted problem to solve, perchance that of the happiest nature that ever bloomed. Let the maiden, with erect soul, walk serenely on her way, accept the hint of each new experience, search in turn all the objects that solicit her eye, that she may learn the power and the charm of her newborn being, which is the kindling of a new dawn in the recesses of space. The fair girl who repels interference by a decided and proud choice of influences, so careless of pleasing, so wilful and lofty, inspires every beholder with somewhat of her own nobleness. The silent heart encourages her; O friend, never strike sail to a fear! Come into port greatly, or sail with God the seas. Not in vain you live, for every passing eye is cheered and refined by the vision.

The characteristic of heroism is its persistency. All men have wandering impulses, fits and starts of generosity. But when you have chosen your part, abide by it, and do not weakly try to reconcile yourself with the world. The heroic cannot be the common, nor the common the heroic. Yet we have the weakness to expect the sympathy of people in those actions whose excellence is that they outrun sympathy and appeal to a tardy justice. If you would serve your brother, because it is fit for you to serve him, do not take back your words when you find that prudent people do not commend you. Adhere to your own act, and congratulate yourself if you have done something strange and extravagant and broken the monotony of a decorous age. It was a high counsel that I once heard given to a young person—"Always do

. . . .

what you are afraid to do." A simple manly character need never make an apology, but should regard its past action with the calmness of Phocion, when he admitted that the event of the battle was happy, yet did not regret his dissuasion from the battle.

There is no weakness or exposure for which we cannot find consolation in the thought—this is a part of my constitution, part of my relation and office to my fellow-creature. Has nature covenanted with me that I should never appear to disadvantage, never make a ridiculous figure? Let us be generous of our dignity as well as of our money. Greatness once and for ever has done with opinion. We tell our charities, not because we wish to be praised for them, not because we think they have great merit, but for our justification. It is a capital blunder; as you discover when another man recites his charities.

To speak the truth, even with some austerity, to live with some rigor of temperance, or some extremes of generosity, seems to be an asceticism which common good-nature would appoint to those who are at ease and in plenty, in sign that they feel a brotherhood with the great multitude of suffering men. And not only need we breathe and exercise the soul by assuming the penalties of abstinence, of debt, of solitude, of unpopularity—but it behooves the wise man to look with a bold eye into those rarer dangers which sometimes invade men, and to familiarize himself with disgusting forms of disease, with sounds of execration, and the vision of violent death.

Times of heroism are generally times of terror, but the day never shines in which this element may not work. The circumstances of man, we say, are historically somewhat better in this country and at this hour than perhaps ever before. More freedom exists for culture. It will not now run against an axe at the first step out of the beaten track of opinion. But whoso is heroic will always find crises to try his edge. Human virtue demands her champions and martyrs, and the trial of persecution always proceeds. It is but the other day that the brave Lovejoy gave his breast to the bullets of a mob, for the rights of free speech and opinion, and died when it was better not to live.

I see not any road of perfect peace which a man can walk but after the counsel of his own bosom. Let him quit too much association, let him go home much, and stablish himself in those courses he approves. The unremitting retention of simple and high sentiments in obscure duties is hardening the character to that temper which will work with honor, if need be in the tumult, or on the scaffold. Whatever outrages have happened to men may befall a man again; and very easily in a republic, if there appear any signs of a decay of religion. Coarse slander, fire, tar and feathers and the gibbet, the youth may freely bring home to his mind and with what sweetness of temper he can, and inquire how fast he can fix his sense of duty, braving such penalties, whenever it may please the next newspaper and a sufficient number of his neighbors to pronounce his opinions incendiary.

It may calm the apprehension of calamity in the most susceptible heart to see how quick a bound Nature has set to the utmost inflection of malice. We rapidly approach a brink over which no enemy can follow us:—

> "Let them rave:
> Thou art quiet in thy grave."

In the gloom of our ignorance of what shall be, in the hour when we are deaf to the higher voices, who does not envy those who have seen safely to an end their manful endeavor? Who that sees the meanness of our politics but inly congratulates Washington that he is long already wrapped in his shroud, and for ever safe; that he was laid sweet in his grave, the hope of humanity not yet subjugated in him? Who does not sometimes envy the good and brave who are no more to suffer from the tumults of the natural world, and await with curious complacency the speedy term of his own conversation with finite nature? And yet the love that will be annihilated sooner than treacherous has already made death impossible, and affirms itself no mortal but a native of the deeps of absolute and inextinguishable being.

THE OVER-SOUL

"But souls that of his own good life partake,
 He loves as his own self; dear as his eye
 They are to Him: He'll never them forsake:
 When they shall die, then God himself shall die:
 They live, they live in blest eternity."

Henry More.

Space is ample, east and west,
But two cannot go abreast,
Cannot travel in it two:
Yonder masterful cuckoo
Crowds every egg out of the nest,
Quick or dead, except its own;
A spell is laid on sod and stone,
Night and Day 've been tampered with,
Every quality and pith
Surcharged and sultry with a power
That works its will on age and hour.

THERE IS a difference between one and another hour of life in their authority and subsequent effect. Our faith comes in moments; our vice is habitual. Yet there is a depth in those brief moments which constrains us to ascribe more reality to them than to all other experiences. For this reason the argument which is always forthcoming to silence those who conceive extraordinary hopes of man, namely the appeal to experience, is for ever invalid and vain. We give up the past to the objector, and yet we hope. He must explain this hope. We grant that human life is mean, but how did we find out that it was mean? What is the ground of this uneasiness of ours; of this old discontent? What is the universal sense of want and ignorance, but the fine innuendo by which the soul makes its enormous claim? Why do men feel that the natural history of man has never been written, but he is always leaving behind what you have said of him, and it becomes old, and books of metaphysics worthless? The philosophy of six thousand years has not searched the chambers and magazines of the soul. In its experiments there has always remained, in the last analysis, a residuum it could not resolve. Man is a stream whose source is hidden. Our being is descending into us from we know not whence. The most exact calculator has no prescience that somewhat incalculable may not balk the very next moment. I am constrained every moment to acknowledge a higher origin for events than the will I call mine.

As with events, so is it with thoughts. When I watch that flowing river, which, out of regions I see not, pours for a season its streams into me, I see that I am a pensioner; not a cause but a surprised spectator of this ethereal water; that I desire and look up and put myself in the attitude of reception, but from some alien energy the visions come.

The Supreme Critic on the errors of the past and the present, and the only prophet of that which must be, is that great nature in which we rest as the earth lies in the soft arms of the atmosphere; that Unity, that Over-Soul, within which every man's particular being is contained and made one with all other; that common heart of which all sincere conversation is the worship, to which all right action is submission; that overpowering reality which confutes our tricks and talents, and constrains every one to pass for what he is, and to speak from his character and not from his tongue, and which evermore tends to pass into our thought and hand and become wisdom and virtue and power and beauty. We live in succession, in division, in parts, in particles. Meantime within man is the soul of the whole; the wise silence; the universal beauty, to which every part and particle is equally related; the eternal ONE. And this deep power in which we exist and whose beatitude is all accessible to us, is not only self-sufficing and perfect in every hour, but the act of seeing and the thing seen, the seer and the spectacle, the subject and the object, are one. We see the world piece by piece, as the sun, the moon, the animal, the tree; but the whole, of which these are the shining parts, is the soul. Only by the vision of that Wisdom can the horoscope of the ages be read, and by falling back on our better thoughts, by yielding to the spirit of prophecy which is innate in every man, we can know what it saith: Every man's words who speaks from that life must sound vain to those who do not dwell in the same thought on their own part. I dare not speak for it. My words do not carry its august sense; they fall short and cold. Only itself can inspire whom it will, and behold! their speech shall be lyrical, and sweet, and universal as the rising of the wind. Yet I desire, even by profane words, if I may not use sacred, to indicate the heaven of this deity and to report what hints I have collected of the transcendent simplicity and energy of the Highest Law.

If we consider what happens in conversation, in reveries, in remorse, in times of passion, in surprises, in the instructions of dreams, wherein often we see ourselves in masquerade—the droll disguises only magnifying and enhancing a real element and forcing it on our distant notice—we shall catch many hints that will broaden and lighten into knowledge of the secret of nature. All goes to show that the soul in man is not an organ, but animates and exercises all the organs; is not a function, like the power of memory, of calculation, of comparison, but uses these as hands and feet; is not a faculty, but a light; is not the intellect or the will, but the master of the intellect and the will; is the background of our being, in which they lie—an immensity not possessed and that cannot be possessed. From within or from behind, a light shines through us upon things and makes us aware that we are nothing, but the light is all. A man is the facade of a temple wherein all wisdom and all good abide. What we commonly call man, the eating, drinking, planting, counting man, does not, as we know him, represent himself, but misrepresents himself. Him we do not respect, but the soul, whose organ he is, would he let it appear through his action, would make our knees bend. When it breathes through his intellect, it is genius; when it breathes through his will, it is virtue; when it flows through his affection, it is love. And the blindness of the intellect begins when it would be something of itself. The weakness of the will begins when the individual would be something of himself. All reform aims in some one particular to let the soul have its way through us; in other words, to engage us to obey.

Of this pure nature every man is at some time sensible. Language cannot paint it with his colors. It is too subtile. It is undefinable, unmeasurable; but we know that it pervades and contains us. We know that all spiritual being is in man. A wise old proverb says, "God comes to see us without bell;" that is, as there is no screen or ceiling between our heads and the infinite heavens, so is there no bar or wall in the soul, where man, the effect, ceases, and God, the cause, begins. The walls are taken away. We lie open on one side to the deeps of spiritual nature, to the attributes of God. Justice we see and know, Love, Freedom, Power. These natures no man ever got above, but they tower over us, and most in the moment when our interests tempt us to wound them.

The sovereignty of this nature whereof we speak is made known by its independency of those limitations which circumscribe us on every hand. The soul circumscribes all things. As I have said, it contradicts all experience. In like manner it abolishes time and space. The influence of the senses has in most men overpowered the mind to that degree that the walls of time and space have come to look real and insurmountable; and to speak with levity of these limits is, in the world, the sign of insanity. Yet time and space are but inverse measures of the force of the soul. The spirit sports with time—

> "Can crowd eternity into an hour,
>   Or stretch an hour to eternity."

We are often made to feel that there is another youth and age than that which is measured from the year of our natural birth. Some thoughts always find us young, and keep us so. Such a thought is the love of the universal and eternal beauty. Every man parts from that contemplation with the feeling that it rather belongs to ages than to mortal life. The least activity of the intellectual powers redeems us in a degree from the conditions of time. In sickness, in languor, give us a strain of poetry or a profound sentence, and we are refreshed; or produce a volume of Plato or Shakspeare, or remind us of their names, and instantly we come into a feeling of longevity. See how the deep divine thought reduces centuries and millenniums, and makes itself present through all ages. Is the teaching of Christ less effective now than it was when first his mouth was opened? The emphasis of facts and persons in my thought has nothing to do with time. And so always the soul's scale is one, the scale of the senses and the understanding is another. Before the revelations of the soul, Time, Space and Nature shrink away. In common speech we refer all things to time, as we habitually refer the immensely sundered stars to one concave sphere. And so we say that the Judgment is distant or near, that the Millennium approaches, that a day of certain political, moral, social reforms is at hand, and the like, when we mean that in the nature of things one of the facts we contemplate is external and fugitive, and the other is permanent and connate with the soul. The things we now esteem fixed shall, one by one, detach themselves like ripe fruit from our experience, and fall. The wind shall blow them none knows whither. The landscape, the figures, Boston, London, are facts as fugitive as any institution past, or any whiff of mist or smoke, and so is society, and so is the world. The soul looketh steadily forwards, creating a world before her, leaving worlds behind her. She has no dates, nor rites, nor persons, nor specialties, nor men. The soul knows only the soul; the web of events is the flowing robe in which she is clothed.

After its own law and not by arithmetic is the rate of its progress to be computed. The soul's advances are not made by gradation, such as can be represented by motion in a straight line, but rather by ascension of state, such as can be represented by metamorphosis—from the egg to the worm, from the worm to the fly. The growths of genius are of a certain total character, that does not advance the elect individual first over John, then Adam, then Richard, and give to each the pain of discovered inferiority—but by every throe of growth the man expands there where he works, passing, at each pulsation, classes, populations, of men. With each divine impulse the mind rends the thin rinds of the visible and finite, and comes out into eternity, and inspires and expires its air. It converses with truths that have always been spoken in the world, and becomes conscious of a closer sympathy with Zeno and Arrian than with persons in the house.

This is the law of moral and of mental gain. The simple rise as by specific levity not into a particular virtue, but into the region of all the virtues. They are in the spirit which contains them all. The soul requires purity, but purity is not it; requires justice, but justice is not that; requires beneficence, but is somewhat better; so that there is a kind of descent and accommodation felt when we leave speaking of moral nature to urge a virtue which it enjoins. To the well-born child all the virtues are natural, and not painfully acquired. Speak to his heart, and the man becomes suddenly virtuous.

Within the same sentiment is the germ of intellectual growth, which obeys the same law. Those who are capable of humility, of justice, of love, of aspiration, stand already on a platform that commands the sciences and arts, speech and poetry, action and grace. For whoso dwells in this moral beatitude already anticipates those special powers which men prize so highly. The lover has no talent, no skill, which passes for quite nothing with his enamored maiden, however little she may possess of related faculty; and the heart which abandons itself to the Supreme Mind finds itself related to all its works, and will travel a royal road to particular knowledges and powers. In ascending to this primary and aboriginal sentiment we have come from our remote station on the circumference instantaneously to the centre of the world, where, as in the closet of God, we see causes, and anticipate the universe, which is but a slow effect.

One mode of the divine teaching is the incarnation of the spirit in a form—in forms, like my own. I live in society; with persons who answer to thoughts in my own mind, or express a certain obedience to the great instincts to which I live. I see its presence to them. I am certified of a common nature; and these other souls, these separated selves, draw me as nothing else can. They stir in me the new emotions we call passion; of love, hatred, fear, admiration, pity; thence come conversation, competition, persuasion, cities and war. Persons are supplementary to the primary teaching of the soul. In youth we are mad for persons. Childhood and youth see all the world in them. But the larger experience of man discovers the identical nature appearing through them all. Persons themselves acquaint us with the impersonal. In all conversation between two persons tacit reference is made, as to a third party, to a common nature. That third party or common nature is not social; it is impersonal; is God. And so in groups where debate is earnest, and especially on high questions, the company become aware that the thought rises to an equal level in all bosoms, that all have a spiritual property in what was said, as well as the sayer. They all become wiser than they were. It arches over them like a temple, this unity of thought in which every heart beats with nobler sense of power and duty, and thinks and acts with unusual solemnity. All are conscious of attaining to a higher self-possession. It shines for all. There is a certain wisdom of humanity which is common to the greatest men with the lowest, and which our ordinary education often labors to silence and obstruct. The mind is one, and the best minds, who love truth for its own sake, think much less of property in truth. They accept it thankfully everywhere, and do not label or stamp it with any man's name, for it is theirs long beforehand, and from eternity. The learned and the studious of thought have no monopoly of wisdom. Their violence of direction in some degree disqualifies them to think truly. We owe many valuable observations to people who are not very acute or profound, and who say the

. . . .

thing without effort which we want and have long been hunting in vain. The action of the soul is oftener in that which is felt and left unsaid than in that which is said in any conversation. It broods over every society, and they unconsciously seek for it in each other. We know better than we do. We do not yet possess ourselves, and we know at the same time that we are much more. I feel the same truth how often in my trivial conversation with my neighbors, that somewhat higher in each of us overlooks this by-play, and Jove nods to Jove from behind each of us.

Men descend to meet. In their habitual and mean service to the world, for which they forsake their native nobleness, they resemble those Arabian sheiks who dwell in mean houses and affect an external poverty, to escape the rapacity of the Pacha, and reserve all their display of wealth for their interior and guarded retirements.

As it is present in all persons, so it is in every period of life. It is adult already in the infant man. In my dealing with my child, my Latin and Greek, my accomplishments and my money stead me nothing; but as much soul as I have avails. If I am wilful, he sets his will against mine, one for one, and leaves me, if I please, the degradation of beating him by my superiority of strength. But if I renounce my will and act for the soul, setting that up as umpire between us two, out of his young eyes looks the same soul; he reveres and loves with me.

The soul is the perceiver and revealer of truth. We know truth when he see it, let sceptic and scoffer say what they choose. Foolish people ask you, when you have spoken what they do not wish to hear, 'How do you know it is truth, and not an error of your own?' We know truth when we see it, from opinion, as we know when we are awake that we are awake. It was a grand sentence of Emanuel Swedenborg, which would alone indicate the greatness of that man's perception—"It is no proof of a man's understanding to be able to affirm whatever he pleases; but to be able to discern that what is true is true, and that what is false is false—this is the mark and character of intelligence." In the book I read, the good thought returns to me, as every truth will, the image of the whole soul. To the bad thought which I find in it, the same soul becomes a discerning, separating sword, and lops it away. We are wiser than we know. If we will not interfere with our thought, but will act entirely, or see how the thing stands in God, we know the particular thing, and every thing, and every man. For the Maker of all things and all persons stands behind us and casts his dread omniscience through us over things.

But beyond this recognition of its own in particular passages of the individual's experience, it also reveals truth. And here we should seek to reinforce ourselves by its very presence, and to speak with a worthier, loftier strain of that advent. For the soul's communication of truth is the highest event in nature, since it then does not give somewhat from itself, but it gives itself, or passes into and becomes that man whom it enlightens; or in proportion to that truth he receives, it takes him to itself.

We distinguish the announcements of the soul, its manifestations of its own nature, by the term *Revelation*. These are always attended by the emotion of the sublime. For this communication is an influx of the Divine mind into our mind. It is an ebb of the individual rivulet before the flowing surges of the sea of life. Every distinct apprehension of this central commandment agitates men with awe and delight. A thrill passes through all men at the reception of new truth, or at the performance of a great action, which comes out of the heart of nature. In these communications the power to see is not separated from the will to do, but the insight proceeds from obedience, and the obedience proceeds from a joyful perception. Every moment when the individual feels himself invaded by it is memorable. By the necessity of our constitution a certain enthusiasm attends the individual's consciousness of that divine presence. The character and duration of this enthusiasm vary with the state of the individual, from an ecstasy and trance and prophetic inspiration—which is its rarer appearance—to the faintest glow of virtuous emotion, in which form it warms, like our household fires, all the families and associations of men, and makes society possible. A certain tendency to insanity has always attended the opening of the religious sense in men, as if they had been "blasted with excess of light." The trances of Socrates, the "union" of Plotinus, the vision of Porphyry, the conversion of Paul, the aurora of Behmen, the convulsions of George Fox and his Quakers, the illumination of Swedenborg, are of this kind. What was in the case of these remarkable persons a ravishment, has, in innumerable instances in common life, been exhibited in less striking manner. Everywhere the history of religion betrays a tendency to enthusiasm. The rapture of the Moravian and Quietist; the opening of the eternal sense of the Word, in the language of the

New Jerusalem Church; the *revival* of the Calvinistic churches; the *experiences* of the Methodists, are varying forms of that shudder of awe and delight with which the individual soul always mingles with the universal soul.

The nature of these revelations is the same; they are perceptions of the absolute law. They are solutions of the soul's own questions. They do not answer the questions which the understanding asks. The soul answers never by words, but by the thing itself that is inquired after.

Revelation is the disclosure of the soul. The popular notion of a revelation is that it is a telling of fortunes. In past oracles of the soul the understanding seeks to find answers to sensual questions, and undertakes to tell from God how long men shall exist, what their hands shall do and who shall be their company, adding names and dates and places. But we must pick no locks. We must check this low curiosity. An answer in words is delusive; it is really no answer to the questions you ask. Do not require a description of the countries towards which you sail. The description does not describe them to you, and tomorrow you arrive there and know them by inhabiting them. Men ask concerning the immortality of the soul, the employments of heaven, the state of the sinner, and so forth. They even dream that Jesus has left replies to precisely these interrogatories. Never a moment did that sublime spirit speak in their *patois*. To truth, justice, love, the attributes of the soul, the idea of immutableness is essentially associated. Jesus, living in these moral sentiments, heedless of sensual fortunes, heeding only the manifestations of these, never made the separation of the idea of duration from the essence of these attributes, nor uttered a syllable concerning the duration of the soul. It was left to his disciples to sever duration from the moral elements, and to teach the immortality of the soul as a doctrine, and maintain it by evidences. The moment the doctrine of the immortality is separately taught, man is already fallen. In the flowing of love, in the adoration of humility, there is no question of continuance. No inspired man ever asks this question or condescends to these evidences. For the soul is true to itself, and the man in whom it is shed abroad cannot wander from the present, which is infinite, to a future which would be finite.

These questions which we lust to ask about the future are a confession of sin. God has no answer for them. No answer in words can reply to a question of things. It is not in an arbitrary "decree of God," but in the nature of man, that a veil shuts down on the facts of to-morrow; for the soul will not have us read any other cipher than that of cause and effect. By this veil which curtains events it instructs the children of men to live in to-day. The only mode of obtaining an answer to these questions of the senses is to forego all low curiosity, and, accepting the tide of being which floats us into the secret of nature, work and live, work and live, and all unawares the advancing soul has built and forged for itself a new condition, and the question and the answer are one.

By the same fire, vital, consecrating, celestial, which burns until it shall dissolve all things into the waves and surges of an ocean of light, we see and know each other, and what spirit each is of. Who can tell the grounds of his knowledge of the character of the several individuals in his circle of friends? No man. Yet their acts and words do not disappoint him. In that man, though he knew no ill of him, he put no trust. In that other, though they had seldom met, authentic signs had yet passed, to signify that he might be trusted as one who had an interest in his own character. We know each other very well—which of us has been just to himself and whether that which we teach or behold is only an inspiration or is our honest effort also.

We are all discerners of spirits. That diagnosis lies aloft in our life or unconscious power. The intercourse of society, its trade, its religion, its friendships, its quarrels, is one wide judicial investigation of character. In full court, or in small committee, or confronted face to face, accuser and accused, men offer themselves to be judged. Against their will they exhibit those decisive trifles by which character is read. But who judges? and what? Not our understanding. We do not read them by learning or craft. No; the wisdom of the wise man consists herein, that he does not judge them; he lets them judge themselves and merely reads and records their own verdict.

By virtue of this inevitable nature, private will is overpowered, and, maugre our efforts or our imperfections, your genius will speak from you, and mine from me. That which we are, we shall teach, not voluntarily but involuntarily. Thoughts come into our minds by avenues which we never left open, and thoughts go out of our minds through avenues which we never voluntarily opened. Character teaches over our head. The infallible index of true progress is found in the tone the man takes. Neither his age, nor his breeding, nor company, nor books, nor actions, nor talents, nor all together can hinder him from being deferential to a higher spirit than his own. If he have not found his home in God, his manners, his forms of speech, the turn of his sentences, the build, shall I say, of all his opinions will involuntarily confess it, let him brave it out how he will. If we have found his centre, the Deity will shine through him, through all the disguises of ignorance, of ungenial temperament, of unfavorable circumstance. The tone of seeking is one, and the tone of having is another.

The great distinction between teachers sacred or literary—between poets like Herbert, and poets like Pope—between philosophers like Spinoza, Kant and Coleridge, and philosophers like Locke, Paley, Mackintosh and Stewart—between men of the world who are reckoned accomplished talkers, and here and there a fervent mystic, prophesying half insane under the infinitude of his thought—is that one class speak *from within*, or from experience, as parties and possessors of the fact; and the other class *from without*, as spectators merely, or perhaps as acquainted with the fact on the evidence of third persons. It is of no use to preach to me from without. I can do that too easily myself. Jesus speaks always from within, and in a degree that transcends all others. In that is the miracle. I believe beforehand that it ought so to be. All men stand continually in the expectation of the appearance of such a teacher. But if a man do not speak from within the veil, where the word is one with that it tells of, let him lowly confess it.

The same Omniscience flows into the intellect and makes what we call genius. Much of the wisdom of the world is not wisdom, and the most illuminated class of men are no doubt superior to literary fame, and are not writers. Among the multitude of scholars and authors we feel no hallowing presence; we are sensible of a knack and skill rather than of inspiration; they have a light and know not whence it comes and call it their own; their talent is some exaggerated faculty, some overgrown member, so that their strength is a disease. In these instances the intellectual gifts do not make the impression of virtue, but almost of vice; and we feel that a man's talents stand in the way of his advancement in truth. But genius is religious. It is a larger imbibing of the common heart. It is not anomalous, but more like and not less like other men. There is in all great poets a wisdom of humanity which is superior to any talents they exercise. The author, the wit, the partisan, the fine gentleman, does not take place of the man. Humanity shines in Homer, in Chaucer, in Spenser, in Shakspeare, in Milton. They are content with truth. They use the positive degree. They seem frigid and phlegmatic to those who have been spiced with the frantic passion and violent coloring of inferior but popular writers. For they are poets by the free course which they allow to the informing soul, which through their eyes beholds again and blesses the things which it hath made. The soul is superior to its knowledge, wiser than any of its works. The great poet makes us feel our own wealth, and then we think less of his compositions. His best communication to our mind is to teach us to despise all he has done. Shakspeare carries us to such a lofty strain of intelligent activity as to suggest a wealth which beggars his own; and we then feel that the splendid works which he has created, and which in other hours we extol as a sort of self-existent poetry, take no stronger hold of real nature than the shadow of a passing traveller on the rock. The inspiration which uttered itself in Hamlet and Lear could utter things as good from day to day for ever. Why then should I make account of Hamlet and Lear, as if we had not the soul from which they fell as syllables from the tongue?

This energy does not descend into individual life on any other condition than entire possession. It comes to the lowly and simple; it comes to whomsoever will put off what is foreign and proud; it comes as insight; it comes as serenity and grandeur. When we see those whom it inhabits, we are apprised of new degrees of greatness. From that inspiration the man comes back with a changed tone. He does not talk with men with an eye to their opinion. He tries them. It requires of us to be plain and true. The vain traveller attempts to embellish his life by quoting my lord and the prince and the countess, who thus said or did to *him*. The ambitious vulgar show you their spoons and brooches and rings, and preserve their cards and compliments. The more cultivated, in their account of their own experience, cull out the pleasing, poetic circumstance—the visit to Rome, the man of genius they saw, the brilliant friend they know; still further on perhaps the gorgeous landscape, the mountain lights, the mountain thoughts they enjoyed yesterday— and so seek to throw a romantic color over their life. But the soul that ascends to worship the great God is plain and true; has no rose-color, no fine friends, no chivalry, no adventures; does not want admiration; dwells in the hour that now is, in the earnest experience of the common day—by reason of the present moment and the mere trifle having become porous to thought and bibulous of the sea of light.

Converse with a mind that is grandly simple, and literature looks like word-catching. The simplest utterances are worthiest to be written, yet are they so cheap and so things of course, that in the infinite riches of the soul it is like gathering a few pebbles off the ground, or bottling a little air in a phial, when the whole earth and the whole atmosphere are ours. Nothing can pass there, or make you one of the circle, but the casting aside your trappings and dealing man to man in naked truth, plain confession and omniscient affirmation.

Souls such as these treat you as gods would, walk as gods in the earth, accepting without any admiration your wit, your bounty, your virtue even—say rather your act of duty, for your virtue they own as their proper blood, royal as themselves, and over-royal, and the father of the gods. But what rebuke their plain fraternal bearing casts on the mutual flattery with which authors solace each other and wound themselves! These flatter not. I do not wonder that these men go to see Cromwell and Christina and Charles the Second and James the First and the Grand Turk. For they are, in their own elevation, the fellows of kings, and must feel the servile tone of conversation in the world. They must always be a godsend to princes, for they confront them, a king to a king, without ducking or concession, and give a high nature the refreshment and satisfaction of resistance, of plain humanity, of even companionship and of new ideas. They leave them wiser and superior men. Souls like these make us feel that sincerity is more excellent than flattery. Deal so plainly with man and woman as to constrain the utmost sincerity and destroy all hope of trifling with you. It is the highest compliment you can pay. Their "highest praising," said Milton, "is not flattery, and their plainest advice is a kind of praising."

Ineffable is the union of man and God in every act of the soul. The simplest person who in his integrity worships God, becomes God; yet for ever and ever the influx of this better and universal self is new and unsearchable. It inspires awe and astonishment. How dear, how soothing to man, arises the idea of God, peopling the lonely place, effacing the scars of our mistakes and disappointments! When we have broken our god of tradition and ceased from our god of rhetoric, then may God fire the heart with his presence. It is the doubling of the heart itself, nay, the infinite enlargement of the heart with a power of growth to a new infinity on every side. It inspires in man an infallible trust. He has not the conviction, but the sight that the best is the true, and may in that thought easily dismiss all particular uncertainties and fears, and adjourn to the sure revelation of time the solution of his private riddles. He is sure that his welfare is dear to the heart of being. In the presence of law to his mind he is overflowed with a reliance so universal that it sweeps away all cherished hopes and the most stable projects of mortal condition in its flood. He believes that he cannot escape from his good. The things that are really for thee gravitate to thee. You are running to seek your friend. Let your feet run, but your mind need not. If you do not find him, will you not acquiesce that it is best you should not find him? for there is a power, which, as it is in you, is in him also, and could therefore very well bring you together, if it were for the best. You are preparing with eagerness to go and render a service to which your talent and your taste invite you, the love of men and the hope of fame. Has it not occurred to you that you have no right to go, unless you are equally willing to be prevented from going? O, believe, as thou livest, that every sound that is spoken over the round world, which thou oughtest to hear, will vibrate on thine ear! Every proverb, every book, every byword that belongs to thee for aid or comfort, shall surely come home through open or winding passages. Every friend whom not thy fantastic will but the great and tender heart in thee craveth, shall lock thee in his embrace. And this because the heart in thee is the heart of all; not a valve, not a wall, not an intersection is there anywhere in nature, but one blood rolls uninterruptedly an endless circulation through all men, as the water of the globe is all one sea, and, truly seen, its tide is one.

Let man then learn the revelation of all nature and all thought to his heart; this, namely; that the Highest dwells with him; that the sources of nature are in his own mind, if the sentiment of duty is there. But if he would know what the great God speaketh, he must 'go into his closet and shut the door,' as Jesus said. God will not make himself manifest to cowards. He must greatly listen to himself, withdrawing himself from all the accents of other men's devotion. Even their prayers are hurtful to him, until he have made his own. Our religion vulgarly stands on numbers of believers. Whenever the appeal is made—no matter how indirectly—to numbers, proclamation is then and there made that religion is not. He that finds God a sweet enveloping thought to him never counts his company. When I sit in that presence, who shall dare to come in? When I rest in perfect humility, when I burn with pure love, what can Calvin or Swedenborg say?

It makes no difference whether the appeal is to numbers or to one. The faith that stands on authority is not faith. The reliance on authority measures the decline of religion, the withdrawal of the soul. The position men have given to Jesus, now for many centuries of history, is a position of authority. It characterizes themselves. It cannot alter the eternal facts. Great is the soul, and plain. It is no flatterer, it is no follower; it never appeals from itself. It believes in itself. Before the immense possibilities of man all mere experience, all past biography, however spotless and sainted, shrinks away. Before that heaven which our presentiments foreshow us, we cannot easily praise any form of life we have seen or read of. We not only affirm that we have few great men, but, absolutely speaking, that we have none; that we have no history, no record of any character or mode of living that entirely contents us. The saints and demigods whom history worships we are constrained to accept with a grain of allowance. Though in our lonely hours we draw a new strength out of their memory, yet, pressed on our attention, as they are by the thoughtless and customary, they fatigue and invade. The soul gives itself, alone, original and pure, to the Lonely, Original and Pure, who, on that condition, gladly inhabits, leads and speaks through it. Then is it glad, young and nimble. It is not wise, but it sees through all things. It is not called religious, but it is innocent. It calls the light its own, and feels that the grass grows and the stone falls by a law inferior to, and dependent on, its nature. Behold, it saith, I am born into the great, the universal mind. I, the imperfect, adore my own Perfect. I am somehow receptive of the great soul, and thereby I do overlook the sun and the stars and feel them to be the fair accidents and effects which change and pass. More and more the surges of everlasting nature enter into me, and I become public and human in my regards and actions. So come I to live in thoughts and act with energies which are immortal. Thus revering the soul, and learning, as the ancient said, that "its beauty is immense," man will come to see that the world is the perennial miracle which the soul worketh, and be

less astonished at particular wonders; he will learn that there is no profane history; that all history is sacred; that the universe is represented in
an atom, in a moment of time. He will weave no longer a spotted life of
shreds and patches, but he will live with a divine unity. He will cease
from what is base and frivolous in his life and be content with all places
and with any service he can render. He will calmly front the morrow
in the negligency of that trust which carries God with it and so hath
already the whole future in the bottom of the heart.

CIRCLES

Nature centres into balls,
And her proud ephemerals,
Fast to surface and outside,
Scan the profile of the sphere;
Knew they what that signified,
A new genesis were here.

THE EYE is the first circle; the horizon which it forms is the second; and throughout nature this primary figure is repeated without end. It is the highest emblem in the cipher of the world. St. Augustine described the nature of God as a circle whose centre was everywhere and its circumference nowhere. We are all our lifetime reading the copious sense of this first of forms. One moral we have already deduced in considering the circular or compensatory character of every human action. Another analogy we shall now trace, that every action admits of being outdone. Our life is an apprenticeship to the truth that around every circle another can be drawn; that there is no end in nature, but every end is a beginning; that there is always another dawn risen on midnoon, and under every deep a lower deep opens.

This fact, as far as it symbolizes the moral fact of the Unattainable, the flying Perfect, around which the hands of man can never meet, at once the inspirer and the condemner of every success, may conveniently serve us to connect many illustrations of human power in every department.

There are no fixtures in nature. The universe is fluid and volatile. Permanence is but a word of degrees. Our globe seen by God is a transparent law, not a mass of facts. The law dissolves the fact and holds it fluid. Our culture is the predominance of an idea which draws after it this train of cities and institutions. Let us rise into another idea; they will disappear. The Greek sculpture is all melted away, as if it had been statues of ice; here and there a solitary figure or fragment remaining, as we see flecks and scraps of snow left in cold dells and mountain clefts in June and July. For the genius that created it creates now somewhat else. The Greek letters last a little longer, but are already passing under the same sentence and tumbling into the inevitable pit which the creation of new thought opens for all that is old. The new continents are built out of the ruins of an old planet; the new races fed out of the decomposition of the foregoing. New arts destroy the old. See the investment of capital in aqueducts, made useless by hydraulics; fortifications, by gunpowder; roads and canals, by railways; sails, by steam; steam by electricity.

You admire this tower of granite, weathering the hurts of so many ages. Yet a little waving hand built this huge wall, and that which builds is better than that which is built. The hand that built can topple it down much faster. Better than the hand and nimbler was the invisible thought which wrought through it; and thus ever, behind the coarse effect, is a fine cause, which, being narrowly seen, is itself the effect of a finer cause. Everything looks permanent until its secret is known. A rich estate appears to women a firm and lasting fact; to a merchant, one easily created out of any materials, and easily lost. An orchard, good tillage, good grounds, seem a fixture, like a gold mine, or a river, to a citizen; but to a large farmer, not much more fixed than the state of the crop. Nature looks provokingly stable and secular, but it has a cause like all the rest; and when once I comprehend that, will these fields stretch so immovably wide, these leaves hang so individually considerable? Permanence is a word of degrees. Every thing is medial. Moons are no more bounds to spiritual power than bat-balls.

The key to every man is his thought. Sturdy and defying though he look, he has a helm which he obeys, which is the idea after which all his facts are classified. He can only be reformed by showing him a new idea which commands his own. The life of man is a self-evolving circle, which, from a ring imperceptibly small, rushes on all sides outwards to new and larger circles, and that without end. The extent to which this generation of circles, wheel without wheel, will go, depends on the force or truth of the individual soul. For it is the inert effort of each thought, having formed itself into a circular wave of circumstance—as for instance an empire, rules of an art, a local usage, a religious rite— to heap itself on that ridge and to solidify and hem in the life. But if the soul is quick and strong it bursts over that boundary on all sides and expands another orbit on the great deep, which also runs up into a high wave, with attempt again to stop and to bind. But the heart refuses to

be imprisoned; in its first and narrowest pulses it already tends outward with a vast force and to immense and innumerable expansions.

Every ultimate fact is only the first of a new series. Every general
law only a particular fact of some more general law presently to disclose itself. There is no outside, no inclosing wall, no circumference to
us. The man finishes his story--how good! how final! how it puts a
new face on all things! He fills the sky. Lo! on the other side rises also
a man and draws a circle around the circle we had just pronounced the
outline of the sphere. Then already is our first speaker not man, but
only a first speaker. His only redress is forthwith to draw a circle outside of his antagonist. And so men do by themselves. The result of
to-day, which haunts the mind and cannot be escaped, will presently be
abridged into a word, and the principle that seemed to explain nature
will itself be included as one example of a bolder generalization. In the
thought of to-morrow there is a power to upheave all thy creed, all the
creeds, all the literatures of the nations, and marshal thee to a heaven
which no epic dream has yet depicted. Every man is not so much a
workman in the world as he is a suggestion of that he should be. Men
walk as prophecies of the next age.

Step by step we scale this mysterious ladder; the steps are actions,
the new prospect is power. Every several result is threatened and
judged by that which follows. Every one seems to be contradicted by
the new; it is only limited by the new. The new statement is always
hated by the old, and, to those dwelling in the old, comes like an abyss
of scepticism. But the eye soon gets wonted to it, for the eye and it are
effects of one cause; then its innocency and benefit appear, and
presently, all its energy spent, it pales and dwindles before the revelation of the new hour.

Fear not the new generalization. Does the fact look crass and material, threatening to degrade thy theory of spirit? Resist it not; it goes
to refine and raise thy theory of matter just as much.

There are no fixtures to men, if we appeal to consciousness. Every
man supposes himself not to be fully understood; and if there is any
truth in him, if he rests at last on the divine soul, I see not how it can
be otherwise. The last chamber, the last closet, he must feel was never
opened; there is always a residuum unknown, unanalyzable. That is,
every man believes that he has a greater possibility.

Our moods do not believe in each other. To-day I am full of

. . . .

thoughts and can write what I please. I see no reason why I should not have the same thought, the same power of expression, to-morrow. What I write, whilst I write it, seems the most natural thing in the world; but yesterday I saw a dreary vacuity in this direction in which now I see so much; and a month hence, I doubt not, I shall wonder who he was that wrote so many continuous pages. Alas for this infirm faith, this will not strenuous, this vast ebb of a vast flow! I am God in nature; I am a weed by the wall.

The continual effort to raise himself above himself, to work a pitch above his last height, betrays itself in a man's relations. We thirst for approbation, yet cannot forgive the approver. The sweet of nature is love; yet if I have a friend I am tormented by my imperfections. The love of me accuses the other party. If he were high enough to slight me, then could I love him, and rise by my affection to new heights. A man's growth is seen in the successive choirs of his friends. For every friend whom he loses for truth, he gains a better. I thought as I walked in the woods and mused on my friends, why should I play with them this game of idolatry? I know and see too well, when not voluntarily blind, the speedy limits of persons called high and worthy. Rich, noble and great they are by the liberality of our speech, but truth is sad. O blessed Spirit, whom I forsake for these, they are not thou! Every personal consideration that we allow costs us heavenly state. We sell the thrones of angels for a short and turbulent pleasure.

How often must we learn this lesson? Men cease to interest us when we find their limitations. The only sin is limitation. As soon as you once come up with a man's limitations, it is all over with him. Has he talents? has he enterprise? has he knowledge? It boots not. Infinitely alluring and attractive was he to you yesterday, a great hope, a sea to swim in; now, you have found his shores, found it a pond, and you care not if you never see it again.

Each new step we take in thought reconciles twenty seemingly discordant facts, as expressions of one law. Aristotle and Plato are reckoned the respective heads of two schools. A wise man will see that Aristotle platonizes. By going one step farther back in thought, discordant opinions are reconciled by being seen to be two extremes of one principle, and we can never go so far back as to preclude a still higher vision.

Beware when the great God lets loose a thinker on this planet.

· ·

Then all things are at risk. It is as when a conflagration has broken out in a great city, and no man knows what is safe, or where it will end. There is not a piece of science but its flank may be turned to-morrow; there is not any literary reputation, not the so-called eternal names of fame, that may not be revised and condemned. The very hopes of man, the thoughts of his heart, the religion of nations, the manners and morals of mankind are all at the mercy of a new generalization. Generalization is always a new influx of the divinity into the mind. Hence the thrill that attends it.

Valor consists in the power of self-recovery, so that a man cannot have his flank turned, cannot be out-generalled, but put him where you will, he stands. This can only be by his preferring truth to his past apprehension of truth, and his alert acceptance of it from whatever quarter; the intrepid conviction that his laws, his relations to society, his Christianity, his world, may at any time be superseded and decease.

There are degrees in idealism. We learn first to play with it academically, as the magnet was once a toy. Then we see in the heyday of youth and poetry that it may be true, that it is true in gleams and fragments. Then its countenance waxes stern and grand, and we see that it must be true. It now shows itself ethical and practical. We learn that God IS; that he is in me; and that all things are shadows of him. The idealism of Berkeley is only a crude statement of the idealism of Jesus, and that again is a crude statement of the fact that all nature is the rapid efflux of goodness executing and organizing itself. Much more obviously is history and the state of the world at any one time directly dependent on the intellectual classification then existing in the minds of men. The things which are dear to men at this hour are so on account of the ideas which have emerged on their mental horizon, and which cause the present order of things, as a tree bears its apples. A new degree of culture would instantly revolutionize the entire system of human pursuits.

Conversation is a game of circles. In conversation we pluck up the *termini* which bound the common of silence on every side. The parties are not to be judged by the spirit they partake and even express under this Pentecost. To-morrow they will have receded from this high-water mark. To-morrow you shall find them stooping under the old pack-saddles. Yet let us enjoy the cloven flame whilst it glows on our walls. When each new speaker strikes a new light, emancipates us from the oppression of the last speaker to oppress us with the greatness and exclusiveness of his own thought, then yields us to another redeemer, we seem to recover our rights, to become men. O, what truths profound and executable only in ages and orbs, are supposed in the announcement of every truth! In common hours, society sits cold and statuesque. We all stand waiting, empty—knowing, possibly, that we can be full, surrounded by mighty symbols which are not symbols to us, but prose and trivial toys. Then cometh the god and converts the statues into fiery men, and by a flash of his eye burns up the veil which shrouded all things, and the meaning of the very furniture, of cup and saucer, of chair and clock and tester, is manifest. The facts which loomed so large in the fogs of yesterday—property, climate, breeding, personal beauty and the like, have strangely changed their proportions. All that we reckoned settled shakes and rattles; and literatures, cities, climates, religions, leave their foundations and dance before our eyes. And yet here again see the swift circumscription! Good as is discourse, silence is better, and shames it. The length of the discourse indicates the distance of thought betwixt the speaker and the hearer. If they were at a perfect understanding in any part, no words would be necessary thereon. If at one in all parts, no words would be suffered.

Literature is a point outside of our hodiernal circle through which a new one may be described. The use of literature is to afford us a platform whence we may command a view of our present life, a purchase by which we may move it. We fill ourselves with ancient learning, install ourselves the best we can in Greek, in Punic, in Roman houses, only that we may wiselier see French, English and American houses and modes of living. In like manner we see literature best from the midst of wild nature, or from the din of affairs, or from a high religion. The field cannot be well seen from within the field. The astronomer must have his diameter of the earth's orbit as a base to find the parallax of any star.

Therefore we value the poet. All the argument and all the wisdom is not in the encyclopædia, or the treatise on metaphysics, or the Body of Divinity, but in the sonnet or the play. In my daily work I incline to repeat my old steps, and do not believe in remedial force, in the power of change and reform. But some Petrarch or Ariosto, filled with the new wine of his imagination, writes me an ode or a brisk romance, full of daring thought and action. He smites and arouses me with his shrill tones, breaks up my whole chain of habits, and I open my eye on my own possibilities. He claps wings to the sides of all the solid old lumber of the world, and I am capable once more of choosing a straight path in theory and practice.

We have the same need to command a view of the religion of the world. We can never see Christianity from the catechism—from the pastures, from a boat in the pond, from amidst the songs of wood-birds we possibly may. Cleansed by the elemental light and wind, steeped in the sea of beautiful forms which the field offers us, we may chance to cast a right glance back upon biography. Christianity is rightly dear to the best of mankind; yet was there never a young philosopher whose breeding had fallen into the Christian church by whom that brave text of Paul's was not specially prized: "Then shall also the Son be subject unto Him who put all things under him, that God may be all in all." Let the claims and virtues of persons be never so great and welcome, the instinct of man presses eagerly onward to the impersonal and illimitable, and gladly arms itself against the dogmatism of bigots with this generous word out of the book itself.

The natural world may be conceived of as a system of concentric circles, and we now and then detect in nature slight dislocations which apprise us that this surface on which we now stand is not fixed, but sliding. These manifold tenacious qualities, this chemistry and vegetation, these metals and animals, which seem to stand there for their own sake, are means and methods only—are words of God, and as fugitive as other words. Has the naturalist or chemist learned his craft, who has explored the gravity of atoms and the elective affinities, who has not yet discerned the deeper law whereof this is only a partial or approximate statement, namely that like draws to like, and that the goods which belong to you gravitate to you and need not be pursued with pains and cost? Yet is that statement approximate also, and not final. Omnipresence is a higher fact. Not through subtle subterranean channels need friend and fact be drawn to their counterpart, but, rightly considered, these things proceed from the eternal generation of the soul. Cause and effect are two sides of one fact.

The same law of eternal procession ranges all that we call the virtues, and extinguishes each in the light of a better. The great man will not be prudent in the popular sense; all his prudence will be so much deduction from his grandeur. But it behooves each to see, when

he sacrifices prudence, to what god he devotes it; if to ease and pleasure, he had better be prudent still; if to a great trust, he can well spare
his mule and panniers who has a winged chariot instead. Geoffrey
draws on his boots to go through the woods, that his feet may be safer
from the bite of snakes; Aaron never thinks of such a peril. In many
years neither is harmed by such an accident. Yet it seems to me that
with every precaution you take against such an evil you put yourself
into the power of the evil. I suppose that the highest prudence is the
lowest prudence. Is this too sudden a rushing from the centre to the
verge of our orbit? Think how many times we shall fall back into pitiful calculations before we take up our rest in the great sentiment, or
make the verge of to-day the new centre. Besides, your bravest sentiment is familiar to the humblest men. The poor and the low have their
way of expressing the last facts of philosophy as well as you. "Blessed
be nothing" and "The worse things are, the better they are" are
proverbs which express the transcendentalism of common life.

One man's justice is another's injustice; one man's beauty another's
ugliness; one man's wisdom another's folly; as one beholds the same
objects from a higher point. One man thinks justice consists in paying
debts, and has no measure in his abhorrence of another who is very
remiss in this duty and makes the creditor wait tediously. But that second man has his own way of looking at things; asks himself, Which
debt must I pay first, the debt to the rich, or the debt to the poor? the
debt of money, or the debt of thought to mankind, of genius to nature?
For you, O broker, there is no other principle but arithmetic. For me,
commerce is of trivial import; love, faith, truth of character, the aspiration of man, these are sacred; nor can I detach one duty, like you,
from all other duties, and concentrate my forces mechanically on the
payment of moneys. Let me live onward; you shall find that, though
slower, the progress of my character will liquidate all these debts without injustice to higher claims. If a man should dedicate himself to the
payment of notes, would not this be injustice? Does he owe no debt
but money? And are all claims on him to be postponed to a landlord's
or a banker's?

There is no virtue which is final; all are initial. The virtues of society are vices of the saint. The terror of reform is the discovery that we
must cast away our virtues, or what we have always esteemed such, into
the same pit that has consumed our grosser vices:—

· ·

> "Forgive his crimes, forgive his virtues too,
>   Those smaller faults, half converts to the right."

It is the highest power of divine moments that they abolish our contritions also. I accuse myself of sloth and unprofitableness day by day; but when these waves of God flow into me I no longer reckon lost time. I no longer poorly compute my possible achievement by what remains to me of the month or the year; for these moments confer a sort of omnipresence and omnipotence which asks nothing of duration, but sees that the energy of the mind is commensurate with the work to be done, without time.

And thus, O circular philosopher, I hear some reader exclaim, you have arrived at a fine Pyrrhonism, at an equivalence and indifferency of all actions, and would fain teach us that *if we are true*, forsooth, our crimes may be lively stones out of which we shall construct the temple of the true God!

I am not careful to justify myself. I own I am gladdened by seeing the predominance of the saccharine principle throughout vegetable nature, and not less by beholding in morals that unrestrained inundation of the principle of good into every chink and hole that selfishness has left open, yea into selfishness and sin itself; so that no evil is pure, nor hell itself without its extreme satisfactions. But lest I should mislead any when I have my own head and obey my whims, let me remind the reader that I am only an experimenter. Do not set the least value on what I do, or the least discredit on what I do not, as if I pretended to settle any thing as true or false. I unsettle all things. No facts are to me sacred; none are profane; I simply experiment, an endless seeker with no Past at my back.

Yet this incessant movement and progression which all things partake could never become sensible to us but by contrast to some principle of fixture or stability in the soul. Whilst the eternal generation of circles proceeds, the eternal generator abides. That central life is somewhat superior to creation, superior to knowledge and thought, and contains all its circles. Forever it labors to create a life and thought as large and excellent as itself, but in vain, for that which is made instructs how to make a better.

Thus there is no sleep, no pause, no preservation, but all things renew, germinate and spring. Why should we import rags and relics into the new hour? Nature abhors the old, and old age seems the only disease; all others run into this one. We call it by many names—fever, intemperance, insanity, stupidity and crime; they are all forms of old age; they are rest, conservatism, appropriation, inertia; not newness, not the way onward. We grizzle every day. I see no need of it. Whilst we converse with what is above us, we do not grow old, but grow young. Infancy, youth, receptive, aspiring, with religious eye looking upward, counts itself nothing and abandons itself to the instruction flowing from all sides. But the man and woman of seventy assume to know all, they have outlived their hope, they renounce aspiration, accept the actual for the necessary and talk down to the young. Let them then become organs of the Holy Ghost; let them be lovers; let them behold truth; and their eyes are uplifted, their wrinkles smoothed, they are perfumed again with hope and power. This old age ought not to creep on a human mind. In nature every moment is new; the past is always swallowed and forgotten; the coming only is sacred. Nothing is secure but life, transition, the energizing spirit. No love can be bound by oath or covenant to secure it against a higher love. No truth so sublime but it may be trivial to-morrow in the light of new thoughts. People wish to be settled; only as far as they are unsettled is there any hope for them.

Life is a series of surprises. We do not guess to-day the mood, the pleasure, the power of to-morrow, when we are building up our being. Of lower states, of acts of routine and sense, we can tell somewhat; but the masterpieces of God, the total growths and universal movements of the soul, he hideth; they are incalculable. I can know that truth is divine and helpful; but how it shall help me I can have no guess, for *so to be* is the sole inlet of *so to know*. The new position of the advancing man has all the powers of the old, yet has them all new. It carries in its bosom all the energies of the past, yet is itself an exhalation of the morning. I cast away in this new moment all my once hoarded knowledge, as vacant and vain. Now for the first time seem I to know any thing rightly. The simplest words—we do not know what they mean except when we love and aspire.

The difference between talents and character is adroitness to keep the old and trodden round, and power and courage to make a new road to new and better goals. Character makes an overpowering present; a cheerful, determined hour, which fortifies all the company by making them see that much is possible and excellent that was not thought of.

Character dulls the impression of particular events. When we see the conqueror we do not think much of any one battle or success. We see that we had exaggerated the difficulty. It was easy to him. The great man is not convulsible or tormentable; events pass over him without much impression. People say sometimes, 'See what I have overcome; see how cheerful I am; see how completely I have triumphed over these black events.' Not if they still remind me of the black event. True conquest is the causing the calamity to fade and disappear as an early cloud of insignificant result in a history so large and advancing.

The one thing which we seek with insatiable desire is to forget ourselves, to be surprised out of our propriety, to lose our sempiternal memory and to do something without knowing how or why; in short to draw a new circle. Nothing great was ever achieved without enthusiasm. The way of life is wonderful; it is by abandonment. The great moments of history are the facilities of performance through the strength of ideas, as the works of genius and religion. "A man," said Oliver Cromwell, "never rises so high as when he knows not whither he is going." Dreams and drunkenness, the use of opium and alcohol are the semblance and counterfeit of this oracular genius, and hence their dangerous attraction for men. For the like reason they ask the aid of wild passions, as in gaming and war, to ape in some manner these flames and generosities of the heart.

INTELLECT

Go, speed the stars of Thought
On to their shining goals—
The sower scatters broad his seed;
The wheat thou strew'st be souls.

EVERY SUBSTANCE is negatively electric to that which stands above it in the chemical tables, positively to that which stands below it. Water dissolves wood and iron and salt; air dissolves water; electric fire dissolves air, but the intellect dissolves fire, gravity, laws, method, and the subtlest unnamed relations of nature in its resistless menstruum. Intellect lies behind genius, which is intellect constructive. Intellect is the simple power anterior to all action or construction. Gladly would I unfold in calm degrees a natural history of the intellect, but what man has yet been able to mark the steps and boundaries of that transparent essence? The first questions are always to be asked, and the wisest doctor is gravelled by the inquisitiveness of a child. How can we speak of the action of the mind under any divisions, as of its knowledge, of its ethics, of its works, and so forth, since it melts will into perception, knowledge into act? Each becomes the other. Itself alone is. Its vision is not like the vision of the eye, but is union with the things known.

Intellect and intellection signify to the common ear consideration of abstract truth. The consideration of time and place, of you and me, of profit and hurt, tyrannize over most men's minds. Intellect separates the fact considered, from *you*, from all local and personal reference, and discerns it as if it existed for its own sake. Heraclitus looked upon the affections as dense and colored mists. In the fog of good and evil affections it is hard for man to walk forward in a straight line. Intellect is void of affection and sees an object as it stands in the light of science, cool and disengaged. The intellect goes out of the individual, floats over its own personality, and regards it as a fact, and not as *I* and *mine*. He who is immersed in what concerns person or place cannot see the problem of existence. This the intellect always ponders. Nature shows all things formed and bound. The intellect pierces the form, overleaps the wall, detects intrinsic likeness between remote things and reduces all things into a few principles.

The making a fact the subject of thought raises it. All that mass of mental and moral phenomena which we do not make objects of voluntary thought, come within the power of fortune; they constitute the circumstance of daily life; they are subject to change, to fear and hope. Every man beholds his human condition with a degree of melancholy. As a ship aground is battered by the waves, so man, imprisoned in mortal life, lies open to the mercy of coming events. But a truth, separated by the intellect, is no longer a subject of destiny. We behold it as a god upraised above care and fear. And so any fact in our life, or any record of our fancies or reflections, disentangled from the web of our unconsciousness, becomes an object impersonal and immortal. It is the past restored, but embalmed. A better art than that of Egypt has taken fear and corruption out of it. It is eviscerated of care. It is offered for science. What is addressed to us for contemplation does not threaten us but makes us intellectual beings.

The growth of the intellect is spontaneous in every expansion. The mind that grows could not predict the times, the means, the mode of that spontaneity. God enters by a private door into every individual. Long prior to the age of reflection is the thinking of the mind. Out of darkness it came insensibly into the marvellous light of to-day. In the period of infancy it accepted and disposed of all impressions from the surrounding creation after its own way. Whatever any mind doth or saith is after a law, and this native law remains over it after it has come to reflection or conscious thought. In the most worn, pedantic, introverted self-tormentor's life, the greatest part is incalculable by him, unforeseen, unimaginable, and must be, until he can take himself up by his own ears. What am I? What has my will done to make me that I am? Nothing. I have been floated into this thought, this hour, this connection of events, by secret currents of might and mind, and my ingenuity and wilfulness have not thwarted, have not aided to an appreciable degree.

Our spontaneous action is always the best. You cannot with your best deliberation and heed come so close to any question as your spontaneous glance shall bring you, whilst you rise from your bed, or walk abroad in the morning after meditating the matter before sleep on the previous night. Our thinking is a pious reception. Our truth of thought is therefore vitiated as much by too violent direction given by our will, as by too great negligence. We do not determine what we will think. We only open our senses, clear away as we can all obstruction from the fact, and suffer the intellect to see. We have little control over our thoughts. We are the prisoners of ideas. They catch us up for moments into their heaven and so fully engage us that we take no thought for the morrow, gaze like children, without an effort to make them our own. By and by we fall out of that rapture, bethink us where we have been, what we have seen, and repeat as truly as we can what we have beheld. As far as we can recall these ecstasies we carry away in the ineffaceable memory the result, and all men and all the ages confirm it. It is called truth. But the moment we cease to report and attempt to correct and contrive, it is not truth.

If we consider what persons have stimulated and profited us, we shall perceive the superiority of the spontaneous or intuitive principle over the arithmetical or logical. The first contains the second, but virtual and latent. We want in every man a long logic; we cannot pardon the absence of it, but it must not be spoken. Logic is the procession or proportionate unfolding of the intuition; but its virtue is as silent method; the moment it would appear as propositions and have a separate value, it is worthless.

In every man's mind, some images, words and facts remain, without effort on his part to imprint them, which others forget, and afterwards these illustrate to him important laws. All our progress is an unfolding, like the vegetable bud. You have first an instinct, then an opinion, then a knowledge, as the plant has root, bud and fruit. Trust the instinct to the end, though you can render no reason. It is vain to hurry it. By trusting it to the end, it shall ripen into truth and you shall know why you believe.

Each mind has its own method. A true man never acquires after college rules. What you have aggregated in a natural manner surprises and delights when it is produced. For we cannot oversee each other's secret. And hence the differences between men in natural endowment are insignificant in comparison with their common wealth. Do you think the porter and the cook have no anecdotes, no experiences, no wonders for you? Everybody knows as much as the savant. The walls of rude minds are scrawled all over with facts, with thoughts. They shall one day bring a lantern and read the inscriptions. Every man, in the

· ·

degree in which he has wit and culture, finds his curiosity inflamed concerning the modes of living and thinking of other men, and especially of those classes whose minds have not been subdued by the drill of school education.

This instinctive action never ceases in a healthy mind, but becomes richer and more frequent in its informations through all states of culture. At last comes the era of reflection, when we not only observe, but take pains to observe; when we of set purpose sit down to consider an abstract truth; when we keep the mind's eye open whilst we converse, whilst we read, whilst we act, intent to learn the secret law of some class of facts.

What is the hardest task in the world? To think. I would put myself in the attitude to look in the eye an abstract truth, and I cannot. I blench and withdraw on this side and on that. I seem to know what he meant who said, No man can see God face to face and live. For example, a man explores the basis of civil government. Let him intend his mind without respite, without rest, in one direction. His best heed long time avails him nothing. Yet thoughts are flitting before him. We all but apprehend, we dimly forebode the truth. We say I will walk abroad, and the truth will take form and clearness to me. We go forth, but cannot find it. It seems as if we needed only the stillness and composed attitude of the library to seize the thought. But we come in, and are as far from it as at first. Then, in a moment, and unannounced, the truth appears. A certain wandering light appears, and is the distinction, the principle, we wanted. But the oracle comes because we had previously laid siege to the shrine. It seems as if the law of the intellect resembled that law of nature by which we now inspire, now expire the breath; by which the heart now draws in, then hurls out the blood—the law of undulation. So now you must labor with your brains, and now you must forbear your activity and see what the great Soul showeth.

The immortality of man is as legitimately preached from the intellections as from the moral volitions. Every intellection is mainly prospective. Its present value is its least. Inspect what delights you in Plutarch, in Shakspeare, in Cervantes. Each truth that a writer acquires is a lantern which he turns full on what facts and thoughts lay already in his mind, and behold, all the mats and rubbish which had littered his garret become precious. Every trivial fact in his private biography

. . . .

becomes an illustration of this new principle, revisits the day, and delights all men by its piquancy and new charm. Men say, Where did he get this? and think there was something divine in his life. But no; they have myriads of facts just as good, would they only get a lamp to ransack their attics withal.

We are all wise. The difference between persons is not in wisdom but in art. I knew, in an academical club, a person who always deferred to me; who, seeing my whim for writing, fancied that my experiences had somewhat superior; whilst I saw that his experiences were as good as mine. Give them to me and I would make the same use of them. He held the old; he holds the new; I had the habit of tacking together the old and the new which he did not use to exercise. This may hold in the great examples. Perhaps, if we should meet Shakspeare we should not be conscious of any steep inferiority; no, but of a great equality— only that he possessed a strange skill of using, of classifying his facts, which we lacked. For notwithstanding our utter incapacity to produce anything like Hamlet and Othello, see the perfect reception this wit and immense knowledge of life and liquid eloquence find in us all.

If you gather apples in the sunshine, or make hay, or hoe corn, and then retire within doors and shut your eyes and press them with your hand, you shall still see apples hanging in the bright light with boughs and leaves thereto, or the tasselled grass, or the corn-flags, and this for five or six hours afterwards. There lie the impressions on the retentive organ, though you knew it not. So lies the whole series of natural images with which your life has made you acquainted, in your memory, though you know it not; and a thrill of passion flashes light on their dark chamber, and the active power seizes instantly the fit image, as the word of its momentary thought.

It is long ere we discover how rich we are. Our history, we are sure, is quite tame: we have nothing to write, nothing to infer. But our wiser years still run back to the despised recollections of childhood, and always we are fishing up some wonderful article out of that pond; until by and by we begin to suspect that the biography of the one foolish person we know is, in reality, nothing less than the miniature paraphrase of the hundred volumes of the Universal History.

In the intellect constructive, which we popularly designate by the word Genius, we observe the same balance of two elements as in intellect receptive. The constructive intellect produces thoughts, sentences,

. . . .

poems, plans, designs, systems. It is the generation of the mind, the marriage of thought with nature. To genius must always go two gifts, the thought and the publication. The first is revelation, always a miracle, which no frequency of occurrence or incessant study can ever familiarize, but which must always leave the inquirer stupid with wonder. It is the advent of truth into the world, a form of thought now for the first time bursting into the universe, a child of the old eternal soul, a piece of genuine and immeasurable greatness. It seems, for the time, to inherit all that has yet existed and to dictate to the unborn. It affects every thought of man and goes to fashion every institution. But to make it available it needs a vehicle or art by which it is conveyed to men. To be communicable it must become picture or sensible object. We must learn the language of facts. The most wonderful inspirations die with their subject if he has no hand to paint them to the senses. The ray of light passes invisible through space and only when it falls on an object is it seen. When the spiritual energy is directed on something outward, then it is a thought. The relation between it and you first makes you, the value of you, apparent to me. The rich inventive genius of the painter must be smothered and lost for want of the power of drawing, and in our happy hours we should be inexhaustible poets if once we could break through the silence into adequate rhyme. As all men have some access to primary truth, so all have some art or power of communication in their head, but only in the artist does it descend into the hand. There is an inequality, whose laws we do not yet know, between two men and between two moments of the same man, in respect to this faculty. In common hours we have the same facts as in the uncommon or inspired, but they do not sit for their portrait; they are not detached, but lie in a web. The thought of genius is spontaneous; but the power of picture or expression, in the most enriched and flowing nature, implies a mixture of will, a certain control over the spontaneous states, without which no production is possible. It is a conversion of all nature into the rhetoric of thought, under the eye of judgment, with a strenuous exercise of choice. And yet the imaginative vocabulary seems to be spontaneous also. It does not flow from experience only or mainly, but from a richer source. Not by any conscious imitation of particular forms are the grand strokes of the painter executed, but by repairing to the fountain-head of all forms in his mind. Who is the first drawing-master? Without instruction we know very well the ideal of the human form. A child knows if an arm or a leg be distorted in a picture; if the attitude be natural or grand or mean; though he has never received any instruction in drawing or heard any conversation on the subject, nor can himself draw with correctness a single feature. A good form strikes all eyes pleasantly, long before they have any science on the subject, and a beautiful face sets twenty hearts in palpitation, prior to all consideration of the mechanical proportions of the features and head. We may owe to dreams some light on the fountain of this skill; for as soon as we let our will go and let the unconscious states ensue, see what cunning draughtsmen we are! We entertain ourselves with wonderful forms of men, of women, of animals, of gardens, of woods and of monsters, and the mystic pencil wherewith we then draw has no awkwardness or inexperience, no meagreness or poverty; it can design well and group well; its composition is full of art, its colors are well laid on and the whole canvas which it paints is lifelike and apt to touch us with terror, with tenderness, with desire and with grief. Neither are the artist's copies from experience ever mere copies, but always touched and softened by tints from this ideal domain.

The conditions essential to a constructive mind do not appear to be so often combined but that a good sentence or verse remains fresh and memorable for a long time. Yet when we write with ease and come out into the free air of thought, we seem to be assured that nothing is easier than to continue this communication at pleasure. Up, down, around, the kingdom of thought has no inclosures, but the Muse makes us free of her city. Well, the world has a million writers. One would think then that good thought would be as familiar as air and water, and the gifts of each new hour would exclude the last. Yet we can count all our good books; nay, I remember any beautiful verse for twenty years. It is true that the discerning intellect of the world is always much in advance of the creative, so that there are many competent judges of the best book, and few writers of the best books. But some of the conditions of intellectual construction are of rare occurrence. The intellect is a whole and demands integrity in every work. This is resisted equally by a man's devotion to a single thought and by his ambition to combine too many.

Truth is our element of life, yet if a man fasten his attention on a single aspect of truth and apply himself to that alone for a long time, the truth becomes distorted and not itself but falsehood; herein resembling the air, which is our natural element and the breath of our nostrils, but if a stream of the same be directed on the body for a time, it causes cold, fever, and even death. How wearisome the grammarian, the phrenologist, the political or religious fanatic, or indeed any possessed mortal whose balance is lost by the exaggeration of a single topic. It is incipient insanity. Every thought is a prison also. I cannot see what you see, because I am caught up by a strong wind and blown so far in one direction that I am out of the hoop of your horizon.

Is it any better if the student, to avoid this offence and to liberalize himself, aims to make a mechanical whole of history, or science, or philosophy, by a numerical addition of all the facts that fall within his vision? The world refuses to be analyzed by addition and subtraction. When we are young we spend much time and pains in filling our notebooks with all definitions of Religion, Love, Poetry, Politics, Art, in the hope that in the course of a few years we shall have condensed into our encyclopædia the net value of all the theories at which the world has yet arrived. But year after year our tables get no completeness, and at last we discover that our curve is a parabola, whose arcs will never meet.

Neither by detachment, neither by aggregation is the integrity of the intellect transmitted to its works, but by a vigilance which brings the intellect in its greatness and best state to operate every moment. It must have the same wholeness which nature has. Although no diligence can rebuild the universe in a model by the best accumulation or disposition of details, yet does the world reappear in miniature in every event, so that all the laws of nature may be read in the smallest fact. The intellect must have the like perfection in its apprehension and in its works. For this reason, an index or mercury of intellectual proficiency is the perception of identity. We talk with accomplished persons who appear to be strangers in nature. The cloud, the tree, the turf, the bird, are not theirs, have nothing of them; the world is only their lodging and table. But the poet, whose verses are to be spheral and complete, is one whom Nature cannot deceive, whatsoever face of strangeness she may put on. He feels a strict consanguinity, and detects more likeness than variety in all her changes. We are stung by the desire for new thought; but when we receive a new thought it is only the old thought with a new face, and though we make it our own we instantly crave another; we are not really enriched. For the truth was in us before it was reflected to us from natural objects; and the profound genius will cast the likeness of all creatures into every product of his wit.

. . . .

But if the constructive powers are rare and it is given to few men to be poets, yet every man is a receiver of this descending holy ghost, and may well study the laws of its influx. Exactly parallel is the whole rule of intellectual duty to the rule of moral duty. A self-denial no less austere than the saint's is demanded of the scholar. He must worship truth, and forego all things for that, and choose defeat and pain, so that his treasure in thought is thereby augmented.

God offers to every mind its choice between truth and repose. Take which you please—you can never have both. Between these, as a pendulum, man oscillates. He in whom the love of repose predominates will accept the first creed, the first philosophy, the first political party he meets—most likely his father's. He gets rest, commodity and reputation; but he shuts the door of truth. He in whom the love of truth predominates will keep himself aloof from all moorings, and afloat. He will abstain from dogmatism, and recognize all the opposite negations between which, as walls, his being is swung. He submits to the inconvenience of suspense and imperfect opinion, but he is a candidate for truth, as the other is not, and respects the highest law of his being.

The circle of the green earth he must measure with his shoes to find the man who can yield him truth. He shall then know that there is somewhat more blessed and great in hearing than in speaking. Happy is the hearing man; unhappy the speaking man. As long as I hear truth I am bathed by a beautiful element and am not conscious of any limits to my nature. The suggestions are thousand-fold that I hear and see. The waters of the great deep have ingress and egress to the soul. But if I speak, I define, I confine and am less. When Socrates speaks Lysis and Menexenus are afflicted by no shame that they do not speak. They also are good. He likewise defers to them, loves them, whilst he speaks. Because a true and natural man contains and is the same truth which an eloquent man articulates; but in the eloquent man, because he can articulate it, it seems something the less to reside, and he turns to these silent beautiful with the more inclination and respect. The ancient sentence said, Let us be silent, for so are the gods. Silence is a solvent that destroys personality, and gives us leave to be great and universal. Every man's progress is through a succession of teachers, each of whom seems at the time to have a superlative influence, but it at last gives place to a new. Frankly let him accept it all. Jesus says, Leave father, mother, house and lands, and follow me. Who leaves all, receives more. This is as true intellectually as morally. Each new mind we approach seems to require an abdication of all our past and present possessions. A new doctrine seems at first a subversion of all our opinions, tastes, and manner of living. Such has Swedenborg, such has Kant, such has Coleridge, such has Hegel or his interpreter Cousin seemed to many young men in this country. Take thankfully and heartily all they can give. Exhaust them, wrestle with them, let them not go until their blessing be won, and after a short season the dismay will be overpast, the excess of influence withdrawn, and they will be no longer an alarming meteor, but one more bright star shining serenely in your heaven and blending its light with all your day.

But whilst he gives himself up unreservedly to that which draws him, because that is his own, he is to refuse himself to that which draws him not, whatsoever fame and authority may attend it, because it is not his own. Entire self-reliance belongs to the intellect. One soul is a counterpoise of all souls, as a capillary column of water is a balance for the sea. It must treat things and books and sovereign genius as itself also a sovereign. If Aeschylus be that man he is taken for, he has not yet done his office when he has educated the learned of Europe for a thousand years. He is now to approve himself a master of delight to me also. If he cannot do that, all his fame shall avail him nothing with me. I were a fool not to sacrifice a thousand Aeschyluses to my intellectual integrity. Especially take the same ground in regard to abstract truth, the science of the mind. The Bacon, the Spinoza, the Hume, Schelling, Kant, or whosoever propounds to you a philosophy of the mind, is only a more or less awkward translator of things in your consciousness which you have also your way of seeing, perhaps of denominating. Say then, instead of too timidly poring into his obscure sense, that he has not succeeded in rendering back to you your consciousness. He has not succeeded; now let another try. If Plato cannot, perhaps Spinoza will. If Spinoza cannot, then perhaps Kant. Anyhow, when at last it is done, you will find it is no recondite, but a simple, natural, common state which the writer restores to you.

But let us end these didactics. I will not, though the subject might provoke it, speak to the open question between Truth and Love. I shall not presume to interfere in the old politics of the skies—"The cherubim know most; the seraphim love most." The gods shall settle their own quarrels. But I cannot recite, even thus rudely, laws of the intellect, without remembering that lofty and sequestered class who have been its prophets and oracles, the high-priesthood of the pure reason, the *Trismegisti*, the expounders of the principles of thought from age to age. When at long intervals we turn over their abstruse pages, wonderful seems the calm and grand air of these few, these great spiritual lords who have walked in the world—these of the old religion—dwelling in a worship which makes the sanctities of Christianity look parvenues and popular; for "persuasion is in soul, but necessity is in intellect." This band of grandees, Hermes, Heraclitus, Empedocles, Plato, Plotinus, Olympiodorus, Proclus, Synesius and the rest, have somewhat so vast in their logic, so primary in their thinking, that it seems antecedent to all the ordinary distinctions of rhetoric and literature, and to be at once poetry and music and dancing and astronomy and mathematics. I am present at the sowing of the seed of the world. With a geometry of sunbeams the soul lays the foundations of nature. The truth and grandeur of their thought is proved by its scope and applicability, for it commands the entire schedule and inventory of things for its illustration. But what marks its elevation and has even a comic look to us, is the innocent serenity with which these babe-like Jupiters sit in their clouds, and from age to age prattle to each other and to no contemporary. Well assured that their speech is intelligible and the most natural thing in the world, they add thesis to thesis, without a moment's heed of the universal astonishment of the human race below, who do not comprehend their plainest argument; nor do they ever relent so much as to insert a popular or explaining sentence, nor testify the least displeasure or petulance at the dulness of their amazed auditory. The angels are so enamored of the language that is spoken in heaven that they will not distort their lips with the hissing and unmusical dialects of men, but speak their own, whether there be any who understand it or not.

ART

Give to barrows, trays and pans
Grace and glimmer of romance,
Bring the moonlight into noon
Hid in gleaming piles of stone;
On the city's pavéd street
Plant gardens lined with lilac sweet,
Let spouting fountains cool the air,
Singing in the sun-baked square.
Let statue, picture, park and hall,
Ballad, flag and festival,
The past restore, the day adorn
And make each morrow a new
   morn.
So shall the drudge in dusty frock
Spy behind the city clock

Retinues of airy kings,
Skirts of angels, starry wings,
His fathers shining in bright fables,
His children fed at heavenly tables.
'T is the privilege of Art
Thus to play its cheerful part,
Man in Earth to acclimate
And bend the exile to his fate,
And, moulded of one element
With the days and firmament,
Teach him on these as stairs to climb
And live on even terms with Time;
Whilst upper life the slender rill
Of human sense doth overfill.

BECAUSE THE SOUL is progressive, it never quite repeats itself, but in every act attempts the production of a new and fairer whole. This appears in works both of the useful and fine arts, if we employ the popular distinction of works according to their aim either at use or beauty. Thus in our fine arts, not imitation but creation is the aim. In landscapes the painter should give the suggestion of a fairer creation than we know. The details, the prose of nature he should omit and give us only the spirit and splendor. He should know that the landscape has beauty for his eye because it expresses a thought which is to him good; and this because the same power which sees through his eyes is seen in that spectacle; and he will come to value the expression of nature and not nature itself, and so exalt in his copy the features that please him. He will give the gloom of gloom and the sunshine of sunshine. In a portrait he must inscribe the character and not the features, and must esteem the man who sits to him as himself only an imperfect picture or likeness of the aspiring original within.

What is that abridgment and selection we observe in all spiritual activity, but itself the creative impulse? for it is the inlet of that higher illumination which teaches to convey a larger sense by simpler symbols. What is a man but nature's finer success in self-explication? What is a man but a finer and compacter landscape than the horizon figures—nature's eclecticism? and what is his speech, his love of painting, love of nature, but a still finer success—all the weary miles and tons of space and bulk left out, and the spirit or moral of it contracted into a musical word, or the most cunning stroke of the pencil?

But the artist must employ the symbols in use in his day and nation to convey his enlarged sense to his fellow-men. Thus the new in art is always formed out of the old. The Genius of the Hour sets his ineffaceable seal on the work and gives it an inexpressible charm for the imagination. As far as the spiritual character of the period overpowers the artist and finds expression in his work, so far it will retain a certain grandeur, and will represent to future beholders the Unknown, the Inevitable, the Divine. No man can quite exclude this element of Necessity from his labor. No man can quite emancipate himself from his age and country, or produce a model in which the education, the religion, the politics, usages and arts of his times shall have no share. Though he were never so original, never so wilful and fantastic, he cannot wipe out of his work every trace of the thoughts amidst which it grew. The very avoidance betrays the usage he avoids. Above his will and out of his sight he is necessitated by the air he breathes and the idea on which he and his contemporaries live and toil, to share the manner of his times, without knowing what that manner is. Now that which is inevitable in the work has a higher charm than individual talent can ever give, inasmuch as the artist's pen or chisel seems to have been held and guided by a gigantic hand to inscribe a line in the history of the human race. This circumstance gives a value to the Egyptian hieroglyphics, to the Indian, Chinese and Mexican idols, however gross and shapeless. They denote the height of the human soul in that hour, and were not fantastic, but sprung from a necessity as deep as the world. Shall I now add that the whole extant product of the plastic arts has herein its highest value, *as history*; as a stroke drawn in the portrait of that fate, perfect and beautiful, according to whose ordinations all beings advance to their beatitude?

Thus, historically viewed, it has been the office of art to educate the perception of beauty. We are immersed in beauty, but our eyes have no clear vision. It needs, by the exhibition of single traits, to assist

. . . .

and lead the dormant taste. We carve and paint, or we behold what is carved and painted, as students of the mystery of Form. The virtue of art lies in detachment, in sequestering one object from the embarrassing variety. Until one thing comes out from the connection of things, there can be enjoyment, contemplation, but no thought. Our happiness and unhappiness are unproductive. The infant lies in a pleasing trance, but his individual character and his practical power depend on his daily progress in the separation of things, and dealing with one at a time. Love and all the passions concentrate all existence around a single form. It is the habit of certain minds to give an all-excluding fulness to the object, the thought, the word they alight upon, and to make that for the time the deputy of the world. These are the artists, the orators, the leaders of society. The power to detach and to magnify by detaching is the essence of rhetoric in the hands of the orator and the poet. This rhetoric, or power to fix the momentary eminency of an object—so remarkable in Burke, in Byron, in Carlyle—the painter and sculptor exhibit in color and in stone. The power depends on the depth of the artist's insight of that object he contemplates. For every object has its roots in central nature, and may of course be so exhibited to us as to represent the world. Therefore each work of genius is the tyrant of the hour and concentrates attention on itself. For the time, it is the only thing worth naming to do that—be it a sonnet, an opera, a landscape, a statue, an oration, the plan of a temple, of a campaign, or of a voyage of discovery. Presently we pass to some other object, which rounds itself into a whole as did the first; for example a well-laid garden; and nothing seems worth doing but the laying out of gardens. I should think fire the best thing in the world, if I were not acquainted with air, and water, and earth. For it is the right and property of all natural objects, of all genuine talents, of all native properties whatsoever, to be for their moment the top of the world. A squirrel leaping from bough to bough and making the wood but one wide tree for his pleasure, fills the eye not less than a lion—is beautiful, self-sufficing, and stands then and there for nature. A good ballad draws my ear and heart whilst I listen, as much as an epic has done before. A dog, drawn by a master, or a litter of pigs, satisfies and is a reality not less than the frescoes of Angelo. From this succession of excellent objects we learn at last the immensity of the world, the opulence of human nature, which can run out to infinitude in any direction. But I also learn that what astonished and fascinated me in the first work, astonished me in the second work also; that excellence of all things is one.

The office of painting and sculpture seems to be merely initial. The best pictures can easily tell us their last secret. The best pictures are rude draughts of a few of the miraculous dots and lines and dyes which make up the ever-changing "landscape with figures" amidst which we dwell. Painting seems to be to the eye what dancing is to the limbs. When that has educated the frame to self-possession, to nimbleness, to grace, the steps of the dancing-master are better forgotten; so painting teaches me the splendor of color and the expression of form, and as I see many pictures and higher genius in the art, I see the boundless opulence of the pencil, the indifferency in which the artist stands free to choose out of the possible forms. If he can draw every thing, why draw any thing? and then is my eye opened to the eternal picture which nature paints in the street, with moving men and children, beggars and fine ladies, draped in red and green and blue and gray; long-haired, grizzled, white-faced, black-faced, wrinkled, giant, dwarf, expanded, elfish—capped and based by heaven, earth and sea.

A gallery of sculpture teaches more austerely the same lesson. As picture teaches the coloring, so sculpture the anatomy of form. When I have seen fine statues and afterwards enter a public assembly, I understand well what he meant who said, "When I have been reading Homer, all men look like giants." I too see that painting and sculpture are gymnastics of the eye, its training to the niceties and curiosities of its function. There is no statue like this living man, with his infinite advantage over all ideal sculpture, of perpetual variety. What a gallery of art have I here! No mannerist made these varied groups and diverse original single figures. Here is the artist himself improvising, grim and glad, at his block. Now one thought strikes him, now another, and with each moment he alters the whole air, attitude and expression of his clay. Away with your nonsense of oil and easels, of marble and chisels; except to open your eyes to the masteries of eternal art, they are hypocritical rubbish.

The reference of all production at last to an aboriginal Power explains the traits common to all works of the highest art—that they are universally intelligible; that they restore to us the simplest states of mind, and are religious. Since what skill is therein shown is the reappearance of the original soul, a jet of pure light, it should produce a similar impression to that made by natural objects. In happy hours, nature appears to us one with art; art perfected—the work of genius. And the individual in whom simple tastes and susceptibility to all the great human influences overpower the accidents of a local and special culture, is the best critic of art. Though we travel the world over to find the beautiful, we must carry it with us, or we find it not. The best of beauty is a finer charm than skill in surfaces, in outlines, or rules of art can ever teach, namely a radiation from the work of art, of human character—a wonderful expression through stone, or canvas, or musical sound, of the deepest and simplest attributes of our nature, and therefore most intelligible at last to those souls which have these attributes. In the sculptures of the Greeks, in the masonry of the Romans, and in the pictures of the Tuscan and Venetian masters, the highest charm is the universal language they speak. A confession of moral nature, of purity, love, and hope, breathes from them all. That which we carry to them, the same we bring back more fairly illustrated in the memory. The traveller who visits the Vatican and passes from chamber to chamber through galleries of statues, vases, sarcophagi and candelabra, through all forms of beauty cut in the richest materials, is in danger of forgetting the simplicity of the principles out of which they all sprung, and that they had their origin from thoughts and laws in his own breast. He studies the technical rules on these wonderful remains, but forgets that these works were not always thus constellated; that they are the contributions of many ages and many countries; that each came out of the solitary workshop of one artist, who toiled perhaps in ignorance of the existence of other sculpture, created his work without other model save life, household life, and the sweet and smart of personal relations, of beating hearts, and meeting eyes; of poverty and necessity and hope and fear. These were his inspirations, and these are the effects he carries home to your heart and mind. In proportion to his force, the artist will find in his work an outlet for his proper character. He must not be in any manner pinched or hindered by his material, but through his necessity of imparting himself the adamant will be wax in his hands, and will allow an adequate communication of himself, in his full stature and proportion. He need not cumber himself with a conventional nature and culture, nor ask what is the mode in Rome or in Paris, but that house and weather and manner of living which poverty and the fate of birth have made at once so odious and so dear, in the gray

unpainted wood cabin, on the corner of a New Hampshire farm, or in
the log-hut of the backwoods, or in the narrow lodging where he has
endured the constraints and seeming of a city poverty, will serve as well
as any other condition as the symbol of a thought which pours itself
indifferently through all.

I remember when in my younger days I had heard of the wonders
of Italian painting, I fancied the great pictures would be great strangers;
some surprising combination of color and form; a foreign wonder, barbaric pearl and gold, like the spontoons and standards of the militia,
which play such pranks in the eyes and imaginations of school-boys. I
was to see and acquire I knew not what. When I came at last to Rome
and saw with eyes the pictures, I found that genius left to novices the
gay and fantastic and ostentatious, and itself pierced directly to the simple and true; that it was familiar and sincere; that it was the old, eternal
fact I had met already in so many forms—unto which I lived; that it
was the plain *you and me* I knew so well—had left at home in so many
conversations. I had had the same experience already in a church at
Naples. There I saw that nothing was changed with me but the place,
and said to myself—'Thou foolish child, hast thou come out hither,
over four thousand miles of salt water, to find that which was perfect to
thee there at home?' That fact I saw again in the Academmia at Naples,
in the chambers of sculpture, and yet again when I came to Rome and
to the paintings of Raphael, Angelo, Sacchi, Titian, and Leonardo da
Vinci. "What, old mole! workest thou in the earth so fast?" It had travelled by my side, that which I fancied I had left in Boston was here in
the Vatican, and again at Milan and at Paris, and made all travelling
ridiculous as a treadmill. I now require this of all pictures, that they
domesticate me, not that they dazzle me. Pictures must not be too picturesque. Nothing astonishes men so much as commonsense and plain
dealing. All great actions have been simple, and all great pictures are.

The Transfiguration, by Raphael, is an eminent example of this
peculiar merit. A calm benignant beauty shines over all this picture,
and goes directly to the heart. It seems almost to call you by name. The
sweet and sublime face of Jesus is beyond praise, yet how it disappoints
all florid expectations! This familiar, simple, home-speaking countenance is as if one should meet a friend. The knowledge of picture
dealers has its value, but listen not to their criticism when your heart
is touched by genius. It was not painted for them, it was painted for

you; for such as had eyes capable of being touched by simplicity and lofty emotions.

Yet when we have said all our fine things about the arts, we must end with a frank confession that the arts, as we know them, are but initial. Our best praise is given to what they aimed and promised, not to the actual result. He has conceived meanly of the resources of man, who believes that the best age of production is past. The real value of the Iliad or the Transfiguration is as signs of power; billows or ripples they are of the stream of tendency; tokens of the everlasting effort to produce, which even in its worst estate the soul betrays. Art has not yet come to its maturity if it do not put itself abreast with the most potent influences of the world, if it is not practical and moral, if it do not stand in connection with the conscience, if it do not make the poor and uncultivated feel that it addresses them with a voice of lofty cheer. There is higher work for Art than the arts. They are abortive births of an imperfect or vitiated instinct. Art is the need to create; but in its essence, immense and universal, it is impatient of working with lame or tied hands, and of making cripples and monsters, such as all pictures and statues are. Nothing less than the creation of man and nature is its end. A man should find in it an outlet for his whole energy. He may paint and carve only as long as he can do that. Art should exhilarate, and throw down the walls of circumstance on every side, awakening in the beholder the same sense of universal relation and power which the work evinced in the artist, and its highest effect is to make new artists.

Already History is old enough to witness the old age and disappearance of particular arts. The art of sculpture is long ago perished to any real effect. It was originally a useful art, a mode of writing, a savage's record of gratitude or devotion, and among a people possessed of a wonderful perception of form this childish carving was refined to the utmost splendor of effect. But it is the game of a rude and youthful people, and not the manly labor of a wise and spiritual nation. Under an oak-tree loaded with leaves and nuts, under a sky full of eternal eyes, I stand in a thoroughfare; but in the works of our plastic arts and especially of sculpture, creation is driven into a corner. I cannot hide from myself that there is a certain appearance of paltriness, as of toys and the trumpery of a theatre, in sculpture. Nature transcends all our moods of thought, and its secret we do not yet find. But the gallery stands at the mercy of our moods, and there is a moment when it becomes frivolous. I do not wonder that Newton, with an attention habitually engaged on the paths of planets and suns, should have wondered what the Earl of Pembroke found to admire in "stone dolls." Sculpture may serve to teach the pupil how deep is the secret of form, how purely the spirit can translate its meanings into that eloquent dialect. But the statue will look cold and false before that new activity which needs to roll through all things, and is impatient of counterfeits and things not alive. Picture and sculpture are the celebrations and festivities of form. But true art is never fixed, but always flowing. The sweetest music is not in the oratorio, but in the human voice when it speaks from its instant life tones of tenderness, truth, or courage. The oratorio has already lost its relation to the morning, to the sun, and the earth, but that persuading voice is in tune with these. All works of art should not be detached, but extempore performances. A great man is a new statue in every attitude and action. A beautiful woman is a picture which drives all beholders nobly mad. Life may be lyric or epic, as well as a poem or a romance.

A true announcement of the law of creation, if a man were found worthy to declare it, would carry art up into the kingdom of nature, and destroy its separate and contrasted existence. The fountains of invention and beauty in modern society are all but dried up. A popular novel, a theatre, or a ball-room makes us feel that we are all paupers in the almshouse of this world, without dignity, without skill or industry. Art is as poor and low. The old tragic Necessity, which lowers on the brows even of the Venuses and the Cupids of the antique, and furnishes the sole apology for the intrusion of such anomalous figures into nature—namely that they were inevitable; that the artist was drunk with a passion for form which he could not resist, and which vented itself in these fine extravagances—no longer dignifies the chisel or the pencil. But the artist and the connoisseur now seek in art the exhibition of their talent, or an asylum from the evils of life. Men are not well pleased with the figure they make in their own imaginations, and they flee to art, and convey their better sense in an oratorio, a statue, or a picture. Art makes the same effort which a sensual prosperity makes; namely to detach the beautiful from the useful, to do up the work as unavoidable, and, hating it, pass on to enjoyment. These solaces and

. . . .

compensations, this division of beauty from use, the laws of nature do not permit. As soon as beauty is sought, not from religion and love but for pleasure, it degrades the seeker. High beauty is no longer attainable by him in canvas or in stone, in sound, or in lyrical construction; an effeminate, prudent, sickly beauty, which is not beauty, is all that can be formed; for the hand can never execute any thing higher than the character can inspire.

The art that thus separates is itself first separated. Art must not be a superficial talent, but must begin farther back in man. Now men do not see nature to be beautiful, and they go to make a statue which shall be. They abhor men as tasteless, dull, and inconvertible, and console themselves with color-bags and blocks of marble. They reject life as prosaic, and create a death which they call poetic. They despatch the day's weary chores, and fly to voluptuous reveries. They eat and drink, that they may afterwards execute the ideal. Thus is art vilified; the name conveys to the mind its secondary and bad senses; it stands in the imagination as somewhat contrary to nature, and struck with death from the first. Would it not be better to begin higher up—to serve the ideal before they eat and drink; to serve the ideal in eating and drinking, in drawing the breath, and in the functions of life? Beauty must come back to the useful arts, and the distinction between the fine and the useful arts be forgotten. If history were truly told, if life were nobly spent, it would be no longer easy or possible to distinguish the one from the other. In nature, all is useful, all is beautiful. It is therefore beautiful because it is alive, moving, reproductive; it is therefore useful because it is symmetrical and fair. Beauty will not come at the call of a legislature, nor will it repeat in England or America its history in Greece. It will come, as always, unannounced, and spring up between the feet of brave and earnest men. It is in vain that we look for genius to reiterate its miracles in the old arts; it is its instinct to find beauty and holiness in new and necessary facts, in the field and road-side, in the shop and mill. Proceeding from a religious heart it will raise to a divine use the railroad, the insurance office, the joint-stock company; our law, our primary assemblies, our commerce, the galvanic battery, the electric jar, the prism, and the chemist's retort; in which we seek now only an economical use. Is not the selfish and even cruel aspect which belongs to our great mechanical works, to mills, railways, and machinery, the effect of the mercenary impulses which these works obey? When its errands are noble and adequate, a steamboat bridging the Atlantic between Old and New England and arriving at its ports with the punctuality of a planet, is a step of man into harmony with nature. The boat at St. Petersburg, which plies along the Lena by magnetism, needs little to make it sublime. When science is learned in love, and its powers are wielded by love, they will appear the supplements and continuations of the material creation.

ESSAYS
SECOND SERIES

[The second book of essays was published in 1844, and soon afterward also in England. The essays had been used in various forms before various publics as lectures, and were completely rewritten for use in the book. This book was better received than its predecessors.]

THE POET

A moody child and wildly wise
Pursued the game with joyful eyes,
Which chose, like meteors, their way,
And rived the dark with private ray:
They overleapt the horizon's edge,
Searched with Apollo's privilege;
Through man, and woman, and sea, and star
Saw the dance of nature forward far;
Through worlds, and races, and terms, and times
Saw musical order, and pairing rhymes.

Olympian bards who sung
Divine ideas below,
Which always find us young,
And always keep us so.

THOSE WHO are esteemed umpires of taste are often persons who have acquired some knowledge of admired pictures or sculptures, and have an inclination for whatever is elegant; but if you inquire whether they are beautiful souls, and whether their own acts are like fair pictures, you learn that they are selfish and sensual. Their cultivation is local, as if you should rub a log of dry wood in one spot to produce fire, all the rest remaining cold. Their knowledge of the fine arts is some study of rules and particulars, or some limited judgment of color or form, which is exercised for amusement or for show. It is a proof of the shallowness of the doctrine of beauty as it lies in the minds of our amateurs, that men seem to have lost the perception of the instant dependence of form upon soul. There is no doctrine of forms in our philosophy. We were put into our bodies, as fire is put into a pan to be carried about; but there is no accurate adjustment between the spirit and the organ, much less is the latter the germination of the former. So in regard to other forms, the intellectual men do not believe in any essential dependence of the material world on thought and volition.

Theologians think it a pretty air-castle to talk of the spiritual meaning of a ship or a cloud, of a city or a contract, but they prefer to come again to the solid ground of historical evidence; and even the poets are contented with a civil and conformed manner of living, and to write poems from the fancy, at a safe distance from their own experience. But the highest minds of the world have never ceased to explore the double meaning, or shall I say the quadruple or the centuple or much more manifold meaning, of every sensuous fact; Orpheus, Empedocles, Heraclitus, Plato, Plutarch, Dante, Swedenborg, and the masters of sculpture, picture and poetry. For we are not pans and barrows, nor even porters of the fire and torch-bearers, but children of the fire, made of it, and only the same divinity transmuted and at two or three removes, when we know least about it. And this hidden truth, that the fountains whence all this river of Time and its creatures floweth are intrinsically ideal and beautiful, draws us to the consideration of the nature and functions of the Poet, or the man of Beauty; to the means and materials he uses, and to the general aspect of the art in the present time.

The breadth of the problem is great, for the poet is representative. He stands among partial men for the complete man, and apprises us not of his wealth, but of the common wealth. The young man reveres men of genius, because, to speak truly, they are more himself than he is. They receive of the soul as he also receives, but they more. Nature enhances her beauty, to the eye of loving men, from their belief that the poet is beholding her shows at the same time. He is isolated among his contemporaries by truth and by his art, but with this consolation in his pursuits, that they will draw all men sooner or later. For all men live by truth and stand in need of expression. In love, in art, in avarice, in politics, in labor, in games, we study to utter our painful secret. The man is only half himself, the other half is his expression.

Notwithstanding this necessity to be published, adequate expression is rare. I know not how it is that we need an interpreter, but the great majority of men seem to be minors, who have not yet come into possession of their own, or mutes, who cannot report the conversation they have had with nature. There is no man who does not anticipate a supersensual utility in the sun and stars, earth and water. These stand and wait to render him a peculiar service. But there is some obstruction or some excess of phlegm in our constitution, which does not suffer them to yield the due effect. Too feeble fall the impressions of nature on us to make us artists. Every touch should thrill. Every man should be so much an artist that he could report in conversation what had befallen him. Yet, in our experience, the rays or appulses have sufficient force to arrive at the senses, but not enough to reach the quick and compel the reproduction of themselves in speech. The poet is the person in whom these powers are in balance, the man without impediment, who sees and handles that which others dream of, traverses the whole scale of experience, and is representative of man, in virtue of being the largest power to receive and to impart.

For the Universe has three children, born at one time, which reappear under different names in every system of thought, whether they be called cause, operation and effect; or, more poetically, Jove, Pluto, Neptune; or, theologically, the Father, the Spirit and the Son; but which we will call here the Knower, the Doer and the Sayer. These stand respectively for the love of truth, for the love of good, and for the love of beauty. These three are equal. Each is that which he is, essentially, so that he cannot be surmounted or analyzed, and each of these three has the power of the others latent in him and his own, patent.

The poet is the sayer, the namer, and represents beauty. He is a sovereign, and stands on the centre. For the world is not painted or adorned, but is from the beginning beautiful; and God has not made some beautiful things, but Beauty is the creator of the universe. Therefore the poet is not any permissive potentate, but is emperor in his own right. Criticism is infested with a cant of materialism, which assumes that manual skill and activity is the first merit of all men, and disparages such as say and do not, overlooking the fact that some men, namely poets, are natural sayers, sent into the world to the end of expression, and confounds them with those whose province is action but who quit it to imitate the sayers. But Homer's words are as costly and admirable to Homer as Agamemnon's victories are to Agamemnon. The poet does not wait for the hero or the sage, but, as they act and think primarily, so he writes primarily what will and must be spoken, reckoning the others, though primaries also, yet, in respect to him, secondaries and servants; as sitters or models in the studio of a painter, or as assistants who bring building-materials to an architect.

For poetry was all written before time was, and whenever we are so finely organized that we can penetrate into that region where the air is music, we hear those primal warblings and attempt to write them down, but we lose ever and anon a word or a verse and substitute something of our own, and thus miswrite the poem. The men of more delicate ear write down these cadences more faithfully, and these transcripts, though imperfect, become the songs of the nations. For nature is as truly beautiful as it is good, or as it is reasonable, and must as much appear as it must be done, or be known. Words and deeds are quite indifferent modes of the divine energy. Words are also actions, and actions are a kind of words.

The sign and credentials of the poet are that he announces that which no man foretold. He is the true and only doctor; he knows and tells; he is the only teller of news, for he was present and privy to the appearance which he describes. He is a beholder of ideas and an utterer of the necessary and causal. For we do not speak now of men of poetical talents, or of industry and skill in metre, but of the true poet. I took part in a conversation the other day concerning a recent writer of lyrics, a man of subtle mind, whose head appeared to be a music-box of delicate tunes and rhythms, and whose skill and command of language we could not sufficiently praise. But when the question arose whether he was not only a lyrist but a poet, we were obliged to confess that he is plainly a contemporary, not an eternal man. He does not stand out of our low limitations, like a Chimborazo under the line, running up from a torrid base through all the climates of the globe, with belts of the herbage of every latitude on its high and mottled sides; but this genius is the landscape-garden of a modern house, adorned with fountains and statues, with well-bred men and women standing and sitting in the walks and terraces. We hear, through all the varied music, the ground-tone of conventional life. Our poets are men of talents who sing, and not the children of music. The argument is secondary, the finish of the verses is primary.

For it is not metres, but a metre-making argument that makes a poem—a thought so passionate and alive that like the spirit of a plant or an animal it has an architecture of its own, and adorns nature with a new thing. The thought and the form are equal in the order of time, but in the order of genesis the thought is prior to the form. The poet has a new thought; he has a whole new experience to unfold; he will tell us how it was with him, and all men will be the richer in his fortune. For the experience of each new age requires a new confession, and the world seems always waiting for its poet. I remember when I was young how much I was moved one morning by tidings that genius had appeared in a youth who sat near me at table. He had left his work and gone rambling none knew whither, and had written hundreds of lines, but could not tell whether that which was in him was therein told; he could tell nothing but that all was changed—man, beast, heaven, earth and sea. How gladly we listened! how credulous! Society seemed to be compromised. We sat in the aurora of a sunrise which was to put out all the stars. Boston seemed to be at twice the distance it had the night before, or was much farther than that. Rome—what was Rome? Plutarch and Shakspeare were in the yellow leaf, and Homer no more should be heard of. It is much to know that poetry has been written this very day, under this very roof, by your side. What! that wonderful spirit has not expired! These stony moments are still sparkling and animated! I had fancied that the oracles were all silent, and nature had spent her fires; and behold! all night, from every pore, these fine auroras have been streaming. Every one has some interest in the advent of the poet, and no one knows how much it may concern him. We know that the secret of the world is profound, but who or what shall be our interpreter, we know not. A mountain ramble, a new style of face, a new person, may put the key into our hands. Of course the value of genius to us is in the veracity of its report. Talent may frolic and juggle; genius realizes and adds. Mankind in good earnest have availed so far in understanding themselves and their work, that the foremost watchman on the peak announces his news. It is the truest word ever spoken, and the phrase will be the fittest, most musical, and the unerring voice of the world for that time.

All that we call sacred history attests that the birth of a poet is the principal event in chronology. Man, never so often deceived, still watches for the arrival of a brother who can hold him steady to a truth until he has made it his own. With what joy I begin to read a poem which I confide in as an inspiration! And now my chains are to be broken; I shall mount above these clouds and opaque airs in which I live—opaque, though they seem transparent—and from the heaven of truth I shall see and comprehend my relations. That will reconcile me to life and renovate nature, to see trifles animated by a tendency, and to know what I am doing. Life will no more be a noise; now I shall see men and women, and know the signs by which they may be discerned from fools and satans. This day shall be better than my birthday: then I became an animal; now I am invited into the science of the real. Such is the hope, but the fruition is postponed. Oftener it falls that this winged man, who will carry me into the heaven, whirls me into mists, then leaps and frisks about with me as it were from cloud to cloud, still affirming that he is bound heavenward; and I, being myself a novice, am slow in perceiving that he does not know the way into the heavens, and is merely bent that I should admire his skill to rise like a fowl or a flying fish, a little way from the ground or the water; but the all-piercing, all-feeding and ocular air of heaven that man shall never inhabit. I tumble down again soon into my old nooks, and lead the life of exaggerations as before, and have lost my faith in the possibility of any guide who can lead me thither where I would be.

But, leaving these victims of vanity, let us, with new hope, observe how nature, by worthier impulses, has insured the poet's fidelity to his office of announcement and affirming, namely by the beauty of things, which becomes a new and higher beauty when expressed. Nature offers all her creatures to him as a picture-language. Being used as a type, a second wonderful value appears in the object, far better than its old value; as the carpenter's stretched cord, if you hold your ear close enough, is musical in the breeze. "Things more excellent than every image," says Jamblichus, "are expressed through images." Things admit of being used as symbols because nature is a symbol, in the whole, and in every part. Every line we can draw in the sand has expression; and there is no body without its spirit or genius. All form is an effect of character; all condition, of the quality of the life; all harmony, of health; and for this reason a perception of beauty should be sympathetic, or proper only to the good. The beautiful rests on the foundations of the necessary. The soul makes the body, as the wise Spenser teaches:—

> "So every spirit, as it is more pure,
>   And hath in it the more of heavenly light,
>   So it the fairer body doth procure
>   To habit in, and it more fairly dight
>   With cheerful grace and amiable sight.
>   For, of the soul, the body form doth take,
>   For soul is form, and doth the body make."

Here we find ourselves suddenly not in a critical speculation but in a holy place, and should go very warily and reverently. We stand before the secret of the world, there where Being passes into Appearance and Unity into Variety.

The Universe is the externization of the soul. Wherever the life is, that bursts into appearance around it. Our science is sensual, and therefore superficial. The earth and the heavenly bodies, physics and chemistry, we sensually treat, as if they were self-existent; but these are the retinue of that Being we have. "The mighty heaven," said Proclus, "exhibits, in its transfigurations, clear images of the splendor of intellectual perceptions; being moved in conjunction with the unapparent periods of intellectual natures." Therefore science always goes abreast with the just elevation of the man, keeping step with religion and metaphysics; or the state of science is an index of our self-knowledge. Since every thing in nature answers to a moral power, if any phenomenon remains brute and dark it is because the corresponding faculty in the observer is not yet active.

No wonder then, if these waters be so deep, that we hover over them with a religious regard. The beauty of the fable proves the importance of the sense; to the poet, and to all others; or, if you please, every man is so far a poet as to be susceptible of these enchantments of nature; for all men have the thoughts whereof the universe is the celebration. I find that the fascination resides in the symbol. Who loves nature? Who does not? Is it only poets, and men of leisure and cultivation, who live with her? No; but also hunters, farmers, grooms and butchers, though they express their affection in their choice of life and not in their choice of words. The writer wonders what the coachman or the hunter values in riding, in horses and dogs. It is not superficial qualities. When you talk with him he holds these at as slight a rate as you. His worship is sympathetic; he has no definitions, but he is commanded in nature by the living power which he feels to be there present. No imitation or playing of these things would content him; he loves the earnest of the north wind, of rain, of stone and wood and iron. A beauty not explicable is dearer than a beauty which we can see to the end of. It is nature the symbol, nature certifying the supernatural, body overflowed by life which he worships with coarse but sincere rites.

The inwardness and mystery of this attachment drive men of every class to the use of emblems. The schools of poets and philosophers are not more intoxicated with their symbols than the populace with theirs. In our political parties, compute the power of badges and emblems. See the great ball which they roll from Baltimore to Bunker Hill! In the political processions, Lowell goes in a loom, and Lynn in a shoe, and Salem in a ship. Witness the cider-barrel, the log-cabin, the hickory-stick, the palmetto, and all the cognizances of party. See the power of national emblems. Some stars, lilies, leopards, a crescent, a lion, an eagle, or other figure which came into credit God knows how, on an old rag of bunting, blowing in the wind on a fort at the ends of the earth, shall make the blood tingle under the rudest or the most conventional exterior. The people fancy they hate poetry, and they are all poets and mystics!

Beyond this universality of the symbolic language, we are apprised of the divineness of this superior use of things, whereby the world is a temple whose walls are covered with emblems, pictures and commandments of the Deity—in this, that there is no fact in nature which does not carry the whole sense of nature; and the distinctions which we make in events and in affairs, of low and high, honest and base, disappear when nature is used as a symbol. Thought makes everything fit for use. The vocabulary of an omniscient man would embrace words and images excluded from polite conversation. What would be base, or even obscene, to the obscene, becomes illustrious, spoken in a new connection of thought. The piety of the Hebrew prophets purges their grossness. The circumcision is an example of the power of poetry to raise the low and offensive. Small and mean things serve as well as great symbols. The meaner the type by which a law is expressed, the more pungent it is, and the more lasting in the memories of men; just as we choose the smallest box or case in which any needful utensil can be carried. Bare lists of words are found suggestive to an imaginative and excited mind; as it is related of Lord Chatham that he was accustomed to read in Bailey's Dictionary when he was preparing to speak in Parliament. The poorest experience is rich enough for all the purposes of expressing thought. Why covet a knowledge of new facts? Day and night, house and garden, a few books, a few actions, serve us as well as would all trades and all spectacles. We are far from having exhausted the significance of the few symbols we use. We can come to use them yet with a terrible simplicity. It does not need that a poem should be long. Every word was once a poem. Every new relation is a new word.

Also we use defects and deformities to a sacred purpose, so expressing our sense that the evils of the world are such only to the evil eye. In the old mythology, mythologists observe, defects are ascribed to divine natures, as lameness to Vulcan, blindness to Cupid, and the like—to signify exuberances.

For as it is dislocation and detachment from the life of God that makes things ugly, the poet, who re-attaches things to nature and the Whole—re-attaching even artificial things and violation of nature, to nature, by a deeper insight—disposes very easily of the most disagreeable facts. Readers of poetry see the factory-village and the railway, and fancy that the poetry of the landscape is broken up by these; for these works of art are not yet consecrated in their reading; but the poet sees them fall within the great Order not less than the beehive or the spider's geometrical web. Nature adopts them very fast into her vital circles, and the gliding train of cars she loves like her own. Besides, in a centred mind, it signifies nothing how many mechanical inventions you exhibit. Though you add millions, and never so surprising, the fact of mechanics has not gained a grain's weight. The spiritual fact remains unalterable, by many or by few particulars; as no mountain is of any appreciable height to break the curve of the sphere. A shrewd country-boy goes to the city for the first time, and the complacent citizen is not satisfied with his little wonder. It is not that he does not see all the fine houses and know that he never saw such before, but he disposes of them as easily as the poet finds place for the railway. The chief value of the new fact is to enhance the great and constant fact of Life, which can dwarf any and every circumstance, and to which the belt of wampum and the commerce of America are alike.

The world being thus put under the mind for verb and noun, the poet is he who can articulate it. For though life is great, and fascinates and absorbs; and though all men are intelligent of the symbols through which it is named; yet they cannot originally use them. We are symbols and inhabit symbols; workmen, work, and tools, words and things, birth and death, all are emblems; but we sympathize with the symbols, and being infatuated with the economical uses of things, we do not know that they are thoughts. The poet, by an ulterior intellectual perception, gives them a power which makes their old use forgotten, and puts eyes and a tongue into every dumb and inanimate object. He perceives the independence of the thought on the symbol, the stability of the thought, the accidency and fugacity of the symbol. As the eyes of Lyncæus were said to see through the earth, so the poet turns the world to glass, and shows us all things in their right series and procession. For through that better perception he stands one step nearer to things, and sees the flowing or metamorphosis; perceives that thought is multiform; that within the form of every creature is a force impelling it to ascend into a higher form; and following with his eyes the life, uses the forms which express that life, and so his speech flows with the flowing of nature. All the facts of the animal economy, sex, nutriment, gestation, birth, growth, are symbols of the passage of the world into the soul of man, to suffer there a change and reappear a new and higher fact. He uses forms according to the life, and not according to the form. This is true science. The poet alone knows astronomy, chemistry, vegetation and animation, for he does not stop at these facts, but employs them as signs. He knows why the plain or meadow of space was strown with these flowers we call suns and moons and stars; why the great deep is adorned with animals, with men, and gods; for in every word he speaks he rides on them as the horses of thought.

By virtue of this science the poet is the Namer or Language-maker, naming things sometimes after their appearance, sometimes after their essence, and giving to every one its own name and not another's, thereby rejoicing the intellect, which delights in detachments or boundary. The poets made all the words, and therefore language is the archives of history, and, if we must say it, a sort of tomb of the muses. For though the origin of most of our words is forgotten, each word was at first a stroke of genius, and obtained currency because for the moment it symbolized the world to the first speaker and to the hearer. The etymologist finds the deadest word to have been once a brilliant picture. Language is fossil poetry. As the limestone of the continent consists of infinite masses of the shells of animalcules, so language is made up of images or tropes, which now, in their secondary use, have long ceased to remind us of their poetic origin. But the poet names the thing because he sees it, or comes one step nearer to it than any other. This expression or naming is not art, but a second nature, grown out of the first, as a leaf out of a tree. What we call nature is a certain self-regulated motion or change; and nature does all things by her own hands, and does not leave another to baptize her but baptizes herself; and this

. . . .

through the metamorphosis again. I remember that a certain poet described it to me thus:—

Genius is the activity which repairs the decays of things, whether wholly or partly of a material and finite kind. Nature, through all her kingdoms, insures herself. Nobody cares for planting the poor fungus; so she shakes down from the gills of one agaric countless spores, any one of which, being preserved, transmits new billions of spores to-morrow or next day. The new agaric of this hour has a chance which the old one had not. This atom of seed is thrown into a new place, not subject to the accidents which destroyed its parent two rods off. She makes a man; and having brought him to ripe age, she will no longer run the risk of losing this wonder at a blow, but she detaches from him a new self, that the kind may be safe from accidents to which the individual is exposed. So when the soul of the poet has come to ripeness of thought, she detaches and sends away from it its poems or songs—a fearless, sleepless, deathless progeny, which is not exposed to the accidents of the weary kingdom of time; a fearless, vivacious offspring, clad with wings (such was the virtue of the soul out of which they came) which carry them fast and far, and infix them irrecoverably into the hearts of men. These wings are the beauty of the poet's soul. The songs, thus flying immortal from their mortal parent, are pursued by clamorous flights of censures, which swarm in far greater numbers and threaten to devour them; but these last are not winged. At the end of a very short leap they fall plump down and rot, having received from the souls out of which they came no beautiful wings. But the melodies of the poet ascend and leap and pierce into the deeps of infinite time.

So far the bard taught me, using his freer speech. But nature has a higher end, in the production of new individuals, than security, namely *ascension*, or the passage of the soul into higher forms. I knew in my younger days the sculptor who made the statue of the youth which stands in the public garden. He was, as I remember, unable to tell directly what made him happy or unhappy, but by wonderful indirections he could tell. He rose one day, according to his habit, before the dawn, and saw the morning break, grand as the eternity out of which it came, and for many days after, he strove to express this tranquillity, and lo! his chisel had fashioned out of marble the form of a beautiful youth, Phosphorus, whose aspect is such that it is said all persons who look on it become silent. The poet also resigns himself to his mood, and that thought which agitated him is expressed, but *alter idem*, in a manner totally new. The expression is organic, or the new type which things themselves take when liberated. As, in the sun, objects paint their images on the retina of the eye, so they, sharing the aspiration of the whole universe, tend to paint a far more delicate copy of their essence in his mind. Like the metamorphosis of things into higher organic forms is their change into melodies. Over everything stands its dæmon or soul, and, as the form of the thing is reflected by the eye, so the soul of the thing is reflected by a melody. The sea, the mountain-ridge, Niagara, and every flower-bed, pre-exist, or super-exist, in pre-cantations, which sail like odors in the air, and when any man goes by with an ear sufficiently fine, he overhears them and endeavors to write down the notes without diluting or depraving them. And herein is the legitimation of criticism, in the mind's faith that the poems are a corrupt version of some text in nature with which they ought to be made to tally. A rhyme in one of our sonnets should not be less pleasing than the iterated nodes of a seashell, or the resembling difference of a group of flowers. The pairing of the birds is an idyl, not tedious as our idyls are; a tempest is a rough ode, without falsehood or rant; a summer, with its harvest sown, reaped and stored, is an epic song, subordinating how many admirably executed parts. Why should not the symmetry and truth that modulate these, glide into our spirits, and we participate the invention of nature?

This insight, which expresses itself by what is called Imagination, is a very high sort of seeing, which does not come by study, but by the intellect being where and what it sees; by sharing the path or circuit of things through forms, and so making them translucid to others. The path of things is silent. Will they suffer a speaker to go with them? A spy they will not suffer; a lover, a poet, is the transcendency of their own nature—him they will suffer. The condition of true naming, on the poet's part, is his resigning himself to the divine aura which breathes through forms, and accompanying that.

It is a secret which every intellectual man quickly learns, that beyond the energy of his possessed and conscious intellect he is capable of a new energy (as of an intellect doubled on itself), by abandonment to the nature of things; that beside his privacy of power as an individual man, there is a great public power on which he can draw, by unlocking, at all risks, his human doors, and suffering the ethereal tides to roll and circulate through him; then he is caught up into the life of the Universe, his speech is thunder, his thought is law, and his words are universally intelligible as the plants and animals. The poet knows that he speaks adequately then only when he speaks somewhat wildly, or "with the flower of the mind"; not with the intellect used as an organ, but with the intellect released from all service and suffered to take its direction from its celestial life; or as the ancients were wont to express themselves, not with intellect alone but with the intellect inebriated by nectar. As the traveller who has lost his way throws his reins on his horse's neck and trusts to the instinct of the animal to find his road, so must we do with the divine animal who carries us through this world. For if in any manner we can stimulate this instinct, new passages are opened for us into nature; the mind flows into and through things hardest and highest, and the metamorphosis is possible.

This is the reason why bards love wine, mead, narcotics, coffee, tea, opium, the fumes of sandalwood and tobacco, or whatever other procurers of animal exhilaration. All men avail themselves of such means as they can, to add this extraordinary power to their normal powers; and to this end they prize conversation, music, pictures, sculpture, dancing, theatres, travelling, war, mobs, fires, gaming, politics, or love, or science, or animal intoxication—which are several coarser or finer quasi-mechanical substitutes for the true nectar, which is the ravishment of the intellect by coming nearer to the fact. These are auxiliaries to the centrifugal tendency of a man, to his passage out into free space, and they help him to escape the custody of that body in which he is pent up, and of that jail-yard of individual relations in which he is enclosed. Hence a great number of such as were professionally expressers of Beauty, as painters, poets, musicians and actors, have been more than others wont to lead a life of pleasure and indulgence; all but the few who received the true nectar; and, as it was a spurious mode of attaining freedom, as it was an emancipation not into the heavens but into the freedom of baser places, they were punished for that advantage they won, by a dissipation and deterioration. But never can any advantage be taken of nature by a trick. The spirit of the world, the great calm presence of the Creator, comes not forth to the sorceries of opium or of wine. The sublime vision comes to the pure and simple soul in a clean and chaste body. That is not an inspiration, which we owe to narcotics, but some counterfeit excitement and fury. Milton says that the lyric poet may drink wine and live generously, but the epic poet, he who shall sing of the gods and their descent unto men, must drink water out of a wooden bowl. For poetry is not 'Devil's wine,' but God's wine. It is with this as it is with toys. We fill the hands and nurseries of our children with all manner of dolls, drums and horses; withdrawing their eyes from the plain face and sufficing objects of nature, the sun and moon, the animals, the water and stones, which should be their toys. So the poet's habit of living should be set on a key so low that the common influences should delight him. His cheerfulness should be the gift of the sunlight; the air should suffice for his inspiration, and he should be tipsy with water. That spirit which suffices quiet hearts, which seems to come forth to such from every dry knoll of sere grass, from every pine stump and half-imbedded stone on which the dull March sun shines, comes forth to the poor and hungry, and such as are of simple taste. If thou fill thy brain with Boston and New York, with fashion and covetousness, and wilt stimulate thy jaded senses with wine and French coffee, thou shalt find no radiance of wisdom in the lonely waste of the pine woods.

If the imagination intoxicates the poet, it is not inactive in other men. The metamorphosis excites in the beholder an emotion of joy. The use of symbols has a certain power of emancipation and exhilaration for all men. We seem to be touched by a wand which makes us dance and run about happily, like children. We are like persons who come out of a cave or cellar into the open air. This is the effect on us of tropes, fables, oracles and all poetic forms. Poets are thus liberating gods. Men have really got a new sense, and found within their world another world, or nest of worlds; for, the metamorphosis once seen, we divine that it does not stop. I will not now consider how much this makes the charm of algebra and the mathematics, which also have their tropes, but it is felt in every definition; as when Aristotle defines *space* to be an immovable vessel in which things are contained; or when Plato defines a *line* to be a flowing point; or *figure* to be a bound of solid; and many the like. What a joyful sense of freedom we have when Vitruvius announces the old opinion of artists that no architect can build any house well who does not know something of anatomy. When

Socrates, in Charmides, tells us that the soul is cured of its maladies by certain incantations, and that these incantations are beautiful reasons, from which temperance is generated in souls; when Plato calls the world an animal, and Timæus affirms that the plants also are animals; or affirms a man to be a heavenly tree, growing with his root, which is his head, upward; and, as George Chapman, following him, writes,

> "So in our tree of man, whose nervie root
> Springs in his top";—

when Orpheus speaks of hoariness as "that white flower which marks extreme old age"; when Proclus calls the universe the statue of the intellect; when Chaucer, in his praise of 'Gentilesse,' compares good blood in mean condition to fire, which, though carried to the darkest house betwixt this and the mount of Caucasus, will yet hold its natural office and burn as bright as if twenty thousand men did it behold; when John saw, in the Apocalypse, the ruin of the world through evil, and the stars fall from heaven as the fig tree casteth her untimely fruit; when Aesop reports the whole catalogue of common daily relations through the masquerade of birds and beasts; we take the cheerful hint of the immortality of our essence and its versatile habit and escapes, as when the gypsies say of themselves "it is in vain to hang them, they cannot die."

The poets are thus liberating gods. The ancient British bards had for the title of their order, "Those who are free throughout the world." They are free, and they make free. An imaginative book renders us much more service at first, by stimulating us through its tropes, than afterward when we arrive at the precise sense of the author. I think nothing is of any value in books excepting the transcendental and extraordinary. If a man is inflamed and carried away by his thought, to that degree that he forgets the authors and the public and heeds only this one dream which holds him like an insanity, let me read his paper, and you may have all the arguments and histories and criticism. All the value which attaches to Pythagoras, Paracelsus, Cornelius Agrippa, Cardan, Kepler, Swedenborg, Schelling, Oken, or any other who introduces questionable facts into his cosmogony, as angels, devils, magic, astrology, palmistry, mesmerism, and so on, is the certificate we have of departure from routine, and that there is a new witness. That also is the best success in conversation, the magic of liberty, which puts the world like a ball in our hands. How cheap even the liberty then seems; how mean to study, when an emotion communicates to the intellect the power to sap and upheave nature; how great the perspective! nations, times, systems, enter and disappear like threads in tapestry of large figure and many colors; dream delivers us to dream, and while the drunkenness lasts we will sell our bed, our philosophy, our religion, in our opulence.

There is good reason why we should prize this liberation. The fate of the poor shepherd, who, blinded and lost in the snowstorm, perishes in a drift within a few feet of his cottage door, is an emblem of the state of man. On the brink of the waters of life and truth, we are miserably dying. The inaccessibleness of every thought but that we are in, is wonderful. What if you come near to it; you are as remote when you are nearest as when you are farthest. Every thought is also a prison; every heaven is also a prison. Therefore we love the poet, the inventor, who in any form, whether in an ode or in an action or in looks and behavior, has yielded us a new thought. He unlocks our chains and admits us to a new scene.

This emancipation is dear to all men, and the power to impart it, as it must come from greater depth and scope of thought, is a measure of intellect. Therefore all books of the imagination endure, all which ascend to that truth that the writer sees nature beneath him, and uses it as his exponent. Every verse or sentence possessing this virtue will take care of its own immortality. The religions of the world are the ejaculations of a few imaginative men.

But the quality of the imagination is to flow, and not to freeze. The poet did not stop at the color or the form, but read their meaning; neither may he rest in this meaning, but he makes the same objects exponents of his new thought. Here is the difference betwixt the poet and the mystic, that the last nails a symbol to one sense, which was a true sense for a moment, but soon becomes old and false. For all symbols are fluxional; all language is vehicular and transitive, and is good, as ferries and horses are, for conveyance, not as farms and houses are, for homestead. Mysticism consists in the mistake of an accidental and individual symbol for an universal one. The morning-redness happens to be the favorite meteor to the eyes of Jacob Behmen, and comes to stand to him for truth and faith; and, he believes, should stand for the

. . . .

same realities to every reader. But the first reader prefers as naturally the symbol of a mother and child, or a gardener and his bulb, or a jeweller polishing a gem. Either of these, or of a myriad more, are equally good to the person to whom they are significant. Only they must be held lightly, and be very willingly translated into the equivalent terms which others use. And the mystic must be steadily told—All that you say is just as true without the tedious use of that symbol as with it. Let us have a little algebra, instead of this trite rhetoric—universal signs, instead of these village symbols —and we shall both be gainers. The history of hierarchies seems to show that all religious error consisted in making the symbol too stark and solid, and was at last nothing but an excess of the organ of language.

Swedenborg, of all men in the recent ages, stands eminently for the translator of nature into thought. I do not know the man in history to whom things stood so uniformly for words. Before him the metamorphosis continually plays. Everything on which his eye rests, obeys the impulses of moral nature. The figs become grapes whilst he eats them. When some of his angels affirmed a truth, the laurel twig which they held blossomed in their hands. The noise which at a distance appeared like gnashing and thumping, on coming nearer was found to be the voice of disputants. The men in one of his visions, seen in heavenly light, appeared like dragons, and seemed in darkness; but to each other they appeared as men, and when the light from heaven shone into their cabin, they complained of the darkness, and were compelled to shut the window that they might see.

There was this perception in him which makes the poet or seer an object of awe and terror, namely that the same man or society of men may wear one aspect to themselves and their companions, and a different aspect to higher intelligences. Certain priests, whom he describes as conversing very learnedly together, appeared to the children who were at some distance, like dead horses; and many the like misappearances. And instantly the mind inquires whether these fishes under the bridge, yonder oxen in the pasture, those dogs in the yard, are immutably fishes, oxen and dogs, or only so appear to me, and perchance to themselves appear upright men; and whether I appear as a man to all eyes. The Brahmins and Pythagoras propounded the same question, and if any poet has witnessed the transformation he doubtless found it in harmony with various experiences. We have all seen changes as considerable in wheat and caterpillars. He is the poet and shall draw us with love and terror, who sees through the flowing vest the firm nature, and can declare it.

I look in vain for the poet whom I describe. We do not with sufficient plainness or sufficient profoundness address ourselves to life, nor dare we chaunt our own times and social circumstance. If we filled the day with bravery, we should not shrink from celebrating it. Time and nature yield us many gifts, but not yet the timely man, the new religion, the reconciler, whom all things await. Dante's praise is that he dared to write his autobiography in colossal cipher, or into universality. We have yet had no genius in America, with tyrannous eye, which knew the value of our incomparable materials, and saw, in the barbarism and materialism of the times, another carnival of the same gods whose picture he so much admires in Homer; then in the Middle Age; then in Calvinism. Banks and tariffs, the newspaper and caucus, Methodism and Unitarianism, are flat and dull to dull people, but rest on the same foundations of wonder as the town of Troy and the temple of Delphi, and are as swiftly passing away. Our log-rolling, our stumps and their politics, our fisheries, our Negroes and Indians, our boats and our repudiations, the wrath of rogues and the pusillanimity of honest men, the northern trade, the southern planting, the western clearing, Oregon and Texas, are yet unsung. Yet America is a poem in our eyes; its ample geography dazzles the imagination, and it will not wait long for metres. If I have not found that excellent combination of gifts in my countrymen which I seek, neither could I aid myself to fix the idea of the poet by reading now and then in Chalmers's collection of five centuries of English poets. These are wits more than poets, though there have been poets among them. But when we adhere to the ideal of the poet, we have our difficulties even with Milton and Homer. Milton is too literary, and Homer too literal and historical.

But I am not wise enough for a national criticism, and must use the old largeness a little longer, to discharge my errand from the muse to the poet concerning his art.

Art is the path of the creator to his work. The paths or methods are ideal and eternal, though few men ever seen them; not the artist himself for years, or for a lifetime, unless he come into the conditions. The painter, the sculptor, the composer, the epic rhapsodist, the orator, all partake one desire, namely to express themselves symmetrically and abundantly, not dwarfishly and fragmentarily. They found or put themselves in certain conditions, as, the painter and sculptor before some impressive human figures; the orator into the assembly of the people; and the others in such scenes as each has found exciting to his intellect; and each presently feels the new desire. He hears a voice, he sees a beckoning. Then he is apprised, with wonder, what herds of dæmons hem him in. He can no more rest; he says, with the old painter, "By God it is in me and must go forth of me." He pursues a beauty, half seen, which flies before him. The poet pours out verses in every solitude. Most of the things he says are conventional, no doubt; but by and by he says something which is original and beautiful. That charms him. He would say nothing else but such things. In our way of talking we say 'That is yours, this is mine;' but the poet knows well that it is not his; that it is as strange and beautiful to him as to you; he would fain hear the like eloquence at length. Once having tasted this immortal ichor, he cannot have enough of it, and as an admirable creative power exists in these intellections, it is of the last importance that these things get spoken. What a little of all we know is said! What drops of all the sea of our science are baled up! and by what accident it is that these are exposed, when so many secrets sleep in nature! Hence the necessity of speech and song; hence these throbs and heart-beatings in the orator, at the door of the assembly, to the end namely that thought may be ejaculated as Logos, or Word.

Doubt not, O poet, but persist. Say 'It is in me, and shall out.' Stand there, balked and dumb, stuttering and stammering, hissed and hooted, stand and strive, until at last rage draw out of thee that *dream*-power which every night shows thee is thine own; a power transcending all limit and privacy, and by virtue of which a man is the conductor of the whole river of electricity. Nothing walks, or creeps, or grows, or exists, which must not in turn arise and walk before him as exponent of his meaning. Comes he to that power, his genius is no longer exhaustible. All the creatures by pairs and by tribes pour into his mind as into a Noah's ark, to come forth again to people a new world. This is like the stock of air for our respiration or for the combustion of our fireplace; not a measure of gallons, but the entire atmosphere if wanted. And therefore the rich poets, as Homer, Chaucer, Shakspeare, and

Raphael, have obviously no limits to their works except the limits of their lifetime, and resemble a mirror carried through the street, ready to render an image of every created thing.

O poet! a new nobility is conferred in groves and pastures, and not in castles or by the sword-blade any longer. The conditions are hard, but equal. Thou shalt leave the world, and know the muse only. Thou shalt not know any longer the times, customs, graces, politics, or opinions of men, but shalt take all from the muse. For the time of towns is tolled from the world by funereal chimes, but in nature the universal hours are counted by succeeding tribes of animals and plants, and by growth of joy on joy. God wills also that thou abdicate a manifold and duplex life, and that thou be content that others speak for thee. Others shall be thy gentlemen and shall represent all courtesy and worldly life for thee; others shall do the great and resounding actions also. Thou shalt lie close hid with nature, and canst not be afforded to the Capitol or the Exchange. The world is full of renunciations and apprenticeships, and this is thine; thou must pass for a fool and a churl for a long season. This is the screen and sheath in which Pan has protected his well-beloved flower, and thou shalt be known only to thine own, and they shall console thee with tenderest love. And thou shalt not be able to rehearse the names of thy friends in thy verse, for an old shame before the holy ideal. And this is the reward; that the ideal shall be real to thee, and the impressions of the actual world shall fall like summer rain, copious, but not troublesome to thy invulnerable essence. Thou shalt have the whole land for thy park and manor, the sea for thy bath and navigation, without tax and without envy; the woods and the rivers thou shalt own, and thou shalt possess that wherein others are only tenants and boarders. Thou true land-lord! sea-lord! air-lord! Wherever snow falls or water flows or birds fly, wherever day and night meet in twilight, wherever the blue heaven is hung by clouds or sown with stars, wherever are forms with transparent boundaries, wherever are outlets into celestial space, wherever is danger, and awe, and love—there is Beauty, plenteous as rain, shed for thee, and though thou shouldst walk the world over, thou shalt not be able to find a condition inopportune or ignoble.

EXPERIENCE

The lords of life, the lords of life—
I saw them pass,
In their own guise,
Like and unlike,
Portly and grim,
Use and Surprise,
Surface and Dream,
Succession swift, and spectral
  Wrong,
Temperament without a tongue,
And the inventor of the game
Omnipresent without name;
Some to see, some to be guessed,
They marched from east to west:
Little man, least of all,
Among the legs of his guardians tall,
Walked about with puzzled look:
Him by the hand dear Nature took;
Dearest Nature, strong and kind,
Whispered, 'Darling, never mind!
To-morrow they will wear another
  face,
The founder thou! these are thy
  race!"

WHERE DO we find ourselves? In a series of which we do not know the extremes, and believe that it has none. We wake and find ourselves on a stair; there are stairs below us, which we seem to have ascended; there are stairs above us, many a one, which go upward and out of sight. But the Genius which according to the old belief stands at the door by which we enter, and gives us the lethe to drink, that we may tell no tales, mixed the cup too strongly, and we cannot shake off the lethargy now at noonday. Sleep lingers all our lifetime about our eyes, as night hovers all day in the boughs of the fir-tree. All things swim and glitter. Our life is not so much threatened as our perception. Ghostlike we glide through nature, and should not know our place again. Did our birth fall in some fit of indigence and frugality in nature, that she was so sparing of her fire and so liberal of her earth that it appears to us that we lack the affirmative principle, and though we have health and reason, yet we have no superfluity of spirit for new creation? We have enough to live and bring the year about, but not an ounce to impart or to invest. Ah that our Genius were a little more of a genius! We are like millers on the lower levels of a stream, when the factories above them have exhausted the water. We too fancy that the upper people must have raised their dams.

    If any of us knew what we were doing, or where we are going, then when we think we best know! We do not know to-day whether we are busy or idle. In times when we thought ourselves indolent, we have afterwards discovered that much was accomplished and much was begun in us. All our days are so unprofitable while they pass, that 't is wonderful where or when we ever got anything of this which we call wisdom, poetry, virtue. We never got it on any dated calendar day. Some heavenly days must have been intercalated somewhere, like those that Hermes won with dice of the Moon, that Osiris might be born. It is said all martyrdoms looked mean when they were suffered. Every ship is a romantic object, except that we sail in. Embark, and the romance quits our vessel and hangs on every other sail in the horizon. Our life looks trivial, and we shun to record it. Men seem to have learned of the horizon the art of perpetual retreating and reference. 'Yonder uplands are rich pasturage, and my neighbor has fertile meadow, but my field,' says the querulous farmer, 'only holds the world together.' I quote another man's saying; unluckily that other withdraws himself in the same way, and quotes me. 'T is the trick of nature thus to degrade to-day; a good deal of buzz, and somewhere a result slipped magically in. Every roof is agreeable to the eye until it is lifted; then we find tragedy and moaning women and hard-eyed husbands and deluges of lethe, and the men ask, 'What's the news?' as if the old were so bad. How many individuals can we count in society? how many actions? how many opinions? So much of our time is preparation, so much is routine, and so much retrospect, that the pith of each man's genius contracts itself to a very few hours. The history of literature—take the net result of Tiraboschi, Warton, or Schlegel—is a sum of very few ideas and of very few original tales; all the rest being variation of these. So in this great society wide lying around us, a critical analysis would find very few spontaneous actions. It is almost all custom and gross sense. There are even few opinions, and these seem organic in the speakers, and do not disturb the universal necessity.

What opium is instilled into all disaster! It shows formidable as we approach it, but there is at last no rough rasping friction, but the most slippery sliding surfaces; we fall soft on a thought; *Ate Dea* is gentle—

"Over men's heads walking aloft,
With tender feet treading so soft."

People grieve and bemoan themselves, but it is not half so bad with them as they say. There are moods in which we court suffering, in the hope that here at least we shall find reality, sharp peaks and edges of truth. But it turns out to be scene-painting and counterfeit. The only thing grief has taught me is to know how shallow it is. That, like all the rest, plays about the surface, and never introduces me into the reality, for contact with which we would even pay the costly price of sons and lovers. Was it Boscovich who found out that bodies never come in contact? Well, souls never touch their objects. An innavigable sea washes with silent waves between us and the things we aim at and converse with. Grief too will make us idealists. In the death of my son, now more than two years ago, I seem to have lost a beautiful estate—no more. I cannot get it nearer to me. If tomorrow I should be informed of the bankruptcy of my principal debtors, the loss of my property would be a great inconvenience to me, perhaps, for many years; but it would leave me as it found me—neither better nor worse. So is it with this calamity; it does not touch me; something which I fancied was a part of me, which could not be torn away without tearing me nor enlarged without enriching me, falls off from me and leaves no scar. It was caducous. I grieve that grief can teach me nothing, nor carry me one step into real nature. The Indian who was laid under a curse that the wind should not blow on him, nor water flow to him, nor fire burn him, is a type of us all. The dearest events are summer-rain, and we the Para coats that shed every drop. Nothing is left us now but death. We look to that with a grim satisfaction, saying, There at least is reality that will not dodge us.

I take this evanescence and lubricity of all objects, which lets them slip through our fingers then when we clutch hardest, to be the most unhandsome part of our condition. Nature does not like to be observed, and likes that we should be her fools and playmates. We may have the sphere for our cricket-ball, but not a berry for our philosophy. Direct strokes she never gave us power to make; all our blows glance, all our hits are accidents. Our relations to each other are oblique and casual.

Dream delivers us to dream, and there is no end to illusion. Life is a train of moods like a string of beads, and as we pass through them they prove to be many-colored lenses which paint the world their own hue, and each shows only what lies in its focus. From the mountain you see the mountain. We animate what we can, and we see only what we animate. Nature and books belong to the eyes that see them. It depends on the mood of the man whether he shall see the sunset or the fine poem. There are always sunsets, and there is always genius; but only a few hours so serene that we can relish nature or criticism. The more or less depends on structure or temperament. Temperament is the iron wire on which the beads are strung. Of what use is fortune or talent to a cold and defective nature? Who cares what sensibility or discrimination a man has at some time shown, if he falls asleep in his chair? or if he laugh and giggle? or if he apologize? or is infected with egotism? or thinks of his dollar? or cannot go by food? or has gotten a child in his boyhood? Of what use is genius, if the organ is too convex or too concave and cannot find a focal distance within the actual horizon of human life? Of what use, if the brain is too cold or too hot, and the man does not care enough for results to stimulate him to experiment, and hold him up in it? or if the web is too finely woven, too irritable by pleasure and pain, so that life stagnates from too much reception without due outlet? Of what use to make heroic vows of amendment, if the same old law-breaker is to keep them? What cheer can the religious sentiment yield, when that is suspected to be secretly dependent on the seasons of the year and the state of the blood? I knew a witty physician who found the creed in the biliary duct, and used to affirm that if there was disease in the liver, the man became a Calvinist, and if that organ was sound, he became a Unitarian. Very mortifying is the reluctant experience that some unfriendly excess or imbecility neutralizes the promise of genius. We see young men who owe us a new world, so readily and lavishly they promise, but they never acquit the debt; they die young and dodge the account; or if they live they lose themselves in the crowd.

Temperament also enters fully into the system of illusions and shuts us in a prison of glass which we cannot see. There is an optical illusion about every person we meet. In truth they are all creatures of given temperament, which will appear in a given character, whose boundaries they will never pass; but we look at them, they seem alive, and we presume there is impulse in them. In the moment it seems impulse; in the year, in the lifetime, it turns out to be a certain uniform tune which the revolving barrel of the music-box must play. Men resist the conclusion in the morning, but adopt it as the evening wears on, that temper prevails over everything of time, place and condition,

. . . .

and is inconsumable in the flames of religion. Some modifications the
moral sentiment avails to impose, but the individual texture holds its
dominion, if not to bias the moral judgments, yet to fix the measure of
activity and of enjoyment.

I thus express the law as it is read from the platform of ordinary
life, but must not leave it without noticing the capital exception. For
temperament is a power which no man willingly hears any one praise
but himself. On the platform of physics we cannot resist the contract-
ing influences of so-called science. Temperament puts all divinity to
rout. I know the mental proclivity of physicians. I hear the chuckle of
the phrenologists. Theoretic kidnappers and slave-drivers, they esteem
each man the victim of another, who winds him round his finger by
knowing the law of his being; and, by such cheap signboards as the
color of his beard or the slope of his occiput, reads the inventory of his
fortunes and character. The grossest ignorance does not disgust like this
impudent knowingness. The physicians say they are not materialists;
but they are—Spirit is matter reduced to an extreme thinness: O *so*
thin! But the definition of *spiritual* should be, *that which is its own evidence*. What notions do they attach to love! what to religion! One
would not willingly pronounce these words in their hearing, and give
them the occasion to profane them. I saw a gracious gentleman who
adapts his conversation to the form of the head of the man he talks
with! I had fancied that the value of life lay in its inscrutable possibilities; in the fact that I never know, in addressing myself to a new
individual, what may befall me. I carry the keys of my castle in my
hand, ready to throw them at the feet of my lord, whenever and in what
disguise soever he shall appear. I know he is in the neighborhood, hidden among vagabonds. Shall I preclude my future by taking a high seat
and kindly adapting my conversation to the shape of heads? When I
come to that, the doctors shall buy me for a cent. 'But, sir, medical history; the report to the Institute; the proven facts!' I distrust the facts
and the inferences. Temperament is the veto or limitation-power in the
constitution, very justly applied to restrain an opposite excess in the
constitution, but absurdly offered as a bar to original equity. When
virtue is in presence, all subordinate powers sleep. On its own level, or
in view of nature, temperament is final. I see not, if one be once caught
in this trap of so-called sciences, any escape for the man from the links
of the chain of physical necessity. Given such an embryo, such a his-

tory must follow. On this platform one lives in a sty of sensualism, and would soon come to suicide. But it is impossible that the creative power should exclude itself. Into every intelligence there is a door which is never closed, through which the creator passes. The intellect, seeker of absolute truth, or the heart, lover of absolute good, intervenes for our succor, and at one whisper of these high powers we awake from ineffectual struggles with this nightmare. We hurl it into its own hell, and cannot again contract ourselves to so base a state.

The secret of the illusoriness is in the necessity of a succession of moods or objects. Gladly we would anchor, but the anchorage is quicksand. This onward trick of nature is too strong for us: *Pero si muove.* When at night I look at the moon and stars, I seem stationary, and they to hurry. Our love of the real draws us to permanence, but health of body consists in circulation, and sanity of mind in variety or facility of association. We need change of objects. Dedication to one thought is quickly odious. We house with the insane, and must humor them; then conversation dies out. Once I took such delight in Montaigne that I thought I should not need any other book; before that, in Shakspeare; then in Plutarch; then in Plotinus; at one time in Bacon; afterwards in Goethe; even in Bettine; but now I turn the pages of either of them languidly, whilst I still cherish their genius. So with pictures; each will bear an emphasis of attention once, which it cannot retain, though we fain would continue to be pleased in that manner. How strongly I have felt of pictures that when you have seen one well, you must take your leave of it; you shall never see it again. I have had good lessons from pictures which I have since seen without emotion or remark. A deduction must be made from the opinion which even the wise express on a new book or occurrence. Their opinion gives me tidings of their mood, and some vague guess at the new fact, but is nowise to be trusted as the lasting relation between that intellect and that thing. The child asks, 'Mamma, why don't I like the story as well as when you told it me yesterday?' Alas! child, it is even so with the oldest cherubim of knowledge. But will it answer thy question to say, Because thou wert born to a whole and this story is a particular? The reason of the pain this discovery causes us (and we make it late in respect to works of art and intellect) is the plaint of tragedy which murmurs from it in regard to persons, to friendship and love.

. . . .

That immobility and absence of elasticity which we find in the arts, we find with more pain in the artist. There is no power of expansion in men. Our friends early appear to us as representatives of certain ideas which they never pass or exceed. They stand on the brink of the ocean of thought and power, but they never take the single step that would bring them there. A man is like a bit of Labrador spar, which has no lustre as you turn it in your hand until you come to a particular angle; then it shows deep and beautiful colors. There is no adaptation or universal applicability in men, but each has his special talent, and the mastery of successful men consists in adroitly keeping themselves where and when that turn shall be oftenest to be practised. We do what we must, and call it by the best names we can, and would fain have the praise of having intended the result which ensues. I cannot recall any form of man who is not superfluous sometimes. But is not this pitiful? Life is not worth the taking, to do tricks in.

Of course it needs the whole society to give the symmetry we seek. The parti-colored wheel must revolve very fast to appear white. Something is earned too by conversing with so much folly and defect. In fine, whoever loses, we are always of the gaining party. Divinity is behind our failures and follies also. The plays of children are nonsense, but very educative nonsense. So it is with the largest and solemnest things, with commerce, government, church, marriage, and so with the history of every man's bread, and the ways by which he is to come by it. Like a bird which alights nowhere, but hops perpetually from bough to bough, is the Power which abides in no man and in no woman, but for a moment speaks from this one, and for another moment from that one.

But what help from these fineries or pedantries? What help from thought? Life is not dialectics. We, I think, in these times, have had lessons enough of the futility of criticism. Our young people have thought and written much on labor and reform and for all that they have written, neither the world nor themselves have got on a step. Intellectual tasting of life will not supersede muscular activity. If a man should consider the nicety of the passage of a piece of bread down his throat, he would starve. At Education Farm the noblest theory of life sat on the noblest figures of young men and maidens, quite powerless and melancholy. It would not rake or pitch a ton of hay; it would not rub down a horse; and the men and maidens it left pale and hungry.

A political orator wittily compared our party promises to western roads, which opened stately enough, with planted trees on either side to tempt the traveller, but soon became narrow and narrower and ended in a squirrel-track and ran up a tree. So does culture with us; it ends in headache. Unspeakably sad and barren does life look to those who a few months ago were dazzled with the splendor of the promise of the times. "There is now no longer any right course of action nor any self-devotion left among the Iranis." Objections and criticism we have had our fill of. There are objections to every course of life and action, and the practical wisdom infers an indifferency, from the omnipresence of objection. The whole frame of things preaches indifferency. Do not craze yourself with thinking, but go about your business anywhere. Life is not intellectual or critical, but sturdy. Its chief good is for well-mixed people who can enjoy what they find, without question. Nature hates peeping, and our mothers speak her very sense when they say, "Children, eat your victuals, and say no more of it." To fill the hour—that is happiness, to fill the hour and leave no crevice for a repentance or an approval. We live amid surfaces, and the true art of life is to skate well on them. Under the oldest mouldiest conventions a man of native force prospers just as well as in the newest world, and that by skill of handling and treatment. He can take hold anywhere. Life itself is a mixture of power and form, and will not bear the least excess of either. To finish the moment, to find the journey's end in every step of the road, to live the greatest number of good hours, is wisdom. It is not the part of men, but of fanatics, or of mathematicians if you will, to say that, the shortness of life considered, it is not worth caring whether for so short a duration we were sprawling in want or sitting high. Since our office is with moments, let us husband them. Five minutes of to-day are worth as much to me as five minutes in the next millennium. Let us be poised, and wise, and our own, to-day. Let us treat the men and women well; treat them as if they were real; perhaps they are. Men live in their fancy, like drunkards whose hands are too soft and tremulous for successful labor. It is a tempest of fancies, and the only ballast I know is a respect to the present hour. Without any shadow of doubt, amidst this vertigo of shows and politics, I settle myself ever the firmer in the creed that we should not postpone and refer and wish, but do broad justice where we are, by whomsoever we deal with, accepting our actual companions and circumstances, however humble or odious, as

the mystic officials to whom the universe has delegated its whole pleasure for us. If these are mean and malignant, their contentment, which
is the last victory of justice, is a more satisfying echo to the heart than
the voice of poets and the casual sympathy of admirable persons. I
think that however a thoughtful man may suffer from the defects and
absurdities of his company, he cannot without affectation deny to any
set of men and women a sensibility to extraordinary merit. The coarse
and frivolous have an instinct of superiority, if they have not a sympathy, and honor it in their blind capricious way with sincere homage.

The fine young people despise life, but in me, and in such as with
me are free from dyspepsia, and to whom a day is a sound and solid
good, it is a great excess of politeness to look scornful and to cry for
company. I am grown by sympathy a little eager and sentimental, but
leave me alone and I should relish every hour and what it brought me,
the potluck of the day, as heartily as the oldest gossip in the bar-room.
I am thankful for small mercies. I compared notes with one of my
friends who expects everything of the universe and is disappointed
when anything is less than the best, and I found that I begin at the
other extreme, expecting nothing, and am always full of thanks for
moderate goods. I accept the clangor and jangle of contrary tendencies.
I find my account in sots and bores also. They give a reality to the cir-
cumjacent picture which such a vanishing meteorous appearance can
ill spare. In the morning I awake and find the old world, wife, babes
and mother, Concord and Boston, the dear old spiritual world and even
the dear old devil not far off. If we will take the good we find, asking
no questions, we shall have heaping measures. The great gifts are not
got by analysis. Everything good is on the highway. The middle region
of our being is the temperate zone. We may climb into the thin and
cold realm of pure geometry and lifeless science, or sink into that of
sensation. Between these extremes is the equator of life, of thought, of
spirit, of poetry—a narrow belt. Moreover, in popular experience everything good is on the highway. A collector peeps into all the
picture-shops of Europe for a landscape of Poussin, a crayon-sketch of
Salvator; but the Transfiguration, the Last Judgment, the Communion
of Saint Jerome, and what are as transcendent as these, are on the walls
of the Vatican, the Uffizi, or the Louvre, where every footman may see
them; to say nothing of Nature's pictures in every street, of sunsets and
sunrises every day, and the sculpture of the human body never absent.

· ·

A collector recently bought at public auction, in London, for one hundred and fifty-seven guineas, an autograph of Shakspeare; but for nothing a school-boy can read Hamlet and can detect secrets of highest concernment yet unpublished therein. I think I will never read any but the commonest books—the Bible, Homer, Dante, Shakspeare and Milton. Then we are impatient of so public a life and planet, and run hither and thither for nooks and secrets. The imagination delights in the woodcraft of Indians, trappers and bee-hunters. We fancy that we are strangers, and not so intimately domesticated in the planet as the wild man and the wild beast and bird. But the exclusion reaches them also; reaches the climbing, flying, gliding, feathered and four-footed man. Fox and woodchuck, hawk and snipe and bittern, when nearly seen, have no more root in the deep world than man, and are just such superficial tenants of the globe. Then the new molecular philosophy shows astronomical interspaces betwixt atom and atom, shows that the world is all outside; it has no inside.

The mid-world is best. Nature, as we know her, is no saint. The lights of the church, the ascetics, Gentoos and corn-eaters, she does not distinguish by any favor. She comes eating and drinking and sinning. Her darlings, the great, the strong, the beautiful, are not children of our law; do not come out of the Sunday School, nor weigh their food, nor punctually keep the commandments. If we will be strong with her strength we must not harbor such disconsolate consciences, borrowed too from the consciences of other nations. We must set up the strong present tense against all the rumors of wrath, past or to come. So many things are unsettled which it is of the first importance to settle; and, pending their settlement, we will do as we do. Whilst the debate goes forward on the equity of commerce, and will not be closed for a century or two, New and Old England may keep shop. Law of copyright and international copyright is to be discussed, and in the interim we will sell our books for the most we can. Expediency of literature, reason of literature, lawfulness of writing down a thought, is questioned; much is to say on both sides, and, while the fight waxes hot, thou, dearest scholar, stick to thy foolish task, add a line every hour, and between whiles add a line. Right to hold land, right of property, is disputed, and the conventions convene, and before the vote is taken, dig away in your garden, and spend your earnings as a waif or godsend to all serene and beautiful purposes. Life itself is a bubble and a scepticism, and a sleep

. . . .

within a sleep. Grant it, and as much more as they will—but thou, God's darling! heed thy private dream; thou wilt not be missed in the scorning and scepticism; there are enough of them; stay there in thy closet and toil until the rest are agreed what to do about it. Thy sickness, they say, and thy puny habit require that thou do this or avoid that, but know that thy life is a flitting state, a tent for a night, and do thou, sick or well, finish that stint. Thou art sick, but shalt not be worse, and the universe, which holds thee dear, shall be the better.

Human life is made up of the two elements, power and form, and the proportion must be invariably kept if we would have it sweet and sound. Each of these elements in excess makes a mischief as hurtful as its defect. Everything runs to excess; every good quality is noxious if unmixed, and, to carry the danger to the edge of ruin, nature causes each man's peculiarity to superabound. Here, among the farms, we adduce the scholars as examples of this treachery. They are nature's victims of expression. You who see the artist, the orator, the poet, too near, and find their life no more excellent than that of mechanics or farmers, and themselves victims of partiality, very hollow and laggard, and pronounce them failures, not heroes, but quacks—conclude very reasonably that these arts are not for man, but are disease. Yet nature will not bear you out. Irresistible nature made men such, and makes legions more of such, every day. You love the boy reading in a book, gazing at a drawing or a cast; yet what are these millions who read and behold, but incipient writers and sculptors? Add a little more of that quality which now reads and sees, and they will seize the pen and chisel. And if one remembers how innocently he began to be an artist, he perceives that nature joined with his enemy. A man is a golden impossibility. The line he must walk is a hair's breadth. The wise through excess of wisdom is made a fool.

How easily, if fate would suffer it, we might keep forever these beautiful limits, and adjust ourselves, once for all, to the perfect calculation of the kingdom of known cause and effect. In the street and in the newspapers, life appears so plain a business that manly resolution and adherence to the multiplication-table through all weathers will insure success. But ah! presently comes a day, or is it only a half-hour, with its angel-whispering—which discomfits the conclusions of nations and of years! To-morrow again every thing looks real and angular, the habitual standards are reinstated, common-sense is as rare as genius—is the basis of genius, and experience is hands and feet to every enterprise; and yet, he who should do his business on this understanding would be quickly bankrupt. Power keeps quite another road than the turnpikes of choice and will; namely the subterranean and invisible tunnels and channels of life. It is ridiculous that we are diplomatists, and doctors, and considerate people; there are no dupes like these. Life is a series of surprises, and would not be worth taking or keeping if it were not. God delights to isolate us every day, and hide from us the past and the future. We would look about us, but with grand politeness he draws down before us an impenetrable screen of purest sky, and another behind us of purest sky. 'You will not remember,' he seems to say, 'and you will not expect.' All good conversation, manners and action come from a spontaneity which forgets usages and makes the moment great. Nature hates calculators; her methods are saltatory and impulsive. Man lives by pulses; our organic movements are such; and the chemical and ethereal agents are undulatory and alternate; and the mind goes antagonizing on, and never prospers but by fits. We thrive by casualties. Our chief experiences have been casual. The most attractive class of people are those who are powerful obliquely and not by the direct stroke; men of genius, but not yet accredited; one gets the cheer of their light without paying too great a tax. Theirs is the beauty of the bird or the morning light, and not of art. In the thought of genius there is always a surprise; and the moral sentiment is well called "the newness," for it is never other; as new to the oldest intelligence as to the young child; "the kingdom that cometh without observation." In like manner, for practical success, there must not be too much design. A man will not be observed in doing that which he can do best. There is a certain magic about his properest action which stupefies your powers of observation, so that though it is done before you, you wist not of it. The art of life has a pudency, and will not be exposed. Every man is an impossibility until he is born; every thing impossible until we see a success. The ardors of piety agree at last with the coldest scepticism—that nothing is of us or our works—that all is of God. Nature will not spare us the smallest leaf of laurel. All writing comes by the grace of God, and all doing and having. I would gladly be moral and keep due metes and bounds, which I dearly love, and allow the most to the will of man; but I have set my heart on honesty in this chapter, and I can see nothing at last, in success or failure, than more or less of vital force supplied from the Eternal. The results of life are uncalculated and uncalculable. The years teach much which the days never know. The persons who compose our company converse, and come and go, and design and execute many things, and somewhat comes of it all, but an unlooked-for result. The individual is always mistaken. He designed many things, and drew in other persons as coadjutors, quarrelled with some or all, blundered much, and something is done; all are a little advanced, but the individual is always mistaken. It turns out somewhat new and very unlike what he promised himself.

The ancients, struck with this irreducibleness of the elements of human life to calculation, exalted Chance into a divinity; but that is to stay too long at the spark, which glitters truly at one point, but the universe is warm with the latency of the same fire. The miracle of life which will not be expounded but will remain a miracle, introduces a new element. In the growth of the embryo, Sir Everard Home I think noticed that the evolution was not from one central point, but coactive from three or more points. Life has no memory. That which proceeds in succession might be remembered, but that which is coexistent, or ejaculated from a deeper cause, as yet far from being conscious, knows not its own tendency. So is it with us, now sceptical or without unity, because immersed in forms and effects all seeming to be of equal yet hostile value, and now religious, whilst in the reception of spiritual law. Bear with these distractions, with this coetaneous growth of the parts; they will one day be members, and obey one will. On that one will, on that secret cause, they nail our attention and hope. Life is hereby melted into an expectation or a religion. Underneath the inharmonious and trivial particulars, is a musical perfection; the Ideal journeying always with us, the heaven without rent or seam. Do but observe the mode of our illumination. When I converse with a profound mind, or if at any time being alone I have good thoughts, I do not at once arrive at satisfactions, as when, being thirsty, I drink water; or go to the fire, being cold; no! but I am at first apprised of my vicinity to a new and excellent region of life. By persisting to read or to think, this region gives further sign of itself, as it were in flashes of light, in sudden discoveries of its profound beauty and repose, as if the clouds that covered it parted at intervals and showed the approaching traveller the inland mountains, with the tranquil eternal meadows spread at their base,

whereon flocks graze and shepherds pipe and dance. But every insight
from this realm of thought is felt as initial, and promises a sequel. I do
not make it; I arrive there, and behold what was there already. I make!
O no! I clap my hands in infantine joy and amazement before the first
opening to me of this august magnificence, old with the love and
homage of innumerable ages, young with the life of life, the sunbright
Mecca of the desert. And what a future it opens! I feel a new heart
beating with the love of the new beauty. I am ready to die out of nature
and be born again into this new yet unapproachable America I have
found in the West:

> "Since neither now nor yesterday began
> These thoughts, which have been ever, nor yet can
> A man be found who their first entrance knew."

If I have described life as a flux of moods, I must now add that there
is that in us which changes not and which ranks all sensations and
states of mind. The consciousness in each man is a sliding scale, which
identifies him now with the First Cause, and now with the flesh of his
body; life above life, in infinite degrees. The sentiment from which it
sprung determines the dignity of any deed, and the question ever is,
not what you have done or forborne, but at whose command you have
done or forborne it.

Fortune, Minerva, Muse, Holy Ghost—these are quaint names, too
narrow to cover this unbounded substance. The baffled intellect must
still kneel before this cause, which refuses to be named—ineffable
cause, which every fine genius has essayed to represent by some
emphatic symbol, as, Thales by water, Anaximenes by air, Anaxagoras
by (Νοῦς) thought, Zoroaster by fire, Jesus and the moderns by love;
and the metaphor of each has become a national religion. The Chinese
Mencius has not been the least successful in his generalization. "I fully
understand language," he said, "and nourish well my vast-flowing
vigor." "I beg to ask what you call vast-flowing vigor?" said his companion. "The explanation," replied Mencius, "is difficult. This vigor
is supremely great, and in the highest degree unbending. Nourish it
correctly and do it no injury, and it will fill up the vacancy between
heaven and earth. This vigor accords with and assists justice and reason, and leaves no hunger." In our more correct writing we give to this

. . . .

generalization the name of Being, and thereby confess that we have arrived as far as we can go. Suffice it for the joy of the universe that we have not arrived at a wall, but at interminable oceans. Our life seems not present so much as prospective; not for the affairs on which it is wasted, but as a hint of this vast-flowing vigor. Most of life seems to be mere advertisement of faculty; information is given us not to sell ourselves cheap; that we are very great. So, in particulars, our greatness is always in a tendency or direction, not in an action. It is for us to believe in the rule, not in the exception. The noble are thus known from the ignoble. So in accepting the leading of the sentiments, it is not what we believe concerning the immortality of the soul or the like, but *the universal impulse to believe*, that is the material circumstance and is the principal fact in the history of the globe. Shall we describe this cause as that which works directly? The spirit is not helpless or needful of mediate organs. It has plentiful powers and direct effects. I am explained without explaining, I am felt without acting, and where I am not. Therefore all just persons are satisfied with their own praise. They refuse to explain themselves, and are content that new actions should do them that office. They believe that we communicate without speech and above speech, and that no right action of ours is quite unaffecting to our friends, at whatever distance; for the influence of action is not to be measured by miles. Why should I fret myself because a circumstance has occurred which hinders my presence where I was expected? If I am not at the meeting, my presence where I am should be as useful to the commonwealth of friendship and wisdom, as would be my presence in that place. I exert the same quality of power in all places. Thus journeys the mighty Ideal before us; it never was known to fall into the rear. No man ever came to an experience which was satiating, but his good is tidings of a better. Onward and onward! In liberated moments we know that a new picture of life and duty is already possible; the elements already exist in many minds around you of a doctrine of life which shall transcend any written record we have. The new statement will comprise the scepticisms as well as the faiths of society, and out of unbeliefs a creed shall be formed. For scepticisms are not gratuitous or lawless, but are limitations of the affirmative statement, and the new philosophy must take them in and make affirmations outside of them, just as much as it must include the oldest beliefs.

It is very unhappy, but too late to be helped, the discovery we have made that we exist. That discovery is called the Fall of Man. Ever afterwards we suspect our instruments. We have learned that we do not see directly, but mediately, and that we have no means of correcting these colored and distorting lenses which we are, or of computing the amount of their errors. Perhaps these subject-lenses have a creative power; perhaps there are no objects. Once we lived in what we saw; now, the rapaciousness of this new power, which threatens to absorb all things, engages us. Nature, art, persons, letters, religions, objects, successively tumble in, and God is but one of its ideas. Nature and literature are subjective phenomena; every evil and every good thing is a shadow which we cast. The street is full of humiliations to the proud. As the fop contrived to dress his bailiffs in his livery and make them wait on his guests at table, so the chagrins which the bad heart gives off as bubbles, at once take form as ladies and gentlemen in the street, shopmen or barkeepers in hotels, and threaten or insult whatever is threatenable and insultable in us. 'T is the same with our idolatries. People forget that it is the eye which makes the horizon, and the rounding mind's eye which makes this or that man a type or representative of humanity, with the name of hero or saint. Jesus, the "providential man," is a good man on whom many people are agreed that these optical laws shall take effect. By love on one part and by forbearance to press objection on the other part, it is for a time settled that we will look at him in the centre of the horizon, and ascribe to him the properties that will attach to any man so seen. But the longest love or aversion has a speedy term. The great and crescive self, rooted in absolute nature, supplants all relative existence and ruins the kingdom of mortal friendship and love. Marriage (in what is called the spiritual world) is impossible, because of the inequality between every subject and every object. The subject is the receiver of Godhead, and at every comparison must feel his being enhanced by that cryptic might. Though not in energy, yet by presence, this magazine of substance cannot be otherwise than felt; nor can any force of intellect attribute to the object the proper deity which sleeps or wakes forever in every subject. Never can love make consciousness and ascription equal in force. There will be the same gulf between every me and thee as between the original and the picture. The universe is the bride of the soul. All private sympathy is particular. Two human beings are like globes, which can touch only in a point, and whilst they remain in contact all other points of each of the spheres are inert; their turn must also come, and the longer a particular union lasts the more energy of appetency the parts not in union acquire.

Life will be imaged, but cannot be divided nor doubled. Any invasion of its unity would be chaos. The soul is not twin-born but the only begotten, and though revealing itself as child in time, child in appearance, is of a fatal and universal power, admitting no co-life. Every day, every act betrays the ill-concealed deity. We believe in ourselves as we do not believe in others. We permit all things to ourselves, and that which we call sin in others is experiment for us. It is an instance of our faith in ourselves that men never speak of crime as lightly as they think; or every man thinks a latitude safe for himself which is nowise to be indulged to another. The act looks very differently on the inside and on the outside; in its quality and in its consequences. Murder in the murderer is no such ruinous thought as poets and romancers will have it; it does not unsettle him or fright him from his ordinary notice of trifles; it is an act quite easy to be contemplated; but in its sequel it turns out to be a horrible jangle and confounding of all relations. Especially the crimes that spring from love seem right and fair from the actor's point of view, but when acted are found destructive of society. No man at last believes that he can be lost, or that the crime in him is as black as in the felon. Because the intellect qualifies in our own case the moral judgments. For there is no crime to the intellect. That is antinomian or hypernomian, and judges law as well as fact. "It is worse than a crime, it is a blunder," said Napoleon, speaking the language of the intellect. To it, the world is a problem in mathematics or the science of quantity, and it leaves out praise and blame and all weak emotions. All stealing is comparative. If you come to absolutes, pray who does not steal? Saints are sad, because they behold sin (even when they speculate) from the point of view of the conscience, and not of the intellect; a confusion of thought. Sin, seen from the thought, is a diminution, or less; seen from the conscience or will, it is pravity or *bad*. The intellect names it shade, absence of light, and no essence. The conscience must feel it as essence, essential evil. This it is not; it has an objective existence, but no subjective.

Thus inevitably does the universe wear our color, and every object fall successively into the subject itself. The subject exists, the subject enlarges; all things sooner or later fall into place. As I am, so I see; use

what language we will, we can never say anything but what we are;
Hermes, Cadmus, Columbus, Newton, Bonaparte, are the mind's ministers. Instead of feeling a poverty when we encounter a great man, let
us treat the newcomer like a travelling geologist who passes through
our estate and shows us good slate, or limestone, or anthracite, in our
brush pasture. The partial action of each strong mind in one direction
is a telescope for the objects on which it is pointed. But every other part
of knowledge is to be pushed to the same extravagance, ere the soul
attains her due sphericity. Do you see that kitten chasing so prettily
her own tail? If you could look with her eyes you might see her surrounded with hundreds of figures performing complex dramas, with
tragic and comic issues, long conversations, many characters, many ups
and downs of fate—and meantime it is only puss and her tail. How
long before our masquerade will end its noise of tambourines, laughter
and shouting, and we shall find it was a solitary performance? A subject
and an object—it takes so much to make the galvanic circuit complete,
but magnitude adds nothing. What imports it whether it is Kepler and
the sphere, Columbus and America, a reader and his book, or puss with
her tail?

It is true that all the muses and love and religion hate these devel-
opments, and will find a way to punish the chemist who publishes in
the parlor the secrets of the laboratory. And we I cannot say too little of
our constitutional necessity of seeing things under private aspects, or
saturated with our humors. And yet is the God the native of these
bleak rocks. That need makes in morals the capital virtue of self-trust.
We must hold hard to this poverty, however scandalous, and by more
vigorous self-recoveries, after the sallies of action, possess our axis more
firmly. The life of truth is cold and so far mournful; but it is not the
slave of tears, contritions and perturbations. It does not attempt
another's work, nor adopt another's facts. It is a main lesson of wisdom to know your own from another's. I have learned that I cannot
dispose of other people's facts; but I possess such a key to my own as
persuades me, against all their denials, that they also have a key to
theirs. A sympathetic person is placed in the dilemma of a swimmer
among drowning men, who all catch at him, and if he give so much as
a leg or a finger they will drown him. They wish to be saved from the
mischiefs of their vices, but not from their vices. Charity would be
wasted on this poor waiting on the symptoms. A wise and hardy physi-

cian will say, *Come out of that*, as the first condition of advice.

In this our talking America we are ruined by our good nature and listening on all sides. This compliance takes away the power of being greatly useful. A man should not be able to look other than directly and forthright. A preoccupied attention is the only answer to the importunate frivolity of other people; an attention, and to an aim which makes their wants frivolous. This is a divine answer, and leaves no appeal and no hard thoughts. In Flaxman's drawing of the Eumenides of Aeschylus, Orestes supplicates Apollo, whilst the Furies sleep on the threshold. The face of the god expresses a shade of regret and compassion, but is calm with the conviction of the irreconcilableness of the two spheres. He is born into other politics, into the eternal and beautiful. The man at his feet asks for his interest in turmoils of the earth, into which his nature cannot enter. And the Eumenides there lying express pictorially this disparity. The god is surcharged with his divine destiny.

Illusion, Temperament, Succession, Surface, Surprise, Reality, Subjectiveness—these are threads on the loom of time, these are the lords of life. I dare not assume to give their order, but I name them as I find them in my way. I know better than to claim any completeness for my picture. I am a fragment, and this is a fragment of me. I can very confidently announce one or another law, which throws itself into relief and form, but I am too young yet by some ages to compile a code. I gossip for my hour concerning the eternal politics. I have seen many fair pictures not in vain. A wonderful time I have lived in. I am not the novice I was fourteen, nor yet seven years ago. Let who will ask, Where is the fruit? I find a private fruit sufficient. This is a fruit—that I should not ask for a rash effect from meditations, counsels and the hiving of truths. I should feel it pitiful to demand a result on this town and county, an overt effect on the instant month and year. The effect is deep and secular as the cause. It works on periods in which mortal lifetime is lost. All I know is reception; I am and I have: but I do not get, and when I have fancied I had gotten anything, I found I did not. I worship with wonder the great Fortune. My reception has been so large, that I am not annoyed by receiving this or that superabundantly. I say to the Genius, if he will pardon the proverb, *In for a mill, in for a million*. When I receive a new gift, I do not macerate my body to make the account square, for if I should die I could not make the account square. The benefit overran the merit the first day, and has overrun the merit ever since. The merit itself, so-called, I reckon part of the receiving.

Also that hankering after an overt or practical effect seems to me an apostasy. In good earnest I am willing to spare this most unnecessary deal of doing. Life wears to me a visionary face. Hardest roughest action is visionary also. It is but a choice between soft and turbulent dreams. People disparage knowing and the intellectual life, and urge doing. I am very content with knowing, if only I could know. That is an august entertainment, and would suffice me a great while. To know a little would be worth the expense of this world. I hear always the law of Adrastia, "that every soul which had acquired any truth, should be safe from harm until another period."

I know that the world I converse with in the city and in the farms, is not the world I think. I observe that difference, and shall observe it. One day I shall know the value and law of this discrepance. But I have not found that much was gained by manipular attempts to realize the world of thought. Many eager persons successively make an experiment in this way, and make themselves ridiculous. They acquire democratic manners, they foam at the mouth, they hate and deny. Worse, I observe that in the history of mankind there is never a solitary example of success—taking their own tests of success. I say this polemically, or in reply to the inquiry, Why not realize your world? But far be from me the despair which prejudges the law by a paltry empiricism; since there never was a right endeavor but it succeeded. Patience and patience, we shall win at the last. We must be very suspicious of the deceptions of the element of time. It takes a good deal of time to eat or to sleep, or to earn a hundred dollars, and a very little time to entertain a hope and an insight which becomes the light of our life. We dress our garden, eat our dinners, discuss the household with our wives, and these things make no impression, are forgotten next week; but, in the solitude to which every man is always returning, he has a sanity and revelations which in his passage into new worlds he will carry with him. Never mind the ridicule, never mind the defeat; up again, old heart?—it seems to say—there is victory yet for all justice; and the true romance which the world exists to realize will be the transformation of genius into practical power.

CHARACTER

The sun set; but set not his hope:
Stars rose; his faith was earlier up:
Fixed on the enormous galaxy,
Deeper and older seemed his eye:
And matched his sufferance sublime
The taciturnity of time.
He spoke, and words more soft than rain
Brought the Age of Gold again:
His action won such reverence sweet,
As hid all measure of the feat.

> Work of his hand
> He nor commends nor grieves:
> Pleads for itself the fact;
> As unrepenting Nature leaves
> Her every act.

I HAVE read that those who listened to Lord Chatham felt that there was something finer in the man than anything which he said. It has been complained of our brilliant English historian of the French Revolution that when he has told all his facts about Mirabeau, they do not justify his estimate of his genius. The Gracchi, Agis, Cleomenes, and others of Plutarch's heroes, do not in the record of facts equal their own fame. Sir Philip Sidney, the Earl of Essex, Sir Walter Raleigh, are men of great figure and of few deeds. We cannot find the smallest part of the personal weight of Washington in the narrative of his exploits. The authority of the name of Schiller is too great for his books. This inequality of the reputation to the works or the anecdotes is not accounted for by saying that the reverberation is longer than the thunder-clap, but somewhat resided in these men which begot an expectation that outran all their performance. The largest part of their power was latent. This is that which we call Character—a reserved force, which acts directly by presence and without means. It is conceived of as a certain undemonstrable force, a Familiar or Genius, by

. . . .

whose impulses the man is guided, but whose counsels he cannot impart; which is company for him, so that such men are often solitary, or if they chance to be social, do not need society but can entertain themselves very well alone. The purest literary talent appears at one time great, at another time small, but character is of a stellar and undiminishable greatness. What others effect by talent or by eloquence, this man accomplishes by some magnetism. "Half his strength he put not forth." His victories are by demonstration of superiority, and not by crossing of bayonets. He conquers because his arrival alters the face of affairs. "O Iole! how did you know that Hercules was a god?" "Because," answered Iole, "I was content the moment my eyes fell on him. When I beheld Theseus, I desired that I might see him offer battle, or at least guide his horses in the chariot-race; but Hercules did not wait for a contest; he conquered whether he stood, or walked, or sat, or whatever thing he did." Man, ordinarily a pendant to events, only half attached, and that awkwardly, to the world he lives in, in these examples appears to share the life of things, and to be an expression of the same laws which control the tides and the sun, numbers and quantities.

But to use a more modest illustration and nearer home, I observe that in our political elections, where this element, if it appears at all, can only occur in its coarsest form, we sufficiently understand its incomparable rate. The people know that they need in their representative much more than talent, namely the power to make his talent trusted. They cannot come at their ends by sending to Congress a learned, acute and fluent speaker, if he be not one who, before he was appointed by the people to represent them, was appointed by Almighty God to stand for a fact—invincibly persuaded of that fact in himself—so that the most confident and the most violent persons learn that here is resistance on which both impudence and terror are wasted, namely faith in a fact. The men who carry their points do not need to inquire of their constituents what they should say, but are themselves the country which they represent; nowhere are its emotions or opinions so instant and true as in them; nowhere so pure from a selfish infusion. The constituency at home hearkens to their words, watches the color of their cheek, and therein, as in a glass, dresses its own. Our public assemblies are pretty good tests of manly force. Our frank countrymen of the west and south have a taste for character, and like to know whether the

New Englander is a substantial man, or whether the hand can pass through him.

The same motive force appears in trade. There are geniuses in trade, as well as in war, or the State, or letters; and the reason why this or that man is fortunate is not to be told. It lies in the man; that is all anybody can tell you about it. See him and you will know as easily why he succeeds, as, if you see Napoleon, you would comprehend his fortune. In the new objects we recognize the old game, the habit of fronting the fact, and not dealing with it at second hand, through the perceptions of somebody else. Nature seems to authorize trade, as soon as you see the natural merchant, who appears not so much a private agent as her factor and Minister of Commerce. His natural probity combines with his insight into the fabric of society to put him above tricks, and he communicates to all his own faith that contracts are of no private interpretation. The habit of his mind is a reference to standards of natural equity and public advantage; and he inspires respect and the wish to deal with him, both for the quiet spirit of honor which attends him, and for the intellectual pastime which the spectacle of so much ability affords. This immensely stretched trade, which makes the capes of the Southern Ocean his wharves and the Atlantic Sea his familiar port, centres in his brain only; and nobody in the universe can make his place good. In his parlor I see very well that he has been at hard work this morning, with that knitted brow and that settled humor, which all his desire to be courteous cannot shake off. I see plainly how many firm acts have been done; how many valiant noes have this day been spoken, when others would have uttered ruinous yeas. I see, with the pride of art and skill of masterly arithmetic and power of remote combination, the consciousness of being an agent and playfellow of the original laws of the world. He too believes that none can supply him, and that a man must be born to trade or he cannot learn it.

This virtue draws the mind more when it appears in action to ends not so mixed. It works with most energy in the smallest companies and in private relations. In all cases it is an extraordinary and incomputable agent. The excess of physical strength is paralyzed by it. Higher natures overpower lower ones by affecting them with a certain sleep. The faculties are locked up, and offer no resistance. Perhaps that is the universal law. When the high cannot bring up the low to itself, it benumbs it, as man charms down the resistance of the lower animals.

Men exert on each other a similar occult power. How often has the influence of a true master realized all the tales of magic! A river of command seemed to run down from his eyes into all those who beheld him, a torrent of strong sad light, like an Ohio or Danube, which pervaded them with his thoughts and colored all events with the hue of his mind. "What means did you employ?" was the question asked of the wife of Concini, in regard to her treatment of Mary of Medici; and the answer was, "Only that influence which every strong mind has over a weak one." Cannot Cæsar in irons shuffle off the irons and transfer them to the person of Hippo or Thraso the turnkey? Is an iron handcuff so immutable a bond? Suppose a slaver on the coast of Guinea should take on board a gang of negroes which should contain persons of the stamp of Toussaint L'Ouverture: or, let us fancy, under these swarthy masks he has a gang of Washingtons in chains. When they arrive at Cuba, will the relative order of the ship's company be the same? Is there nothing but rope and iron? Is there no love, no reverence? Is there never a glimpse of right in a poor slave-captain's mind; and cannot these be supposed available to break or elude or in any manner overmatch the tension of an inch of iron ring?

This is a natural power, like light and heat, and all nature cooperates with it. The reason why we feel one man's presence and do not feel another's is as simple as gravity. Truth is the summit of being; justice is the application of it to affairs. All individual natures stand in a scale, according to the purity of this element in them. The will of the pure runs down from them into other natures, as water runs down from a higher into a lower vessel. This natural force is no more to be withstood than any other natural force. We can drive a stone upward for a moment into the air, but it is yet true that all stones will forever fall; and whatever instances can be quoted of unpunished theft, or of a lie which somebody credited, justice must prevail, and it is the privilege of truth to make itself believed. Character is this moral order seen through the medium of an individual nature. An individual is an encloser. Time and space, liberty and necessity, truth and thought, are left at large no longer. Now, the universe is a close or pound. All things exist in the man tinged with the manners of his soul. With what quality is in him he infuses all nature that he can reach; nor does he tend to lose himself in vastness, but, at how long a curve soever, all his regards return into his own good at last. He animates all he can, and he sees only what he animates. He encloses the world, as the patriot does his country, as a material basis for his character, and a theatre for action. A healthy soul stands united with the Just and the True, as the magnet arranges itself with the pole; so that he stands to all beholders like a transparent object betwixt them and the sun, and whoso journeys towards the sun, journeys towards that person. He is thus the medium of the highest influence to all who are not on the same level. Thus men of character are the conscience of the society to which they belong.

The natural measure of this power is the resistance of circumstances. Impure men consider life as it is reflected in opinions, events and persons. They cannot see the action until it is done. Yet its moral element preexisted in the actor, and its quality as right or wrong it was easy to predict. Everything in nature is bipolar, or has a positive and a negative pole. There is a male and a female, a spirit and a fact, a north and a south. Spirit is the positive, the event is the negative. Will is the north, action the south pole. Character may be ranked as having its natural place in the north. It shares the magnetic currents of the system. The feeble souls are drawn to the south or negative pole. They look at the profit or hurt of the action. They never behold a principle until it is lodged in a person. They do not wish to be lovely, but to be loved. Men of character like to hear of their faults; the other class do not like to hear of faults; they worship events; secure to them a fact, a connection, a certain chain of circumstances, and they will ask no more. The hero sees that the event is ancillary; it must follow him. A given order of events has no power to secure to him the satisfaction which the imagination attaches to it; the soul of goodness escapes from any set of circumstances; whilst prosperity belongs to a certain mind, and will introduce that power and victory which is its natural fruit, into any order of events. No change of circumstances can repair a defect of character. We boast our emancipation from many superstitions; but if we have broken any idols it is through a transfer of the idolatry. What have I gained, that I no longer immolate a bull to Jove or to Neptune, or a mouse to Hecate; that I do not tremble before the Eumenides, or the Catholic Purgatory, or the Calvinistic Judgment-day—if I quake at opinion, the public opinion as we call it; or at the threat of assault, or contumely, or bad neighbors, or poverty, or mutilation, or at the rumor of revolution, or of murder? If I quake, what matters it what I quake at? Our proper vice takes form in one or another shape, according to the sex, age, or temperament of the person, and, if we are capable of fear, will readily find terrors. The covetousness or the malignity which saddens me when I ascribe it to society, is my own. I am always environed by myself. On the other part, rectitude is a perpetual victory, celebrated not by cries of joy but by serenity, which is joy fixed or habitual. It is disgraceful to fly to events for confirmation of our truth and worth. The capitalist does not run every hour to the broker to coin his advantages into current money of the realm; he is satisfied to read in the quotations of the market that his stocks have risen. The same transport which the occurrence of the best events in the best order would occasion me, I must learn to taste purer in the perception that my position is every hour meliorated, and does already command those events I desire. That exultation is only to be checked by the foresight of an order of things so excellent as to throw all our prosperities into the deepest shade.

The face which character wears to me is self-sufficingness. I revere the person who is riches; so that I cannot think of him as alone, or poor, or exiled, or unhappy, or a client, but as perpetual patron, benefactor and beatified man. Character is centrality, the impossibility of being displaced or overset. A man should give us a sense of mass. Society is frivolous, and shreds its day into scraps, its conversation into ceremonies and escapes. But if I go to see an ingenious man I shall think myself poorly entertained if he give me nimble pieces of benevolence and etiquette; rather he shall stand stoutly in his place and let me apprehend, if it were only his resistance; know that I have encountered a new and positive quality; great refreshment for both of us. It is much that he does not accept the conventional opinions and practices. That non-conformity will remain a goad and remembrancer, and every inquirer will have to dispose of him, in the first place. There is nothing real or useful that is not a seat of war. Our houses ring with laughter and personal and critical gossip, but it helps little. But the uncivil, unavailable man, who is a problem and a threat to society, whom it cannot let pass in silence but must either worship or hate— and to whom all parties feel related, both the leaders of opinion and the obscure and eccentric—he helps; he puts America and Europe in the wrong, and destroys the scepticism which says, 'Man is a doll, let us eat and drink, 't is the best we can do,' by illuminating the untried and unknown. Acquiescence in the establishment and appeal to the public, indicate infirm faith, heads which are not clear, and which must see a house built before they can comprehend the plan of it. The wise man not only leaves out of his thought the many, but leaves out the few. Fountains, the self-moved, the absorbed, the commander because he is commanded, the assured, the primary—they are good; for these announce the instant presence of supreme power.

Our action should rest mathematically on our substance. In nature there are no false valuations. A pound of water in the ocean-tempest has no more gravity than in a midsummer pond. All things work exactly according to their quality and according to their quantity; attempt nothing they cannot do, except man only. He has pretension; he wishes and attempts things beyond his force. I read in a book of English memoirs, "Mr. Fox (afterwards Lord Holland) said, he must have the Treasury; he had served up to it, and would have it." Xenophon and his Ten Thousand were quite equal to what they attempted, and did it; so equal, that it was not suspected to be a grand and inimitable exploit. Yet there stands that fact unrepeated, a high-water mark in military history. Many have attempted it since, and not been equal to it. It is only on reality that any power of action can be based. No institution will be better than the institutor. I knew an amiable and accomplished person who undertook a practical reform, yet I was never able to find in him the enterprise of love he took in hand. He adopted it by ear and by the understanding from the books he had been reading. All his action was tentative, a piece of the city carried out into the fields, and was the city still, and no new fact, and could not inspire enthusiasm. Had there been something latent in the man, a terrible undemonstrated genius agitating and embarrassing his demeanor, we had watched for its advent. It is not enough that the intellect should see the evils and their remedy. We shall still postpone our existence, nor take the ground to which we are entitled, whilst it is only a thought and not a spirit that incites us. We have not yet served up to it.

These are properties of life, and another trait is the notice of incessant growth. Men should be intelligent and earnest. They must also make us feel that they have a controlling happy future opening before them, whose early twilights already kindle in the passing hour. The hero is misconceived and misreported; he cannot therefore wait to unravel any man's blunders; he is again on his road, adding new powers and honors to his domain and new claims on your heart, which will bankrupt you if you have loitered about the old things and have not kept your relation to him by adding to your wealth. New actions are the only apologies and explanations of old ones which the noble can bear to offer or to receive. If your friend has displeased you, you shall not sit down to consider it, for he has already lost all memory of the passage, and has doubled his power to serve you, and ere you can rise up again will burden you with blessings.

We have no pleasure in thinking of a benevolence that is only measured by its works. Love is inexhaustible, and if its estate is wasted, its granary emptied, still cheers and enriches, and the man, though he sleep, seems to purify the air and his house to adorn the landscape and strengthen the laws. People always recognize this difference. We know who is benevolent, by quite other means than the amount of subscription to soup-societies. It is only low merits that can be enumerated. Fear, when your friends say to you what you have done well, and say it through; but when they stand with uncertain timid looks of respect and half-dislike, and must suspend their judgment for years to come, you may begin to hope. Those who live to the future must always appear selfish to those who live to the present. Therefore it was droll in the good Riemer, who has written memoirs of Goethe, to make out a list of his donations and good deeds, as, so many hundred thalers given to Stilling, to Hegel, to Tischbein; a lucrative place found for Professor Voss, a post under the Grand Duke for Herder, a pension for Meyer, two professors recommended to foreign universities; etc., etc. The longest list of specifications of benefit would look very short. A man is a poor creature if he is to be measured so. For all these of course are exceptions, and the rule and hodiurnal life of a good man is benefaction. The true charity of Goethe is to be inferred from the account he gave Dr. Eckermann of the way in which he had spent his fortune. "Each bon mot of mine has cost a purse of gold. Half a million of my own money, the fortune I inherited, my salary and the large income derived from my writings for fifty years back, have been expended to instruct me in what I now know. I have besides seen," etc.

I own it is but poor chat and gossip to go to enumerate traits of this simple and rapid power, and we are painting the lightning with charcoal; but in these long nights and vacations I like to console myself so. Nothing but itself can copy it. A word warm from the heart enriches me. I surrender at discretion. How death-cold is literary genius before this fire of life! These are the touches that reanimate my heavy soul and give it eyes to pierce the dark of nature. I find, where I thought myself poor, there was I most rich. Thence comes a new intellectual exaltation, to be again rebuked by some new exhibition of character. Strange alternation of attraction and repulsion! Character repudiates intellect, yet excites it; and character passes into thought, is published so, and then is ashamed before new flashes of moral worth.

Character is nature in the highest form. It is of no use to ape it or to contend with it. Somewhat is possible of resistance, and of persistence, and of creation, to this power, which will foil all emulation.

This masterpiece is best where no hands but nature's have been laid on it. Care is taken that the greatly-destined shall slip up into life in the shade, with no thousand-eyed Athens to watch and blazon every new thought, every blushing emotion of young genius. Two persons lately, very young children of the most high God, have given me occasion for thought. When I explored the source of their sanctity and charm for the imagination, it seemed as if each answered, 'From my non-conformity; I never listened to your people's law, or to what they call their gospel, and wasted my time. I was content with the simple rural poverty of my own; hence this sweetness; my work never reminds you of that—is pure of that.' And nature advertises me in such persons that in democratic America she will not be democratized. How cloistered and constitutionally sequestered from the market and from scandal! It was only this morning that I sent away some wild flowers of these wood-gods. They are a relief from literature—these fresh draughts from the sources of thought and sentiment; as we read, in an age of polish and criticism, the first lines of written prose and verse of a nation. How captivating is their devotion to their favorite books, whether Aeschylus, Dante, Shakspeare, or Scott, as feeling that they have a stake in that book; who touches that, touches them—and especially the total solitude of the critic, the Patmos of thought from which he writes, in unconsciousness of any eyes that shall ever read this writing. Could they dream on still, as angels, and not wake to comparisons and to be flattered! Yet some natures are too good to be spoiled by praise, and wherever the vein of thought reaches down into the profound, there is no danger from vanity. Solemn friends will warn them of the danger of the head's being turned by the flourish of trumpets, but they can afford to smile. I remember the indignation of an eloquent

Methodist at the kind admonitions of a Doctor of Divinity—'My friend, a man can neither be praised nor insulted.' But forgive the counsels; they are very natural. I remember the thought which occurred to me when some ingenious and spiritual foreigners came to America, was, Have you been victimized in being brought hither?—or, prior to that, answer me this, 'Are you victimizable?'

As I have said, Nature keeps these sovereignties in her own hands, and however pertly our sermons and disciplines would divide some share of credit, and teach that the laws fashion the citizen, she goes her own gait and puts the wisest in the wrong. She makes very light of gospels and prophets, as one who has a great many more to produce and no excess of time to spare on any one. There is a class of men, individuals of which appear at long intervals, so eminently endowed with insight and virtue that they have been unanimously saluted as divine, and who seem to be an accumulation of that power we consider. Divine persons are character born, or, to borrow a phrase from Napoleon, they are victory organized. They are usually received with ill-will, because they are new and because they set a bound to the exaggeration that has been made of the personality of the last divine person. Nature never rhymes her children, nor makes two men alike. When we see a great man we fancy a resemblance to some historical person, and predict the sequel of his character and fortune; a result which he is sure to disappoint. None will ever solve the problem of his character according to our prejudice, but only in his own high unprecedented way. Character wants room; must not be crowded on by persons nor be judged from glimpses got in the press of affairs or on few occasions. It needs perspective, as a great building. It may not, probably does not, form relations rapidly and we should not require rash explanation, either on the popular ethics, or on our own, of its action.

I look on Sculpture as history. I do not think the Apollo and the Jove impossible in flesh and blood. Every trait which the artist recorded in stone he had seen in life, and better than his copy. We have seen many counterfeits, but we are born believers in great men. How easily we read in old books, when men were few, of the smallest action of the patriarchs. We require that a man should be so large and columnar in the landscape, that it should deserve to be recorded that he arose, and girded up his loins, and departed to such a place. The most credible pictures are those of majestic men who prevailed at their entrance, and convinced the senses; as happened to the eastern magian who was sent to test the merits of Zertusht or Zoroaster. "When the Yunani sage arrived at Balkh, the Persians tell us, Gushtasp appointed a day on which the Mobeds of every country should assemble, and a golden chair was placed for the Yunani sage. Then the beloved of Yezdam, the prophet Zertusht, advanced into the midst of the assembly. The Yunani sage, on seeing that chief, said, 'This form and this gait cannot lie, and nothing but truth can proceed from them.'" Plato said it was impossible not to believe in the children of the gods, "though they should speak without probable or necessary arguments." I should think myself very unhappy in my associates if I could not credit the best things in history. "John Bradshaw," says Milton, "appears like a consul, from whom the fasces are not to depart with the year; so that not on the tribunal only, but throughout his life, you would regard him as sitting in judgment upon kings." I find it more credible, since it is anterior information, that one man should *know heaven*, as the Chinese say, than that so many men should know the world. "The virtuous prince confronts the gods, without any misgiving. He waits a hundred ages till a sage comes, and does not doubt. He who confronts the gods, without any misgivings, knows heaven; he who waits a hundred ages until a sage comes, without doubting, knows men. Hence the virtuous prince moves, and for ages shows empire the way." But there is no need to seek remote examples. He is a dull observer whose experience has not taught him the reality and force of magic, as well as of chemistry. The coldest precisian cannot go abroad without encountering inexplicable influences. One man fastens an eye on him and the graves of the memory render up their dead; the secrets that make him wretched either to keep or to betray must be yielded; another, and he cannot speak, and the bones of his body seem to lose their cartilages; the entrance of a friend adds grace, boldness and eloquence to him; and there are persons he cannot choose but remember who gave a transcendent expansion to his thought, and kindled another life in his bosom.

What is so excellent as strict relations of amity, when they spring from this deep root? The sufficient reply to the skeptic who doubts the power and the furniture of man, is in that possibility of joyful intercourse with persons, which makes the faith and practice of all reasonable men. I know nothing which life has to offer so satisfying as the profound good understanding which can subsist, after much

exchange of good offices, between two virtuous men, each of whom is
sure of himself and sure of his friend. It is a happiness which postpones
all other gratifications, and makes politics, and commerce, and
churches, cheap. For when men shall meet as they ought, each a benefactor, a shower of stars, clothed with thoughts, with deeds, with
accomplishments, it should be the festival of nature which all things
announce. Of such friendship, love in the sexes is the first symbol, as
all other things are symbols of love. Those relations to the best men,
which, at one time, we reckoned the romances of youth, become, in the
progress of the character, the most solid enjoyment.

If it were possible to live in right relations with men!—if we could
abstain from asking anything of them, from asking their praise, or help,
or pity, and content us with compelling them through the virtue of the
eldest laws! Could we not deal with a few persons—with one person—
after the unwritten statutes, and make an experiment of their efficacy?
Could we not pay our friend the compliment of truth, of silence, of for-
bearing? Need we be so eager to seek him? If we are related, we shall
meet. It was a tradition of the ancient world that no metamorphosis
could hide a god from a god; and there is a Greek verse which runs—

"The Gods are to each other not unknown."

Friends also follow the laws of divine necessity; they gravitate to each
other, and cannot otherwise:—

When each the other shall avoid,
Shall each by each be most enjoyed.

Their relation is not made, but allowed. The gods must seat themselves
without seneschal in our Olympus, and as they can install themselves
by seniority divine. Society is spoiled if pains are taken, if the associates
are brought a mile to meet. And if it be not society, it is a mischievous,
low, degrading jangle, though made up of the best. All the greatness
of each is kept back and every foible in painful activity, as if the
Olympians should meet to exchange snuff-boxes.

Life goes headlong. We chase some flying scheme, or we are
hunted by some fear or command behind us. But if suddenly we
encounter a friend, we pause; our heat and hurry look foolish enough;

now pause, now possession is required, and the power to swell the moment from the resources of the heart. The moment is all, in all noble relations.

A divine person is the prophecy of the mind; a friend is the hope of the heart. Our beatitude waits for the fulfilment of these two in one. The ages are opening this moral force. All force is the shadow or symbol of that. Poetry is joyful and strong as it draws its inspiration thence. Men write their names on the world as they are filled with this. History has been mean; our nations have been mobs; we have never seen a man: that divine form we do not yet know, but only the dream and prophecy of such: we do not know the majestic manners which belong to him, which appease and exalt the beholder. We shall one day see that the most private is the most public energy, that quality atones for quantity, and grandeur of character acts in the dark, and succors them who never saw it. What greatness has yet appeared is beginnings and encouragements to us in this direction. The history of those gods and saints which the world has written and then worshipped, are documents of character. The ages have exulted in the manners of a youth who owed nothing to fortune, and who was hanged at the Tyburn of his nation, who, by the pure quality of his nature, shed an epic splendor around the facts of his death which has transfigured every particular into an universal symbol for the eyes of mankind. This great defeat is hitherto our highest fact. But the mind requires a victory to the senses; a force of character which will convert judge, jury, soldier and king; which will rule animal and mineral virtues, and blend with the courses of sap, of rivers, of winds, of stars, and of moral agents.

If we cannot attain at a bound to these grandeurs, at least let us do them homage. In society, high advantages are set down to the possessor as disadvantages. It requires the more wariness in our private estimates. I do not forgive in my friends the failure to know a fine character and to entertain it with thankful hospitality. When at last that which we have always longed for is arrived and shines on us with glad rays out of that far celestial land, then to be coarse, then to be critical and treat such a visitant with the jabber and suspicion of the streets, argues a vulgarity that seems to shut the doors of heaven. This is confusion, this the right insanity, when the soul no longer knows its own, nor where its allegiance, its religion, are due. Is there any religion but this, to know that wherever in the wide desert of being the holy sentiment we cherish has opened into a flower, it blooms for me? if none sees it, I see it; I am aware, if I alone, of the greatness of the fact. Whilst it blooms, I will keep sabbath or holy time, and suspend my gloom and my folly and jokes. Nature is indulged by the presence of this guest. There are many eyes that can detect and honor the prudent and household virtues; there are many that can discern Genius on his starry track, though the mob is incapable; but when that love which is all-suffering, all-abstaining, all-inspiring, which has vowed to itself that it will be a wretch and also a fool in this world sooner than soil its white hands by any compliances, comes into our streets and houses— only the pure and aspiring can know its face, and the only compliment they can pay it is to own it.

MANNERS

"How near to good is what is fair!
Which we no sooner see,
But with the lines and outward air
Our senses taken be.

Again yourselves compose,
And now put all the aptness on
Of Figure, that Proportion
Or Color can disclose;
That if those silent arts were lost,
Design and Picture, they might boast
From you a newer ground,
Instructed by the heightening sense
Of dignity and reverence
In their true motions found."

Ben Jonson.

HALF THE WORLD, it is said, knows not how the other half live. Our Exploring Expedition saw the Feejee islanders getting their dinner off human bones; and they are said to eat their own wives and children. The husbandry of the modern inhabitants of Gournou (west of old Thebes) is philosophical to a fault. To set up their housekeeping nothing is requisite but two or three earthen pots, a stone to grind meal, and a mat which is the bed. The house, namely a tomb, is ready without rent or taxes. No rain can pass through the roof, and there is no door, for there is no want of one, as there is nothing to lose. If the house do not please them, they walk out and enter another, as there are several hundreds at their command. "It is somewhat singular," adds Belzoni, to whom we owe this account, "to talk of happiness among people who live in sepulchres, among the corpses and rags of an ancient nation which they know nothing of." In the deserts of Borgoo the rock-Tibboos still dwell in caves, like cliff-swallows, and the language of these negroes is compared by their neighbors to the shrieking of bats and to the whistling of birds. Again, the Bornoos have no proper names; individuals are called after their height, thickness, or other accidental quality, and have nicknames merely. But the sale, the dates, the ivory, and the gold, for which these horrible regions are visited, find their way into countries where the purchaser and consumer can hardly be ranked in one race with these cannibals and man-stealers; countries where man serves himself with metals, wood, stone, glass, gum, cotton, silk and wool; honors himself with architecture; writes laws, and contrives to execute his will through the hands of many nations; and, especially, establishes a select society, running through all the countries of intelligent men, a self-constituted aristocracy, or fraternity of the best, which, without written law or exact usage of any kind, perpetuates itself, colonizes every new-planted island and adopts and makes its own whatever personal beauty or extraordinary native endowment anywhere appears.

What fact more conspicuous in modern history than the creation of the gentleman? Chivalry is that, and loyalty is that, and in English literature half the drama, and all the novels, from Sir Philip Sidney to Sir Walter Scott, paint this figure. The word *gentleman*, which, like the word *Christian*, must hereafter characterize the present and the few preceding centuries by the importance attached to it, is a homage to personal and incommunicable properties. Frivolous and fantastic additions have got associated with the name, but the steady interest of mankind in it must be attributed to the valuable properties which it designates. An element which unites all the most forcible persons of every country, makes them intelligible and agreeable to each other, and is somewhat so precise that it is at once felt if an individual lack the masonic sign—cannot be any casual product, but must be an average result of the character and faculties universally found in men. It seems a certain permanent average; as the atmosphere is a permanent composition, whilst so many gases are combined only to be decompounded. *Comme il faut*, is the Frenchman's description of good society: *as we must be*. It is a spontaneous fruit of talents and feelings of precisely that class who have most vigor, who take the lead in the world of this hour, and though far from pure, far from constituting the gladdest and highest tone of human feeling, it is as good as the whole society permits it to be. It is made of the spirit, more than of the talent of men, and is a compound result into which every great force enters as an ingredient, namely virtue, wit, beauty, wealth and power.

There is something equivocal in all the words in use to express the excellence of manners and social cultivation, because the quantities are fluxional, and the last effect is assumed by the senses as the cause. The word *gentleman* has not any correlative abstract to express the quality. *Gentility* is mean, and *gentilesse* is obsolete. But we must keep alive in the vernacular the distinction between *fashion*, a word of narrow and often sinister meaning, and the heroic character which *the gentleman* imports. The usual words, however, must be respected; they will be found to contain the root of the matter. The point of distinction in all this class of names, as courtesy, chivalry, fashion, and the like, is that the flower and fruit, not the grain of the tree, are contemplated. It is beauty which is the aim this time, and not worth. The result is now in question, although our words intimate well enough the popular feeling that the appearance supposes a substance. The gentleman is a man of truth, lord of his own actions, and expressing that lordship in his behavior; not in any manner dependent and servile, either on persons, or opinions, or possessions. Beyond this fact of truth and real force, the word denotes good-nature or benevolence: manhood first, and then gentleness. The popular notion certainly adds a condition of ease and fortune; but that is a natural result of personal force and love, that they should possess and dispense the goods of the world. In times of violence, every eminent person must fall in with many opportunities to approve his stoutness and worth; therefore every man's name that emerged at all from the mass in the feudal ages rattles in our ear like a flourish of trumpets. But personal force never goes out of fashion. That is still paramount to-day, and in the moving crowd of good society the men of valor and reality are known and rise to their natural place. The competition is transferred from war to politics and trade, but the personal force appears readily enough in these new arenas.

Power first, or no leading class. In politics and in trade, bruisers and pirates are of better promise than talkers and clerks. God knows that all sorts of gentlemen knock at the door; but whenever used in strictness and with any emphasis, the name will be found to point at original energy. It describes a man standing in his own right and working after untaught methods. In a good lord there must first be a good animal, at least to the extent of yielding the incomparable advantage of animal spirits. The ruling class must have more, but they must have these, giving in every company the sense of power, which makes things easy to be done which daunt the wise. The society of the energetic class, in their friendly and festive meetings, is full of courage and of attempts which intimidate the pale scholar. The courage which girls exhibit is like a battle of Lundy's Lane, or a sea-fight. The intellect relies on memory to make some supplies to face these extemporaneous squadrons. But memory is a base mendicant with basket and badge, in the presence of these sudden masters. The rulers of society must be up to the work of the world, and equal to their versatile office: men of the right Cæsarian pattern, who have great range of affinity. I am far from believing the timid maxim of Lord Falkland ("that for ceremony there must go two to it; since a bold fellow will go through the cunningest forms"), and am of opinion that the gentleman is the bold fellow whose forms are not to be broken through; and only that plenteous nature is rightful master which is the complement of whatever person it converses with. My gentleman gives the law where he is; he will outpray saints in chapel, outgeneral veterans in the field, and outshine all courtesy in the hall. He is good company for pirates and good with academicians; so that it is useless to fortify yourself against him; he has the private entrance to all minds, and I could as easily exclude myself, as him. The famous gentleman of Asia and Europe have been of this strong type; Saladin, Sapor, the Cid, Julius Cæsar, Scipio, Alexander, Pericles, and the lordliest personages. They sat very carelessly in their chairs, and were too excellent themselves, to value any condition at a high rate.

A plentiful fortune is reckoned necessary, in the popular judgment, to the completion of this man of the world; and it is a material deputy which walks through the dance which the first has led. Money is not essential, but this wide affinity is, which transcends the habits of clique and caste and makes itself felt by men of all classes. If the aristocrat is only valid in fashionable circles and not with truckmen, he will never be a leader in fashion; and if the man of the people cannot speak on equal terms with the gentleman, so that the gentleman shall perceive that he is already really of his own order, he is not to be feared. Diogenes, Socrates, and Epaminondas, are gentlemen of the best blood who have chosen the condition of poverty when that of wealth was equally open to them. I use these old names, but the men I speak of are my contemporaries. Fortune will not supply to every generation one of these well-appointed knights, but every collection of men furnishes some example of the class; and the politics of this country, and the trade of every town, are controlled by these hardy and irresponsible doers, who have invention to take the lead, and a broad sympathy which puts them in fellowship with crowds, and makes their action popular.

The manners of this class are observed and caught with devotion by men of taste. The association of these masters with each other and with men intelligent of their merits, is mutually agreeable and stimulating. The good forms, the happiest expressions of each, are repeated and adopted. By swift consent everything superfluous is dropped, everything graceful is renewed. Fine manners show themselves formidable to the uncultivated man. They are a subtler science of defence to parry and intimidate; but once matched by the skill of the other party, they drop the point of the sword—points and fences disappear, and the youth finds himself in a more transparent atmosphere, wherein life is a less troublesome game, and not a misunderstanding rises between the players. Manners aim to facilitate life, to get rid of impediments and bring the man pure to energize. They aid our dealing and conversation as a railway aids travelling, by getting rid of all avoidable obstructions of the road and leaving nothing to be conquered but pure space. These forms very soon become fixed, and a fine sense of propriety is cultivated with the more heed that it becomes a badge of social and civil distinctions. Thus grows up Fashion, an equivocal semblance, the most puissant, the most fantastic and frivolous, the most feared and followed, and which morals and violence assault in vain.

There exists a strict relation between the class of power and the exclusive and polished circles. The last are always filled or filling from the first. The strong men usually give some allowance even to the petulances of fashion, for that affinity they find in it. Napoleon, child of the revolution, destroyer of the old noblesse, ever ceased to court the Faubourg St. Germain; doubtless with the feeling that fashion is a homage to men of his stamp. Fashion, though in a strange way, represents all manly virtue. It is virtue gone to seed: it is a kind of posthumous honor. It does not often caress the great, but the children of the great: it is a hall of the Past. It usually sets its face against the great of this hour. Great men are not commonly in its halls; they are absent in the field: they are working, not triumphing. Fashion is made up of their children; of those who through the value and virtue of somebody, have acquired lustre to their name, marks of distinction, means of cultivation and generosity, and in their physical organization a certain health and excellence which secure to them, if not the highest power to work, yet high power to enjoy. The class of power, the working heroes, the Cortez, the Nelson, the Napoleon, see that this is the festivity and permanent celebration of such as they; that fashion is funded talent; is Mexico, Marengo and Trafalgar beaten out thin; that the brilliant names of fashion run back to just such busy names as their own, fifty or sixty years ago. They are the sowers, their sons shall be the reapers, and *their* sons, in the ordinary course of things, must yield the possession of the harvest to new competitors with keener eyes and stronger frames. The city is recruited from the country. In the year 1805, it is said, every legitimate monarch in Europe was imbecile. The city would have died out, rotted and exploded, long ago, but that it was reinforced from the fields. It is only country which came to town day before yesterday that is city and court to-day.

Aristocracy and fashion are certain inevitable results. These mutual selections are indestructible. If they provoke anger in the least favored class, and the excluded majority revenge themselves on the excluding minority by the strong hand and kill them, at once a new class finds itself at the top, as certainly as cream rises in a bowl of milk: and if the people should destroy class after class, until two men only were left, one of these would be the leader and would be involuntarily served and copied by the other. You may keep this minority out of sight and out of mind, but it is tenacious of life, and is one of the estates of the realm. I am the more struck with this tenacity when I see its work. It respects the administration of such unimportant matters, that we should not look for any durability in its rule. We sometimes meet men under some strong moral influence, as a patriotic, a literary, a religious movement, and feel that the moral sentiment rules man and nature. We think all other distinctions and ties will be slight and fugitive, this of caste or fashion for example; yet come from year to year and see how permanent that is, in this Boston or New York life of man, where too it has not the least countenance from the law of the land. Not in Egypt or in India a firmer or more impassable line. Here are associations whose ties go over and under and through it, a meeting of merchants, a military corps, a college class, a fire-club, a professional association, a political, a religious convention; the persons seem to draw inseparably near; yet, that assembly once dispersed, its members will not in the year meet again. Each returns to his degree in the scale of good society, porcelain remains porcelain, and earthen earthen. The objects of fashion may be frivolous, or fashion may be objectless, but the nature of this union and selection can be neither frivolous nor accidental. Each man's rank in that perfect graduation depends on some symmetry in his structure or some agreement in his structure to the symmetry of society. Its doors unbar instantaneously to a natural claim of their own kind. A natural gentleman finds his way in, and will keep the oldest patrician out who has lost his intrinsic rank. Fashion understands itself; good-breeding and personal superiority of whatever country readily fraternize with those of every other. The chiefs of savage tribes have distinguished themselves in London and Paris by the purity of their tournure.

To say what good of fashion we can, it rests on reality, and hates nothing so much as pretenders; to exclude and mystify pretenders and send them into everlasting 'Coventry,' is its delight. We contemn in turn every other gift of men of the world; but the habit even in little and the least matters of not appealing to any but our own sense of propriety, constitutes the foundation of all chivalry. There is almost no kind of self-reliance, so it be sane and proportioned, which fashion does not occasionally adopt and give it the freedom of its saloons. A sainted soul is always elegant, and, if it will, passes unchallenged into the most guarded ring. But so will Jock the teamster pass, in some crisis that brings him thither, and find favor, as long as his head is not giddy with the new circumstance, and the iron shoes do not wish to dance in waltzes and cotillons. For there is nothing settled in manners, but the laws of behavior yield to the energy of the individual. The maiden at her first ball, the countryman at a city dinner, believes that there is a ritual according to which every act and compliment must be performed, or the failing party must be cast out of this presence. Later they learn that good sense and character make their own forms every moment, and speak or abstain, take wine or refuse it, stay or go, sit in a chair or sprawl with children on the floor, or stand on their head, or what else soever, in a new and aboriginal way; and that strong will is always in fashion, let who will be unfashionable. All that fashion demands is composure and self-content. A circle of men perfectly well-bred would be a company of sensible persons in which every man's native manners and character appeared. If the fashionist have not this quality, he is nothing. We are such lovers of self-reliance that we excuse in a man many sins if he will show us a complete satisfaction in his position, which asks no leave to be, of mine, or any man's good opinion. But any deference to some eminent man or woman of the world, forfeits all privilege of nobility. He is an underling: I have nothing to do with him; I will speak with his master. A man should not go where he cannot carry his whole sphere or society with him—not bodily, the whole circle of his friends, but atmospherically. He should preserve in a new company the same attitude of mind and reality of relation which his daily associates draw him to, else he is shorn of his best beams, and will be an orphan in the merriest club. "If you could see Vich Ian Vohr with his tail on!" But Vich Ian Vohr must always carry his belongings in some fashion, if not added as honor, then severed as disgrace.

There will always be in society certain persons who are mercuries of its approbation, and whose glance will at any time determine for the curious their standing in the world. These are the chamberlains of the lesser gods. Accept their coldness as an omen of grace with the loftier deities, and allow them all their privilege. They are clear in their office, nor could they be thus formidable without their own merits. But do not measure the importance of this class by their pretension, or imagine that a fop can be the dispenser of honor and shame. They pass also at their just rate; for how can they otherwise, in circles which exist as a sort of herald's office for the sifting of character?

As the first thing man requires of man is reality, so that appears in all the forms of society. We pointedly, and by name, introduce the parties to each other. Know you before all heaven and earth, that this is Andrew, and this is Gregory—they look each other in the eye; they grasp each other's hand, to identify and signalize each other. It is a great satisfaction. A gentleman never dodges; his eyes look straight forward, and he assures the other party, first of all, that he has been met. For what is it that we seek, in so many visits and hospitalities? Is it your draperies, pictures and decorations? Or do we not insatiably ask, Was a man in the house? I may easily go into a great household where there is much substance, excellent provision for comfort, luxury and taste, and yet not encounter there any Amphitryon who shall subordinate these appendages. I may go into a cottage, and find a farmer who feels that he is the man I have come to see, and fronts me accordingly. It was therefore a very natural point of old feudal etiquette that a gentleman who received a visit, though it were of his sovereign, should not leave his roof, but should wait his arrival at the door of his house. No house, though it were the Tuileries or the Escurial, is good for anything without a master. And yet we are not often gratified by this hospitality. Everybody we know surrounds himself with a fine house, fine books, conservatory, gardens, equipage and all manner of toys, as screens to interpose between himself and his guest. Does it not seem as if man was of a very sly, elusive nature, and dreaded nothing so much as a full rencontre front to front with his fellow? It were unmerciful, I know, quite to abolish the use of these screens, which are of eminent convenience, whether the guest is too great or too little. We call together many friends who keep each other in play, or by luxuries and ornaments we amuse the young people, and guard our retirement. Or if perchance a searching realist comes to our gate, before whose eye we have no care to stand, then again we run to our curtain, and hide ourselves as Adam at the voice of the Lord God in the garden. Cardinal Caprara, the Pope's legate at Paris, defended himself from the glances of Napoleon by an immense pair of green spectacles. Napoleon remarked them, and speedily managed to rally them off: and yet Napoleon, in his turn, was not great enough, with eight hundred thousand troops at his back, to face a pair of freeborn eyes, but fenced himself with etiquette and within triple barriers of reserve; and, as all the world knows from Madame de Staël, was wont, when he found himself observed, to discharge his face of all expression. But emperors and rich men are by no means the most skilful masters of good manners. No rent-roll nor army-list can dignify skulking and dissimulation; and the first point of courtesy must always be truth, as really all the forms of good-breeding point that way.

I have just been reading, in Mr. Hazlitt's translation, Montaigne's account of his journey into Italy, and am struck with nothing more agreeably than the self-respecting fashions of the time. His arrival in each place, the arrival of a gentleman of France, is an event of some consequence. Wherever he goes he pays a visit to whatever prince or gentleman of note resides upon his road, as a duty to himself and to civilization. When he leaves any house in which he has lodged for a few weeks, he causes his arms to be painted and hung up as a perpetual sign to the house, as was the custom of gentlemen.

The complement of this graceful self-respect, and that of all the points of good-breeding I most require and insist upon, is deference. I like that every chair should be a throne, and hold a king. I prefer a tendency to stateliness to an excess of fellowship. Let the incommunicable objects of nature and the metaphysical isolation of man teach us independence. Let us not be too much acquainted. I would have a man enter his house through a hall filled with heroic and sacred sculptures, that he might not want the hint of tranquillity and self-poise. We should meet each morning as from foreign countries, and, spending the day together, should depart at night, as into foreign countries. In all things I would have the island of a man inviolate. Let us sit apart as the gods, talking from peak to peak all round Olympus. No degree of affection need invade this religion. This is myrrh and rosemary to keep the other sweet. Lovers should guard their strangeness. If they forgive too much, all slides into confusion and meanness. It is easy to push this deference to a Chinese etiquette; but coolness and absence of heat and haste indicate fine qualities. A gentleman makes no noise; a lady is serene. Proportionate is our disgust at those invaders who fill a studious house with blast and running, to secure some paltry convenience. Not less I dislike a low sympathy of each with his neighbor's needs. Must we have a good understanding with one another's palates? as foolish people who have lived long together know when each wants salt or sugar. I pray my companion, if he wishes for bread, to ask me for bread, and if he wishes for sassafras or arsenic, to ask me for them, and not to hold out his plate as if I knew already. Every natural function can be dignified by deliberation and privacy. Let us leave hurry to slaves. The compliments and ceremonies of our breeding should recall, however remotely, the grandeur of our destiny.

The flower of courtesy does not well bide handling, but if we dare to open another leaf and explore what parts go to its confirmation, we shall find also an intellectual quality. To the leaders of men, the brain as well as the flesh and the heart must furnish a proportion. Defect in manners is usually the defect of fine perceptions. Men are too coarsely made for the delicacy of beautiful carriage and customs. It is not quite sufficient to good-breeding, a union of kindness and independence. We imperatively require a perception of, and a homage to beauty in our companions. Other virtues are in request in the field and workyard, but a certain degree of taste is not to be spared in those we sit with. I could better eat with one who did not respect the truth or the laws than with a sloven and unpresentable person. Moral qualities rule the world, but at short distances the senses are despotic. The same discrimination of fit and fair runs out if with less rigor, into all parts of life. The average spirit of the energetic class is good sense, acting under certain limitations and to certain ends. It entertains every natural gift. Social in its nature, it respects everything which tends to unite men. It delights in measure. The love of beauty is mainly the love of measure or proportion. The person who screams, or uses the superlative degree, or converses with heat, puts whole drawing-rooms to flight. If you wish to be loved, love measure. You must have genius or a prodigious usefulness if you will hide the want of measure. This perception comes in to polish and perfect the parts of the social instrument. Society will pardon much to genius and special gifts, but, being in its nature a convention, it loves what is conventional, or what belongs to coming together. That makes the good and bad of manners, namely what helps or hinders fellowship. For fashion is not good sense absolute, but relative; not good sense private, but good sense entertaining company. It hates corners and sharp points of character, hates quarrelsome, egotistical, solitary and gloomy people; hates whatever can interfere with total blending of parties; whilst it values all peculiarities as in the highest degree refreshing, which can consist with good fellowship. And besides the general infusion of with to heighten civility, the direct splendor of intellectual power is ever welcome in fine society as the costliest addition to its rule and its credit.

The dry light must shine in to adorn our festival, but it must be tempered and shaded, or that will also offend. Accuracy is essential to beauty, and quick perceptions to politeness, but not too quick perceptions. One may be too punctual and too precise. He must leave the omniscience of business at the door, when he comes into the palace of beauty. Society loves creole natures, and sleepy languishing manners, so that they cover sense, grace and good-will: the air of drowsy strength, which disarms criticism; perhaps because such a person seems to reserve himself for the best of the game, and not spend himself on surfaces; an ignoring eye, which does not see the annoyances, shifts and inconveniences that cloud the brow and smother the voice of the sensitive.

Therefore besides personal force and so much perception as constitutes unerring taste, society demands in its patrician class another
element already intimated, which it significantly terms good-nature—
expressing all degrees of generosity, from the lowest willingness and
faculty to oblige, up to the heights of magnanimity and love. Insight we
must have, or we shall run against one another and miss the way to our
food; but intellect is selfish and barren. The secret of success in society is a certain heartiness and sympathy. A man who is not happy in
the company cannot find any word in his memory that will fit the occasion. All his information is a little impertinent. A man who is happy
there, finds in every turn of the conversation equally lucky occasions for
the introduction of that which he has to say. The favorites of society,
and what it calls *whole souls*, are able men and of more spirit than wit,
who have no uncomfortable egotism, but who exactly fill the hour and
the company; contented and contenting, at a marriage or a funeral, a
ball or a jury, a water-party or a shooting-match. England, which is
rich in gentlemen, furnished, in the beginning of the present century,
a good model of that genius which the world loves, in Mr. Fox, who
added to his great abilities the most social disposition and real love of
men. Parliamentary history has few better passages than the debate in
which Burke and Fox separated in the House of Commons; when Fox
urged on his old friend the claims of old friendship with such tenderness that the house was moved to tears. Another anecdote is so close
to my matter, that I must hazard the story. A tradesman who had long
dunned him for a note of three hundred guineas, found him one day
counting gold, and demanded payment. "No," said Fox, "I owe this
money to Sheridan; it is a debt of honor; if an accident should happen
to me, he has nothing to show." "Then," said the creditor, "I change
my debt into a debt of honor," and tore the note in pieces. Fox thanked
the man for his confidence and paid him, saying, "his debt was of older
standing, and Sheridan must wait." Lover of liberty, friend of the Hindoo, friend of the African slave, he possessed a great personal
popularity; and Napoleon said of him on the occasion of his visit to
Paris, in 1805, "Mr. Fox will always hold the first place in an assembly at the Tuileries."

We may easily seem ridiculous in our eulogy of courtesy whenever
we insist on benevolence as its foundation. The painted phantasm
Fashion rises to cast a species of derision on what we say. But I will

neither be driven from some allowance to fashion as a symbolic institution, nor from the belief that love is the basis of courtesy. We must
obtain *that*, if we can; but by all means we must affirm this. Life owes
much of its spirit to these sharp contrasts. Fashion, which affects to be
honor, is often, in all men's experience, only a ballroom code. Yet so
long as it is the highest circle in the imagination of the best heads on
the planet, there is something necessary and excellent in it; for it is not
to be supposed that men have agreed to be the dupes of anything preposterous; and the respect which these mysteries inspire in the most
rude and sylvan characters, and the curiosity with which details of high
life are read, betray the universality of the love of cultivated manners.
I know that a comic disparity would be felt, if we should enter the
acknowledged 'first circles' and apply these terrific standards of justice,
beauty and benefit to the individuals actually found there. Monarchs
and heroes, sages and lovers, these gallants are not. Fashion has many
classes and many rules of probation and admission, and not the best
alone. There is not only the right of conquest, which genius pretends—
the individual demonstrating his natural aristocracy best of the
best—but less claims will pass for the time; for Fashion loves lions, and
points like Circe to her horned company. This gentleman is this afternoon arrived from Denmark; and that is my Lord Ride, who came
yesterday from Bagdat; here is Captain Friese, from Cape Turnagain;
and Captain Symmes, from the interior of the earth; and Monsieur
Jovaire, who came down this morning in a balloon; Mr. Hobnail, the
reformer; and Reverend Jul Bat, who has converted the whole torrid
zone in his Sunday school; and Signor Torre del Greco, who extinguished Vesuvius by pouring into it the Bay of Naples; Spahi, the
Persian ambassador; and Tul Wil Shan, the exiled nabob of Nepaul,
whose saddle is the new moon. But these are monsters of one day, and
to-morrow will be dismissed to their holes and dens; for in these rooms
every chair is waited for. The artist, the scholar, and, in general, the
clerisy, win their way up into these places and get represented here,
somewhat on this footing of conquest. Another mode is to pass through
all the degrees, spending a year and a day in St. Michael's Square,
being steeped in Cologne water, and perfumed, and dined, and introduced, and properly grounded in all the biography and politics and
anecdotes of the boudoirs.

Yet these fineries may have grace and wit. Let there be grotesque sculpture about the gates and offices of temples. Let the creed and commandments even have the saucy homage of parody. The forms of politeness universally express benevolence in superlative degrees. What if they are in the mouths of selfish men, and used as means of selfishness? What if the false gentleman almost bows the true out of the world? What if the gentleman contrives so to address his companion as civilly to exclude all others from his discourse, and also to make them feel excluded? Real service will not lose its nobleness. All generosity is not merely French and sentimental; nor is it to be concealed that living blood and a passion of kindness does at last distinguish God's gentleman from Fashion's. The epitaph of Sir Jenkin Grout is not wholly unintelligible to the present age: "Here lies Sir Jenkin Grout, who loved his friend and persuaded his enemy: what his mouth ate, his hand paid for: what his servants robbed, he restored: if a woman gave him pleasure, he supported her in pain: he never forgot his children; and whoso touched his finger, drew after it his whole body." Even the line of heroes is not utterly extinct. There is still ever some admirable person in plain clothes, standing on the wharf, who jumps in to rescue a drowning man; there is still some absurd inventor of charities; some guide and comforter of runaway slaves; some friend of Poland; some Philhellene; some fanatic who plants shade-trees for the second and third generation, and orchards when he is grown old; some well-concealed piety; some just man happy in an ill fame; some youth ashamed of the favors of fortune and impatiently casting them on other shoulders. And these are the centres of society, on which it returns for fresh impulses. These are the creators of Fashion, which is an attempt to organize beauty of behavior. The beautiful and the generous are, in the theory, the doctors and apostles of this church: Scipio, and the Cid, and Sir Philip Sidney, and Washington, and every pure and valiant heart who worshipped Beauty by word and by deed. The persons who constitute the natural aristocracy are not found in the actual aristocracy, or only on its edge; as the chemical energy of the spectrum is found to be greatest just outside of the spectrum. Yet that is the infirmity of the seneschals, who do not know their sovereign when he appears. The theory of society supposes the existence and sovereignty of these. It divines afar off their coming. It says with the elder gods—

> "As Heaven and Earth are fairer far
>   Than Chaos and blank Darkness, though once chiefs;
>   And as we show beyond that Heaven and Earth
>   In form and shape compact and beautiful; . . .
>   So on our heels a fresh perfection treads,
>   A power more strong in beauty, born of us
>   And fated to excel us, as we pass
>   In glory that old Darkness. . . .
>   . . . For 't is the eternal law
>   That first in beauty shall be first in might."

Therefore, within the ethnical circle of good society there is a narrower and higher circle, concentration of its light, and flower of courtesy, to which there is always a tacit appeal of pride and reference, as to its inner and imperial court; the parliament of love and chivalry. And this is constituted of those persons in whom heroic dispositions are native; with the love of beauty, the delight in society, and the power to embellish the passing day. If the individuals who compose the purest circles of aristocracy in Europe, the guarded blood of centuries, should pass in review, in such manner as that we could at leisure and critically inspect their behavior, we might find no gentleman and no lady; for although excellent specimens of courtesy and high-breeding would gratify us in the assemblage, in the particulars we should detect offence. Because elegance comes of no breeding, but of birth. There must be romance of character, or the most fastidious exclusion of impertinencies will not avail. It must be genius which takes that direction: it must be not courteous, but courtesy. High behavior is as rare in fiction as it is in fact. Scott is praised for the fidelity with which he painted the demeanor and conversation of the superior classes. Certainly, kings and queens, nobles and great ladies, had some right to complain of the absurdity that had been put in their mouths before the days of Waverley; but neither does Scott's dialogue bear criticism. His lords brave each other in smart epigrammatic speeches, but the dialogue is in costume, and does not please on the second reading: it is not warm with life. In Shakspeare alone the speakers do not strut and bridle, the dialogue is easily great, and he adds to so many titles that of being the best-bred man in England and in Christendom. Once or twice in a lifetime we are permitted to enjoy the charm of noble manners, in the presence of a man or woman who have no bar in their nature, but whose character emanates freely in their word and gesture. A beautiful form is better than a beautiful face; a beautiful behavior is better than a beautiful form: it gives a higher pleasure than statues or pictures; it is the finest of the fine arts. A man is but a little thing in the midst of the objects of nature, yet, by the moral quality radiating from his countenance he may abolish all considerations of magnitude, and in his manners equal the majesty of the world. I have seen an individual whose manners, though wholly within the conventions of elegant society, were never learned there, but were original and commanding and held out protection and prosperity; one who did not need the aid of a court-suit, but carried the holiday in his eye; who exhilarated the fancy by flinging wide the doors of new modes of existence; who shook off the captivity of etiquette, with happy, spirited bearing, good-natured and free as Robin Hood; yet with the port of an emperor, if need be— calm, serious and fit to stand the gaze of millions.

The open air and the fields, the street and public chambers are the places where Man executes his will; let him yield or divide the sceptre at the door of the house. Woman, with her instinct of behavior, instantly detects in man a love of trifles, any coldness or imbecility, or, in short, any want of that large, flowing and magnanimous deportment which is indispensable as an exterior in the hall. Our American institutions have been friendly to her, and at this moment I esteem it a chief felicity of this country, that it excels in women. A certain awkward consciousness of inferiority in the men may give rise to the new chivalry in behalf of Woman's Rights. Certainly let her be as much better placed in the laws and in social forms as the most zealous reformer can ask, but I confide so entirely in her inspiring and musical nature, that I believe only herself can show us how she shall be served. The wonderful generosity of her sentiments raises her at times into heroical and godlike regions, and verifies the pictures of Minerva, Juno, or Polymnia; and by the firmness with which she treads her upward path, she convinces the coarsest calculators that another road exists than that which their feet know. But besides those who make good in our imagination the place of muses and of Delphic Sibyls, are there not women who fill our vase with wine and roses to the brim, so that the wine runs over and fills the house with perfume; who inspire us with courtesy;

who unloose our tongues and we speak; who anoint our eyes and we see? We say things we never thought to have said; for once, our walls of habitual reserve vanished and left us at large; we were children playing with children in a wide field of flowers. Steep us, we cried, in these influences, for days, for weeks, and we shall be sunny poets and will write out in many-colored words the romance that you are. Was it Hafiz or Firdousi that said of his Persian Lilla, She was an elemental force, and astonished me by her amount of life, when I saw her day after day radiating, every instant, redundant joy and grace on all around her? She was a solvent powerful to reconcile all heterogeneous persons into one society: like air or water, an element of such a great range of affinities that it combines readily with a thousand substances. Where she is present all others will be more than they are wont. She was a unit and whole, so that whatsoever she did, became her. She had too much sympathy and desire to please, than that you could say her manners were marked with dignity, yet no princess could surpass her clear and erect demeanor on each occasion. She did not study the Persian grammar, nor the books of the seven poets, but all the poems of the seven seemed to be written upon her. For though the bias of her nature was not to thought, but to sympathy, yet was she so perfect in her own nature as to meet intellectual persons by the fulness of her heart, warming them by her sentiments; believing, as she did, that by dealing nobly with all, all would show themselves noble.

I know that this Byzantine pile of chivalry or Fashion, which seems so fair and picturesque to those who look at the contemporary facts for science or for entertainment, is not equally pleasant to all spectators. The constitution of our society makes it a giant's castle to the ambitious youth who have not found their names enrolled in its Golden Book, and whom it has excluded from its coveted honors and privileges. They have yet to learn that its seeming grandeur is shadowy and relative: it is great by their allowance; its proudest gates will fly open at the approach of their courage and virtue. For the present distress, however, of those who are predisposed to suffer from the tyrannies of this caprice, there are easy remedies. To remove your residence a couple of miles, or at most four, will commonly relieve the most extreme susceptibility. For the advantages which fashion values are plants which thrive in very confines localities, in a few streets namely. Out of this precinct they go for nothing; are of no use in the farm, in the forest, in the market, in war, in the nuptial society, in the literary or scientific circle, at sea, in friendship, in the heaven of thought or virtue.

But we have lingered long enough in these painted courts. The worth of the thing signified must vindicate our taste for the emblem. Everything that is called fashion and courtesy humbles itself before the cause and fountain of honor, creator of titles and dignities, namely the heart of love. This is the royal blood, this the fire, which, in all countries and contingencies, will work after its kind and conquer and expand all that approaches it. This gives new meanings to every fact. This impoverishes the rich, suffering no grandeur but its own. What is rich? Are you rich enough to help anybody? To succour the unfashionable and the eccentric? rich enough to make the Canadian in his wagon, the itinerant with his consul's paper which commends him "To the charitable," the swarthy Italian with his few broken words of English, the lame pauper hunted by overseers from town to town, even the poor insane or besotted wreck of man or woman, feel the noble exception of your presence and your house from the general bleakness and stoniness; to make such feel that they were greeted with a voice which made them both remember and hope? What is vulgar but to refuse the claim on acute and conclusive reasons? What is gentle, but to allow it, and give their heart and yours one holiday from the national caution? Without the rich heart, wealth is an ugly beggar. The king of Schiraz could not afford to be so bountiful as the poor Osman who dwelt at his gate. Osman had a humanity so broad and deep that although his speech was so bold and free with the Koran as to disgust all the dervishes, yet was there never a poor outcast, eccentric, or insane man, some fool who had cut off his beard, or who had been mutilated under a vow, or had a pet madness in his brain, but fled at once to him; that great heart lay there so sunny and hospitable in the centre of the country, that it seemed as if the instinct of all sufferers drew them to his side. And the madness which he harbored he did not share. Is not this to be rich? this only to be rightly rich?

But I shall hear without pain that I play the courtier very ill, and talk of that which I do not well understand. It is easy to see that what is called by distinction society and fashion has good laws as well as bad, has much that is necessary, and much that is absurd. Too good for banning, and too bad for blessing, it reminds us of a tradition of the pagan mythology, in any attempt to settle its character. 'I overheard Jove, one day,' said Silenus, 'talking of destroying the earth; he said it had failed; they were all rogues and vixens, who went from bad to worse, as fast as the days succeeded each other. Minerva said she hoped not; they were only ridiculous little creatures, with this odd circumstance, that they had a blur, or indeterminate aspect, seen far or seen near; if you called them bad, they would appear so; if you called them good, they would appear so; and there was no one person or action among them which would not puzzle her owl, much more all Olympus, to know whether it was fundamentally bad or good.'

GIFTS

Gifts of one who loved me—
'T was high time they came;
When he ceased to love me,
Time they stopped for shame.

IT IS SAID that the world is in a state of bankruptcy; that the world owes the world more than the world can pay, and ought to go into chancery and be sold. I do not think this general insolvency, which involves in some sort all the population, to be the reason of the difficulty experienced at Christmas and New Year and other times, in bestowing gifts; since it is always so pleasant to be generous, though very vexatious to pay debts. But the impediment lies in the choosing. If at any time it comes into my head that a present is due from me to somebody, I am puzzled what to give, until the opportunity is gone. Flowers and fruits are always fit presents; flowers, because they are a proud assertion that a ray of beauty outvalues all the utilities of the world. Those gay natures contrast with the somewhat stern countenance of ordinary nature: they are like music heard out of a work-house. Nature does not cocker us; we are children, not pets; she is not fond; everything is dealt to us without fear or favor, after severe universal laws. Yet these delicate flowers look like the frolic and interference of love and beauty. Men use to tell us that we love flattery even though we are not deceived by it, because it shows that we are of importance enough to be courted. Something like that pleasure, the flowers give us: what am I to whom these sweet hints are addressed? Fruits are acceptable gifts, because they are the flower of commodities, and admit of fantastic values being attached to them. If a man should send to me to come a hundred miles to visit him and should set before me a basket of fine summer-fruit, I should think there was some proportion between the labor and the reward.

For common gifts, necessity makes pertinences and beauty every day, and one is glad when an imperative leaves him no option; since if the man at the door have no shoes, you have not to consider whether you could procure him a paint-box. And as it is always pleasing to see a man eat bread, or drink water, in the house or out of doors, so it is always a great satisfaction to supply these first wants. Necessity does everything well. In our condition of universal dependence it seems heroic to let the petitioner be the judge of his necessity, and to give all that is asked, though at great inconvenience. If it be a fantastic desire, it is better to leave to others the office of punishing him. I can think of many parts I should prefer playing to that of the Furies. Next to things of necessity, the rule for a gift, which one of my friends prescribed, is that we might convey to some person that which properly belonged to his character, and was easily associated with him in thought. But our tokens of compliment and love are for the most part barbarous. Rings and other jewels are not gifts, but apologies for gifts. The only gift is a portion of thyself. Thou must bleed for me. Therefore the poet brings his poem; the shepherd, his lamb; the farmer, corn; the miner, a gem; the sailor, coral and shells; the painter, his picture; the girl, a handkerchief of her own sewing. This is right and pleasing, for it restores society in so far to the primary basis, when a man's biography is conveyed in his gift, and every man's wealth is an index of his merit. But it is a cold lifeless business when you go to the shops to buy me something which does not represent your life and talent, but a goldsmith's. This is fit for kings, and rich men who represent kings, and a false state of property, to make presents of gold and silver stuffs, as a kind of symbolical sin-offering, or payment of blackmail.

The law of benefits is a difficult channel, which requires careful sailing, or rude boats. It is not the office of a man to receive gifts. How dare you give them? We wish to be self-sustained. We do not quite forgive a giver. The hand that feeds us is in some danger of being bitten. We can receive anything from love, for that is a way of receiving it from ourselves; but not from any one who assumes to bestow. We sometimes hate the meat which we eat, because there seems something of degrading dependence in living by it:

> "Brother, if Jove to thee a present make,
> Take heed that from his hands thou nothing take."

We ask the whole. Nothing less will content us. We arraign society if it do not give us, besides earth and fire and water, opportunity, love, reverence and objects of veneration.

He is a good man who can receive a gift well. We are either glad or sorry at a gift, and both emotions are unbecoming. Some violence I think is done, some degradation borne, when I rejoice or grieve at a gift. I am sorry when my independence is invaded or when a gift comes from such as do not know my spirit, and so the act is not supported; and if the gift pleases me overmuch, then I should be ashamed that the donor should read my heart, and see that I love his commodity, and not him. The gift, to be true, must be the flowing of the giver unto me, correspondent to my flowing unto him. When the waters are at level, then my goods pass to him, and his to me. All his are mine, all mine his. I say to him, How can you give me this pot of oil or this flagon of wine when all your oil and wine is mine, which belief of mine this gift seems to deny? Hence the fitness of beautiful, not useful things, for gifts. This giving is flat usurpation, and therefore when the beneficiary is ungrateful, as all beneficiaries hate all Timons, not at all considering the value of the gift but looking back to the greater store it was taken from—I rather sympathize with the beneficiary than with the anger of my lord Timon. For the expectation of gratitude is mean, and is continually punished by the total insensibility of the obliged person. It is a great happiness to get off without injury and heart-burning from one who has had the ill-luck to be served by you. It is a very onerous business, this of being served, and the debtor naturally wishes to give you a slap. A golden text for these gentlemen is that which I so admire in the Buddhist, who never thanks, and who says, "Do not flatter your benefactors."

The reason of these discords I conceive to be that there is no commensurability between a man and any gift. You cannot give anything to a magnanimous person. After you have served him he at once puts you in debt by his magnanimity. The service a man renders his friend is trivial and selfish compared with the service he knows his friend stood in readiness to yield him, alike before he had begun to serve his friend, and now also. Compared with that good-will I bear my friend, the benefit it is in my power to render him seems small. Besides, our action on each others good as well as evil, is so incidental and at random that we can seldom hear the acknowledgments of any person who would thank us for a benefit, without some shame and humiliation. We can rarely strike a direct stroke, but must be content with an oblique one; we seldom have the satisfaction of yielding a direct benefit which is directly received. But rectitude scatters favors on every side without knowing it, and receives with wonder the thanks of all people.

I fear to breathe any treason against the majesty of love, which is the genius and god of gifts, and to whom we must not affect to prescribe. Let him give kingdoms of flower-leaves indifferently. There are persons from whom we always expect fairy-tokens; let us not cease to expect them. This is prerogative, and not to be limited by our municipal rules. For the rest, I like to see that we cannot be bought and sold. The best of hospitality and of generosity is also not in the will, but in fate. I find that I am not much to you: you do not need me; you do not feel me; then am I thrust out of doors, though you proffer me house and lands. No services are of any value, but only likeness. When I have attempted to join myself to others by services, it proved an intellectual trick—no more. They eat your service like apples, and leave you out. But love them, and they feel you and delight in you all the time.

NATURE

The rounded world is fair to see,
Nine times folded in mystery:
Though baffled seers cannot impart
The secret of its laboring heart,
Throb thine with Nature's throbbing breast,
And all is clear from east to west.
Spirit that lurks each form within
Beckons to spirit of its kin;
Self-kindled every atom glows,
And hints the future which it owes.

THERE ARE DAYS which occur in this climate, at almost any season of
the year, wherein the world reaches its perfection; when the air, the
heavenly bodies and the earth, make a harmony, as if nature would
indulge her offspring; when, in these bleak upper sides of the planet,
nothing is to desire that we have heard of the happiest latitudes, and we
bask in the shining hours of Florida and Cuba; when everything that
has life gives sign of satisfaction, and the cattle that lie on the ground
seem to have great and tranquil thoughts. These halcyons may be
looked for with a little more assurance in that pure October weather
which we distinguish by the name of the Indian summer. The day,
immeasurably long, sleeps over the broad hills and warm wide fields.
To have lived through all its sunny hours, seems longevity enough.
The solitary places do not seem quite lonely. At the gates of the forest, the surprised man of the world is forced to leave his city estimates
of great and small, wise and foolish. The knapsack of custom falls off
his back with the first step he takes into these precincts. Here is sanctity which shames our religions, and reality which discredits our heroes.
Here we find Nature to be the circumstance which dwarfs every other
circumstance, and judges like a god all men that come to her. We have
crept out of our close and crowded houses into the night and morning,
and we see what majestic beauties daily wrap us in their bosom. How
willingly we would escape the barriers which render them comparatively impotent, escape the sophistication and second thought, and

suffer nature to intrance us. The tempered light of the woods is like a perpetual morning, and is stimulating and heroic. The anciently-reported spells of these places creep on us. The stems of pines, hemlocks and oaks almost gleam like iron on the excited eye. The incommunicable trees begin to persuade us to live with them, and quit our life of solemn trifles. Here no history, or church, or state, is interpolated on the divine sky and the immortal year. How easily we might walk onward into the opening landscape, absorbed by new pictures and by thoughts fast succeeding each other, until by degrees the recollection of home was crowded out of the mind, all memory obliterated by the tyranny of the present, and we were led in triumph by nature.

These enchantments are medicinal, they sober and heal us. These are plain pleasures, kindly and native to us. We come to our own, and make friends with matter, which the ambitious chatter of the schools would persuade us to despise. We never can part with it; the mind loves its old home: as water to our thirst, so is the rock, the ground, to our eyes and hands and feet. It is firm water; it is cold flame; what health, what affinity! Ever an old friend, ever like a dear friend and brother when we chat affectedly with strangers, comes in this honest face, and takes a grave liberty with us, and shames us out of our nonsense. Cities give not the human senses room enough. We go out daily and nightly to feed the eyes on the horizon, and require so much scope, just as we need water for our bath. There are all degrees of natural influence, from these quarantine powers of nature, up to her dearest and gravest ministrations to the imagination and the soul. There is the bucket of cold water from the spring, the wood-fire to which the chilled traveller rushes for safety—and there is the sublime moral of autumn and of noon. We nestle in nature, and draw our living as parasites from her roots and grains, and we receive glances from the heavenly bodies, which call us to solitude and foretell the remotest future. The blue zenith is the point in which romance and reality meet. I think if we should be rapt away into all that and dream of heaven, and should converse with Gabriel and Uriel, the upper sky would be all that would remain of our furniture.

It seems as if the day was not wholly profane in which we have given heed to some natural object. The fall of snowflakes in a still air, preserving to each crystal its perfect form; the blowing of sleet over a wide sheet of water, and over plains; the waving rye-field; the mimic waving of acres of houstonia, whose innumerable florets whiten and ripple before the eye; the reflections of trees and flowers in glassy lakes; the musical, steaming, odorous south wind, which converts all trees to wind-harps; the crackling and spurting of hemlock in the flames, or of pine logs which yield glory to the walls and faces in the sitting-room— these are the music and pictures of the most ancient religion. My house stands in low land, with limited outlook, and on the skirt of the village. But I go with my friend to the shore of our little river, and with one stroke of the paddle I leave the village politics and personalities, yes, and the world of villages and personalities, behind, and pass into a delicate realm of sunset and moonlight, too bright almost for spotted man to enter without novitiate and probation. We penetrate bodily this incredible beauty; we dip our hands in this painted element; our eyes are bathed in these lights and forms. A holiday, a villeggiatura, a royal revel, the proudest, most heart-rejoicing festival that valor and beauty, power and taste, ever decked and enjoyed, establishes itself on the instant. These sunset clouds, these delicately emerging stars, with their private and ineffable glances, signify it and proffer it. I am taught the poorness of our invention, the ugliness of towns and palaces. Art and luxury have early learned that they must work as enhancement and sequel to this original beauty. I am over-instructed for my return. Henceforth I shall be hard to please. I cannot go back to toys. I am grown expensive and sophisticated. I can no longer live without elegance, but a countryman shall be my master of revels. He who knows the most; he who knows what sweets and virtues are in the ground, the waters, the plants, the heavens, and how to come at these enchantments, is the rich and royal man. Only as far as the masters of the world have called in nature to their aid, can they reach the height of magnificence. This is the meaning of their hanging-gardens, villas, garden-houses, islands, parks and preserves, to back their faulty personality with these strong accessories. I do not wonder that the landed interest should be invincible in the State with these dangerous auxiliaries. These bribe and invite, not kings, not palaces, not men, not women, but these tender and poetic stars, eloquent of secret promises. We heard what the rich man said, we knew of his villa, his grove, his wine and his company, but the provocation and point of the invitation came out of these beguiling stars. In their soft glances I see what men strove to realize in some Versailles, or Paphos, or Ctesiphon. Indeed, it is the magical lights of the horizon and the blue sky for the background which save all our works of art, which were otherwise bawbles. When the rich tax the poor with servility and obsequiousness, they should consider the effect of men reputed to be the possessors of nature, on imaginative minds. Ah! if the rich were rich as the poor fancy riches! A boy hears a military band play on the field at night, and he has kings and queens and famous chivalry palpably before him. He hears the echoes of a horn in a hill country, in the Notch Mountains, for example, which converts the mountains into an Aeolian harp—and this supernatural *tiralira* restores to him the Dorian mythology, Apollo, Diana, and all divine hunters and huntresses. Can a musical note be so lofty, so haughtily beautiful! To the poor young poet, thus fabulous is his picture of society; he is loyal; he respects the rich; they are rich for the sake of his imagination; how poor his fancy would be, if they were not rich! That they have some high-fenced grove which they call a park; that they live in larger and better-garnished saloons than he has visited, and go in coaches, keeping only the society of the elegant, to watering-places and to distant cities—these make the groundwork from which he has delineated estates of romance compared with which their actual possessions are shanties and paddocks. The muse herself betrays her son, and enhances the gifts of wealth and well-born beauty by a radiation out of the air, and clouds, and forests that skirt the road—a certain haughty favor, as if from patrician genii to patricians, a kind of aristocracy in nature, a prince of the power of the air.

The moral sensibility which makes Edens and Tempes so easily, may not be always found, but the material landscape is never far off. We can find these enchantments without visiting the Como Lake, or the Madeira Islands. We exaggerate the praises of local scenery. In every landscape the point of astonishment is the meeting of the sky and the earth, and that is seen from the first hillock as well as from the top of the Alleghanies. The stars at night stoop down over the brownest, homeliest common with all the spiritual magnificence which they shed on the Campagna, or on the marble deserts of Egypt. The uprolled clouds and the colors of morning and evening will transfigure maples and alders. The difference between landscape and landscape is small, but there is great difference in the beholders. There is nothing so wonderful in any particular landscape as the necessity of being beautiful under which every landscape lies. Nature cannot be surprised in undress. Beauty breaks in everywhere.

But it is very easy to outrun the sympathy of readers on this topic, which schoolmen called *natura naturata*, or nature passive. One can hardly speak directly of it without excess. It is as easy to broach in mixed companies what is called "the subject of religion." A susceptible person does not like to indulge his tastes in this kind without the apology of some trivial necessity: he goes to see a wood-lot, or to look at the crops, or to fetch a plant or a mineral from a remote locality, or he carries a fowling-piece or a fishing-rod. I suppose this shame must have a good reason. A dilettanteism in nature is barren and unworthy. The fop of fields is no better than his brother of Broadway. Men are naturally hunters and inquisitive of wood-craft, and I suppose that such a gazetteer as woodcutters and Indians should furnish facts for, would take place in the most sumptuous drawing-rooms of all the "Wreaths" and "Flora's chaplets" of the bookshops; yet ordinarily, whether we are too clumsy for so subtle a topic, or from whatever cause, as soon as men begin to write on nature, they fall into euphuism. Frivolity is a most unfit tribute to Pan, who ought to be represented in the mythology as the most continent of gods. I would not be frivolous before the admirable reserve and prudence of time, yet I cannot renounce the rights of returning often to this old topic. The multitude of false churches accredits the true religion. Literature, poetry, science are the homage of man to this unfathomed secret, concerning which no sane man can affect an indifference or incuriosity. Nature is loved by what is best in us. It is loved as the city of God, although, or rather because there is no citizen. The sunset is unlike anything that is underneath it: it wants men. And the beauty of nature must always seem unreal and mocking, until the landscape has human figures that are as good as itself. If there were good men, there would never be this rapture in nature. If the king is in the palace, nobody looks at the walls. It is when he is gone, and the house is filled with grooms and gazers, that we turn from the people to find relief in the majestic men that are suggested by the pictures and the architecture. The critics who complain of the sickly separation of the beauty of nature from the thing to be done, must consider that our hunting of the picturesque is inseparable from our protest against false society. Man is fallen; nature is erect, and serves as a differential thermometer, detecting the presence or absence of the divine

sentiment in man. By fault of our dulness and selfishness we are looking up to nature, but when we are convalescent, nature will look up to
us. We see the foaming brook with compunction: if our own life flowed
with the right energy, we should shame the brook. The stream of zeal
sparkles with real fire, and not with reflex rays of sun and moon.
Nature may be as selfishly studied as trade. Astronomy to the selfish
becomes astrology; psychology, mesmerism (with intent to show where
our spoons are gone); and anatomy and physiology become phrenology
and palmistry.

But taking timely warning, and leaving many things unsaid on this
topic, let us not longer omit our homage to the Efficient Nature, *natura
naturans*, the quick cause before which all forms flee as the driven
snows; itself secret, its works driven before it in flocks and multitudes
(as the ancients represented nature by Proteus, a shepherd) and in
undescribable variety. It publishes itself in creatures, reaching from
particles and spiculæ through transformation on transformation to the
highest symmetries, arriving at consummate results without a shock or
a leap. A little heat, that is a little motion, is all that differences the
bald, dazzling white and deadly cold poles of the earth from the prolific
tropical climates. All changes pass without violence, by reason of the
two cardinal conditions of boundless space and boundless time. Geology has initiated us into the secularity of nature; and taught us to
disuse our dame-school measures, and exchange our Mosaic and Ptolemaic schemes for her large style. We knew nothing rightly, for want
of perspective. Now we learn what patient periods must round themselves before the rock is formed; then before the rock is broken, and
the first lichen race has disintegrated the thinnest external plate into
soil, and opened the door for the remote Flora, Fauna, Ceres, and
Pomona to come in. How far off yet is the trilobite! how far the
quadruped! how inconceivably remote is man! All duly arrive, and then
race after race of men. It is a long way from granite to the oyster; farther yet to Plato and the preaching of the immortality of the soul. Yet
all must come, as surely as the first atom has two sides.

Motion or change and identity or rest are the first and second
secrets of nature: Motion and Rest. The whole code of her laws may be
written on the thumbnail, or the signet of a ring. The whirling bubble
on the surface of a brook admits us to the secret of the mechanics of the
sky. Every shell on the beach is a key to it. A little water made to rotate

in a cup explains the formation of the simpler shells; the addition of matter from year to year arrives at last at the most complex forms; and yet so poor is nature with all her craft, that from the beginning to the end of the universe she has but one stuff—but one stuff with its two ends, to serve up all her dream-like variety. Compound it how she will, star, sand, fire, water, tree, man, it is still one stuff, and betrays the same properties.

Nature is always consistent, though she feigns to contravene her own laws. She keeps her laws, and seems to transcend them. She arms and equips an animal to find its place and living in the earth, and at the same time she arms and equips another animal to destroy it. Space exists to divide creatures; but by clothing the sides of a bird with a few feathers she gives him a petty omnipresence. The direction is forever onward, but the artist still goes back for materials and begins again with the first elements on the most advanced stage: otherwise all goes to ruin. If we look at her work, we seem to catch a glance of a system in transition. Plants are the young of the world, vessels of health and vigor; but they grope ever upward towards consciousness; the trees are imperfect men, and seem to bemoan their imprisonment, rooted in the ground. The animal is the novice and probationer of a more advanced order. The men, though young, having tasted the first drop from the cup of thought, are already dissipated; the maples and ferns are still uncorrupt; yet no doubt when they come to consciousness they too will curse and swear. Flowers so strictly belong to youth that we adult men soon come to feel that their beautiful generations concern not us: we have had our day; now let the children have theirs. The flowers jilt us, and we are old bachelors with our ridiculous tenderness.

Things are so strictly related, that according to the skill of the eye, from any one object the parts and properties of any other may be predicted. If we had eyes to see it, a bit of stone from the city wall would certify us of the necessity that man must exist, as readily as the city. That identity makes us all one, and reduces to nothing great intervals on our customary scale. We talk of deviations from natural life, as if artificial life were not also natural. The smoothest curled courtier in the boudoirs of a palace has an animal nature, rude and aboriginal as a white bear, omnipotent to its own ends, and is directly related, there amid essences and billets-doux, to Himmaleh mountain-chains and the axis of the globe. If we consider how much we are nature's, we need not be superstitious about towns, as if that terrific or benefic force did not find us there also, and fashion cities. Nature, who made the mason, made the house. We may easily hear too much of rural influences. The cool disengaged air of natural objects makes them enviable to us, chafed and irritable creatures with red faces, and we think we shall be as grand as they if we camp out and eat roots; but let us be men instead of woodchucks and the oak and the elm shall gladly serve us, though we sit in chairs of ivory on carpets of silk.

This guiding identity runs through all the surprises and contrasts of the piece, and characterizes every law. Man carries the world in his head, the whole astronomy and chemistry suspended in a thought. Because the history of nature is charactered in his brain, therefore is he the prophet and discoverer of her secrets. Every known fact in natural science was divined by the presentiment of somebody, before it was actually verified. A man does not tie his shoe without recognizing laws which bind the farthest regions of nature: moon, plant, gas, crystal, are concrete geometry and numbers. Common sense knows its own, and recognizes the fact at first sight in chemical experiment. The common sense of Franklin, Dalton, Davy and Black is the same common sense which made the arrangements which now it discovers.

If the identity expresses organized rest, the counter action runs also into organization. The astronomers said, 'Give us matter and a little motion and we will construct the universe. It is not enough that we should have matter, we must also have a single impulse, one shove to launch the mass and generate the harmony of the centrifugal and centripetal forces. Once heave the ball from the hand, and we can show how all this mighty order grew.' 'A very unreasonable postulate,' said the metaphysicians, 'and a plain begging of the question. Could you not prevail to know the genesis of projection, as well as the continuation of it?' Nature, meanwhile, had not waited for the discussion, but, right or wrong, bestowed the impulse, and the balls rolled. It was no great affair, a mere push, but the astronomers were right in making much of it, for there is no end to the consequences of the act. That famous aboriginal push propagates itself through all the balls of the system, and through every atom of every ball; through all the races of creatures, and through the history and performance of every individual. Exaggeration is in the course of things. Nature sends no creature, no man into the world without adding a small excess of his proper quality. Given the planet, it is still necessary to add the impulse; so to every creature nature added a little violence of direction in its proper path, a shove to put it on its way; in every instance a slight generosity, a drop too much. Without electricity the air would rot, and without this violence of direction which men and women have, without a spice of bigot and fanatic, no excitement, no efficiency. We aim above the mark to hit the mark. Every act hath some falsehood of exaggeration in it. And when now and then comes along some sad, sharp-eyed man, who sees how paltry a game is played, and refuses to play, but blabs the secret; how then? is the bird flown? O no, the wary Nature sends a new troop of fairer forms, of lordlier youths, with a little more excess of direction to hold them fast to their several aim; makes them a little wrong-headed in that direction in which they are rightest, and on goes the game again with new whirl, for a generation or two more. The child with his sweet pranks, the fool of his senses, commanded by every sight and sound, without any power to compare and rank his sensations, abandoned to a whistle or a painted chip, to a lead dragoon or a gingerbread-dog, individualizing everything, generalizing nothing, delighted with every new thing, lies down at night overpowered by the fatigue which this day of continual pretty madness has incurred. But Nature has answered her purpose with the curly, dimpled lunatic. She has tasked every faculty, and has secured the symmetrical growth of the bodily frame by all these attitudes and exertions—an end of the first importance, which could not be trusted to any care less perfect than her own. This glitter, this opaline lustre plays round the top of every toy to his eye to insure his fidelity, and he is deceived to his good. We are made alive and kept alive by the same arts. Let the stoics say what they please, we do not eat for the good of living, but because the meat is savory and the appetite is keen. The vegetable life does not content itself with casting from the flower or the tree a single seed, but it fills the air and earth with a prodigality of seeds, that, if thousands perish, thousands may plant themselves; that hundreds may come up, that tens may live to maturity; that at least one may replace the parent. All things betray the same calculated profusion. The excess of fear with which the animal frame is hedged round, shrinking from cold, starting at sight of a snake or at a sudden noise, protects us, through a multitude of groundless alarms, from some one real danger at last. The lover seeks in marriage his private felicity and perfection, with no prospective end; and nature hides in his happiness her own end, namely progeny, or the perpetuity of the race.

But the craft with which the world is made, runs also into the mind and character of men. No man is quite sane; each has a vein of folly in his composition, a slight determination of blood to the head, to make sure of holding him hard to some one point which nature had taken to heart. Great causes are never tried on their merits; but the cause is reduced to particulars to suit the size of the partisans, and the contention is ever hottest on minor matters. Not less remarkable is the overfaith of each man in the importance of what he has to do or say. The poet, the prophet, has a higher value for what he utters than any hearer, and therefore it gets spoken. The strong, self-complacent Luther declares with an emphasis not to be mistaken, that "God himself cannot do without wise men." Jacob Behmen and George Fox betray their egotism in the pertinacity of their controversial tracts, and James Naylor once suffered himself to be worshipped as the Christ. Each prophet comes presently to identify himself with his thought, and to esteem his hat and shoes sacred. However this may discredit such persons with the judicious, it helps them with the people, as it gives heat, pungency and publicity to their words. A similar experience is not infrequent in private life. Each young and ardent person writes a diary, in which, when the hours of prayer and penitence arrive, he inscribes his soul. The pages thus written are to him burning and fragrant; he reads them on his knees by midnight and by the morning star; he wets them with his tears; they are sacred; too good for the world, and hardly yet to be shown to the dearest friend. This is the man-child that is born to the soul, and her life still circulates in the babe. The umbilical cord has not yet been cut. After some time has elapsed, he begins to wish to admit his friend to this hallowed experience, and with hesitation, yet with firmness, exposes the pages to his eye. Will they not burn his eyes? The friend coldly turns them over, and passes from the writing to conversation, with easy transition, which strikes the other party with astonishment and vexation. He cannot suspect the writing itself. Days and nights of fervid life, of communion with angels of darkness and of light have engraved their shadowy characters on their tear-stained book. He suspects the intelligence or the heart of his friend. Is there then no friend? He cannot yet credit that one may have impressive experience and yet may not know how to put his private fact into literature: and perhaps the discovery that wisdom has other tongues and ministers than we, that though we should hold our peace the truth would not the less be spoken, might check injuriously the flames of our zeal. A man can only speak so long as he does not feel his speech to be partial and inadequate. It is partial, but he does not see it to be so whilst he utters it. As soon as he is released from the instinctive and particular and sees its partiality, he shuts his mouth in disgust. For no man can write anything who does not think that what he writes is for the time the history of the world; or do anything well who does not esteem his work to be of importance. My work may be of none, but I must not think it of none, or I shall not do it with impunity.

In like manner, there is throughout nature something mocking, something that leads us on and on, but arrives nowhere; keeps no faith with us. All promise outruns the performance. We live in a system of approximations. Every end is prospective of some other end, which is also temporary; a round and final success nowhere. We are encamped in nature, not domesticated. Hunger and thirst lead us on to eat and to drink; but bread and wine, mix and cook them how you will, leave us hungry and thirsty, after the stomach is full. It is the same with all our arts and performances. Our music, our poetry, our language itself are not satisfactions, but suggestions. The hunger for wealth, which reduces the planet to a garden, fools the eager pursuer. What is the end sought? Plainly to secure the ends of good sense and beauty from the intrusion of deformity or vulgarity of any kind. But what an operose method! What a train of means to secure a little conversation! This palace of brick and stone, these servants, this kitchen, these stables, horses and equipage, this bank-stock and file of mortgages; trade to all the world, country-house and cottage by the waterside, all for a little conversation, high, clear and spiritual! Could it not be had as well by beggars on the highway? No, all these things came from successive efforts of these beggars to remove friction from the wheels of life, and give opportunity. Conversation, character, were the avowed ends; wealth was good as it appeased the animal cravings, cured the smoky chimney, silenced the creaking door, brought friends together in a warm and quiet room, and kept the children and the dinner-table in a different apartment. Thought, virtue, beauty, were the ends; but it was known that men of thought and virtue sometimes had the headache, or

. . . .

wet feet, or could lose good time whilst the room was getting warm in winter days. Unluckily, in the exertions necessary to remove these inconveniences, the main attention has been diverted to this object; the old aims have been lost sight of, and to remove friction has come to be the end. That is the ridicule of rich men; and Boston, London, Vienna, and now the governments generally of the world, are cities and governments of the rich; and the masses are not men, but poor men, that is, men who would be rich; this is the ridicule of the class, that they arrive with pains and sweat and fury nowhere; when all is done, it is for nothing. They are like one who has interrupted the conversation of a company to make his speech, and now has forgotten what he went to say. The appearance strikes the eye everywhere of an aimless society, of aimless nations. Were the ends of nature so great and cogent as to exact this immense sacrifice of men?

Quite analogous to the deceits in life, there is, as might be expected, a similar effect on the eye from the face of external nature. There is in woods and waters a certain enticement and flattery, together with a failure to yield a present satisfaction. This disappointment is felt in every landscape. I have seen the softness and beauty of the summer clouds floating feathery overhead, enjoying, as it seemed, their height and privilege of motion, whilst yet they appeared not so much the drapery of this place and hour, as forelooking to some pavilions and gardens of festivity beyond. It is an odd jealousy, but the poet finds himself not near enough to his object. The pine-tree, the river, the bank of flowers before him does not seem to be nature. Nature is still elsewhere. This or this is but outskirt and a far-off reflection and echo of the triumph that has passed by and is now at its glancing splendor and heyday, perchance in the neighboring fields, or, if you stand in the field, then in the adjacent woods. The present object shall give you this sense of stillness that follows a pageant which has just gone by. What splendid distance, what recesses of ineffable pomp and loveliness in the sunset! But who can go where they are, or lay his hand or plant his foot thereon? Off they fall from the round world forever and ever. It is the same among the men and women as among the silent trees; always a referred existence, an absence, never a presence and satisfaction. Is it that beauty can never be grasped? in persons and in landscape is equally inaccessible? The accepted and betrothed lover has lost the wildest charm of his maiden in her acceptance of him. She was heaven whilst he pursued her as a star: she cannot be heaven if she stoops to such a one as he.

What shall we say of this omnipresent appearance of that first projectile impulse, of this flattery and balking of so many well-meaning creatures? Must we not suppose somewhere in the universe a slight treachery and derision? Are we not engaged to a serious resentment of this use that is made of us? Are we tickled trout, and fools of nature? One look at the face of heaven and earth lays all petulance at rest, and soothes us to wiser convictions. To the intelligent, nature converts itself into a vast promise, and will not be rashly explained. Her secret is untold. Many and many an Oedipus arrives; he has the whole mystery teeming in his brain. Alas! the same sorcery has spoiled his skill; no syllable can he shape on his lips. Her mighty orbit vaults like the fresh rainbow into the deep, but no archangel's wing was yet strong enough to follow it and report of the return of the curve. But it also appears that our actions are seconded and disposed to greater conclusions than we designed. We are escorted on every hand through life by spiritual agents, and a beneficent purpose lies in wait for us. We cannot bandy words with Nature, or deal with her as we deal with persons. If we measure our individual forces against hers we may easily feel as if we were the sport of an insuperable destiny. But if, instead of identifying ourselves with the work, we feel that the soul of the Workman streams through us, we shall find the peace of the morning dwelling first in our hearts, and the fathomless powers of gravity and chemistry, and, over them, of life, preexisting within us in their highest form.

The uneasiness which the thought of our helplessness in the chain of causes occasions us, results from looking too much at one condition of nature, namely, Motion. But the drag is never taken from the wheel. Wherever the impulse exceeds, the Rest or Identity insinuates its compensation. All over the wide fields of earth grows the prunella or self-heal. After every foolish day we sleep off the fumes and furies of its hours; and though we are always engaged with particulars, and often enslaved to them, we bring with us to every experiment the innate universal laws. These, while they exist in the mind as ideas, stand around us in nature forever embodied, a present sanity to expose and cure the insanity of men. Our servitude to particulars betrays us into a hundred foolish expectations. We anticipate a new era from the invention of a locomotive, or a balloon; the new engine brings with it the old checks. They say that by electro-magnetism your salad shall be grown from the seed whilst your fowl is roasting for dinner; it is a symbol of our modern aims and endeavors, of our condensation and acceleration of objects; but nothing is gained; nature cannot be cheated; man's life is but seventy salads long, grow they swift or grow they slow. In these checks and impossibilities, however, we find our advantage, not less than in the impulses. Let the victory fall where it will, we are on that side. And the knowledge that we traverse the whole scale of being, from the centre to the poles of nature, and have some stake in every possibility, lends that sublime lustre to death, which philosophy and religion have too outwardly and literally striven to express in the popular doctrine of the immortality of the soul. The reality is more excellent than the report. Here is no ruin, no discontinuity, no spent ball. The divine circulations never rest nor linger. Nature is the incarnation of a thought, and turns to a thought again, as ice becomes water and gas. The word is mind precipitated, and the volatile essence is forever escaping again into the state of free thought. Hence the virtue and pungency of the influence on the mind of natural objects, whether inorganic or organized. Man imprisoned, man crystallized, man vegetative, speaks to man impersonated. That power which does not respect quantity, which makes the whole and the particle its equal channel, delegates its smile to the morning, and distils its essence into every drop of rain. Every moment instructs, and every object; for wisdom is infused into every form. It has been poured into us as blood; it convulsed us as pain; it slid into us as pleasure; it enveloped us in dull, melancholy days, or in days of cheerful labor; we did not guess its essence until after a long time.

POLITICS

Gold and iron are good
To buy iron and gold;
All earth's fleece and food
For their like are sold.
Boded Merlin wise,
Proved Napoleon great—
Nor kind nor coinage buys
Aught above its rate.
Fear, Craft and Avarice
Cannot rear a State.
Out of dust to build
What is more than dust—
Walls Amphion piled

Phœbus stablish must.
When the Muses nine
With the Virtues meet,
Find to their design
An Atlantic seat,
By green orchard boughs
Fended from the heat,
Where the statesman ploughs
Furrow for the wheat;
When the Church is social worth,
When the state-house is the hearth,
Then the perfect State is come,
The republican at home.

IN DEALING with the State we ought to remember that its institutions are not aboriginal, though they existed before we were born; that they are not superior to the citizen; that every one of them was once the act of a single man; every law and usage was a man's expedient to meet a particular case; that they all are imitable, all alterable; we may make as good, we may make better. Society is an illusion to the young citizen. It lies before him in rigid repose, with certain names, men and institutions rooted like oak-trees to the centre, round which all arrange themselves the best they can. But the old statesman knows that society is fluid; there are no such roots and centres, but any particle may suddenly become the centre of the movement and compel the system to gyrate round it; as every man of strong will, like Pisistratus or Cromwell, does for a time, and every man of truth like Plato or Paul, does forever. But politics rest on necessary foundations, and cannot be treated with levity. Republics abound in young civilians who believe that the laws make the city, that grave modifications of the policy and modes of living and employments of the population, that commerce, education and religion may be voted in or out; and that any measure, though it were absurd, may be imposed on a people if only you can get

378

sufficient voices to make it a law. But the wise know that foolish legislation is a rope of sand which perishes in the twisting; that the State must follow and not lead the character and progress of the citizen; the strongest usurper is quickly got rid of; and they only who build on Ideas, build for eternity; and that the form of government which prevails is the expression of what cultivation exists in the population which permits it. The law is only a memorandum. We are superstitious, and esteem the statute somewhat: so much life as it has in the character of living men is its force. The statute stands there to say, Yesterday we agreed so and so, but how feel ye this article to-day? Our statute is a currency which we stamp with our own portrait: it soon becomes unrecognizable, and in process of time will return to the mint. Nature is not democratic, nor limited-monarchical, but despotic, and will not be fooled or abated of any jot of her authority by the pertest of her sons; and as fast as the public mind is opened to more intelligence, the code is seen to be brute and stammering. It speaks not articulately, and must be made to. Meantime the education of the general mind never stops. The reveries of the true and simple are prophetic. What the tender poetic youth dreams, and prays, and paints to-day, but shuns the ridicule of saying aloud, shall presently be the resolutions of public bodies; then shall be carried as grievance and bill of rights through conflict and war, and then shall be triumphant law and establishment for a hundred years, until it gives place in turn to new prayers and pictures. The history of the State sketches in coarse outline the progress of thought, and follows at a distance the delicacy of culture and of aspiration.

The theory of politics which has possessed the mind of men, and which they have expressed the best they could in their laws and in their revolutions, considers persons and property as the two objects for whose protection government exists. Of persons, all have equal rights, in virtue of being identical in nature. This interest of course with its whole power demands a democracy. Whilst the rights of all as persons are equal, in virtue of their access to reason, their rights in property are very unequal. One man owns his clothes, and another owns a country. This accident, depending primarily on the skill and virtue of the parties, of which there is every degree, and secondarily on patrimony, falls unequally, and its rights of course are unequal. Personal rights, universally the same, demand a government framed on the ratio of the census;

property demands a government framed on the ratio of owners and of owning. Laban, who has flocks and herds, wishes them looked after by an officer on the frontiers, lest the Midianites shall drive them off; and pays a tax to that end. Jacob has no flocks or herds and no fear of the Midianites, and pays no tax to the officer. It seemed fit that Laban and Jacob should have equal rights to elect the officer who is to defend their persons, but that Laban and not Jacob should elect the officer who is to guard the sheep and cattle. And if question arise whether additional officers or watch-towers should be provided, must not Laban and Isaac, and those who must sell part of their herds to buy protection for the rest, judge better of this, and with more right, than Jacob, who, because he is a youth and a traveller, eats their bread and not his own?

In the earliest society the proprietors made their own wealth, and so long as it comes to the owners in the direct way, no other opinion would arise in any equitable community than that property should make the law for property, and persons the law for persons.

But property passes through donation or inheritance to those who do not create it. Gift, in one case, makes it as really the new owner's, as labor made it the first owner's: the other case, of patrimony, the law makes an ownership which will be valid in each man's view according to the estimate which he sets on the public tranquillity.

It was not, however, found easy to embody the readily admitted principle that property should make law for property, and persons for persons, since persons and property mixed themselves in every transaction. At last it seemed settled that the rightful distinction was that the proprietors should have more elective franchise than non-proprietors, on the Spartan principle of "calling that which is just, equal; not that which is equal, just."

That principle no longer looks so self-evident as it appeared in former times, partly because doubts have arisen whether too much weight had not been allowed in the laws to property, and such a structure given to our usages as allowed the rich to encroach on the poor, and to keep them poor; but mainly because there is an instinctive sense, however obscure and yet inarticulate, that the whole constitution of property, on its present tenures, is injurious, and its influence on persons deteriorating and degrading; that truly the only interest for the consideration of the State is persons; that property will always follow persons; that the highest end of government is the culture of men; and that if men can be educated, the institutions will share their improvement and the moral sentiment will write the law of the land.

If it be not easy to settle the equity of this question, the peril is less when we take note of our natural defences. We are kept by better guards than the vigilance of such magistrates as we commonly elect. Society always consists in greatest part of young and foolish persons. The old, who have seen through the hypocrisy of courts and statesmen, die and leave no wisdom to their sons. They believe their own newspaper, as their fathers did at their age. With such an ignorant and deceivable majority, States would soon run to ruin, but that there are limitations beyond which the folly and ambition of governors cannot go. Things have their laws, as well as men; and things refuse to be trifled with. Property will be protected. Corn will not grow unless it is planted and manured; but the farmer will not plant or hoe it unless the chances are a hundred to one that he will cut and harvest it. Under any forms, persons and property must and will have their just sway. They exert their power, as steadily as matter its attraction. Cover up a pound of earth never so cunningly, divide and subdivide it; melt it to liquid, convert it to gas; it will always weigh a pound; it will always attract and resist other matter by the full virtue of one pound weight: and the attributes of a person, his wit and his moral energy, will exercise, under any law or extinguishing tyranny, their proper force, if not overtly, then covertly; if not for the law, then against it; if not wholesomely, then poisonously; with right, or by might.

The boundaries of personal influence it is impossible to fix, as persons are organs of moral or supernatural force. Under the dominion of an idea which possesses the minds of multitudes, as civil freedom, or the religious sentiment, the powers of persons are no longer subjects of calculation. A nation of men unanimously bent on freedom or conquest can easily confound the arithmetic of statists, and achieve extravagant actions, out of all proportion to their means; as the Greeks, the Saracens, the Swiss, the Americans, and the French have done.

In like manner to every particle of property belongs its own attraction. A cent is the representative of a certain quantity of corn or other commodity. Its value is in the necessities of the animal man. It is so much warmth, so much bread, so much water, so much land. The law may do what it will with the owner of property; its just power will still attach to the cent. The law may in a mad freak say that all shall have power except the owners of property; they shall have no vote. Never-theless, by a higher law, the property will, year after year, write every statute that respects property. The non-proprietor will be the scribe of the proprietor. What the owners wish to do, the whole power of prop-erty will do, either through the law or else in defiance of it. Of course I speak of all the property, not merely of the great estates. When the rich are outvoted, as frequently happens, it is the joint treasury of the poor which exceeds their accumulations. Every man owns something, if it is only a cow, or a wheelbarrow, or his arms, and so has that property to dispose of.

The same necessity which secures the rights of person and property against the malignity or folly of the magistrate, determines the form and methods of governing, which are proper to each nation and to its habit of thought, and nowise transferable to other states of society. In this country we are very vain of our political institutions, which are sin-gular in this, that they sprung, within the memory of living men, from the character and condition of the people, which they still express with sufficient fidelity—and we ostentatiously prefer them to any other in history. They are not better, but only fitter for us. We may be wise in asserting the advantage in modern times of the democratic form, but to other states of society, in which religion consecrated the monarchical, that and not this was expedient. Democracy is better for us, because the religious sentiment of the present time accords better with it. Born democrats, we are nowise qualified to judge of monarchy, which, to our fathers living in the monarchical idea, was also relatively right. But our institutions, though in coincidence with the spirit of the age, have not any exemption from the practical defects which have discredited other forms. Every actual State is corrupt. Good men must not obey the laws too well. What satire on government can equal the severity of censure conveyed in the word *politic*, which now for ages has signified *cunning*, intimating that the State is a trick?

The same benign necessity and the same practical abuse appear in the parties, into which each State divides itself, of opponents and defenders of the administration of the government. Parties are also founded on instincts, and have better guides to their own humble aims than the sagacity of their leaders. They have nothing perverse in their origin, but rudely mark some real and lasting relation. We might as wisely reprove the east wind or the frost, as a political party, whose members, for the most part, could give no account of their position, but stand for the defence of those interests in which they find themselves. Our quarrel with them begins when they quit this deep natural ground at the bidding of some leader, and obeying personal considerations, throw themselves into the maintenance and defence of points nowise belonging to their system. A party is perpetually corrupted by personality. Whilst we absolve the association from dishonesty, we cannot extend the same charity to their leaders. They reap the rewards of the docility and zeal of the masses which they direct. Ordinarily our parties are parties of circumstance, and not of principle; as the planting interest in conflict with the commercial; the party of capitalists and that of operatives: parties which are identical in their moral character, and which can easily change ground with each other in the support of many of their measures. Parties of principle, as, religious sects, or the party of free-trade, of universal suffrage, of abolition of slavery, of abolition of capital punishment—degenerate into personalities, or would inspire enthusiasm. The vice of our leading parties in this country (which may be cited as a fair specimen of these societies of opinion) is that they do not plant themselves on the deep and necessary grounds to which they are respectively entitled, but lash themselves to fury in the carrying of some local and momentary measure, nowise useful to the commonwealth. Of the two great parties which at this hour almost share the nation between them, I should say that one has the best cause, and the other contains the best men. The philosopher, the poet, or the religious man, will of course wish to cast his vote with the democrat, for free-trade, for wide suffrage, for the abolition of legal cruelties in the penal code, and for facilitating in every manner the access of the young and the poor to the sources of wealth and power. But he can rarely accept the persons whom the so-called popular party propose to him as representatives of these liberalities. They have not at heart the ends which give to the name of democracy what hope and virtue are in it. The spirit of our American radicalism is destructive and aimless: it is not loving; it has no ulterior and divine ends, but is destructive only out of hatred and selfishness. On the other side, the conservative party, composed of the most moderate, able and cultivated part of the population, is timid, and merely defensive of property. It vindicates no right, it aspires to no real good, it brands no crime, it proposes no generous policy; it does not build, nor write, nor cherish the arts, nor foster religion, nor establish schools, nor encourage science, nor emancipate the slave, nor befriend the poor, or the Indian, or the immigrant. From neither party, when in power, has the world any benefit to expect in science, art, or humanity, at all commensurate with the resources of the nation.

I do not for these defects despair of our republic. We are not at the mercy of any waves of chance. In the strife of ferocious parties, human nature always finds itself cherished; as the children of the convicts at Botany Bay are found to have as healthy a moral sentiment as other children. Citizens of feudal states are alarmed at our democratic institutions lapsing into anarchy, and the older and more cautious among ourselves are learning from Europeans to look with some terror at our turbulent freedom. It is said that in our license of construing the Constitution, and in the despotism of public opinion, we have no anchor; and one foreign observer thinks he has found the safeguard in the sanctity of Marriage among us; and another thinks he has found it in our Calvinism. Fisher Ames expressed the popular security more wisely, when he compared a monarchy and a republic saying that a monarchy is a merchantman, which sails well, but will sometimes strike on a rock and go to the bottom; whilst a republic is a raft, which would never sink, but then your feet are always in water. No forms can have any dangerous importance whilst we are befriended by the laws of things. It makes no difference how many tons' weight of atmosphere presses on our heads, so long as the same pressure resists it within the lungs. Augment the mass a thousand-fold, it cannot begin to crush us, as long as reaction is equal to action. The fact of two poles, of two forces, centripetal and centrifugal, is universal, and each force by its own activity develops the other. Wild liberty develops iron conscience. Want of liberty, by strengthening law and decorum, stupefies conscience. 'Lynch-law' prevails only where there is greater hardihood and self-subsistency in the leaders. A mob cannot be a permanency; everybody's interest requires that it should not exist, and only justice satisfies all.

We must trust infinitely to the beneficent necessity which shines through all laws. Human nature expresses itself in them as characteristically as in statues, or songs, or railroads; and an abstract of the codes of nations would be a transcript of the common conscience. Governments have their origin in the moral identity of men. Reason for one

. . . .

is seen to be reason for another, and for every other. There is a middle measure which satisfies all parties, be they never so many or so resolute for their own. Every man finds a sanction for his simplest claims and deeds, in decisions of his own mind, which he calls Truth and Holiness. In these decisions all the citizens find a perfect agreement, and only in these; not in what is good to eat, good to wear, good use of time, or what amount of land or of public aid each is entitled to claim. This truth and justice men presently endeavor to make application of to the measuring of land, the apportionment of service, the protection of life and property. Their first endeavors, no doubt, are very awkward. Yet absolute right is the first governor; or, every government is an impure theocracy. The idea after which each community is aiming to make and mend its law, is the will of the wise man. The wise man it cannot find in nature, and it makes awkward but earnest efforts to secure his government by contrivance; as by causing the entire people to give their voices on every measure; or by a double choice to get the representation of the whole; or by a selection of the best citizens; or to secure the advantages of efficiency and internal peace by confiding the government to one, who may himself select his agents. All forms of government symbolize an immortal government, common to all dynasties and independent of numbers, perfect where two men exist, perfect where there is only one man.

Every man's nature is a sufficient advertisement to him of the character of his fellows. My right and my wrong is their right and their wrong. Whilst I do what is fit for me, and abstain from what is unfit, my neighbor and I shall often agree in our means, and work together for a time to one end. But whenever I find my dominion over myself not sufficient for me, and undertake the direction of him also, I overstep the truth, and come into false relations to him. I may have so much more skill or strength than he that he cannot express adequately his sense of wrong, but it is a lie, and hurts like a lie both him and me. Love and nature cannot maintain the assumption; it must be executed by a practical lie, namely by force. This undertaking for another is the blunder which stands in colossal ugliness in the governments of the world. It is the same thing in numbers, as in a pair, only not quite so intelligible. I can see well enough a great difference between my setting myself down to a self-control, and my going to make somebody else act after my views; but when a quarter of the human race assume to tell me what I must do, I may be too much disturbed by the circumstances to see so clearly the absurdity of their command. Therefore all public ends look vague and quixotic beside private ones. For any laws but those which men make for themselves are laughable. If I put myself in the place of my child, and we stand in one thought and see that things are thus or thus, that perception is law for him and me. We are both there, both act. But if, without carrying him into the thought, I look over into his plot, and, guessing how it is with him, ordain this or that, he will never obey me. This is the history of governments—one man does something which is to bind another. A man who cannot be acquainted with me, taxes me; looking from afar at me ordains that a part of my labor shall go to this or that whimsical end—not as I, but as he happens to fancy. Behold the consequence. Of all debts men are least willing to pay the taxes. What a satire is this on government! Everywhere they think they get their money's worth, except for these.

Hence the less government we have the better—the fewer laws, and the less confided power. The antidote to this abuse of formal government is the influence of private character, the growth of the Individual; the appearance of the principal to supersede the proxy; the appearance of the wise man; of whom the existing government is, it must be owned, but a shabby imitation. That which all things tend to educe; which freedom, cultivation, intercourse, revolutions, go to form and deliver, is character; that is the end of Nature, to reach unto this coronation of her king. To educate the wise man the State exists, and with the appearance of the wise man the State expires. The appearance of character makes the State unnecessary. The wise man is the State. He needs no army, fort, or navy—he loves men too well; no bribe, or feast, or palace, to draw friends to him; no vantage ground, no favorable circumstance. He needs no library, for he has not done thinking; no church, for he is a prophet; no statute-book, for he has the lawgiver; no money, for he is value; no road, for he is at home where he is; no experience, for the life of the creator shoots through him, and looks from his eyes. He has no personal friends, for he who has the spell to draw the prayer and piety of all men unto him needs not husband and educate a few to share with him a select and poetic life. His relation to men is angelic; his memory is myrrh to them; his presence, frankincense and flowers.

We think our civilization near its meridian, but we are yet only at the cock-crowing and the morning star. In our barbarous society the influence of character is in its infancy. As a political power, as the rightful lord who is to tumble all rulers from their chairs, its presence is hardly yet suspected. Malthus and Ricardo quite omit it; the Annual Register is silent; in the Conversations' Lexicon it is not set down; the President's Message, the Queen's Speech, have not mentioned it; and yet it is never nothing. Every thought which genius and piety throw into the world, alters the world. The gladiators in the lists of power feel, through all their frocks of force and simulation, the presence of worth. I think the very strife of trade and ambition is confession of this divinity; and successes in those fields are the poor amends, the fig-leaf with which the shamed soul attempts to hide its nakedness. I find the like unwilling homage in all quarters. It is because we know how much is due from us that we are impatient to show some petty talent as a substitute for worth. We are haunted by a conscience of this right to grandeur of character, and are false to it. But each of us has some talent, can do somewhat useful, or graceful, or formidable, or amusing, or lucrative. That we do, as an apology to others and to ourselves for not reaching the mark of a good and equal life. But it does not satisfy us, whilst we thrust it on the notice of our companions. It may throw dust in their eyes, but does not smooth our own brow, or give us the tranquillity of the strong when we walk abroad. We do penance as we go. Our talent is a sort of expiation, and we are constrained to reflect on our splendid moment with a certain humiliation, as somewhat too fine, and not as one act of many acts, a fair expression of our permanent energy. Most persons of ability meet in society with a kind of tacit appeal. Each seems to say, 'I am not all here.' Senators and presidents have climbed so high with pain enough, not because they think the place specially agreeable, but as an apology for real worth, and to vindicate their manhood in our eyes. This conspicuous chair is their compensation to themselves for being of a poor, cold, hard nature. They must do what they can. Like one class of forest animals, they have nothing but a prehensile tail; climb they must, or crawl. If a man found himself so rich-natured that he could enter into strict relations with the best persons and make life serene around him by the dignity and sweetness of his behavior, could he afford to circumvent the favor of the caucus and the press, and covet relations so hollow and pompous as those of a politician? Surely nobody would be a charlatan who could afford to be sincere.

The tendencies of the times favor the idea of self-government, and leave the individual, for all code, to the rewards and penalties of his own constitution; which work with more energy than we believe whilst we depend on artificial restraints. The movement in this direction has been very marked in modern history. Much has been blind and discreditable, but the nature of the revolution is not affected by the vices of the revolters; for this is a purely moral force. It was never adopted by any party in history, neither can be. It separates the individual from all party, and unites him at the same time to the race. It promises a recognition of higher rights than those of personal freedom, or the security of property. A man has a right to be employed, to be trusted, to be loved, to be revered. The power of love, as the basis of a State, has never been tried. We must not imagine that all things are lapsing into confusion if every tender protestant be not compelled to bear his part in certain social conventions; nor doubt that roads can be built, letters carried, and the fruit of labor secured, when the government of force is at an end. Are our methods now so excellent that all competition is hopeless? could not a nation of friends even devise better ways? On the other hand, let not the most conservative and timid fear anything from a premature surrender of the bayonet and the system of force. For, according to the order of nature, which is quite superior to our will, it stands thus; there will always be a government of force where men are selfish; and when they are pure enough to abjure the code of force they will be wise enough to see how these public ends of the post-office, of the highway, of commerce and the exchange of property, of museums and libraries, of institutions of art and science can be answered.

We live in a very low state of the world, and pay unwilling tribute to governments founded on force. There is not, among the most religious and instructed men of the most religious and civil nations, a reliance on the moral sentiment and a sufficient belief in the unity of things, to persuade them that society can be maintained without artificial restraints, as well as the solar system; or that the private citizen might be reasonable and a good neighbor, without the hint of a jail or a confiscation. What is strange too, there never was in any man sufficient faith in the power of rectitude to inspire him with the broad design of renovating the State on the principle of right and love. All those who have pretended this design have been partial reformers, and have admitted in some manner the supremacy of the bad State. I do not call to mind a single human being who has steadily denied the authority of the laws, on the simple ground of his own moral nature. Such designs, full of genius and full of faith as they are, are not entertained except avowedly as air-pictures. If the individual who exhibits them dare to think them practicable, he disgusts scholars and churchmen; and men of talent and women of superior sentiments cannot hide their contempt. Not the less does nature continue to fill the heart of youth with suggestions of this enthusiasm, and there are now men—if indeed I can speak in the plural number—more exactly, I will say, I have just been conversing with one man, to whom no weight of adverse experience will make it for a moment appear impossible that thousands of human beings might exercise towards each other the grandest and simplest sentiments, as well as a knot of friends, or a pair of lovers.

NOMINALIST AND REALIST

In countless upward-striving waves
The moon-drawn tide-wave strives:
In thousand far-transplanted grafts
The parent fruit survives;
So, in the new-born millions,
The perfect Adam lives.
Not less are summer mornings dear
To every child they wake,
And each with novel life his sphere
Fills for his proper sake.

I CANNOT often enough say that a man is only a relative and representative nature. Each is a hint of the truth, but far enough from being that truth which yet he quite newly and inevitably suggests to us. If I seek it in him I shall not find it. Could any man conduct into me the pure stream of that which he pretends to be! Long afterwards I find that quality elsewhere which he promised me. The genius of the Platonists is intoxicating to the student, yet how few particulars of it can I detach from all their books. The man momentarily stands for the thought, but will not bear examination; and a society of men will cursorily represent well enough a certain quality and culture, for example, chivalry or beauty of manners; but separate them and there is no gentleman and no lady in the group. The least hint sets us on the pursuit of a character which no man realizes. We have such exorbitant eyes that on seeing the smallest arc we complete the curve, and when the curtain is lifted from the diagram which it seemed to veil, we are vexed to find that no more was drawn than just that fragment of an arc which we first beheld. We are greatly too liberal in our construction of each other's faculty and promise. Exactly what the parties have already done they shall do again; but that which we inferred from their nature and inception, they will not do. That is in nature, but not in them. That happens in the world, which we often witness in a public debate. Each of the speakers expresses himself imperfectly; no one of them hears much that another says, such is the preoccupation of mind of each; and the audience, who have only to hear and not to speak, judge very wisely and superiorly how wrongheaded and unskilful is each of the debaters to his own affair. Great men or men of great gifts you shall easily find, but symmetrical men never. When I meet a pure intellectual force or a generosity of affection, I believe here then is man; and am presently mortified by the discovery that this individual is no more available to his own or to the general ends than his companions; because the power which drew my respect is not supported by the total symphony of his talents. All persons exist to society by some shining trait of beauty or utility which they have. We borrow the proportions of the man from that one fine feature, and finish the portrait symmetrically; which is false, for the rest of his body is small or deformed. I observe a person who makes a good public appearance, and conclude thence the perfection of his private character, on which this is based; but he has no private character. He is a graceful cloak or lay-figure for holidays. All our poets, heroes and saints, fail utterly in some one or in many parts to satisfy our idea, fail to draw our spontaneous interest, and so leave us without any hope of realization but in our own future. Our exaggeration of all fine characters arises from the fact that we identify each in turn with the soul. But there are no such men as we fable; no Jesus, nor Pericles, nor Cæsar, nor Angelo, nor Washington, such as we have made. We consecrate a great deal of nonsense because it was allowed by great men. There is none without his foible. I believe that if an angel should come to chant the chorus of the moral law, he would eat too much gingerbread, or take liberties with private letters, or do some precious atrocity. It is bad enough that our geniuses cannot do anything useful, but it is worse that no man is fit for society who has fine traits. He is admired at a distance, but he cannot come near without appearing a cripple. The men of fine parts protect themselves by solitude, or by courtesy, or by satire, or by an acid worldly manner; each concealing as he best can his incapacity for useful association, but they want either love or self-reliance.

Our native love of reality joins with this experience to teach us a little reserve, and to dissuade a too sudden surrender to the brilliant qualities of persons. Young people admire talents or particular excellences; as we grow older we value total powers and effects, as the impression, the quality, the spirit of men and things. The genius is all. The man, it is his system: we do not try a solitary word or act, but his habit. The acts which you praise, I praise not, since they are departures from his faith, and are mere compliances. The magnetism which arranges tribes and races in one polarity is alone to be respected; the men are steel-filings. Yet we unjustly select a particle, and say, 'O steel-filing number one! what heart-drawings I feel to thee! what prodigious virtues are these of thine! how constitutional to thee, and incommunicable!' Whilst we speak the loadstone is withdrawn; down falls our filing in a heap with the rest, and we continue our mummery to the wretched shaving. Let us go for universals; for the magnetism, not for the needles. Human life and its persons are poor empirical pretensions. A personal influence is an *ignis fatuus*. If they say it is great, it is great; if they say it is small, it is small; you see it, and you see it not, by turns; it borrows all its size from the momentary estimation of the speakers: the Will-of-the-wisp vanishes if you go too near, vanishes if you go too far, and only blazes at one angle. Who can tell if Washington be a great man or no? Who can tell if Franklin be? Yes, or any but the twelve, or six, or three great gods of fame? And they too loom and fade before the eternal.

We are amphibious creatures, weaponed for two element, having two sets of faculties, the particular and the catholic. We adjust our instrument for general observation, and sweep the heavens as easily as we pick out a single figure in the terrestrial landscape. We are practically skilful in detecting elements for which we have no place in our theory, and no name. Thus we are very sensible of an atmospheric influence in men and in bodies of men, not accounted for in an arithmetical addition of all their measurable properties. There is a genius of a nation, which is not to be found in the numerical citizens, but which characterizes the society. England, strong, punctual, practical, well-spoken England I should not find if I should go to the island to seek it. In the parliament, in the play-house, at dinner-tables, I might see a great number of rich, ignorant, book-read, conventional, proud men—many old women—and not anywhere the Englishman who made the good speeches, combined the accurate engines, and did the bold and nervous deeds. It is even worse in America, where, from the intellectual quickness of the race, the genius of the country is more splendid in its promise and more slight in its performance. Webster cannot do the work of Webster. We conceive distinctly enough the French, the Spanish, the German genius, and it is not the less real that perhaps we should not meet in either of those nations a single individual who corresponded with the type. We infer the spirit of the nation in great measure from the language, which is a sort of monument to which each forcible individual in a course of many hundred years has contributed a stone. And, universally, a good example of this social force is the veracity of language, which cannot be debauched. In any controversy concerning morals, an appeal may be made with safety to the sentiments which the language of the people expresses. Proverbs, words and grammar-inflections convey the public sense with more purity and precision than the wisest individual.

In the famous dispute with the Nominalists, the Realists had a good deal of reason. General ideas are essences. They are our gods: they round and ennoble the most partial and sordid way of living. Our proclivity to details cannot quite degrade our life and divest it of poetry. The day-laborer is reckoned as standing at the foot of the social scale, yet he is saturated with the laws of the world. His measures are the hours; morning and night, solstice and equinox, geometry, astronomy and all the lovely accidents of nature play through his mind. Money, which represents the prose of life, and which is hardly spoken of in parlors without an apology, is, in its effects and laws, as beautiful as roses. Property keeps the accounts of the world, and is always moral. The property will be found where the labor, the wisdom and the virtue have been in nations, in classes and (the whole life-time considered, with the compensations) in the individual also. How wise the world appears, when the laws and usages of nations are largely detailed, and the completeness of the municipal system is considered! Nothing is left out. If you go into the markets and the custom-houses, the insurers' and notaries' offices, the offices of sealers of weights and measures, of inspection of provisions—it will appear as if one man had made it all. Wherever you go, a wit like your own has been before you, and has realized its thought. The Eleusinian mysteries, the Egyptian architecture, the Indian astronomy, the Greek sculpture, show that there always were seeing and knowing men in the planet. The world is full of masonic ties, of guilds, of secret and public legions of honor; that of scholars, for example; and that of gentlemen, fraternizing with the upper class of every country and every culture.

I am very much struck in literature by the appearance that one person wrote all the books; as if the editor of a journal planted his body of reporters in different parts of the field of action, and relieved some by others from time to time; but there is such equality and identity both of judgment and point of view in the narrative that it is plainly the work of one all-seeing, all-hearing gentleman. I looked into Pope's Odyssey yesterday: it is as correct and elegant after our canon of to-day as if it were newly written. The modernness of all good books seems to give me an existence as wide as man. What is well done I feel as if I did; what is ill done I reck not of. Shakspeare's passages of passion (for example, in Lear and Hamlet) are in the very dialect of the present year. I am faithful again to the whole over the members in my use of books. I find the most pleasure in reading a book in a manner least flattering to the author. I read Proclus, and sometimes Plato, as I might read a dictionary, for a mechanical help to the fancy and the imagination. I read for the lustres, as if one should use a fine picture in a chromatic experiment, for its rich colors. 'T is not Proclus, but a piece of nature and fate that I explore. It is a greater joy to see the author's author, than himself. A higher pleasure of the same kind I found lately at a concert, where I went to hear Handel's Messiah. As the master overpowered the littleness and incapableness of the performers and made them conductors of his electricity, so it was easy to observe what efforts nature was making, through so many hoarse, wooden and imperfect persons, to produce beautiful voices, fluid and soul-guided men and women. The genius of nature was paramount at the oratorio.

This preference of the genius to the parts is the secret of that deification of art, which is found in all superior minds. Art, in the artist, is proportion, or a habitual respect to the whole by an eye loving beauty in details. And the wonder and charm of it is the sanity in insanity which it denotes. Proportion is almost impossible to human beings. There is no one who does not exaggerate. In conversation, men are encumbered with personality, and talk too much. In modern sculpture, picture and poetry, the beauty is miscellaneous; the artist works here and there and at all points, adding and adding, instead of unfolding the unit of his thought. Beautiful details we must have, or no artist; but they must be means and never other. The eye must not lose sight for a moment of the purpose. Lively boys write to their ear and eye, and the cool reader finds nothing but sweet jingles in it. When they grow older, they respect the argument.

We obey the same intellectual integrity when we study in exceptions the law of the world. Anomalous facts, as the never quite obsolete rumors of magic and demonology, and the new allegations of phrenologists and neurologists, are of ideal use. They are good indications. Homœopathy is insignificant as an art of healing, but of great value as criticism on the hygeia or medical practice of the time. So with Mesmerism, Swedenborgism, Fourierism, and the Millennial Church; they are poor pretensions enough, but good criticism on the science, philosophy and preaching of the day. For these abnormal insights of the adepts ought to be normal, and things of course.

All things show us that on every side we are very near to the best. It seems not worth while to execute with too much pains some one intellectual, or æsthetical, or civil feat, when presently the dream will scatter, and we shall burst into universal power. The reason of idleness and of crime is the deferring of our hopes. Whilst we are waiting we beguile the time with jokes, with sleep, with eating and with crimes.

Thus we settle it in our cool libraries, that all the agents with which we deal are subalterns, which we can well afford to let pass, and life will be simpler when we live at the centre and flout the surfaces. I wish to speak with all respect of persons, but sometimes I must pinch myself to keep awake and preserve the due decorum. They melt so fast into each other that they are like grass and trees, and it needs an effort to treat them as individuals. Though the uninspired man certainly finds persons a conveniency in household matters, the divine man does not respect them; he sees them as a rack of clouds, or a fleet of ripples which the wind drives over the surface of the water. But this is flat rebellion. Nature will not be Buddhist: she resents generalizing, and insults the philosopher in every moment with a million of fresh particulars. It is all idle talking: as much as a man is a whole, so is he also a part; and it were partial not to see it. What you say in your pompous distribution only distributes you into your class and section. You have not got rid of parts by denying them, but are the more partial. You are one thing, but Nature is *one thing and the other thing*, in the same moment. She will not remain orbed in a thought, but rushes into persons; and when each person, inflamed to a fury of personality, would conquer all things to his poor crotchet, she raises up against him another person, and by many persons incarnates again a sort of whole.

She will have all. Nick Bottom cannot play all the parts, work it how he may; there will be somebody else, and the world will be round. Everything must have its flower or effort at the beautiful, coarser or finer according to its stuff. They relieve and recommend each other, and the sanity of society is a balance of a thousand insanities. She punishes abstractionists, and will only forgive an induction which is rare and casual. We like to come to a height of land and see the landscape, just as we value a general remark in conversation. But it is not the intention of Nature that we should live by general views. We fetch fire and water, run about all day among the shops and markets, and get our clothes and shoes made and mended, and are the victims of these details; and once in a fortnight we arrive perhaps at a rational moment. If we were not thus infatuated, if we saw the real from hour to hour, we should not be here to write and to read, but should have been burned or frozen long ago. She would never get anything done, if she suffered Admirable Crichtons and universal geniuses. She loves better a wheelwright who dreams all night of wheels, and a groom who is part of his horse; for she is full of work, and these are her hands. As the frugal farmer takes care that his cattle shall eat down the rowen, and swine shall eat the waste of his house, and poultry shall pick the crumbs—so our economical mother dispatches a new genius and habit of mind into every district and condition of existence, plants an eye wherever a new ray of light can fall, and gathering up into some man every property in the universe, establishes thousandfold occult mutual attractions among her offspring, that all this wash and waste of power may be imparted and exchanged.

Great dangers undoubtedly accrue from this incarnation and distribution of the godhead, and hence Nature has her maligners, as if she were Circe; and Alphonso of Castile fancied he could have given useful advice. But she does not go unprovided; she has hellebore at the bottom of the cup. Solitude would ripen a plentiful crop of despots. The recluse thinks of men as having his manner, or as not having his manner; and as having degrees of it, more and less. But when he comes into a public assembly he sees that men have very different manners from his own, and in their way admirable. In his childhood and youth he has had many checks and censures, and thinks modestly enough of his own endowment. When afterwards he comes to unfold it in propitious circumstance, it seems the only talent; he is delighted with his success, and accounts himself already the fellow of the great. But he goes into a mob, into a banking house, into a mechanic's shop, into a mill, into a laboratory, into a ship, into a camp, and in each new place he is no better than an idiot; other talents take place, and rule the hour. The rotation which whirls every leaf and pebble to the meridian, reaches to every gift of man, and we all take turns at the top.

For Nature, who abhors mannerism, has set her heart on breaking up all styles and tricks, and it is so much easier to do what one has done before than to do a new thing, that there is a perpetual tendency to a set mode. In every conversation, even the highest, there is a certain trick, which may be soon learned by an acute person, and then that particular style continued indefinitely. Each man too is a tyrant in tendency, because he would impose his idea on others; and their trick is their natural defence. Jesus would absorb the race; but Tom Paine or the coarsest blasphemer helps humanity by resisting this exuberance of power. Hence the immense benefit of party in politics, as it reveals faults of character in a chief, which the intellectual force of the persons, with ordinary opportunity and not hurled into aphelion by hatred, could not have seen. Since we are all so stupid, what benefit that there should be two stupidities! It is like that brute advantage so essential to astronomy, of having the diameter of the earth's orbit for a base of its triangles. Democracy is morose, and runs to anarchy, but in the State and in the schools it is indispensable to resist the consolidation of all men into a few men. If John was perfect, why are you and I alive? As long as any man exists, there is some need of him; let him fight for his own. A new poet has appeared; a new character approached us; why should we refuse to eat bread until we have found his regiment and section in our old army-files? Why not a new man? Here is a new enterprise of Brook Farm, of Skeneateles, of Northampton: why so impatient to baptize them Essenes, or Port-Royalists, or Shakers, or by any known and effete name? Let it be a new way of living. Why have only two or three ways of life, and not thousands? Every man is wanted, and no man is wanted much. We came this time for condiments, not for corn. We want the great genius only for joy; for one star more in our constellation, for one tree more in our grove. But he thinks we wish to belong to him, as he wishes to occupy us. He greatly mistakes us. I think I have done well if I have acquired a new word from a good author; and my business with him is to find my own, though it were only to melt him down into an epithet or an image for daily use:

"Into paint will I grind thee, my bride!"

To embroil the confusion and make it impossible to arrive at any general statement—when we have insisted on the imperfection of individuals, our affections and our experience urge that every individual is entitled to honor, and a very generous treatment is sure to be repaid. A recluse sees only two or three persons, and allows them all their room; they spread themselves at large. The statesman looks at many, and compares the few habitually with others, and these look less. Yet are they not entitled to this generosity of reception? and is not munificence the means of insight? For though gamesters say that the cards beat all the players, though they were never so skilful, yet in the contest we are now considering, the players are also the game, and share the power of the cards. If you criticise a fine genius, the odds are that you are out of your reckoning, and instead of the poet, are censuring your own caricature of him. For there is somewhat spheral and infinite in every man, especially in every genius, which, if you can come very near him, sports with all your limitations. For rightly every man is a channel through which heaven floweth, and whilst I fancied I was criticising him, I was censuring or rather terminating my own soul. After taxing Goethe as a courtier, artificial, unbelieving, worldly—I took up this book of Helena, and found him an Indian of the wilderness, a piece of pure nature like an apple or an oak, large as morning or night, and virtuous as a brier-rose.

But care is taken that the whole tune shall be played. If we were not kept among surfaces, everything would be large and universal; now the excluded attributes burst in on us with the more brightness that they have been excluded. "Your turn now, my turn next," is the rule of the game. The universality being hindered in its primary form, comes in the secondary form of *all sides*; the points come in succession to the meridian, and by the speed of rotation a new whole is formed. Nature keeps herself whole and her representation complete in the experience of each mind. She suffers no seat to be vacant in her college. It is the secret of the world that all things subsist and do not die, but only retire a little from sight and afterwards return again. Whatever does not concern us is concealed from us. As soon as a person is no longer related to our present well-being, he is concealed, or dies, as we say. Really, all things and persons are related to us, but according to our nature they act on us not at once but in succession, and we are made aware of their presence one at a time. All persons, all things which we have known, are here present, and many more than we see; the world is full. As the ancient said, the world is a plenum or solid; and if we saw all things that really surround us we should be imprisoned and unable to move. For though nothing is impassable to the soul, but all things are pervious to it and like highways, yet this is only whilst the soul does not see them. As soon as the soul sees any object, it stops before that object. Therefore the divine Providence which keeps the universe open in every direction to the soul, conceals all the furniture and all the persons that do not concern a particular soul, from the senses of that individual. Through solidest eternal things the man finds his road as if they did not subsist, and does not once suspect their being. As soon as he needs a new object, suddenly he beholds it, and no longer attempts to pass through it, but takes another way. When he has exhausted for the time the nourishment to be drawn from any one person or thing, that object is withdrawn from his observation, and though still in his immediate neighborhood, he does not suspect its presence. Nothing is dead: men feign themselves dead, and endure mock funerals and mournful obituaries, and there they stand looking out of the window, sound and well, in some new and strange disguise. Jesus is not dead; he is very well alive: nor John, nor Paul, nor Mahomet, nor Aristotle; at times we believe we have seen them all, and could easily tell the names under which they go.

If we cannot make voluntary and conscious steps in the admirable science of universals, let us see the parts wisely, and infer the genius of nature from the best particulars with a becoming charity. What is best in each kind is an index of what should be the average of that thing. Love shows me the opulence of nature, by disclosing to me in my friend a hidden wealth, and I infer an equal depth of good in every other direction. It is commonly said by farmers that a good pear or apple costs no more time or pains to rear than a poor one; so I would have no work of art, no speech, or action, or thought, or friend, but the best.

The end and the means, the gamester and the game—life is made up of the intermixture and reaction of these two amicable powers, whose marriage appears beforehand monstrous, as each denies and tends to abolish the other. We must reconcile the contradictions as we can, but their discord and their concord introduce wild absurdities into our thinking and speech. No sentence will hold the whole truth, and the only way in which we can be just, is by giving ourselves the lie; Speech is better than silence; silence is better than speech;—All things are in contact; every atom has a sphere of repulsion;—Things are, and are not, at the same time;—and the like. All the universe over, there is but one thing, this old Two-Face, creator-creature, mind-matter, right-wrong, of which any proposition may be affirmed or denied. Very fitly therefore I assert that every man is a partialist; that nature secures him as an instrument by self-conceit, preventing the tendencies to religion and science; and now further assert, that, each man's genius being nearly and affectionately explored, he is justified in his individuality, as his nature is found to be immense; and now I add that every man is a universalist also, and, as our earth, whilst it spins on its own axis, spins all the time around the sun through the celestial spaces, so the least of its rational children, the most dedicated to his private affair, works out, though as it were under a disguise, the universal problem. We fancy men are individuals; so are pumpkins; but every pumpkin in the field goes through every point of pumpkin history. The rabid democrat, as soon as he is senator and rich man, has ripened beyond possibility of sincere radicalism, and unless he can resist the sun, he must be conservative the remainder of his days. Lord Eldon said in his old age that "if he were to begin life again, he would be damned but he would begin as agitator."

We hide this universality if we can, but it appears at all points. We are as ungrateful as children. There is nothing we cherish and strive to draw to us but in some hour we turn and rend it. We keep a running fire of sarcasm at ignorance and the life of the senses; then goes by, perchance, a fair girl, a piece of life, gay and happy, and making the commonest offices beautiful by the energy and heart with which she does them; and seeing this we admire and love her and them, and say, 'Lo! a genuine creature of the fair earth, not dissipated or too early ripened by books, philosophy, religion, society, or care!' insinuating a

· ·

treachery and contempt for all we had so long loved and wrought in ourselves and others.

If we could have any security against moods! If the profoundest prophet could be holden to his words, and the hearer who is ready to sell all and join the crusade could have any certificate that to-morrow his prophet shall not unsay his testimony! But the Truth sits veiled there on the Bench, and never interposes an adamantine syllable; and the most sincere and revolutionary doctrine, put as if the ark of God were carried forward some furlongs, and planted there for the succor of the world, shall in a few weeks be coldly set aside by the same speaker, as morbid; "I thought I was right, but I was not," and the same immeasurable credulity demanded for new audacities. If we were not of all opinions! if we did not in any moment shift the platform on which we stand, and look and speak from another! if there could be any regulation, any 'one-hour-rule,' that a man should never leave his point of view without sound of trumpet. I am always insincere, as always knowing there are other moods.

How sincere and confidential we can be, saying all that lies in the mind, and yet go away feeling that all is yet unsaid, from the incapacity of the parties to know each other, although they use the same words! My companion assumes to know my mood and habit of thought, and we go on from explanation to explanation until all is said which words can, and we leave matters just as they were at first, because of that vicious assumption. Is it that every man believes every other to be an incurable partialist, and himself a universalist? I talked yesterday with a pair of philosophers; I endeavored to show my good men that I liked everything by turns and nothing long; that I loved the centre, but doated on the superficies; that I loved man, if men seemed to me mice and rats; that I revered saints, but woke up glad that the old pagan world stood its ground and died hard; that I was glad of men of every gift and nobility, but would not live in their arms. Could they but once understand that I loved to know that they existed, and heartily wished them God-speed, yet, out of my poverty of life and thought, had no word or welcome for them when they came to see me, and could well consent to their living in Oregon for any claim I felt on them—it would be a great satisfaction.

NEW ENGLAND REFORMERS

LECTURE READ BEFORE THE SOCIETY IN AMORY
HALL, ON SUNDAY, MARCH 3, 1844

In the suburb,in the town,
On the railway, in the square,
Came a beam of goodness down
Doubling daylight everywhere:
Peace now each for malice takes,
Beauty for his sinful weeds,
For the angel Hope aye makes
Him an angel whom she leads.

WHOEVER has had opportunity of acquaintance with society in New England during the last twenty-five years, with those middle and with those leading sections that may constitute any just representation of the character and aim of the community, will have been struck with the great activity of thought and experimenting. His attention must be commanded by the signs that the Church, or religious party, is falling from the Church nominal, and is appearing in temperance and non-resistance societies; in movements of abolitionists and of socialists; and in very significant assemblies called Sabbath and Bible Conventions; composed of ultraists, of seekers, of all the soul of the soldiery of dissent, and meeting to call in question the authority of the Sabbath, of the priesthood, and of the Church. In these movements nothing was more remarkable than the discontent they begot in the movers. The spirit of protest and of detachment drove the members of these Conventions to bear testimony against the Church, and immediately afterwards to declare their discontent with these Conventions, their independence of their colleagues, and their impatience of the methods whereby they were working. They defied each other, like a congress of kings, each of whom had a realm to rule, and a way of his own that made concert unprofitable. What a fertility of projects for the salvation of the world! One apostle thought all men should go to farming, and another that no man should buy or sell, that the use of money was

402

the cardinal evil; another that the mischief was in our diet, that we eat and drink damnation. These made unleavened bread, and were foes to the death to fermentation. It was in vain urged by the housewife that God made yeast, as well as dough, and loves fermentation just as dearly as he loves vegetation; that fermentation develops the saccharine element in the grain, and makes it more palatable and more digestible. No; they wish the pure wheat, and will die but it shall not ferment. Stop, dear Nature, these incessant advances of thine; let us scotch these ever-rolling wheels! Others attacked the system of agriculture, the use of animal manures in farming, and the tyranny of man over brute nature; these abuses polluted his food. The ox must be taken from the plough and the horse from the cart, the hundred acres of the farm must be spaded, and the man must walk, wherever boats and locomotives will not carry him. Even the insect world was to be defended—that had been too long neglected, and a society for the protection of ground-worms, slugs and mosquitos was to be incorporated without delay. With these appeared the adepts of homœopathy, of hydropathy, of mesmerism, of phrenology, and their wonderful theories of the Christian miracles! Others assailed particular vocations, as that of the lawyer, that of the merchant, of the manufacturer, of the clergyman, of the scholar. Others attacked the institution of marriage as the fountain of social evils. Others devoted themselves to the worrying of churches and meetings for public worship; and the fertile forms of antinomianism among the elder puritans seemed to have their match in the plenty of the new harvest of reform.

With this din of opinion and debate there was a keener scrutiny of institutions and domestic life than any we had known; there was sincere protesting against existing evils, and there were changes of employment dictated by conscience. No doubt there was plentiful vaporing, and cases of backsliding might occur. But in each of these movements emerged a good result, a tendency to the adoption of simpler methods, and an assertion of the sufficiency of the private man. Thus it was directly in the spirit and genius of the age, what happened in one instance when a church censured and threatened to excommunicate one of its members on account of the somewhat hostile part to the church which his conscience led him to take in the anti-slavery business; the threatened individual immediately excommunicated the church, in a public and formal process. This has been several times repeated; it was excellent when it was done the first time, but of course loses all value when it is copied. Every project in the history of reform, no matter how violent and surprising, is good when it is the dictate of a man's genius and constitution, but very dull and suspicious when adopted from another. It is right and beautiful in any man to say, 'I will take this coat, or this book, or this measure of corn of yours'— in whom we see the act to be original, and to flow from the whole spirit and faith of him; for then that taking will have a giving as free and divine; but we are very easily disposed to resist the same generosity of speech when we miss originality and truth to character in it.

There was in all the practical activities of New England for the last quarter of a century, a gradual withdrawal of tender consciences from the social organizations. There is observable throughout, the contest between mechanical and spiritual methods, but with a steady tendency of the thoughtful and virtuous to a deeper belief and reliance on spiritual facts.

In politics, for example, it is easy to see the progress of dissent. The country is full of rebellion; the country is full of kings. Hands off! let there be no control and no interference in the administration of the affairs of this kingdom of me. Hence the growth of the doctrine and of the party of Free Trade, and the willingness to try that experiment, in the face of what appear incontestable facts. I confess, the motto of the Globe newspaper is so attractive to me that I can seldom find much appetite to read what is below it in its columns: "The world is governed too much." So the country is frequently affording solitary examples of resistance to the government, solitary nullifiers, who throw themselves on their reserved rights; nay, who have reserved all their rights; who reply to the assessor and to the clerk of court that they do not know the State, and embarrass the courts of law by non-juring and the commander-in-chief of the militia by non-resistance.

The same disposition to scrutiny and dissent appeared in civil, festive, neighborly, and domestic society. A restless, prying, conscientious criticism broke out in unexpected quarters. Who gave me the money with which I bought my coat? Why should professional labor and that of the counting-house be paid so disproportionately to the labor of the porter and wood-sawyer? This whole business of Trade gives me to pause and think, as it constitutes false relations between men; inasmuch as I am prone to count myself relieved of any responsibility to behave well and nobly to that person whom I pay with money; whereas if I had not that commodity, I should be put on my good behavior in all companies, and man would be a benefactor to man, as being himself his only certificate that he had a right to those aids and services which each asked of the other. Am I not too protected a person? is there not a wide disparity between the lot of me and the lot of thee, my poor brother, my poor sister? Am I not defrauded of my best culture in the loss of those gymnastics which manual labor and the emergencies of poverty constitute? I find nothing healthful or exalting in the smooth conventions of society; I do not like the close air of saloons. I begin to suspect myself to be a prisoner, though treated with all this courtesy and luxury. I pay a destructive tax in my conformity.

The same insatiable criticism may be traced in the efforts for the reform of Education. The popular education has been taxed with a want of truth and nature. It was complained that an education to things was not given. We are students of words: we are shut up in schools, and colleges, and recitation-rooms, for ten or fifteen years, and come out at last with a bag of wind, a memory of words, and do not know a thing. We cannot use our hands, or our legs, or our eyes, or our arms. We do not know an edible root in the woods, we cannot tell our course by the stars, nor the hour of the day by the sun. It is well if we can swim and skate. We are afraid of a horse, of a cow, of a dog, of a snake, of a spider. The Roman rule was to teach a boy nothing that he could not learn standing. The old English rule was, 'All summer in the field, and all winter in the study.' And it seems as if a man should learn to plant, or to fish, or to hunt, that he might secure his subsistence at all events, and not be painful to his friends and fellow-men. The lessons of science should be experimental also. The sight of a planet through a telescope is worth all the course on astronomy; the shock of the electric spark in the elbow, outvalues all the theories; the taste of the nitrous oxide, the firing of an artificial volcano, are better than volumes of chemistry.

One of the traits of the new spirit is the inquisition it fixed on our scholastic devotion to the dead languages. The ancient languages, with great beauty of structure, contain wonderful remains of genius, which draw, and always will draw, certain like-minded men—Greek men, and Roman men—in all countries, to their study; but by a wonderful drowsiness of usage they had exacted the study of *all* men. Once (say two centuries ago), Latin and Greek had a strict relation to all the science and culture there was in Europe, and the Mathematics had a momentary importance at some era of activity in physical science. These things became stereotyped as *education*, as the manner of men is. But the Good Spirit never cared for the colleges, and though all men and boys were now drilled in Latin, Greek and Mathematics, it had quite left these shells high and dry on the beach, and was now creating and feeding other matters at other ends of the world. But in a hundred high schools and colleges this warfare against common-sense still goes on. Four, or six, or ten years, the pupil is parsing Greek and Latin, and as soon as he leaves the University, as it is ludicrously styled, he shuts those books for the last time. Some thousands of young men are graduated at our colleges in this country every year, and the persons who, at forty years, still read Greek, can all be counted on your hand. I never met with ten. Four or five persons I have seen who read Plato.

But is not this absurd, that the whole liberal talent of this country should be directed in its best years on studies which lead to nothing? What was the consequence? Some intelligent persons said or thought, 'Is that Greek and Latin some spell to conjure with, and not words of reason? If the physician, the lawyer, the divine, never use it to come at their ends, I need never learn it to come at mine. Conjuring is gone out of fashion, and I will omit this conjugating, and go straight to affairs.' So they jumped the Greek and Latin, and read law, medicine, or sermons, without it. To the astonishment of all, the self-made men took even ground at once with the oldest of the regular graduates, and in a few months the most conservative circles of Boston and New York had quite forgotten who of their gownsmen was college-bred, and who was not.

One tendency appears alike in the philosophical speculation and in the rudest democratical movements, through all the petulance and all the puerility, the wish, namely, to cast aside the superfluous and arrive at short methods; urged, as I suppose, by an intuition that the human spirit is equal to all emergencies, alone, and that man is more often injured than helped by the means he uses.

I conceive this gradual casting off of material aids, and the indication of growing trust in the private self-supplied powers of the individual, to be the affirmative principle of the recent philosophy, and that it is feeling its own profound truth and is reaching forward at this very hour to the happiest conclusions. I readily concede that in this, as in every period of intellectual activity, there has been a noise of denial and protest; much was to be resisted, much was to be got rid of by those who were reared in the old, before they could begin to affirm and to construct. Many a reformer perishes in his removal of rubbish; and that makes the offensiveness of the class. They are partial; they are not equal to the work they pretend. They lose their way; in the assault on the kingdom of darkness they expend all their energy on some accidental evil, and lose their sanity and power of benefit. It is of little moment that one or two or twenty errors of our social system be corrected, but of much that the man be in his senses.

The criticism and attack on institutions, which we have witnessed, has made one thing plain, that society gains nothing whilst a man, not himself renovated, attempts to renovate things around him: he has become tediously good in some particular but negligent or narrow in the rest; and hypocrisy and vanity are often the disgusting result.

It is handsomer to remain in the establishment better than the establishment, and conduct that in the best manner, than to make a sally against evil by some single improvement, without supporting it by a total regeneration. Do not be so vain of your one objection. Do you think there is only one? Alas! my good friend, there is no part of society or of life better than any other part. All our things are right and wrong together. The wave of evil washes all our institutions alike. Do you complain of our Marriage? Our marriage is no worse than our education, our diet, our trade, our social customs. Do you complain of the laws of Property? It is a pedantry to give such importance to them. Can we not play the game of life with these counters, as well as with those? in the institution of property, as well as out of it? Let into it the new and renewing principle of love, and property will be universality. No one gives the impression of superiority to the institution, which he must give who will reform it. It makes no difference what you say, you must make me feel that you are aloof from it; by your natural and supernatural advantages do easily see to the end of it—do see how man can do without it. Now all men are on one side. No man deserves to be heard against property. Only Love, only an Idea, is against property as we hold it.

I cannot afford to be irritable and captious, nor to waste all my time in attacks. If I should go out of church whenever I hear a false sentiment I could never stay there five minutes. But why come out? the street is as false as the church, and when I get to my house, or to my manners, or to my speech, I have not got away from the lie. When we see an eager assailant of one of these wrongs, a special reformer, we feel like asking him, What right have you, sir, to your one virtue? Is virtue piecemeal? This is a jewel amidst the rags of a beggar.

In another way the right will be vindicated. In the midst of abuses, in the heart of cities, in the aisles of false churches, alike in one place and in another—wherever, namely, a just and heroic soul finds itself, there it will do what is next at hand, and by the new quality of character it shall put forth it shall abrogate that old condition, law, or school in which it stands, before the law of its own mind.

If partiality was one fault of the movement party, the other defect was their reliance on Association. Doubts such as those I have intimated drove many good persons to agitate the questions of social reform. But the revolt against the spirit of commerce, the spirit of aristocracy, and the inveterate abuses of cities, did not appear possible to individuals; and to do battle against numbers they armed themselves with numbers, and against concert they relied on new concert.

Following or advancing beyond the ideas of St. Simon, of Fourier, and of Owen, three communities have already been formed in Massachusetts on kindred plans, and many more in the country at large. They aim to give every member a share in the manual labor, to give an equal reward to labor and to talent, and to unite a liberal culture with an education to labor. The scheme offers, by the economies of associated labor and expense, to make every member rich, on the same amount of property that, in separate families, would leave every member poor. These new associations are composed of men and women of superior talents and sentiments; yet it may easily be questioned whether such a community will draw, except in its beginnings, the able and the good; whether those who have energy will not prefer their chance of superiority and power in the world, to the humble certainties of the association; whether such a retreat does not promise to become an asylum to those who have tried and failed, rather than a field to the strong; and whether the members will not necessarily be fractions of men, because each finds that he cannot enter it without some compromise. Friendship and association are very fine things, and a grand phalanx of the best of the human race, banded for some catholic object; yes, excellent; but remember that no society can ever be so large as one man. He, in his friendship, in his natural and momentary associations, doubles or multiplies himself; but in the hour in which he mortgages himself to two or ten or twenty, he dwarfs himself below the stature of one.

But the men of less faith could not thus believe, and to such, concert appears the sole specific of strength. I have failed, and you have failed, but perhaps together we shall not fail. Our housekeeping is not satisfactory to us, but perhaps a phalanx, a community, might be. Many of us have differed in opinion, and we could find no man who could make the truth plain, but possibly a college, or an ecclesiastical council, might. I have not been able either to persuade my brother or to prevail on myself to disuse the traffic or the potation of brandy, but perhaps a pledge of total abstinence might effectually restrain us. The candidate my party votes for is not to be trusted with a dollar, but he will be honest in the Senate, for we can bring public opinion to bear on him. Thus concert was the specific in all cases. But concert is neither better nor worse, neither more nor less potent, than individual force. All the men in the world cannot make a statue walk and speak, cannot make a drop of blood, or a blade of grass, any more than one man can. But let there be one man, let there be truth in two men, in ten men, then is concert for the first time possible; because the force which moves the world is a new quality, and can never be furnished by adding whatever quantities of a different kind. What is the use of the concert of the false and the disunited? There can be no concert in two, where there is no concert in one. When the individual is not *individual*, but is dual; when his thoughts look one way and his actions another; when his faith is traversed by his habits; when his will, enlightened by reason, is warped by his sense; when with one hand he rows and with the other backs water, what concert can be?

I do not wonder at the interest these projects inspire. The world is awaking to the idea of union, and these experiments show what it is thinking of. It is and will be magic. Men will live and communicate, and plough, and reap, and govern, as by added ethereal power, when once they are united; as in a celebrated experiment, by expiration and respiration exactly together, four persons lift a heavy man from the ground by the little finger only, and without sense of weight. But this

. . . .

union must be inward, and not one of covenants, and is to be reached by a reverse of the methods they use. The union is only perfect when all the uniters are isolated. It is the union of friends who live in different streets or towns. Each man, if he attempts to join himself to others, is on all sides cramped and diminished of his proportion; and the stricter the union the smaller and the more pitiful he is. But leave him alone, to recognize in every hour and place the secret soul; he will go up and down doing the works of a true member, and, to the astonishment of all, the work will be done with concert, though no man spoke. Government will be adamantine without any governor. The union must be ideal in actual individualism.

I pass to the indication in some particulars of that faith in man, which the heart is preaching to us in these days, and which engages the more regard, from the consideration that the speculations of one generation are the history of the next following.

In alluding just now to our system of education, I spoke of the deadness of its details. But it is open to graver criticism than the palsy of its members: it is a system of despair. The disease with which the human mind now labors is want of faith. Men do not believe in a power of education. We do not think we can speak to divine sentiments in man, and we do not try. We renounce all high aims. We believe that the defects of so many perverse and so many frivolous people who make up society, are organic, and society is a hospital of incurables. A man of good sense but of little faith, whose compassion seemed to lead him to church as often as he went there, said to me that "he liked to have concerts, and fairs, and churches, and other public amusements go on." I am afraid the remark is too honest, and comes from the same origin as the maxim of the tyrant, "If you would rule the world quietly, you must keep it amused." I notice too that the ground on which eminent public servants urge the claims of popular education is fear; 'This country is filling up with thousands and millions of voters, and you must educate them to keep them from our throats.' We do not believe that any education, any system of philosophy, any influence of genius, will ever give depth of insight to a superficial mind. Having settled ourselves into this infidelity, our skill is expended to procure alleviations, diversion, opiates. We adorn the victim with manual skill, his tongue with languages, his body with inoffensive and comely manners. So have we cunningly hid the tragedy of limitation and inner death we cannot avert. Is it strange that society should be devoured by a secret melancholy which breaks through all its smiles and all its gayety and games?

But even one step farther our infidelity has gone. It appears that some doubt is felt by good and wise men whether really the happiness and probity of men is increased by the culture of the mind in those disciplines to which we give the name of education. Unhappily too the doubt comes from scholars, from persons who have tried these methods. In their experience the scholar was not raised by the sacred thoughts amongst which he dwelt, but used them to selfish ends. He was a profane person, and became a showman, turning his gifts to a marketable use, and not to his own sustenance and growth. It was found that the intellect could be independently developed, that is, in separation from the man, as any single organ can be invigorated, and the result was monstrous. A canine appetite for knowledge was generated, which must still be fed but was never satisfied, and this knowledge, not being directed on action, never took the character of substantial, humane truth, blessing those whom it entered. It gave the scholar certain powers of expression, the power of speech, the power of poetry, of literary art, but it did not bring him to peace or to beneficence.

When the literary class betray a destitution of faith, it is not strange that society should be disheartened and sensualized by unbelief. What remedy? Life must be lived on a higher plane. We must go up to a higher platform, to which we are always invited to ascend; there, the whole aspect of things changes. I resist the scepticism of our education and of our educated men. I do not believe that the differences of opinion and character in men are organic. I do not recognize, beside the class of the good and the wise, a permanent class of sceptics, or a class of conservatives, or of malignants, or of materialists. I do not believe in two classes. You remember the story of the poor woman who importuned King Philip of Macedon to grant her justice, which Philip refused: the woman exclaimed, "I appeal:" the king, astonished, asked to whom she appealed: the woman replied, "From Philip drunk to Philip sober." The text will suit me very well. I believe not in two classes of men, but in man in two moods, in Philip drunk and Philip sober. I think, according to the good-hearted word of Plato, "Unwillingly the soul is deprived of truth." Iron conservative, miser, or thief, no man is but by a supposed necessity which he tolerates by shortness or torpidity of sight. The soul lets no man go without some visitations and holidays of a diviner presence. It would be easy to show, by a narrow scanning of any man's biography, that we are not so wedded to our paltry performances of every kind but that every man has at intervals the grace to scorn his performances, in comparing them with his belief of what he should do; that he puts himself on the side of his enemies, listening gladly to what they say of him, and accusing himself of the same things.

What is it men love in Genius, but its infinite hope, which degrades all it has done? Genius counts all its miracles poor and short. Its own idea is never executed. The Iliad, the Hamlet, the Doric column, the Roman arch, the Gothic minster, the German anthem, when they are ended, the master casts behind him. How sinks the song in the waves of melody which the universe pours over his soul! Before that gracious Infinite out of which he drew these few strokes, how mean they look, though the praises of the world attend them. From the triumphs of his art he turns with desire to this greater defeat. Let those admire who will. With silent joy he sees himself to be capable of a beauty that eclipses all which his hands have done; all which human hands have ever done.

Well, we are all the children of genius, the children of virtue—and feel their inspirations in our happier hours. Is not every man sometimes a radical in politics? Men are conservatives when they are least vigorous, or when they are most luxurious. They are conservatives after dinner, or before taking their rest; when they are sick, or aged. In the morning, or when their intellect or their conscience has been aroused; when they hear music, or when they read poetry, they are radicals. In the circle of the rankest tories that could be collected in England, Old or New, let a powerful and stimulating intellect, a man of great heart and mind act on them, and very quickly these frozen conservators will yield to the friendly influence, these hopeless will begin to hope, these haters will begin to love, these immovable statues will begin to spin and revolve. I cannot help recalling the fine anecdote which Warton relates of Bishop Berkeley, when he was preparing to leave England with his plan of planting the gospel among the American savages. "Lord Bathurst told me that the members of the Scriblerus Club being met at his house at dinner, they agreed to rally Berkeley, who was also his guest, on his scheme at Bermudas. Berkeley, having listened to the many lively things they had to say, begged to be heard in his turn, and displayed his plan with such an astonishing and animating force of eloquence and enthusiasm that they were struck dumb, and, after some pause, rose up all together with earnestness, exclaiming, 'Let us set out with him immediately.'" Men in all ways are better than they seem. They like flattery for the moment, but they know the truth for their own. It is a foolish cowardice which keeps us from trusting them and speaking to them rude truth. They resent your honesty for an instant, they will thank you for it always. What is it we heartily wish of each other? Is it to be pleased and flattered? No, but to be convicted and exposed, to be shamed out of our nonsense of all kinds, and made men of, instead of ghosts and phantoms. We are weary of gliding ghostlike through the world, which is itself so slight and unreal. We crave a sense of reality, though it comes in strokes of pain. I explain so—by this manlike love of truth—those excesses and errors into which souls of great vigor, but not equal insight, often fall. They feel the poverty at the bottom of all the seeming affluence of the world. They know the speed with which they come straight through the thin masquerade, and conceive a disgust at the indigence of nature: Rousseau, Mirabeau, Charles Fox, Napoleon, Byron—and I could easily add names nearer home, of raging riders, who drive their steeds so hard, in the violence of living to forget its illusion: they would know the worst, and tread the floors of hell. The heroes of ancient and modern fame, Cimon, Themistocles, Alcibiades, Alexander, Cæsar, have treated life and fortune as a game to be well and skilfully played, but the stake not to be so valued but that any time it could be held as a trifle light as air, and thrown up. Cæsar, just before the battle of Pharsalia, discourses with the Egyptian priest concerning the fountains of the Nile, and offers to quit the army, the empire, and Cleopatra, if he will show him those mysterious sources.

The same magnanimity shows itself in our social relations, in the preference, namely, which each man gives to the society of superiors over that of his equals. All that a man has will he give for right relations with his mates. All that he has will he give for an erect demeanor in every company and on each occasion. He aims at such things as his neighbors prize, and gives his days and nights, his talents and his heart, to strike a good stroke, to acquit himself in all men's sight as a man. The consideration of an eminent citizen, of a noted merchant, of a man of mark in his profession; a naval and military honor, a general's commission, a marshal's baton, a ducal coronet, the laurel of poets, and, anyhow procured, the acknowledgment of eminent merit—have this lustre for each candidate that they enable him to walk erect and unashamed in the presence of some persons before whom he felt himself inferior. Having raised himself to this rank, having established his equality with class after class of those with whom he would live well, he still finds certain others before whom he cannot possess himself, because they have somewhat fairer, somewhat grander, somewhat purer, which extorts homage of him. Is his ambition pure? then will his laurels and his possessions seem worthless: instead of avoiding these men who make his fine gold dim, he will cast all behind him and seek their society only, woo and embrace this his humiliation and mortification, until he shall know why his eye sinks, his voice is husky, and his brilliant talents are paralyzed in this presence. He is sure that the soul which gives the lie to all things will tell none. His constitution will not mislead him. If it cannot carry itself as it ought, high and unmatchable in the presence of any man; if the secret oracles whose whisper makes the sweetness and dignity of his life do here withdraw and accompany him no longer—it is time to undervalue what he has valued, to dispossess himself of what he has acquired, and with Cæsar to take in his hand the army, the empire and Cleopatra, and say, "All these will I relinquish, if you will show me the fountains of the Nile." Dear to us are those who love us; the swift moments we spend with them are a compensation for a great deal of misery; they enlarge our life; but dearer are those who reject us as unworthy, for they add another life: they build a heaven before us whereof we had not dreamed, and thereby supply to us new powers out of the recesses of the spirit, and urge us to new and unattempted performances.

As every man at heart wishes the best and not inferior society, wishes to be convicted of his error and to come to himself—so he wishes that the same healing should not stop in his thought, but should penetrate his will or active power. The selfish man suffers more from his selfishness than he from whom that selfishness withholds some important benefit. What he most wishes is to be lifted to some higher platform, that he may see beyond his present fear the transalpine good, so that his fear, his coldness, his custom may be broken up like fragments of ice, melted and carried away in the great stream of good will. Do you ask my aid? I also wish to be a benefactor. I wish more to be a benefactor and servant than you wish to be served by me; and surely the greatest good fortune that could befall me is precisely to be so moved by you that I should say, 'Take me and all mine, and use me and mine freely to your ends!' for I could not say it otherwise than because a great enlargement had come to my heart and mind, which made me superior to my fortunes. Here we are paralyzed with fear; we hold on to our little properties, house and land, office and money, for the bread which they have in our experience yielded us, although we confess that our being does not flow through them. We desire to be made great; we desire to be touched with that fire which shall command this ice to stream, and make our existence a benefit. If therefore we start objections to your project, O friend of the slave, or friend of the poor or of the race, understand well that it is because we wish to drive you to drive us into your measures. We wish to hear ourselves confuted. We are haunted with a belief that you have a secret which it would highliest advantage us to learn, and we would force you to impart it to us, though it should bring us to prison or to worse extremity.

Nothing shall warp me from the belief that every man is a lover of truth. There is no pure lie, no pure malignity in nature. The entertainment of the proposition of depravity is the last profligacy and profanation. There is no scepticism, no atheism but that. Could it be received into common belief, suicide would unpeople the planet. It has had a name to live in some dogmatic theology, but each man's innocence and his real liking of his neighbor have kept it a dead letter. I remember standing at the polls one day when the anger of the political contest gave a certain grimness to the faces of the independent electors, and a good man at my side, looking on the people, remarked, "I am satisfied that the largest part of these men, on either side, mean to vote right." I suppose considerate observers, looking at the masses of men in their blameless and in their equivocal actions, will assent, that in spite of selfishness and frivolity, the general purpose in the great number of persons is fidelity. The reason why any one refuses his assent to your opinion, or his aid to your benevolent design, is in you: he refuses to accept you as a bringer of truth, because though you think you have it, he feels that you have it not. You have not given him the authentic sign.

If it were worth while to run into details this general doctrine of the latent but ever soliciting Spirit, it would be easy to adduce illustration in particulars of a man's equality to the Church, of his equality to the

State, and of his equality to every other man. It is yet in all men's memory that, a few years ago, the liberal churches complained that the Calvinistic church denied to them the name of Christian. I think the complaint was confession: a religious church would not complain. A religious man, like Behmen, Fox, or Swedenborg, is not irritated by wanting the sanction of the Church, but the Church feels the accusation of his presence and belief.

It only needs that a just man should walk in our streets to make it appear how pitiful and inartificial a contrivance is our legislation. The man whose part is taken and who does not wait for society in anything, has a power which society cannot choose but feel. The familiar experiment called the hydrostatic paradox, in which a capillary column of water balances the ocean, is a symbol of the relation of one man to the whole family of men. The wise Dandamis, on hearing the lives of Socrates, Pythagoras and Diogenes read, "judged them to be great men every way, excepting that they were too much subjected to the reverence of the laws, which to second and authorize, true virtue must abate very much of its original vigor."

And as a man is equal to the Church and equal to the State, so he is equal to every other man. The disparities of power in men are superficial; and all frank and searching conversation, in which a man lays himself open to his brother, apprises each of their radical unity. When two persons sit and converse in a thoroughly good understanding, the remark is sure to be made, See how we have disputed about words! Let a clear, apprehensive mind, such as every man knows among his friends, converse with the most commanding poetic genius, I think it would appear that there was no inequality such as men fancy, between them; that a perfect understanding, a like receiving, a like perceiving, abolished differences; and the poet would confess that his creative imagination gave him no deep advantage, but only the superficial one that he could express himself and the other could not; that his advantage was a knack, which might impose on indolent men but could not impose on lovers of truth; for they know the tax of talent, or what a price of greatness the power of expression too often pays. I believe it is the conviction of the purest men that the net amount of man and man does not much vary. Each is incomparably superior to his companion in some faculty. His want of skill in other directions has added to his fitness for his own work. Each seems to have some compensation yielded to him by his infirmity, and every hinderance operates as a concentration of his force.

These and the like experiences intimate that man stands in strict connection with a higher fact never yet manifested. There is power over and behind us, and we are the channels of its communications. We seek to say thus and so, and over our head some spirit sits which contradicts what we say. We would persuade our fellow to this or that; another self within our eyes dissuades him. That which we keep back, this reveals. In vain we compose our faces and our words; it holds uncontrollable communication with the enemy, and he answers civilly to us, but believes the spirit. We exclaim, 'There's a traitor in the house!' but at last it appears that he is the true man, and I am the traitor. This open channel to the highest life is the first and last reality, so subtle, so quiet, yet so tenacious, that although I have never expressed the truth, and although I have never heard the expression of it from any other, I know that the whole truth is here for me. What if I cannot answer your questions? I am not pained that I cannot frame a reply to the question, What is the operation we call Providence? There lies the unspoken thing, present, omnipresent. Every time we converse we seek to translate it into speech, but whether we hit or whether we miss, we have the fact. Every discourse is an approximate answer: but it is of small consequence that we do not get it into verbs and nouns, whilst it abides for contemplation forever.

If the auguries of the prophesying heart shall make themselves good in time, the man who shall be born, whose advent men and events prepare and foreshow, is one who shall enjoy his connection with a higher life, with the man within man; shall destroy distrust by his trust, shall use his native but forgotten methods, shall not take counsel of flesh and blood, but shall rely on the Law alive and beautiful which works over our heads and under our feet. Pitiless, it avails itself of our success when we obey it, and of our ruin when we contravene it. Men are all secret believers in it, else the word justice would have no meaning: they believe that the best is the true; that right is done at last; or chaos would come. It rewards actions after their nature, and not after the design of the agent. 'Work,' it saith to man, 'in every hour, paid or unpaid, see only that thou work, and thou canst not escape the reward: whether thy work be fine or coarse, planting corn or writing epics, so only it be honest work, done to thine own approbation, it shall earn a reward to the senses as well as to the thought: no matter how often defeated, you are born to victory. The reward of a thing well done, is to have done it.'

As soon as a man is wonted to look beyond surfaces, and to see how this high will prevails without an exception or an interval, he settles himself into serenity. He can already rely on the laws of gravity, that every stone will fall where it is due; the good globe is faithful, and carries us securely through the celestial spaces, anxious or resigned, we need not interfere to help it on: and he will learn one day the mild lesson they teach, that our own orbit is all our task, and we need not assist the administration of the universe. Do not be so impatient to set the town right concerning the unfounded pretensions and the false reputation of certain men of standing. They are laboring harder to set the town right concerning themselves, and will certainly succeed. Suppress for a few days your criticism on the insufficiency of this or that teacher or experimenter, and he will have demonstrated his insufficiency to all men's eyes. In like manner, let a man fall into the divine circuits, and he is enlarged. Obedience to his genius is the only liberating influence. We wish to escape from subjection and a sense of inferiority, and we make self-denying ordinances, we drink water, we eat grass, we refuse the laws, we go to jail: it is all in vain; only by obedience to his genius, only by the freest activity in the way constitutional to him, does an angel seem to arise before a man and lead him by the hand out of all the wards of the prison.

That which befits us, embosomed in beauty and wonder as we are, is cheerfulness and courage, and the endeavor to realize our aspirations. The life of man is the true romance, which when it is valiantly conducted will yield the imagination a higher joy than any fiction. All around us what powers are wrapped up under the coarse mattings of custom, and all wonder prevented. It is so wonderful to our neurologists that a man can see without his eyes, that it does not occur to them that it is just as wonderful that he should see with them; and that is ever the difference between the wise and the unwise: the latter wonders at what is unusual, the wise man wonders at the usual. Shall not the heart which has received so much, trust the Power by which it lives? May it not quit other leadings, and listen to the Soul that has guided it so gently and taught it so much, secure that the future will be worthy of the past?

PLATO; OR, THE PHILOSOPHER

[*This essay, like the one that follows it, is from* Representative Men, *which was published in 1850. The chapters in that book were originally given as a series of lectures in Boston in 1845-46, and were delivered before the Manchester Athenaeum in England in 1847-48. The chapters not included in this volume are: "Uses of Great Men," "Swedenborg; or, The Mystic," "Montaigne; or, The Skeptic," "Shakspeare; or, The Poet," and "Goethe; or, The Writer."*]

PLATO; OR, THE PHILOSOPHER

AMONG SECULAR BOOKS, Plato only is entitled to Omar's fanatical compliment to the Koran, when he said, "Burn the libraries; for their value is in this book." These sentences contain the culture of nations; these are the corner-stone of schools; these are the fountain-head of literatures. A discipline it is in logic, arithmetic, taste, symmetry, poetry, language, rhetoric, ontology, morals or practical wisdom. There was never such range of speculation. Out of Plato come all things that are still written and debated among men of thought. Great havoc makes he among our originalities. We have reached the mountain from which all these drift boulders were detached. The Bible of the learned for twenty-two hundred years, every brisk young man who says in succession fine things to each reluctant generation—Boethius, Rabelais, Erasmus, Bruno, Locke, Rousseau, Alfieri, Coleridge—is some reader of Plato, translating into the vernacular, wittily, his good things. Even the men of grander proportion suffer some deduction from the misfortune (shall I say?) of coming after this exhausting generalizer. St. Augustine, Copernicus, Newton, Behmen, Swedenborg, Goethe, are likewise his debtors and must say after him. For it is fair to credit the broadest generalizer with all the particulars deducible from his thesis.

Plato is philosophy, and philosophy, Plato—at once the glory and the shame of mankind, since neither Saxon nor Roman have availed to add any idea to his categories. No wife, no children had he, and the thinkers of all civilized nations are his posterity and are tinged with his mind. How many great men Nature is incessantly sending up out of night, to be *his* men—Platonists! the Alexandrians, a constellation of genius; the Elizabethans, not less; Sir Thomas More, Henry More, John Hales, John Smith, Lord Bacon, Jeremy Taylor, Ralph Cudworth, Sydenham, Thomas Taylor; Marcilius Ficinus and Picus Mirandola. Calvinism is in his Phædo: Christianity is in it. Mahometanism draws all its philosophy, in its hand-book of morals, the Akhlak-y-Jalaly, from him. Mysticism finds in Plato all its texts. This citizen of a town in Greece is no villager nor patriot. An Englishman reads and says, 'how

English!' a German—'how Teutonic!' an Italian—'how Roman and how Greek!' As they say that Helen of Argos had that universal beauty that every body felt related to her, so Plato seems to a reader in New England an American genius. His broad humanity transcends all sectional lines.

This range of Plato instructs us what to think of the vexed question concerning his reputed works—what are genuine, what spurious. It is singular that wherever we find a man higher by a whole head than any of his contemporaries, it is sure to come into doubt what are his real works. Thus Homer, Plato, Raffaelle, Shakspeare. For these men magnetize their contemporaries, so that their companions can do for them what they can never do for themselves; and the great man does thus live in several bodies, and write, or paint or act, by many hands; and after some time it is not easy to say what is the authentic work of the master and what is only of his school.

Plato, too, like every great man, consumed his own times. What is a great man but one of great affinities, who takes up into himself all arts, sciences, all knowables, as his food? He can spare nothing; he can dispose of every thing. What is not good for virtue, is good for knowledge. Hence his contemporaries tax him with plagiarism. But the inventor only knows how to borrow; and society is glad to forget the innumerable laborers who ministered to this architect, and reserves all its gratitude for him. When we are praising Plato, it seems we are praising quotations from Solon and Sophron and Philolaus. Be it so. Every book is a quotation; and every house is a quotation out of all forests and mines and stone quarries; and every man is a quotation from all his ancestors. And this grasping inventor puts all nations under contribution.

Plato absorbed the learning of his times—Philolaus, Timæus, Heraclitus, Parmenides, and what else; then his master, Socrates; and finding himself still capable of a larger synthesis—beyond all example then or since—he travelled into Italy, to gain what Pythagoras had for him; then into Egypt, and perhaps still farther East, to import the other element, which Europe wanted, into the European mind. This breadth entitles him to stand as the representative of philosophy. He says, in the Republic, "Such a genius as philosophers must of necessity have, is wont but seldom in all its parts to meet in one man, but its different parts generally spring up in different persons." Every man who would do anything well, must come to it from a higher ground. A philosopher must be more than a philosopher. Plato is clothed with the powers of a poet, stands upon the highest place of the poet, and (though I doubt he wanted the decisive gift of lyric expression), mainly is not a poet because he chose to use the poetic gift to an ulterior purpose.

Great geniuses have the shortest biographies. Their cousins can tell you nothing about them. They lived in their writings, and so their house and street life was trivial and commonplace. If you would know their tastes and complexions, the most admiring of their readers most resembles them. Plato especially has no external biography. If he had lover, wife, or children, we hear nothing of them. He ground them all into paint. As a good chimney burns its smoke, so a philosopher converts the value of all his fortunes into his intellectual performances.

He was born 427 B. C., about the time of the death of Pericles; was of patrician connection in his times and city, and is said to have had an early inclination for war, but, in his twentieth year, meeting with Socrates, was easily dissuaded from this pursuit and remained for ten years his scholar, until the death of Socrates. He then went to Megara, accepted the invitations of Dion and of Dionysius to the court of Sicily, and went thither three times, though very capriciously treated. He travelled into Italy; then into Egypt, where he stayed a long time; some say three—some say thirteen years. It is said he went farther, into Babylonia: this is uncertain. Returning to Athens, he gave lessons in the Academy to those whom his fame drew thither; and died, as we have received it, in the act of writing, at eighty-one years.

But the biography of Plato is interior. We are to account for the supreme elevation of this man in the intellectual history of our race— how it happens that in proportion to the culture of men they become his scholars; that, as our Jewish Bible has implanted itself in the table-talk and household life of every man and woman in the European and American nations, so the writings of Plato have preoccupied every school of learning, every lover of thought, every church, every poet— making it impossible to think, on certain levels, except through him. He stands between the truth and every man's mind, and has almost impressed language and the primary forms of thought with his name and seal. I am struck, in reading him, with the extreme modernness of his style and spirit. Here is the germ of that Europe we know so well, in its long history of arts and arms; here are all its traits, already discernible in the mind of Plato—and in none before him. It has spread itself since into a hundred histories, but has added no new element. This perpetual modernness is the measure of merit in every work of art; since the author of it was not misled by any thing short-lived or local, but abode by real and abiding traits. How Plato came thus to be Europe, and philosophy, and almost literature, is the problem to solve.

This could not have happened without a sound, sincere and catholic man, able to honor, at the same time, the ideal, or laws of the mind, and fate, or the order of nature. The first period of a nation, as of an individual, is the period of unconscious strength. Children cry, scream and stamp with fury, unable to express their desires. As soon as they can speak and tell their want and the reason of it, they become gentle. In adult life, whilst the perceptions are obtuse, men and women talk vehemently and superlatively, blunder and quarrel: their manners are full of desperation; their speech is full of oaths. As soon as, with culture, things have cleared up a little, and they see them no longer in lumps and masses but accurately distributed, they desist from that weak vehemence and explain their meaning in detail. If the tongue had not been framed for articulation, man would still be a beast in the forest. The same weakness and want, on a higher plane, occurs daily in the education of ardent young men and women. 'Ah! you don't understand me; I have never met with any one who comprehends me:' and they sigh and weep, write verses and walk alone—fault of power to express their precise meaning. In a month or two, through the favor of their good genius, they meet some one so related as to assist their volcanic estate, and, good communication being once established, they are thenceforward good citizens. It is ever thus. The progress is to accuracy, to skill, to truth, from blind force.

There is a moment in the history of every nation, when, proceeding out of this brute youth, the perceptive powers reach their ripeness and have not yet become microscopic: so that man, at that instant, extends across the entire scale, and, with his feet still planted on the immense forces of night, converses by his eyes and brain with solar and stellar creation. That is the moment of adult health, the culmination of power.

Such is the history of Europe, in all points; and such in philosophy. Its early records, almost perished, are of the immigrations from Asia, bringing with them the dreams of barbarians; a confusion of crude notions of morals and of natural philosophy, gradually subsiding through the partial insight of single teachers.

Before Pericles came the Seven Wise Masters, and we have the beginnings of geometry, metaphysics and ethics: then the partialists—deducing the origin of things from flux or water, or from air, or from fire, or from mind. All mix with these causes mythologic pictures. At last comes Plato, the distributor, who needs no barbaric paint, or tattoo, or whooping; for he can define. He leaves with Asia the vast and superlative; he is the arrival of accuracy and intelligence. "He shall be as a god to me, who can rightly divide and define."

This defining is philosophy. Philosophy is the account which the human mind gives to itself of the constitution of the world. Two cardinal facts lie forever at the base; the one, and the two. 1. Unity, or Identity; and, 2. Variety. We unite all things by perceiving the law which pervades them; by perceiving the superficial differences and the profound resemblances. But every mental act—this very perception of identity or oneness, recognizes the difference of things. Oneness and otherness. It is impossible to speak or to think without embracing both.

The mind is urged to ask for one cause of many effects; then for the cause of that; and again the cause, diving still into the profound: self-assured that it shall arrive at an absolute and sufficient one—a one that shall be all. "In the midst of the sun is the light, in the midst of the light is truth, and in the midst of truth is the imperishable being," say the Vedas. All philosophy, of East and West, has the same centripetence. Urged by an opposite necessity, the mind returns from the one to that which is not one, but other or many; from cause to effect; and affirms the necessary existence of variety, the self-existence of both, as each is involved in the other. These strictly-blended elements it is the problem of thought to separate and to reconcile. Their existence is mutually contradictory and exclusive; and each so fast slides into the other that we can never say what is one, and what it is not. The Proteus is as nimble in the highest as in the lowest grounds; when we contemplate the one, the true, the good—as in the surfaces and extremities of matter.

In all nations there are minds which incline to dwell in the conception of the fundamental Unity. The raptures of prayer and ecstasy of devotion lose all being in one Being. This tendency finds its highest expression in the religious writings of the East, and chiefly in the Indian Scriptures, in the Vedas, the Bhagavat Geeta, and the Vishnu Purana. Those writings contain little else than this idea, and they rise to pure and sublime strains in celebrating it.

The Same, the Same: friend and foe are of one stuff; the plough-man, the plough and the furrow are of one stuff; and the stuff is such and so much that the variations of form are unimportant. "You are fit" (says the supreme Krishna to a sage) "to apprehend that you are not distinct from me. That which I am, thou art, and that also is this world, with its gods and heroes and mankind. Men contemplate distinctions, because they are stupefied with ignorance." "The words *I* and *mine* constitute ignorance. What is the great end of all, you shall now learn from me. It is soul—one in all bodies, pervading, uniform, perfect, preeminent over nature, exempt from birth, growth and decay, omnipresent, made up of true knowledge, independent, unconnected with unrealities, with name, species and the rest, in time past, present and to come. The knowledge that this spirit, which is essentially one, is in one's own and in all other bodies, is the wisdom of one who knows the unity of things. As one diffusive air, passing through the perforations of a flute, is distinguished as the notes of a scale, so the nature of the Great Spirit is single, though its forms be manifold, arising from the consequences of acts. When the difference of the investing form, as that of god or the rest, is destroyed, there is no distinction." "The whole world is but a manifestation of Vishnu, who is identical with all things, and is to be regarded by the wise as not differing from, but as the same as themselves. I neither am going nor coming; nor is my dwelling in any one place; nor art thou, thou; nor are others, others; nor am I, I." As if he had said, 'All is for the soul, and the soul is Vishnu; and animals and stars are transient paintings; and light is whitewash; and durations are deceptive; and form is imprisonment; and heaven itself a decoy.' That which the soul seeks is resolution into being above form, out of Tartarus and out of heaven—liberation from nature.

If speculation tends thus to a terrific unity, in which all things are absorbed, action tends directly backwards to diversity. The first is the course or gravitation of mind; the second is the power of nature. Nature is the manifold. The unity absorbs, and melts or reduces. Nature opens and creates. These two principles reappear and interpenetrate all things, all thought; the one, the many. One is being; the other, intellect: one is necessity; the other, freedom: one, rest; the other, motion: one, power; the other, distribution: one, strength; the other, pleasure: one, consciousness; the other, definition: one, genius; the other, talent: one, earnestness; the other, knowledge: one, possession; the other, trade: one, caste; the other, culture: one, king; the other, democracy: and, if we dare carry these generalizations a step higher, and name the last tendency of both, we might say, that the end of the one is escape from organization—pure science; and the end of the other is the highest instrumentality, or use of means, or executive deity.

Each student adheres, by temperament and by habit, to the first or to the second of these gods of the mind. By religion, he tends to unity; by intellect, or by the senses, to the many. A too rapid unification, and an excessive appliance to parts and particulars, are the twin dangers of speculation.

To this partiality the history of nations corresponded. The country of unity, of immovable institutions, the seat of a philosophy delighting in abstractions, of men faithful in doctrine and in practice to the idea of a deaf, unimplorable, immense fate, is Asia; and it realizes this faith in the social institution of caste. On the other side, the genius of Europe is active and creative: it resists caste by culture; its philosophy was a discipline; it is a land of arts, inventions, trade, freedom. If the East loved infinity, the West delighted in boundaries.

European civility is the triumph of talent, the extension of system, the sharpened understanding, adaptive skill, delight in forms, delight in manifestation, in comprehensible results. Pericles, Athens, Greece, had been working in this element with the joy of genius not yet chilled by any foresight of the detriment of an excess. They saw before them no sinister political economy; no ominous Malthus; no Paris or London; no pitiless subdivision of classes—the doom of the pin-makers, the doom of the weavers, of dressers, of stockingers, of carders, of spinners, of colliers; no Ireland; no Indian caste, superinduced by the efforts of Europe to throw it off. The understanding was in its health and prime. Art was in its splendid novelty. They cut the Pentelican marble as if it were snow, and their perfect works in architecture and sculpture seemed things of course, not more difficult than the completion of a new ship at the Medford yards or new mills at Lowell. These things are in course, and may be taken for granted. The Roman legion,

. . . .

Byzantine legislation, English trade, the saloons of Versailles, the cafés of Paris, the steam-mill, steamboat, steam-coach, may all be seen in perspective; the town-meeting, the ballot-box, the newspaper and cheap press.

Meantime, Plato, in Egypt and in Eastern pilgrimages, imbibed the idea of one Deity, in which all things are absorbed. The unity of Asia and the detail of Europe; the infinitude of the Asiatic soul and the defining, result-loving, machine-making, surface-seeking, opera-going Europe—Plato came to join, and, by contact, to enhance the energy of each. The excellence of Europe and Asia are in his brain. Metaphysics and natural philosophy expressed the genius of Europe; he substructs the religion of Asia, as the base.

In short, a balanced soul was born, perceptive of the two elements. It is as easy to be great as to be small. The reason why we do not at once believe in admirable souls is because they are not in our experience. In actual life, they are so rare as to be incredible; but primarily there is not only no presumption against them, but the strongest presumption in favor of their appearance. But whether voices were heard in the sky, or not; whether his mother or his father dreamed that the infant man-child was the son of Apollo; whether a swarm of bees settled on his lips, or not—a man who could see two sides of a thing was born. The wonderful synthesis so familiar in nature; the upper and the under side of the medal of Jove; the union of impossibilities, which reappears in every object; its real and its ideal power—was now also transferred entire to the consciousness of a man.

The balanced soul came. If he loved abstract truth, he saved himself by propounding the most popular of all principles, the absolute good, which rules rulers, and judges the judge. If he made transcendental distinctions, he fortified himself by drawing all his illustrations from sources disdained by orators and polite conversers; from mares and puppies; from pitchers and soup-ladles; from cooks and criers; the shops of potters, horse-doctors, butchers and fishmongers. He cannot forgive in himself a partiality, but is resolved that the two poles of thought shall appear in his statement. His argument and his sentence are self-poised and spherical. The two poles appear; yes, and become two hands, to grasp and appropriate their own.

Every great artist has been such by synthesis. Our strength is transitional, alternating; or, shall I say, a thread of two strands. The

sea-shore, sea seen from shore, shore seen from sea; the taste of two
metals in contact; and our enlarged powers at the approach and at the
departure of a friend; the experience of poetic creativeness, which is not
found in staying at home, nor yet in travelling, but in transitions from
one to the other, which must therefore be adroitly managed to present
as much transitional surface as possible; this command of two elements
must explain the power and the charm of Plato. Art expresses the one
or the same by the different. Thought seeks to know unity in unity;
poetry to show it by variety; that is, always by an object or symbol.
Plato keeps the two vases, one of æther and one of pigment, at his side,
and invariably uses both. Things added to things, as statistics, civil history, are inventories. Things used as language are inexhaustibly
attractive. Plato turns incessantly the obverse and the reverse of the
medal of Jove.

To take an example: The physical philosophers had sketched each
his theory of the world; the theory of atoms, of fire, of flux, of spirit;
theories mechanical and chemical in their genius. Plato, a master of
mathematics, studious of all natural laws and causes, feels these, as second causes, to be no theories of the world but bare inventories and lists.
To the study of nature he therefore prefixes the dogma—"Let us
declare the cause which led the Supreme Ordainer to produce and compose the universe. He was good; and he who is good has no kind of
envy. Exempt from envy, he wished that all things should be as much
as possible like himself. Whosoever, taught by wise men, shall admit
this as the prime cause of the origin and foundation of the world, will
be in the truth." "All things are for the sake of the good, and it is the
cause of every thing beautiful." This dogma animates and impersonates
his philosophy.

The synthesis which makes the character of his mind appears in
all his talents. Where there is great compass of wit, we usually find
excellencies that combine easily in the living man, but in description
appear incompatible. The mind of Plato is not to be exhibited by a
Chinese catalogue, but is to be apprehended by an original mind in the
exercise of its original power. In him the freest abandonment is united
with the precision of a geometer. His daring imagination gives him the
more solid grasp of facts; as the birds of highest flight have the
strongest alar bones. His patrician polish, his intrinsic elegance, edged
by an irony so subtle that it stings and paralyzes, adorn the soundest

health and strength of frame. According to the old sentence, "If Jove should descend to the earth, he would speak in the style of Plato."

With this palatial air there is, for the direct aim of several of his works and running through the tenor of them all, a certain earnestness, which mounts, in the Republic and in the Phædo, to piety. He has been charged with feigning sickness at the time of the death of Socrates. But the anecdotes that have come down from the times attest his manly interference before the people in his master's behalf, since even the savage cry of the assembly to Plato is preserved; and the indignation towards popular government, in many of his pieces, expresses a personal exasperation. He has a probity, a native reverence for justice and honor, and a humanity which makes him tender for the superstitions of the people. Add to this, he believes that poetry, prophecy and the high insight are from a wisdom of which man is not master; that the gods never philosophize, but by a celestial mania these miracles are accomplished. Horsed on these winged steeds, he sweeps the dim regions, visits worlds which flesh cannot enter; he saw the souls in pain, he hears the doom of the judge, he beholds the penal metempsychosis, the Fates, with the rock and shears, and hears the intoxicating hum of their spindle.

But his circumspection never forsook him. One would say he has read the inscription on the gates of Busyrane—"Be bold;" and on the second gate—"Be bold, be bold, and everymore be bold;" and then again had paused well at the third gate—"Be not too bold." His strength is like the momentum of a falling planet, and his discretion the return of its due and perfect curve—so excellent is his Greek love of boundary and his skill in definition. In reading logarithms one is not more secure than in following Plato in his flights. Nothing can be colder than his head, when the lightnings of his imagination are playing in the sky. He has finished his thinking before he brings it to the reader, and he abounds in the surprises of a literary master. He has that opulence which furnishes, at every turn, the precise weapon he needs. As the rich man wears no more garments, drives no more horses, sits in no more chambers than the poor—but has that one dress, or equipage, or instrument, which is fit for the hour and the need; so Plato, in his plenty, is never restricted, but has the fit word. There is indeed no weapon in all the armory of wit which he did not possess and use— epic, analysis, mania, intuition, music, satire and irony, down to the customary and polite. His illustrations are poetry and his jests illustrations. Socrates' profession of obstetric art is good philosophy; and his finding that word "cookery," and "adulatory art," for rhetoric, in the Gorgias, does us as a substantial service still. No orator can measure in effect with him who can give good nicknames.

What moderation and understatement and checking his thunder in mid volley! He has good-naturedly furnished the courtier and citizen with all that can be said against the schools. "For philosophy is an elegant thing, if any one modestly meddles with it; but if he is conversant with it more than is becoming, it corrupts the man." He could well afford to be generous—he, who from the sunlike centrality and reach of his vision, had a faith without cloud. Such as his perception, was his speech: he plays with the doubt and makes the most of it: he paints and quibbles; and by and by comes a sentence that moves the sea and land. The admirable earnest comes not only at intervals, in the perfect yes and no of the dialogue, but in bursts of light. "I, therefore, Callicles, am persuaded by these accounts, and consider how I may exhibit my soul before the judge in a healthy condition. Wherefore, disregarding the honors that most men value, and looking to the truth, I shall endeavor in reality to live as virtuously as I can; and when I die, to die so. And I invite all other men, to the utmost of my power; and you too I in turn invite to this contest, which, I affirm, surpasses all contests here."

He is a great average man; one who, to the best thinking, adds a proportion and equality in his faculties, so that men see in him their own dreams and glimpses made available and made to pass for what they are. A great common-sense is his warrant and qualification to be the world's interpreter. He has reason, as all the philosophic and poetic class have: but he has also what they have not—this strong solving sense to reconcile his poetry with the appearances of the world, and build a bridge from the streets of cities to the Atlantis. He omits never this graduation, but slopes his thought, however picturesque the precipice on one side, to an access from the plain. He never writes in ecstasy, or catches us up into poetic raptures.

Plato apprehended the cardinal facts. He could prostrate himself on the earth and cover his eyes whilst he adored that which cannot be numbered, or gauged, or known, or named: that of which every thing can be affirmed and denied: that "which is entity and nonentity." He called it super-essential. He even stood ready, as in the Parmenides, to demonstrate that it was so—that this Being exceeded the limits of intellect. No man ever more fully acknowledged the Ineffable. Having paid his homage, as for the human race, to the Illimitable, he then stood erect, and for the human race affirmed, 'And yet things are knowable!'—that is, the Asia in his mind was first heartily honored—the ocean of love and power, before form, before will, before knowledge, the Same, the Good, the One; and now, refreshed and empowered by this worship, the instinct of Europe, namely, culture, returns; and he cries, 'Yet things are knowable!' They are knowable, because being from one, things correspond. There is a scale; and the correspondence of heaven to earth, of matter to mind, of the part to the whole, is our guide. As there is a science of stars, called astronomy; a science of quantities, called mathematics; a science of qualities, called chemistry; so there is a science of sciences—I call it Dialectic—which is the Intellect discriminating the false and the true. It rests on the observation of identity and diversity; for to judge is to unite to an object the notion which belongs to it. The sciences, even the best—mathematics and astronomy—are like sportsmen, who seize whatever prey offers, even without being able to make any use of it. Dialectic must teach the use of them. "This is of that rank that no intellectual man will enter on any study for its own sake, but only with a view to advance himself in that one sole science which embraces all."

"The essence or peculiarity of man is to comprehend a whole; or that which in the diversity of sensations can be comprised under a rational unity." "The soul which has never perceived the truth, cannot pass into the human form." I announce to men the Intellect. I announce the good of being interpenetrated by the mind that made nature: this benefit, namely, that it can understand nature, which it made and maketh. Nature is good, but intellect is better: as the lawgiver is before the law-receiver. I give you joy, O sons of men! that truth is altogether wholesome; that we have hope to search out what might be the very self of everything. The misery of man is to be baulked of the sight of essence and to be stuffed with conjectures; but the supreme good is reality; the supreme beauty is reality; and all virtue and all felicity depend on this science of the real: for courage is nothing else than knowledge; the fairest fortune that can befall man is to be guided by his dæmon to that which is truly his own. This also is the essence of justice—to attend every one his own: nay, the notion of virtue is not to be arrived at except through direct contemplation of the divine essence. Courage then! for "the persuasion that we must search that which we do not know, will render us, beyond comparison, better, braver and more industrious than if we thought it impossible to discover what we do not know, and useless to search for it." He secures a position not to be commanded, by his passion for reality; valuing philosophy only as it is the pleasure of conversing with real being.

Thus, full of the genius of Europe, he said, *Culture*. He saw the institutions of Sparta and recognized, more genially one would say than any since, the hope of education. He delighted in every accomplishment, in every graceful and useful and truthful performance; above all in the splendors of genius and intellectual achievement. "The whole of life, O Socrates," said Glauco, "is, with the wise, the measure of hearing such discourses as these." What a price he sets on the feats of talent, on the powers of Pericles, of Isocrates, of Parmenides! What price above price on the talents themselves! He called the several faculties, gods, in his beautiful personation. What value he gives to the art of gymnastic in education; what to geometry; what to music; what to astronomy, whose appeasing and medicinal power he celebrates! In the Timæus he indicates the highest employment of the eyes. "By us it is asserted that God invented and bestowed sight on us for this purpose— that on surveying the circles of intelligence in the heavens, we might properly employ those of our own minds, which, though disturbed when compared with the others that are uniform, are still allied to their circulations; and that having thus learned, and being naturally possessed of a correct reasoning faculty, we might, by imitating the uniform revolutions of divinity, set right our own wanderings and blunders." And in the Republic—"By each of these disciplines a certain organ of the soul is both purified and reanimated which is blinded and buried by studies of another kind; an organ better worth saving than ten thousand eyes, since truth is perceived by this alone."

He said, Culture; but he first admitted its basis, and gave immeasurably the first place to advantages of nature. His patrician tastes laid stress on the distinctions of birth. In the doctrine of the organic character and disposition is the origin of caste. "Such as were fit to govern, into their composition the informing Deity mingled gold; into the mil-

. . . .

itary, silver; iron and brass for husbandmen and artificers." The East confirms itself, in all ages, in this faith. The Koran is explicit on this point of caste. "Men have their metal, as of gold and silver. Those of you who were the worthy ones in the state of ignorance, will be the worthy ones in the state of faith, as soon as you embrace it." Plato was not less firm. "Of the five orders of things, only four can be taught to the generality of men." In the Republic he insists on the temperaments of the youth, as first of the first.

A happier example of the stress laid on nature is in the dialogue with the young Theages, who wishes to receive lessons from Socrates. Socrates declares that if some have grown wise by associating with him, no thanks are due to him; but, simply, whilst they were with him they grew wise, not because of him; he pretends not to know the way of it. "It is adverse to many, nor can those be benefited by associating with me whom the Dæmon opposes; so that it is not possible for me to live with these. With many however he does not prevent me from convers-ing, who yet are not at all benefited by associating with me. Such, O Theages, is the association with me; for, if it pleases the God, you will make great and rapid proficiency: you will not, if he does not please. Judge whether it is not safer to be instructed by some one of those who have power over the benefit which they impart to men, than by me, who benefit or not, just as it may happen." As if he had said, 'I have no system. I cannot be answerable for you. You will be what you must. If there is love between us, inconceivably delicious and profitable will our intercourse be; if not, your time is lost and you will only annoy me. I shall seem to you stupid, and the reputation I have, false. Quite above us, beyond the will of you or me, is this secret affinity or repulsion laid. All my good is magnetic, and I educate, not by lessons, but by going about my business.'

He said, Culture; he said, Nature; and he failed not to add, 'There is also the divine.' There is no thought in any mind but it quickly tends to convert itself into a power and organizes a huge instrumentality of means. Plato, lover of limits, loved the illimitable, saw the enlargement and nobility which come from truth itself and good itself, and attempted as if on the part of the human intellect, once for all to do it adequate homage—homage fit for the immense soul to receive, and yet homage becoming the intellect to render. He said then, 'Our faculties run out into infinity, and return to us thence. We can define but a little way; but here is a fact which will not be skipped, and which to shut our eyes upon is suicide. All things are in a scale; and, begin where we will, ascend and ascend. All things are symbolical; and what we call results are beginnings.'

A key to the method and completeness of Plato is his twice bisected line. After he has illustrated the relation between the absolute good and true and the forms of the intelligible world, he says: "Let there be a line cut in two unequal parts. Cut again each of these two main parts—one representing the visible, the other the intelligible world—and let these two new sections represent the bright part and the dark part of each of these worlds. You will have, for one of the sections of the visible world, images, that is, both shadows and reflections—for the other section, the objects of these images, that is, plants, animals, and the works of art and nature. Then divide the intelligible world in like manner; the one section will be of opinions and hypotheses, and the other section of truths." To these four sections, the four operations of the soul correspond—conjecture, faith, understanding, reason. As every pool reflects the image of the sun, so every thought and thing restores us an image and creature of the supreme Good. The universe is perforated by a million channels for his activity. All things mount and mount.

All his thought has this ascension; in Phædrus, teaching that beauty is the most lovely of all things, exciting hilarity and shedding desire and confidence through the universe wherever it enters, and it enters in some degree into all things—but that there is another, which is as much more beautiful than beauty as beauty is than chaos; namely, wisdom, which our wonderful organ of sight cannot reach unto, but which, could it be seen, would ravish us with its perfect reality. He has the same regard to it as the source of excellence in works of art. When an artificer he says, in the fabrication of any work, looks to that which always subsists according *to the same*; and, employing a model of this kind, expresses its idea and power in his work—it must follow that his production should be beautiful. But when he beholds that which is born and dies, it will be far from beautiful.

Thus ever: the Banquet is a teaching in the same spirit, familiar now to all the poetry and to all the sermons of the world, that the love of the sexes is initial, and symbolizes at a distance the passion of the soul for that immense lake of beauty it exists to seek. This faith in the Divinity is never out of mind, and constitutes the ground of all his dog-

mas. Body cannot teach wisdom—God only. In the same mind he constantly affirms that virtue cannot be taught; that it is not a science, but
an inspiration; that the greatest goods are produced to us through
mania and are assigned to us by a divine gift.

This leads me to that central figure which he has established in his
Academy as the organ through which every considered opinion shall
be announced, and whose biography he has likewise so labored that the
historic facts are lost in the light of Plato's mind. Socrates and Plato
are the double star which the most powerful instruments will not
entirely separate. Socrates again, in his traits and genius, is the best
example of that synthesis which constitutes Plato's extraordinary power.
Socrates, a man of humble stem, but honest enough; of the commonest history; of a personal homeliness so remarkable as to be a cause of
wit in others—the rather that his broad good nature and exquisite taste
for a joke invited the sally, which was sure to be paid. The players personated him on the stage; the potters copied his ugly face on their stone
jugs. He was a cool fellow, adding to his humor a perfect temper and
a knowledge of his man, be he who he might whom he talked with,
which laid the companion open to certain defeat in any debate—and in
debate he immoderately delighted. The young men are prodigiously
fond of him and invite him to their feasts, whither he goes for conversation. He can drink, too; has the strongest head in Athens; and after
leaving the whole party under the table, goes away as if nothing had
happened, to begin new dialogues with somebody that is sober. In
short, he was what our countrypeople call *an old one.*

He affected a good many citizen-like tastes, was monstrously fond
of Athens, hated trees, never willingly went beyond the walls, knew the
old characters, valued the bores and philistines, thought every thing in
Athens a little better than anything in any other place. He was plain
as a Quaker in habit and speech, affected low phrases, and illustrations
from cocks and quails, soup-pans and sycamore-spoons, grooms and
farriers, and unnamable offices—especially if he talked with any
superfine person. He had a Franklin-like wisdom. Thus he showed one
who was afraid to go on foot to Olympia, that it was no more than his
daily walk within doors, if continuously extended, would easily reach.

Plain old uncle as he was, with his great ears, an immense talker—
the rumor ran that on one or two occasions, in the war with Bœotia, he
had shown a determination which had covered the retreat of a troop;

and there was some story that under cover of folly, he had, in the city government, when one day he chanced to hold a seat there, evinced a courage in opposing singly the popular voice, which had well-nigh ruined him. He is very poor; but then he is hardy as a soldier, and can live on a few olives; usually, in the strictest sense, on bread and water, except when entertained by his friends. His necessary expenses were exceedingly small, and no one could live as he did. He wore no under garment; his upper garment was the same for summer and winter, and he went barefooted; and it is said that to procure the pleasure, which he loves, of talking at his ease all day with the most elegant and cultivated young men, he will now and then return to his shop and carve statues, good or bad, for sale. However that be, it is certain that he had grown to delight in nothing else than this conversation; and that, under his hypocritical pretence of knowing nothing, he attacks and brings down all the fine speakers, all the fine philosophers of Athens, whether natives or strangers from Asia Minor and the islands. Nobody can refuse to talk with him, he is so honest and really curious to know; a man who was willingly confuted if he did not speak the truth, and who willingly confuted others asserting what was false; and not less pleased when confuted than when confuting; for he thought not any evil happened to men of such a magnitude as false opinion respecting the just and unjust. A pitiless disputant, who knows nothing, but the bounds of whose conquering-intelligence no man had ever reached; whose temper was imperturbable; whose dreadful logic was always leisurely and sportive; so careless and ignorant as to disarm the wariest and draw them, in the pleasantest manner, into horrible doubts and confusion. But he always knew the way out; knew it, yet would not tell it. No escape; he drives them to terrible choices by his dilemmas, and tosses the Hippiases and Gorgiases with their grand reputations, as a boy tosses his balls. The tyrannous realist!—Meno has discoursed a thousand times, at length, on virtue, before many companies, and very well, as it appeared to him; but at this moment he cannot even tell what it is—this cramp-fish of a Socrates has so bewitched him.

This hard-headed humorist, whose strange conceits, drollery and *bonhommie* diverted the young patricians, whilst the rumor of his sayings and quibbles gets abroad every day—turns out, in the sequel, to have a probity as invincible as his logic, and to be either insane, or at least, under cover of this play, enthusiastic in his religion. When accused before the judges of subverting the popular creed, he affirms the immortality of the soul, the future reward and punishment; and refusing to recant, in a caprice of the popular government was condemned to die, and sent to the prison. Socrates entered the prison and took away all ignominy from the place, which could not be a prison whilst he was there. Crito bribed the jailer; but Socrates would not go out by treachery. "Whatever inconvenience ensue, nothing is to be preferred before justice. These things I hear like pipes and drums, whose sound makes me deaf to every thing you say." The fame of this prison, the fame of the discourses there and the drinking of the hemlock are one of the most precious passages in the history of the world.

The rare coincidence, in one ugly body, of the droll and the martyr; the keen street and market debater with the sweetest saint known to any history at that time, had forcibly struck the mind of Plato, so capacious of these contrasts; and the figure of Socrates by a necessity placed itself in the foreground of the scene, as the fittest dispenser of the intellectual treasures he had to communicate. It was a rare fortune that this Aesop of the mob and this robed scholar should meet, to make each other immortal in their mutual faculty. The strange synthesis in the character of Socrates capped the synthesis in the mind of Plato. Moreover by this means he was able, in the direct way and without envy to avail himself of the wit and weight of Socrates, to which unquestionably his own debt was great; and these derived again their principal advantage from the perfect art of Plato.

It remains to say that the defect of Plato in power is only that which results inevitably from his quality. He is intellectual in his aim; and therefore, in expression, literary. Mounting into heaven, diving into the pit, expounding the laws of the state, the passion of love, the remorse of crime, the hope of the parting soul—he is literary, and never otherwise. It is almost the sole deduction from the merit of Plato that his writings have not—what is no doubt incident to this regnancy of intellect in his work—the vital authority which the screams of prophets and the sermons of unlettered Arabs and Jews possess. There is an interval; and to cohesion, contact is necessary.

I know not what can be said in reply to this criticism but that we have come to a fact in the nature of things: an oak is not an orange. The qualities of sugar remain with sugar, and those of salt with salt.

In the second place, he has not a system. The dearest defenders and disciples are at fault. He attempted a theory of the universe, and his theory is not complete or self-evident. One man thinks he means this, and another that; he has said one thing in one place, and the reverse of it in another place. He is charged with having failed to make the transition from ideas to matter. Here is the world, sound as a nut, perfect, not the smallest piece of chaos left, never a stitch nor an end, not a mark of haste, or botching, or second thought; but the theory of the world is a thing of shreds and patches.

The longest wave is quickly lost in the sea. Plato would willingly have a Platonism, a known and accurate expression for the world, and it should be accurate. It shall be the world passed through the mind of Plato—nothing less. Every atom shall have the Platonic tinge; every atom, every relation or quality you knew before, you shall know again and find here, but now ordered; not nature, but art. And you shall feel that Alexander indeed overran, with men and horses, some countries of the planet; but countries, and things of which countries are made, elements, planet itself, laws of planet and of men, have passed through this man as bread into his body, and become no longer bread, but body: so all this mammoth morsel has become Plato. He has clapped copyright on the world. This is the ambition of individualism. But the mouthful proves too large. *Boa constrictor* has good will to eat it, but he is foiled. He falls abroad in the attempt; and biting, gets strangled: the bitten world holds the biter fast by his own teeth. There he perishes: unconquered nature lives on and forgets him. So it fares with all: so must it fare with Plato. In view of eternal nature, Plato turns out to be philosophical exercitations. He argues on this side and on that. The acutest German, the lovingest disciple, could never tell what Platonism was; indeed, admirable texts can be quoted on both sides of every great question from him.

These things we are forced to say if we must consider the effort of Plato or of any philosopher to dispose of nature—which will not be disposed of. No power of genius has ever yet had the smallest success in explaining existence. The perfect enigma remains. But there is an injustice in assuming this ambition for Plato. Let us not seem to treat with flippancy his venerable name. Men, in proportion to their intellect, have admitted his transcendent claims. The way to know him is to compare him, not with nature, but with other men. How many ages have gone by, and he remains unapproached! A chief structure of human wit, like Karnac, or the mediæval cathedrals, or the Etrurian remains, it requires all the breath of human faculty to know it. I think it is trueliest seen when seen with the most respect. His sense deepens, his merits multiply, with study. When we say, Here is a fine collection of fables; or when we praise the style, or the common sense, or arithmetic, we speak as boys, and much of our impatient criticism of the dialectic, I suspect, is no better.

The criticism is like our impatience of miles, when we are in a hurry; but it is still best that a mile should have seventeen hundred and sixty yards. The great-eyed Plato proportioned the lights and shades after the genius of our life.

PLATO: NEW READINGS

THE publication, in Mr. Bohn's "Serial Library," of the excellent translations of Plato, which we esteem one of the chief benefits the cheap press has yielded, gives us an occasion to take hastily a few more notes of the elevation and bearings of this fixed star; or to add a bulletin, like the journals, of *Plato at the latest dates*.

Modern science, by the extent of its generalization, has learned to indemnify the student of man for the defects of individuals by tracing growth and ascent in races; and, by the simple expedient of lighting up the vast background, generates a feeling of complacency and hope. The human being has the saurian and the plant in his rear. His arts and sciences, the easy issue of his brain, look glorious when prospectively beheld from the distant brain of ox, crocodile and fish. It seems as if nature, in regarding the geologic night behind her, when, in five or six millenniums, she had turned out five or six men, as Homer, Phidias, Menu and Columbus, was no wise discontented with the result. These samples attested the virtue of the tree. These were a clear amelioration of trilobite and saurus, and a good basis for further proceeding. With this artist, time and space are cheap, and she is insensible to what you say of tedious preparation. She waited tranquilly the flowing periods of paleontology, for the hour to be struck when man should arrive. Then periods must pass before the motion of the earth can be suspected; then before the map of the instincts and the cultivable powers can be drawn. But as of races, so the succession of individual men is fatal and beautiful, and Plato has the fortune in the history of mankind to mark an epoch.

Plato's fame does not stand on a syllogism, or on any masterpieces of the Socratic reasoning, or on any thesis, as for example the immortality of the soul. He is more than an expert, or a schoolman, or a geometer, or the prophet of a peculiar message. He represents the privilege of the intellect, the power, namely, of carrying up every fact to successive platforms and so disclosing in every fact a germ of expansion. These expansions are in the essence of thought. The naturalist would never help us to them by any discoveries of the extent of the universe, but is as poor when cataloguing the resolved nebula of Orion, as when measuring the angles of an acre. But the Republic of Plato, by these expansions, may be said to require and so to anticipate the astronomy of Laplace. The expansions are organic. The mind does not create what it perceives, any more than the eye creates the rose. In ascribing to Plato the merit of announcing them, we only say, Here was a more complete man, who could apply to nature the whole scale of the senses, the understanding and the reason. These expansions or extensions consist in continuing the spiritual sight where the horizon falls on our natural vision, and by this second sight discovering the long lines of law which shoot in every direction. Everywhere he stands on a path which has no end, but runs continuously round the universe. Therefore every word becomes an exponent of nature. Whatever he looks upon discloses a second sense, and ulterior senses. His perception of the generation of contraries, of death out of life and life out of death—that law by which, in nature, decomposition is recomposition, and putrefaction and cholera are only signals of a new creation; his discernment of the little in the large and the large in the small; studying the state in the citizen and the citizen in the state; and leaving it doubtful whether he exhibited the Republic as an allegory on the education of the private soul; his beautiful definitions of ideas, of time, of form, of figure, of the line, sometimes hypothetically given, as his defining of virtue, courage, justice, temperance; his love of the apologue, and his apologues themselves; the cave of Trophonius; the ring of Gyges; the charioteer and two horses; the golden, silver, brass and iron temperaments; Theuth and Thamus; and the visions of Hades and the Fates—fables which have imprinted themselves in the human memory like the signs of the zodiac; his soliform eye and his boniform soul; his doctrine of assimilation; his doctrine of reminiscence; his clear vision of the laws of return, or reaction, which secure instant justice throughout the universe, instanced everywhere, but specially in the doctrine, "what comes from God to us, returns from us to God," and in Socrates' belief that the laws below are sisters of the laws above.

More striking examples are his moral conclusions. Plato affirms the coincidence of science and virtue; for vice can never know itself and virtue, but virtue knows both itself and vice. The eye attested that justice was best, as long as it was profitable; Plato affirms that it is profitable throughout; that the profit is intrinsic, though the just conceal his justice from gods and men; that it is better to suffer injustice than to do it; that the sinner ought to covet punishment; that the lie was more hurtful than homicide; and that ignorance, or the involuntary lie, was more calamitous than involuntary homicide; that the soul is unwillingly deprived of true opinions, and that no man sins willingly; that the order or proceeding of nature was from the mind to the body, and, though a sound body cannot restore an unsound mind, yet a good soul can, by its virtue, render the body the best possible. The intelligent have a right over the ignorant, namely, the right of instructing them. The right punishment of one out of tune is to make him play in tune; the fine which the good, refusing to govern, ought to pay, is, to be governed by a worse man; that his guards shall not handle gold and silver, but shall be instructed that there is gold and silver in their souls, which will make men willing to give them every thing which they need.

This second sight explains the stress laid on geometry. He saw that the globe of earth was not more lawful and precise than was the supersensible; that a celestial geometry was in place there, as a logic of lines and angles here below; that the world was throughout mathematical; the proportions are constant of oxygen, azote and lime; there is just so much water and slate and magnesia; not less are the proportions constant of the moral elements.

This eldest Goethe, hating varnish and falsehood, delighted in revealing the real at the base of the accidental; in discovering connection, continuity and representation everywhere, hating insulation; and appears like the god of wealth among the cabins of vagabonds, opening power and capability in everything he touches. Ethical science was new and vacant when Plato could write thus: "Of all whose arguments are left to the men of the present time, no one has ever yet condemned injustice, or praised justice, otherwise than as respects the repute, honors and emoluments arising therefrom; while, as respects either of them in itself, and subsisting by its own power in the soul of the possessor, and concealed both from gods and men, no one has yet sufficiently investigated, either in poetry or prose writings—how, namely, that injustice is the greatest of all the evils that the soul has within it, and justice the greatest good."

His definition of ideas, as what is simple, permanent, uniform and self-existent, forever discriminating them from the notions of the understanding, marks an era in the world. He was born to behold the self-evolving power of spirit, endless, generator of new ends; a power which is the key at once to the centrality and the evanescence of things. Plato is so centred that he can well spare all his dogmas. Thus the fact of knowledge and ideas reveals to him the fact of eternity; and the doctrine of reminiscence he offers as the most probable particular explication. Call that fanciful—it matters not: the connection between our knowledge and the abyss of being is still real, and the explication must be not less magnificent.

He has indicated every eminent point in speculation. He wrote on the scale of the mind itself, so that all things have symmetry in his tablet. He put in all the past, without weariness, and descended into detail with a courage like that he witnessed in nature. One would say that his forerunners had mapped out each a farm or a district or an island, in intellectual geography, but that Plato first drew the sphere. He domesticates the soul in nature: man is the microcosm. All the circles of the visible heaven represent as many circles in the rational soul. There is no lawless particle, and there is nothing casual in the action of the human mind. The names of things, too, are fatal, following the nature of things. All the gods of the Pantheon are, by their names, significant of a profound sense. The gods are the ideas. Pan is speech, or manifestation; Saturn, the contemplative; Jove, the regal soul; and Mars, passion. Venus is proportion; Calliope, the soul of the world; Aglaia, intellectual illustration.

These thoughts, in sparkles of light, had appeared often to pious and to poetic souls; but this well-bred, all-knowing Greek geometer comes with command, gathers them all up into rank and gradation, the Euclid of holiness, and marries the two parts of nature. Before all men, he saw the intellectual values of the moral sentiment. He describes his own ideal, when he paints, in Timæus, a god leading things from disorder into order. He kindled a fire so truly in the centre that we see the sphere illuminated, and can distinguish poles, equator and lines of latitude, every arc and node: a theory so averaged, so modulated, that you would say the winds of ages had swept through this rhythmic structure, and not that it was the brief extempore blotting of one short-lived scribe. Hence it has happened that a very well-marked class of souls, namely those who delight in giving a spiritual, that is, an ethico-intellectual expression to every truth, by exhibiting an ulterior end which is yet legitimate to it—are said to Platonize. Thus, Michael Angelo is a Platonist in his sonnets: Shakspeare is a Platonist when he writes—

> "Nature is made better by no mean,
> But nature makes that mean,"

or—

> "He, that can endure
> To follow with allegiance a fallen lord,
> Does conquer him that did his master conquer,
> And earns a place in the story."

Hamlet is a pure Platonist, and 't is the magnitude only of Shakspeare's proper genius that hinders him from being classed as the most eminent of this school. Swedenborg, throughout his prose poem of "Conjugal Love," is a Platonist.

His subtlety commended him to men of thought. The secret of his popular success is the moral aim which endeared him to mankind. "Intellect," he said, "is king of heaven and of earth; " but in Plato, intellect is always moral. His writings have also the sempiternal youth of poetry. For their arguments, most of them, might have been couched in sonnets: and poetry has never soared higher than in the Timæus and the Phædrus. As the poet, too, he is only contemplative. He did not, like Pythagoras, break himself with an institution. All his painting in the Republic must be esteemed mythical, with intent to bring out, sometimes in violent colors, his thought. You cannot institute, without peril of charlatanism.

It was a high scheme, his absolute privilege for the best (which, to make emphatic, he expressed by community of women), as the premium which he would set on grandeur. There shall be exempts of two kinds: first, those who by demerit have put themselves below protection—outlaws; and secondly, those who by eminence of nature and desert are out of the reach of your rewards. Let such be free of the city and above the law. We confide them to themselves; let them do with us as they will. Let none presume to measure the irregularities of Michael Angelo and Socrates by village scales.

In his eighth book of the Republic, he throws a little mathematical dust in our eyes. I am sorry to see him, after such noble superiorities, permitting the lie to governors. Plato plays Providence a little with the baser sort, as people allow themselves with their dogs and cats.

NAPOLEON; OR, THE MAN OF THE WORLD

NAPOLEON; OR, THE MAN OF THE WORLD

AMONG THE EMINENT PERSONS of the nineteenth century, Bonaparte is far the best known and the most powerful; and owes his predominance to the fidelity with which he expresses the tone of thought and belief, the aims of the masses of active and cultivated men. It is Swedenborg's theory that every organ is made up of homogeneous particles; or as it is sometimes expressed, every whole is made of similars; that is, the lungs are composed of infinitely small lungs; the liver, of infinitely small livers; the kidney, of little kidneys, etc. Following this analogy, if any man is found to carry with him the power and affections of vast numbers, if Napoleon is France, if Napoleon is Europe, it is because the people whom he sways are little Napoleons.

In our society there is a standing antagonism between the conservative and the democratic classes; between those who have made their fortunes, and the young and the poor who have fortunes to make; between the interests of dead labor—that is, the labor of hands long ago still in the grave, which labor is now entombed in money stocks, or in land and buildings owned by idle capitalists—and the interests of living labor, which seeks to possess itself of land and buildings and money stocks. The first class is timid, selfish, illiberal, hating innovation, and continually losing numbers by death. The second class is selfish also, encroaching, bold, self-relying, always outnumbering the other and recruiting its numbers every hour by births. It desires to keep open every avenue to the competition of all, and to multiply avenues: the class of business men in America, in England, in France and throughout Europe; the class of industry and skill. Napoleon is its representative. The instinct of active, brave, able men, throughout the middle class every where, has pointed out Napoleon as the incarnate Democrat. He had their virtues and their vices; above all, he had their spirit or aim. That tendency is material, pointing at a sensual success and employing the richest and most various means to that end; conversant with mechanical powers, highly intellectual, widely and

. . . .

accurately learned and skilful, but subordinating all intellectual and spiritual forces into means to a material success. To be the rich man, is the end. "God has granted," says the Koran, "to every people a prophet in its own tongue." Paris and London and New York, the spirit of commerce, of money and material power, were also to have their prophet; and Bonaparte was qualified and sent.

Every one of the million readers of anecdotes or memoirs or lives of Napoleon, delights in the page, because he studies in it his own history. Napoleon is thoroughly modern, and, at the highest point of his fortunes, has the very spirit of the newspapers. He is no saint—to use his own word, "no capuchin," and he is no hero, in the high sense. The man in the street finds in him the qualities and powers of other men in the street. He finds him, like himself, by birth a citizen, who, by very intelligible merits, arrived at such a commanding position that he could indulge all those tastes which the common man possesses but is obliged to conceal and deny: good society, good books, fast travelling, dress, dinners, servants without number, personal weight, the execution of his ideas, the standing in the attitude of a benefactor to all persons about him, the refined enjoyments of pictures, statues, music, palaces and conventional honors—precisely what is agreeable to the heart of every man in the nineteenth century, this powerful man possessed.

It is true that a man of Napoleon's truth of adaptation to the mind of the masses around him, becomes not merely representative but actually a monopolizer and usurper of other minds. Thus Mirabeau plagiarized every good thought, every good word that was spoken in France. Dumont relates that he sat in the gallery of the Convention and heard Mirabeau make a speech. It struck Dumont that he could fit it with a peroration, which he wrote in pencil immediately, and showed it to Lord Elgin, who sat by him. Lord Elgin approved it, and Dumont, in the evening, showed it to Mirabeau. Mirabeau read it, pronounced it admirable, and declared he would incorporate it into his harangue to-morrow, to the Assembly. "It is impossible." said Dumont, "as, unfortunately, I have shown it to Lord Elgin." "If you have shown it to Lord Elgin and to fifty persons beside, I shall still speak it to-morrow:" and he did speak it with much effect, at the next day's session. For Mirabeau, with his overpowering personality, felt that these things which his presence inspired were as much his own as if he had said them, and that his adoption of them gave them their weight. Much more absolute and centralizing was the successor to Mirabeau's popularity and to much more than his predominance in France. Indeed, a man of Napoleon's stamp almost ceases to have a private speech and opinion. He is so largely receptive, and is so placed, that he comes to be a bureau for all the intelligence, wit and power of the age and country. He gains the battle; he makes the code; he makes the system of weights and measures; he levels the Alps; he builds the road. All distinguished engineers, savants, statists, report to him: so likewise do all good heads in every kind: he adopts the best measures, sets his stamp on them, and not these alone, but on every happy and memorable expression. Every sentence spoken by Napoleon and every line of his writing, deserves reading, as it is the sense of France.

Bonaparte was the idol of common men because he had in transcendent degree the qualities and powers of common men. There is a certain satisfaction in coming down to the lowest ground of politics, for we get rid of cant and hypocrisy. Bonaparte wrought, in common with that great class he represented, for power and wealth—but Bonaparte, specially, without any scruple as to the means. All the sentiments which embarrass men's pursuit of these objects, he set aside. The sentiments were for women and children. Fontanes, in 1804, expressed Napoleon's own sense, when in behalf of the Senate he addressed him—"Sire, the desire of perfection is the worst disease that ever afflicted the human mind." The advocates of liberty and of progress are "ideologists"—a word of contempt often in his mouth—"Necker is an ideologist:" "Lafayette is an ideologist."

An Italian proverb, too well known, declares that "if you would succeed, you must not be too good." It is an advantage, within certain limits, to have renounced the dominion of the sentiments of piety, gratitude and generosity; since what was an impassable bar to us, and still is to others, becomes a convenient weapon for our purposes; just as the river which was a formidable barrier, winter transforms into the smoothest of roads.

Napoleon renounced, once for all, sentiments and affections, and would help himself with his hands and his head. With him is no miracle and no magic. He is a worker in brass, in iron, in wood, in earth, in roads, in buildings, in money and in troops, and a very consistent and wise master-workman. He is never weak and literary, but acts with the solidity and the precision of natural agents. He has not lost his native sense and sympathy with things. Men give way before such a man, as before natural events. To be sure there are men enough who are immersed in things, as farmers, smiths, sailors and mechanics generally; and we know how real and solid such men appear in the presence of scholars and grammarians: but these men ordinarily lack the power of arrangement, and are like hands without a head. But Bonaparte superadded to this mineral and animal force, insight and generalization, so that men saw in him combined the natural and the intellectual power, as if the sea and land had taken flesh and begun to cipher. Therefore the land and sea seem to presuppose him. He came unto his own and they received him. This ciphering operative knows what he is working with and what is the product. He knew the properties of gold and iron, of wheels and ships, of troops and diplomatists, and required that each should do after its kind.

The art of war was the game in which he exerted his arithmetic. It consisted, according to him, in having always more forces than the enemy, on the point where the enemy is attacked, or where he attacks: and his whole talent is strained by endless manœuvre and evolution, to march always on the enemy at an angle, and destroy his forces in detail. It is obvious that a very small force, skilfully and rapidly manœuvring so as always to bring two men against one at the point of engagement, will be an overmatch for a much larger body of men.

The times, his constitution and his early circumstances combined to develop this pattern democrat. He had the virtues of his class and the conditions for their activity. That common-sense which no sooner respects any end than it finds the means to effect it; the delight in the use of means; in the choice, simplification and combining of means; the directness and thoroughness of his work; the prudence with which all was seen and the energy with which all was done, make him the natural organ and head of what I may almost call, from its extent, the *modern* party.

Nature must have far the greatest share in every success, and so in his. Such a man was wanted, and such a man was born; a man of stone and iron, capable of sitting on horseback sixteen or seventeen hours, of going many days together without rest or food except by snatches, and with the speed and spring of a tiger in action; a man not embarrassed by any scruples; compact, instant, selfish, prudent, and of a perception which did not suffer itself to be baulked or misled by any pretences of others, or any superstition or any heat or haste of his own. "My hand of iron," he said, "was not at the extremity of my arm, it was immediately connected with my head." He respected the power of nature and fortune, and ascribed to it his superiority, instead of valuing himself, like inferior men, on his opinionativeness, and waging war with nature. His favorite rhetoric lay in allusion to his star; and he pleased himself, as well as the people, when he styled himself the "Child of Destiny." "They charge me," he said, "with the commission of great crimes: men of my stamp do not commit crimes. Nothing has been more simple than my elevation, 't is in vain to ascribe it to intrigue or crime; it was owing to the peculiarity of the times and to my reputation of having fought well against the enemies of my country. I have always marched with the opinion of great masses and with events. Of what use then would crimes be to me?" Again he said, speaking of his son, "My son can not replace me; I could not replace myself. I am the creature of circumstances."

He had a directness of action never before combined with so much comprehension. He is a realist, terrific to all talkers and confused truth-obscuring persons. He sees where the matter hinges, throws himself on the precise point of resistance, and slights all other considerations. He is strong in the right manner, namely by insight. He never blundered into victory, but won his battles in his head before he won them on the field. His principal means are in himself. He asks counsel of no other. In 1796 he writes to the Directory: "I have conducted the campaign without consulting any one. I should have done no good if I had been under the necessity of conforming to the notions of another person. I have gained some advantages over superior forces and when totally destitute of every thing, because, in the persuasion that your confidence was reposed in me, my actions were as prompt as my thoughts."

History is full, down to this day, of the imbecility of kings and governors. They are a class of persons much to be pitied, for they know not what they should do. The weavers strike for bread, and the king and his ministers, knowing not what to do, meet them with bayonets. But Napoleon understood his business. Here was a man who in each moment and emergency knew what to do next. It is an immense comfort and refreshment to the spirits, not only of kings, but of citizens. Few men have any next; they live from hand to mouth, without plan, and are ever at the end of their line, and after each action wait for an impulse from abroad. Napoleon had been the first man of the world, if his ends had been purely public. As he is, he inspires confidence and vigor by the extraordinary unity of his action. He is firm, sure, self-denying, self-postponing, sacrificing every thing—money, troops, generals, and his own safety also, to his aim; not misled, like common adventurers, by the splendor of his own means. "Incidents ought not to govern policy," he said, "but policy, incidents." "To be hurried away by every event is to have no political system at all." His victories were only so many doors, and he never for a moment lost sight of his way onward, in the dazzle and uproar of the present circumstance. He knew what to do, and he flew to his mark. He would shorten a straight line to come at his object. Horrible anecdotes may no doubt be collected from his history, of the price at which he bought his successes; but he must not therefore be set down as cruel, but only as one who knew no impediment to his will; not bloodthirsty, not cruel—but woe to what thing or person stood in his way! Not bloodthirsty, but not sparing of blood—and pitiless. He saw only the object: the obstacle must give way. "Sire, General Clarke can not combine with General Junot, for the dreadful fire of the Austrian battery."—"Let him carry the battery."—"Sire, every regiment that approaches the heavy artillery is sacrificed: Sire, what orders?"—"Forward, forward!" Seruzier, a colonel of artillery, gives, in his "Military Memoirs," the following sketch of a scene after the battle of Austerlitz.—"At the moment in which the Russian army was making its retreat, painfully, but in good order, on the ice of the lake, the Emperor Napoleon came riding at full speed toward the artillery. 'You are losing time,' he cried; 'fire upon those masses; they must be engulfed: fire upon the ice!' The order remained unexecuted for ten minutes. In vain several officers and myself were placed on the slope of a hill to produce the effect: their balls and mine rolled upon the ice without breaking it up. Seeing that, I tried a simple method of elevating light howitzers. The almost perpendicular fall of the heavy projectiles produced the desired effect. My method was immediately followed by the adjoining batteries, and in less than no time we buried" some "thousands of Russians and Austrians under the waters of the lake."

In the plenitude of his resources, every obstacle seemed to vanish. "There shall be no Alps," he said; and he built his perfect roads, climbing by graded galleries their steepest precipices, until Italy was as open to Paris as any town in France. He laid his bones to, and wrought for his crown. Having decided what was to be done, he did that with might and main. He put out all his strength. He risked every thing and spared nothing, neither ammunition, nor money, nor troops, nor generals, nor himself.

We like to see every thing do its office after its kind, whether it be a milch-cow or a rattlesnake; and if fighting be the best mode of adjusting national differences (as large majorities of men seem to agree), certainly Bonaparte was right in making it thorough. The grand principle of war, he said, was that an army ought always to be ready, by day and by night and at all hours, to make all the resistance it is capable of making. He never economized his ammunition, but, on a hostile position, rained a torrent of iron—shells, balls, grape-shot—to annihilate all defence. On any point of resistance he concentrated squadron on squadron in overwhelming numbers until it was swept out of existence. To a regiment of horse-chasseurs at Lobenstein, two days before the battle of Jena, Napoleon said, "My lads, you must not fear death; when soldiers brave death, they drive him into the enemy's ranks." In the fury of assault, he no more spared himself. He went to the edge of his possibility. It is plain that in Italy he did what he could, and all that he could. He came, several times, within an inch of ruin; and his own person was all but lost. He was flung into the marsh at Arcola. The Austrians were between him and his troops, in the *mêlée*, and he was brought off with desperate efforts. At Lonato, and at other places, he was on the point of being taken prisoner. He fought sixty battles. He had never enough. Each victory was a new weapon. "My power would fall, were I not to support it by new achievements. Conquest has made me what I am, and conquest must maintain me." He felt, with every wise man, that as much life is needed for conservation as for creation. We are always in peril, always in a bad plight, just on the edge of destruction and only to be saved by invention and courage.

This vigor was guarded and tempered by the coldest prudence and punctuality. A thunderbolt in the attack, he was found invulnerable in his intrenchments. His very attack was never the inspiration of courage, but the result of calculation. His idea of the best defence consists in being still the attacking party. "My ambition," he says, "was great, but was of a cold nature." In one of his conversations with Las Cases, he remarked, "As to the moral courage, I have rarely met with the two-o'clock-in-the-morning kind: I mean unprepared courage; that which is necessary on an unexpected occasion, and which, in spite of the most unforeseen events, leaves full freedom of judgment and decision:" and he did not hesitate to declare that he was himself eminently endowed with this two-o'clock-in-the-morning courage, and that he had met with few persons equal to himself in this respect.

Every thing depended on the nicety of his combinations, and the stars were not more punctual than his arithmetic. His personal attention descended to the smallest particulars. "At Montebello, I ordered Kellermann to attack with eight hundred horse, and with these he separated the six thousand Hungarian grenadiers, before the very eyes of the Austrian cavalry. This cavalry was half a league off and required a quarter of an hour to arrive on the field of action, and I have observed that it is always these quarters of an hour that decide the fate of a battle." "Before he fought a battle, Bonaparte thought little about what he should do in case of success, but a great deal about what he should do in case of a reverse of fortune." The same prudence and good sense mark all his behavior. His instructions to his secretary at the Tuileries are worth remembering. "During the night, enter my chamber as seldom as possible. Do not awake me when you have any good news to communicate; with that there is no hurry. But when you bring bad news, rouse me instantly, for then there is not a moment to be lost." It was a whimsical economy of the same kind which dictated his practice, when general in Italy, in regard to his burdensome correspondence. He directed Bourrienne to leave all letters unopened for three weeks, and then observed with satisfaction how large a part of the correspondence had thus disposed of itself and no longer required an answer. His achievement of business was immense, and enlarges the known powers of man. There have been many working kings, from Ulysses to William of Orange, but none who accomplished a tithe of this man's performance.

To these gifts of nature, Napoleon added the advantage of having been born to a private and humble fortune. In his later days he had the weakness of wishing to add to his crowns and badges the prescription of aristocracy; but he knew his debt to his austere education, and made no secret of his contempt for the born kings, and for "the hereditary asses," as he coarsely styled the Bourbons. He said that "in their exile they had learned nothing, and forgot nothing." Bonaparte had passed through all the degrees of military service, but also was citizen before he was emperor, and so has the key to citizenship. His remarks and estimates discover the information and justness of measurement of the middle class. Those who had to deal with him found that he was not to be imposed upon, but could cipher as well as another man. This appears in all parts of his Memoirs, dictated at St. Helena. When the expenses of the empress, of his household, of his palaces, had accumulated great debts, Napoleon examined the bills of the creditors himself, detected overcharges and errors, and reduced the claims by considerable sums.

His grand weapon, namely the millions whom he directed, he owed to the representative character which clothed him. He interests us as he stands for France and for Europe; and he exists as captain and king only as far as the Revolution, or the interest of the industrious masses, found an organ and a leader in him. In the social interests, he knew the meaning and value of labor, and threw himself naturally on that side. I like an incident mentioned by one of his biographers at St. Helena. "When walking with Mrs. Balcombe, some servants, carrying heavy boxes, passed by on the road, and Mrs. Balcombe desired them, in rather an angry tone, to keep back. Napoleon interfered, saying 'Respect the burden, Madame.'" In the time of the empire he directed attention to the improvement and embellishment of the markets of the capital. "The market-place," he said, "is the Louvre of the common people." The principal works that have survived him are his magnificent roads. He filled the troops with his spirit, and a sort of freedom and companionship grew up between him and them, which the forms of his court never permitted between the officers and himself. They performed, under his eye, that which no others could do. The best document of his relation to his troops is the order of the day on the morning of the battle of Austerlitz, in which Napoleon promises the troops that he will keep his person out of reach of fire. This declaration, which is the reverse of that ordinarily made by generals and sovereigns on the eve of a battle, sufficiently explains the devotion of the army to their leader.

But though there is in particulars this identity between Napoleon and the mass of the people, his real strength lay in their conviction that he was their representative in his genius and aims, not only when he courted, but when he controlled, and even when he decimated them by his conscriptions. He knew, as well as any Jacobin in France, how to philosophize on liberty and equality; and when allusion was made to the precious blood of centuries, which was spilled by the killing of the Duc d'Enghien, he suggested, "Neither is my blood ditch-water." The people felt that no longer the throne was occupied and the land sucked of its nourishment, by a small class of legitimates, secluded from all community with the children of the soil, and holding the ideas and superstitions of a long-forgotten state of society. Instead of that vampyre, a man of themselves held, in the Tuileries, knowledge and ideas like their own, opening of course to them and their children all places of power and trust. The day of sleepy, selfish policy, ever narrowing the means and opportunities of young men, was ended, and a day of expansion and demand was come. A market for all the powers and productions of man was opened; brilliant prizes glittered in the eyes of youth and talent. The old, iron-bound, feudal France was changed into a young Ohio or New York; and those who smarted under the immediate rigors of the new monarch, pardoned them as the necessary severities of the military system which had driven out the oppressor. And even when the majority of the people had begun to ask whether they had really gained any thing under the exhausting levies of men and money of the new master, the whole talent of the country, in every rank and kindred, took his part and defended him as its natural patron In 1814, when advised to rely on the higher classes, Napoleon said to those around him, "Gentlemen, in the situation in which I stand, my only nobility is the rabble of the Faubourgs."

Napoleon met this natural expectation. The necessity of his position required a hospitality to every sort of talent, and its appointment to trusts; and his feeling went along with this policy. Like every superior person, he undoubtedly felt a desire for men and compeers, and a wish to measure his power with other masters, and an impatience of fools and underlings. In Italy, he sought for men and found none. "Good God!" he said, "how rare men are! There are eighteen millions in Italy, and I have with difficulty found two—Dandolo and Melzi." In later years, with larger experience, his respect for mankind was not increased. In a moment of bitterness he said to one of his oldest friends, "Men deserve the contempt with which they inspire me. I have only to put some gold-lace on the coat of my virtuous republicans and they immediately become just what I wish them." This impatience at levity was, however, an oblique tribute of respect to those able persons who commanded his regard not only when he found them friends and coadjutors but also when they resisted his will. He could not confound Fox and Pitt, Carnot, Lafayette and Bernadotte, with the danglers of his court; and in spite of the detraction which his systematic egotism dictated toward the great captains who conquered with and for him, ample acknowledgments are made by him to Lannes, Duroc, Kleber, Dessaix, Massena, Murat, Ney and Augereau. If he felt himself their patron and the founder of their fortunes, as when he said "I made my generals out of mud"—he could not hide his satisfaction in receiving from them a seconding and support commensurate with the grandeur of his enterprise. In the Russian campaign he was so much impressed by the courage and resources of Marshal Ney, that he said, "I have two hundred millions in my coffers, and I would give them all for Ney." The characters which he has drawn of several of his marshals are discriminating, and though they did not content the insatiable vanity of French officers, are no doubt substantially just. And in fact every species of merit was sought and advanced under his government. "I know," he said, "the depth and draught of water of every one of my generals." Natural power was sure to be well received at his court. Seventeen men in his time were raised from common soldiers to the rank of king, marshal, duke, or general; and the crosses of his Legion of Honor were given to personal valor, and not to family connexion. "When soldiers have been baptized in the fire of a battlefield, they have all one rank in my eyes."

When a natural king becomes a titular king, every body is pleased and satisfied. The Revolution entitled the strong populace of the Faubourg St. Antoine, and every horse-boy and powder-monkey in the army, to look on Napoleon as flesh of his flesh and the creature of *his* party; but there is something in the success of grand talent which enlists an universal sympathy. For in the prevalence of sense and spirit over stupidity and malversation, all reasonable men have an interest; and as intellectual beings we feel the air purified by the electric shock, when material force is overthrown by intellectual energies. As soon as we are removed out of the reach of local and accidental partialities, Man feels that Napoleon fights for him; these are honest victories; this strong steam-engine does our work. Whatever appeals to the imagination, by transcending the ordinary limits of human ability, wonderfully encour-

ages and liberates us. This capacious head, revolving and disposing
sovereignly trains of affairs, and animating such multitudes of agents;
this eye, which looked through Europe; this prompt invention; this
inexhaustible resource—what events! what romantic pictures! what
strange situations!—when spying the Alps, by a sunset in the Sicilian
sea; drawing up his army for battle in sight of the Pyramids, and saying
to his troops, "From the tops of those pyramids, forty centuries look
down on you;" fording the Red Sea; wading in the gulf of the Isthmus
of Suez. On the shore of Ptolemais, gigantic projects agitated him.
"Had Acre fallen, I should have changed the face of the world." His
army, on the night of the battle of Austerlitz, which was the anniversary of his inauguration as Emperor, presented him with a bouquet of
forty standards taken in the fight. Perhaps it is a little puerile, the pleasure he took in making these contrasts glaring; as when he pleased
himself with making kings wait in his antechambers, at Tilsit, at Paris
and at Erfurt.

We can not, in the universal imbecility, indecision and indolence of
men, sufficiently congratulate ourselves on this strong and ready actor,
who took occasion by the beard, and showed us how much may be
accomplished by the mere force of such virtues as all men possess in
less degrees; namely, by punctuality, by personal attention, by courage
and thoroughness. "The Austrians," he said, "do not know the value of
time." I should cite him, in his earlier years, as a model of prudence.
His power does not consist in any wild or extravagant force; in any
enthusiasm like Mahomet's, or singular power of persuasion; but in the
exercise of common-sense on each emergency, instead of abiding by
rules and customs. The lesson he teaches is that which vigor always
teaches—that there is always room for it. To what heaps of cowardly
doubts is not that man's life an answer. When he appeared it was the
belief of all military men that there could be nothing new in war; as it
is the belief of men to-day that nothing new can be undertaken in politics, or in church, or in letters, or in trade, or in farming, or in our
social manners and customs; and as it is at all times the belief of society
that the world is used up. But Bonaparte knew better than society; and
moreover knew that he knew better. I think all men know better than
they do; know that the institutions we so volubly commend are go-carts
and baubles; but they dare not trust their presentiments. Bonaparte
relied on his own sense, and did not care a bean for other people's. The

world treated his novelties just as it treats everybody's novelties—made infinite objection, mustered all the impediments; but he snapped his finger at their objections. "What creates great difficulty," he remarks, "in the profession of the land-commander, is the necessity of feeding so many men and animals. If he allows himself to be guided by the commissaries he will never stir, and all his expeditions will fail." An example of his common-sense is what he says of the passage of the Alps in winter, which all writers, one repeating after the other, had described as impracticable. "The winter," says Napoleon, "is not the most unfavorable season for the passage of lofty mountains. The snow is then firm, the weather settled, and there is nothing to fear from avalanches, the real and only danger to be apprehended in the Alps. On these high mountains there are often very fine days in December, of a dry cold, with extreme calmness in the air." Read his account, too, of the way in which battles are gained. "In all battles a moment occurs when the bravest troops, after having made the greatest efforts, feel inclined to run. That terror proceeds from a want of confidence in their own courage, and it only requires a slight opportunity, a pretence, to restore confidence to them. The art is, to give rise to the opportunity and to invent the pretence. At Arcola I won the battle with twenty-five horsemen. I seized that moment of lassitude, gave every man a trumpet, and gained the day with this handful. You see that two armies are two bodies which meet and endeavor to frighten each other; a moment of panic occurs, and that moment must be turned to advantage. When a man has been present in many actions, he distinguishes that moment without difficulty: it is as easy as casting up an addition."

This deputy of the nineteenth century added to his gifts a capacity for speculation on general topics. He delighted in running through the range of practical, of literary and of abstract questions. His opinion is always original and to the purpose. On the voyage to Egypt he liked, after dinner, to fix on three or four persons to support a proposition, and as many to oppose it. He gave a subject, and the discussions turned on questions of religion, the different kinds of government, and the art of war. One day he asked whether the planets were inhabited. On another, what was the age of the world. Then he proposed to consider the probability of the destruction of the globe, either by water or by fire: at another time, the truth or fallacy of presentiments, and the interpretation of dreams. He was very fond of talking of religion. In

1806 he conversed with Fournier, bishop of Montpellier, on matters of theology. There were two points on which they could not agree, viz. that of hell, and that of salvation out of the pale of the church. The Emperor told Josephine that he disputed like a devil on these two points, on which the bishop was inexorable. To the philosophers he readily yielded all that was proved against religion as the work of men and time, but he would not hear of materialism. One fine night, on deck, amid a clatter of materialism, Bonaparte pointed to the stars, and said, "You may talk as long as you please, gentlemen, but who made all that?" He delighted in the conversation of men of science, particularly of Monge and Berthollet; but the men of letters he slighted; they were "manufacturers of phrases." Of medicine too he was fond of talking, and with those of its practitioners whom he most esteemed—with Corvisart at Paris, and with Antonomarchi at St. Helena. "Believe me," he said to the last, "we had better leave off all these remedies: life is a fortress which neither you nor I know any thing about. Why throw obstacles in the way of its defence? Its own means are superior to all the apparatus of your laboratories. Corvisart candidly agreed with me that all your filthy mixtures are good for nothing. Medicine is a collection of uncertain prescriptions, the results of which, taken collectively, are more fatal than useful to mankind. Water, air and cleanliness are the chief articles in my pharmacopœia."

His memoirs, dictated to Count Montholon and General Gourgaud at St. Helena, have great value, after all the deduction that it seems is to be made from them on account of his known disingenuousness. He has the good-nature of strength and conscious superiority. I admire his simple, clear narrative of his battles—good as Cæsar's; his good-natured and sufficiently respectful account of Marshal Wurmser and his other antagonists; and his own equality as a writer to his varying subject. The most agreeable portion is the Campaign in Egypt.

He had hours of thought and wisdom. In intervals of leisure, either in the camp or the palace, Napoleon appears as a man of genius direct-ing on abstract questions the native appetite for truth and the impatience of words he was wont to show in war. He could enjoy every play of invention, a romance, a *bon mot*, as well as a stratagem in a campaign. He delighted to fascinate Josephine and her ladies, in a dim-lighted apartment, by the terrors of a fiction to which his voice and dramatic power lent every addition.

I call Napoleon the agent or attorney of the middle class of modern society; of the throng who fill the markets, shops, counting-houses, manufactories, ships, of the modern world, aiming to be rich. He was the agitator, the destroyer of prescription, the internal improver, the liberal, the radical, the inventor of means, the opener of doors and markets, the subverter of monopoly and abuse. Of course the rich and aristocratic did not like him. England, the centre of capital, and Rome and Austria, centres of tradition and genealogy, opposed him. The consternation of the dull and conservative classes, the terror of the foolish old men and old women of the Roman conclave, who in their despair took hold of any thing, and would cling to red-hot iron—the vain attempts of statists to amuse and deceive him, of the emperor of Austria to bribe him; and the instinct of the young, ardent and active men every where, which pointed him out as the giant of the middle class, make his history bright and commanding. He had the virtues of the masses of his constituents: he had also their vices. I am sorry that the brilliant picture has its reverse. But that is the fatal quality which we discover in our pursuit of wealth, that it is treacherous, and is bought by the breaking or weakening of the sentiments; and it is inevitable that we should find the same fact in the history of this champion, who proposed to himself simply a brilliant career, without any stipulation or scruple concerning the means.

Bonaparte was singularly destitute of generous sentiments. The highest-placed individual in the most cultivated age and population of the world—he has not the merit of common truth and honesty. He is unjust to his generals; egotistic and monopolizing; meanly stealing the credit of their great actions from Kellermann, from Bernadotte; intriguing to involve his faithful Junot in hopeless bankruptcy, in order to drive him to a distance from Paris, because the familiarity of his manners offends the new pride of his throne. He is a boundless liar. The official paper, his "Moniteur," and all his bulletins, are proverbs for saying what he wished to be believed; and worse—he sat, in his premature old age, in his lonely island, coldly falsifying facts and dates and characters, and giving to history a theatrical *éclat*. Like all Frenchmen he has a passion for stage effect. Every action that breathes of generosity is poisoned by this calculation. His star, his love of glory, his doctrine of the immortality of the soul, are all French. "I must dazzle and astonish. If I were to give the liberty of the press, my power could not last three days." To make a great noise is his favorite design. "A great reputation is a great noise: the more there is made, the farther off it is heard. Laws, institutions, monuments, nations, all fall; but the noise continues, and resounds in after ages." His doctrine, of immortality is simply fame. His theory of influence is not flattering. "There are two levers for moving men—interest and fear. Love is a silly infatuation, depend upon it. Friendship is but a name. I love nobody. I do not even love my brothers: perhaps Joseph a little, from habit, and because he is my elder; and Duroc, I love him too; but why?—because his character pleases me: he is stern and resolute, and I believe the fellow never shed a tear. For my part I know very well that I have no true friends. As long as I continue to be what I am, I may have as many pretended friends as I please. Leave sensibility to women; but men should be firm in heart and purpose, or they should have nothing to do with war and government." He was thoroughly unscrupulous. He would steal, slander, assassinate, drown and poison, as his interest dictated. He had no generosity, but mere vulgar hatred; he was intensely selfish; he was perfidious; he cheated at cards; he was a prodigious gossip, and opened letters, and delighted in his infamous police, and rubbed his hands with joy when he had intercepted some morsel of intelligence concerning the men and women about him, boasting that "he knew every thing;" and interfered with the cutting the dresses of the women; and listened after the hurrahs and the compliments of the street, incognito. His manners were coarse. He treated women with low familiarity. He had the habit of pulling their ears and pinching their cheeks when he was in good humor, and of pulling the ears and whiskers of men, and of striking and horse-play with them, to his last days. It does not appear that he listened at keyholes, or at least that he was caught at it. In short, when you have penetrated through all the circles of power and splendor, you were not dealing with a gentleman, at last; but with an impostor and a rogue; and he fully deserves the epithet of *Jupiter Scapin*, or a sort of Scamp Jupiter.

In describing the two parties into which modern society divides itself—the democrat and the conservative—I said, Bonaparte represents the democrat, or the party of men of business, against the stationary or conservative party. I omitted then to say, what is material to the statement, namely that these two parties differ only as young and old. The democrat is a young conservative; the conservative is an old democrat. The aristocrat is the democrat ripe and gone to seed—because both parties stand on the one ground of the supreme value of property, which one endeavors to get, and the other to keep. Bonaparte may be said to represent the whole history of this party, its youth and its age; yes, and with poetic justice its fate, in his own. The counter-revolution, the counter-party, still waits for its organ and representative, in a lover and a man of truly public and universal aims.

Here was an experiment, under the most favorable conditions, of the powers of intellect without conscience. Never was such a leader so endowed and so weaponed; never leader found such aids and followers. And what was the result of this vast talent and power, of these immense armies, burned cities, squandered treasures, immolated millions of men, of this demoralized Europe? It came to no result. All passed away like the smoke of his artillery, and left no trace. He left France smaller, poorer, feebler, than he found it; and the whole contest for freedom was to be begun again. The attempt was in principle suicidal. France served him with life and limb and estate, as long as it could identify its interest with him; but when men saw that after victory was another war; after the destruction of armies, new conscriptions; and they who had toiled so desperately were never nearer to the reward—they could not spend what they had earned, nor repose on their down-beds, nor strut in their châteaux—they deserted him. Men found that his absorbing egotism was deadly to all other men. It resembled the torpedo, which inflicts a succession of shocks on any one who takes hold of it, producing spasms which contract the muscles of the hand, so that the man can not open his fingers; and the animal inflicts new and more violent shocks, until he paralyzes and kills his victim. So this exorbitant egotist narrowed, impoverished and absorbed the power and existence of those who served him; and the universal cry of France and of Europe in 1814 was, "Enough of him;" "*Assez de Bonaparte.*"

It was not Bonaparte's fault. He did all that in him lay to live and thrive without moral principle. It was the nature of things, the eternal law of man and of the world which baulked and ruined him; and the result, in a million experiments, will be the same. Every experiment, by multitudes or by individuals, that has a sensual and selfish aim, will fail. The pacific Fourier will be as inefficient as the pernicious Napoleon. As long as our civilization is essentially one of property, of fences, of exclusiveness, it will be mocked by delusions. Our riches will leave us sick; there will be bitterness in our laughter, and our wine will burn our mouth. Only that good profits which we can taste with all doors open, and which serves all men.

ENGLISH TRAITS

[*Emerson first visited England in 1833 at a time when he was in low spirits and poor health. His first wife had just died. One of his brothers had just broken down from over-work. He had just resigned his pulpit in Boston and had to find a new career. Since he had published nothing, he was unknown in England. He made an effort to seek out writers there in whom he was interested—especially Wordsworth, Coleridge and Carlyle. His second visit occurred in 1847 by invitation from people who had read his books and wanted to see him. During the winter he lectured extensively in England and Scotland, and had an opportunity to meet a great many people. After his return to America he read lectures on English traits. In 1856, he published the book of that title.*]

ENGLISH TRAITS

CHAPTER I
FIRST VISIT TO ENGLAND

I HAVE BEEN twice to England. In 1833, on my return from a short tour in Sicily, Italy and France, I crossed from Boulogne and landed in London at the Tower stairs. It was a dark Sunday morning; there were few people in the streets, and I remember the pleasure of that first walk on English ground, with my companion, an American artist, from the Tower up through Cheapside and the Strand to a house in Russell Square, whither we had been recommended to good chambers. For the first time for many months we were forced to check the saucy habit of travellers' criticism, as we could no longer speak aloud in the streets without being understood. The shop-signs spoke our language; our country names were on the door-plates, and the public and private buildings wore a more native and wonted front.

Like most young men at that time, I was much indebted to the men of Edinburgh and of the Edinburgh Review—to Jeffrey, Mackintosh, Hallam, and to Scott, Playfair and De Quincey; and my narrow and desultory reading had inspired the wish to see the faces of three or four writers—Coleridge, Wordsworth, Landor, De Quincey, and the latest and strongest contributor to the critical journals, Carlyle; and I suppose if I had sifted the reasons that led me to Europe, when I was ill and was advised to travel, it was mainly the attraction of these persons. If Goethe had been still living I might have wandered into Germany also. Besides those I have named (for Scott was dead), there was not in Britain the man living whom I cared to behold, unless it were the Duke of Wellington, whom I afterwards saw at Westminster Abbey at the funeral of Wilberforce. The young scholar fancies it happiness enough to live with people who can give an inside to the world; without reflecting that they are prisoners, too, of their own thought, and cannot apply themselves to yours. The conditions of literary success are almost destructive of the best social power, as they do not leave that frolic liberty which only can encounter a companion on the best terms. It is probable you left some obscure comrade at a tavern, or in the farms, with right mother-wit and equality to life, when you crossed sea and land to play bo-peep with celebrated scribes. I have, however, found writers superior to their books, and I cling to my first belief that a strong head will dispose fast enough of these impediments and give one the satisfaction of reality, the sense of having been met, and a larger horizon.

On looking over the diary of my journey in 1833, I find nothing to publish in my memoranda of visits to places. But I have copied the few notes I made of visits to persons, as they respect parties quite too good and too transparent to the whole world to make it needful to affect any prudery of suppression about a few hints of those bright personalities.

At Florence, chief among artists I found Horatio Greenough, the American sculptor. His face was so handsome and his person so well formed that he might be pardoned, if, as was alleged, the face of his Medora and the figure of a colossal Achilles in clay, were idealizations of his own. Greenough was a superior man, ardent and eloquent, and all his opinions had elevation and magnanimity. He believed that the Greeks had wrought in schools or fraternities—the genius of the master imparting his design to his friends and inflaming them with it, and when his strength was spent, a new hand with equal heat continued the work; and so by relays, until it was finished in every part with equal fire. This was necessary in so refractory a material as stone; and he thought art would never prosper until we left our shy jealous ways and worked in society as they. All his thoughts breathed the same generosity. He was an accurate and a deep man. He was a votary of the Greeks, and impatient of Gothic art. His paper on Architecture, published in 1843, announced in advance the leading thoughts of Mr. Ruskin on the *morality* in architecture, notwithstanding the antagonism in their views of the history of art. I have a private letter from him—later, but respecting the same period—in which he roughly sketches his own theory. "Here is my theory of structure: A scientific arrangement of spaces and forms to functions and to site; an emphasis of features proportioned to their *gradated* importance in function; color and ornament to be decided and arranged and varied by strictly organic laws, having a distinct reason for each decision; the entire and immediate banishment of all make-shift and make-believe."

Greenough brought me, through a common friend, an invitation

from Mr. Landor, who lived at San Domenica di Fiesole. On the 15th
May I dined with Mr. Landor. I found him noble and courteous, living
in a cloud of pictures at his Villa Gherardesca, a fine house commanding a beautiful landscape. I had inferred from his books, or magnified
from some anecdotes, an impression of Achillean wrath—an untamable
petulance. I do not know whether the imputation were just or not, but
certainly on this May day his courtesy veiled that haughty mind and he
was the most patient and gentle of hosts. He praised the beautiful
cyclamen which grows all about Florence; he admired Washington;
talked of Wordsworth, Byron, Massinger, Beaumont and Fletcher. To
be sure, he is decided in his opinions, likes to surprise, and is well content to impress, if possible, his English whim upon the immutable past.
No great man ever had a great son, if Philip and Alexander be not an
exception; and Philip he calls the greater man. In art, he loves the
Greeks, and in sculpture, them only. He prefers the Venus to everything else, and, after that, the head of Alexander, in the gallery here.
He prefers John of Bologna to Michael Angelo; in painting, Raffaelle,
and shares the growing taste for Perugino and the early masters. The
Greek histories he thought the only good; and after them, Voltaire's. I
could not make him praise Mackintosh, nor my more recent friends;
Montaigne very cordially—and Charron also, which seemed undiscrim-
inating. He thought Degerando indebted to "Lucas on Happiness" and
"Lucas on Holiness"! He pestered me with Southey; but who is
Southey?

He invited me to breakfast on Friday. On Friday I did not fail to
go, and this time with Greenough. He entertained us at once with reciting half a dozen hexameter lines of Julius Cæsar's!—from Donatus, he
said. He glorified Lord Chesterfield more than was necessary, and
undervalued Burke, and undervalued Socrates; designated as three of
the greatest of men, Washington, Phocion and Timoleon—much as our
pomologists, in their lists, select the three or the six best pears "for a
small orchard;"—and did not even omit to remark the similar termina-
tion of their names. "A great man," he said, "should make great
sacrifices and kill his hundred oxen without knowing whether they
would be consumed by gods and heroes, or whether the flies would eat
them." I had visited Professor Amici, who had shown me his microscopes, magnifying (it was said) two thousand diameters; and I spoke of
the uses to which they were applied. Landor despised entomology, yet,

in the same breath, said, "the sublime was in a grain of dust." I suppose I teased him about recent writers, but he professed never to have
heard of Herschel, *not even by name*. One room was full of pictures,
which he likes to show, especially one piece, standing before which he
said "he would give fifty guineas to the man that would swear it was a
Domenichino." I was more curious to see his library, but Mr. H——,
one of the guests, told me that Mr. Landor gives away his books and
has never more than a dozen at a time in his house.

Mr. Landor carries to its height the love of freak which the English
delight to indulge, as if to signalize their commanding freedom. He has
a wonderful brain, despotic, violent and inexhaustible, meant for a soldier, by what chance converted to letters; in which there is not a style
nor a tint not known to him, yet with an English appetite for action
and heroes. The thing done avails, and not what is said about it. An
original sentence, a step forward, is worth more than all the censures.
Landor is strangely undervalued in England; usually ignored and sometimes savagely attacked in the Reviews. The criticism may be right or
wrong, and is quickly forgotten; but year after year the scholar must
still go back to Landor for a multitude of elegant sentences; for wisdom, wit, and indignation that are unforgettable.

From London, on the 5th August, I went to Highgate, and wrote a
note to Mr. Coleridge, requesting leave to pay my respects to him. It
was near noon. Mr. Coleridge sent a verbal message that he was in bed,
but if I would call after one o'clock he would see me. I returned at one,
and he appeared, a short, thick old man, with bright blue eyes and fine
clear complexion; leaning on his cane. He took snuff freely, which
presently soiled his cravat and neat black suit. He asked whether I
knew Allston, and spoke warmly of his merits and doings when he
knew him in Rome; what a master of the Titianesque he was, etc., etc.
He spoke of Dr. Channing. It was an unspeakable misfortune that he
should have turned out a Unitarian after all. On this, he burst into a
declamation on the folly and ignorance of Unitarianism—its high
unreasonableness; and taking up Bishop Waterland's book, which lay
on the table, he read with vehemence two or three pages written by
himself in the fly-leaves—passages, too, which, I believe, are printed
in the Aids to Reflection. When he stopped to take breath, I interposed
that "whilst I highly valued all his explanations, I was bound to tell

. . . .

him that I was born and bred a Unitarian." "Yes," he said, "I supposed
so;" and continued as before. It was a wonder that after so many ages
of unquestioning acquiescence in the doctrine of St. Paul—the doctrine
of the Trinity, which was also according to Philo Judæus the doctrine
of the Jews before Christ—this handful of Priestleians should take on
themselves to deny it, etc., etc. He was very sorry that Dr. Channing, a
man to whom he looked up—no, to say that he looked *up* to him would
be to speak falsely, but a man whom he looked *at* with so much interest—should embrace such views. When he saw Dr. Channing he had
hinted to him that he was afraid he loved Christianity for what was
lovely and excellent—he loved the good in it, and not the true—"And I
tell you, sir, that I have known ten persons who loved the good, for one
person who loved the true; but it is a far greater virtue to love the true
for itself alone, than to love the good for itself alone." He (Coleridge)
knew all about Unitarianism perfectly well, because he had once been
a Unitarian and knew what quackery it was. He had been called "the
rising star of Unitarianism." He went on defining, or rather refining:
"The Trinitarian doctrine was realism; the idea of God was not essential, but super-essential;" talked of *trinism* and *tetrakism* and much
more, of which I only caught this, "that the will was that by which a
person is a person; because, if one should push me in the street, and
so I should force the man next me into the kennel, I should at once
exclaim, I did not do it, sir, meaning it was not my will." And this also,
that "if you should insist on your faith here in England, and I on mine,
mine would be the hotter side of the fagot."

I took advantage of a pause to say that he had many readers of all
religious opinions in America, and I proceeded to inquire if the
"extract" from the Independent's pamphlet, in the third volume of the
Friend, were a veritable quotation. He replied that it was really taken
from a pamphlet in his possession entitled "A Protest of one of the
Independents," or something to that effect. I told him how excellent I
thought it and how much I wished to see the entire work. "Yes," he
said, "the man was a chaos of truths, but lacked the knowledge that
God was a God of order. Yet the passage would no doubt strike you
more in the quotation than in the original, for I have filtered it."

When I rose to go, he said, "I do not know whether you care about
poetry, but I will repeat some verses I lately made on my baptismal

anniversary," and he recited with strong emphasis, standing, ten or twelve lines beginning—

"Born unto God in Christ—"

He inquired where I had been travelling; and on learning that I had been in Malta and Sicily, he compared one island with the other, repeating what he had said to the Bishop of London when he returned from that country, that Sicily was an excellent school of political economy; for, in any town there, it only needed to ask what the government enacted, and reverse that, to know what ought to be done; it was the most felicitously opposite legislation to anything good and wise. There were only three things which the government had brought into that garden of delights, namely, itch, pox and famine. Whereas in Malta, the force of law and mind was seen, in making that barren rock of semi-Saracen inhabitants the seat of population and plenty. Going out, he showed me in the next apartment a picture of Allston's, and told me that Montague, a picture-dealer, once came to see him, and glancing towards this, said, "Well, you have got a picture!" thinking it the work of an old master; afterwards, Montague, still talking with his back to the canvas, put up his hand and touched it, and exclaimed, "By Heaven! this picture is not ten years old:"—so delicate and skilful was that man's touch.

I was in his company for about an hour, but find it impossible to recall the largest part of his discourse, which was often like so many printed paragraphs in his book—perhaps the same—so readily did he fall into certain commonplaces. As I might have foreseen, the visit was rather a spectacle than a conversation, of no use beyond the satisfaction of my curiosity. He was old and preoccupied, and could not bend to a new companion and think with him.

From Edinburgh I went to the Highlands. On my return I came from Glasgow to Dumfries, and being intent on delivering a letter which I had brought from Rome, inquired for Craigen puttock. It was a farm in Nithsdale, in the parish of Dunscore, sixteen miles distant. No public coach passed near it, so I took a private carriage from the inn. I found the house amid desolate heathery hills, where the lonely scholar nourished his mighty heart. Carlyle was a man from his youth, an author who did not need to hide from his readers, and as absolute a man of the world, unknown and exiled on that hill-farm, as if holding on his own terms what is best in London. He was tall and gaunt, with a cliff-like brow, self-possessed and holding his extraordinary powers of conversation in easy command; clinging to his northern accent with evident relish; full of lively anecdote and with a streaming humor which floated every thing he looked upon. His talk playfully exalting the familiar objects, put the companion at once into an acquaintance with his Lars and Lemurs, and it was very pleasant to learn what was predestined to be a pretty mythology. Few were the objects and lonely the man; "not a person to speak to within sixteen miles except the minister of Dunscore;" so that books inevitably made his topics.

He had names of his own for all the matters familiar to his discourse. Blackwood's was the "sand magazine;" Fraser's nearer approach to possibility of life was the "mud magazine;" a piece of road near by, that marked some failed enterprise, was the "grave of the last sixpence." When too much praise of any genius annoyed him he professed hugely to admire the talent shown by his pig. He had spent much time and contrivance in confining the poor beast to one enclosure in his pen, but pig, by great strokes of judgment, had found out how to let a board down, and had foiled him. For all that he still thought man the most plastic little fellow in the planet, and he liked Nero's death, "*Qualis artifex pereo!*" better than most history. He worships a man that will manifest any truth to him. At one time he had inquired and read a good deal about America. Landor's principle was mere rebellion; and *that* he feared was the American principle. The best thing he knew of that country was that in it a man can have meat for his labor. He had read in Stewart's book that when he inquired in a New York hotel for the Boots, he had been shown across the street and had found Mungo in his own house dining on roast turkey.

We talked of books. Plato he does not read, and he disparaged Socrates; and, when pressed, persisted in making Mirabeau a hero. Gibbon he called the "splendid bridge from the old world to the new." His own reading had been multifarious. Tristram Shandy was one of his first books after Robinson Crusoe, and Robertson's America an early favorite. Rousseau's Confessions had discovered to him that he was not a dunce; and it was now ten years since he had learned German, by the advice of a man who told him he would find in that language what he wanted.

He took despairing or satirical views of literature at this moment; recounted the incredible sums paid in one year by the great booksellers for puffing. Hence it comes that no newspaper is trusted now, no books are bought, and the booksellers are on the eve of bankruptcy.

He still returned to English pauperism, the crowded country, the selfish abdication by public men of all that public persons should perform. Government should direct poor men what to do. Poor Irish folk come wandering over these moors. My dame makes it a rule to give to every son of Adam bread to eat, and supplies his wants to the next house. But here are thousands of acres which might give them all meat, and nobody to bid these poor Irish go to the moor and till it. They burned the stacks and so found a way to force the rich people to attend to them.

We went out to walk over long hills, and looked at Criffel, then without his cap, and down into Wordsworth's country. There we sat down and talked of the immortality of the soul. It was not Carlyle's fault that we talked on that topic, for he had the natural disinclination of every nimble spirit to bruise itself against walls, and did not like to place himself where no step can be taken. But he was honest and true, and cognizant of the subtile links that bind ages together, and saw how every event affects all the future. "Christ died on the tree; that built Dunscore kirk yonder; that brought you and me together. Time has only a relative existence."

He was already turning his eyes towards London with a scholar's appreciation. London is the heart of the world, he said, wonderful only from the mass of human beings. He liked the huge machine. Each keeps its own round. The baker's boy brings muffins to the window at a fixed hour every day, and that is all the Londoner knows or wishes to know on the subject. But it turned out good men. He named certain individuals, especially one man of letters, his friend, the best mind he knew, whom London had well served.

On the 28th August I went to Rydal Mount, to pay my respects to Mr. Wordsworth. His daughters called in their father, a plain, elderly, white-haired man, not prepossessing, and disfigured by green goggles. He sat down, and talked with great simplicity. He had just returned from a journey. His health was good but he had broken a tooth by a fall, when walking with two lawyers, and had said that he was glad it did not happen forty years ago; whereupon they had praised his philosophy.

He had much to say of America, the more that it gave occasion for his favorite topic—that society is being enlightened by a superficial tuition, out of all proportion to its being restrained by moral culture. Schools do no good. Tuition is not education. He thinks more of the education of circumstances than of tuition. 'T is not question whether there are offences of which the law takes cognizance, but whether there are offences of which the law does not take cognizance. Sin is what he fears—and how society is to escape without gravest mischiefs from this source. He has even said, what seemed a paradox, that they needed a civil war in America, to teach the necessity of knitting the social ties stronger. "There may be," he said, "in America some vulgarity in manner, but that's not important. That comes of the pioneer state of things. But I fear they are too much given to the making of money; and secondly, to politics; that they make political distinction the end and not the means. And I fear they lack a class of men of leisure—in short, of gentlemen—to give a tone of honor to the community. I am told that things are boasted of in the second class of society there, which, in England—God knows, are done in England every day,—but would never be spoken of. In America I wish to know not how many churches or schools, but what newspapers? My friend Colonel Hamilton, at the foot of the hill, who was a year in America, assures me that the newspapers are atrocious, and accuse members of Congress of stealing spoons!" He was against taking off the tax on newspapers in England—which the reformers represent as a tax upon knowledge—for this reason, that they would be inundated with base prints. He said he talked on political aspects, for he wished to impress on me and all good Americans to cultivate the moral, the conservative, etc., etc., and never to call into action the physical strength of the people, as had just now been done in England in the Reform Bill—a thing prophesied by Delolme. He alluded once or twice to his conversation with Dr. Channing, who had recently visited him (laying his hand on a particular chair in which the Doctor had sat).

The conversation turned on books. Lucretius he esteems a far higher poet than Virgil; not in his system, which is nothing, but in his

. . . .

power of illustration. Faith is necessary to explain anything and to reconcile the foreknowledge of God with human evil. Of Cousin (whose
lectures we had all been reading in Boston), he knew only the name.

I inquired if he had read Carlyle's critical articles and translations.
He said he thought him sometimes insane. He proceeded to abuse
Goethe's Wilhelm Meister heartily. It was full of all manner of forni-
cation. It was like the crossing of flies in the air. He had never gone
farther than the first part; so disgusted was he that he threw the book
across the room. I deprecated this wrath, and said what I could for the
better parts of the book, and he courteously promised to look at it
again. Carlyle he said wrote most obscurely. He was clever and deep,
but he defied the sympathies of every body. Even Mr. Coleridge wrote
more clearly, though he had always wished Coleridge would write more
to be understood. He led me out into his garden, and showed me the
gravel walk in which thousands of his lines were composed. His eyes
are much inflamed. This is no loss except for reading, because he never
writes prose, and of poetry he carries even hundreds of lines in his head
before writing them. He had just returned from a visit to Staffa, and
within three days had made three sonnets on Fingal's Cave, and was
composing a fourth when he was called in to see me. He said, "If you
are interested in my verses perhaps you will like to hear these lines." I
gladly assented, and he recollected himself for a few moments and then
stood forth and repeated, one after the other, the three entire sonnets
with great animation. I fancied the second and third more beautiful
than his poems are wont to be. The third is addressed to the flowers,
which, he said, especially the ox-eye daisy, are very abundant on the
top of the rock. The second alludes to the name of the cave, which is
"Cave of Music;" the first to the circumstance of its being visited by
the promiscuous company of the steamboat.

This recitation was so unlooked for and surprising—he, the old
Wordsworth, standing apart, and reciting to me in a garden-walk, like
a school-boy declaiming—that I at first was near to laugh; but recollecting myself, that I had come thus far to see a poet and he was
chanting poems to me, I saw that he was right and I was wrong, and
gladly gave myself up to hear. I told him how much the few printed
extracts had quickened the desire to possess his unpublished poems.
He replied he never was in haste to publish; partly because he corrected

a good deal, and every alteration is ungraciously received after printing; but what he had written would be printed, whether he lived or died. I said Tintern Abbey appeared to be the favorite poem with the public, but more contemplative readers preferred the first books of the Excursion, and the Sonnets. He said, "Yes, they are better." He preferred such of his poems as touched the affections, to any others; for whatever is didactic—what theories of society, and so on—might perish quickly; but whatever combined a truth with an affection was χτῆμα ἐζ ἀεί, good to-day and good forever. He cited the sonnet, On the feelings of a highminded Spaniard, which he preferred to any other (I so understood him), and the Two Voices; and quoted, with evident pleasure, the verses addressed To the Skylark. In this connection he said of the Newtonian theory that it might yet be superseded and forgotten; and Dalton's atomic theory.

When I prepared to depart he said he wished to show me what a common person in England could do, and he led me into the enclosure of his clerk, a young man to whom he had given this slip of ground, which was laid out, or its natural capabilities shown, with much taste. He then said he would show me a better way towards the inn; and he walked a good part of a mile, talking and ever and anon stopping short to impress the word or the verse, and finally parted from me with great kindness and returned across the fields.

Wordsworth honored himself by his simple adherence to truth, and was very willing not to shine; but he surprised by the hard limits of his thought. To judge from a single conversation, he made the impression of a narrow and very English mind; of one who paid for his rare elevation by general tameness and conformity. Off his own beat, his opinions were of no value. It is not very rare to find persons loving sympathy and ease, who expiate their departure from the common in one direction, by their conformity in every other.

CHAPTER II

VOYAGE TO ENGLAND

THE OCCASION of my second visit to England was an invitation from some Mechanics' Institutes in Lancashire and Yorkshire, which separately are organized much in the same way as our New England Lyceums, but in 1847 had been linked into a "Union," which embraced twenty or thirty towns and cities and presently extended into the middle counties and northward into Scotland. I was invited, on liberal terms, to read a series of lectures in them all. The request was urged with every kind suggestion and every assurance of aid and comfort, by friendliest parties in Manchester, who, in the sequel, amply redeemed their word. The remuneration was equivalent to the fees at that time paid in this country for the like services. At all events it was sufficient to cover any travelling expenses, and the proposal offered an excellent opportunity of seeing the interior of England and Scotland, by means of a home and a committee of intelligent friends awaiting me in every town.

I did not go very willingly. I am not a good traveller, nor have I found that long journeys yield a fair share of reasonable hours. But the invitation was repeated and pressed at a moment of more leisure and when I was a little spent by some unusual studies. I wanted a change and a tonic, and England was proposed to me. Besides, there were at least the dread attraction and salutary influences of the sea. So I took my berth in the packet-ship Washington Irving and sailed from Boston, Tuesday, October 5, 1847.

On Friday at noon we had only made one hundred and thirty-four miles. A nimble Indian would have swum as far; but the captain affirmed that the ship would show us in time all her paces, and we crept along through the floating drift of boards, logs and chips, which the rivers of Maine and New Brunswick pour into the sea after a freshet.

At last, on Sunday night, after doing one day's work in four, the storm came, the winds blew, and we flew before a northwester which strained every rope and sail. The good ship darts through the water all day, all night, like a fish; quivering with speed, gliding through liquid leagues, sliding from horizon to horizon. She has passed Cape Sable; she has reached the Banks; the land-birds are left; gulls, haglets, ducks, petrels, swim, dive and hover around; no fishermen; she has passed the Banks, left five sail behind her far on the edge of the west at sundown, which were far east of us at morn—though they say at sea a stern chase is a long race—and still we fly for our lives. The shortest sea-line from Boston to Liverpool is 2850 miles. This a steamer keeps, and saves 150

· ·

miles. A sailing ship can never go in a shorter line than 3000, and usually it is much longer. Our good master keeps his kites up to the last moment, studding-sails alow and aloft, and by incessant straight steering, never loses a rod of way. Watchfulness is the law of the ship—watch on watch, for advantage and for life. Since the ship was built, it seems, the master never slept but in his day-clothes whilst on board. "There are many advantages," says Saadi, "in sea-voyaging, but security is not one of them." Yet in hurrying over these abysses, whatever dangers we are running into, we are certainly running out of the risks of hundreds of miles every day, which have their own chances of squall, collision, sea-stroke, piracy, cold and thunder. Hour for hour, the risk on a steamboat is greater; but the speed is safety, or twelve days of danger instead of twenty-four.

Our ship was registered 750 tons, and weighed perhaps, with all her freight, 1500 tons. The mainmast, from the deck to the top-button, measured 115 feet; the length of the deck from stem to stern, 155. It is impossible not to personify a ship; every body does, in every thing they say—she behaves well; she minds her rudder; she swims like a duck; she runs her nose into the water; she looks into a port. Then that wonderful *esprit de corps* by which we adopt into our self-love every thing we touch, makes us all champions of her sailing qualities.

The conscious ship hears all the praise. In one week she has made 1467 miles, and now, at night, seems to hear the steamer behind her, which left Boston to-day at two; has mended her speed and is flying before the gray south wind eleven and a half knots the hour. The sea-fire shines in her wake and far around wherever a wave breaks. I read the hour, 9h. 45′, on my watch by this light. Near the equator you can read small print by it; and the mate describes the phosphoric insects, when taken up in a pail, as shaped like a Carolina potato.

I find the sea-life an acquired taste, like that for tomatoes and olives. The confinement, cold, motion, noise and odor are not to be dispensed with. The floor of your room is sloped at an angle of twenty or thirty degrees, and I waked every morning with the belief that some one was tipping up my berth. Nobody likes to be treated ignominiously, upset, shoved against the side of the house, rolled over, suffocated with bilge, mephitis and stewing oil. We get used to these annoyances at last, but the dread of the sea remains longer. The sea is masculine, the type of active strength. Look, what egg-shells are drift-

· ·

ing all over it, each one, like ours, filled with men in ecstasies of terror, alternating with cockney conceit, as the sea is rough or smooth. Is this sad-colored circle an eternal cemetery? In our graveyards we scoop a pit, but this aggressive water opens mile-wide pits and chasms and makes a mouthful of a fleet. To the geologist the sea is the only firmament; the land is in perpetual flux and change, now blown up like a tumor, now sunk in a chasm, and the registered observations of a few hundred years find it in a perpetual tilt, rising and falling. The sea keeps its old level; and 't is no wonder that the history of our race is so recent, if the roar of the ocean is silencing our traditions. A rising of the sea, such as has been observed, say an inch in a century, from east to west on the land, will bury all the towns, monuments, bones and knowledge of mankind, steadily and insensibly. If it is capable of these great and secular mischiefs, it is quite as ready at private and local damage; and of this no landsman seems so fearful as the seaman. Such discomfort and such danger as the narratives of the captain and mate disclose are bad enough as the costly fee we pay for entrance to Europe; but the wonder is always new that any sane man can be a sailor. And here on the second day of our voyage, stepped out a little boy in his shirt-sleeves, who had hid himself whilst the ship was in port, in the bread-closet, having no money and wishing to go to England. The sailors have dressed him in Guernsey frock, with a knife in his belt, and he is climbing nimbly about after them;—"likes the work first-rate, and if the captain will take him, means now to come back again in the ship." The mate avers that this is the history of all sailors; nine out of ten are runaway boys; and adds that all of them are sick of the sea, but stay in it out of pride. Jack has a life of risks, incessant abuse and the worst pay. It is a little better with the mate and not very much better with the captain. A hundred dollars a month is reckoned high pay. If sailors were contented, if they had not resolved again and again not to go to sea any more, I should respect them.

Of course the inconveniences and terrors of the sea are not of any account to those whose minds are preoccupied. The water-laws, arctic frost, the mountain, the mine, only shatter cockneyism; every noble activity makes room for itself. A great mind is a good sailor, as a great heart is. And the sea is not slow in disclosing inestimable secrets to a good naturalist.

'T is a good rule in every journey to provide some piece of liberal study to rescue the hours which bad weather, bad company and taverns steal from the best economist. Classics which at home are drowsily read, have a strange charm in a country inn, or in the transom of a merchant brig. I remember that some of the happiest and most valuable hours I have owed to books, passed, many years ago, on shipboard. The worst impediment I have found at sea is the want of light in the cabin.

We found on board the usual cabin library; Basil Hall, Dumas, Dickens, Bulwer, Balzac and Sand were our sea-gods. Among the passengers there was some variety of talent and profession; we exchanged our experiences and all learned something. The busiest talk with leisure and convenience at sea, and sometimes a memorable fact turns up, which you have long had a vacant niche for, and seize with the joy of a collector. But, under the best conditions, a voyage is one of the severest tests to try a man. A college examination is nothing to it. Sea-days are long—these lack-lustre, joyless days which whistled over us; but they were few—only fifteen, as the captain counted, sixteen according to me. Reckoned from the time when we left soundings, our speed was such that the captain drew the line of his course in red ink on his chart, for the encouragement or envy of future navigators.

It has been said that the King of England would consult his dignity by giving audience to foreign ambassadors in the cabin of a man-of-war. And I think the white path of an Atlantic ship the right avenue to the palace front of this seafaring people, who for hundreds of years claimed the strict sovereignty of the sea, and exacted toll and the striking sail from the ships of all other peoples. When their privilege was disputed by the Dutch and other junior marines, on the plea that you could never anchor on the same wave, or hold property in what was always flowing, the English did not stick to claim the channel, or bottom of all the main: "As if," said they, "we contended for the drops of the sea, and not for its situation, or the bed of those waters. The sea is bounded by his majesty's empire."

As we neared the land, its genius was felt. This was inevitably the British side. In every man's thought arises now a new system, English sentiments, English loves and fears, English history and social modes. Yesterday every passenger had measured the speed of the ship by watching the bubbles over the ship's bulwarks. To-day, instead of bubbles, we measure by Kinsale, Cork, Waterford and Ardmore. There lay the green shore of Ireland, like some coast of plenty. We could see towns, towers, churches, harvests; but the curse of eight hundred years we could not discern.

CHAPTER III
LAND

ALFIERI THOUGHT Italy and England the only countries worth living in; the former because there Nature vindicates her rights and triumphs over the evils inflicted by the governments; the latter because art conquers nature and transforms a rude, ungenial land into a paradise of comfort and plenty. England is a garden. Under an ash-colored sky, the fields have been combed and rolled till they appear to have been finished with a pencil instead of a plough. The solidity of the structures that compose the towns speaks the industry of ages. Nothing is left as it was made. Rivers, hills, valleys, the sea itself, feel the hand of a master. The long habitation of a powerful and ingenious race has turned every rood of land to its best use, has found all the capabilities, the arable soil, the quarriable rock, the highways, the byways, the fords, the navigable waters; and the new arts of intercourse meet you every where; so that England is a huge phalanstery, where all that man wants is provided within the precinct. Cushioned and comforted in every manner, the traveller rides as on a cannon-ball, high and low, over rivers and towns, through mountains in tunnels of three or four miles, at near twice the speed of our trains; and reads quietly the Times newspaper, which, by its immense correspondence and reporting seems to have machinized the rest of the world for his occasion.

The problem of the traveller landing at Liverpool is, Why England is England? What are the elements of that power which the English hold over other nations? If there be one test of national genius universally accepted, it is success; and if there be one successful country in the universe for the last millennium, that country is England.

A wise traveller will naturally choose to visit the best of actual nations; and an American has more reasons than another to draw him to Britain. In all that is done or begun by the Americans towards right thinking or practice, we are met by a civilization already settled and overpowering. The culture of the day, the thoughts and aims of men, are English thoughts and aims. A nation considerable for a thousand years since Egbert, it has, in the last centuries, obtained the ascendent, and stamped the knowledge, activity and power of mankind with its impress. Those who resist it do not feel it or obey it less. The Russian in his snows is aiming to be English. The Turk and Chinese also are making awkward efforts to be English. The practical common-sense of modern society, the utilitarian direction which labor, laws, opinion, religion take, is the natural genius of the British mind. The influence of France is a constituent of modern civility, but not enough opposed to the English for the most wholesome effect. The American is only the continuation of the English genius into new conditions, more or less propitious.

See what books fill our libraries. Every book we read, every biography, play, romance, in whatever form, is still English history and manners. So that a sensible Englishman once said to me, "As long as you do not grant us copyright, we shall have the teaching of you."

But we have the same difficulty in making a social or moral estimate of England, that the sheriff finds in drawing a jury to try some cause which has agitated the whole community and on which every body finds himself an interested party. Officers, jurors, judges have all taken sides. England has inoculated all nations with her civilization, intelligence and tastes; and to resist the tyranny and prepossession of the British element, a serious man must aid himself by comparing with it the civilizations of the farthest east and west, the old Greek, the Oriental, and, much more, the ideal standard; if only by means of the very impatience which English forms are sure to awaken in independent minds.

Besides, if we will visit London, the present time is the best time, as some signs portend that it has reached its highest point. It is observed that the English interest us a little less within a few years; and hence the impression that the British power has culminated, is in solstice, or already declining.

As soon as you enter England, which, with Wales, is no larger than the State of Georgia, this little land stretches by an illusion to the dimensions of an empire. Add South Carolina, and you have more than an equivalent for the area of Scotland. The innumerable details, the crowded succession of towns, cities, cathedrals, castles and great and decorated estates, the number and power of the trades and guilds, the military strength and splendor, the multitudes of rich and of remarkable people, the servants and equipages—all these catching the eye and never allowing it to pause, hide all boundaries by the impression of magnificence and endless wealth.

I reply to all the urgencies that refer me to this and that object indispensably to be seen—Yes, to see England well needs a hundred years; for what they told me was the merit of Sir John Soane's Museum, in London—that it was well packed and well saved—is the merit of England—it is stuffed full, in all corners and crevices, with towns, towers, churches, villas, palaces, hospitals and charity-houses. In the history of art it is a long way from a cromlech to York minster; yet all the intermediate steps may still be traced in this all-preserving island.

The territory has a singular perfection. The climate is warmer by many degrees than it is entitled to by latitude. Neither hot nor cold, there is no hour in the whole year when one cannot work. Here is no winter, but such days as we have in Massachusetts in November, a temperature which makes no exhausting demand on human strength, but allows the attainment of the largest stature. Charles the Second said, "It invited men abroad more days in the year and more hours in the day than another country." Then England has all the materials of a working country except wood. The constant rain—a rain with every tide, in some parts of the island—keeps its multitude of rivers full and brings agricultural production up to the highest point. It has plenty of water, of stone, of potter's clay, of coal, of salt and of iron. The land naturally abounds with game; immense heaths and downs are paved with quails, grouse and woodcock, and the shores are animated by water-birds. The rivers and the surrounding sea spawn with fish; there are salmon for the rich and sprats and herrings for the poor. In the northern lochs, the herring are in innumerable shoals; at one season, the country people say, the lakes contain one part water and two parts fish.

The only drawback on this industrial conveniency is the darkness of its sky. The night and day are too nearly of a color. It strains the eyes to read and to write. Add the coal smoke. In the manufacturing towns, the fine soot or *blacks* darken the day, give white sheep the color of black sheep, discolor the human saliva, contaminate the air, poison many plants and corrode the monuments and buildings.

The London fog aggravates the distempers of the sky, and some times justifies the epigram on the climate by an English wit "in a fine day, looking up a chimney; in a foul day, looking down one." A gentleman in Liverpool told me that he found he could do without a fire in his parlor about one day in the year. It is however pretended that the enormous consumption of coal in the island is also felt in modifying the general climate.

Factitious climate, factitious position. England resembles a ship in its shape, and if it were one, its best admiral could not have worked it or anchored it in a more judicious or effective position. Sir John Herschel said, "London is the centre of the terrene globe." The shopkeeping nation, to use a shop word, has a *good stand*. The old Venetians pleased themselves with the flattery that Venice was in 45°, midway between the poles and the line; as if that were an imperial centrality. Long of old, the Greeks fancied Delphi the navel of the earth, in their favorite mode of fabling the earth to be an animal. The Jews believed Jerusalem to be the centre. I have seen a kratometric chart designed to show that the city of Philadelphia was in the same thermic belt, and by inference in the same belt of empire, as the cities of Athens, Rome and London. It was drawn by a patriotic Philadelphian, and was examined with pleasure, under his showing, by the inhabitants of Chestnut Street. But when carried to Charleston, to New Orleans and to Boston, it somehow failed to convince the ingenious scholars of all those capitals.

But England is anchored at the side of Europe, and right in the heart of the modern world. The sea, which, according to Virgil's famous line, divided the poor Britons utterly from the world, proved to be the ring of marriage with all nations. It is not down in the books—it is written only in the geologic strata—that fortunate day when a wave of the German Ocean burst the old isthmus which joined Kent and Cornwall to France, and gave to this fragment of Europe its impregnable sea-wall, cutting off an island of eight hundred miles in length, with an irregular breadth reaching to three hundred miles; a territory large enough for independence, enriched with every seed of national power, so near that it can see the harvests of the continent, and so far that who would cross the strait must be an expert mariner, ready for tempests. As America, Europe and Asia lie, these Britons have precisely the best commercial position in the whole planet, and are sure of a market for all the goods they can manufacture. And to make these advantages avail, the river Thames must dig its spacious outlet to the sea from the heart of the kingdom, giving road and landing to innumerable ships, and all the conveniency to trade that a people so skilful and sufficient in economizing water-front by docks, warehouses and lighters required. When James the First declared his purpose of punishing London by removing his Court, the Lord Mayor replied that "in removing his royal presence from his lieges, they hoped he would leave them the Thames."

In the variety of surface, Britain is a miniature of Europe, having plain, forest, marsh, river, seashore, mines in Cornwall; caves in Matlock and Derbyshire; delicious landscape in Dovedale, delicious sea-view at Tor Bay, Highlands in Scotland, Snowdon in Wales, and in Westmoreland and Cumberland a pocket Switzerland, in which the lakes and mountains are on a sufficient scale to fill the eye and touch the imagination. It is a nation conveniently small. Fontenelle thought that nature had sometimes a little affectation; and there is such an artificial completeness in this nation of artificers as if there were a design from the beginning to elaborate a bigger Birmingham. Nature held counsel with herself and said, 'My Romans are gone. To build my new empire, I will choose a rude race, all masculine, with brutish strength. I will not grudge a competition of the roughest males. Let buffalo gore buffalo, and the pasture to the strongest! For I have work that requires the best will and sinew. Sharp and temperate northern breezes shall blow, to keep that will alive and alert. The sea shall disjoin the people from others, and knit them to a fierce nationality. It shall give them markets on every side. Long time I will keep them on their feet, by poverty, border-wars, seafaring, sea-risks and the stimulus of gain. An island—but not so large, the people not so many as to glut the great markets and depress one another, but proportioned to the size of Europe and the continents.'

With its fruits, and wares, and money, must its civil influence radiate. It is a singular coincidence to this geographic centrality, the spiritual centrality which Emanuel Swedenborg ascribes to the people. "For the English nation, the best of them are in the centre of all Christians, because they have interior intellectual light. This appears conspicuously in the spiritual world. This light they derive from the liberty of speaking and writing, and thereby of thinking."

CHAPTER IV

RACE

AN INGENIOUS ANATOMIST has written a book to prove that races are imperishable, but nations are pliant political constructions, easily changed or destroyed. But this writer did not found his assumed races on any necessary law, disclosing their ideal or metaphysical necessity; nor did he on the other hand count with precision the existing races and settle the true bounds; a point of nicety, and the popular test of the theory. The individuals at the extremes of divergence in one race of men are as unlike as the wolf to the lapdog. Yet each variety shades down imperceptibly into the next, and you cannot draw the line where a race begins or ends. Hence every writer makes a different count. Blumenbach reckons five races; Humboldt three; and Mr. Pickering, who lately in our Exploring Expedition thinks he saw all the kinds of men that can be on the planet, makes eleven.

The British Empire is reckoned to contain (in 1848) 222,000,000 souls—perhaps a fifth of the population of the globe; and to comprise a territory of 5,000,000 square miles. So far have British people predominated. Perhaps forty of these millions are of British stock. Add the United States of America, which reckon (in the same year), exclusive of slaves, 20,000,000 of people, on a territory of 3,000,000 square miles, and in which the foreign element, however considerable, is rapidly assimilated, and you have a population of English descent and language of 60,000,000, and governing a population of 245,000,000 souls.

The British census proper reckons twenty-seven and a half millions in the home countries. What makes this census important is the quality of the units that compose it. They are free forcible men, in a country where life is safe and has reached the greatest value. They give the bias to the current age; and that, not by chance or by mass, but by their character and by the number of individuals among them of personal ability. It has been denied that the English have genius. Be it as it may, men of vast intellect have been born on their soil, and they have made or applied the principal inventions. They have sound bodies and supreme endurance in war and in labor. The spawning force of the race has sufficed to the colonization of great parts of the world; yet it remains to be seen whether they can make good the exodus of millions from Great Britain, amounting in 1852 to more than a thousand a day. They have assimilating force, since they are imitated by their foreign subjects; and they are still aggressive and propagandist, enlarging the dominion of their arts and liberty. Their laws are hospitable, and slavery does not exist under them. What oppression exists is incidental and temporary; their success is not sudden or fortunate, but they have maintained constancy and self-equality for many ages.

Is this power due to their race, or to some other cause? Men hear gladly of the power of blood or race. Every body likes to know that his advantages cannot be attributed to air, soil, sea, or to local wealth, as mines and quarries, nor to laws and traditions, nor to fortune; but to superior brain, as it makes the praise more personal to him.

We anticipate in the doctrine of race something like that law of physiology that whatever bone, muscle, or essential organ is found in one healthy individual, the same part or organ may be found in or near the same place in its congener; and we look to find in the son every mental and moral property that existed in the ancestor. In race, it is not the broad shoulders, or litheness, or stature that give advantage, but a symmetry that reaches as far as to the wit. Then the miracle and renown begin. Then first we care to examine the pedigree, and copy heedfully the training—what food they ate, what nursing, school, and exercises they had, which resulted in this mother-wit, delicacy of thought and robust wisdom. How came such men as King Alfred, and Roger Bacon, William of Wykeham, Walter Raleigh, Philip Sidney, Isaac Newton, William Shakspeare, George Chapman, Francis Bacon, George Herbert, Henry Vane, to exist here? What made these delicate natures? was it the air? was it the sea? was it the parentage? For it is certain that these men are samples of their contemporaries. The hearing ear is always found close to the speaking tongue, and no genius can long or often utter any thing which is not invited and gladly entertained by men around him.

It is race, is it not, that puts the hundred millions of India under the dominion of a remote island in the north of Europe? Race avails much, if that be true which is alleged, that all Celts are Catholics and all Saxons are Protestants; that Celts love unity of power, and Saxons the representative principle. Race is a controlling influence in the Jew, who, for two millenniums, under every climate, has preserved the same

. . . .

character and employments. Race in the negro is of appalling importance. The French in Canada, cut off from all intercourse with the
parent people, have held their national traits. I chanced to read Tacitus On the Manners of the Germans, not long since, in Missouri and
the heart of Illinois, and I found abundant points of resemblance
between the Germans of the Hercynian forest, and our *Hoosiers*, *Suck-
ers* and *Badgers* of the American woods.

But whilst race works immortally to keep its own, it is resisted by
other forces. Civilization is a re-agent, and eats away the old traits. The
Arabs of to-day are the Arabs of Pharaoh; but the Briton of to-day is
a very different person from Cassibelaunus or Ossian. Each religious
sect has its physiognomy. The Methodists have acquired a face; the
Quakers, a face; the nuns, a face. An Englishman will pick out a dis-
senter by his manners. Trades and professions carve their own lines on
face and form. Certain circumstances of English life are not less effective; as personal liberty; plenty of food; good ale and mutton; open
market or good wages for every kind of labor; high bribes to talent and
skill; the island life, or the million opportunities and outlets for expanding and misplaced talent; readiness of combination among themselves
for politics or for business; strikes; and sense of superiority founded on
habit of victory in labor and in war: and the appetite for superiority
grows by feeding.

It is easy to add to the counteracting forces to race. Credence is a
main element. 'T is said that the views of nature held by any people
determine all their institutions. Whatever influences add to mental or
moral faculty, take men out of nationality as out of other conditions,
and make the national life a culpable compromise.

These limitations of the formidable doctrine of race suggest others
which threaten to undermine it, as not sufficiently based. The fixity or
inconvertibleness of races as we see them is a weak argument for the
eternity of these frail boundaries, since all our historical period is a
point to the duration in which nature has wrought. Any the least and
solitariest fact in our natural history, such as the melioration of fruits
and of animal stocks, has the worth of a power in the opportunity of
geologic periods. Moreover, though we flatter the self-love of men and
nations by the legend of pure races, all our experience is of the gradation and resolution of races, and strange resemblances meet us
everywhere. It need not puzzle us that Malay and Papuan, Celt and

Roman, Saxon and Tartar should mix, when we see the rudiments of tiger and baboon in our human form, and know that the barriers of races are not so firm but that some spray sprinkles us from the antediluvian seas.

The low organizations are simplest; a mere mouth, a jelly, or a straight worm. As the scale mounts, the organizations become complex. We are piqued with pure descent, but nature loves inoculation. A child blends in his face the faces of both parents and some feature from every ancestor whose face hangs on the wall. The best nations are those most widely related; and navigation, as effecting a world-wide mixture, is the most potent advancer of nations.

The English composite character betrays a mixed origin. Everything English is a fusion of distant and antagonistic elements. The language is mixed; the names of men are of different nations—three languages, three or four nations—the currents of thought are counter: contemplation and practical skill; active intellect and dead conservatism; world-wide enterprise and devoted use and wont; aggressive freedom and hospitable law with bitter class-legislation; a people scattered by their wars and affairs over the face of the whole earth, and homesick to a man; a country of extremes—dukes and chartists, Bishops of Durham and naked heathen colliers—nothing can be praised in it without damning exceptions, and nothing denounced without salvos of cordial praise.

Neither do this people appear to be of one stem, but collectively a better race than any from which they are derived. Nor is it easy to trace it home to its original seats. Who can call by right names what races are in Britain? Who can trace them historically? Who can discriminate them anatomically, or metaphysically?

In the impossibility of arriving at satisfaction on the historical question of race, and—come of whatever disputable ancestry—the indisputable Englishman before me, himself very well marked, and nowhere else to be found—I fancied I could leave quite aside the choice of a tribe as his lineal progenitors. Defoe said in his wrath, "the Englishman was the mud of all races." I incline to the belief that, as water, lime and sand make mortar, so certain temperaments marry well, and, by well-managed contrarieties, develop as drastic a character as the English. On the whole it is not so much a history of one or of certain tribes of Saxons, Jutes, or Frisians, coming from one place and genetically identical, as it is an anthology of temperaments out of them all. Certain temperaments suit the sky and soil of England, say eight or ten or twenty varieties, as, out of a hundred pear-trees, eight or ten suit the soil of an orchard and thrive—whilst all the unadapted temperaments die out.

The English derive their pedigree from such a range of nationalities that there needs sea-room and land-room to unfold the varieties of talent and character. Perhaps the ocean serves as a galvanic battery, to distribute acids at one pole and alkalies at the other. So England tends to accumulate her liberals in America, and her conservatives at London. The Scandinavians in her race still hear in every age the murmurs of their mother, the ocean; the Briton in the blood hugs the homestead still.

Again, as if to intensate the influences that are not of race, what we think of when we talk of English traits really narrows itself to a small district. It excludes Ireland and Scotland and Wales, and reduces itself at last to London, that is, to those who come and go thither. The portraits that hang on the walls in the Academy Exhibition at London, the figures in Punch's drawings of the public men or of the club-houses, the prints in the shop-windows, are distinctive English, and not American, no, nor Scotch, nor Irish: but 't is a very restricted nationality. As you go north into the manufacturing and agricultural districts, and to the population that never travels; as you go into Yorkshire, as you enter Scotland, the world's Englishman is no longer found. In Scotland there is a rapid loss of all grandeur of mien and manners; a provincial eagerness and acuteness appear; the poverty of the country makes itself remarked, and a coarseness of manners; and, among the intellectual, is the insanity of dialectics. In Ireland are the same climate and soil as in England, but less food, no right relation to the land, political dependence, small tenantry and an inferior or misplaced race.

These queries concerning ancestry and blood may be well allowed, for there is no prosperity that seems more to depend on the kind of man than British prosperity. Only a hardy and wise people could have made this small territory great. We say, in a regatta or yacht-race, that if the boats are anywhere nearly matched, it is the man that wins. Put the best sailing-master into either boat, and he will win.

Yet it is fine for us to speculate in face of unbroken traditions, though vague and losing themselves in fable. The traditions have got

· ·

footing, and refuse to be disturbed. The kitchen-clock is more convenient than sidereal time. We must use the popular category, as we do
the Linnæan classification, for convenience, and not as exact and final.
Otherwise we are presently confounded when the best-settled traits of
one race are claimed by some new ethnologist as precisely characteristic of the rival tribe.

I found plenty of well-marked English types, the ruddy complexion
fair and plump, robust men, with faces cut like a die, and a strong
island speech and accent; a Norman type, with the complacency that
belongs to that constitution. Others who might be Americans, for any
thing that appeared in their complexion or form; and their speech was
much less marked and their thought much less bound. We will call
them Saxons. Then the Roman has implanted his dark complexion in
the trinity or quaternity of bloods.

1. The sources from which tradition derives their stock are mainly
three. And first they are of the oldest blood of the world—the Celtic.
Some peoples are deciduous or transitory. Where are the Greeks?
Where the Etrurians? Where the Romans? But the Celts or Sidonides
are an old family, of whose beginning there is no memory, and their
end is likely to be still more remote in the future; for they have
endurance and productiveness. They planted Britain, and gave to the
seas and mountains names which are poems and imitate the pure voices
of nature. They are favorably remembered in the oldest records of
Europe. They had no violent feudal tenure, but the husband-man
owned the land. They had an alphabet, astronomy, priestly culture and
a sublime creed. They have a hidden and precarious genius. They made
the best popular literature of the Middle Ages in the songs of Merlin
and the tender and delicious mythology of Arthur.

2. The English come mainly from the Germans, whom the
Romans found hard to conquer in two hundred and ten years—say
impossible to conquer, when one remembers the long sequel—a people about whom in the old empire the rumor ran there was never any
that meddled with them that repented it not.

3. Charlemagne, halting one day in a town of Narbonnese Gaul,
looked out of a window and saw a fleet of Northmen cruising in the
Mediterranean. They even entered the port of the town where he was,
causing no small alarm and sudden manning and arming of his galleys.
As they put out to sea again, the emperor gazed long after them, his

. . . .

eyes bathed in tears. "I am tormented with sorrow," he said, "when I foresee the evils they will bring on my posterity." There was reason for these Xerxes' tears. The men who have built a ship and invented the rig, cordage, sail, compass and pump; the working in and out of port, have acquired much more than a ship. Now arm them and every shore is at their mercy. For if they have not numerical superiority where they anchor, they have only to sail a mile or two to find it. Bonaparte's art of war, namely of concentrating force on the point of attack, must always be theirs who have the choice of the battle-ground. Of course they come into the fight from a higher ground of power than the land-nations; and can engage them on shore with a victorious advantage in the retreat. As soon as the shores are sufficiently peopled to make piracy a losing business, the same skill and courage are ready for the service of trade.

The Heimskringla, or Sagas of the Kings of Norway, collected by Snorro Sturleson, is the Iliad and Odyssey of English history. Its portraits, like Homer's, are strongly individualized. The Sagas describe a monarchical republic like Sparta. The government disappears before the importance of citizens. In Norway, no Persian masses fight and perish to aggrandize a king, but the actors are bonders or landholders, every one of whom is named and personally and patronymically described, as the king's friend and companion. A sparse population gives this high worth to every man. Individuals are often noticed as very handsome persons, which trait only brings the story nearer to the English race. Then the solid material interest predominates, so dear to English understanding, wherein the association is logical, between merit and land. The heroes of the Sagas are not the knights of South Europe. No vaporing of France and Spain has corrupted them. They are substantial farmers whom the rough times have forced to defend their properties. They have weapons which they use in a determined manner, by no means for chivalry, but for their acres. They are people considerably advanced in rural arts, living amphibiously on a rough coast, and drawing half their food from the sea and half from the land. They have herds of cows, and malt, wheat, bacon, butter and cheese. They fish in the fiord and hunt the deer. A king among these farmers has a varying power, sometimes not exceeding the authority of a sheriff. A king was maintained, much as in some of our country districts a winter-school-master is quartered, a week here, a week there, and a fortnight on the

· ·

next farm—on all the farms in rotation. This the king calls going into guest-quarters; and it was the only way in which, in a poor country, a poor king with many retainers could be kept alive when he leaves his own farm to collect his dues through the kingdom.

These Norsemen are excellent persons in the main, with good sense, steadiness, wise speech and prompt action. But they have a singular turn for homicide; their chief end of man is to murder or to be murdered; oars, scythes, harpoons, crowbars, peat-knives and hay-forks are tools valued by them all the more for their charming aptitude for assassinations. A pair of kings, after dinner, will divert themselves by thrusting each his sword through the other's body, as did Yngve and Alf. Another pair ride out on a morning for a frolic, and finding no weapon near, will take the bits out of their horses' mouths and crush each other's heads with them, as did Alric and Eric. The sight of a tent-cord or a cloak-string puts them on hanging somebody, a wife, or a husband, or, best of all, a king. If a farmer has so much as a hay-fork, he sticks it into a King Dag. King Ingiald finds it vastly amusing to burn up half a dozen kings in a hall, after getting them drunk. Never was poor gentleman so surfeited with life, so furious to be rid of it, as the Northman. If he cannot pick any other quarrel, he will get himself comfortably gored by a bull's horns, like Egil, or slain by a land-slide, like the agricultural King Onund. Odin died in his bed, in Sweden; but it was a proverb of ill condition to die the death of old age. King Hake of Sweden cuts and slashes in battle, as long as he can-stand, then orders his war-ship, loaded with his dead men and their weapons, to be taken out to sea, the tiller shipped and the sails spread; being left alone he sets fire to some tar-wood and lies down contented on deck. The wind blew off the land, the ship flew, burning in clear flame, out between the islets into the ocean, and there was the right end of King Hake.

The early Sagas are sanguinary and piratical; the later are of a noble strain. History rarely yields us better passages than the conversation between King Sigurd the Crusader and King Eystein his brother, on their respective merits—one the soldier, and the other a lover of the arts of peace.

But the reader of the Norman history must steel himself by holding fast the remote compensations which result from animal vigor. As the old fossil world shows that the first steps of reducing the chaos were confided to saurians and other huge and horrible animals, so the foundations of the new civility were to be laid by the most savage men.

The Normans came out of France into England worse men than they went into it one hundred and sixty years before. They had lost their own language and learned the Romance or barbarous Latin of the Gauls, and had acquired with the language, all the vices it had names for. The conquest has obtained in the chronicles the name of the "memory of sorrow." Twenty thousand thieves landed at Hastings. These founders of the House of Lords were greedy and ferocious dragons, sons of greedy and ferocious pirates. They were all alike, they took everything they could carry, they burned, harried, violated, tortured and killed, until everything English was brought to the verge of ruin. Such however is the illusion of antiquity and wealth, that decent and dignified men now existing boast their descent from these filthy thieves, who showed a far juster conviction of their own merits, by assuming for their types the swine, goat, jackal, leopard, wolf and snake, which they severally resembled.

England yielded to the Danes and Northmen in the tenth and eleventh centuries, and was the receptacle into which all the mettle of that strenuous population was poured. The continued draught of the best men in Norway, Sweden and Denmark to these piratical expeditions exhausted those countries, like a tree which bears much fruit when young, and these have been second-rate powers ever since. The power of the race migrated and left Norway void. King Olaf said, "When King Harold, my father, went westward to England, the chosen men in Norway followed him; but Norway was so emptied then, that such men have not since been to find in the country, nor especially such a leader as King Harold was for wisdom and bravery."

It was a tardy recoil of these invasions, when, in 1801, the British government sent Nelson to bombard the Danish forts in the Sound, and, in 1807, Lord Cathcart, at Copenhagen, took the entire Danish fleet, as it lay in the basins, and all the equipments from the Arsenal, and carried them to England. Konghelle, the town where the kings of Norway, Sweden and Denmark were wont to meet, is now rented to a private English gentleman for a hunting ground.

It took many generations to trim and comb and perfume the first boat-load of Norse pirates into royal highnesses and most noble

Knights of the Garter; but every sparkle of ornament dates back to the Norse boat. There will be time enough to mellow this strength into civility and religion. It is a medical fact that the children of the blind see; the children of felons have a healthy conscience. Many a mean, dastardly boy is, at the age of puberty, transformed into a serious and generous youth.

The mildness of the following ages has not quite effaced these traits of Odin; as the rudiment of a structure matured in the tiger is said to be still found unabsorbed in the Caucasian man. The nation has a tough, acrid, animal nature, which centuries of churching and civilizing have not been able to sweeten. Alfieri said "the crimes of Italy were the proof of the superiority of the stock"; and one may say of England that this watch moves on a splinter of adamant. The English uncultured are a brutal nation. The crimes recorded in their calendars leave nothing to be desired in the way of cold malignity. Dear to the English heart is a fair stand-up fight. The brutality of the manners in the lower class appears in the boxing, bear-baiting, cock-fighting, love of executions, and in the readiness for a set-to in the streets, delightful to the English of all classes. The costermongers of London streets hold cowardice in loathing: "We must work our fists well; we are all handy with our fists." The public schools are charged with being bear-gardens of brutal strength, and are liked by the people for that cause. The fagging is a trait of the same quality. Medwin, in the Life of Shelley, relates that at a military school they rolled up a young man in a snowball, and left him so in his room while the other cadets went to church—and crippled him for life. They have retained impressment, deck-flogging, army-flogging, and school-flogging. Such is the ferocity of the army discipline that a soldier, sentenced to flogging, sometimes prays that his sentence may be commuted to death. Flogging, banished from the armies of Western Europe, remains here by the sanction of the Duke of Wellington. The right of the husband to sell the wife has been retained down to our times. The Jews have been the favorite victims of royal and popular persecution. Henry III mortgaged all the Jews in the kingdom to his brother the Earl of Cornwall, as security for money which he borrowed. The torture of criminals, and the rack for extorting evidence, were slowly disused. Of the criminal statutes, Sir Samuel Romilly said, "I have examined the codes of all nations, and ours is the worst, and worthy of the Anthropophagi." In the last session

(1848), the House of Commons was listening to the details of flogging and torture practised in the jails.

As soon as this land, thus geographically posted, got a hardy people into it, they could not help becoming the sailors and factors of the globe. From childhood, they dabbled in water, they swam like fishes, their playthings were boats. In the case of the ship-money, the judges delivered it for law, that "England being an island, the very midland shires therein are all to be accounted maritime"; and Fuller adds, "the genius even of landlocked counties driving the natives with a maritime dexterity." As early as the conquest, it is remarked, in explanation of the wealth of England, that its merchants trade to all countries.

The English at the present day have great vigor of body and endurance. Other countrymen look slight and undersized beside them, and invalids. They are bigger men than the Americans. I suppose a hundred English taken at random out of the street would weigh a fourth more than so many Americans. Yet, I am told, the skeleton is not larger. They are round, ruddy and handsome; at least the whole bust is well formed, and there is a tendency to stout and powerful frames. I remarked the stoutness on my first landing at Liverpool; porter, drayman, coachman, guard—what substantial, respectable, grandfatherly figures, with costume and manners to suit. The American has arrived at the old mansion-house and finds himself among uncles, aunts and grandsires. The pictures on the chimney-tiles of his nursery were pictures of these people. Here they are in the identical costumes and air which so took him.

It is the fault of their forms that they grow stocky, and the women have that disadvantage—few tall, slender figures of flowing shape, but stunted and thickset persons. The French say that the Englishwomen have two left hands. But in all ages they are a handsome race. The bronze monuments of crusaders lying cross-legged in the Temple Church at London, and those in Worcester and in Salisbury cathedrals, which are seven hundred years old, are of the same type as the best youthful heads of men now in England—please by beauty of the same character, an expression blending good-nature, valor and refinement, and mainly by that uncorrupt youth in the face of manhood, which is daily seen in the streets of London.

Both branches of the Scandinavian race are distinguished for beauty. The anecdote of the handsome captives which Saint Gregory found at Rome, A.D. 600, is matched by the testimony of the Norman chroniclers, five centuries later, who wondered at the beauty and long flowing hair of the young English captives. Meantime the Heimskringla has frequent occasion to speak of the personal beauty of its heroes. When it is considered what humanity, what resources of mental and moral power the traits of the blonde race betoken, its accession to empire marks a new and finer epoch, wherein the old mineral force shall be subjugated at last by humanity and shall plough in its furrow henceforward. It is not a final race, once a crab always crab—but a race with a future.

On the English face are combined decision and nerve with the fair complexion, blue eyes and open and florid aspect. Hence the love of truth, hence the sensibility, the fine perception and poetic construction. The fair Saxon man, with open front and honest meaning, domestic, affectionate, is not the wood out of which cannibal, or inquisitor, or assassin is made, but he is moulded for law, lawful trade, civility, marriage, the nurture of children, for colleges, churches, charities and colonies.

They are rather manly than warlike. When the war is over, the mask falls from the affectionate and domestic tastes, which make them women in kindness. This union of qualities is fabled in their national legend of "Beauty and the Beast," or, long before, in the Greek legend of Hermaphrodite. The two sexes are co-present in the English mind. I apply to Britannia, queen of seas and colonies, the words in which her latest novelist portrays his heroine; "She is as mild as she is game, and as game as she is mild." The English delight in the antagonism which combines in one person the extremes of courage and tenderness. Nelson, dying at Trafalgar, sends his love to Lord Collingwood, and like an innocent schoolboy that goes to bed, says "Kiss me, Hardy," and turns to sleep. Lord Collingwood, his comrade, was of a nature the most affectionate and domestic. Admiral Rodney's figure approached to delicacy and effeminacy, and he declared himself very sensible to fear, which he surmounted only by considerations of honor and public duty. Clarendon says the Duke of Buckingham was so modest and gentle, that some courtiers attempted to put affronts on him, until they found that this modesty and effeminacy was only a mask for the most terrible determination. And Sir Edward Parry said of Sir John Franklin, that "if he found Wellington Sound open, he explored it; for he was a man who never turned his back on a danger, yet of that tenderness that he would not brush away a mosquito." Even for their highwaymen the same virtue is claimed, and Robin Hood comes described to us as *mitissimus prædonum*; the gentlest thief. But they know where their war-dogs lie. Cromwell, Blake, Marlborough, Chatham, Nelson and Wellington are not to be trifled with, and the brutal strength which lies at the bottom of society, the animal ferocity of the quays and cockpits, the bullies of the costermongers of Shoreditch, Seven Dials and Spitalfields, they know how to wake up.

They have a vigorous health and last well into middle and old age. The old men are as red as roses, and still handsome. A clear skin, a peach-bloom complexion and good teeth are found all over the island. They use a plentiful and nutritious diet. The operative cannot subsist on water-cresses. Beef, mutton, wheat-bread and malt-liquors are universal among the first-class laborers. Good feeding is a chief point of national pride among the vulgar, and in their caricatures they represent the Frenchman as a poor, starved body. It is curious that Tacitus found the English beer already in use among the Germans: "They make from barley or wheat a drink corrupted into some resemblance to wine." Lord Chief Justice Fortescue, in Henry VI's time says, "The inhabitants of England drink no water, unless at certain times on a religious score and by way of penance." The extremes of poverty and ascetic penance, it would seem, never reach cold water in England. Wood the antiquary, in describing the poverty and maceration of Father Lacey, an English Jesuit, does not deny him beer. He says, "His bed was under a thatching, and the way to it up a ladder; his fare was coarse; his drink, of a penny a gawn, or gallon."

They have more constitutional energy than any other people. They think, with Henri Quatre, that manly exercises are the foundation of that elevation of mind which gives one nature ascendant over another; or with the Arabs, that the days spent in the chase are not counted in the length of life. They box, run, shoot, ride, row, and sail from pole to pole. They eat and drink and live jolly in the open air, putting a bar of solid sleep between day and day. They walk and ride as fast as they can, their head bent forward, as if urged on some pressing affair. The French say that Englishmen in the street always walk straight before them like mad dogs. Men and women walk with infatuation. As soon as he can handle a gun, hunting is the fine art of every Englishman of condition. They are the most voracious people of prey that ever existed. Every season turns out the aristocracy into the country to shoot and fish. The more vigorous run out of the island to America, to Asia, to Africa and Australia, to hunt with fury by gun, by trap, by harpoon, by lasso, with dog, with horse, with elephant or with dromedary, all the game that is in nature. These men have written the game-books of all countries, as Hawker, Scrope, Murray, Herbert, Maxwell, Cumming and a host of travellers. The people at home are addicted to boxing, running, leaping and rowing matches.

I suppose the dogs and horses must be thanked for the fact that the men have muscles almost as tough and supple as their own. If in every efficient man there is first a fine animal, in the English race it is of the best breed, a wealthy, juicy, broad-chested creature, steeped in ale and good cheer and a little overloaded by his flesh. Men of animal nature rely, like animals, on their instincts. The Englishman associates well with dogs and horses. His attachment to the horse arises from the courage and address required to manage it. The horse finds out who is afraid of it, and does not disguise its opinion. Their young boiling clerks and lusty collegians like the company of horses better than the company of professors. I suppose the horses are better company for them. The horse has more uses than Buffon noted. If you go into the streets, every driver in 'bus or dray is a bully, and if I wanted a good troop of soldiers, I should recruit among the stables. Add a certain degree of refinement to the vivacity of these riders, and you obtain the precise quality which makes the men and women of polite society formidable.

They come honestly by their horsemanship, with *Hengst* and *Horsa* for their Saxon founders. The other branch of their race had been Tartar nomads. The horse was all their wealth. The children were fed on mares' milk. The pastures of Tartary were still remembered by the tenacious practice of the Norsemen to eat horseflesh at religious feasts. In the Danish invasions the marauders seized upon horses where they landed, and were at once converted into a body of expert cavalry.

At one time this skill seems to have declined. Two centuries ago the English horse never performed any eminent service beyond the seas; and the reason assigned was that the genius of the English hath always more inclined them to foot-service, as pure and proper manhood, without any mixture; whilst in a victory on horseback, the credit ought to be divided betwixt the man and his horse. But in two hundred years a change has taken place. Now, they boast that they understand horses better than any other people in the world, and that their horses are become their second selves.

"William the Conqueror being," says Camden, "better affected to beasts than to men, imposed heavy fines and punishments on those that should meddle with his game." The Saxon Chronicle says "he loved the tall deer as if he were their father." And rich Englishmen have followed his example, according to their ability, ever since, in encroaching on the tillage and commons with their game-preserves. It is a proverb in England that it is safer to shoot a man than a hare. The severity of the game-laws certainly indicates an extravagant sympathy of the nation with horses and hunters. The gentlemen are always on horseback, and have brought horses to an ideal perfection; the English racer is a factitious breed. A score or two of mounted gentlemen may frequently be seen running like centaurs down a hill nearly as steep as the roof of a house. Every inn-room is lined with pictures of races; telegraphs communicate, every hour, tidings of the heats from Newmarket and Ascot; and the House of Commons adjourns over the "Derby Day."

CHAPTER V

ABILITY

THE SAXON and the Northman are both Scandinavians. History does not allow us to fix the limits of the application of these names with any accuracy, but from the residence of a portion of these people in France, and from some effect of that powerful soil on their blood and manners, the Norman has come popularly to represent in England the aristocratic, and the Saxon the democratic principle. And though, I doubt not, the nobles are of both tribes, and the workers of both, yet we are forced to use the names a little mythically, one to represent the workers and the other the enjoyer.

The island was a prize for the best race. Each of the dominant races tried its fortune in turn. The Phœnician, the Celt and the Goth had already got in. The Roman came, but in the very day when his fortune culminated. He looked in the eyes of a new people that was to supplant his own. He disembarked his legions, erected his camps and towers—presently he heard bad news from Italy, and worse and worse, every year; at last, he made a handsome compliment of roads and walls, and departed. But the Saxon seriously settled in the land, builded, tilled, fished and traded, with German truth and adhesiveness. The Dane came and divided with him. Last of all the Norman or French-Dane arrived, and formally conquered, harried and ruled the kingdom. A century later it came out that the Saxon had the most bottom and longevity, had managed to make the victor speak the language and accept the law and usage of the victim; forced the baron to dictate Saxon terms to Norman kings; and, step by step, got all the essential securities of civil liberty invented and confirmed. The genius of the race and the genius of the place conspired to this effect. The island is lucrative to free labor, but not worth possession on other terms. The race was so intellectual that a feudal or military tenure could not last longer than the war. The power of the Saxon-Danes, so thoroughly beaten in the war that the name of English and villein were synonymous, yet so vivacious as to extort charters from the kings, stood on the strong personality of these people. Sense and economy must rule in a world which is made of sense and economy, and the banker, with his seven per cent., drives the earl out of his castle. A nobility of soldiers cannot keep down a commonalty of shrewd scientific persons. What signifies a pedigree of a hundred links, against a cotton-spinner with steam in his mill; or against a company of broad-shouldered Liverpool merchants, for whom Stephenson and Brunel are contriving locomotives and a tubular bridge?

These Saxons are the hands of mankind. They have the taste for toil, a distaste for pleasure or repose, and the telescopic appreciation of distant gain. They are the wealth-makers—and by dint of mental faculty which has its own conditions. The Saxon works after liking, or only for himself; and to set him at work and to begin to draw his monstrous values out of barren Britain, all dishonor, fret and barrier must be removed, and then his energies begin to play.

The Scandinavian fancied himself surrounded by Trolls—a kind of goblin men with vast power of work and skilful production—divine stevedores, carpenters, reapers, smiths and masons, swift to reward every kindness done them, with gifts of gold and silver. In all English history this dream comes to pass. Certain Trolls or working brains, under the names of Alfred, Bede, Caxton, Bracton, Camden, Drake, Selden, Dugdale, Newton, Gibbon, Brindley, Watt, Wedgwood, dwell in the troll-mounts of Britain and turn the sweat of their face to power and renown.

If the race is good, so is the place. Nobody landed on this spellbound island with impunity. The enchantments of barren shingle and rough weather transformed every adventurer into a laborer. Each vagabond that arrived bent his neck to the yoke of gain, or found the air too tense for him. The strong survived, the weaker went to the ground. Even the pleasure-hunters and sots of England are of a tougher texture. A hard temperament had been formed by Saxon and Saxon-Dane, and such of these French or Normans as could reach it were naturalized in every sense.

All the admirable expedients or means hit upon in England must be looked at as growths or irresistible offshoots of the expanding mind of the race. A man of that brain thinks and acts thus; and his neighbor, being afflicted with the same kind of brain, though he is rich and called a baron or a duke, thinks the same thing, and is ready to allow the justice of the thought and act in his retainer or tenant, though sorely against his baronial or ducal will.

The island was renowned in antiquity for its breed of mastiffs, so fierce that when their teeth were set you must cut their heads off to part them. The man was like his dog. The people have that nervous bilious temperament which is known by medical men to resist every means employed to make its possessor subservient to the will of others. The English game is main force to main force, the planting of foot to foot, fair play and open field—a rough tug without trick or dodging, till one or both come to pieces. King Ethelwald spoke the language of his race when he planted himself at Wimborne and said he "would do one of two things, or there live, or there lie." They hate craft and subtlety. They neither poison, nor waylay, nor assassinate; and when they have pounded each other to a poultice, they will shake hands and be friends for the remainder of their lives.

You shall trace these Gothic touches at school, at country fairs, at the hustings and in parliament. No artifice, no breach of truth and plain dealing—not so much as secret ballot, is suffered in the island. In parliament, the tactics of the opposition is to resist every step of the government by a pitiless attack: and in a bargain, no prospect of advantage is so dear to the merchant as the thought of being tricked is mortifying.

Sir Kenelm Digby, a courtier of Charles and James, who won the sea-fight of Scanderoon, was a model Englishman in his day. "His person was handsome and gigantic, he had so graceful elocution and noble address, that, had he been dropt out of the clouds in any part of the world, he would have made himself respected: he was skilled in six tongues, and master of arts and arms." Sir Kenelm wrote a book, Of Bodies and of Souls, in which he propounds, that "syllogisms do breed, or rather are all the variety of man's life. They are the steps by which we walk in all our businesses. Man, as he is man, doth nothing else but weave such chains. Whatsoever, he doth, swarving from this work, he doth as deficient from the nature of man: and, if he do aught beyond this, by breaking out into divers sorts of exterior actions, he findeth, nevertheless, in this linked sequel of simplest discourses, the art, the cause, the rule, the bounds and the model of it."

There spoke the genius of the English people. There is a necessity on them to be logical. They would hardly greet the good that did not logically fall—as if it excluded their own merit, or shook their understandings. They are jealous of minds that have much facility of association, from an instinctive fear that the seeing many relations to their thought might impair this serial continuity and lucrative concentration. They are impatient of genius, or of minds addicted to contemplation, and cannot conceal their contempt for sallies of thought, however lawful, whose steps they cannot count by their wonted rule. Neither do they reckon better a syllogism that ends in syllogism. For they have a supreme eye to facts, and theirs is a logic that brings salt to soup, hammer to nail, oar to boat; the logic of cooks, carpenters and chemists, following the sequence of nature, and one on which words make no impression. Their mind is not dazzled by its own means, but locked and bolted to results. They love men who, like Samuel Johnson, a doctor in the schools, would jump out of his syllogism the instant his major proposition was in danger, to save that at all hazards. Their practical vision is spacious, and they can hold many threads without entangling them. All the steps they orderly take; but with the high logic of never confounding the minor and major proposition; keeping their eye on their aim, in all the complicity and delay incident to the several series of means they employ. There is room in their minds for this and that—a science of degrees. In the courts the independence of the judges and the loyalty of the suitors are equally excellent. In parliament they have hit on that capital invention of freedom, a constitutional opposition. And when courts and parliament are both deaf, the plaintiff is not silenced. Calm, patient, his weapon of defence from year to year is the obstinate reproduction of the grievance, with calculations and estimates. But, meantime, he is drawing numbers and money to his opinion, resolved that if all remedy fails, right of revolution is at the bottom of his charter-box. They are bound to see their measure carried, and stick to it through ages of defeat.

Into this English logic, however, an infusion of justice enters, not so apparent in other races—a belief in the existence of two sides, and the resolution to see fair play. There is on every question an appeal from the assertion of the parties to the proof of what is asserted. They kiss the dust before a fact. Is it a machine, is it a charter, is it a boxer in the ring, is it a candidate on the hustings—the universe of Englishmen will suspend their judgment until the trial can be had. They are not to be led by a phrase, they want a working plan, a working machine, a working constitution, and will sit out the trial and abide by the issue and reject all preconceived theories. In politics they put blunt questions, which must be answered; Who is to pay the taxes? What will you do for trade? What for corn? What for the spinner?

This singular fairness and its results strike the French with surprise. Philip de Commines says, "Now, in my opinion, among all the sovereignties I know in the world, that in which the public good is best attended to, and the least violence exercised on the people, is that of England." Life is safe, and personal rights; and what is freedom without security? whilst, in France, "fraternity," "equality," and "indivisible unity" are names for assassination. Montesquieu said, "England is the freest country in the world. If a man in England had as many enemies as hair on his head, no harm would happen to him."

Their self-respect, their faith in causation, and their realistic logic or coupling of means to ends, have given them the leadership of the modern world. Montesquieu said, "No people have true common-sense but those who are born in England." This common-sense is a perception of all the conditions of our earthly existence; of laws that can be stated, and of laws that cannot be stated, or that are learned only by practice, in which allowance for friction is made. They are impious in their skepticism of theory, and in high departments they are cramped and sterile. But the unconditional surrender to facts, and the choice of means to reach their ends, are as admirable as with ants and bees.

The bias of the nation is a passion for utility. They love the lever, the screw and pulley, the Flanders draught-horse, the waterfall, windmills, tide-mills; the sea and the wind to bear their freight ships. More than the diamond Koh-i-noor, which glitters among their crown jewels, they prize that dull pebble which is wiser than a man, whose poles turn themselves to the poles of the world, and whose axis is parallel to the axis of the world. Now, their toys are steam and galvanism. They are heavy at the fine arts, but adroit at the coarse; not good in jewelry or mosaics, but the best iron-masters, colliers, wool-combers and tanners in Europe. They apply themselves to agriculture, to draining, to resisting encroachments of sea, wind, travelling sands, cold and wet sub-soil; to fishery, to manufacture of indispensable staples—salt, plumbago, leather, wool, glass, pottery and brick—to bees and silkworms—and by their steady combinations they succeed. A manufacturer sits down to dinner in a suit of clothes which was wool on a sheep's back at sunrise. You dine with a gentleman on venison, pheasant, quail, pigeons, poultry, mushrooms and pine-apples, all the growth of his estate. They are neat husbands for ordering all their tools pertaining to house and field. All are well kept. There is no want and no waste. They study use and fitness in their building, in the order of their dwellings and in their dress. The Frenchman invented the ruffle; the Englishman added the shirt. The Englishman wears a sensible coat buttoned to the chin, of rough but solid and lasting texture. If he is a lord, he dresses a little worse than a commoner. They have diffused the taste for plain substantial hats, shoes and coats through Europe. They think him the best dressed man whose dress is so fit for his use that you cannot notice or remember to describe it.

They secure the essentials in their diet, in their arts and manufactures. Every article of cutlery shows, in its shape, thought and long experience of workmen. They put the expense in the right place, as, in their sea-steamers, in the solidity of the machinery and the strength of the boat. The admirable equipment of their arctic ships carries London to the pole. They build roads, aqueducts; warm and ventilate houses. And they have impressed their directness and practical habit on modern civilization.

In trade, the Englishman believes that nobody breaks who ought not to break; and that if he do not make trade everything, it will make him nothing; and acts on this belief. The spirit of system, attention to details, and the subordination of details, or the not driving things too finely (which is charged on the Germans), constitute that dispatch of business which makes the mercantile power of England.

In war, the Englishman looks to his means. He is of the opinion of Civilis, his German ancestor, whom Tacitus reports as holding that "the gods are on the side of the strongest"—a sentence which Bonaparte unconsciously translated, when he said that "he had noticed that Providence always favored the heaviest battalion." Their military science propounds that if the weight of the advancing column is greater than that of the resisting, the latter is destroyed. Therefore, Wellington, when he came to the army in Spain, had every man weighed, first with accoutrements, and then without; believing that the force of an army depended on the weight and power of the individual soldiers, in spite of cannon. Lord Palmerston told the House of Commons that more care is taken of the health and comfort of English troops than of any other troops in the world; and that hence the English can put more men into the rank, on the day of action, on the field of battle, than any other army. Before the bombardment of the Danish forts in the Baltic, Nelson spent day after day, himself, in the boats, on the exhausting service of sounding the channel. Clerk of Eldin's celebrated manœuvre of breaking the line of sea-battle, and Nelson's feat of *doubling*, or stationing his ships one on the outer bow, and another on the outer quarter of each of the enemy's, were only translations into naval tactics of Bonaparte's rule of concentration. Lord Collingwood was accustomed to tell his men that if they could fire three well-directed broadsides in five minutes, no vessel could resist them; and from constant practice they came to do it in three minutes and a half.

But conscious that no race of better men exists, they rely most on the simplest means, and do not like ponderous and difficult tactics, but delight to bring the affair hand to hand; where the victory lies with the strength, courage and endurance of the individual combatants. They adopt every improvement in rig, in motor, in weapons, but they fundamentally believe that the best stratagem in naval war is to lay your ship close alongside of the enemy's ship and bring all your guns to bear on him, until you or he go to the bottom. This is the old fashion, which never goes out of fashion, neither in nor out of England.

It is not usually a point of honor, nor a religious sentiment, and never any whim, that they will shed their blood for; but usually property, and right measured by property, that breeds revolution. They have no Indian taste for a tomahawk-dance, no French taste for a badge or a proclamation. The Englishman is peaceably minding his business and earning his day's wages. But if you offer to lay hand on his day's wages, on his cow, or his right in common, or his shop, he will fight to the Judgment. Magna-charta, jury-trial, *habeas-corpus*, star-chamber, ship-money, Popery, Plymouth colony, American Revolution, are all questions involving a yeoman's right to his dinner, and except as touching that, would not have lashed the British nation to rage and revolt.

Whilst they are thus instinct with a spirit of order and of calculation, it must be owned they are capable of larger views; but the indulgence is expensive to them, costs great crises, or accumulations of mental power. In common, the horse works best with blinders. Nothing is more in the line of English thought than our unvarnished Connecticut question, "Pray, sir, how do you get your living when you are at home?" The questions of freedom, of taxation, of privilege, are money questions. Heavy fellows, steeped in beer and fleshpots, they are hard of hearing and dim of sight. Their drowsy minds need to be flagellated by war and trade and politics and persecution. They cannot well read a principle, except by the light of fagots and of burning towns.

Tacitus says of the Germans, "Powerful only in sudden efforts, they are impatient of toil and labor." This highly destined race, if it had not somewhere added the chamber of patience to its brain, would not have built London. I know not from which of the tribes and temperaments that went to the composition of the people this tenacity was supplied, but they clinch every nail they drive. They have no running for luck, and no immoderate speed. They spend largely on their fabric, and await the slow return. Their leather lies tanning seven years in the vat. At Rogers's mills, in Sheffield, where I was shown the process of making a razor and a penknife, I was told there is no luck in making good steel; that they make no mistakes, every blade in the hundred and in the thousand is good. And that is characteristic of all their work—no more is attempted than is done.

When Thor and his companions arrive at Utgard, he is told that "nobody is permitted to remain here, unless he understand some art,

. . . .

and excel in it all other men." The same question is still put to the posterity of Thor. A nation of laborers, every man is trained to some one
art or detail and aims at perfection in that; not content unless he has
something in which he thinks he surpasses all other men. He would
rather not do anything at all than not do it well. I suppose no people
have such thoroughness—from the highest to the lowest, every man
meaning to be master of his art.

"To show capacity," a Frenchman described as the end of a speech
in debate: "No," said an Englishman, "but to set your shoulder at the
wheel—to advance the business." Sir Samuel Romilly refused to speak
in popular assemblies, confining himself to the House of Commons,
where a measure can be carried by a speech. The business of the House
of Commons is conducted by a few persons, but these are hard-worked.
Sir Robert Peel "knew the Blue Books by heart." His colleagues and
rivals carry Hansard in their heads. The high civil and legal offices are
not beds of ease, but posts which exact frightful amounts of mental
labor. Many of the great leaders, like Pitt, Canning, Castlereagh,
Romilly, are soon worked to death. They are excellent judges in England of a good worker, and when they find one, like Clarendon, Sir
Philip Warwick, Sir William Coventry, Ashley, Burke, Thurlow,
Mansfield, Pitt, Eldon, Peel, or Russell, there is nothing too good or
too high for him.

They have a wonderful heat in the pursuit of a public aim. Private
persons exhibit, in scientific and antiquarian researches, the same pertinacity as the nation showed in the coalitions in which it yoked Europe
against the empire of Bonaparte, one after the other defeated, and still
renewed, until the sixth hurled him from his seat.

Sir John Herschel, in completion of the work of his father, who had
made the catalogue of the stars of the northern hemisphere, expatriated
himself for years at the Cape of Good Hope, finished his inventory of
the southern heaven, came home, and redacted it in eight years more—
a work whose value does not begin until thirty years have elapsed, and
thenceforward a record to all ages of the highest import. The Admiralty sent out the Arctic expeditions year after year, in search of Sir
John Franklin, until at last they have threaded their way through polar
pack and Behring's Straits and solved the geographical problem. Lord
Elgin, at Athens, saw the imminent ruin of the Greek remains, set up
his scaffoldings, in spite of epigrams, and, after five years' labor to col-

lect them, got his marbles on ship-board. The ship struck a rock and
went to the bottom. He had them all fished up by divers, at a vast
expense, and brought to London; not knowing that Haydon, Fuseli and
Canova, and all good heads in all the world, were to be his applaud-
ers. In the same spirit, were the excavation and research by Sir Charles
Fellowes for the Xanthian monument, and of Layard for his Nineveh
sculptures.

The nation sits in the immense city they have builded, a London
extended into every man's mind, though he live in Van Dieman's Land
or Capetown. Faithful performance of what is undertaken to be performed, they honor in themselves, and exact in others, as certificate of
equality with themselves. The modern world is theirs. They have made
and make it day by day. The commercial relations of the world are so
intimately drawn to London, that every dollar on earth contributes to
the strength of the English government. And if all the wealth in the
planet should perish by war or deluge, they know themselves competent
to replace it.

They have approved their Saxon blood, by their sea-going qualities; their descent from Odin's smiths, by their hereditary skill in
working in iron; their British birth, by husbandry and immense wheat
harvests;. and justified their occupancy of the centre of habitable land,
by their supreme ability and cosmopolitan spirit. They have tilled,
builded, forged, spun and woven. They have made the island a thoroughfare, and London a shop, a law-court, a record-office and scientific
bureau, inviting to strangers; a sanctuary to refugees of every political
and religious opinion; and such a city that almost every active man, in
any nation, finds himself at one time or other forced to visit it.

In every path of practical activity they have gone even with the
best. There is no secret of war in which they have not shown mastery.
The steam-chamber of Watt, the locomotive of Stephenson, the cot-
ton-mule of Roberts, perform the labor of the world. There is no
department of literature, of science, or of useful art, in which they have
not produced a first-rate book. It is England whose opinion is waited
for on the merit of a new invention, an improved science. And in the
complications of the trade and politics of their vast empire, they have
been equal to every exigency, with counsel and with conduct. Is it their
luck, or is it the chambers of their brain—it is their commercial advantage that whatever light appears in better method or happy invention,

breaks out *in their race*. They are a family to which a destiny attaches, and the Banshee has sworn that a male heir shall never be wanting. They have a wealth of men to fill important posts, and the vigilance of party criticism insures the selection of a competent person.

A proof of the energy of the British people is the highly artificial construction of the whole fabric. The climate and geography, I said, were factitious, as if the hands of man had arranged the conditions. The same character pervades the whole kingdom. Bacon said, "Rome was a state not subject to paradoxes"; but England subsists by antagonisms and contradictions. The foundations of its greatness are the rolling waves; and from first to last it is a museum of anomalies. This foggy and rainy country furnishes the world with astronomical observations. Its short rivers do not afford water-power, but the land shakes under the thunder of the mills. There is no gold-mine of any importance, but there is more gold in England than in all other countries. It is too far north for the culture of the vine, but the wines of all countries are in its docks. The French Comte de Lauraguais said, "No fruit ripens in England but a baked apple"; but oranges and pine-apples are as cheap in London as in the Mediterranean. The Mark-Lane Express, or the Custom House Returns, bear out to the letter the vaunt of Pope—

> "Let India boast her palms, nor envy we
> The weeping amber, nor the spicy tree,
> While, by our oaks, those precious loads are borne
> And realms commanded which those trees adorn."

The native cattle are extinct, but the island is full of artificial breeds. The agriculturist Bakewell created sheep and cows and horses to order, and breeds in which every thing was omitted but what is economical. The cow is sacrificed to her bag, the ox to his sirloin. Stall-feeding makes sperm-mills of the cattle, and converts the stable to a chemical factory. The rivers, lakes and ponds, too much fished, or obstructed by factories, are artificially filled with the eggs of salmon, turbot and herring.

Chat Moss and the fens of Lincolnshire and Cambridgeshire are unhealthy and too barren to pay rent. By cylindrical tiles and gutta-percha tubes, five millions of acres of bad land have been drained and put on equality with the best, for rape-culture and grass. The climate too, which was already believed to have become milder and drier by the enormous consumption of coal, is so far reached by this new action, that fogs and storms are said to disappear. In due course, all England will be drained and rise a second time out of the waters. The latest step was to call in the aid of steam to agriculture. Steam is almost an Englishman. I do not know but they will send him to Parliament next, to make laws. He weaves, forges, saws, pounds, fans, and now he must pump, grind, dig and plough for the farmer. The markets created by the manufacturing population have erected agriculture into a great thriving and spending industry. The value of the houses in Britain is equal to the value of the soil. Artificial aids of all kinds are cheaper than the natural resources. No man can afford to walk, when the par-liamentary-train carries him for a penny a mile. Gas-burners are cheaper than daylight in numberless floors in the cities. All the houses in London buy their water. The English trade does not exist for the exportation of native products, but on its manufactures, or the making well every thing which is ill-made elsewhere. They make ponchos for the Mexican, bandannas for the Hindoo, ginseng for the Chinese, beads for the Indian, laces for the Flemings, telescopes for astronomers, can-nons for kings.

The Board of Trade caused the best models of Greece and Italy to be placed within the reach of every manufacturing population. They caused to be translated from foreign languages and illustrated by elab-orate drawings, the most approved works of Munich, Berlin and Paris. They have ransacked Italy to find new forms, to add a grace to the products of their looms, their potteries and their foundries.

The nearer we look, the more artificial is their social system. Their law is a network of fictions. Their property, a scrip or certificate of right to interest on money that no man ever saw. Their social classes are made by statute. Their ratios of power and representation are his-torical and legal. The last Reform-bill took away political power from a mound, a ruin and a stone wall, whilst Birmingham and Manchester, whose mills paid for the wars of Europe, had no representative. Purity in the elective Parliament is secured by the purchase of seats. Foreign power is kept by armed colonies; power at home, by a standing army of police. The pauper lives better than the free laborer, the thief better than the pauper, and the transported felon better than the one under imprisonment. The crimes are factitious; as smuggling, poaching, non-

conformity, heresy and treason. The sovereignty of the seas is maintained by the impressment of seamen. "The impressment of seamen,"
said Lord Eldon, "is the life of our navy." Solvency is maintained by
means of a national debt, on the principle, "If you will not lend me the
money, how can I pay you?" For the administration of justice, Sir
Samuel Romilly's expedient for clearing the arrears of business in
Chancery was, the Chancellor's staying away entirely from his court.
Their system of education is factitious. The Universities galvanize dead
languages into a semblance of life. Their church is artificial. The manners and customs of society are artificial—made-up men with made-up
manners—and thus the whole is Birminghamized, and we have a nation
whose existence is a work of art—a cold, barren, almost arctic isle being
made the most fruitful, luxurious and imperial land in the whole earth.

Man in England submits to be a product of political economy. On
a bleak moor a mill is built, a banking-house is opened, and men come
in as water in a sluice-way, and towns and cities rise. Man is made as
a Birmingham button. The rapid doubling of the population dates from
Watt's steam-engine. A landlord who owns a province says, "The tenantry are unprofitable; let me have sheep." He unroofs the houses and
ships the population to America. The nation is accustomed to the
instantaneous creation of wealth. It is the maxim of their economists,
"that the greater part in value of the wealth now existing in England
has been produced by human hands within the last twelve months."
Meantime, three or four days' rain will reduce hundreds to starving in
London.

One secret of their power is their mutual good understanding. Not
only good minds are born among them, but all the people have good
minds. Every nation has yielded some good wit, if, as has chanced to
many tribes, only one. But the intellectual organization of the English
admits a communicableness of knowledge and ideas among them all.
An electric touch by any of their national ideas, melts them into one
family and brings the hoards of power which their individuality is
always hiving, into use and play for all. Is it the smallness of the country, or is it the pride and affection of race—they have solidarity, or
responsibleness, and trust in each other.

Their minds, like wool, admit of a dye which is more lasting than
the cloth. They embrace their cause with more tenacity than their life.
Though not military, yet every common subject by the poll is fit to

make a soldier of. These private, reserved, mute family-men can adopt a public end with all their heat, and this strength of affection makes the romance of their heroes. The difference of rank does not divide the national heart. The Danish poet Oehlenschläger complains that who writes in Danish writes to two hundred readers. In Germany there is one speech for the learned, and another for the masses, to that extent that, it is said, no sentiment or phrase from the works of any great German writer is ever heard among the lower classes. But in England, the language of the noble is the language of the poor. In Parliament, in pulpits, in theatres, when the speakers rise to thought and passion, the language becomes idiomatic; the people in the street best understand the best words. And their language seems drawn from the Bible, the Common Law and the works of Shakspeare, Bacon, Milton, Pope, Young, Cowper, Burns and Scott. The island has produced two or three of the greatest men that ever existed, but they were not solitary in their town time. Men quickly embodied what Newton found out, in Greenwich observatories and practical navigation. The boys know all that Hutton knew of strata, or Dalton of atoms, or Harvey of blood-vessels; and these studies, once dangerous, are in fashion. So what is invented or known in agriculture, or in trade, or in war, or in art, or in literature and antiquities. A great ability, not amassed on a few giants, but poured into the general mind, so that each of them could at a pinch stand in the shoes of the other; and they are more bound in character than differenced in ability or in rank. The laborer is a possible lord. The lord is a possible basket-maker. Every man carries the English system in his brain, knows what is confided to him and does therein the best he can. The chancellor carries England on his mace, the midshipman at the point of his dirk, the smith on his hammer, the cook in the bowl of his spoon; the postilion cracks his whip for England, and the sailor times his oars to "God save the King!" The very felons have their pride in each other's English stanchness. In politics and in war they hold together as by hooks of steel. The charm in Nelson's history is the unselfish greatness, the assurance of being supported to the uttermost by those whom he supports to the uttermost. Whilst they are some ages ahead of the rest of the world in the art of living; whilst in some directions they do not represent the modern spirit but constitute it—this vanguard of civility and power they coldly hold, marching in phalanx, lockstep, foot after foot, file after file of heroes, ten thousand deep.

CHAPTER VI

MANNERS

I FIND the Englishman to be him of all men who stands firmest in his shoes. They have in themselves what they value in their horses—mettle and bottom. On the day of my arrival at Liverpool, a gentleman, in describing to me the Lord Lieutenant of Ireland, happened to say, "Lord Clarendon has pluck like a cock and will fight till he dies"; and what I heard first I heard last, and the one thing the English value is *pluck*. The word is not beautiful, but on the quality they signify by it the nation is unanimous. The cabmen have it; the merchants have it; the bishops have it; the women have it; the journals have it; the Times newspaper they say is the pluckiest thing in England, and Sydney Smith had made it a proverb that little Lord John Russell, the minister, would take the command of the Channel fleet to-morrow.

They require you to dare to be of your own opinion, and they hate the practical cowards who cannot in affairs answer directly yes or no. They dare to displease, nay, they will let you break all the commandments, if you do it natively and with spirit. You must be somebody; then you may do this or that, as you will.

Machinery has been applied to all work, and carried to such perfection that little is left for the men but to mind the engines and feed the furnaces. But the machines require punctual service, and as they never tire, they prove too much for their tenders. Mines, forges, mills, breweries, railroads, steam-pump, steam-plough, drill of regiments, drill of police, rule of court and shop-rule have operated to give a mechanical regularity to all the habit and action of men. A terrible machine has possessed itself of the ground, the air, the men and women, and hardly even thought is free.

The mechanical might and organization requires in the people constitution and answering spirits; and he who goes among them must have some weight of metal. At last, you take your hint from the fury of life you find, and say, one thing is plain, this is no country for faint-hearted people: don't creep about diffidently; make up your mind; take your own course, and you shall find respect and furtherance.

It requires, men say, a good constitution to travel in Spain. I say as much of England, for other cause, simply on account of the vigor and brawn of the people. Nothing but the most serious business could give one any counterweight to these Baresarks, though they were only to order eggs and muffins for their breakfast. The Englishman speaks with all his body. His elocution is stomachic—as the American's is labial. The Englishman is very petulant and precise about his accommodation at inns and on the roads; a quiddle about his toast and his chop and every species of convenience, and loud and pungent in his expressions of impatience at any neglect. His vivacity betrays itself at all points, in his manners, in his respiration, and the inarticulate noises he makes in clearing the throat—all significant of burly strength. He has stamina; he can take the initiative in emergencies. He has that *aplomb* which results from a good adjustment of the moral and physical nature and the obedience of all the powers to the will; as if the axes of his eyes were united to his backbone, and only moved with the trunk.

This vigor appears in the incuriosity and stony neglect, each of every other. Each man walks, eats, drinks, shaves, dresses, gesticulates, and, in every manner acts and suffers without reference to the bystanders, in his own fashion, only careful not to interfere with them or annoy them; not that he is trained to neglect the eyes of his neighbors—he is really occupied with his own affair and does not think of them. Every man in this polished country consults only his convenience, as much as a solitary pioneer in Wisconsin. I know not where any personal eccentricity is so freely allowed, and no man gives himself any concern with it. An Englishman walks in a pouring rain, swinging his closed umbrella like a walking-stick; wears a wig, or a shawl, or a saddle, or stands on his head, and no remark is made. And as he has been doing this for several generations, it is now in the blood.

In short, every one of these islanders is an island himself, safe, tranquil, incommunicable. In a company of strangers you would think him deaf; his eyes never wander from his table and newspaper. He is never betrayed into any curiosity or unbecoming emotion. They have all been trained in one severe school of manners, and never put off the harness. He does not give his hand. He does not let you meet his eye. It is almost an affront to look a man in the face without being introduced. In mixed or in select companies they do not introduce persons; so that a presentation is a circumstance as valid as a contract. Introductions are sacraments. He withholds his name. At the hotel, he is hardly willing to whisper it to the clerk at the book-office. If he give you his private address on a card, it is like an avowal of friendship; and his bearing, on being introduced, is cold, even though he is seeking your acquaintance and is studying how he shall serve you.

It was an odd proof of this impressive energy, that in my lectures I hesitated to read and threw out for its impertinence many a disparaging phrase which I had been accustomed to spin about poor, thin, unable mortals; so much had the fine physique and the personal vigor of this robust race worked on my imagination.

I happened to arrive in England at the moment of a commercial crisis. But it was evident that let who will fail, England will not. These people have sat here a thousand years, and here will continue to sit. They will not break up, or arrive at any desperate revolution, like their neighbors; for they have as much energy, as much continence of character as they ever had. The power and possession which surround them are their own creation, and they exert the same commanding industry at this moment.

They are positive, methodical, cleanly and formal, loving routine and conventional ways; loving truth and religion, to be sure, but inexorable on points of form. All the world praises the comfort and private appointments of an English inn, and of English households. You are sure of neatness and of personal decorum. A Frenchman may possibly be clean; an Englishman is conscientiously clean. A certain order and complete propriety is found in his dress and in his belongings.

Born in a harsh and wet climate, which keeps him indoors whenever he is at rest, and being of an affectionate and loyal temper, he dearly loves his house. If he is rich, he buys a demesne and builds a hall; if he is in middle condition, he spares no expense on his house. Without, it is all planted; within, it is wainscoted, carved, curtained, hung with pictures and filled with good furniture. 'T is a passion which survives all others, to deck and improve it. Hither he brings all that is rare and costly, and with the national tendency to sit fast in the same spot for many generations, it comes to be, in the course of time, a museum of heirlooms, gifts and trophies of the adventures and exploits of the family. He is very fond of silver plate, and though he have no gallery of portraits of his ancestors, he has of their punch-bowls and porringers. Incredible amounts of plate are found in good houses, and the poorest have some spoon or saucepan, gift of a godmother, saved out of better times.

An English family consists of a few persons, who, from youth to age, are found revolving within a few feet of each other, as if tied by some invisible ligature, tense as that cartilage which we have seen attaching the two Siamese. England produces under favorable conditions of ease and culture the finest women in the world. And as the men are affectionate and true-hearted, the women inspire and refine them. Nothing can be more delicate without being fantastical, nothing more firm and based in nature and sentiment, than the courtship and mutual carriage of the sexes. The song of 1596 says, "The wife of every Englishman is counted blest." The sentiment of Imogen in Cymbeline is copied from English nature; and not less the Portia of Brutus, the Kate Percy and the Desdemona. The romance does not exceed the height of noble passion in Mrs. Lucy Hutchinson, or in Lady Russell, or even as one discerns through the plain prose of Pepys's Diary, the sacred habit of an English wife. Sir Samuel Romilly could not bear the death of his wife. Every class has its noble and tender examples.

Domesticity is the taproot which enables the nation to branch wide and high. The motive and end of their trade and empire is to guard the independence and privacy of their homes. Nothing so much marks their manners as the concentration on their household ties. This domesticity is carried into court and camp. Wellington governed India and Spain and his own troops, and fought battles, like a good family-man, paid his debts, and though general of an army in Spain, could not stir abroad for fear of public creditors. This taste for house and parish merits has of course its doting and foolish side. Mr. Cobbett attributes the huge popularity of Perceval, prime minister in 1810, to the fact that he was wont to go to church every Sunday, with a large quarto gilt prayer-book under one arm, his wife hanging on the other, and followed by a long brood of children.

They keep their old customs, costumes, and pomps, their wig and mace, sceptre and crown. The Middle Ages still lurk in the streets of London. The Knights of the Bath take oath to defend injured ladies; the gold-stick-in-waiting survives. They repeated the ceremonies of the eleventh century in the coronation of the present Queen. A hereditary tenure is natural to them. Offices, farms, trades and traditions descend so. Their leases run for a hundred and a thousand years. Terms of service and partnership are lifelong, or are inherited. "Holdship has been with me," said Lord Eldon, "eight-and-twenty years, knows all my

business and books." Antiquity of usage is sanction enough. Wordsworth says of the small freeholders of Westmoreland, "Many of these
humble sons of the hills had a consciousness that the land which they
tilled had for more than five hundred years been possessed by men of
the same name and blood." The ship-carpenter in the public yards, my
lord's gardener and porter, have been there for more than a hundred
years, grandfather, father, and son.

The English power resides also in their dislike of change. They
have difficulty in bringing their reason to act, and on all occasions use
their memory first. As soon as they have rid themselves of some
grievance and settled the better practice, they make haste to fix it as a
finality, and never wish to hear of alteration more.

Every Englishman is an embryonic chancellor: his instinct is to
search for a precedent. The favorite phrase of their law is, "a custom
whereof the memory of man runneth not back to the contrary." The
barons say, *"Nolumus mutari"*; and the cockneys stifle the curiosity of
the foreigner on the reason of any practice with "Lord, sir, it was
always so." They hate innovation. Bacon told them, Time was the right
reformer; Chatham, that "confidence was a plant of slow growth"; Canning, to "advance with the times"; and Wellington, that "habit was ten
times nature." All their statesmen learn the irresistibility of the tide of
custom, and have invented many fine phrases to cover this slowness of
perception and prehensility of tail.

A sea-shell should be the crest of England, not only because it represents a power built on the waves, but also the hard finish of the men.
The Englishman is finished like a cowry or a murex. After the spire
and the spines are formed, or with the formation, a juice exudes and a
hard enamel varnishes every part. The keeping of the proprieties is as
indispensable as clean linen. No merit quite countervails the want of
this whilst this sometimes stands in lieu of all. " 'T is in bad taste," is
the most formidable word an Englishman can pronounce. But this
japan costs them dear. There is a prose in certain Englishmen which
exceeds in wooden deadness all rivalry with other countrymen. There is
a knell in the conceit and externality of their voice, which seems to say,
Leave all hope behind. In this Gibraltar of propriety, mediocrity gets
intrenched and consolidated and founded in adamant. An Englishman
of fashion is like one of those souvenirs, bound in gold vellum, enriched
with delicate engravings on thick hotpressed-paper, fit for the hands of

ladies and princes, but with nothing in it worth reading or remembering.

A severe decorum rules the court and the cottage. When Thalberg
the pianist was one evening performing before the Queen at Windsor,
in a private party, the Queen accompanied him with her voice. The circumstance took air, and all England shuddered from sea to sea. The
indecorum was never repeated. Cold, repressive manners prevail. No
enthusiasm is permitted except at the opera. They avoid every thing
marked. They require a tone of voice that excites no attention in the
room. Sir Philip Sidney is one of the patron saints of England, of whom
Wotton said, "His wit was the measure of congruity."

Pretension and vaporing are once for all distasteful. They keep to
the other extreme of low tone in dress and manners. They avoid pretension and go right to the heart of the thing. They hate nonsense,
sentimentalism and high-flown expression; they use a studied plainness.
Even Brummel, their fop, was marked by the severest simplicity in
dress. They value themselves on the absence of every thing theatrical in
the public business, and on conciseness and going to the point, in private affairs.

In an aristocratical country like England, not the Trial by Jury, but
the dinner, is the capital institution. It is the mode of doing honor to a
stranger, to invite him to eat—and has been for many hundred years.
"And they think," says the Venetian traveller of 1500, "no greater
honor can be conferred or received, than to invite others to eat with
them, or to be invited themselves, and they would sooner give five or
six ducats to provide an entertainment for a person, than a groat to
assist him in any distress." It is reserved to the end of the day, the fam-
ily-hour being generally six, in London, and if any company is
expected, one or two hours later. Every one dresses for dinner, in his
own house, or in another man's. The guests are expected to arrive
within half an hour of the time fixed by card of invitation, and nothing but death or mutilation is permitted to detain them. The English
dinner is precisely the model on which our own are constructed in the
Atlantic cities. The company sit one or two hours before the ladies
leave the table. The gentlemen remain over their wine an hour longer,
and rejoin the ladies in the drawing-room and take coffee. The dress-
dinner generates a talent of table-talk which reaches great perfection:
the stories are so good that one is sure they must have been often told

before, to have got such happy turns. Hither come all manner of clever projects, bits of popular science, of practical intervention, of miscellaneous humor; political, literary and personal news; railroads, horses, diamonds, agriculture, horticulture, pisciculture and wine.

English stories, *bon mots* and the recorded table-talk of their wits, are as good as the best of the French. In America, we are apt scholars, but have not yet attained the same perfection: for the range of nations from which London draws, and the steep contrasts of condition, create the picturesque in society, as broken country makes picturesque landscape; whilst our prevailing equality makes a prairie tameness: and secondly, because the usage of a dress-dinner every day at dark has a tendency to hive and produce to advantage every thing good. Much attrition has worn every sentence into a bullet. Also one meets now and then with polished men who know every thing, have tried every thing, and can do every thing, and are quite superior to letters and science. What could they not, if only they would?

CHAPTER VII

TRUTH

THE TEUTONIC TRIBES have a national singleness of heart, which contrasts with the Latin races. The German name has a proverbial significance of sincerity and honest meaning. The arts bear testimony to it. The faces of clergy and laity in old sculptures and illuminated missals are charged with earnest belief. Add to this hereditary rectitude the punctuality and precise dealing which commerce creates, and you have the English truth and credit. The government strictly performs its engagements. The subjects do not understand trifling on its part. When any breach of promise occurred, in the old days of prerogative, it was resented by the people as an intolerable grievance. And in modern times, any slipperiness in the government of political faith, or any repudiation or crookedness in matters of finance, would bring the whole nation to a committee of inquiry and reform. Private men keep their promises, never so trivial. Down goes the flying word on the tablets, and is indelible as Domesday Book.

Their practical power rests on their national sincerity. Veracity derives from instinct, and marks superiority in organization. Nature has endowed some animals with cunning, as a compensation for strength withheld; but it has provoked the malice of all others, as if avengers of public wrong. In the nobler kinds, where strength could be afforded, her races are loyal to truth, as truth is the foundation of the social state. Beasts that make no truce with man, do not break faith with each other. 'T is said that the wolf, who makes a *cache* of his prey and brings his fellows with him to the spot, if, on digging, it is not found, is instantly and unresistingly torn in pieces. English veracity seems to result on a sounder animal structure, as if they could afford it. They are blunt in saying what they think, sparing of promises, and they require plain dealing of others. We will not have to do with a man in a mask. Let us know the truth. Draw a straight line, hit whom and where it will. Alfred, whom the affection of the nation makes the type of their race, is called by a writer at the Norman Conquest, the *truth-speaker; Alueredus veridicus*. Geoffrey of Monmouth says of King Aurelius, uncle of Arthur, that "above all things he hated a lie." The Northman Guttorm said to King Olaf, "It is royal work to fulfil royal words." The mottoes of their families are monitory proverbs, as, *Fare fac*—Say, do—of the Fairfaxes; Say and seal, of the house of Fiennes; *Vero nil verius*, of the De Veres. To be king of their word is their pride. When they unmask cant, they say, "The English of this is," etc.; and to give the lie is the extreme insult. The phrase of the lowest of the people is "honor-bright," and their vulgar praise, "His word is as good as his bond." They hate shuffling and equivocation, and the cause is damaged in the public opinion, on which any paltering can be fixed. Even Lord Chesterfield, with his French breeding, when he came to define a gentleman, declared that truth made his distinction; and nothing ever spoken by him would find so hearty a suffrage from his nation. The Duke of Wellington, who had the best right to say so, advises the French General Kellermann that he may rely on the parole of an English officer. The English, of all classes, value themselves on this trait, as distinguishing them from the French, who, in the popular belief, are more polite than true. An Englishman understates, avoids the superlative, checks himself in compliments, alleging that in the French language one cannot speak without lying.

They love reality in wealth, power, hospitality, and do not easily learn to make a show, and take the world as it goes. They are not fond of ornaments, and if they wear them, they must be gems. They read

. . . .

gladly in old Fuller that a lady in the reign of Elizabeth "would have as patiently digested a lie, as the wearing of false stones or pendants of counterfeit pearl." They have the earth-hunger, or preference for property in land, which is said to mark the Teutonic nations. They build of stone: public and private buildings are massive and durable. In comparing their ships' houses and public offices with the American, it is commonly said that they spend a pound where we spend a dollar. Plain rich clothes, plain rich equipage, plain rich finish throughout their house and belongings mark the English truth.

They confide in each other—English believes in English. The French feel the superiority of this probity. The Englishman is not springing a trap for his admiration, but is honestly minding his business. The Frenchman is vain. Madame de Staël says that the English irritated Napoleon, mainly because they have found out how to unite success with honesty. She was not aware how wide an application her foreign readers would give to the remark. Wellington discovered the ruin of Bonaparte's affairs, by his own probity. He augured ill of the empire as soon as he saw that it was mendacious and lived by war. If war do not bring in its sequel new trade, better agriculture and manufactures, but only games, fireworks and spectacles—no prosperity could support it; much less a nation decimated for conscripts and out of pocket, like France. So he drudged for years on his military works at Lisbon, and from this base at last extended his gigantic lines to Waterloo, believing in his countrymen and their syllogisms above all the rhodomontade of Europe.

At a St. George's festival, in Montreal, where I happened to be a guest since my return home, I observed that the chairman complimented his compatriots, by saying, "they confided that wherever they met an Englishman, they found a man who would speak the truth." And one cannot think this festival fruitless, if, all over the world, on the 23d of April, wherever two or three English are found, they meet to encourage each other in the nationality of veracity.

In the power of saying rude truth, sometimes in the lion's mouth, no men surpass them. On the king's birthday, when each bishop was expected to offer the king a purse of gold, Latimer gave Henry VIII a copy of the Vulgate, with a mark at the passage, "Whoremongers and adulterers God will judge"; and they so honor stoutness in each other that the king passed it over. They are tenacious of their belief and cannot easily change their opinions to suit the hour. They are like ships with too much head on to come quickly about, nor will prosperity or even adversity be allowed to shake their habitual view of conduct. Whilst I was in London, M. Guizot arrived there on his escape from Paris, in February, 1848. Many private friends called on him. His name was immediately proposed as an honorary member of the Athenæum. M. Guizot was blackballed. Certainly they knew the distinction of his name. But the Englishman is not fickle. He had really made up his mind now for years as he read his newspaper, to hate and despise M. Guizot; and the altered position of the man as an illustrious exile and a guest in the country, makes no difference to him, as it would instantly to an American.

They require the same adherence, thorough conviction and reality, in public men. It is the want of character which makes the low reputation of the Irish members. "See them," they said, "one hundred and twenty-seven all voting like sheep, never proposing any thing, and all but four voting the income tax"—which was an ill-judged concession of the government, relieving Irish property from the burdens charged on English.

They have a horror of adventurers in or out of Parliament. The ruling passion of Englishmen in these days is a terror of humbug. In the same proportion they value honesty, stoutness, and adherence to your own. They like a man committed to his objects. They hate the French, as frivolous; they hate the Irish, as aimless; they hate the Germans, as professors. In February, 1848, they said, Look, the French king and his party fell for want of a shot; they had not conscience to shoot, so entirely was the pith and heart of monarchy eaten out.

They attack their own politicians every day, on the same grounds, as adventurers. They love stoutness in standing for your right, in declining money or promotion that costs any concession. The barrister refuses the silk gown of Queen's Counsel, if his junior have it one day earlier. Lord Collingwood would not accept his medal for victory on 14 February, 1797, if he did not receive one for victory on 1st June, 1794; and the long withholden medal was accorded. When Castlereagh dissuaded Lord Wellington from going to the king's levee until the unpopular Cintra business had been explained, he replied, "You furnish me a reason for going. I will go to this, or I will never go to a king's levee." The radical mob at Oxford cried after the tory Lord Eldon,

"There's old Eldon; cheer him; he never ratted." They have given the parliamentary nickname of *Trimmers* to the timeservers, whom English character does not love.

They are very liable in their politics to extraordinary delusions; thus to believe what stands recorded in the gravest books, that the movement of 10 April, 1848, was urged or assisted by foreigners: which, to be sure, is paralleled by the democratic whimsy in this country which I have noticed to be shared by men sane on other points, that the English are at the bottom of the agitation of slavery, in American politics: and then again by the French popular legends on the subject of *perfidious Albion*. But suspicion will make fools of nations as of citizens.

A slow temperament makes them less rapid and ready than other countrymen, and has given occasion to the observation that English wit comes afterwards—which the French denote as *esprit d'escalier*. This dulness makes their attachment to home and their adherence in all foreign countries to home habits. The Englishman who visits Mount Etna will carry his tea-kettle to the top. The old Italian author of the "Relation of England" (in 1500), says, "I have it on the best information, that, when the war is actually ranging most furiously, they will seek for good eating and all their other comforts, without thinking what harm might befall them." Then their eyes seem to be set at the bottom of a tunnel, and they affirm the one small fact they know, with the best faith in the world that nothing else exists. And as their own belief in guineas is perfect, they readily, on all occasions, apply the pecuniary argument as final. Thus when the Rochester rappings began to be heard of in England, a man deposited £100 in a sealed box in the Dublin Bank, and then advertised in the newspapers to all somnambulists, mesmerizers and others, that whoever could tell him the number of his note should have the money. He let it lie there six months, the newspapers now and then, at his instance, stimulating the attention of the adepts; but none could ever tell him; and he said, "Now let me never be bothered more with this proven lie." It is told of a good Sir John that he heard a case stated by counsel, and made up his mind; then the counsel for the other side taking their turn to speak, he found himself so unsettled and perplexed that he exclaimed, "So help me God! I will never listen to evidence again." Any number of delightful examples of this English stolidity are the anecdotes of Europe. I knew a very worthy man—a magistrate, I believe he was, in the town of

· ·

Derby—who went to the opera to see Malibran. In one scene, the heroine was to rush across a ruined bridge. Mr. B. arose and mildly yet
firmly called the attention of the audience and the performers to the
fact that, in his judgment, the bridge was unsafe! This English stolidity
contrasts with French wit and tact. The French, it is commonly said,
have greatly more influence in Europe than the English. What influence the English have is by brute force of wealth and power; that of
the French by affinity and talent. The Italian is subtle, the Spaniard
treacherous: tortures, it is said, could never wrest from an Egyptian the
confession of a secret. None of these traits belong to the Englishman.
His choler and conceit force everything out. Defoe, who knew his countrymen well, says of them—

> "In close intrigue, their faculty's but weak,
> For generally whate'er they know, they speak,
> And often their own counsels undermine
> By mere infirmity without design;
> From whence, the learned say, it doth proceed,
> That English treasons never can succeed;
> For they're so open-hearted, you may know
> Their own most secret thoughts, and others' too."

CHAPTER VIII

CHARACTER

THE ENGLISH RACE are reputed morose. I do not know that they have
sadder brows than their neighbors of northern climates. They are sad
by comparison with the singing and dancing nations: not sadder, but
slow and staid, as finding their joys at home. They, too, believe that
where there is no enjoyment of life there can be no vigor and art in
speech or thought; that your merry heart goes all the way, your sad one
tires in a mile. This trait of gloom has been fixed on them by French
travellers, who, from Froissart, Voltaire, Le Sage, Mirabeau, down to
the lively journalists of the *feuilletons*, have spent their wit on the
solemnity of their neighbors. The French say, gay conversation is
unknown in their island. The Englishman finds no relief from reflection, except in reflection. When he wishes for amusement, he goes to

work. His hilarity is like an attack of fever. Religion, the theatre and the reading the books of his country all feed and increase his natural melancholy. The police does not interfere with public diversions. It thinks itself bound in duty to respect the pleasures and rare gayety of this inconsolable nation; and their well-known courage is entirely attributable to their disgust of life.

I suppose their gravity of demeanor and their few words have obtained this reputation. As compared with the Americans, I think them cheerful and contented. Young people in this country are much more prone to melancholy. The English have a mild aspect and a ringing cheerful voice. They are large-natured and not so easily amused as the southerners, and are among them as grown people among children, requiring war, or trade, or engineering, or science, instead of frivolous games. They are proud and private, and even if disposed to recreation, will avoid an open garden. They sported sadly; *ils s'amusaient tristement, selon la coutume de leur pays*, said Froissart; and I suppose never nation built their party-walls so thick, or their garden-fences so high. Meat and wine produce no effect on them. They are just as cold, quiet and composed, at the end, as at the beginning of dinner.

The reputation of taciturnity they have enjoyed for six or seven hundred years; and a kind of pride in bad public speaking is noted in the House of Commons, as if they were willing to show that they did not live by their tongues, or thought they spoke well enough if they had the tone of gentlemen. In mixed company they shut their mouths. A Yorkshire mill-owner told me he had ridden more than once all the way from London to Leeds, in the first-class carriage, with the same persons, and no word exchanged. The club-houses were established to cultivate social habits, and it is rare that more than two eat together, and oftenest one eats alone. Was it then a stroke of humor in the serious Swedenborg, or was it only his pitiless logic, that made him shut up the English souls in a heaven by themselves?

They are contradictorily described as sour, splenetic and stubborn—and as mild, sweet and sensible. The truth is they have great range and variety of character. Commerce sends abroad multitudes of different classes. The choleric Welshman, the fervid Scot, the bilious resident in the East or West Indies, are wide of the perfect behavior of the educated and dignified man of family. So is the burly farmer; so is the country squire, with his narrow and violent life. In every inn is the

Commercial-Room, in which 'travellers,' or bagmen who carry patterns and solicit orders for the manufacturers, are wont to be entertained. It easily happens that this class should characterize England to the foreigner, who meets them on the road and at every public house, whilst the gentry avoid the taverns, or seclude themselves whilst in them.

But these classes are the right English stock, and may fairly show the national qualities, before yet art and education have dealt with them. They are good lovers, good haters, slow but obstinate admirers, and in all things very much steeped in their temperament, like man hardly awaked from deep sleep, which they enjoy. Their habits and instincts cleave to nature. They are of the earth, earthy; and of the sea, as the sea-kinds, attached to it for what it yields them, and not from any sentiment. They are full of coarse strength, rude exercise, butcher's meat and sound sleep; and suspect any poetic insinuation or any hint for the conduct of life which reflects on this animal existence, as if somebody were fumbling at the umbilical cord and might stop their supplies. They doubt a man's sound judgment if he does not eat with appetite, and shake their heads if he is particularly chaste. Take them as they come, you shall find in the common people a surly indifference, sometimes gruffness and ill temper; and in minds of more power, magazines of inexhaustible war, challenging.

> "The ruggedest hour that time and spite dare bring
> To frown upon the enraged Northumberland."

They are headstrong believers and defenders of their opinion, and not less resolute in maintaining their whim and perversity. Hezekiah Woodward wrote a book against the Lord's Prayer. And one can believe that Burton, the Anatomist of Melancholy, having predicted from the stars the hour of his death, slipped the knot himself round his own neck, not to falsify his horoscope.

Their looks bespeak an invincible stoutness: they have extreme difficulty to run away, and will die game. Wellington said of the young coxcombs of the Life-Guards, delicately brought up, "But the puppies fight well"; and Nelson said of his sailors, "They really mind shot no more than peas." Of absolute stoutness no nation has more or better examples. They are good at storming redoubts, at boarding frigates, at dying in the last ditch, or any desperate service which has daylight and honor in it; but not, I think, at enduring the rack, or any passive obedience, like jumping off a castle-roof at the word of a czar. Being both vascular and highly organized, so as to be very sensible of pain; and intellectual, so as to see reason and glory in a matter.

Of that constitutional force which yields the supplies of the day, they have the more than enough; the excess which creates courage on fortitude, genius in poetry, invention in mechanics, enterprise in trade, magnificence in wealth, splendor in ceremonies, petulance and projects in youth. The young men have a rude health which runs into peccant humors. They drink brandy like water, cannot expend their quantities of waste strength on riding, hunting, swimming and fencing, and run into absurd frolics with the gravity of the Eumenides. They stoutly carry into every nook and corner of the earth their turbulent sense; leaving no lie uncontradicted; no pretension unexamined. They chew hasheesh; cut themselves with poisoned creases; swing their hammock in the boughs of the Bohon Upas; taste every poison; buy every secret; at Naples they put St. Januarius's blood in an alembic; they saw a hole into the head of the "winking Virgin," to know why she winks; measure with an English footrule every cell of the Inquisition, every Turkish caaba, every Holy of holies; translate and send to Bentley the arcanum bribed and bullied away from shuddering Brahmins; and measure their own strength by the terror they cause. These travellers are of every class, the best and the worst; and it may easily happen that those of rudest behavior are taken notice of and remembered. The Saxon melancholy in the vulgar rich and poor appears as gushes of ill-humor, which every check exasperates into sarcasm and vituperation. There are multitudes of rude young English who have the self-sufficiency and bluntness of their nation, and who, with their disdain of the rest of mankind and with this indigestion and choler, have made the English traveller a proverb for uncomfortable and offensive manners. It was no bad description of the Briton generically, what was said two hundred years ago of one particular Oxford scholar: "He was a very bold man, uttered any thing that came into his mind, not only among his companions, but in public coffee-houses, and would often speak his mind of particular persons then accidentally present, without examining the company he was in; for which he was often reprimanded and several times threatened to be kicked and beaten."

The common Englishman is prone to forget a cardinal article in the bill of social rights, that every man has a right to his own ears. No man can claim to usurp more than a few cubic feet of the audibilities of a public room, or to put upon the company with the loud statement of his crotchets or personalities.

But it is in the deep traits of race that the fortunes of nations are written, and however derived—whether a happier tribe or mixture of tribes, the air, or what circumstance that mixed for them the golden mean of temperament—here exists the best stock in the world, broad-fronted, broad-bottomed, best for depth, range and equability; men of aplomb and reserves, great range and many moods, strong instincts, yet apt for culture; war-class as well as clerks; earls and tradesmen; wise minority, as well as foolish majority; abysmal temperament, hiding wells of wrath, and glooms on which no sunshine settles, alternated with a common sense and humanity which hold them fast to every piece of cheerful duty; making this temperament a sea to which all storms are superficial; a race to which their fortunes flow, as if they alone had the elastic organization at once fine and robust enough for dominion; as if the burly inexpressive, now mute and contumacious, now fierce and sharp-tongued dragon, which once made the island light with his fiery breath, had bequeathed his ferocity to his conqueror. They hide virtues under vices, or the semblance of them. It is the mis-shapen hairy Scandinavian troll again, who lifts the cart out of the mire, or threshes

> "The corn
> That ten day-laborers could not end,"

but it is done in the dark and with muttered maledictions. He is a churl with a soft place in his heart, whose speech is a brash of bitter waters, but who loves to help you at a pinch. He says no, and serves you, and your thanks disgust him. Here was lately a cross-grained miser, odd and ugly, resembling in countenance the portrait of Punch with the laugh left out; rich by his own industry; sulking in a lonely house; who never gave a dinner to any man and disdained all courtesies: yet as true a worshipper of beauty in form and color as ever existed, and profusely pouring over the cold mind of his countrymen creations of grace and truth, removing the reproach of sterility from English art, catching from their savage climate every fine hint, and importing into their galleries

. . . .

every tint and trait of sunnier cities and skies; making an era in painting; and when he saw that the splendor of one of his pictures in the
Exhibition dimmed his rival's that hung next it, secretly took a brush
and blackened his own.

They do not wear their heart in their sleeve for daws to peck at.
They have that phlegm or staidness which it is a compliment to disturb. "Great men," said Aristotle, "are always of a nature originally
melancholy." 'T is the habit of a mind which attaches to abstractions
with a passion which gives vast results. They dare to displease, they
do not speak to expectation. They like the sayers of No, better than
the sayers of Yes. Each of them has an opinion which he feels it
becomes him to express all the more that it differs from yours. They
are meditating opposition. This gravity is inseparable from minds of
great resources.

There is an English hero superior to the French, the German, the
Italian, or the Greek. When he is brought to the strife with fate, he sacrifices a richer material possession, and on more purely metaphysical
grounds. He is there with his own consent, face to face with fortune,
which he defies. On deliberate choice and from grounds of character, he
has elected his part to live and die for, and dies with grandeur. This
race has added new elements to humanity and has a deeper root in the
world.

They have great range of scale, from ferocity to exquisite refinement. With larger scale, they have great retrieving power. After
running each tendency to an extreme, they try another tack with equal
heat. More intellectual than other races, when they live with other races
they do not take their language, but bestow their own. They subsidize
other nations, and are not subsidized. They proselyte, and are not pros-
elyted. They assimilate other races to themselves, and are not
assimilated. The English did not calculate the conquest of the Indies. It
fell to their character. So they administer, in different parts of the
world, the codes of every empire and race; in Canada, old French law;
in the Mauritius, the Code Napoléon; in the West Indies, the edicts of
the Spanish Cortes; in the East Indies, the Laws of Menu; in the Isle of
Man, of the Scandanivian Thing; at the Cape of Good Hope, of the
old Netherlands; and in the Ionian Islands, the Pandects of Justinian.

They are very conscious of their advantageous position in history.
England is the lawgiver, the patron, the instructor, the ally. Compare

the tone of the French and of the English press: the first querulous, captious, sensitive about English opinion; the English press never timorous about French opinion, but arrogant and contemptuous.

They are testy and headstrong through an excess of will and bias; churlish as men sometimes please to be who do not forget a debt, who ask no favors and who will do what they like with their own. With education and intercourse, these asperities wear off and leave the good-will pure. If anatomy is reformed according to national tendencies, I suppose the spleen will hereafter be found in the Englishman, not found in the American, and differencing the one from the other. I anticipate another anatomical discovery, that this organ will be found to be cortical and caducous; that they are superficially morose, but at last tender-hearted, herein differing from Rome and the Latin nations. Nothing savage, nothing mean resides in the English heart. They are subject to panics of credulity and of rage, but the temper of the nation, however disturbed, settles itself soon and easily, as, in this temperate zone, the sky after whatever storms clears again, and serenity is its normal condition.

A saving stupidity masks and protects their perception, as the curtain of the eagle's eye. Our swifter Americans, when they first deal with English, pronounce them stupid; but, later, do them justice as people who wear well, or hide their strength. To understand the power of performance that is in their finest wits, in the patient Newton, or in the versatile transcendent poets, or in the Dugdales, Gibbons, Hallams, Eldons and Peels, one should see how English day-laborers hold out. High and low, they are of an unctuous texture. There is an adipocere in their constitution, as if they had oil also for their mental wheels and could perform vast amounts of work without damaging themselves.

Even the scale of expense on which people live, and to which scholars and professional men conform, proves the tension of their muscle, when vast numbers are found who can each lift this enormous load. I might even add, their daily feasts argue a savage vigor of body.

No nation was ever so rich in able men; "Gentlemen," as Charles I said of Strafford, "whose abilities might make a prince rather afraid than ashamed in the greatest affairs of state;" men of such temper, that, like Baron Vere, "had one seen him returning from a victory, he would by his silence have suspected that he had lost the day; and, had he beheld him in a retreat, he would have collected him a conqueror by the cheerfulness of his spirit."

The following passage from the "Heimskringla" might almost stand as a portrait of the modern Englishman—"Haldor was very stout and strong and remarkably handsome in appearances. King Harold gave him this testimony, that he, among all his men, cared least about doubtful circumstances, whether they betokened danger or pleasure; for whatever turned up, he was never in higher nor in lower spirits, never slept less nor more on account of them, nor ate nor drank but according to his custom. Haldor was not a man of many words, but short in conversation, told his opinion bluntly and was obstinate and hard: and this could not please the king, who had many clever people about him, zealous in his service. Haldor remained a short time with the king, then came to Iceland, where he took up his abode in Hiardaholt and dwelt in that farm to a very advanced age."

The national temper, in the civil history, is not flashy or whiffling. The slow, deep English mass smoulders with fire, which at last sets all its borders in flame. The wrath of London is not French wrath, but has a long memory, and, in its hottest heat, a register and rule.

Half their strength they put not forth. They are capable of a sublime resolution, and if hereafter the war of races, often predicted, and making itself a war of opinions also (a question of despotism and liberty coming from Eastern Europe), should menace the English civilization, these sea-kings may take once again to their floating castles and find a new home and a second millennium of power in their colonies.

The stability of England is the security of the modern world. If the English race were as mutable as the French, what reliance? But the English stand for liberty. The conservative, money-loving, lord-loving English are yet liberty-loving; and so freedom is safe: for they have more personal force than any other people. The nation always resist the immoral action of their government. They think humanely on the affairs of France, of Turkey, of Poland, of Hungary, of Schleswig Holstein, though overborne by the statecraft of the rulers at last.

Does the early history of each tribe show the permanent bias, which, though not less potent, is masked as the tribe spreads its activity into colonies, commerce, codes, arts, letters? The early history shows it, as the musician plays the air which he proceeds to conceal in a tempest of variations. In Alfred, in the Northmen, one may read the genius of the English society, namely that private life is the place of honor. Glory, a career, and ambition, words familiar to the longitude of Paris, are seldom heard in English speech. Nelson wrote from their hearts his homely telegraph, "England expects every man to do his duty."

For actual service, for the dignity of a profession, or to appease diseased or inflamed talent, the army and navy may be entered (the worst boys doing well in the navy); and the civil service in departments where serious official work is done; and they hold in esteem the barrister engaged in the severer studies of the law. But the calm, sound and most British Briton shrinks from public life as charlatanism, and respects an economy founded on agriculture, coal-mines, manufactures or trade, which secures an independence through the creation of real values.

They wish neither to command nor obey, but to be kings in their own houses. They are intellectual and deeply enjoy literature; they like well to have the world served up to them in books, maps, models, and every mode of exact information, and, though not creators in art, they value its refinement. They are ready for leisure, can direct and fill their own day, nor need so much as others the constraint of a necessity. But the history of the nation discloses, at every turn, this original predilection for private independence, and however this inclination may have been disturbed by the bribes with which their vast colonial power has warped men out of orbit, the inclination endures, and forms and reforms the laws, letters, manners and occupations. They choose that welfare which is compatible with the commonwealth, knowing that such alone is stable; as wise merchants prefer investments in the three per cents.

CHAPTER IX

COCKAYNE

THE ENGLISH are a nation of humorists. Individual right is pushed to the uttermost bound compatible with public order. Property is so perfect that it seems the craft of that race, and not to exist elsewhere. The king cannot step on an acre which the peasant refuses to sell. A testator endows a dog or a rookery, and Europe cannot interfere with his absurdity. Every individual has his particular way of living, which he pushes

. . . .

to folly, and the decided sympathy of his compatriots is engaged to back up Mr. Crump's whim by statutes and chancellors and horse-guards. There is no freak so ridiculous but some Englishman has attempted to immortalize by money and law. British citizenship is as omnipotent as Roman was. Mr. Cockayne is very sensible of this. The pursy man means by freedom the right to do as he pleases, and does wrong in order to feel his freedom, and makes a conscience of persisting in it.

He is intensely patriotic, for his country is so small. His confidence in the power and performance of his nation makes him provokingly incurious about other nations. He dislikes foreigners. Swedenborg, who lived much in England, notes "the similitude of minds among the English, in consequence of which they contract familiarity with friends who are of that nation, and seldom with others; and they regard foreigners as one looking through a telescope from the top of a palace regards those who dwell or wander about out of the city." A much older traveller, the Venetian who wrote the "Relation of England," in 1500, says: "The English are great lovers of themselves and of every thing belonging to them. They think that there are no other men than themselves and no other world but England; and whenever they see a handsome foreigner, they say that he looks like an Englishman and it is a great pity he should not be an Englishman; and whenever they partake of any delicacy with a foreigner, they ask him whether such a thing is made in his country." When he adds epithets of praise, his climax is, "So English"; and when he wishes to pay you the highest compliment, he says, "I should not know you from an Englishman." France is, by its natural contrast, a kind of blackboard on which English character draws its own traits in chalk. This arrogance habitually exhibits itself in allusions to the French. I suppose that all men of English blood in America, Europe or Asia, have a secret feeling of joy that they are not French natives. Mr. Coleridge is said to have given public thanks to God, at the close of a lecture, that he had defended him from being able to utter a single sentence in the French language. I have found that Englishmen have such a good opinion of England, that the ordinary phrases in all good society, of postponing or disparaging one's own things in talking with a stranger, are seriously mistaken by them for an insuppressible homage to the merits of their nation; and the New Yorker or Pennsylvanian who modestly laments the disadvantage of a new country, log-huts and savages, is surprised by the instant and unfeigned commiseration of the whole company, who plainly account all the world out of England a heap of rubbish.

The same insular limitation pinches his foreign politics. He sticks to his traditions and usages, and, so help him God! he will force his island by-laws down the throat of great countries, like India, China, Canada, Australia, and not only so, but impose Wapping on the Congress of Vienna and trample down all nationalities with his taxed boots. Lord Chatham goes for liberty and no taxation without representation—for that is British law; but not a hobnail shall they dare make in America, but buy their nails in England—for that also is British law; and the fact that British commerce was to be re-created by the independence of America, took them all by surprise.

In short, I am afraid that English nature is so rank and aggressive as to be a little incompatible with every other. The world is not wide enough for two.

But beyond this nationality, it must be admitted, the island offers a daily worship to the old Norse god Brage, celebrated among our Scandinavian forefathers for his eloquence and majestic air. The English have a steady courage that fits them for great attempts and endurance: they have also a petty courage, through which every man delights in showing himself for what he is and in doing what he can; so that in all companies, each of them has too good an opinion of himself to imitate anybody. He hides no defect of his form, features, dress, connection, or birthplace, for he thinks every circumstance belonging to him comes recommended to you. If one of them have a bald, or a red, or a green head, or bow legs, or a scar, or mark, or a paunch, or a squeaking or a raven voice, he has persuaded himself that there is something modish and becoming in it, and that it sits well on him.

But nature makes nothing in vain, and this little superfluity of self-regard in the English brain is one of the secrets of their power and history. It sets every man on being and doing what he really is and can. It takes away a dodging, skulking, secondary air, and encourages a frank and manly bearing, so that each man makes the most of himself and loses no opportunity for want of pushing. A man's personal defects will commonly have, with the rest of the world, precisely that importance which they have to himself. If he makes light of them, so will other men. We all find in these a convenient metre of character, since a

. . . .

little man would be ruined by the vexation. I remember a shrewd politician, in one of our western cities, told me that "he had known several successful statesmen made by their foible." And another, an ex-governor of Illinois, said to me, "If the man knew anything, he would sit in a corner and be modest; but he is such an ignorant peacock that he goes bustling up and down and hits on extraordinary discoveries."

There is also this benefit in brag, that the speaker is unconsciously expressing his own ideal. Humor him by all means, draw it all out and hold him to it. Their culture generally enables the travelled English to avoid any ridiculous extremes of this self-pleasing, and to give it an agreeable air. Then the natural disposition is fostered by the respect which they find entertained in the world for English ability. It was said of Louis XIV, that his gait and air were becoming enough in so great a monarch, yet would have been ridiculous in another man; so the prestige of the English name warrants a certain confident bearing, which a Frenchman or Belgian could not carry. At all events, they feel themselves at liberty to assume the most extraordinary tone on the subject of English merits.

An English lady on the Rhine hearing a German speaking of her party as foreigners, exclaimed, "No, we are not foreigners; we are English; it is you that are foreigners." They tell you daily in London the story of the Frenchman and Englishman who quarrelled. Both were unwilling to fight, but their companions put them up to it; at last it was agreed that they should fight alone, in the dark, and with pistols: the candles were put out, and the Englishman, to make sure not to hit any body, fired up the chimney—and brought down the Frenchman. They have no curiosity about foreigners, and answer any information you may volunteer with "Oh, Oh!" until the informant makes up his mind that they shall die in their ignorance, for any help he will offer. There are really no limits to this conceit, though brighter men among them make painful efforts to be candid.

The habit of brag runs through all classes, from the "Times" newspaper through politicians and poets, through Wordsworth, Carlyle, Mill and Sydney Smith, down to the boys of Eton. In the gravest treatise on political economy, in a philosophical essay, in books of science, one is surprised by the most innocent exhibition of unflinching nationality. In a tract on Corn, a most amiable and accomplished gentleman writes thus: "Though Britain, according to Bishop Berkeley's idea, were surrounded by a wall of brass ten thousand cubits in height, still she would as far excel the rest of the globe in riches, as she now does both in this secondary quality and in the more important ones of freedom, virtue and science."

The English dislike the American structure of society, whilst yet trade, mills, public education and Chartism are doing what they can to create in England the same social condition. America is the paradise of the economists; is the favorable exception invariably quoted to the rules of ruin; but when he speaks directly of the Americans the islander forgets his philosophy and remembers his disparaging anecdotes.

But this childish patriotism costs something, like all narrowness. The English sway of their colonies has no root of kindness. They govern by their arts and ability; they are more just than kind; and whenever an abatement of their power is felt, they have not conciliated the affection on which to rely.

Coarse local distinctions, as those of nation, province or town, are useful in the absence of real ones; but we must not insist on these accidental lines. Individual traits are always triumphing over national ones. There is no fence in metaphysics discriminating Greek, or English, or Spanish science. Aesop and Montaigne, Cervantes and Saadi are men of the world; and to wave our own flag at the dinner table or in the University is to carry the boisterous dulness of a fire-club into a polite circle. Nature and destiny are always on the watch for our follies. Nature trips us up when we strut; and there are curious examples in history on this very point of national pride.

George of Cappadocia, born at Epiphania in Cilicia, was a low parasite who got a lucrative contract to supply the army with bacon. A rogue and informer, he got rich and was forced to run from justice. He saved his money, embraced Arianism, collected a library, and got promoted by a faction to the episcopal throne of Alexandria. When Julian came, A.D. 361, George was dragged to prison; the prison was burst open by the mob and George was lynched, as he deserved. And this precious knave became, in good time, Saint George of England, patron of chivalry, emblem of victory and civility and the pride of the best blood of the modern world.

Strange, that the solid truth-speaking Briton should derive from an impostor. Strange, that the New World should have no better luck—

that broad America must wear the name of a thief. Amerigo Vespucci, the pickle-dealer at Seville, who went out, in 1499, a subaltern with Hojeda, and whose highest naval rank was boatswain's mate in an expedition that never sailed, managed in this lying world to supplant Columbus and baptize half the earth with his own dishonest name. Thus nobody can throw stones. We are equally badly off in our founders; and the false pickle-dealer is an offset to the false bacon-seller.

CHAPTER X

WEALTH

THERE is no country in which so absolute a homage is paid to wealth. In America there is a touch of shame when a man exhibits the evidences of large property, as if after all it needed apology. But the Englishman has pure pride in his wealth, and esteems it a final certificate. A coarse logic rules throughout all English souls—if you have merit, can you not show it by your good clothes and coach and horses? How can a man be a gentleman without a pipe of wine? Haydon says, "There is a fierce resolution to make every man live according to the means he possesses." There is a mixture of religion in it. They are under the Jewish law, and read with sonorous emphasis that their days shall be long in the land, they shall have sons and daughters, flocks and herds, wine and oil. In exact proportion is the reproach of poverty. They do not wish to be represented except by opulent men. An Englishman who has lost his fortune is said to have died of a broken heart. The last term of insult is, "a beggar." Nelson said, "The want of fortune is a crime which I can never get over." Sydney Smith said, "Poverty is infamous in England." And one of their recent writers speaks, in reference to a private and scholastic life, of "the grave moral deterioration which follows an empty exchequer." You shall find this sentiment, if not so frankly put, yet deeply implied in the novels and romances of the present century, and not only in these, but in biography and in the votes of public assemblies, in the tone of the preaching and in the table-talk.

I was lately turning over Wood's *Athenæ Oxonienses*, and looking naturally for another standard in a chronicle of the scholars of Oxford for two hundred years. But I found the two disgraces in that, as in most English books, are, first, disloyalty to Church and State, and second, to be born poor, or to come to poverty. A natural fruit of England is the brutal political economy. Malthus finds no cover laid at Nature's table for the laborer's son. In 1809, the majority in Parliament expressed itself by the language of Mr. Fuller in the House of Commons, "If you do not like the country, damn you, you can leave it." When Sir S. Romilly proposed his bill forbidding parish officers to bind children apprentices at a greater distance than forty miles from their home, Peel opposed, and Mr. Wortley said, "though, in the higher ranks, to cultivate family affections was a good thing, it was not so among the lower orders. Better take them away from those who might deprave them. And it was highly injurious to trade to stop binding to manufacturers, as it must raise the price of labor and of manufactured goods."

The respect for truth of facts in England is equalled only by the respect for wealth. It is at once the pride of art of the Saxon, as he is a wealth-maker, and his passion for independence. The Englishman believes that every man must take care of himself, and has himself to thank if he do not mend his condition. To pay heir debts is their national point of honor. From the Exchequer and the East India House to the huckster's shop, every thing prospers because it is solvent. The British armies are solvent and pay for what they take. The British empire is solvent; for in spite of the huge national debt, the valuation mounts. During the war from 1789 to 1815, whilst they complained that they were taxed within an inch of their lives, and by dint of enormous taxes were subsidizing all the continent against France, the English were growing rich every year faster than any people ever grew before. It is their maxim that the weight of taxes must be calculated, not by what is taken, but by what is left. Solvency is in the ideas and mechanism of an Englishman. The Crystal Palace is not considered honest until it pays; no matter how much convenience, beauty, or *éclat*, it must be self-supporting. They are contented with slower steamers, as long as they know that swifter boats lose money. They proceed logically by the double method of labor and thrift. Every household exhibits an exact economy, and nothing of that uncalculated headlong expenditure which families use in America. If they cannot pay, they do not buy; for they have no presumption of better fortunes next year, as our people have; and they say without shame, I cannot afford it. Gentlemen do not hesitate to ride in the second-class cars, or in the second cabin. An economist, or a man who can proportion his means and his ambition, or bring the year round with expenditure which expresses his character without embarrassing one day of his future, is already a master of life, and a freeman. Lord Burleigh writes to his son that "one ought never to devote more than two thirds of his income to the ordinary expenses of life, since the extraordinary will be certain to absorb the other third."

The ambition to create value evokes every kind of ability; government becomes a manufacturing corporation, and every house a mill. The headlong bias to utility will let no talent lie in a napkin—if possible will teach spiders to weave silk stockings. An Englishman, while he eats and drinks no more or not much more than another man, labors three times as many hours in the course of a year as another European; or, his life as a workman is three lives. He works fast. Everything in England is at a quick pace. They have reinforced their own productivity by the creation of that marvellous machinery which differences this age from any other age.

It is a curious chapter in modern history, the growth of the machine-shop. Six hundred years ago, Roger Bacon explained the precession of the equinoxes, the consequent necessity of the reform of the calendar; measured the length of the year; invented gunpowder; and announced (as if looking from his lofty cell, over five centuries, into ours) that "machines can be constructed to drive ships more rapidly than a whole galley of rowers could do; nor would they need anything but a pilot to steer them. Carriages also might be constructed to move with an incredible speed, without the aid of any animal. Finally, it would not be impossible to make machines which by means of a suit of wings should fly in the air in the manner of birds." But the secret slept with Bacon. The six hundred years have not yet fulfilled his words. Two centuries ago the sawing of timber was done by hand; the carriage wheels ran on wooden axles; the land was tilled by wooden ploughs. And it was to little purpose that they had pit-coal, or that looms were improved, unless Watt and Stephenson had taught them to work force-pumps and power-looms by steam. The great strides were all taken within the last hundred years. The Life of Sir Robert Peel, in his day the model Englishman, very properly has, for a frontispiece, a drawing of the spinning-jenny, which wove the web of his fortunes. Hargreaves invented the spinning-jenny, and died in a work-house. Arkwright improved the invention, and the machine dispensed with the work of ninety-nine men; that is, one spinner could do as much work as one hundred had done before. The loom was improved further. But the men would sometimes strike for wages and combine against the masters, and, about 1829-30, much fear was felt lest the trade would be drawn away by these interruptions and the emigration of the spinners to Belgium and the United States. Iron and steel are very obedient. Whether it were not possible to make a spinner that would not rebel, nor mutter, nor scowl, nor strike for wages, nor emigrate? At the solicitation of the masters, after a mob and riot at Staley Bridge, Mr. Roberts of Manchester undertook to create this peaceful fellow, instead of the quarrelsome fellow God had made. After a few trials, he succeeded, and in 1830 procured a patent for his self-acting mule; a creation, the delight of mill-owners, and "destined," they said, "to restore order among the industrious classes"; a machine requiring only a child's hand to piece the broken yarns. As Arkwright had destroyed domestic spinning, so Roberts destroyed the factory spinner. The power of machinery in Great Britain, in mills, has been computed to be equal to 600,000,000 men, one man being able by the aid of steam to do the work which required two hundred and fifty men to accomplish fifty years ago. The production has been commensurate. England already had this laborious race, rich soil, water, wood, coal, iron and favorable climate. Eight hundred years ago commerce had made it rich, and it was recorded, "England is the richest of all the northern nations." The Norman historians recite that "in 1067, William carried with him into Normandy, from England, more gold and silver than had ever before been seen in Gaul." But when, to this labor and trade and these native resources was added this goblin of steam, with his myriad arms, never tired, working night and day everlastingly, the amassing of property has run out of all figures. It makes the motor of the last ninety years. The steam-pipe has added to her population and wealth the equivalent of four or five Englands. Forty thousand ships are entered in Lloyd's lists. The yield of wheat has gone on from 2,000,000 quarters in the time of the Stuarts, to 13,000,000 in 1854. A thousand million of pounds sterling are said to compose the floating money of commerce. In 1848, Lord John Russell stated that the people of this country had laid out £300,000,000 of capital in rail-

· ·

ways, in the last four years. But a better measure than these sounding figures is the estimate that there is wealth enough in England to support the entire population in idleness for one year.

The wise, versatile, all-giving machinery makes chisels, roads, locomotives, telegraphs. Whitworth divides a bar to a millionth of an inch. Steam twines huge cannon into wreaths, as easily as it braids straw, and vies with the volcanic forces which twisted the strata. It can clothe shingle mountains with ship-oaks, make sword-blades that will cut gun-barrels in two. In Egypt, it can plant forests, and bring rain after three thousand years. Already it is ruddering the balloon, and the next war will be fought in the air. But another machine more potent in England than steam is the Bank. It votes an issue of bills, population is stimulated and cities rise; it refuses loans, and emigration empties the country; trade sinks; revolutions break out; kings are dethroned. By these new agents our social system is moulded. By dint of steam and of money, war and commerce are changed. Nations have lost their old omnipotence; the patriotic tie does not hold. Nations are getting obsolete, we go and live where we will. Steam has enabled men to choose what law they will live under. Money makes place for them. The telegraph is a limp band that will hold the Fenris-wolf of war. For now that a telegraph line runs through France and Europe from London, every message it transmits makes stronger by one thread the band which war will have to cut.

The introduction of these elements gives new resources to existing proprietors. A sporting duke may fancy that the state depends on the House of Lords, but the engineer sees that every stroke of the steam-piston gives value to the duke's land, fills it with tenants; doubles, quadruples, centuples the duke's capital, and creates new measures and new necessities for the culture of his children. Of course it draws the nobility into the competition, as stockholders in the mine, the canal, the railway, in the application of steam to agriculture, and sometimes into trade. But it also introduces large classes into the same competition; the old energy of the Norse race arms itself with these magnificent powers; new men prove an overmatch for the land-owner, and the mill buys out the castle. Scandinavian Thor, who once forged his bolts in icy Hecla and built galleys by lonely fiords, in England has advanced with the times, has shorn his beard, enters Parliament, sits down at a desk in the India House and lends Miöllnir to Birmingham for a steam-hammer.

The creation of wealth in England in the last ninety years is a main fact in modern history. The wealth of London determines prices all over the globe. All things precious, or useful, or amusing, or intoxicating, are sucked into this commerce and floated to London. Some English private fortunes reach, and some exceed a million of dollars a year. A hundred thousand palaces adorn the island. All that can feed the senses and passions, all that can succor the talent or arm the hands of the intelligent middle class, who never spare in what they buy for their own consumption; all that can aid science, gratify taste, or soothe comfort, is in open market. Whatever is excellent and beautiful in civil, rural, or ecclesiastic architecture, in fountain, garden, or grounds—the English noble crosses sea and land to see and to copy at home. The taste and science of thirty peaceful generations; the gardens which Evelyn planted; the temples and pleasure-houses which Inigo Jones and Christopher Wren built; the wood that Gibbons carved; the taste of foreign and domestic artists, Shenstone, Pope, Brown, Loudon, Paxton—are in the vast auction, and the hereditary principle heaps on the owner of to-day the benefit of ages of owners. The present possessors are to the full as absolute as any of their fathers in choosing and procuring what they like. This comfort and splendor, the breadth of lake and mountain, tillage, pasture and park, sumptuous castle and modern villa—all consist with perfect order. They have no revolutions; no horse-guards dictating to the crown; no Parisian *poissardes* and barricades; no mob: but drowsy habitude, daily dress-dinners, wine and ale and beer and gin and sleep.

With this power of creation and this passion for independence, property has reached an ideal perfection. It is felt and treated as the national life-blood. The laws are framed to give property the securest possible basis, and the provisions to lock and transmit it have exercised the cunningest heads in a profession which never admits a fool. The rights of property nothing but felony and treason can override. The house is a castle which the king cannot enter. The Bank is a strong box to which the king has no key. Whatever surly sweetness possession can give, is tasted in England to the dregs. Vested rights are awful things, and absolute possession gives the smallest freeholder identity of interest with the duke. High stone fences and padlocked garden-gates announce the absolute will of the owner to be alone. Every whim of exaggerated egotism is put into stone and iron, into silver and gold, with costly deliberation and detail.

An Englishman hears that the Queen Dowager wishes to establish some claim to put her park paling a rod forward into his grounds, so as to get a coachway and save her a mile to the avenue. Instantly he transforms his paling into stone-masonry, solid as the walls of Cuma, and all Europe cannot prevail on him to sell or compound for an inch of the land. They delight in a freak as the proof of their sovereign freedom. Sir Edward Boynton, at Spic Park at Cadenham, on a precipice of incomparable prospect, built a house like a long barn, which had not a window on the prospect side. Strawberry Hill of Horace Walpole, Fonthill Abbey of Mr. Beckford, were freaks; and Newstead Abbey became one in the hands of Lord Byron.

But the proudest result of this creation has been the great and refined forces it has put at the disposal of the private citizen. In the social world an Englishman to-day has the best lot. He is a king in a plain coat. He goes with the most powerful protection, keeps the best company, is armed by the best education, is seconded by wealth; and his English name and accidents are like a flourish of trumpets announcing him. This, with his quiet style of manners, gives him the power of a sovereign without the inconveniences which belong to that rank. I much prefer the condition of an English gentleman of the better class to that of any potentate in Europe—whether for travel, or for opportunity of society, or for access to means of science or study, or for mere comfort and easy healthy relation to people at home.

Such as we have seen is the wealth of England; a mighty mass, and made good in whatever details we care to explore. The cause and spring of it is the wealth of temperament in the people. The wonder of Britain is this plenteous nature. Her worthies are ever surrounded by as good men as themselves; each is a captain a hundred strong, and that wealth of men is represented again in the faculty of each individual—that he has waste strength, power to spare. The English are so rich and seem to have established a tap-root in the bowels of the planet, because they are constitutionally fertile and creative.

But a man must keep an eye on his servants, if he would not have them rule him. Man is a shrewd inventor and is ever taking the hint of a new machine from his own structure, adapting some secret of his own anatomy in iron, wood and leather to some required function in the work of the world. But it is found that the machine unmans the user. What he gains in making cloth, he loses in general power. There should be temperance in making cloth, as well as in eating. A man should not be a silk-worm, nor a nation a tent of caterpillars. The robust rural Saxon degenerates in the mills to the Leicester stockinger, to the imbecile Manchester spinner—far on the way to be spiders and needles. The incessant repetition of the same hand-work dwarfs the man, robs him of his strength, wit and versatility, to make a pin-polisher, a buckle-maker, or any other specialty; and presently, in a change of industry, whole towns are sacrificed like ant-hills, when the fashion of shoe-strings supersedes buckles, when cotton takes the place of linen, or railways of turnpikes, or when commons are enclosed by landlords. Then society is admonished of the mischief of the division of labor, and that the best political economy is care and culture of men; for in these crises all are ruined except such as are proper individuals, capable of thought and of new choice and the application of their talent to new labor. Then again come in new calamities. England is aghast at the disclosure of her fraud in the adulteration of food, of drugs and of almost every fabric in her mills and shops; finding that milk will not nourish, nor sugar sweeten, nor bread satisfy, nor pepper bite the tongue, nor glue stick. In true England all is false and forged. This too is the reaction of machinery, but of the larger machinery of commerce. 'T is not, I suppose, want of probity, so much as the tyranny of trade, which necessitates a perpetual competition of underselling, and that again a perpetual deterioration of the fabric.

The machinery has proved, like the balloon, unmanageable, and flies away with the aeronaut. Steam from the first hissed and screamed to warn him; it was dreadful with its explosion, and crushed the engineer. The machinist has wrought and watched, engineers and firemen without number have been sacrificed in learning to tame and guide the monster. But harder still it has proved to resist and rule the dragon Money, with his paper wings. Chancellors and Boards of Trade, Pitt, Peel and Robinson and their Parliaments and their whole generation adopted false principles, and went to their graves in the belief that they were enriching the country which they were impoverishing. They congratulated each other on ruinous expedients. It is rare to find a merchant who knows why a crisis occurs in trade, why prices rise or fall, or who knows the mischief of paper-money. In the culmination of national prosperity, in the annexation of countries; building of ships, depots, towns; in the influx of tons of gold and silver; amid the chuckle of chancellors and financiers, it was found that bread rose to famine prices, that the yeoman was forced to sell his cow and pig, his tools and his acre of land; and the dreadful barometer of the poor-rates was touching the point of ruin. The poor-rate was sucking in the solvent classes and forcing an exodus of farmers and mechanics. What befalls from the violence of financial crises befalls daily in the violence of artificial legislation.

Such a wealth has England earned, ever new, bounteous and augmenting. But the question recurs, does she take the step beyond, namely to the wise use, in view of the supreme wealth of nations? We estimate the wisdom of nations by seeing what they did with their surplus capital. And, in view of these injuries, some compensation has been attempted in England. A part of the money earned returns to the brain to buy schools, libraries, bishops, astronomers, chemists and artists with; and a part to repair the wrongs of this intemperate weaving, by hospitals, savings-banks, Mechanics' Institutes, public grounds and other charities and amenities. But the antidotes are frightfully inadequate, and the evil requires a deeper cure, which time and a simpler social organization must supply. At present she does not rule her wealth. She is simply a good England, but no divinity, or wise and instructed soul. She too is in the stream of fate, one victim more in a common catastrophe.

But being in the fault, she has the misfortune of greatness to be held as the chief offender. England must be held responsible for the despotism of expense. Her prosperity, the splendor which so much manhood and talent and perseverance has thrown upon vulgar aims, is the very argument of materialism. Her success strengthens the hands of base wealth. Who can propose to youth poverty and wisdom, when mean gain has arrived at the conquest of letters and arts; when English success has grown out of the very renunciation of principles, and the dedication to outsides? A civility of trifles, of money and expense, an erudition of sensation takes place, and the putting as many impediments as we can between the man and his objects. Hardly the bravest among them have the manliness to resist it successfully. Hence it has come that not the aims of a manly life, but the means of meeting a certain ponderous expense, is that which is to be considered by a youth in England emerging from his minority. A large family is reckoned a misfortune. And it is a consolation in the death of the young, that a source of expense is closed.

CHAPTER XI

ARISTOCRACY

THE FEUDAL CHARACTER of the English state, now that it is getting obsolete, glares a little, in contrast with the democratic tendencies. The inequality of power and property shocks republican nerves. Palaces, halls, villas, walled parks, all over England, rival the splendor of royal seats. Many of the halls, like Haddon or Kedleston, are beautiful desolations. The proprietor never saw them, or never lived in them. Primogeniture built these sumptuous piles, and I suppose it is the sentiment of every traveller, as it was mine, It was well to come ere these were gone. Primogeniture is a cardinal rule of English property and institutions. Laws, customs, manners, the very persons and faces, affirm it.

The frame of society is aristocratic, the taste of the people is loyal. The estates, names and manners of the nobles flatter the fancy of the people and conciliate the necessary support. In spite of broken faith, stolen charters and the devastation of society by the profligacy of the court, we take sides as we read for the loyal England and King Charles's "return to his right" with his Cavaliers—knowing what a heartless trifler he is, and what a crew of God-forsaken robbers they are. The people of England knew as much. But the fair idea of a settled government connecting itself with heraldic names, with the written and oral history of Europe, and, at last, with the Hebrew religion and the oldest traditions of the world, was too pleasing a vision to be shattered by a few offensive realities and the politics of shoe-makers and costermongers. The hopes of the commoners take the same direction with the interest of the patricians. Every man who becomes rich buys land and does what he can to fortify the nobility, into which he hopes to rise. The Anglican clergy are identified with the aristocracy. Time and law have made the joining and moulding perfect in every part. The Cathedrals, the Universities, the national music, the popular romances, conspire to uphold the heraldry which the current politics of the day are sapping. The taste of the people is conservative. They are proud of the castles, and of the language and symbol of chivalry. Even the word *lord* is the luckiest style that is used in any language to designate a patrician. The superior education and manners of the nobles recommend them to the country.

The Norwegian pirate got what he could and held it for his eldest son. The Norman noble, who was the Norwegian pirate baptized, did likewise. There was this advantage of Western over Oriental nobility, that this was recruited from below. English history is aristocracy with the doors open. Who has courage and faculty, let him come in. Of course the terms of admission to this club are hard and high. The selfishness of the nobles comes in aid of the interest of the nation to require signal merit. Piracy and war gave place to trade, politics and letters; the war-lord to the law-lord; the law-lord to the merchant and the mill-owner; but the privilege was kept, whilst the means of obtaining it were changed.

The foundations of these families lie deep in Norwegian exploits by sea and Saxon sturdiness on land. All nobility in its beginnings was somebody's natural superiority. The things these English have done were not done without peril of life, nor without wisdom and conduct; and the first hands, it may be presumed, were often challenged to show their right to their honors, or yield them to better men. "He that will be a head, let him be a bridge," said the Welsh chief Benegridran, when he carried all his men over the river on his back. "He shall have the book," said the mother of Alfred, "who can read it"; and Alfred won it by that title: and I make no doubt that feudal tenure was no sinecure, but baron, knight and tenant often had their memories refreshed, in regard to the service by which they held their lands. The De Veres, Bohuns, Mowbrays and Plantagenets were not addicted to contemplation. The Middle Age adorned itself with proofs of manhood and devotion. Of Richard Beauchamp, Earl of Warwick, the Emperor told Henry V that no Christian king had such another knight for wisdom, nurture and manhood, and caused him to be named, "Father of curtesie." "Our success in France," says the historian, "lived and died with him."

The war-lord earned his honors, and no donation of land was large, as long as it brought the duty of protecting it, hour by hour, against a terrible enemy. In France and in England the nobles were, down to a late day, born and bred to war: and the duel, which in peace still held them to the risks of war, diminished the envy that in trading and studious nations would else have pried into their title. They were looked on as men who played high for a great stake.

Great estates are not sinecures, if they are to be kept great. A creative economy is the fuel of magnificence. In the same line of Warwick, the successor next but one to Beauchamp was the stout earl of Henry VI and Edward IV. Few esteemed themselves in the mode, whose heads were not adorned with the black ragged staff, his badge. At his house in London, six oxen were daily eaten at a breakfast, and every tavern was full of his meat, and who had any acquaintance in his family should have as much boiled and roast as he could carry on a long dagger.

The new age brings new qualities into request; the virtues of pirates gave way to those of planters, merchants, senators and scholars. Comity, social talent and fine manners, no doubt, have had their part also. I have met somewhere with a historiette, which, whether more or less true in its particulars, carries a general truth. "How came the Duke of Bedford by his great landed estates? His ancestor having travelled on the continent, a lively, pleasant man, became the companion of a foreign prince wrecked on the Dorsetshire coast, where Mr. Russell lived. The prince recommended him to Henry VIII, who; liking his company, gave him a large share of the plundered church lands."

The pretence is that the noble is of unbroken descent from the Norman, and has never worked for eight hundred years. But the fact is otherwise. Where is Bohun? where is De Vere? The lawyer, the farmer, the silk-mercer lies *perdu* under the coronet, and winks to the antiquary to say nothing; especially skilful lawyers, nobody's sons, who did some piece of work at a nice moment for government and were rewarded with ermine.

The national tastes of the English do not lead them to the life of the courtier, but to secure the comfort and independence of their homes. The aristocracy are marked by their predilection for country-life. They are called the county-families. They have often no residence in London and only go thither a short time, during the season, to see the opera; but they concentrate the love and labor of many generations on the building, planting and decoration of their homesteads. Some of

them are too old and too proud to wear titles, or, as Sheridan said of
Coke, "disdain to hide their head in a coronet"; and some curious
examples are cited to show the stability of English families. Their
proverb is, that fifty miles from London, a family will last a hundred
years; at a hundred miles, two hundred years; and so on; but I doubt
that steam, the enemy of time as well as of space, will disturb these
ancient rules. Sir Henry Wotton says of the first Duke of Buckingham,
"He was born at Brookeby in Leicestershire, where his ancestors had
chiefly continued about the space of four hundred years, rather without obscurity, than with any great lustre." Wraxall says that in 1781,
Lord Surrey, afterwards Duke of Norfolk, told him that when the year
1783 should arrive, he meant to give a grand festival to all the descen-
dants of the body of Jockey of Norfolk, to mark the day when the
dukedom should have remained three hundred years in their house,
since its creation by Richard III. Pepys tells us, in writing of an Earl
Oxford, in 1666, that the honor had now remained in that name and
blood six hundred years.

This long descent of families and this cleaving through ages to the
same spot of ground, captivates the imagination. It has too a connection
with the names of the towns and districts of the country.

The names are excellent—an atmosphere of legendary melody
spread over the land. Older than all epics and histories which clothe a
nation, this undershirt sits close to the body. What history too, and what
stores of primitive and savage observation it enfolds! Cambridge is the
bridge of the Cam; Sheffield the field of the river Sheaf; Leicester the
castra, or camp, of the Lear, or Leir (now Soar); Rochdale, of the Roch;
Exeter or Excester, the *castra* of the Ex; Exmouth, Dartmouth, Sid-
mouth, Teignmouth, the mouths of the Ex, Dart, Sid and Teign rivers.
Waltham is strong town; Radcliffe is red cliff; and so on—a sincerity
and use in naming very striking to an American, whose country is white-
washed all over by unmeaning names, the cast-off clothes of the country
from which its emigrants came; or named at a pinch from a psalm-tune.
But the English are those "barbarians" of Jamblichus, who "are stable in
their manners, and firmly continue to employ the same words, which
also are dear to the gods."

'T is an old sneer that the Irish peerage drew their names from
playbooks. The English lords do not call their lands after their own
names, but call themselves after their lands, as if the man represented

the country that bred him; and they rightly wear the token of the glebe that gave them birth, suggesting that the tie is not cut, but that there in London—the crags of Argyle, the kail of Cornwall, the downs of Devon, the iron of Wales, the days of Stafford are neither forgetting nor forgotten, but know the man who was born by them and who, like the long line of his fathers, has carried that crag, that shore, dale, fen, or woodland, in his blood and manners. It has, too, the advantage of suggesting responsibleness. A susceptible man could not wear a name which represented in a strict sense a city or a county of England, without hearing in it a challenge to duty and honor.

The predilection of the patricians for residence in the country, combined with the degree of liberty possessed by the peasant, makes the safety of the English hall. Mirabeau wrote prophetically from England, in 1784, "If revolution break out in France, I tremble for the aristocracy: their châteaux will be reduced to ashes and their blood be spilt in torrents. The English tenant would defend his lord to the last extremity." The English go to their estates for grandeur. The French live at court, and exile themselves to their estates for economy. As they do not mean to live with their tenants, they do not conciliate them, but wring from them the last sous. Evelyn writes from Blois, in 1644: "The wolves are here in such numbers, that they often come and take children out of the streets; yet will not the Duke, who is sovereign here, permit them to be destroyed."

In evidence of the wealth amassed by ancient families, the traveller is shown the palaces in Piccadilly, Burlington House, Devonshire House, Lansdowne House in Berkshire Square, and lower down in the city, a few noble houses which still withstand in all their amplitude the encroachment of streets. The Duke of Bedford includes or included a mile square in the heart of London, where the British Museum, once Montague House, now stands, and the land occupied by Woburn Square, Bedford Square, Russell Square. The Marquis of Westminster built within a few years the series of squares called Belgravia. Stafford House is the noblest palace in London. Northumberland House holds its place by Charing Cross. Chesterfield House remains in Audley Street. Sion House and Holland House are in the suburbs. But most of the historical houses are masked or lost in the modern uses to which trade or charity has converted them. A multitude of town palaces contain inestimable galleries of art.

In the country, the size of private estates is more impressive. From Barnard Castle I rode on the highway twenty-three miles from High Force, a fall of the Tees, towards Darlington, past Raby Castle, through the estate of the Duke of Cleveland. The Marquis of Breadalbane rides out of his house a hundred miles in a straight line to the sea, on his own property. The Duke of Sutherland owns the County of Sutherland, stretching across Scotland from sea to sea. The Duke of Devonshire, besides his other estates, owns 96,000 acres in the County of Derby. The Duke of Richmond has 40,000 acres at Goodwood and 300,000 at Gordon Castle. The Duke of Norfolk's park in Sussex is fifteen miles in circuit. An agriculturist bought lately the island of Lewis, in Hebrides, containing 500,000 acres. The possessions of the Earl of Lonsdale gave him eight seats in Parliament. This is the Heptarchy again; and before the Reform of 1832, one hundred and fifty-four persons sent three hundred and seven members to Parliament. The borough-mongers governed England.

These large domains are growing larger. The great estates are absorbing the small freeholds. In 1786 the soil of England was owned by 250,000 corporations and proprietors; and in 1822, by 32,000. These broad estates find room in this narrow island. All over England, scattered at short intervals among ship-yards, mills, mines and forges, are the paradises of the nobles, where the livelong repose and refinement are heightened by the contrast with the roar of industry and necessity, out of which you have stepped aside.

I was surprised to observe the very small attendance usually in the House of Lords. Out of five hundred and seventy-three peers, on ordinary days only twenty or thirty. Where are they? I asked. "At home on their estates, devoured by *ennui*, or in the Alps, or up the Rhine, in the Harz Mountains, or in Egypt, or in India, on the Ghauts." But, with such interests at stake, how can these men afford to neglect them? "O," replied my friend, "why should they work for themselves, when every man in England works for them and will suffer before they come to harm?" The hardest radical instantly uncovers and changes his tone to a lord. It was remarked, on the 10th April, 1848 (the day of the Chartist demonstration), that the upper classes were for the first time actively interesting themselves in their own defence, and men of rank were sworn special constables with the rest. "Besides, why need they sit out the debate? Has not the Duke of Wellington, at this moment, their proxies—the proxies of fifty peers—in his pocket, to vote for them if there be an emergency?"

It is however true that the existence of the House of Peers as a branch of the government entitles them to fill half the Cabinet; and their weight of property and station gives them a virtual nomination of the other half; whilst they have their share in the subordinate offices, as a school of training. This monopoly of political power has given them their intellectual and social eminence in Europe. A few law lords and a few political lords take the brunt of public business. In the army, the nobility fill a large part of the high commissions, and give to these a tone of expense and splendor and also of exclusiveness. They have borne their full share of duty and danger in this service, and there are few noble families which have not paid, in some of their members, the debt of life or limb in the sacrifices of the Russian war. For the rest, the nobility have the lead in matters of state and of expense; in questions of taste, in social usages, in convivial and domestic hospitalities. In general, all that is required of them is to sit securely, to preside at public meetings, to countenance charities and to give the example of that decorum so dear to the British heart.

If one asks, in the critical spirit of the day, what service this class have rendered?—uses appear, or they would have perished long ago. Some of these are easily enumerated, others more subtle make a part of unconscious history. Their institution is one step in the progress of society. For a race yields a nobility in some form, however we name the lords, as surely as it yields women.

The English nobles are high-spirited, active, educated men, born to wealth and power, who have run through every country and kept in every country the best company, have seen every secret of art and nature, and, when men of any ability or ambition, have been consulted in the conduct of every important action. You cannot wield great agencies without lending yourself to them, and when it happens that the spirit of the earl meets his rank and duties, we have the best examples of behavior. Power of any kind readily appears in the manners; and beneficent power *le talent de bien faire*, gives a majesty which cannot be concealed or resisted.

These people seem to gain as much as they lose by their position. They survey society as from the top of St. Paul's, and if they never hear plain truth from men, they see the best of everything, in every kind, and they see things so grouped and amassed as to infer easily the sum and genius, instead of tedious particularities. Their good behavior deserves all its fame, and they have that simplicity and that air of repose which are the finest ornament of greatness.

The upper classes have only birth, say the people here, and not thoughts. Yes, but they have manners, and it is wonderful how much talent runs into manners nowhere—and never so much as in England. They have the sense of superiority, the absence of all the ambitious effort which disgusts in the aspiring classes, a pure tone of thought and feeling, and the power to command, among their other luxuries, the presence of the most accomplished men in their festive meetings.

Loyalty is in the English a sub-religion. They wear the laws as ornaments, and walk by their faith in their painted May-Fair as if among the forms of gods. The economist of 1855 who asks, Of what use are the lords? may learn of Franklin to ask, Of what use is a baby? They have been a social church proper to inspire sentiments mutually honoring the lover and the loved. Politeness is the ritual of society, as prayers are of the church, a school of manners, and a gentle blessing to the age in which it grew. 'T is a romance adorning English life with a larger horizon; a midway heaven, fulfilling to their sense their fairy tales and poetry. This, just as far as the breeding of the nobleman really made him brave, handsome, accomplished and great-hearted.

On general grounds, whatever tends to form manners or to finish men, has a great value. Every one who has tasted the delight of friendship will respect every social guard which our manners can establish, tending to secure from the intrusion of frivolous and distasteful people. The jealousy of every class to guard itself is a testimony to the reality they have found in life. When a man once knows that he has done justice to himself, let him dismiss all terrors of aristocracy as superstitions, so far as he is concerned. He who keeps the door of a mine, whether of cobalt, or mercury, or nickel, or plumbago, securely knows that the world cannot do without him. Everybody who is real is open and ready for that which is also real.

Besides, these are they who make England that strongbox and museum it is; who gather and protect works of art, dragged from amidst burning cities and revolutionary countries, and brought hither out of all the world. I look with respect at houses six, seven, eight hundred, or, like Warwick Castle, nine hundred years old. I pardoned high park-fences, when I saw that besides does and pheasants, these have preserved Arundel marbles, Townley galleries, Howard and Spenserian libraries, Warwick and Portland vases, Saxon manuscripts, monastic architectures, millennial trees, and breeds of cattle elsewhere extinct. In these manors after the frenzy of war and destruction subsides a little, the antiquary finds the frailest Roman jar or crumbling Egyptian mummy-case, without so much as a new layer of dust, keeping the series of history unbroken and waiting for its interpreter, who is sure to arrive. These lords are the treasurers and librarians of mankind, engaged by their pride and wealth to this function.

Yet there were other works for British dukes to do. George Loudon, Quintinye, Evelyn, had taught them to make gardens. Arthur Young, Bakewell and Mechi have made them agricultural. Scotland was a camp until the day of Culloden. The Dukes of Athol, Sutherland, Buccleugh and the Marquis of Breadalbane have introduced the rape-culture, the sheep-farm, wheat, drainage, the plantation of forests, the artificial replenishment of lakes and ponds with fish, the renting of game-preserves. Against the cry of the old tenantry and the sympathetic cry of the English press, they have rooted out and planted anew, and now six millions of people live, and live better, on the same land that fed three millions.

The English barons, in every period, have been grave and great, after the estimate and opinion of their times. The grand old halls scattered up and down in England, are dumb vouchers to the state and broad hospitality of their ancient lords. Shakspeare's portraits of good Duke Humphrey, of Warwick, of Northumberland, of Talbot, were drawn in strict consonance with the traditions. A sketch of the Earl of Shrewsbury, from the pen of Queen Elizabeth's archbishop Parker; Lord Herbert of Cherbury's autobiography; the letters and essays of Sir Philip Sidney; the anecdotes preserved by the antiquaries Fuller and Collins; some glimpses at the interiors of noble houses, which we owe to Pepys and Evelyn; the details which Ben Jonson's masques (performed at Kenilworth, Althorpe, Belvoir and other noble houses), record or suggest; down to Aubrey's passages of the life of Hobbes in the house of the Earl of Devon, are favorable pictures of a romantic style of manners. Penshurst still shines for us, and its Christmas revels, "where logs not burn, but men." At Wilton House the "Arcadia" was written, amidst conversations with Fulke Greville, Lord Brooke, a man of no vulgar mind, as his own poems declare him. I must hold Ludlow Castle an honest house, for which Milton's "Comus" was written, and the company nobly bred which performed it with knowledge and sympathy. In the roll of nobles are found poets, philosophers, chemists, astronomers, also men of solid virtues and of lofty sentiments; often they have been the friends and patrons of genius and learning, and especially of the fine arts; and at this moment, almost every great house has its sumptuous picture-gallery.

Of course there is another side to this gorgeous show. Every victory was the defeat of a party only less worthy. Castles are proud things, but 't is safest to be outside of them. War is a foul game, and yet war is not the worst part of aristocratic history. In later times, when the baron, educated only for war, with his brains paralyzed by his stomach, found himself idle at home, he grew fat and wanton and a sorry brute. Grammont, Pepys and Evelyn show the kennels to which the king and court went in quest of pleasure. Prostitutes taken from the theatres were made duchesses, their bastards dukes and earls. "The young men sat uppermost, the old serious lords were out of favor." The discourse that the king's companions had with him was "poor and frothy." No man who valued his head might do what these pot-companions familiarly did with the king. In logical sequence of these dignified revels, Pepys can tell the beggarly shifts to which the king was reduced, who could not find paper at his council table, and "no handkerchers" in his wardrobe, "and but three bands to his neck," and the linen-draper and the stationer were out of pocket and refusing to trust him, and the baker will not bring bread any longer. Meantime the English Channel was swept and London threatened by the Dutch fleet, manned too by English sailors, who, having been cheated of their pay for years by the king, enlisted with the enemy.

The Selwyn correspondence, in the reign of George III, discloses a rottenness in the aristocracy which threatened to decompose the state. The sycophancy and sale of votes and honor, for place and title; lewdness, gaming, smuggling, bribery and cheating; the sneer at the childish indiscretion of quarrelling with ten thousand a year; the want of ideas; the splendor of the titles, and the apathy of the nation, are instructive, and make the reader pause and explore the firm bounds which confined these vices to a handful of rich men. In the reign of the Fourth George,

. . . .

things do not seem to have mended, and the rotten debauchee let down from a window by an inclined plane into his coach to take the air, was a scandal to Europe which the ill fame of his queen and of his family did nothing to retrieve.

Under the present reign the perfect decorum of the Court is thought to have put a check on the gross vices of the aristocracy; yet gaming, racing, drinking and mistresses bring them down, and the democrat can still gather scandals, if he will. Dismal anecdotes abound, verifying the gossip of the last generation, of dukes served by bailiffs, with all their plate in pawn; of great lords living by the showing of their houses, and of an old man wheeled in his chair from room to room, whilst his chambers are exhibited to the visitor for money; of ruined dukes and earls living in exile for debt. The historic names of the Buckinghams, Beauforts, Marlboroughs and Hertfords have gained no new lustre, and now and then darker scandals break out, ominous as the new chapters added under the Orleans dynasty to the "Causes Célèbres" in France. Even peers who are men of worth and public spirit are overtaken and embarrassed by their vast expense. The respectable Duke of Devonshire, willing to be the Mæcenas and Lucullus of his island, is reported to have said that he cannot live at Chatsworth but one month in the year. Their many houses eat them up. They cannot sell them, because they are entailed. They will not let them, for pride's sake, but keep them empty, aired, and the grounds mown and dressed, at a cost of four or five thousand pounds a year. The spending is for a great part in servants, in many houses exceeding a hundred.

Most of them are only chargeable with idleness, which, because it squanders such vast power of benefit, has the mischief of crime. "They might be little Providences on earth," said my friend, "and they are, for the most part, jockeys and fops." Campbell says, "Acquaintance with the nobility, I could never keep up. It requires a life of idleness, dressing and attendance on their parties." I suppose too that a feeling of self-respect is driving cultivated men out of this society, as if the noble were slow to receive the lessons of the times and had not learned to disguise his pride of place. A man of wit, who is also one of the celebrities of wealth and fashion, confessed to his friend that he could not enter their houses without being made to feel that they were great lords, and he a low plebeian. With the tribe of *artistes*, including the musical tribe, the patrician morgue keeps no terms, but excludes them. When Julia Grisi and Mario sang at the houses of the Duke of Wellington and other grandees, a cord was stretched between the singer and the company.

When every noble was a soldier, they were carefully bred to great personal prowess. The education of a soldier is a simpler affair than that of an earl in the nineteenth century. And this was very seriously pursued; they were expert in every species of equitation, to the most dangerous practices, and this down to the accession of William of Orange. But graver men appear to have trained their sons for civil affairs. Elizabeth extended her thought to the future; and Sir Philip Sidney in his letter to his brother, and Milton and Evelyn, gave plain and hearty counsel. Already too the English noble and squire were preparing for the career of the country-gentleman and his peaceable expense. They went from city to city, learning receipts to make perfumes, sweet powders, pomanders, antidotes, gathering seeds, gems, coins and divers curiosities, preparing for a private life thereafter, when they should take pleasure in these recreations.

All advantages given to absolve the young patrician from intellectual labor are of course mistaken. "In the university, noblemen are exempted from the public exercises for the degree, etc., by which they attain a degree called *honorary*. At the same time, the fees they have to pay for matriculation, and on all other occasions, are much higher." Fuller records "the observation of foreigners, that Englishmen, by making their children gentlemen before they are men, cause they are so seldom wise men." This cockering justifies Dr. Johnson's bitter apology for primogeniture, that "it makes but one fool in a family."

The revolution in society has reached this class. The great powers of industrial art have no exclusion of name or blood. The tools of our time, namely steam, ships, printing, money and popular education, belong to those who can handle them; and their effect has been that advantages once confined to men of family are now open to the whole middle class. The road that grandeur levels for his coach, toil can travel in his cart.

This is more manifest every day, but I think it is true throughout English history. English history, wisely read, is the vindication of the brain of that people. Here at last were climate and condition friendly to the working faculty. Who now will work and dare, shall rule. This is

the charter, or the chartism, which fogs and seas and rains proclaimed—that intellect and personal force should make the law; that
industry and administrative talent should administer; that work should
wear the crown. I know that not this, but something else is pretended.
The fiction with which the noble and the bystander equally please
themselves is that the former is of unbroken descent from the Norman,
and so has never worked for eight hundred years. All the families are
new, but the name is old, and they have made a covenant with their
memories not to disturb it. But the analysis of the peerage and gentry
shows the rapid decay and extinction of old families, the continual
recruiting of these from new blood. The doors, though ostentatiously
guarded, are really open, and hence the power of the bribe. All the barriers to rank only whet the thirst and enhance the prize. "Now," said
Nelson, when clearing for battle, "a peerage, or Westminster Abbey!"
"I have no illusion left," said Sydney Smith, "but the Archbishop of
Canterbury." "The lawyers," said Burke, "are only birds of passage in
this House of Commons," and then added, with a new figure, "they
have their best bower anchor in the House of Lords."

Another stride that has been taken appears in the perishing of heraldry. Whilst the privileges of nobility are passing to the middle class,
the badge is discredited and the titles of lordship are getting musty and
cumbersome. I wonder that sensible men have not been already impatient of them. They belong, with wigs, powder and scarlet coats, to an
earlier age and may be advantageously consigned, with paint and tatoo,
to the dignitaries of Australia and Polynesia.

A multitude of English, educated at the universities, bred into their
society with manners, ability and the gifts of fortune, are every day
confronting the peers on a footing of equality, and outstripping them,
as often, in the race of honor and influence. That cultivated class is
large and ever enlarging. It is computed that, with titles and without,
there are seventy thousand of these people coming and going in London, who make up what is called high society. They cannot shut their
eyes to the fact that an untitled nobility possess all the power without
the inconveniences that belong to rank, and the rich Englishman goes
over the world at the present day, drawing more than all the advantages which the strongest of his kings could command.

CHAPTER XII

UNIVERSITIES

OF BRITISH UNIVERSITIES, Cambridge has the most illustrious names on its list. At the present day too, it has the advantage of Oxford, counting in its *alumni* a greater number of distinguished scholars. I regret that I had but a single day wherein to see King's College Chapel, the beautiful lawns and gardens of the colleges, and a few of its gownsmen.

But I availed myself of some repeated invitations to Oxford, where I had introductions to Dr. Daubeny, Professor of Botany, and to the Regius Professor of Divinity, as well as to a valued friend, a Fellow of Oriel, and went thither on the last day of March, 1848. I was the guest of my friend in Oriel, was housed close upon that college, and I lived on college hospitalities.

My new friends showed me their cloisters, the Bodleian Library, the Randolph Gallery, Merton Hall and the rest. I saw several faithful, high-minded young men, some of them in the mood of making sacrifices for peace of mind—a topic, of course, on which I had no counsel to offer. Their affectionate and gregarious ways reminded me at once of the habits of *our* Cambridge men, though I imputed to these English an advantage in their secure and polished manners. The halls are rich with oaken wainscoting and ceiling. The pictures of the founders hang from the walls; the tables glitter with plate. A youth came forward to the upper table and pronounced the ancient form of grace before meals, which, I suppose, has been in use here for ages, *Benedictus, benedicat; benedicitur, benedicatur.*

It is a curious proof of the English use and wont, or of their good nature, that these young men are locked up every night at nine o'clock, and the porter at each hall is required to give the name of any belated student who is admitted after that hour. Still more descriptive is the fact that out of twelve hundred young men, comprising the most spirited of the aristocracy, a duel has never occurred.

Oxford is old, even in England, and conservative. Its foundations date from Alfred and even from Arthur, if, as is alleged, the Pheryllt of the Druids had a seminary here. In the reign of Edward I, it is pretended, here were thirty thousand students; and nineteen most noble foundations were then established. Chaucer found it as firm as if it had always stood; and it is, in British story, rich with great names, the school of the island and the link of England to the learned of Europe. Hither came Erasmus, with delight, in 1497. Albericus Gentilis, in 1580, was relieved and maintained by the university. Albert Alaskie, a noble Polonian, Prince of Sirad, who visited England to admire the wisdom of Queen Elizabeth, was entertained with stage-plays in the Refectory of Christ-Church in 1583. Isaac Casaubon, coming from Henri Quatre of France by invitation of James I, was admitted to Christ-Church, in July, 1613. I saw the Ashmolean Museum, whither Elias Ashmole in 1682 sent twelve cart-loads of rarities. Here indeed was the Olympia of all Antony Wood's and Aubrey's games and heroes, and every inch of ground has its lustre. For Wood's *Athenæ Oxonienses,* or calendar of the writers of Oxford for two hundred years, is a lively record of English manners and merits, and as much a national monument as Purchas's Pilgrims or Hansard's Register. On every side, Oxford is redolent of age and authority. Its gates shut of themselves against modern innovation. It is still governed by the statutes of Archbishop Laud. The books in Merton Library are still chained to the wall. Here, on August 27, 1660, John Milton's *Pro Populo Anglicano Defensio* and *Iconoclastes* were committed to the flames. I saw the school-court or quadrangle where, in 1683, the Convocation caused the Leviathan of Thomas Hobbes to be publicly burnt. I do not know whether this learned body have yet heard of the Declaration of American Independence, or whether the Ptolemaic astronomy does not still hold its ground against the novelties of Copernicus.

As many sons, almost so many benefactors. It is usual for a nobleman, or indeed for almost every wealthy student, on quitting college to leave behind him some article of plate; and gifts of all values, from a hall or a fellowship or a library, down to a picture or a spoon, are continually accruing, in the course of a century. My friend Doctor J. gave me the following anecdote. In Sir Thomas Lawrence's collection at London were the cartoons of Raphael and Michael Angelo. This inestimable prize was offered to Oxford University for seven thousand pounds. The offer was accepted, and the committee charged with the affair had collected three thousand pounds, when, among other friends, they called on Lord Eldon. Instead of a hundred pounds, he surprised them by putting down his name for three thousand pounds. They told him they should now very easily raise the remainder. "No," he said, "your men have probably already contributed all they can spare; I can as well give the rest:" and he withdrew his cheque for three thousand, and wrote four thousand pounds. I saw the whole collection in April, 1848.

In the Bodleian Library, Dr. Bandinel showed me the manuscript Plato, of the date of A.D. 896, brought by Dr. Clarke from Egypt; a manuscript Virgil of the same century; the first Bible printed at Mentz (I believe in 1450); and a duplicate of the same, which had been deficient in about twenty leaves at the end. But one day, being in Venice, he bought a room full of books and manuscripts—every scrap and fragment—for four thousand louis d'ors, and had the doors locked and sealed by the consul. On proceeding afterwards to examine his purchase, he found the twenty deficient pages of his Mentz Bible, in perfect order; brought them to Oxford with the rest of his purchase, and placed them in the volume; but has too much awe for the Providence that appears in bibliography also, to suffer the reunited parts to be re-bound. The oldest building here is two hundred years younger than the frail manuscript brought by Dr. Clarke from Egypt. No candle or fire is ever lighted in the Bodleian. Its catalogue is the standard catalogue on the desk of every library in Oxford. In each several college they underscore in red ink on this catalogue the titles of books contained in the library of that college—the theory being that the Bodleian has all books. This rich library spent during the last year (1847), for the purchase of books, £1668.

The logical English train a scholar as they train an engineer. Oxford is a Greek factory, as Wilton mills weave carpet and Sheffield grinds steel. They know the use of a tutor, as they know the use of a horse; and they draw the greatest amount of benefit out of both. The reading men are kept, by hard walking, hard riding and measured eating and drinking, at the top of their condition, and two days before the examination, do no work, but lounge, ride, or run, to be fresh on the college doomsday. Seven years' residence is the theoretic period for a master's degree. In point of fact, it has long been three years' residence, and four years more of standing. This "three years" is about twenty-one months in all.

"The whole expense," says Professor Sewel, "of ordinary college tuition at Oxford, is about sixteen guineas a year." But this plausible statement may deceive a reader unacquainted with the fact that the principal teaching relied on is private tuition. And the expenses of private tuition are reckoned at from £50 to £70 a year, or $1000 for the whole course of three years and a half. At Cambridge, $750 a year is economical, and $1500 not extravagant.

The number of students and of residents, the dignity of the authorities, the value of the foundations, the history and the architecture, the known sympathy of entire Britain in what is done there, justify a dedication to study in the undergraduate such as cannot easily be in America, where his college is half suspected by the Freshman to be insignificant in the scale beside trade and politics. Oxford is a little aristocracy in itself, numerous and dignified enough to rank with other estates in the realm; and where fame and secular promotion are to be had for study, and in a direction which has the unanimous respect of all cultivated nations.

This aristocracy, of course, repairs its own losses; fills places, as they fall vacant, from the body of students. The number of fellowships at Oxford is 540, averaging £200 a year, with lodging and diet at the college. If a young American, loving learning and hindered by poverty, were offered a home, a table, the walks and the library in one of these academical palaces, and a thousand dollars a year, as long as he chose to remain a bachelor, he would dance for joy. Yet these young men thus happily placed, and paid to read, are impatient of their few checks, and many of them preparing to resign their fellowships. They shuddered at the prospect of dying a Fellow, and they pointed out to me a paralytic old man, who was assisted into the hall. As the number of undergraduates at Oxford is only about 1200 or 1300, and many of these are never competitors, the chance of a fellowship is very great. The income of the nineteen colleges is conjectured at £150,000 a year.

The effect of this drill is the radical knowledge of Greek and Latin and of mathematics, and the solidity and taste of English criticism. Whatever luck there may be in this or that award, an Eton captain can write Latin longs and shorts, can turn the Court-Guide into hexameters, and it is certain that a Senior Classic can quote correctly from the Corpus Poetarum and is critically learned in all the humanities. Greek erudition exists on the Isis and Cam, whether the Maud man or the Brasenose man be properly ranked or not; the atmosphere is loaded with Greek learning; the whole river has reached a certain height, and kills all that growth of weeds which this Castalian water kills. The

English nature takes culture kindly. So Milton thought. It refines the Norseman. Access to the Greek mind lifts his standard of taste. He has enough to think of, and, unless of an impulsive nature, is indisposed from writing or speaking, by the fulness of his mind and the new severity of his taste. The great silent crowd of thoroughbred Grecians always known to be around him, the English writer cannot ignore. They prune his orations and point his pen. Hence the style and tone of English journalism. The men have learned accuracy and comprehension, logic, and pace, or speed of working. They have bottom, endurance, wind. When born with good constitutions, they make those eupeptic studying-mills, the cast-iron men, the dura ilia, whose powers of performance compare with ours as the steam-hammer with the music-box—Cokes, Mansfields, Seldens and Bentleys, and when it happens that a superior brain puts a rider on this admirable horse we obtain those masters of the world who combine the highest energy in affairs with a supreme culture.

It is contended by those who have been bred at Eton, Harrow, Rugby and Westminster, that the public sentiment within each of those schools is high-toned and manly; that, in their playgrounds, courage is universally admired, meanness despised, manly feelings and generous conduct are encouraged: that an unwritten code of honor deals to the spoiled child of rank and to the child of upstart wealth, an even-handed justice, purges their nonsense out of both and does all that can be done to make them gentlemen.

Again, at the universities, it is urged that all goes to form what England values as the flower of its national life—a well-educated gentleman. The German Huber, in describing to his countrymen the attributes of an English gentleman, frankly admits that "in Germany, we have nothing of the kind. A gentleman must possess a political character, an independent and public position, or at least the right of assuming it. He must have average opulence, either of his own, or in his family. He should also have bodily activity and strength, unattainable by our sedentary life in public offices. The race of English gentlemen presents an appearance of manly vigor and form not elsewhere to be found among an equal number of persons. No other nation produces the stock. And in England, it has deteriorated. The university is a decided presumption in any man's favor. And so eminent are the members that a glance at the calendars will show that in all the world

. . . .

one cannot be in better company than on the books of one of the larger Oxford or Cambridge colleges."

These seminaries are finishing schools for the upper classes, and not for the poor. The useful is exploded. The definition of a public school is "a school which excludes all that could fit a man for standing behind a counter."

No doubt, the foundations have been perverted. Oxford, which equals in wealth several of the smaller European states, shuts up the lectureships which were made "public for all men thereunto to have concourse"; mis-spends the revenues bestowed for such youths "as should be most meet for towardness, poverty and painfulness"; there is gross favoritism; many chairs and many fellowships are made beds of ease; and it is likely that the university will know how to resist and make inoperative the terrors of parliamentary inquiry; no doubt their learning is grown obsolete—but Oxford also has its merits, and I found here also proof of the national fidelity and thoroughness. Such knowledge as they prize they possess and impart. Whether in course or by indirection, whether by a cramming tutor or by examiners with prizes and foundational scholarships, education, according to the English notion of it, is arrived at. I looked over the Examination Papers of the year 1848, for the various scholarships and fellowships, the Lusby, the Hertford, the Dean-Ireland and the University (copies of which were kindly given me by a Greek professor), containing the tasks which many competitors had victoriously performed, and I believed they would prove too severe tests for the candidates for a Bachelor's degree in Yale or Harvard. And in general, here was proof of a more searching study in the appointed directions, and the knowledge pretended to be conveyed was conveyed. Oxford sends out yearly twenty or thirty very able men and three or four hundred well-educated men.

The diet and rough exercise secure a certain amount of old Norse power. A fop will fight, and in exigent circumstances will play the manly part. In seeing these youths I believed I saw already an advantage in vigor and color and general habit, over their contemporaries in the American colleges. No doubt much of the power and brilliancy of the reading-men is merely constitutional or hygienic. With a hardier habit and resolute gymnastics, with five miles more walking, or five ounces less eating, or with a saddle and gallop of twenty miles a day, with skating and rowing-matches, the American would arrive at as robust exegesis and cheery and hilarious tone. I should readily concede these advantages, which it would be easy to acquire, if I did not find also that they read better than we, and write better.

English wealth falling on their school and university training, makes a systematic reading of the best authors, and to the end of a knowledge how the things whereof they treat really stand: whilst pamphleteer or journalist, reading for an argument for a party, or reading to write, or at all events for some by-end imposed on them, must read meanly and fragmentarily. Charles I said that he understood English law as well as a gentleman ought to understand it.

Then they have access to books; the rich libraries collected at every one of many thousands of houses, give an advantage not to be attained by a youth in this country, when one thinks how much more and better may be learned by a scholar who, immediately on hearing of a book, can consult it, than by one who is on the quest, for years, and reads inferior books because he cannot find the best.

Again, the great number of cultivated men keep each other up to a high standard. The habit of meeting well-read and knowing men teaches the art of omission and selection.

Universities are of course hostile to geniuses, which, seeing and using ways of their own, discredit the routine: as churches and monasteries persecute youthful saints. Yet we all send our sons to college, and though he be a genius, the youth must take his chance. The university must be retrospective. The gale that gives direction to the vanes on all its towers blows out of antiquity. Oxford is a library, and the professors must be librarians. And I should as soon think of quarrelling with the janitor for not magnifying his office by hostile sallies into the street, like the Governor of Kertch or Kinburn, as of quarrelling with the professors for not admiring the young neologists who pluck the beards of Euclid and Aristotle, or for not attempting themselves to fill their vacant shelves as original writers.

It is easy to carp at colleges, and the college, if we will wait for it, will have its own turn. Genius exists there also, but will not answer a call of a committee of the House of Commons. It is rare, precarious, eccentric and darkling. England is the land of mixture and surprise, and when you have settled it that the universities are moribund, out comes a poetic influence from the heart of Oxford, to mould the opinions of cities, to build their houses as simply as birds their nests, to give veracity to art and charm mankind, as an appeal to moral order always must. But besides this restorative genius, the best poetry of England of this age, in the old forms, comes from two graduates at Cambridge.

CHAPTER XIII

RELIGION

NO PEOPLE at the present day can be explained by their national religion. They do not feel responsible for it; it lies far outside of them. Their loyalty to truth and their labor and expenditure rest on real foundations, and not on a national church. And English life, it is evident, does not grow out of the Athanasian creed, or the Articles, or the Eucharist. It is with religion as with marriage. A youth marries in haste; afterwards, when his mind is opened to the reason of the conduct of life, he is asked what he thinks of the institution of marriage and of the right relations of the sexes? 'I should have much to say,' he might reply, 'if the question were open, but I have a wife and children, and all question is closed for me.' In the barbarous days of a nation, some cultus is formed or imported; altars are built, tithes are paid, priests ordained. The education and expenditure of the country take that direction, and when wealth, refinement, great men, and ties to the world supervene, its prudent men say, Why fight against Fate, or lift these absurdities which are now mountainous? Better find some niche or crevice in this mountain of stone which religious ages have quarried and carved, wherein to bestow yourself, than attempt anything ridiculously and dangerously above your strength, like removing it.

In seeing old castles and cathedrals, I sometimes say, as to-day in front of Dundee Church tower, which is eight hundred years old, 'This was built by another and a better race than any that now look on it.' And plainly there has been great power of sentiment at work in this island, of which these buildings are the proofs; as volcanic basalts show the work of fire which has been extinguished for ages. England felt the full heat of the Christianity which fermented Europe, and drew, like the chemistry of fire, a firm line between barbarism and culture. The power of the religious sentiment put an end to human sacrifices, checked appetite, inspired the crusades, inspired resistance to tyrants, inspired self-respect, set bounds to serfdom and slavery, founded liberty, created the religious architecture—York, Newstead, Westminster, Fountains Abbey, Ripon, Beverley and Dundee—works to which the key is lost, with the sentiment which created them; inspired the English Bible, the liturgy, the monkish histories, the chronicle of Richard of Devizes. The priest translated the Vulgate, and translated the sanctities of old hagiology into English virtues on English ground. It was a certain affirmative or aggressive state of the Caucasian races. Man awoke refreshed by the sleep of ages. The violence of the northern savages exasperated Christianity into power. It lived by the love of the people. Bishop Wilfrid manumitted two hundred and fifty serfs, whom he found attached to the soil. The clergy obtained respite from labor for the boor on the Sabbath and on church festivals. "The lord who compelled his boor to labor between sunset on Saturday and sunset on Sunday, forfeited him altogether." The priest came out of the people and sympathized with his class. The church was the mediator, check and democratic principle, in Europe. Latimer, Wicliffe, Arundel, Cobham, Antony Parsons, Sir Harry Vane, George Fox, Penn, Bunyan are the democrats, as well as the saints of their times. The Catholic Church, thrown on this toiling, serious people, has made in fourteen centuries a massive system, close fitted to the manners and genius of the country, at once domestical and stately. In the long time, it has blended with everything in heaven above and the earth beneath. It moves through a zodiac of feasts and fasts, names every day of the year, every town and market and headland and monument, and has coupled itself with the almanac, that no court can be held, no field ploughed, no horse shod, without some leave from the church. All maxims of prudence or shop or farm are fixed and dated by the church. Hence its strength in the agricultural districts. The distribution of land into parishes enforces a church sanction to every civil privilege; and the gradation of the clergy—prelates for the rich and curates for the poor—with the fact that a classical education has been secured to the clergyman, makes them "the link which unites the sequestered peasantry with the intellectual advancement of the age."

The English Church has many certificates to show of humble effective service in humanizing the people, in cheering and refining men, feeding, healing and educating. It has the seal of martyrs and confessors; the noblest books; a sublime architecture; a ritual marked by the same secular merits, nothing cheap or purchasable.

From this slow-grown church important reactions proceed; much for culture, much for giving a direction to the nation's affection and will to-day. The carved and pictured chapel—its entire surface animated with image and emblem—made the parish-church a sort of book and Bible to the people's eye.

Then, when the Saxon instinct had secured a service in the vernacular tongue, it was the tutor and university of the people. In York minster, on the day of the enthronization of the new archbishop, I heard the service of evening prayer read and chanted in the choir. It was strange to hear the pretty pastoral of the betrothal of Rebecca and Isaac, in the morning of the world, read with circumstantiality in York minster, on the 13th January, 1848, to the decorous English audience, just fresh from the Times newspaper and their wine, and listening with all the devotion of national pride. That was binding old and new to some purpose. The reverence for the Scriptures is an element of civilization, for thus has the history of the world been preserved and is preserved. Here in England every day a chapter of Genesis, and a leader in the Times.

Another part of the same service on this occasion was not insignificant. Handel's coronation anthem, *God save the King*, was played by Dr. Camidge on the organ, with sublime effect. The minster and the music were made for each other. It was a hint of the part the church plays as a political engine. From his infancy, every Englishman is accustomed to hear daily prayers for the Queen, for the royal family and the Parliament, by name; and this lifelong consecration cannot be without influence on his opinions.

The universities also are parcel of the ecclesiastical system, and their first design is to form the clergy. Thus the clergy for a thousand years have been the scholars of the nation.

The national temperament deeply enjoys the unbroken order and tradition of its church; the liturgy, ceremony, architecture; the sober grace, the good company, the connection with the throne and with history, which adorn it. And whilst it endears itself thus to men of more taste than activity, the stability of the English nation is passionately enlisted to its support, from its inextricable connection with the cause of public order, with politics and with the funds.

Good churches are not built by bad men; at least there must be probity and enthusiasm somewhere in the society. These minsters were neither built nor filled by atheists. No church has had more learned, industrious or devoted men; plenty of "clerks and bishops, who, out of their gowns, would turn their backs on no man." Their architecture still glows with faith in immortality. Heats and genial periods arrive in history, or, shall we say, plenitudes of Divine Presence, by which high tides are caused in the human spirit, and great virtues and talents appear, as in the eleventh, twelfth, thirteenth, and again in the sixteenth and seventeenth centuries, when the nation was full of genius and piety.

But the age of the Wicliffes, Cobhams, Arundels, Beckets; of the Latimers, Mores, Cranmers; of the Taylors, Leightons, Herberts; of the Sherlocks and Butlers, is gone. Silent revolutions in opinion have made it impossible that men like these should return, or find a place in their once sacred stalls. The spirit that dwelt in this church has glided away to animate other activities, and they who come to the old shrines find apes and players rustling the old garments.

The religion of England is part of good-breeding. When you see on the continent the well-dressed Englishman come into his ambassador's chapel and put his face for silent prayer into his smooth-brushed hat, you cannot help feeling how much national pride prays with him, and the religion of a gentleman. So far is he from attaching any meaning to the words, that he believes himself to have done almost the generous thing, and that it is very condescending in him to pray to God. A great duke said on the occasion of a victory, in the House of Lords, that he thought the Almighty God had not been well used by them, and that it would become their magnanimity, after so great successes, to take order that a proper acknowledgment be made. It is the church of the gentry, but it is not the church of the poor. The operatives do not own it, and gentlemen lately testified in the House of Commons that in their lives they never saw a poor man in a ragged coat inside a church.

The torpidity on the side of religion of the vigorous English understanding shows how much wit and folly can agree in one brain. Their religion is a quotation; their church is a doll; and any examination is interdicted with screams of terror. In good company you expect them to laugh at the fanaticism of the vulgar; but they do not; they are the vulgar.

The English, in common perhaps with Christendom in the nineteenth century, do not respect power, but only performance; value ideas only for an economic result. Wellington esteems a saint only as far as he can be an army chaplain: "Mr. Briscoll, by his admirable conduct and good sense, got the better of Methodism, which had appeared among the soldiers and once among the officers." They value a philosopher as they value an apothecary who brings bark or a drench; and inspiration is only some blow-pipe, or a finer mechanical aid.

I suspect that there is in an Englishman's brain a valve that can be closed at pleasure, as an engineer shuts off steam. The most sensible and well-informed men possess the power of thinking just so far as the bishop in religious matters, and as the chancellor of the exchequer in politics. They talk with courage and logic, and show you magnificent results, but the same men who have brought free trade or geology to their present standing, look grave and lofty and shut down their valve as soon as the conversation approaches the English Church. After that, you talk with a box-turtle.

The action of the university, both in what is taught and in the spirit of the place, is directed more on producing an English gentleman, than a saint or a psychologist. It ripens a bishop, and extrudes a philosopher. I do not know that there is more cabalism in the Anglican than in other churches, but the Anglican clergy are identified with the aristocracy. They say here, that if you talk with a clergyman, you are sure to find him well-bred, informed and candid: he entertains your thought or your project with sympathy and praise. But if a second clergyman come in, the sympathy is at an end: two together are inaccessible to your thought, and whenever it comes to action, the clergyman invariably sides with his church.

The Anglican Church is marked by the grace and good sense of its forms, by the manly grace of its clergy. The gospel it preaches is 'By taste are ye saved.' It keeps the old structures in repair, spends a world of money in music and building, and in buying Pugin and architectural literature. It has a general good name for amenity and mildness. It is not in ordinary a persecuting church; it is not inquisitorial, not even inquisitive; is perfectly well-bred, and can shut its eyes on all proper occasions. If you let it alone, it will let you alone. But its instinct is hostile to all change in politics, literature, or social arts. The church has not been the founder of the London University, of the Mechanics' Institutes, of the Free School, of whatever aims at diffusion of knowledge. The Platonists of Oxford are as bitter against this heresy, as Thomas Taylor.

. . . .

The doctrine of the Old Testament is the religion of England. The first leaf of the New Testament it does not open. It believes in a Providence which does not treat with levity a pound sterling. They are neither transcendentalists nor Christians. They put up no Socratic prayer, much less any saintly prayer for the Queen's mind; ask neither for light nor right, but say bluntly, "Grant her in health and wealth long to live." And one traces this Jewish prayer in all English private history, from the prayers of King Richard, in Richard of Devizes' Chronicle, to those in the diaries of Sir Samuel Romilly and of Haydon the painter. "Abroad with my wife," writes Pepys piously, "the first time that ever I rode in my own coach; which do make my heart rejoice and praise God, and pray him to bless it to me, and continue it." The bill for the naturalization of the Jews (in 1753) was resisted by petitions from all parts of the kingdom, and by petition from the city of London, reprobating this bill, as "tending extremely to the dishonor of the Christian religion, and extremely injurious to the interests and commerce of the kingdom in general, and of the city of London in particular."

But they have not been able to congeal humanity by act of Parliament. "The heavens journey still and sojourn not," and arts, wars, discoveries and opinion go onward at their own pace. The new age has new desires, new enemies, new trades, new charities, and reads the Scriptures with new eyes. The chatter of French politics, the steam-whistle, the hum of the mill and the noise of embarking emigrants had quite put most of the old legends out of mind; so that when you came to read the liturgy to a modern congregation, it was almost absurd in its unfitness, and suggested a masquerade of old costumes.

No chemist has prospered in the attempt to crystallize a religion. It is endogenous, like the skin and other vital organs. A new statement every day. The prophet and apostle knew this, and the nonconformist confutes the conformists, by quoting the texts they must allow. It is the condition of a religion to require religion for its expositor. Prophet and apostle can only be rightly understood by prophet and apostle. The statesman knows that the religious element will not fail, any more than the supply of fibrine and chyle; but it is in its nature constructive, and will organize such a church as it wants. The wise legislator will spend on temples, schools, libraries, colleges, but will shun the enriching of priests. If in any manner he can leave the election and paying of the priest to the people, he will do well. Like the Quakers, he may resist the separation of a class of priests, and create opportunity and expectation in the society to run to meet natural endowment in this kind. But when wealth accrues to a chaplaincy, a bishopric, or rectorship, it requires moneyed men for its stewards, who will give it another direction than to the mystics of their day. Of course, money will do after its kind, and will steadily work to unspiritualize and unchurch the people to whom it was bequeathed. The class certain to be excluded from all preferment are the religious—and driven to other churches; which is nature's *vis medicatrix*.

The curates are ill paid, and the prelates are overpaid. This abuse draws into the church the children of the nobility and other unfit persons who have a taste for expense. Thus a bishop is only a surpliced merchant. Through his lawn I can see the bright buttons of the shopman's coat glitter. A wealth like that of Durham makes almost a premium on felony. Brougham, in a speech in the House of Commons on the Irish elective franchise, said, "How will the reverend bishops of the other house be able to express their due abhorrence of the crime of perjury, who solemnly declare in the presence of God that when they are called upon to accept a living, perhaps of £4000 a year, at that very instant they are moved by the Holy Ghost to accept the office and administration thereof, and for no other reason whatever?" The modes of initiation are more damaging than customhouse oaths. The Bishop is elected by the Dean and Prebends of the cathedral. The Queen sends these gentlemen a *congé d'élire*, or leave to elect; but also sends them the name of the person whom they are to elect. They go into the cathedral, chant and pray and beseech the Holy Ghost to assist them in their choice; and, after these invocations, invariably find that the dictates of the Holy Ghost agree with the recommendations of the Queen.

But you must pay for conformity. All goes well as long as you run with conformists. But you, who are an honest man in other particulars, know that there is alive somewhere a man whose honesty reaches to this point also that he shall not kneel to false gods, and on the day when you meet him, you sink into the class of counterfeits. Besides, this succumbing has grave penalties. If you take in a lie, you must take in all that belongs to it. England accepts this ornamented national church, and it glazes the eyes, bloats the flesh, gives the voice a stertorous clang, and clouds the understanding of the receivers.

The English Church, undermined by German criticism, had nothing left but tradition; and was led logically back to Romanism. But that was an element which only hot heads could breathe: in view of the educated class, generally, it was not a fact to front the sun; and the alienation of such men from the church became complete.

Nature, to be sure, had her remedy. Religious persons are driven out of the Established Church into sects, which instantly rise to credit and hold the Establishment in check. Nature has sharper remedies, also. The English, abhorring change in all things, abhorring it most in matters of religion, cling to the last rag of form, and are dreadfully given to cant. The English (and I wish it were confined to them, but 't is a taint in the Anglo-Saxon blood in both hemispheres)—the English and the Americans cant beyond all other nations. The French relinquish all that industry to them. What is so odious as the polite bows to God, in our books and newspapers? The popular press is flagitious in the exact measure of its sanctimony, and the religion of the day is a theatrical Sinai, where the thunders are supplied by the property-man. The fanaticism and hypocrisy create satire. Punch finds an inexhaustible material. Dickens writes novels on Exeter-Hall humanity. Thackeray exposes the heartless high life. Nature revenges herself more summarily by the heathenism of the lower classes. Lord Shaftesbury calls the poor thieves together and reads sermons to them, and they call it 'gas.' George Borrow summons the Gypsies to hear his discourse on the Hebrews in Egypt, and reads to them the Apostles' Creed in Romany. "When I had concluded," he says, "I looked around me. The features of the assembly were twisted, and the eyes of all turned upon me with a frightful squint; not an individual present but squinted; the genteel Pepa, the good-humored Chicharona, the Cosdami, all squinted; the Gypsy jockey squinted worst of all."

The church at this moment is much to be pitied. She has nothing left but possession. If a bishop meets an intelligent gentleman and reads fatal interrogations in his eyes, he has no resource but to take wine with him. False position introduces cant, perjury, simony and ever a lower class of mind and character into the clergy: and, when the hierarchy is afraid of science and education, afraid of piety, afraid of tradition and afraid of theology, there is nothing left but to quit a church which is no longer one.

But the religion of England—is it the Established Church? no; is it the sects? no; they are only perpetuations of some private man's dissent, and are to the Established Church as cabs are to a coach, cheaper and more convenient, but really the same thing. Where dwells the religion? Tell me first where dwells electricity, or motion, or thought, or gesture. They do not dwell or stay at all. Electricity cannot be made fast, mortared up and ended, like London Monument or the Tower, so that you shall know where to find it, and keep it fixed, as the English do with their things, forevermore; it is passing, glancing, gesticular; it is a traveller, a newness, a surprise, a secret, which perplexes them and puts them out. Yet, if religion be the doing of all good, and for its sake the suffering of all evil, *souffrir de tout le monde, et ne faire souffrir personne*, that divine secret has existed in England from the days of Alfred to those of Romilly, of Clarkson and of Florence Nightingale, and in thousands who have no fame.

CHAPTER XIV

LITERATURE

A STRONG COMMON SENSE, which it is not easy to unseat or disturb, marks the English mind for a thousand years: a rude strength newly applied to thought, as of sailors and soldiers who had lately learned to read. They have no fancy, and never are surprised into a covert or witty word, such as pleased the Athenians and Italians, and was convertible into a fable not long after; but they delight in strong earthy expression, not mistakable, coarsely true to the human body, and, though spoken among princes, equally fit and welcome to the mob. This homeliness, veracity and plain style appear in the earliest extant works and in the latest. It imports into songs and ballads the smell of the earth, the breath of cattle, and, like a Dutch painter, seeks a household charm, though by pails and pans. They ask their constitutional utility in verse. The kail and herrings are never out of sight. The poet nimbly recovers himself from every sally of the imagination. The English muse loves the farmyard, the lane and market. She says, with De Staël, "I tramp in the mire with wooden shoes, whenever they would force me into the clouds." For the Englishman has accurate perceptions; takes hold of things by the right end, and there is no slipperiness in his grasp. He loves the axe, the spade, the oar, the gun, the steam-pipe: he has built the engine he uses. He is materialist, economical, mercantile. He must be treated with sincerity and reality; with muffins, and not the promise of muffins; and prefers his hot chop, with perfect security and convenience in the eating of it, to the chances of the amplest and Frenchiest bill of fare, engraved on embossed paper. When he is intellectual, and a poet or a philosopher, he carries the same hard truth and the same keen machinery into the mental sphere. His mind must stand on a fact. He will not be baffled, or catch at clouds, but the mind must have a symbol palpable and resisting. What he relishes in Dante is the vise-like tenacity with which he holds a mental image before the eyes, as if it were a scutcheon painted on a shield. Byron "liked something craggy to break his mind upon." A taste for plain strong speech, what is called a biblical style, marks the English. It is in Alfred and the Saxon Chronicle and in the Sagas of the Northmen. Latimer was homely. Hobbes was perfect in the "noble vulgar speech." Donne, Bunyan, Milton, Taylor, Evelyn, Pepys, Hooker, Cotton and the translators wrote it. How realistic or materialistic in treatment of his subject is Swift. He describes his fictitious persons as if for the police. Defoe has no insecurity or choice. Hudibras has the same hard mentality—keeping the truth at once to the senses and to the intellect.

It is not less seen in poetry. Chaucer's hard painting of his Canterbury pilgrims satisfies the senses. Shakspeare, Spenser and Milton, in their loftiest ascents, have this national grip and exactitude of mind. This mental materialism makes the value of England transcendental genius; in these writers and in Herbert, Henry More, Donne and Sir Thomas Browne. The Saxon materialism and narrowness, exalted into the sphere of intellect, makes the very genius of Shakspeare and Milton. When it reaches the pure element, it treads the clouds as securely as the adamant. Even in its elevations materialistic, its poetry is common sense inspired; or iron raised to white heat.

The marriage of the two qualities is in their speech. It is a tacit rule of the language to make the frame or skeleton of Saxon words, and, when elevation or ornament is sought, to interweave Roman, but sparingly; nor is a sentence made of Roman words alone, without loss of strength. The children and laborers use the Saxon unmixed. The Latin unmixed is abandoned to the colleges and Parliament. Mixture is a secret of the English island; and, in their dialect, the male principle is the Saxon, the female, the Latin; and they are combined in every dis-

. . . .

course. A good writer, if he has indulged in a Roman roundness, makes haste to chasten and nerve his period by English monosyllables.

When the Gothic nations came into Europe they found it lighted with the sun and moon of Hebrew and of Greek genius. The tablets of their brain, long kept in the dark, were finely sensible to the double glory. To the images from this twin source (of Christianity and art), the mind became fruitful as by the incubation of the Holy Ghost. The English mind flowered in every faculty. The commonest sense was surprised and inspired. For two centuries England was philosophic, religious, poetic. The mental furniture seemed of larger scale: the memory capacious like the storehouse of the rains. The ardor and endurance of study, the boldness and facility of their mental construction, their fancy and imagination and easy spanning of vast distances of thought, the enterprise or accosting of new subjects, and, generally, the easy exertion of power—astonish, like the legendary feats of Guy of Warwick. The union of Saxon precision and Oriental soaring, of which Shakspeare is the perfect example, is shared in less degree by the writers of two centuries. I find not only the great masters out of all rivalry and reach, but the whole writing of the time charged with a masculine force and freedom.

There is a hygienic simpleness, rough vigor and closeness to the matter in hand even in the second and third class of writers; and, I think, in the common style of the people, as one finds it in the citation of wills, letters and public documents; in proverbs and forms of speech. The more hearty and sturdy expression may indicate that the savageness of the Norseman was not all gone. Their dynamic brains hurled off their words as the revolving stone hurls off scraps of grit. I could cite from the seventeenth century sentences and phrases of edge not to be matched in the nineteenth. Their poets by simple force of mind equalized themselves with the accumulated science of ours. The country gentlemen had a posset or drink they called October; and the poets, as if by this hint, knew how to distil the whole season into their autumnal verses: and as nature, to pique the more, sometimes works up deformities into beauty in some rare Aspasia or Cleopatra; and as the Greek art wrought many a vase or column, in which too long or too lithe, or nodes, or pits and flaws are made a beauty of—so these were so quick and vital that they could charm and enrich by mean and vulgar objects.

. . . .

A man must think that age well taught and thoughtful, by which masques and poems, like those of Ben Jonson, full of heroic sentiment in a manly style, were received with favor. The unique fact in literary history, the unsurprised reception of Shakspeare—the reception proved by his making his fortune; and the apathy proved by the absence of all contemporary panegyric—seems to demonstrate an elevation in the mind of the people. Judge of the splendor of a nation by the insignificance of great individuals in it. The manner in which they learned Greek and Latin, before our modern facilities were yet ready; without dictionaries, grammars, or indexes, by lectures of a professor, followed by their own searchings—required a more robust memory, and cooperation of all the faculties; and their scholars, Camden, Usher, Selden, Mede, Gataker, Hooker, Taylor, Burton, Bentley, Brian Walton, acquired the solidity and method of engineers.

The influence of Plato tinges the British genius. Their minds loved analogy; were cognizant of resemblances, and climbers on the staircase of unity. 'T is a very old strife between those who elect to see identity and those who elect to see discrepancies; and it renews itself in Britain. The poets, of course, are of one part; the men of the world, of the other. But Britain had many disciples of Plato—More, Hooker, Bacon, Sidney, Lord Brooke, Herbert, Browne, Donne, Spenser, Chapman, Milton, Crashaw, Norris, Cudworth, Berkeley, Jeremy Taylor.

Lord Bacon has the English duality. His centuries of observations on useful science, and his experiments, I suppose, were worth nothing. One hint of Franklin, or Watt, or Dalton, or Davy, or any one who had a talent for experiment, was worth all his lifetime of exquisite trifles. But he drinks of a diviner stream, and marks the influx of idealism into England. Where that goes, is poetry, health and progress. The rules of its genesis or its diffusion are not known. That knowledge, if we had it, would supersede all that we call science of the mind. It seems an affair of race, or of meta-chemistry—the vital point being, how far the sense of unity, or instinct of seeking resemblances, predominated. For wherever the mind takes a step, it is to put itself at one with a larger class, discerned beyond the lesser class with which it has been conversant. Hence, all poetry and all affirmative action comes.

Bacon, in the structure of his mind, held of the analogists, of the idealists, or (as we popularly say, naming from the best example) Platonists. Whoever discredits analogy and requires heaps of facts before any theories can be attempted, has no poetic power, and nothing original or beautiful will be produced by him. Locke is as surely the influx of decomposition and of prose, as Bacon and the Platonists of growth. The Platonic is the poetic tendency, the so-called scientific is the negative and poisonous. 'T is quite certain that Spenser, Burns, Byron and Wordsworth will be Platonists, and that the dull men will be Lockists. Then politics and commerce will absorb from the educated class men of talents without genius, precisely because such have no resistance.

Bacon, capable of ideas, yet devoted to ends, required in his map of the mind, first of all, universality, or *prima philosophia*; the receptacle for all such profitable observations and axioms as fall not within the compass of any of the special parts of philosophy, but are more common and of a higher stage. He held this element essential: it is never out of mind: he never spares rebukes for such as neglect it; believing that no perfect discovery can be made in a flat or level, but you must ascend to a higher science. "If any man thinketh philosophy and universality to be idle studies, he doth not consider that all professions are from thence served and supplied; and this I take to be a great cause that has hindered the progression of learning, because these fundamental knowledges have been studied but in passage." He explained himself by giving various quaint examples of the summary or common laws of which each science has its own illustration. He complains that "he finds this part of learning very deficient, the profounder sort of wits drawing a bucket now and then for their own use, but the spring-head unvisited. This was the *dry light* which did scorch and offend most men's watery natures." Plato had signified the same sense, when he said, "All the great arts require a subtle and speculative research into the law of nature, since loftiness of thought and perfect mastery over every subject seem to be derived from some such source as this. This Pericles had, in addition to a great natural genius. For, meeting with Anaxagoras, who was a person of this kind, he attached himself to him, and nourished himself with sublime speculations on the absolute intelligence; and imported thence into the oratorical art whatever could be useful to it."

A few generalizations always circulate in the world, whose authors we do not rightly know, which astonish, and appear to be avenues to vast kingdoms of thought, and these are in the world *constants*, like the Copernican and Newtonian theories in physics. In England these may be traced usually to Shakspeare, Bacon, Milton, or Hooker, even to Van Helmont and Behmen, and do all have a kind of filial retrospect to Plato and the Greeks. Of this kind is Lord Bacon's sentence, that "Nature is commanded by obeying her"; his doctrine of poetry, which "accommodates the shows of things to the desires of the mind," or the Zoroastrian definition of poetry, mystical, yet exact, "apparent pictures of unapparent natures"; Spenser's creed that "soul is form, and doth the body make"; the theory of Berkeley, that we have no certain assurance of the existence of matter; Doctor Samuel Clarke's argument for theism from the nature of space and time; Harrington's political rule that power must rest on land—a rule which requires to be liberally interpreted; the theory of Swedenborg, so cosmically applied by him, that the man makes his heaven and hell; Hegel's study of civil history, as the conflict of ideas and the victory of the deeper thought; the identity-philosophy of Schelling, couched in the statement that "all difference is quantitative." So the very announcement of the theory of gravitation, of Kepler's three harmonic laws, and even of Dalton's doctrine of definite proportions, finds a sudden response in the mind, which remains a superior evidence to empirical demonstrations. I cite these generalizations, some of which are more recent, merely to indicate a class. Not these particulars, but the mental plane or the atmosphere from which they emanate was the home and element of the writers and readers in what we loosely call the Elizabethan age (say, in literary history, the period from 1575 to 1625), yet a period almost short enough to justify Ben Jonson's remark on Lord Bacon—"About his time, and within his view, were born all the wits that could honor a nation, or help study."

Such richness of genius had not existed more than once before. These heights could not be maintained. As we find stumps of vast trees in our exhausted soils, and have received traditions of their ancient fertility to tillage, so history reckons epochs in which the intellect of famed races became effete. So it fared with English genius. These heights were followed by a meanness and a descent of the mind into lower levels; the loss of wings; no high speculation. Locke, to whom the meaning of ideas was unknown, became the type of philosophy, and his "understanding" the measure, in all nations, of the English intellect. His countrymen forsook the lofty sides of Parnassus, on which they had once walked with echoing steps, and disused the studies once so beloved; the powers of thought fell into neglect. The later English want the faculty of Plato and Aristotle, of grouping men in natural classes by an insight of general laws, so deep that the rule is deduced with equal precision from few subjects, or from one, as from multitudes of lives. Shakspeare is supreme in that, as in all the great mental energies. The Germans generalize: the English cannot interpret the German mind. German science comprehends the English. The absence of the faculty in England is shown by the timidity which accumulates mountains of facts, as a bad general wants myriads of men and miles of redoubts to compensate the inspirations of courage and conduct.

The English shrink from a generalization. "They do not look abroad into universality, or they draw only a bucketful at the fountain of the First Philosophy for their occasion, and do not go to the spring-head." Bacon, who said this, is almost unique among his countrymen in that faculty; at least among the prose-writers. Milton, who was the stair or high table-land to let down the English genius from the summits of Shakspeare, used this privilege sometimes in poetry, more rarely in prose. For a long interval afterwards, it is not found. Burke was addicted to generalizing, but his was a shorter line; as his thoughts have less depth, they have less compass. Hume's abstractions are not deep or wise. He owes his fame to one keen observation, that no copula had been detected between any cause and effect, either in physics or in thought; that the term cause and effect was loosely or gratuitously applied to what we know only as consecutive, not at all as causal. Doctor Johnson's written abstractions have little value; the tone of feeling in them makes their chief worth.

Mr. Hallam, a learned and elegant scholar, has written the history of European literature for three centuries—a performance of great ambition, inasmuch as a judgment was to be attempted on every book. But his eye does not reach to the ideal standards: the verdicts are all dated from London; all new thought must be cast into the old moulds. The expansive element which creates literature is steadily denied. Plato is resisted, and his school. Hallam is uniformly polite, but with deficient sympathy; writes with resolute generosity, but is unconscious of the deep worth which lies in the mystics, and which often outvalues as a seed of power and a source of revolution all the correct writers and shining reputations of their day. He passes in silence, or dismisses with a kind of contempt, the profounder masters: a lover of ideas is not only uncongenial, but unintelligible. Hallam inspires respect by his knowledge and fidelity, by his manifest love of good books, and he lifts himself to own better than almost any the greatness of Shakspeare, and better than Johnson he appreciates Milton. But in Hallam, or in the firmer intellectual nerve of Mackintosh, one still finds the same type of English genius. It is wise and rich, but it lives on its capital. It is retrospective. How can it discern and hail the new forms that are looming up on the horizon, new and gigantic thoughts which cannot dress themselves out of any old wardrobe of the past?

The essays, the fiction and the poetry of the day have the like municipal limits. Dickens, with preternatural apprehension of the language of manners and the varieties of street life; with pathos and laughter, with patriotic and still enlarging generosity, writes London tracts. He is a painter of English details, like Hogarth; local and temporary in his tints and style, and local in his aims. Bulwer, an industrious writer, with occasional ability, is distinguished for his reverence of intellect as a temporality, and appeals to the worldly ambition of the student. His romances tend to fan these low flames. Their novelists despair of the heart. Thackeray finds that God has made no allowance for the poor thing in his universe—more's the pity, he thinks—but 't is not for us to be wiser; we must renounce ideals and accept London.

The brilliant Macaulay, who expresses the tone of the English governing classes of the day, explicitly teaches that *good* means good to eat, good to wear, material commodity; that the glory of modern philosophy is its direction on "fruit"; to yield economical inventions; and that its merit is to avoid ideas and avoid morals. He thinks it the distinctive merit of the Baconian philosophy in its triumph over the old Platonic, its disentangling the intellect from theories of the all-Fair and all-Good, and pinning it down to the making a better sick chair and a better wine-whey for an invalid—this not ironically, but in good faith—that, "solid advantage," as he calls it, meaning always sensual benefit, is the only good. The eminent benefit of astronomy is the better navigation it creates to enable the fruit-ships to bring home their lemons and wine to the London grocer. It was a curious result, in which the civility and religion of England for a thousand years ends in denying morals and reducing the intellect to a sauce-pan. The critic hides his skepticism under the English cant of practical. To convince the reason, to touch the conscience, is romantic pretension. The fine arts fall to the ground. Beauty, except as luxurious commodity, does not exist. It is very certain, I may say in passing, that if Lord Bacon had been only the sensualist his critic pretends, he would never have acquired the fame which now entitles him to this patronage. It is because he had imagination, the leisures of the spirit, and basked in an element of contemplation out of all modern English atmospheric gauges, that he is impressive to the imaginations of men and has become a potentate not to be ignored. Sir David Brewster sees the high place of Bacon, without finding Newton indebted to him, and thinks it a mistake. Bacon occupies it by specific gravity or levity, not by any feat he did, or by any tutoring more or less of Newton, etc., but as an effect of the same cause which showed itself more pronounced afterwards in Hooke, Boyle and Halley.

Coleridge, a catholic mind, with a hunger for ideas; with eyes looking before and after to the highest bards and sages, and who wrote and spoke the only high criticism in his time, is one of those who save England from the reproach of no longer possessing the capacity to appreciate what rarest wit the island has yielded. Yet the misfortune of his life, his vast attempts but most inadequate performings, failing to accomplish any one masterpiece—seems to mark the closing of an era. Even in him, the traditional Englishman was too strong for the philosopher, and he fell into *accommodations*; and as Burke had striven to idealize the English State, so Coleridge 'narrowed his mind' in the attempt to reconcile the Gothic rule and dogma of the Anglican Church, with eternal ideas. But for Coleridge, and a lurking taciturn minority uttering itself in occasional criticism, oftener in private discourse, one would say that in Germany and in America is the best mind in England rightly respected. It is the surest sign of national decay, when the Brahmins can no longer read or understand the Brahminical philosophy.

In the decomposition and asphyxia that followed all this materialism, Carlyle was driven by his disgust at the pettiness and the cant, into the preaching of Fate. In comparison with all this rottenness, any check, any cleansing, though by fire, seemed desirable and beautiful. He saw little difference in the gladiators, or "the causes" for which they combated; the one comfort was, that they were all going speedily into the abyss together. And his imagination, finding no nutriment in any creation, avenged itself by celebrating the majestic beauty of the laws of decay. The necessities of mental structure force all minds into a few categories; and where impatience of the tricks of men makes Nemesis amiable, and builds altars to the negative Deity, the inevitable recoil is to heroism or the gallantry of the private heart, which decks its immolation with glory, in the unequal combat of will against fate.

Wilkinson, the editor of Swedenborg, the annotator of Fourier and the champion of Hahnemann, has brought to metaphysics and to physiology a native vigor, with a catholic perception of relations, equal to the highest attempts, and a rhetoric like the armory of the invincible knights of old. There is in the action of his mind a long Atlantic roll not known except in deepest waters, and only lacking what ought to accompany such powers, a manifest centrality. If his mind does not rest in immovable biases, perhaps the orbit is larger and the return is not yet: but a master should inspire a confidence that he will adhere to his convictions and give his present studies always the same high place.

It would be easy to add exceptions to the limitary tone of English thought, and much more easy to adduce examples of excellence in particular veins; and if, going out of the region of dogma, we pass into that of general culture, there is no end to the graces and amenities, wit, sensibility and erudition of the learned class. But the artificial succor which marks all English performance appears in letters also: much of their æsthetic production is antiquarian and manufactured, and literary reputations have been achieved by forcible men, whose relation to literature was purely accidental, but who were driven by tastes and modes they found in vogue into their several careers. So, at this moment, every ambitious young man studies geology: so members of Parliament are made, and churchmen.

The bias of Englishmen to practical skill has reacted on the national mind. They are incapable of an inutility, and respect the five mechanic powers even in their song. The voice of their modern muse has a slight hint of the steam-whistle, and the poem is created as an ornament and finish of their monarchy, and by no means as the bird of a new morning which forgets the past world in the full enjoyment of that which is forming. They are with difficulty ideal; they are the most conditioned men, as if, having the best conditions, they could not bring themselves to forfeit them. Every one of them is a thousand years old and lives by his memory: and when you say this, they accept it as praise.

. . . .

Nothing comes to the book-shops but politics, travels, statistics, tabulation and engineering; and even what is called philosophy and letters is mechanical in its structure, as if inspiration had ceased, as if no vast hope, no religion, no song of joy, no wisdom, no analogy existed any more. The tone of colleges and of scholars and of literary society has this mortal air. I seem to walk on a marble floor, where nothing will grow. They exert every variety of talent on a lower ground and may be said to live and act in a sub-mind. They have lost all commanding views in literature, philosophy and science. A good Englishman shuts himself out of three fourths of his mind and confines himself to one fourth. He has learning, good sense, power of labor, and logic; but a faith in the laws of the mind like that of Archimedes; a belief like that of Euler and Kepler, that experience must follow and not lead the laws of the mind; a devotion to the theory of politics like that of Hooker and Milton and Harrington, the modern English mind repudiates.

I fear the same fault lies in their science, since they have known how to make it repulsive and bereave nature of its charm—though perhaps the complaint flies wider, and the vice attaches to many more than to British physicists. The eye of the naturalist must have a scope like nature itself, a susceptibility to all impressions, alive to the heart as well as to the logic of creation. But English science puts humanity to the door. It wants the connection which is the test of genius. The science is false by not being poetic. It isolates the reptile or mollusk it assumes to explain; whilst reptile or mollusk only exists in system, in relation. The poet only sees it as an inevitable step in the path of the Creator. But, in England, one hermit finds this fact, and another finds that, and lives and dies ignorant of its value. There are great exceptions, of John Hunter, a man of ideas; perhaps of Robert Brown, the botanist; and of Richard Owen, who has imported into Britain the German homologies, and enriched science with contributions of his own, adding sometimes the divination of the old masters to the unbroken power of labor in the English mind. But for the most part the natural science in England is out of its loyal alliance with morals, and is as void of imagination and free play of thought as conveyancing. It stands in strong contrast with the genius of the Germans, those semi-Greeks, who love analogy, and, by means of their height of view, preserve their enthusiasm and think for Europe.

. . . .

No hope, no sublime augury cheers the student, no secure striding from experiment onward to a foreseen law, but only a casual dipping here and there, like diggers in California "prospecting for a placer" that will pay. A horizon of brass of the diameter of his umbrella shuts down around his senses. Squalid contentment with conventions, satire at the names of philosophy and religion, parochial and shop-till politics, and idolatry of usage, betray the ebb of life and spirit. As they trample on nationalities to reproduce London and Londoners in Europe and Asia, so they fear the hostility of ideas, of poetry, of religion—ghosts which they cannot lay; and, having attempted to domesticate and dress the Blessed Soul itself in English broadcloth and gaiters, they are tormented with fear that herein lurks a force that will sweep their system away. The artists say, "Nature puts them out"; the scholars have become unideal. They parry earnest speech with banter and levity; they laugh you down, or they change the subject. "The fact is," say they over their wine, "all that about liberty, and so forth, is gone by; it won't do any longer." The practical and comfortable oppress them with inexorable claims, and the smallest fraction of power remains for heroism and poetry. No poet dares murmur of beauty out of the precinct of his rhymes. No priest dares hint at a Providence which does not respect English utility. The island is a roaring volcano of fate, of material values, of tariffs and laws of repression, glutted markets and low prices.

In the absence of the highest aims, of the pure love of knowledge and the surrender to nature, there is the suppression of the imagination, the priapism of the senses and the understanding; we have the factitious instead of the natural; tasteless expense, arts of comfort, and the rewarding as an illustrious inventor whosoever will contrive one impediment more to interpose between the man and his objects.

Thus poetry is degraded and made ornamental. Pope and his school wrote poetry fit to put round frosted cake. What did Walter Scott write without stint? a rhymed traveller's guide to Scotland. And the libraries of verses they print have this Birmingham character. How many volumes of well-bred metre we must jingle through, before we can be filled, taught, renewed! We want the miraculous; the beauty which we can manufacture at no mill—can give no account of; the beauty of which Chaucer and Chapman had the secret. The poetry of course is low and prosaic; only now and then, as in Wordsworth, conscientious; or in Byron, passional; or in Tennyson, factitious. But if I should count the poets who have contributed to the Bible of existing England sentences of guidance and consolation which are still glowing and effective—how few! Shall I find my heavenly bread in the reigning poets? Where is great design in modern English poetry? The English have lost sight of the fact that poetry exists to speak the spiritual law, and that no wealth of description or of fancy is yet essentially new and out of the limits of prose, until this condition is reached. Therefore the grave old poets, like the Greek artists, heeded their designs, and less considered the finish. It was their office to lead to the divine sources, out of which all this, and much more, readily springs; and, if this religion is in the poetry, it raises us to some purpose and we can well afford some staidness or hardness, or want of popular tune in the verses.

The exceptional fact of the period is the genius of Wordsworth. He had no master but nature and solitude. "He wrote a poem," says Landor, "without the aid of war." His verse is the voice of sanity in a worldly and ambitious age. One regrets that his temperament was not more liquid and musical. He has written longer than he was inspired. But for the rest, he has no competitor.

Tennyson is endowed precisely in points where Wordsworth wanted. There is no finer ear, nor more command of the keys of language. Color, like the dawn, flows over the horizon from his pencil, in waves so rich that we do not miss the central form. Through all his refinements, too, he has reached the public—a certificate of good sense and general power, since he who aspires to be the English poet must be as large as London, not in the same kind as London, but in his own kind. But he wants a subject, and climbs no mount of vision to bring its secrets to the people. He contents himself with describing the Englishman as he is, and proposes no better. There are all degrees in poetry and we must be thankful for every beautiful talent. But it is only a first success, when the ear is gained. The best office of the best poets has been to show how low and uninspired was their general style, and that only once or twice they have struck the high chord.

That expansiveness which is the essence of the poetic element, they have not. It was no Oxonian, but Hafiz, who said, "Let us be crowned with roses, let us drink wine, and break up the tiresome old roof of heaven into new forms." A stanza of the song of nature the Oxonian has no ear for, and he does not value the salient and curative influence of intellectual action, studious of truth without a by-end.

By the law of contraries, I look for an irresistible taste for Orientalism in Britain. For a self-conceited modish life, made up of trifles, clinging to a corporeal civilization, hating ideas, there is no remedy like the Oriental largeness. That astonishes and disconcerts English decorum. For once, there is thunder it never heard, light it never saw, and power which trifles with time and space. I am not surprised then to find an Englishman like Warren Hastings, who had been struck with the grand style of thinking in the Indian writings, deprecating the prejudices of his countrymen while offering them a translation of the Bhagvat. "Might I, an unlettered man, venture to prescribe bounds to the latitude of criticism, I should exclude, in estimating the merit of such a production, all rules drawn from the ancient or modern literature of Europe, all references to such sentiments or manners as are become the standards of propriety for opinion and action in our own modes, and, equally, all appeals to our revealed tenets of religion and moral duty." He goes to bespeak indulgence to "ornaments of fancy unsuited to our taste, and passages elevated to a tract of sublimity into which our habits of judgment will find it difficult to pursue them."

Meantime, I know that a retrieving power lies in the English race which seems to make any recoil possible; in other words, there is at all times a minority of profound minds existing in the nation, capable of appreciating every soaring of intellect and every hint of tendency. While the constructive talent seems dwarfed and superficial, the criticism is often in the noblest tone and suggests the presence of the invisible gods. I can well believe what I have often heard, that there are two nations in England; but it is not the Poor and the Rich, nor is it the Normans and Saxons, nor the Celt and the Goth. These are each always becoming the other; for Robert Owen does not exaggerate the power of circumstance. But the two complexions, or two styles of mind—the perceptive class, and the practical finality class—are ever in counterpoise, interacting mutually: one in hopeless minorities; the other in huge masses; one studious, contemplative, experimenting; the other, the ungrateful pupil, scornful of the source whilst availing itself of the knowledge for gain; these two nations, of genius and of animal force, though the first consist of only a dozen souls and the second of twenty millions, forever by their discord and their accord yield the power of the English State.

CHAPTER XV

THE "TIMES"

THE POWER of the newspaper is familiar in America and in accordance with our political system. In England, it stands in antagonism with the feudal institutions, and it is all the more beneficent succor against the secretive tendencies of a monarchy. The celebrated Lord Somers "knew of no good law proposed and passed in his time, to which the public papers had not directed his attention." There is no corner and no night. A relentless inquisition drags every secret to the day, turns the glare of this solar microscope on every malfaisance, so as to make the public a more terrible spy than any foreigner; and no weakness can be taken advantage of by an enemy, since the whole people are already forewarned. Thus England rids herself of those incrustations which have been the ruin of old states. Of course, this inspection is feared. No antique privilege, no comfortable monopoly, but sees surely that its days are counted; the people are familiarized with the reason of reform, and, one by one, take away every argument of the obstructives. "So your grace likes the comfort of reading the newspapers," said Lord Mansfield to the Duke of Northumberland; "mark my words; you and I shall not live to see it, but this young gentleman (Lord Eldon) may, or it may be a little later; but a little sooner or later, these newspapers will most assuredly write the dukes of Northumberland out of their titles and possessions, and the country out of its king." The tendency in England towards social and political institutions like those of America, is inevitable, and the ability of its journals is the driving force.

England is full of manly, clever, well-bred men who possess the talent of writing off-hand pungent paragraphs, expressing with clearness and courage their opinion on any person or performance. Valuable or not, it is a skill that is rarely found, out of the English journals. The English do this, as they write poetry, as they ride and box, by being educated to it. Hundreds of clever Praeds and Freres and Froudes and Hoods and Hooks and Maginns and Mills and Macaulays, make poems, or short essays for a journal, as they make speeches in Parliament and on the hustings, or as they shoot and ride. It is a quite accidental and arbitrary direction of their general ability. Rude health and spirits, an Oxford education and the habits of society are implied, but not a ray of genius. It comes of the crowded state of the professions, the violent interest which all men take in politics, the facility of experimenting in the journals, and high pay.

The most conspicuous result of this talent is the Times newspaper. No power in England is more felt, more feared, or more obeyed. What you read in the morning in that journal, you shall hear in the evening in all society. It has ears everywhere, and its information is earliest, completest and surest. It has risen, year by year, and victory by victory, to its present authority. I asked one of its old contributors whether it had once been abler than it is now? "Never," he said; "these are its palmiest days." It has shown those qualities which are dear to Englishmen, unflinching adherence to its objects, prodigal intellectual ability and a towering assurance, backed by the perfect organization in its printing-house and its world-wide network of correspondence and reports. It has its own history and famous trophies. In 1820, it adopted the cause of Queen Caroline, and carried it against the king. It adopted a poor-law system, and almost alone lifted it through. When Lord Brougham was in power, it decided against him, and pulled him down. It declared war against Ireland, and conquered it. It adopted the League against the Corn Laws, and, when Cobden had begun to despair, it announced his triumph. It denounced and discredited the French Republic of 1848, and checked every sympathy with it in England, until it had enrolled 200,000 special constables to watch the Chartists and make them ridiculous on the 10th April. It first denounced and then adopted the new French Empire, and urged the French Alliance and its results. It has entered into each municipal, literary and social question, almost with a controlling voice. It has done bold and seasonable service in exposing frauds which threatened the commercial community. Meantime, it attacks its rivals by perfecting its printing machinery, and will drive them out of circulation: for the only limit to the circulation of The Times is the impossibility of printing copies fast enough; since a daily paper can only be new and seasonable for a few hours. It will kill all but that paper which is diametrically in opposition; since many papers, first and last, have lived by their attacks on the leading journal.

The late Mr. Walter was printer of The Times, and had gradually arranged the whole *matériel* of it in perfect system. It is told that when he demanded a small share in the proprietary and was refused, he said,

"As you please, gentlemen; and you may take away The Times from this office when you will; I shall publish The New Times next Monday morning." The proprietors, who had already complained that his charges for printing were excessive, found that they were in his power, and gave him whatever he wished.

I went one day with a good friend to The Times office, which was entered through a pretty garden-yard in Printing-House Square. We walked with some circumspection, as if we were entering a powder-mill; but the door was opened by a mild old woman, and, by dint of some transmission of cards, we were at last conducted into the parlor of Mr. Morris, a very gentle person, with no hostile appearances. The statistics are now quite out of date, but I remember he told us that the daily printing was then 35,000 copies; that on the 1st March, 1848, the greatest number ever printed—54,000—were issued; that, since February, the daily circulation had increased by 8000 copies. The old press they were then using printed five or six thousand sheets per hour; the new machine, for which they were then building an engine, would print twelve thousand per hour. Our entertainer confided us to a courteous assistant to show us the establishment, in which, I think, they employed a hundred and twenty men. I remember I saw the reporters' room, in which they redact their hasty stenographs, but the editor's room, and who is in it, I did not see, though I shared the curiosity of mankind respecting it.

The staff of The Times has always been made up of able men. Old Walter, Sterling, Bacon, Barnes, Alsiger, Horace Twiss, Jones Lloyd, John Oxenford, Mr. Mosely, Mr. Bailey, have contributed to its renown in their special departments. But it has never wanted the first pens for occasional assistance. Its private information is inexplicable, and recalls the stories of Fouché's police, whose omniscience made it believed that the Empress Josephine must be in his pay. It has mercantile and political correspondents in every foreign city, and its expresses outrun the despatches of the government. One hears anecdotes of the rise of its servants, as of the functionaries of the India House. I was told of the dexterity of one of its reporters, who, finding himself, on one occasion, where the magistrates had strictly forbidden reporters, put his hands into his coat-pocket, and with pencil in one hand and tablet in the other, did his work.

The influence of this journal is a recognized power in Europe, and,

of course, none is more conscious of it than its conductors. The tone
of its articles has often been the occasion of comment from the official
organs of the continental courts, and sometimes the ground of diplo-
matic complaint. 'What would The Times say?' is a terror in Paris, in
Berlin, in Vienna, in Copenhagen and in Nepaul. Its consummate discretion and success exhibit the English skill of combination. The daily
paper is the work of many hands, chiefly, it is said, of young men
recently from the University, and perhaps reading law in chambers in
London. Hence the academic elegance and classic allusion which adorns
its columns. Hence, too, the heat and gallantry of its onset. But the
steadiness of the aim suggests the belief that this fire is directed and
fed by older engineers; as if persons of exact information, and with settled views of policy, supplied the writers with the basis of fact and the
object to be attained, and availed themselves of their younger energy
and eloquence to plead the cause. Both the council and the executive
departments gain by this division. Of two men of equal ability, the one
who does not write but keeps his eye on the course of public affairs,
will have the higher judicial wisdom. But the parts are kept in concert,
all the articles appear to proceed from a single will. The Times never
disapproves of what itself has said, or cripples itself by apology for the
absence of the editor, or the indiscretion of him who held the pen. It
speaks out bluff and bold, and sticks to what it says. It draws from any
number of learned and skilful contributors; but a more learned and skilful person supervises, corrects, and co-ordinates. Of this closet, the
secret does not transpire. No writer is suffered to claim the authorship
of any paper; everything good, from whatever quarter, comes out edi-
torially; and thus, by making the paper everything and those who write
it nothing, the character and the awe of the journal gain.

The English like it for its complete information. A statement of
fact in The Times is as reliable as a citation from Hansard. Then they
like its independence; they do not know, when they take it up, what
their paper is going to say: but, above all, for the nationality and confidence of its tone. It thinks for them all; it is their understanding and
day's ideal daguerreotyped. When I see them reading its columns, they
seem to me becoming every moment more British. It has the national
courage, not rash and petulant, but considerate and determined. No
dignity or wealth is a shield from its assault. It attacks a duke as readily as a policeman, and with the most provoking airs of condescension.

. . . .

It makes rude work with the Board of Admiralty. The Bench of Bishops is still less safe. One bishop fares badly for his rapacity, and another for his bigotry, and a third for his courtliness. It addresses occasionally a hint to Majesty itself, and sometimes a hint which is taken. There is an air of freedom even in their advertising columns, which speaks well for England to a foreigner. On the days when I arrived in London in 1847, I read, among the daily announcements, one offering a reward of fifty pounds to any person who would put a nobleman, described by name and title, late a member of Parliament, into any county jail in England, he having been convicted of obtaining money under false pretences.

Was never such arrogancy as the tone of this paper. Every slip of an Oxonian or Cantabrigian who writes his first leader assumes that we subdued the earth before we sat down to write this particular Times. One would think the world was on its knees to The Times office for its daily breakfast. But this arrogance is calculated. Who would care for it, if it "surmised," or "dared to confess," or "ventured to predict," etc.? No; *it is so*, and so it shall be.

The morality and patriotism of The Times claim only to be representative, and by no means ideal. It gives the argument, not of the majority, but of the commanding class. Its editors know better than to defend Russia, or Austria, or English vested rights, on abstract grounds. But they give a voice to the class who at the moment take the lead; and they have an instinct for finding where the power now lies, which is eternally shifting its banks. Sympathizing with, and speaking for the class that rules the hour, yet being apprised of every ground-swell, every Chartist resolution, every Church squabble, every strike in the mills, they detect the first tremblings of change. They watch the hard and bitter struggles of the authors of each liberal movement, year by year; watching them only to taunt and obstruct them—until, at last, when they see that these have established their fact, that power is on the point of passing to them, they strike in with the voice of a monarch, astonish those whom they succor as much as those whom they desert, and make victory sure. Of course the aspirants see that The Times is one of the goods of fortune, not to be won but by winning their cause.

Punch is equally an expression of English good sense, as the London Times. It is the comic version of the same sense. Many of its caricatures are equal to the best pamphlets, and will convey to the eye

. . . .

in an instant the popular view which was taken of each turn of public affairs. Its sketches are usually made by masterly hands, and sometimes with genius; the delight of every class, because uniformly guided by that taste which is tyrannical in England. It is a new trait of the nineteenth century, that the wit and humor of England—as in Punch, so in the humorists, Jerrold, Dickens, Thackeray, Hood—have taken the direction of humanity and freedom.

The Times, like every important institution, shows the way to a better. It is a living index of the colossal British power. Its existence honors the people who dare to print all they know, dare to know all the facts and do not wish to be flattered by hiding the extent of the public disaster. There is always safety in valor. I wish I could add that this journal aspired to deserve the power it wields, by guidance of the public sentiment to the right. It is usually pretended, in Parliament and elsewhere, that the English press has a high tone—which it has not. It has an imperial tone, as of a powerful and independent nation. But, as with other empires, its tone is prone to be official, and even officinal. The Times shares all the limitations of the governing classes, and wishes never to be in a minority. If only it dared to cleave to the right, to show the right to be the only expedient, and feed its batteries from the central heart of humanity, it might not have so many men of rank among its contributors, but genius would be its cordial and invincible ally; it might now and then bear the brunt of formidable combinations, but no journal is ruined by wise courage. It would be the natural leader of British reform; its proud function, that of being the voice of Europe, the defender of the exile and patriot against despots, would be more effectually discharged; it would have the authority which is claimed for that dream of good men not yet come to pass, an International Congress; and the least of its victories would be to give to England a new millennium of beneficent power.

CHAPTER XVI

STONEHENGE

IT HAD BEEN AGREED between my friend Mr. Carlyle and me, that before I left England we should make an excursion together to Stonehenge, which neither of us had seen; and the project pleased my fancy with the double attraction of the monument and the companion. It seemed a bringing together of extreme points, to visit the oldest religious monument in Britain in company with her latest thinker, and one whose influence may be traced in every contemporary book. I was glad to sum up a little my experiences, and to exchange a few reasonable words on the aspects of England with a man on whose genius I set a very high value, and who had as much penetration and as severe a theory of duty as any person in it. On Friday, 7th July, we took the South Western Railway through Hampshire to Salisbury, where we found a carriage to convey us to Amesbury. The fine weather and my friend's local knowledge of Hampshire, in which he is wont to spend a part of every summer, made the way short. There was much to say, too, of the travelling Americans and their usual objects in London. I thought it natural that they should give some time to works of art collected here which they cannot find at home, and a little to scientific clubs and museums, which, at this moment, make London very attractive. But my philosopher was not contented. Art and 'high art' is a favorite target for his wit. "Yes, *Kunst* is a great delusion, and Goethe and Schiller wasted a great deal of good time on it:"—and he thinks he discovers that old Goethe found this out, and, in his later writings, changed his tone. As soon as men begin to talk of art, architecture and antiquities, nothing good comes of it. He wishes to go through the British Museum in silence, and thinks a sincere man will see something and say nothing. In these days, he thought, it would become an architect to consult only the grim necessity, and say, 'I can build you a coffin for such dead persons as you are, and for such dead purposes as you have, but you shall have no ornament.' For the science, he had if possible even less tolerance, and compared the *savants* of Somerset House to the boy who asked Confucius "how many stars in the sky?" Confucius replied, "he minded things near him:" then said the boy, "how many hairs are in your eyebrows?" Confucius said, "he didn't know and didn't care."

Still speaking of the Americans, Carlyle complained that they dislike the coldness and exclusiveness of the English, and run away to France and go with their countrymen and are amused, instead of manfully staying in London, and confronting Englishmen and acquiring their culture, who really have much to teach them.

I told Carlyle that I was easily dazzled, and was accustomed to concede readily all that an Englishman would ask; I saw everywhere in the country proofs of sense and spirit, and success of every sort: I like the people; they are as good as they are handsome; they have everything and can do everything; but meantime, I surely know that as soon as I return to Massachusetts I shall lapse at once into the feeling, which the geography of America inevitably inspires, that we play the game with immense advantage; that there and not here is the seat and centre of the British race; and that no skill or activity can long compete with the prodigious natural advantages of that country, in the hands of the same race; and that England, an old and exhausted island, must one day be contented, like other parents, to be strong only in her children. But this was a proposition which no Englishman of whatever condition can easily entertain.

We left the train at Salisbury and took a carriage to Amesbury, passing by Old Sarum, a bare, treeless hill, once containing the town which sent two members to Parliament—now, not a hut; and, arriving at Amesbury, stopped at the George Inn. After dinner we walked to Salisbury Plain. On the broad downs, under the gray sky, not a house was visible, nothing but Stonehenge, which looked like a group of brown dwarfs in the wide expanse—Stonehenge and the barrows, which rose like green bosses about the plain, and a few hayricks. On the top of a mountain, the old temple would not be more impressive. Far and wide a few shepherds with their flocks sprinkled the plain, and a bagman drove along the road. It looked as if the wide margin given in this crowded isle to this primeval temple were accorded by the veneration of the British race to the old egg out of which all their ecclesiastical structures and history had proceeded. Stonehenge is a circular colonnade with a diameter of a hundred feet, and enclosing a second and a third colonnade within. We walked round the stones and clambered over them, to wont ourselves with their strange aspect and groupings, and found a nook sheltered from the wind among them, where Carlyle lighted his cigar. It was pleasant to see that just this simplest of all simple structures—two upright stones and a lintel laid across—had long outstood all later churches and all history, and were like what is most permanent on the face of the planet: these, and the barrows—mere mounds (of which there are a hundred and sixty within a circle of three miles about Stonehenge), like the same mound on the plain of Troy, which still makes good to the passing mariner on Hellespont, the vaunt of Homer and the fame of Achilles. Within the enclosure grow buttercups, nettles, and all around, wild thyme, daisy, meadowsweet, gold-enrod thistle and the carpeting grass. Over us, larks were soaring and singing—as my friend said, "the larks which were hatched last year, and the wind which was hatched many thousand years ago." We counted and measured by paces the biggest stones, and soon knew as much as any man can suddenly know of the inscrutable temple. There are ninety-four stones, and there were once probably one hundred and sixty. The temple is circular and uncovered, and the situation fixed astronomically—the grand entrances, here and at Abury, being placed exactly northeast, "as all the gates of the old cavern temples are." How came the stones here? for these *sarsens*, or Druidical sandstones, are not found in this neighborhood. The *sacrificial stone*, as it is called, is the only one in all these blocks that can resist the action of fire, and as I read in the books, must have been brought one hundred and fifty miles.

On almost every stone we found the marks of the mineralogist's hammer and chisel. The nineteen smaller stones of the inner circle are of granite. I, who had just come from Professor Sedgwick's Cambride Museum of megatheria and mastodons, was ready to maintain that some cleverer elephants or mylodonta had borne off and laid these rocks one on another. Only the good beasts must have known how to cut a well-wrought tenon and mortise, and to smooth the surface of some of the stones. The chief mystery is, that any mystery should have been allowed to settle on so remarkable a monument, in a country on which all the muses have kept their eyes now for eighteen hundred years. We are not yet too late to learn much more than is known of this structure. Some diligent Fellowes or Layard will arrive, stone by stone, at the whole history, by that exhaustive British sense and perseverance, so whimsical in its choice of objects, which leaves its own Stonehenge or Choir Gaur to the rabbits, whilst it opens pyramids and uncovers Nineveh. Stonehenge, in virtue of the simplicity of its plan and its good preservation, is as if new and recent; and, a thousand years hence, men will thank this age for the accurate history. We walked in and out and took again and again a fresh look at the uncanny stones. The old sphinx put our petty differences of nationality out of sight. To these conscious stones we two pilgrims were alike known and near. We could equally well revere their old British meaning. My philosopher was subdued and gentle. In this quiet house of destiny he happens to say, "I plant cypresses wherever I go, and if I am in search of pain, I cannot go wrong." The spot, the gray blocks and their rude order, which refuses to be disposed of, suggested to him the flight of ages and the succession of religions. The old times of England impress Carlyle much: he reads little, he says, in these last years, but *Acta Sanctorum*; the fifty-three volumes of which are in the London Library. He finds all English history therein. He can see, as he reads, the old Saint of Iona sitting there and writing, a man to men. The *Acta Sanctorum* show plainly that the men of those times believed in God and in the immortality of the soul, as their abbeys and cathedrals testify: now, even the puritanism is all gone. London is pagan. He fancied that greater men had lived in England than any of her writers; and, in fact, about the time when those writers appeared, the last of these were already gone.

We left the mound in the twilight, with the design to return the next morning, and coming back two miles to our inn we were met by little showers, and late as it was, men and women were out attempting to protect their spread windows. The grass grows rank and dark in the showery England. At the inn, there was only milk for one cup of tea. When we called for more, the girl brought us three drops. My friend was annoyed, who stood for the credit of an English inn, and still more the next morning, by the dog-cart, sole procurable vehicle, in which we were to be sent to Wilton. I engaged the local antiquary, Mr. Brown, to go with us to Stonehenge, on our way, and show us what he knew of the "astronomical" and "sacrificial" stones. I stood on the last, and he pointed to the upright, or rather, inclined stone, called the "astronomical," and bade me notice that its top ranged with the sky-line. "Yes." Very well. Now, at the summer solstice, the sun rises exactly over the top of that stone, and, at the Druidical temple at Abury, there is also an astronomical stone, in the same relative position.

In the silence of tradition, this one relation to science becomes an important clew; but we were content to leave the problem with the rocks. Was this the "Giants' Dance," which Merlin brought from Killaraus, in Ireland, to be Uther Pendragon's monument to the British nobles whom Hengist slaughtered here, as Geoffrey of Monmouth relates? or was it a Roman work, as Inigo Jones explained to King James; or identical in design and style with the East Indian temples of the sun, as Davies in the Celtic Researches maintains? Of all the writers, Stukeley is the best. The heroic antiquary, charmed with the geometric perfections of his ruin, connects it with the oldest monuments and religion of the world, and with the courage of his tribe, does not stick to say, "the Deity who made the world by the scheme of Stonehenge." He finds that the *cursus* on Salisbury Plain stretches across the downs like a line of latitude upon the globe, and the meridian line of Stonehenge passes exactly through the middle of this *cursus*. But here is the high point of the theory: the Druids had the magnet; laid their courses by it; their cardinal points in Stonehenge, Ambresbury, and elsewhere, which vary a little from true east and west, followed the variations of the compass. The Druids were Phœnicians. The name of the magnet is *lapis Heracleus*, and Hercules was the god of the Phœnicians. Hercules, in the legend, drew his bow at the sun, and the sun-god gave him a golden cup, with which he sailed over the ocean. What was this, but a compass-box? This cup or little boat, in which the magnet was made to float on water and so show the north, was probably its first form, before it was suspended on a pin. But science was an *arcanum*, and, as Britain was a Phœnician secret, so they kept their compass a secret, and it was lost with the Tyrian commerce. The golden fleece again, of Jason, was the compass—a bit of loadstone, easily supposed to be the only one in the world, and therefore naturally awakening the cupidity and ambition of the young heroes of a maritime nation to join in an expedition to obtain possession of this wise stone. Hence the fable that the ship Argo was loquacious and oracular. There is also some curious coincidence in the names. Apollodorus makes *Magnes* the son of *Aeolus*, who married *Nais*. On hints like these, Stukeley builds again the grand colonnade into historic harmony, and computing backward by the known variations of the compass, bravely assigns the year 406 before Christ for the date of the temple.

For the difficulty of handling and carrying stones of this size, the like is done in all cities, every day, with no other aid than horse-power. I chanced to see, a year ago, men at work on the substructure of a house in Bowdoin Square, in Boston, swinging a block of granite of the size of the largest of the Stonehenge columns, with an ordinary derrick. The men were common masons, with paddies to help, nor did they think they were doing anything remarkable. I suppose there were as good men a thousand years ago. And we wonder how Stonehenge was built and forgotten. After spending half an hour on the spot, we set forth in our dog-cart over the downs for Wilton, Carlyle not suppressing some threats and evil omens on the proprietors, for keeping these broad plains a wretched sheep-walk when so many thousands of English men were hungry and wanted labor. But I heard afterwards that it is not an economy to cultivate this land, which only yields one crop on being broken up, and is then spoiled.

We came to Wilton and to Wilton Hall—the renowned seat of the Earls of Pembroke, a house known to Shakspeare and Massinger, the frequent home of Sir Philip Sidney, where he wrote the Arcadia; where he conversed with Lord Brooke, a man of deep thought, and a poet, who caused to be engraved on his tombstone, "Here lies Fulke Greville, Lord Brooke, the friend of Sir Philip Sidney." It is now the property of the Earl of Pembroke, and the residence of his brother, Sidney Herbert, Esq., and is esteemed a noble specimen of the English manor-hall. My friend had a letter from Mr. Herbert to his housekeeper, and the house was shown. The state drawing-room is a double cube, 30 feet high, by 30 feet wide, by 60 feet long: the adjoining room is a single cube, of 30 feet every way. Although these apartments and the long library were full of good family portraits, Vandykes and other; and though there were some good pictures, and a quadrangle cloister full of antique and modern statuary—to which Carlyle, catalogue in hand, did all too much justice—yet the eye was still drawn to the windows, to a magnificent lawn, on which grew the finest cedars in England. I had not seen more charming grounds. We went out, and walked over the estate. We crossed a bridge built by Inigo Jones, over a stream of which the gardener did not know the name (Qu. Alph?); watched the deer; climbed to the lonely sculptured summer-house, on a hill backed by a wood; came down into the Italian garden and into a French pavilion garnished with French busts; and so again to the house, where we found a table laid for us with bread, meats, peaches, grapes and wine.

On leaving Wilton House, we took the coach for Salisbury. The Cathedral, which was finished six hundred years ago, has even a spruce and modern air, and its spire is the highest in England. I know not why, but I had been more struck with one of no fame, at Coventry, which rises three hundred feet from the ground, with the lightness of a mullein plant, and not at all implicated with the church. Salisbury is now esteemed the culmination of the Gothic art in England, as the buttresses are fully unmasked and honestly detailed from the sides of the pile. The interior of the Cathedral is obstructed by the organ in the

. . . .

middle, acting like a screen. I know not why in real architecture the hunger of the eye for length of line is so rarely gratified. The rule of art is that a colonnade is more beautiful the longer it is, and that *ad infinitum*. And the nave of a church is seldom so long that it need be divided by a screen.

We loitered in the church, outside the choir, whilst service was said. Whilst we listened to the organ, my friend remarked, the music is good, and yet not quite religious, but somewhat as if a monk were panting to some fine Queen of Heaven. Carlyle was unwilling, and we did not ask to have the choir shown us, but returned to our inn, after seeing another old church of the place. We passed in the train Clarendon Park, but could see little but the edge of a wood, though Carlyle had wished to pay closer attention to the birthplace of the Decrees of Clarendon. At Bishopstoke we stopped, and found Mr. H., who received us in his carriage, and took us to his house at Bishops Waltham.

On Sunday we had much discourse, on a very rainy day. My friends asked, whether there were any Americans?—any with an American idea—any theory of the right future of that country? Thus challenged, I bethought myself neither of caucuses nor congress, neither of presidents nor of cabinet-ministers, nor of such as would make of America another Europe. I thought only of the simplest and purest minds; I said, "Certainly yes—but those who hold it are fanatics of a dream which I should hardly care to relate to your English ears, to which it might be only ridiculous—and yet it is the only true." So I opened the dogma of no-government and non-resistance, and anticipated the objections and the fun, and procured a kind of hearing for it. I said, it is true that I have never seen in any country a man of sufficient valor to stand for this truth, and yet it is plain to me that no less valor than this can command my respect. I can easily see the bankruptcy of the vulgar musket-worship—though great men be musket-worshippers—and 't is certain as God liveth, the gun that does not need another gun, the law of love and justice alone, can effect a clean revolution. I fancied that one or two of my anecdotes made some impression on Carlyle, and I insisted that the manifest absurdity of the view to English feasibility could make no difference to a gentleman; that as to our secure tenure of our mutton-chop and spinach in London or in Boston, the soul might quote Talleyrand, *"Monsieur, je n'en vois pas la nécessité."* As I had thus taken in the conversation the saint's part, when dinner was announced, Carlyle refused to go out before me—"he was altogether too wicked." I planted my back against the wall, and our host wittily rescued us from the dilemma, by saying he was the wickedest and would walk out first, then Carlyle followed, and I went last.

On the way to Winchester, whither our host accompanied us in the afternoon, my friends asked many questions respecting American landscapes, forests, houses—my house, for example. It is not easy to answer these queries well. There, I thought, in America, lies nature sleeping, overgrowing, almost conscious, too much by half for man in the picture, and so giving a certain tristesse, like the rank vegetation of swamps and forests seen at night, steeped in dews and rains, which it loves; and on it man seems not able to make much impression. There, in that great sloven continent, in high Alleghany pastures, in the sea-wide sky-skirted prairie, still sleeps and murmurs and hides the great mother, long since driven away from the trim hedge-rows and over-cultivated garden of England. And, in England, I am quite too sensible of this. Every one is on his good behavior and must be dressed for dinner at six. So I put off my friends with very inadequate details, as best I could.

Just before entering Winchester we stopped at the Church of Saint Cross, and after looking through the quaint antiquity, we demanded a piece of bread and a draught of beer, which the founder, Henry de Blois, in 1136, commanded should be given to every one who should ask it at the gate. We had both, from the old couple who take care of the church. Some twenty people every day, they said, make the same demand. This hospitality of seven hundred years' standing did not hinder Carlyle from pronouncing a malediction on the priest who receives £2000 a year, that were meant for the poor, and spends a pittance on this small-beer and crumbs.

In the Cathedral I was gratified, at least by the ample dimensions. The length of line exceeds that of any other English church; being 556 feet, by 250 in breadth of transept. I think I prefer this church to all I have seen, except Westminster and York. Here was Canute buried, and here Alfred the Great was crowned and buried, and here the Saxon kings; and, later, in his own church, William of Wykeham. It is very old: part of the crypt into which we went down and saw the Saxon and

Norman arches of the old church on which the present stands, was built fourteen or fifteen hundred years ago. Sharon Turner, in his History of the Anglo-Saxons, says, "Alfred was buried at Winchester, in the Abbey he had founded there, but his remains were removed by Henry I to the new Abbey in the meadows at Hyde, on the northern quarter of the city, and laid under the high altar. The building was destroyed at the Reformation, and what is left of Alfred's body now lies covered by modern buildings, or buried in the ruins of the old." William of Wykeham's shrine tomb was unlocked for us, and Carlyle took hold of the recumbent statue's marble hands and patted them affectionately, for he rightly values the brave man who built Windsor and this Cathedral and the School here and New College at Oxford. But it was growing late in the afternoon. Slowly we left the old house, and parting with our host, we took the train for London.

CHAPTER XVII
PERSONAL

IN THESE COMMENTS on an old journey, now revised after seven busy years have much changed men and things in England, I have abstained from reference to persons, except in the last chapter and in one or two cases where the fame of the parties seemed to have given the public a property in all that concerned them. I must further allow myself a few notices, if only as an acknowledgment of debts that cannot be paid. My journeys were cheered by so much kindness from new friends, that my impression of the island is bright with agreeable memories both of public societies and of households: and, what is nowhere better found than in England, a cultivated person fitly surrounded by a happy home, with

"Honor, love, obedience, troops of friends,"

is of all institutions the best. At the landing in Liverpool I found my Manchester correspondent awaiting me, a gentleman whose kind reception was followed by a train of friendly and effective attentions which never rested whilst I remained in the country. A man of sense and of letters, the editor of a powerful local journal, he added to solid virtues an infinite sweetness and *bonhommie*. There seemed a pool of honey about his heart which lubricated all his speech and action with fine jets of mead. An equal good fortune attended many later accidents of my journey, until the sincerity of English kindness ceased to surprise. My visit fell in the fortunate days when Mr. Bancroft was the American Minister in London, and at his house, or through his good offices, I had easy access to excellent persons and to privileged places. At the house of Mr. Carlyle, I met persons eminent in society and in letters. The privileges of the Athenæum and of the Reform Clubs were hospitably opened to me, and I found much advantage in the circles of the "Geologic," the "Antiquarian" and the "Royal" Societies. Every day in London gave me new opportunities of meeting men and women who give splendor to society. I saw Rogers, Hallam, Macaulay, Milnes, Milman, Barry Cornwall, Dickens, Thackeray, Tennyson, Leigh Hunt, D'Israeli, Helps, Wilkinson, Bailey, Kenyon and Forster: the younger poets, Clough, Arnold and Patmore; and among the men of science, Robert Brown, Owen, Sedgwick, Faraday, Buckland, Lyell, De la Beche, Hooker, Carpenter, Babbage and Edward Forbes. It was my privilege also to converse with Miss Baillie, with Lady Morgan, with Mrs. Jameson and Mrs. Somerville. A finer hospitality made many private houses not less known and dear. It is not in distinguished circles that wisdom and elevated characters are usually found, or, if found, they are not confined thereto; and my recollections of the best hours go back to private conversations in different parts of the kingdom, with persons little known. Nor am I insensible to the courtesy which frankly opened to me some noble mansions, if I do not adorn my page with their names. Among the privileges of London, I recall with pleasure two or three signal days, one at Kew, where Sir William Hooker showed me all the riches of the vast botanic garden; one at the Museum, where Sir Charles Fellowes explained in detail the history of his Ionic trophy-monument; and still another, on which Mr. Owen accompanied my countryman Mr. H. and myself through the Hunterian Museum.

The like frank hospitality, bent on real service, I found among the great and the humble, wherever I went; in Birmingham, in Oxford, in Leicester, in Nottingham, in Sheffield, in Manchester, in Liverpool. At Edinburgh, through the kindness of Dr. Samuel Brown, I made the acquaintance of De Quincey, of Lord Jeffrey, of Wilson, of Mrs. Crowe, of the Messrs. Chambers, and of a man of high character and genius, the short-lived painter, David Scott.

At Ambleside in March, 1848, I was for a couple of days the guest of Miss Martineau, then newly returned from her Egyptian tour. On Sunday afternoon I accompanied her to Rydal Mount. And as I have recorded a visit to Wordsworth, many years before, I must not forget this second interview. We found Mr. Wordsworth asleep on the sofa. He was at first silent and indisposed, as an old man suddenly waked before he had ended his nap; but soon became full of talk on the French news. He was nationally bitter on the French; bitter on Scotchmen, too. No Scotchman, he said, can write English. He detailed the two models, on one or the other of which all the sentences of the historian Robertson are framed. Nor could Jeffrey, nor the Edinburgh Reviewers write English, nor can * * *, who is a pest to the English tongue. Incidentally he added, Gibbon cannot write English. The Edinburgh Review wrote what would tell and what would sell. It had however changed the tone of its literary criticism from the time when a certain letter was written to the editor by Coleridge. Mrs. W. had the Editor's answer in her possession. Tennyson he thinks a right poetic genius, though with some affectation. He had thought an elder brother of Tennyson at first the better poet, but must now reckon Alfred the true one. . . . In speaking of I know not what style, he said, "to be sure, it was the manner, but then you know the matter always comes out of the manner." . . . He thought Rio Janeiro the best place in the world for a great capital city. . . . We talked of English national character. I told him it was not creditable that no one in all the country knew anything of Thomas Taylor, the Platonist, whilst in every American library his translations are found. I said, If Plato's Republic were published in England as a new book to-day, do you think it would find any readers?—he confessed it would not: "And yet," he added after a pause, with that complacency which never deserts a true-born Englishman, "and yet we have embodied it all."

His opinions of French, English, Irish and Scotch, seemed rashly formulized from little anecdotes of what had befallen himself and members of his family, in a diligence or stagecoach. His face sometimes lighted up, but his conversation was not marked by special force or elevation. Yet perhaps it is a high compliment to the cultivation of the English generally, when we find such a man not distinguished. He had a healthy look, with a weather-beaten face, his face corrugated, especially the large nose.

Miss Martineau, who lived near him, praised him to me not for his poetry, but for thrift and economy; for having afforded to his country-neighbors an example of a modest household where comfort and culture were secured without any display. She said that in his early housekeeping at the cottage where he first lived, he was accustomed to offer his friends bread and plainest fare; if they wanted anything more, they must pay him for their board. It was the rule of the house. I replied that it evinced English pluck more than any anecdote I knew. A gentleman in the neighborhood told the story of Walter Scott's staying once for a week with Wordsworth, and slipping out every day, under pretence of a walk, to the Swan Inn for a cold cut and porter; and one day passing with Wordsworth the inn, he was betrayed by the landlord's asking him if he had come for his porter. Of course this trait would have another look in London, and there you will hear from different literary men that Wordsworth had no personal friend, that he was not amiable, that he was parsimonious, etc. Landor, always generous, says that he never praised anybody. A gentleman in London showed me a watch that once belonged to Milton, whose initials are engraved on its face. He said he once showed this to Wordsworth, who took it in one hand, then drew out his own watch and held it up with the other, before the company, but no one making the expected remark, he put back his own in silence. I do not attach much importance to the disparagement of Wordsworth among London scholars. Who reads him well will know that in following the strong bent of his genius, he was careless of the many, careless also of the few, self-assured that he should "create the taste by which he is to be enjoyed." He lived long enough to witness the revolution he had wrought, and to "see what he foresaw." There are torpid places in his mind, there is something hard and sterile in his poetry, want of grace and variety, want of due catholicity and cosmopolitan scope: he had conformities to English politics and traditions; he had egotistic puerilities in the choice and treatment of his subjects; but let us say of him that, alone in his time, he treated the human mind well, and with an absolute trust. His adherence to his poetic creed rested on real inspirations. The Ode on Immortality is the high-water mark which the intellect has reached in this age. New means were employed, and new realms added to the empire of the muse, by his courage.

CHAPTER XVIII

RESULT

ENGLAND is the best of actual nations. It is no ideal framework, it is an old pile built in different ages, with repairs, additions and makeshifts; but you see the poor best you have got. London is the epitome of our times, and the Rome of to-day. Broad-fronted, broad-bottomed Teutons, they stand in solid phalanx foursquare to the points of compass; they constitute the modern world, they have earned their vantage ground and held it through ages of adverse possession. They are well marked and differing from other leading races. England is tenderhearted. Rome was not. England is not so public in its bias; private life is its place of honor. Truth in private life, untruth in public, marks these home-loving men. Their political conduct is not decided by general views, but by internal intrigues and personal and family interest. They cannot readily see beyond England. The history of Rome and Greece, when written by their scholars, degenerates into English party pamphlets. They cannot see beyond England, nor in England can they transcend the interests of the governing classes. "English principles" mean a primary regard to the interests of property. England, Scotland and Ireland combine to check the colonies. England and Scotland combine to check Irish manufactures and trade. England rallies at home to check Scotland. In England, the strong classes check the weaker. In the home population of near thirty millions, there are but one million voters. The Church punishes dissent, punishes education. Down to a late day, marriages performed by dissenters were illegal. A bitter class-legislation gives power to those who are rich enough to buy a law. The game-laws are a proverb of oppression. Pauperism incrusts and clogs the state, and in hard times becomes hideous. In bad seasons, the porridge was diluted. Multitudes lived miserably by shell-fish and sea-ware. In cities, the children are trained to beg, until they shall be old enough to rob. Men and women were convicted of poisoning scores of children for burial-fees. In Irish districts, men deteriorated in size and shape, the nose sunk, the gums were exposed, with diminished brain and brutal form. During the Australian emigration, multitudes were rejected by the commissioners as being too emaciated for useful colonists. During the Russian war, few of those that offered as recruits were found up to the medical standard, though it had been reduced.

The foreign policy of England, though ambitious and lavish of money, has not often been generous or just. It has a principal regard to the interest of trade, checked however by the aristocratic bias of the ambassador, which usually puts him in sympathy with the continental Courts. It sanctioned the partition of Poland, it betrayed Genoa, Sicily, Parma, Greece, Turkey, Rome and Hungary.

Some public regards they have. They have abolished slavery in the West Indies and put an end to human sacrifices in the East. At home they have a certain statute hospitality. England keeps open doors, as a trading country must, to all nations. It is one of their fixed ideas, and wrathfully supported by their laws in unbroken sequence for a thousand years. In *Magne Charta* it was ordained that all "merchants shall have safe and secure conduct to go out and come into England, and to stay there, and to pass as well by land as by water, to buy and sell by the ancient allowed customs, without any evil toll, except in time of war, or when they shall be of any nation at war with us." It is a statute and obliged hospitality and peremptorily maintained. But this shop-rule had one magnificent effect. It extends its cold unalterable courtesy to political exiles of every opinion, and is a fact which might give additional light to that portion of the planet seen from the farthest star. But this perfunctory hospitality puts no sweetness into their unaccommodating manners, no check on that puissant nationality which makes their existence incompatible with all that is not English.

What we must say about a nation is a superficial dealing with symptoms. We cannot go deep enough into the biography of the spirit who never throws himself entire into one hero, but delegates his energy in parts or spasms to vicious and defective individuals. But the wealth of the source is seen in the plenitude of English nature. What variety of power and talent; what facility and plenteousness of knighthood, lordship, ladyship, royalty, loyalty; what a proud chivalry is indicated in "Collins's Peerage," through eight hundred years! What dignity resting on what reality and stoutness! What courage in war, what sinew in labor, what cunning workmen, what inventors and engineers, what seamen and pilots, what clerks and scholars! No one man and no few men can represent them. It is a people of myriad personalities.

Their many-headedness is owing to the advantageous position of the middle class, who are always the source of letters and science. Hence the vast plenty of their æsthetic production. As they are many-headed, so they are many-nationed: their colonization annexes archipelagoes and continents, and their speech seems destined to be the universal language of men. I have noted the reserve of power in the English temperament. In the island, they never let out all the length of all the reins, there is no Berserker rage, no abandonment or ecstasy of will or intellect, like that of the Arabs in the time of Mahomet, or like that which intoxicated France in 1789. But who would see the uncoiling of that tremendous spring, the explosion of their well-husbanded forces, must follow the swarms which pouring now for two hundred years from the British islands, have sailed and rode and traded and planted through all climates, mainly following the belt of empire, the temperate zones, carrying the Saxon seed, with its instinct for liberty and law, for arts and for thought—acquiring under some skies a more electric energy than the native air allows—to the conquest of the globe. Their colonial policy, obeying the necessities of a vast empire, has become liberal. Canada and Australia have been contented with substantial independence. They are expiating the wrongs of India by benefits; first, in works for the irrigation of the peninsula, and roads, and telegraphs; and secondly, in the instruction of the people, to qualify them for self-government, when the British power shall be finally called home.

Their mind is in a state of arrested development—a divine cripple like Vulcan; a blind *savant* like Huber and Sanderson. They do not occupy themselves on matters of general and lasting import, but on a corporeal civilization, on goods that perish in the using. But they read with good intent, and what they learn they incarnate. The English mind turns every abstraction it can receive into a portable utensil, or a working institution. Such is their tenacity and such their practical turn, that they hold all they gain. Hence we say that only the English race can be trusted with freedom—freedom which is double-edged and dangerous to any but the wise and robust. The English designate the kingdoms emulous of free institutions, as the sentimental nations. Their culture is not an outside varnish, but is thorough and secular in families and the race. They are oppressive with their temperament, and all the more that they are refined. I have sometimes seen them walk with my countrymen when I was forced to allow them every advantage, and their companions seemed bags of bones.

There is cramp limitation in their habit of thought, sleepy routine, and a tortoise's instinct to hold hard to the ground with his claws, lest he should be thrown on his back. There is a drag of inertia which resists reform in every shape—law-reform, army-reform, extension of suffrage, Jewish franchise, Catholic emancipation—the abolition of slavery, of impressment, penal code and entails. They praise this drag, under the formula that it is the excellence of the British constitution that no law can anticipate the public opinion. These poor tortoises must hold hard, for they feel no wings sprouting at their shoulders. Yet somewhat divine warms at their heart and waits a happier hour. It hides in their sturdy will. "Will," said the old philosophy, "is the measure of power," and personality is the token of this race. *Quid vult valde vult.* What they do they do with a will. You cannot account for their success by their Christianity, commerce, charter, common law, Parliament, or letters, but by the contumacious sharp-tongued energy of English *naturel,* with a poise impossible to disturb, which makes all these its instruments. They are slow and reticent, and are like a dull good horse which lets every nag pass him, but with whip and spur will run down every racer in the field. They are right in their feeling, though wrong in their speculation.

The feudal system survives in the steep inequality of property and privilege, in the limited franchise, in the social barriers which confine patronage and promotion to a caste, and still more in the submissive ideas pervading these people. The fagging of the schools is repeated in the social classes. An Englishman shows no mercy to those below him in the social scale, as he looks for none from those above him; any forbearance from his superiors surprises him, and they suffer in his good opinion. But the feudal system can be seen with less pain on large historical grounds. It was pleaded in mitigation of the rotten borough, that it worked well, that substantial justice was done. Fox, Burke, Pitt, Erskine, Wilberforce, Sheridan, Romilly, or whatever national man, were by this means sent to Parliament, when their return by large constituencies would have been doubtful. So now we say that the right measures of England are the men it bred; that it has yielded more able men in five hundred years than any other nation; and, though we must not play Providence and balance the chances of producing ten great men against the comfort of ten thousand mean men, yet retrospectively, we may strike the balance and prefer one Alfred, one Shakspeare, one Milton, one Sidney, one Raleigh, one Wellington, to a million foolish democrats.

The American system is more democratic, more humane; yet the American people do not yield better or more able men, or more inventions or books or benefits than the English. Congress is not wiser or better than Parliament. France has abolished its suffocating old *régime*, but is not recently marked by any more wisdom or virtue.

The power of performance has not been exceeded—the creation of value. The English have given importance to individuals, a principal end and fruit of every society. Every man is allowed and encouraged to be what he is, and is guarded in the indulgence of his whim. "Magna Charta," said Rushworth, "is such a fellow that he will have no sovereign." By this general activity and by this sacredness of individuals, they have in seven hundred years evolved the principles of freedom. It is the land of patriots, martyrs, sages and bards, and if the ocean out of which it emerged should wash it away, it will be remembered as an island famous for immortal laws, for the announcements of original right which make the stone tables of liberty.

CHAPTER XIX
SPEECH AT MANCHESTER

A FEW DAYS after my arrival at Manchester, in November, 1847, the Manchester Athenæum gave its annual Banquet in the Free-Trade Hall. With other guests, I was invited to be present and to address the company. In looking over recently a newspaper-report of my remarks, I incline to reprint it, as fitly expressing the feeling with which I entered England, and which agrees well enough with the more deliberate results of better acquaintance recorded in the foregoing pages. Sir Archibald Alison, the historian, presided, and opened the meeting with a speech. He was followed by Mr. Cobden, Lord Brackley and others, among whom was Mr. Cruikshank, one of the contributors to Punch. Mr. Dickens's letter of apology for his absence was read. Mr. Jerrold, who had been announced, did not appear. On being introduced to the meeting I said—

Mr. Chairman and Gentlemen: It is pleasant to me to meet this great and brilliant company, and doubly pleasant to see the faces of so many distinguished persons on this platform. But I have known all these persons already. When I was at home, they were as near to me as they are to you. The arguments of the League and its leader are known to all the friends of free trade. The gayeties and genius, the political, the social, the parietal wit of Punch go duly every fortnight to every boy and girl in Boston and New York. Sir, when I came to sea, I found the History of Europe, by Sir A. Alison, on the ship's cabin table, the property of the captain—a sort of programme or play-bill to tell the seafaring New Englander what he shall find on his landing here. And as for Dombey, sir, there is no land where paper exists to print on, where it is not found; no man who can read, that does not read it, and, if he cannot, he finds some charitable pair of eyes that can, and hears it.

But these things are not for me to say; these compliments, though true, would better come from one who felt and understood these merits more. I am not here to exchange civilities with you, but rather to speak of that which I am sure interests these gentlemen more than their own praises; of that which is good in holidays and working-days, the same in one century and in another century. That which lures a solitary American in the woods with the wish to see England, is the moral peculiarity of the Saxon race—its commanding sense of right and wrong, the love and devotion to that—this is the imperial trait, which arms them with the sceptre of the globe. It is this which lies at the foundation of that aristocratic character, which certainly wanders into strange vagaries, so that its origin is often lost sight of, but which, if it should lose this, would find itself paralyzed; and in trade and in the mechanic's shop, gives that honesty in performance, that thoroughness and solidity of work which is a national characteristic. This conscience is one element, and the other is that loyal adhesion, that habit of friendship, that homage of man to man, running through all classes— the electing of worthy persons to a certain fraternity, to acts of kindness and warm and stanch support, from year to year, from youth to age—which is alike lovely and honorable to those who render and those who receive it; which stands in strong contrast with the superficial attachments of other races, their excessive courtesy and short-lived connection.

You will think me very pedantic, gentlemen, but holiday though it be, I have not the smallest interest in any holiday except as it celebrates real and not pretended joys; and I think it just, in this time of gloom and commercial disaster, of affliction and beggary in these districts, that, on these very accounts I speak of, you should not fail to keep your literary anniversary. I seem to hear you say, that for all that is come and gone yet, we will not reduce by one chaplet or one oak-leaf the braveries of our annual feast. For I must tell you, I was given to understand in my childhood that the British island from which my forefathers came was no lotus-garden, no paradise of serene sky and roses and music and merriment all the year round, no, but a cold, foggy, mournful country, where nothing grew well in the open air but robust men and virtuous women, and these of a wonderful fibre and endurance; that their best parts were slowly revealed; their virtues did not come out until they quarrelled; they did not strike twelve the first time; good lovers, good haters, and you could know little about them till you had seen them long, and little good of them till you had seen them in action; that in prosperity they were moody and dumpish, but in adversity they were grand. Is it not true, sir, that the wise ancients did not praise the ship parting with flying colors from the port, but only that brave sailor which came back with torn sheets and battered sides, stript of her banners, but having ridden out the storm? And so, gentlemen, I feel in regard to this aged England, with the possessions, honors and trophies, and also with the infirmities of a thousand years gathering around her, irretrievably committed as she now is to many old customs which cannot be suddenly changed; pressed upon by the transitions of trade and new and all incalculable modes, fabrics, arts, machines and competing populations. I see her not dispirited, not weak, but well remembering that she has seen dark days before—indeed with a kind of instinct that she sees a little better in a cloudy day, and that in storm of battle and calamity she has a secret vigor and a pulse like a cannon. I see her in her old age, not decrepit, but young and still daring to believe in her power of endurance and expansion. Seeing this, I say, All hail! mother of nations, mother of heroes, with strength still equal to the time; still wise to entertain and swift to execute the policy which mind and heart of mankind requires in the present hour, and thus only hospitable to the foreigner and truly a home to the thoughtful and generous who are born in the soil. So be it! so let it be! If it be not so, if the courage of England goes with the chances of a commercial crisis, I will go back to the capes of Massachusetts and my own Indian stream, and say to my countrymen, the old race are all gone, and the elasticity and hope of mankind must henceforth remain on the Alleghany ranges, or nowhere.

CONDUCT OF LIFE

[Conduct of Life *was published in 1860. Most of the material in this book had served as a course of lectures, first in Pittsburgh in 1851, later in Boston and then at various places throughout the country. By this time Emerson was well known everywhere in America and was in constant demand. He was traveling extensively in the East and in the Middle West, which was then a raw and growing part of the country. The period between his return from England in 1848 and the publication of this book in 1860 was full of great political unrest and Emerson was unwillingly drawn into it.* Conduct of Life *was well received and sold rapidly. Selected for this volume are the essays* "Wealth" *and* "Culture."]

WEALTH

Who shall tell what did befall,
Far away in time, when once,
Over the lifeless ball,
Hung idle stars and suns?
What god the element obeyed?
Wings of what wind the lichen bore,
Wafting the puny seeds of power,
Which, lodged in rock, the rock
     abrade?
And well the primal pioneer
Knew the strong task to it assigned,
Patient through Heaven's enormous
     year
To build in matter home for mind.
From air the creeping centuries drew
The matted thicket low and wide,
This must the leaves of ages strew
The granite slab to clothe and hide,
Ere wheat can wave its golden
     pride.
What smiths, and in what furnace,
     rolled
(In dizzy æons dim and mute
The reeling brain can ill compute)
Copper and iron, lead, and gold?
What oldest star the fame can save
Of races perishing to pave
The planet with a floor of lime?
Dust is their pyramid and mole:
Who saw what ferns and palms
     were pressed
Under the tumbling mountain's
     breast,

In the safe herbal of the coal?
But when the quarried means were
     piled,
All is waste and worthless, till
Arrives the wise selecting will,
And, out of slime and chaos, Wit
Draws the threads of fair and fit.
Then temples rose, and towns, and
     marts,
The shop of toil, the hall of arts;
Then flew the sail across the seas
To feed the North from tropic trees;
The storm-wind wove, the torrent
     span,
Where they were bid the rivers ran;
New slaves fulfilled the poet's
     dream,
Galvanic wire, strong-shouldered
     steam.
Then docks were built, and crops
     were stored,
And ingots added to the hoard.
But, though light-headed man forget,
Remembering Matter pays her debt:
Still, through her motes and masses,
     draw
Electric thrills and ties of Law,
Which bind the strengths of Nature
     wild
To the conscience of a child.

As soon as a stranger is introduced into any company, one of the first questions which all wish to have answered, is, How does that man get his living? And with reason. He is no whole man until he knows how to earn a blameless livelihood. Society is barbarous until every industrious man can get his living without dishonest customs.

Every man is a consumer, and ought to be a producer. He fails to make his place good in the world unless he not only pays his debt but also adds something to the common wealth. Nor can he do justice to his genius without making some larger demand on the world than a bare subsistence. He is by constitution expensive, and needs to be rich.

Wealth has its source in applications of the mind to nature, from the rudest strokes of spade and axe up to the last secrets of art. Intimate ties subsist between thought and all production; because a better order is equivalent to vast amounts of brute labor. The forces and the resistances are nature's, but the mind acts in bringing things from where they abound to where they are wanted; in wise combining; in directing the practice of the useful arts, and in the creation of finer values by fine art, by eloquence, by song, or the reproductions of memory. Wealth is in applications of mind to nature; and the art of getting rich consists not in industry, much less in saving, but in a better order, in timeliness, in being at the right spot. One man has stronger arms or longer legs; another sees by the course of streams and growth of markets where land will be wanted, makes a clearing to the river, goes to sleep and wakes up rich. Steam is no stronger now than it was a hundred years ago; but is put to better use. A clever fellow was acquainted with the expansive force of steam; he also saw the wealth of heat and grass rotting in Michigan. Then he cunningly screws on the steam-pipe to the wheat-crop. Puff now, O Steam! The steam puffs and expands as before, but this time it is dragging all Michigan at its back to hungry New York and hungry England. Coal lay in ledges under the ground since the Flood, until a laborer with pick and windlass brings it to the surface. We may well call it black diamonds. Every basket is power and civilization. For coal is a portable climate. It carries the heat of the tropics to Labrador and the polar circle; and it is the means of transporting itself whithersoever it is wanted. Watt and Stephenson whispered in the ear of mankind their secret, that *a half-ounce of coal will draw two tons a mile*, and coal carries coal, by rail and by boat, to make Canada as warm as Calcutta; and with its comfort brings its industrial power.

. . . .

When the farmer's peaches are taken from under the tree and carried into town, they have a new look and a hundredfold value over the fruit which grew on the same bough and lies fulsomely on the ground. The craft of the merchant is this bringing a thing from where it abounds to where it is costly.

Wealth begins in a tight roof that keeps the rain and wind out; in a good pump that yields you plenty of sweet water; in two suits of clothes, so to change your dress when you are wet; in dry sticks to burn, in a good double-wick lamp, and three meals; in a horse or a locomotive to cross the land, in a boat to cross the sea; in tools to work with, in books to read; and so in giving on all sides by tools and auxiliaries the greatest possible extension to our powers; as if it added feet and hands and eyes and blood, length to the day, and knowledge and good will.

Wealth begins with these articles of necessity. And here we must recite the iron law which nature thunders in these northern climates. First she requires that each man should feed himself. If happily his fathers have left him no inheritance, he must go to work, and by making his wants less or his gains more, he must draw himself out of that state of pain and insult in which she forces the beggar to lie. She gives him no rest until this is done; she starves, taunts and torments him, takes away warmth, laughter, sleep, friends and daylight, until he has fought his way to his own loaf. Then, less peremptorily but still with sting enough, she urges him to the acquisition of such things as belong to him. Every warehouse and shop-window, every fruit-tree, every thought of every hour opens a new want to him which it concerns his power and dignity to gratify. It is of no use to argue the wants down: the philosophers have laid the greatness of man in making his wants few, but will a man content himself with a hut and a handful of dried pease? He is born to be rich. He is thoroughly related; and is tempted out by his appetites and fancies to the conquest of this and that piece of nature, until he finds his well-being in the use of his planet, and of more planets than his own. Wealth requires, besides the crust of bread and the roof—the freedom of the city, the freedom of the earth, travelling, machinery, the benefits of science, music and fine arts, the best culture and the best company. He is the rich man who can avail himself of all men's faculties. He is the richest man who knows how to draw a benefit from the labors of the greatest number of men, of men in distant countries and in past times. The same correspondence that is between thirst in the stomach and water in the spring, exists between the whole of man and the whole of nature. The elements offer their service to him. The sea, washing the equator and the poles, offers its perilous aid and the power and empire that follow it—day by day to his craft and audacity. "Beware of me," it says, "but if you can hold me, I am the key to all the lands." Fire offers, on its side, an equal power. Fire, steam, lightning, gravity, ledges of rock, mines of iron, lead, quicksilver, tin and gold; forests of all woods; fruits of all climates; animals of all habits; the powers of tillage; the fabrics of his chemic laboratory; the webs of his loom; the masculine draught of his locomotive; the talismans of the machine-shop; all grand and subtile things, minerals, gases, ethers, passions, war, trade, government—are his natural playmates, and according to the excellence of the machinery in each human being is his attraction for the instruments he is to employ. The world is his tool-chest, and he is successful, or his education is carried on just so far, as is the marriage of his faculties with nature, or the degree in which he takes up things into himself.

The strong race is strong on these terms. The Saxons are the merchants of the world; now, for a thousand years, the leading race, and by nothing more than their quality of personal independence, and in its special modification, pecuniary independence. No reliance for bread and games on the government; no clanship, no patriarchal style of living by the revenues of a chief, no marrying-on, no system of clientship suits them; but every man must pay his scot. The English are prosperous and peaceable, with their habit of considering that every man must take care of himself and has himself to thank if he do not maintain and improve his position in society.

The subject of economy mixes itself with morals, inasmuch as it is a peremptory point of virtue that a man's independence be secured. Poverty demoralizes. A man in debt is so far a slave, and Wall Street thinks it easy for a *millionaire* to be a man of his word, a man of honor, but that in failing circumstances no man can be relied on to keep his integrity. And when one observes in the hotels and palaces of our Atlantic capitals the habit of expense, the riot of the senses, the absence of bonds, clanship, fellow-feeling of any kind—he feels that when a man or a woman is driven to the wall, the chances of integrity are frightfully diminished; as if virtue were coming to be a luxury which few could afford, or, as Burke said, "at a market almost too high for humanity." He may fix his inventory of necessities and of enjoyments on what scale he pleases, but if he wishes the power and privilege of thought, the chalking out his own career and having society on his own terms, he must bring his wants within his proper power to satisfy.

The manly part is to do with might and main what you can do. The world is full of fops who never did anything and who had persuaded beauties and men of genius to wear their fop livery; and these will deliver the fop opinion, that it is not respectable to be seen earning a living; that it is much more respectable to spend without earning; and this doctrine of the snake will come also from the elect sons of light; for wise men are not wise at all hours, and will speak five times from their taste or their humor, to once from their reason. The brave workman, who might betray his feeling of it in his manners, if he do not succumb in his practice, must replace the grace or elegance forfeited, by the merit of the work done. No matter whether he makes shoes, or statues, or laws. It is the privilege of any human work which is well done to invest the doer with a certain haughtiness. He can well afford not to conciliate, whose faithful work will answer for him. The mechanic at his bench carries a quiet heart and assured manners, and deals on even terms with men of any condition. The artist has made his picture so true that it disconcerts criticism. The statue is so beautiful that it contracts no stain from the market, but makes the market a silent gallery for itself. The case of the young lawyer was pitiful to disgust—a paltry matter of buttons or tweezer-cases; but the determined youth saw in it an aperture to insert his dangerous wedges, made the insignificance of the thing forgotten, and gave fame by his sense and energy to the name and affairs of the Tittleton snuff-box factory.

Society in large towns is babyish, and wealth is made a toy. The life of pleasure is so ostentatious that a shallow observer must believe that this is the agreed best use of wealth, and, whatever is pretended, it ends in cosseting. But if this were the main use of surplus capital, it would bring us to barricades, burned towns and tomahawks, presently. Men of sense esteem wealth to be the assimilation of nature to themselves, the converting of the sap and juices of the planet to the incarnation and nutriment of their design. Power is what they want, not candy—power to execute their design, power to give legs and feet, form and actuality to their thought; which, to a clear-sighted man, appears the end for which the universe exists, and all its resources might be well applied. Columbus thinks that the sphere is a problem for practical navigation as well as for closet geometry, and looks on all kings and peoples as cowardly landsmen until they dare fit him out. Few men on the planet have more truly belonged to it. But he was forced to leave much of his map blank. His successors inherited his map, and inherited his fury to complete it.

So the men of the mine, telegraph, mill, map and survey—the monomaniacs who talk up their project in marts and offices and entreat men to subscribe—how did our factories get built? how did North America get netted with iron rails, except by the importunity of these orators who dragged all the prudent men in? Is party the madness of many for the gain of a few? This *speculative* genius is the madness of a few for the gain of the world. The projectors are sacrificed, but the public is the gainer. Each of these idealists, working after his thought, would make it tyrannical, if he could. He is met and antagonized by other speculators as hot as he. The equilibrium is preserved by these counteractions, as one tree keeps down another in the forest, that it may not absorb all the sap in the ground. And the supply in nature of rail-road-presidents, copper-miners, grand-junctioners, smoke-burners, fire-annihilators, etc., is limited by the same law which keeps the proportion in the supply of carbon, of alum, and of hydrogen.

To be rich is to have a ticket of admission to the master-works and chief men of each race. It is to have the sea, by voyaging; to visit the mountains, Niagara, the Nile, the desert, Rome, Paris, Constantinople; to see galleries, libraries, arsenals, manufactories. The reader of Humboldt's Cosmos follows the marches of a man whose eyes, ears and mind are armed by all the science, arts and implements which mankind have anywhere accumulated, and who is using these to add to the stock. So it is with Denon, Beckford, Belzoni, Wilkinson, Layard, Kane, Lepsius and Livingstone. "The rich man," says Saadi, "is everywhere expected and at home." The rich take up something more of the world into man's life. They include the country as well as the town, the ocean-side, the White Hills, the Far West and the old European homesteads of man, in their notion of available material. The world is his who has money to go over it. He arrives at the seashore and a sumptuous ship has floored and carpeted for him the stormy Atlantic, and made it a luxurious hotel, amid the horrors of tempests. The Persians say, " 'T is the same to him who wears a shoe, as if the whole earth were covered with leather."

Kings are said to have long arms, but every man should have long arms, and should pluck his living, his instruments, his power and his knowing, from the sun, moon and stars. Is not then the demand to be rich legitimate? Yet I have never seen a rich man. I have never seen a man as rich as all men ought to be, or with an adequate command of nature. The pulpit and the press have many commonplaces denouncing the thirst for wealth; but if men should take these moralists at their word and leave off aiming to be rich, the moralists would rush to rekindle at all hazards this love of power in the people, lest civilization should be undone. Men are urged by their ideas to acquire the command over nature. Ages derive a culture from the wealth of Roman Cæsars, Leo Tenths, magnificent Kings of France, Grand Dukes of Tuscany, Dukes of Devonshire, Townleys, Vernons and Peels, in England; or whatever great proprietors. It is the interest of all men that there should be Vaticans and Louvres full of noble works of art; British Museums, and French Gardens of Plants, Philadelphia Academies of Natural History, Bodleian, Ambrosian, Royal, Congressional Libraries. It is the interest of all that there should be Exploring Expeditions; Captain Cooks to voyage round the world, Rosses, Franklins, Richardsons and Kanes, to find the magnetic and the geographic poles. We are all richer for the measurement of a degree of latitude on the earth's surface. Our navigation is safer for the chart. How intimately our knowledge of the system of the Universe rests on that!—and a true economy in a state or an individual will forget its frugality in behalf of claims like these.

Whilst it is each man's interest that not only ease and convenience of living, but also wealth or surplus product should exist somewhere, it need not be in his hands. Often it is very undesirable to him. Goethe said well, "Nobody should be rich but those who understand it." Some men are born to own, and can animate all their possessions. Others cannot: their owning is not graceful; seems to be a compromise of their character; they seem to steal their own dividends. They should own who can administer, not they who hoard and conceal; not they who, the greater proprietors they are, are only the greater beggars, but they whose work carves out work for more, opens a path for all. For he is the rich man in whom the people are rich, and he is the poor man in whom the people are poor; and how to give all access to the master-pieces of art and nature, is the problem of civilization. The socialism of our day has done good service in setting men on thinking how certain civilizing benefits, now only enjoyed by the opulent, can be enjoyed by all. For example, the providing to each man the means and apparatus of science and of the arts. There are many articles good for occasional use, which few men are able to own. Every man wishes to see the ring of Saturn, the satellites and belts of Jupiter and Mars, the mountains and craters in the moon; yet how few can buy a telescope! and of those, scarcely one would like the trouble of keeping it in order and exhibiting it. So of electrical and chemical apparatus, and many the like things. Every man may have occasion to consult books which he does not care to possess, such as cyclopedias, dictionaries, tables, charts, maps and other public documents; pictures also of birds, beasts, fishes, shells, trees, flowers, whose names he desires to know.

There is a refining influence from the arts of Design on a prepared mind which is as positive as that of music, and not to be supplied from any other source. But pictures, engravings, statues and casts, beside their first cost, entail expenses, as of galleries and keepers for the exhibition; and the use which any man can make of them is rare, and their value too is much enhanced by the numbers of men who can share their enjoyment. In the Greek cities it was reckoned profane that any person should pretend a property in a work of art, which belonged to all who could behold it. I think sometimes, could I only have music on my own terms; could I live in a great city and know where I could go whenever I wished the ablution and inundation of musical waves—that were a bath and a medicine.

If properties of this kind were owned by states, towns and lyceums, they would draw the bonds of neighborhood closer. A town would exist to an intellectual purpose. In Europe, where the feudal forms secure the permanence of wealth in certain families, those families buy and preserve these things and lay them open to the public. But in America, where democratic institutions divide every estate into small portions after a few years, the public should step into the place of these proprietors, and provide this culture and inspiration for the citizens.

Man was born to be rich, or inevitably grows rich by the use of his faculties; by the union of thought with nature. Property is an intellectual production. The game requires coolness, right reasoning, promptness and patience in the players. Cultivated labor drives out brute labor. An infinite number of shrewd men, in infinite years, have arrived at certain best and shortest ways of doing, and this accumulated skill in arts, cultures, harvestings, curings, manufactures, navigations, exchanges, constitutes the worth of our world to-day.

Commerce is a game of skill, which every man cannot play, which few men can play well. The right merchant is one who has the just average of faculties we call *common-sense*; a man of a strong affinity for facts, who makes up his decision on what he has seen. He is thoroughly persuaded of the truths of arithmetic. There is always a reason, *in the man*, for his good or bad fortune, and so in making money. Men talk as if there were some magic about this, and believe in magic, in all parts of life. He knows that all goes on the old road, pound for pound, cent for cent—for every effect a perfect cause—and that good luck is another name for tenacity of purpose. He insures himself in every transaction, and likes small and sure gains. Probity and closeness to the facts are the basis, but the masters of the art add a certain long arithmetic. The problem is to combine many and remote operations with the accuracy and adherence to the facts which is easy in near and small transactions; so to arrive at gigantic results, without any compromise of safety. Napoleon was fond of telling the story of the Marseilles banker who said to his visitor, surprised at the contrast between the splendor of the banker's château and hospitality and the meanness of the counting-room in which he had seen him—"Young man, you are too young to understand how masses are formed; the true and only power, whether composed of money, water or men; it is all alike; a mass is an immense centre of motion, but it must be begun, it must be kept up"—and he might have added that the way in which it must be begun and kept up is by obedience to the law of particles.

Success consists in close appliance to the laws of the world, and since those laws are intellectual and moral, an intellectual and moral obedience. Political Economy is as good a book wherein to read the life of man and the ascendancy of laws over all private and hostile influences, as any Bible which has come down to us.

Money is representative, and follows the nature and fortunes of the owner. The coin is a delicate meter of civil, social and moral changes. The farmer is covetous of his dollar, and with reason. It is no waif to him. He knows how many strokes of labor it represents. His bones ache

with the days' work that earned it. He knows how much land it represents—how much rain, frost and sunshine. He knows that, in the
dollar, he gives you so much discretion and patience, so much hoeing
and threshing. Try to lift his dollar; you must lift all that weight. In the
city, where money follows the skit of a pen or a lucky rise in exchange,
it comes to be looked on as light. I wish the farmer held it dearer, and
would spend it only for real bread; force for force.

The farmer's dollar is heavy and the clerk's is light and nimble;
leaps out of his pocket; jumps on to card and faro-tables: but still more
curious is its susceptibility to metaphysical changes. It is the finest
barometer of social storms, and announces revolutions.

Every step of civil advancement makes every man's dollar worth
more. In California, the country where it grew—what would it buy? A
few years since, it would buy a shanty, dysentery, hunger, bad company and crime. There are wide countries, like Siberia, where it would
buy little else to-day than some petty mitigation of suffering. In Rome
it will buy beauty and magnificence. Forty years ago, a dollar would
not buy much in Boston. Now it will buy a great deal more in our old
towns, thanks to railroads, telegraphs, steamers, and the contemporaneous growth of New York and the whole country. Yet there are many
goods appertaining to a capital city which are not yet purchasable here,
no, not with a mountain of dollars. A dollar in Florida is not worth a
dollar in Massachusetts. A dollar is not value, but representative of
value, and, at last, of moral values. A dollar is rated for the corn it will
buy, or to speak strictly, not for the corn or house-room, but for Athenian corn, and Roman house-room—for the wit, probity and power
which we eat bread and dwell in houses to share and exert. Wealth is
mental; wealth is moral. The value of a dollar is, to buy just things; a
dollar goes on increasing in value with all the genius and all the virtue
of the world. A dollar in a university is worth more than a dollar in a
jail; in a temperate, schooled, law-abiding community than in some sink
of crime, where dice, knives and arsenic are in constant play.

The Bank-Note Detector is a useful publication. But the current
dollar, silver or paper, is itself the detector of the right and wrong
where it circulates. Is it not instantly enhanced by the increase of
equity? If a trader refuses to sell his vote, or adheres to some odious
right, he makes so much more equity in Massachusetts; and every acre
in the state is more worth, in the hour of his action. If you take out of

State Street the ten honestest merchants and put in ten roguish persons controlling the same amount of capital, the rates of insurance will indicate it; the soundness of banks will show it; the highways will be less secure; the schools will feel it, the children will bring home their little dose of the poison; the judge will sit less firmly on the bench, and his decisions be less upright; he has lost so much support and constraint, which all need; and the pulpit will betray it, in a laxer rule of life. An apple-tree, if you take out every day for a number of days a load of loam and put in a load of sand about its roots, will find it out. An apple-tree is a stupid kind of creature, but if this treatment be pursued for a short time I think it would begin to mistrust something. And if you should take out of the powerful class engaged in trade a hundred good men and put in a hundred bad, or, what is just the same thing, introduce a demoralizing institution, would not the dollar, which is not much stupider than an apple-tree, presently find it out? The value of a dollar is social, as it is created by society. Every man who removes into this city with any purchasable talent or skill in him, gives to every man's labor in the city a new worth. If a talent is anywhere born into the world, the community of nations is enriched; and much more with a new degree of probity. The expense of crime, one of the principal charges of every nation, is so far stopped. In Europe, crime is observed to increase or abate with the price of bread. If the Rothschilds at Paris do not accept bills, the people at Manchester, at Paisley, at Birmingham are forced into the highway, and landlords are shot down in Ireland. The police-records attest it. The vibrations are presently felt in New York, New Orleans and Chicago. Not much otherwise the economical power touches the masses through the political lords. Rothschild refuses the Russian loan, and there is peace and the harvests are saved. He takes it, and there is war and an agitation through a large portion of mankind, with every hideous result, ending in revolution and a new order.

Wealth brings with it its own checks and balances. The basis of political economy is non-interference. The only safe rule is found in the self-adjusting meter of demand and supply. Do not legislate. Meddle, and you snap the sinews with your sumptuary laws. Give no bounties, make equal laws, secure life and property, and you need not give alms. Open the doors of opportunity to talent and virtue and they will do themselves justice, and property will not be in bad hands. In a free and just commonwealth, property rushes from the idle and imbecile to the industrious, brave and persevering.

The laws of nature play through trade, as a toy-battery exhibits the effects of electricity. The level of the sea is not more surely kept than is the equilibrium of value in society by the demand and supply; and artifice or legislation punishes itself by reactions, gluts and bankruptcies. The sublime laws play indifferently through atoms and galaxies. Whoever knows what happens in the getting and spending of a loaf of bread and a pint of beer, that no wishing will change the rigorous limits of pints and penny loaves; that for all that is consumed so much less remains in the basket and pot, but what is gone out of these is not wasted, but well spent, if it nourish his body and enable him to finish his task—knows all of political economy that the budgets of empires can teach him. The interest of petty economy is this symbolization of the great economy; the way in which a house and a private man's methods tally with the solar system and the laws of give and take, throughout nature; and however wary we are of the falsehoods and petty tricks which we suicidally play off on each other, every man has a certain satisfaction whenever his dealing touches on the inevitable facts; when he sees that things themselves dictate the price, as they always tend to do, and, in large manufactures, are seen to do. Your paper is not fine or coarse enough—is too heavy, or too thin. The manufacturer says he will furnish you with just that thickness or thinness you want; the pattern is quite indifferent to him; here is his schedule—any variety of paper, as cheaper or dearer, with the prices annexed. A pound of paper costs so much, and you may have it made up in any pattern you fancy.

There is in all our dealings a self-regulation that supersedes chaffering. You will rent a house, but must have it cheap. The owner can reduce the rent, but so he incapacitates himself from making proper repairs, and the tenant gets not the house he would have, but a worse one; besides that, a relation a little injurious is established between landlord and tenant. You dismiss your laborer, saying, "Patrick, I shall send for you as soon as I cannot do without you." Patrick goes off contented, for he knows that the weeds will grow with the potatoes, the vines must be planted, next week, and however unwilling you may be, the cantaloupes, crook-necks and cucumbers will send for him. Who but must wish that all labor and value should stand on the same simple and surly market? If it is the best of its kind, it will. We must have joiner, locksmith, planter, priest, poet, doctor, cook, weaver, ostler; each in turn, through the year.

If a St. Michael's pear sells for a shilling, it costs a shilling to raise it. If, in Boston, the best securities offer twelve per cent. for money, they have just six per cent. of insecurity. You may not see that the fine pear costs you a shilling, but it costs the community so much. The shilling represents the number of enemies the pear has, and the amount of risk in ripening it. The price of coal shows the narrowness of the coal-field, and a compulsory confinement of the miners to a certain district. All salaries are reckoned on contingent as well as on actual services. "If the wind were always southwest by west," said the skipper, "women might take ships to sea." One might say that all things are of one price; that nothing is cheap or dear, and that the apparent disparities that strike us are only a shopman's trick of concealing the damage in your bargain. A youth coming into the city from his native New Hampshire farm, with its hard fare still fresh in his remembrance, boards at a first-class hotel, and believes he must somehow have outwitted Dr. Franklin and Malthus, for luxuries are cheap. But he pays for the one convenience of a better dinner, by the loss of some of the richest social and educational advantages. He has lost what guards! what incentives! He will perhaps find by and by that he left the Muses at the door of the hotel, and found the Furies inside. Money often costs too much, and power and pleasure are not cheap. The ancient poet said, "The gods sell all things at a fair price."

There is an example of the compensations in the commercial history of this country. When the European wars threw the carrying-trade of the world, from 1800 to 1812, into American bottoms, a seizure was now and then made of an American ship. Of course the loss was serious to the owner, but the country was indemnified; for we charged threepence a pound for carrying cotton, sixpence for tobacco, and so on; which paid for the risk and loss, and brought into the country an immense prosperity, early marriages, private wealth, the building of cities and of states; and after the war was over, we received compensation over and above, by treaty, for all the seizures. Well, the Americans grew rich and great. But the pay-day comes round. Britain, France and Germany, which our extraordinary profits had impoverished, send out, attracted by the fame of our advantages, first their thousands, then their

. . . .

millions of poor people, to share the crop. At first we employ them, and increase our prosperity; but in the artificial system of society and of protected labor, which we also have adopted and enlarged, there come presently checks and stoppages. Then we refuse to employ these poor men. But they will not be so answered. They go into the poor-rates, and though we refuse wages, we must now pay the same amount in the form of taxes. Again, it turns out that the largest proportion of crimes are committed by foreigners. The cost of the crime and the expense of courts and of prisons we must bear, and the standing army of preventive police we must pay. The cost of education of the posterity of this great colony, I will not compute. But the gross amount of these costs will begin to pay back what we thought was a net gain from our transatlantic customers of 1800. It is vain to refuse this payment. We cannot get rid of these people, and we cannot get rid of their will to be supported. That has become an inevitable element of our politics; and, for their votes, each of the dominant parties courts and assists them to get it executed. Moreover, we have to pay, not what would have contented them at home, but what they have learned to think necessary here; so that opinion, fancy and all manner of moral considerations complicate the problem.

There are few measures of economy which will bear to be named without disgust; for the subject is tender and we may easily have too much of it, and therein resembles the hideous animalcules of which our bodies are built up—which, offensive in the particular, yet compose valuable and effective masses. Our nature and genius force us to respect ends, whilst we use means. We must use the means, and yet, in our most accurate using somehow screen and cloak them, as we can only give them any beauty by a reflection of the glory of the end. That is the good head, which serves the end and commands the means. The rabble are corrupted by their means; the means are too strong for them, and they desert their end.

1. The first of these measures is that each man's expense must proceed from his character. As long as your genius buys, the investment is safe, though you spend like a monarch. Nature arms each man with some faculty which enables him to do easily some feat impossible to any other, and thus makes him necessary to society. This native determination guides his labor and his spending. He wants an equipment of

. . . .

means and tools proper to his talent. And to save on this point were to neutralize the special strength and helpfulness of each mind. Do your work, respecting the excellence of the work, and not its acceptableness. This is so much economy that, rightly read, it is the sum of economy. Profligacy consists not in spending years of time or chests of money—but in spending them off the line of your career. The crime which bankrupts men and states is job-work—declining from your main design, to serve a turn here or there. Nothing is beneath you, if it is in the direction of your life; nothing is great or desirable if it is off from that. I think we are entitled here to draw a straight line and say that society can never prosper but must always be bankrupt, until every man does that which he was created to do.

Spend for your expense, and retrench the expense which is not yours. Allston the painter was wont to say that he built a plain house, and filled it with plain furniture, because he would hold out no bribe to any to visit him who had not similar tastes to his own. We are sympathetic, and, like children, want everything we see. But it is a large stride to independence, when a man, in the discovery of his proper talent, has sunk the necessity for false expenses. As the betrothed maiden by one secure affection is relieved from a system of slaveries—the daily inculcated necessity of pleasing all—so the man who has found what he can do, can spend on that and leave all other spending. Montaigne said, "When he was a younger brother, he went brave in dress and equipage, but afterward his château and farms might answer for him." Let a man who belongs to the class of nobles, those namely who have found out that they can do something, relieve himself of all vague squandering on objects not his. Let the realist not mind appearances. Let him delegate to others the costly courtesies and decorations of social life. The virtues are economists, but some of the vices are also. Thus, next to humility, I have noticed that pride is a pretty good husband. A good pride is, as I reckon it, worth from five hundred to fifteen hundred a year. Pride is handsome, economical; pride eradicates so many vices, letting none subsist but itself, that it seems as if it were a great gain to exchange vanity for pride. Pride can go without domestics, without fine clothes, can live in a house with two rooms, can eat potato, purslain, beans, lyed corn, can work on the soil, can travel afoot, can talk with poor men, or sit silent well contented in fine saloons. But vanity costs money, labor, horses, men, women, health and peace, and is still nothing at last; a long way leading nowhere. Only one drawback; proud people are intolerably selfish, and the vain are gentle and giving.

Art is a jealous mistress, and if a man have a genius for painting, poetry, music, architecture or philosophy, he makes a bad husband and an ill provider, and should be wise in season and not fetter himself with duties which will embitter his days and spoil him for his proper work. We had in this region, twenty years ago, among our educated men, a sort of Arcadian fanaticism, a passionate desire to go upon the land and unite farming to intellectual pursuits. Many effected their purpose and made the experiment, and some became downright ploughmen; but all were cured of their faith that scholarship and practical farming (I mean, with one's own hands) could be united.

With brow bent, with firm intent, the pale scholar leaves his desk to draw a freer breath and get a juster statement of his thought, in the garden-walk. He stoops to pull up a purslain or a dock that is choking the young corn, and finds there are two; close behind the last is a third; he reaches out his hand to a fourth, behind that are four thousand and one. He is heated and untuned, and by and by wakes up from his idiot dream of chickweed and red-root, to remember his morning thought, and to find that with his adamantine purposes he has been duped by a dandelion. A garden is like those pernicious machineries we read of every month in the newspapers, which catch a man's coat-skirt or his hand and draw in his arm, his leg and his whole body to irresistible destruction. In an evil hour he pulled down his wall and added a field to his homestead. No land is bad, but land is worse. If a man own land, the land owns him. Now let him leave home, if he dare. Every tree and graft, every hill of melons, row of corn, or quickset hedge; all he has done and all he means to do, stand in his way like duns, when he would go out of his gate. The devotion to these vines and trees he finds poisonous. Long free walks, a circuit of miles, free his brain and serve his body. Long marches are no hardship to him. He believes he composes easily on the hills. But this pottering in a few square yards of garden is dispiriting and drivelling. The smell of the plants has drugged him and robbed him of energy. He finds a catalepsy in his bones. He grows peevish and poor-spirited. The genius of reading and of gardening are antagonistic, like resinous and vitreous electricity. One is concentrative in sparks and shocks; the other is diffuse strength; so that each disqualifies its workman for the other's duties.

. . . .

An engraver, whose hands must be of an exquisite delicacy of stroke, should not lay stone walls. Sir David Brewster gives exact instructions for microscopic observation: "Lie down on your back, and hold the single lens and object over your eye," etc., etc. How much more the seeker of abstract truth, who needs periods of isolation and rapt concentration and almost a going out of the body to think!

2. Spend after your genius, *and by system.* Nature goes by rule, not by sallies and saltations. There must be system in the economies. Saving and unexpensiveness will not keep the most pathetic family from ruin, nor will bigger incomes make free spending safe. The secret of success lies never in the amount of money, but in the relation of income to outgo; as, after expense has been fixed at a certain point, then new and steady rills of income, though never so small, being added, wealth begins. But in ordinary, as means increase, spending increases faster, so that large incomes, in England and elsewhere, are found not to help matters—the eating quality of debt does not relax its voracity. When the cholera is in the potato, what is the use of planting larger crops? In England, the richest country in the universe, I was assured by shrewd observers that great lords and ladies had no more guineas to give away than other people; that liberality with money is as rare and as immediately famous a virtue as it is here. Want is a growing giant whom the coat of Have was never large enough to cover. I remember in Warwickshire to have been shown a fair manor, still in the same name as in Shakspeare's time The rent-roll I was told is some fourteen thousand pounds a year; but when the second son of the late proprietor was born, the father was perplexed how to provide for him. The eldest son must inherit the manor; what to do with this supernumerary? He was advised to breed him for the Church and to settle him in the rectorship which was in the gift of the family; which was done. It is a general rule in that country that bigger incomes do not help anybody. It is commonly observed that a sudden wealth, like a prize drawn in a lottery or a large bequest to a poor family, does not permanently enrich. They have served no apprenticeship to wealth, and with the rapid wealth come rapid claims which they do not know how to deny, and the treasure is quickly dissipated.

A system must be in every economy, or the best single expedients are of no avail. A farm is a good thing when it begins and ends with itself, and does not need a salary or a shop to eke it out. Thus, the cat-

tle are a main link in the chain-ring. If the non-conformist or æsthetic
farmer leaves out the cattle and does not also leave out the want which
the cattle must supply, he must fill the gap by begging or stealing.
When men now alive were born, the farm yielded everything that was
consumed on it. The farm yielded no money, and the farmer got on
without. If he fell sick, his neighbors came in to his aid; each gave a
day's work, or a half day; or lent his yoke of oxen, or his horse, and
kept his work even; hoed his potatoes, mowed his hay, reaped his rye;
well knowing that no man could afford to hire labor without selling his
land. In autumn a farmer could sell an ox or a hog and get a little
money to pay taxes withal. Now, the farmer buys almost all he consumes—tinware, cloth, sugar, tea, coffee, fish, coal, railroad tickets and
newspapers.

A master in each art is required, because the practice is never with
still or dead subjects, but they change in your hands. You think farm
buildings and broad acres a solid property; but its value is flowing like
water. It requires as much watching as if you were decanting wine from
a cask. The farmer knows what to do with it, stops every leak, turns
all the streamlets to one reservoir and decants wine; but a blunderhead
comes out of Cornhill, tries his hand, and it all leaks away. So is it with
granite streets or timber townships as with fruit or flowers. Nor is any
investment so permanent that it can be allowed to remain without
incessant watching, as the history of each attempt to lock up an inheritance through two generations for an unborn inheritor may show.

When Mr. Cockayne takes a cottage in the country, and will keep
his cow, he thinks a cow is a creature that is fed on hay and gives a
pail of milk twice a day. But the cow that he buys gives milk for three
months; then her bag dries up. What to do with a dry cow? who will
buy her? Perhaps he bought also a yoke of oxen to do his work; but
they get blown and lame. What to do with blown and lame oxen? The
farmer fats his after the spring work is done, and kills them in the fall.
But how can Cockayne, who has no pastures, and leaves his cottage
daily in the cars at business hours, be pothered with fatting and killing
oxen? He plants trees; but there must be crops, to keep the trees in
ploughed land. What shall be the crops? He will have nothing to do
with trees, but will have grass. After a year or two the grass must be
turned up and ploughed; now what crops? Credulous Cockayne!

3. Help comes in the custom of the country, and the rule of *Impera*

. . . .

parendo. The rule is not to dictate nor to insist on carrying out each of your schemes by ignorant wilfulness, but to learn practically the secret spoken from all nature, that things themselves refuse to be mismanaged, and will show to the watchful their own law. Nobody need stir hand or foot. The custom of the country will do it all. I know not how to build or to plant; neither how to buy wood, nor what to do with the house-lot, the field, or the wood-lot, when bought. Never fear; it is all settled how it shall be, long beforehand, in the custom of the country— whether to sand or whether to clay it, when to plough, and how to dress, whether to grass or to corn; and you cannot help or hinder it. Nature has her own best mode of doing each thing, and she has somewhere told it plainly, if we will keep our eyes and ears open. If not, she will not be slow in undeceiving us when we prefer our own way to hers. How often we must remember the art of the surgeon, which, in replacing the broken bone, contents itself with releasing the parts from false position; they fly into place by the action of the muscles. On this art of nature all our arts rely.

Of the two eminent engineers in the recent construction of railways in England, Mr. Brunel went straight from terminus to terminus, through mountains, over streams, crossing highways, cutting ducal estates in two, and shooting through this man's cellar and that man's attic window, and so arriving at his end, at great pleasure to geometers, but with cost to his company. Mr. Stephenson on the contrary, believing that the river knows the way, followed his valley as implicitly as our Western Railroad follows the Westfield River, and turned out to be the safest and cheapest engineer. We say the cows laid out Boston. Well, there are worse surveyors. Every pedestrian in our pastures has frequent occasion to thank the cows for cutting the best path through the thicket and over the hills; and travellers and Indians know the value of a buffalo-trail, which is sure to be the easiest possible pass through the ridge.

When a citizen fresh from Dock Square or Milk Street comes out and buys land in the country, his first thought is to a fine outlook from his windows; his library must command a western view; a sunset every day, bathing the shoulder of Blue Hills, Wachusett, and the peaks of Monadnoc and Uncanoonuc. What, thirty acres, and all this magnificence for fifteen hundred dollars! It would be cheap at fifty thousand. He proceeds at once, his eyes dim with tears of joy, to fix the spot for his cornerstone. But the man who is to level the ground thinks it will take many hundred loads of gravel to fill the hollow to the road. The stonemason who should build the well thinks he shall have to dig forty feet; the baker doubts he shall never like to drive up to the door; the practical neighbor cavils at the position of the barn; and the citizen comes to know that his predecessor the farmer built the house in the right spot for the sun and wind, the spring, and water-drainage, and the convenience to the pasture, the garden, the field and the road. So Dock Square yields the point, and things have their own way. Use has made the farmer wise, and the foolish citizen learns to take his counsel. From step to step he comes at last to surrender at discretion. The farmer affects to take his orders; but the citizen says, You may ask me as often as you will, and in what ingenious forms, for an opinion concerning the mode of building my wall, or sinking my well, or laying out my acre, but the ball will rebound to you. These are matters on which I neither know nor need to know anything. These are questions which you and not I shall answer.

Not less within doors a system settles itself, paramount and tyrannical over master and mistress, servant and child, cousin and acquaintance. 'T is in vain that genius or virtue or energy of character strive and cry against it. This is fate. And 't is very well that the poor husband reads in a book of a new way of living, and resolves to adopt it at home; let him go home and try it, if he dare.

4. Another point of economy is to look for seed of the same kind as you sow, and not to hope to buy one kind with another kind. Friendship buys friendship; justice, justice; military merit, military success. Good husbandry finds wife, children and household. The good merchant, large gains, ships, stocks and money. The good poet, fame and literary credit; but not either, the other. Yet there is commonly a confusion of expectations on these points. Hotspur lives for the moment, praises himself for it, and despises Furlong, that he does not. Hotspur of course is poor, and Furlong a good provider. The odd circumstance is that Hotspur thinks it a superiority in himself, this improvidence, which ought to be rewarded with Furlong's lands.

I have not at all completed my design. But we must not leave the topic without casting one glance into the interior recesses. It is a doctrine of philosophy that man is a being of degrees; that there is nothing in the world which is not repeated in his body, his body being a sort of miniature or summary of the world; then that there is nothing in his body which is not repeated as in a celestial sphere in his mind; then, there is nothing in his brain which is not repeated in a higher sphere in his moral system.

5. Now these things are so in nature. All things ascend, and the royal rule of economy is that it should ascend also, or, whatever we do must always have a higher aim. Thus it is a maxim that money is another kind of blood, *Pecunia alter sanguis*: or, the estate of a man is only a larger kind of body, and admits of regimen analogous to his bodily circulations. So there is no maxim of the merchant which does not admit of an extended sense, *e.g.*, "Best use of money is to pay debts"; "Every business by itself"; "Best time is present time"; "The right investment is in tools of your trade"; and the like. The counting-room maxims liberally expounded are laws of the universe. The merchant's economy is a coarse symbol of the soul's economy. It is to spend for power and not for pleasure. It is to invest income; that is to say, to take up particulars into generals; days into integral eras—literary, emotive, practical—of its life, and still to ascend in its investment. The merchant has but one rule, *absorb and invest*; he is to be capitalist; the scraps and filings must be gathered back into the crucible; the gas and smoke must be burned, and earnings must not go to increase expense, but to capital again. Well, the man must be capitalist. Will he spend his income, or will he invest? His body and every organ is under the same law. His body is a jar in which the liquor of life is stored. Will he spend for pleasure? The way to ruin is short and facile. Will he not spend but hoard for power? It passes through the sacred fermentations, by that law of nature whereby everything climbs to higher platforms, and bodily vigor becomes mental and moral vigor. The bread he eats is first strength and animal spirits; it becomes, in higher laboratories, imagery and thought; and in still higher results, courage and endurance. This is the right compound interest; this is capital doubled, quadrupled, centupled; man raised to his highest power.

The true thrift is always to spend on the higher plane; to invest and invest, with keener avarice, that he may spend in spiritual creation and not in augmenting animal existence. Nor is the man enriched, in repeating the old experiments of animal sensation; nor unless through new powers and ascending pleasures he knows himself by the actual experience of higher good to be already on the way to the highest.

CULTURE

Can rules or tutors educate
The semigod whom we await?
He must be musical,
Tremulous, impressional,
Alive to gentle influence
Of landscape and of sky,
And tender to the spirit-touch
Of man's or maiden's eye:
But, to his native centre fast,
Shall into Future fuse the Past,
And the world's flowing fates in
    his own mould recast.

THE WORD of ambition at the present day is Culture. Whilst all the world is in pursuit of power, and of wealth as a means of power, culture corrects the theory of success. A man is the prisoner of his power. A topical memory makes him an almanac; a talent for debate, a disputant; skill to get money makes him a miser, that is, a beggar. Culture reduces these inflammations by invoking the aid of other powers against the dominant talent, and by appealing to the rank of powers. It watches success. For performance, nature has no mercy, and sacrifices the performer to get it done; makes a dropsy or a tympany of him. If she wants a thumb, she makes one at the cost of arms and legs, and any excess of power in one part is usually paid for at once by some defect in a contiguous part.

Our efficiency depends so much on our concentration, that nature usually in the instances where a marked man is sent into the world, overloads him with bias, sacrificing his symmetry to his working power. It is said a man can write but one book; and if a man have a defect, it is apt to leave its impression on all his performances. If she creates a policeman like Fouché, he is made up of suspicions and of plots to circumvent them. "The air," said Fouché, "is full of poniards." The physician Sanctorius spent his life in a pair of scales, weighing his food. Lord Coke valued Chaucer highly because the Canon Yeoman's Tale illustrates the statute fifth Hen. IV chap. 4, against alchemy. I saw a man who believed the principal mischiefs in the English state were derived from the devotion to musical concerts. A freemason, not long since, set out to explain to this country that the principal cause of the success of General Washington was the aid he derived from the freemasons.

But worse than the harping on one string, nature has secured individualism by giving the private person a high conceit of his weight in the system. The pest of society is egotists. There are dull and bright, sacred and profane, coarse and fine egotists. It is a disease that like influenza falls on all constitutions. In the distemper known to physicians as *chorea*, the patient sometimes turns round and continues to spin slowly on one spot. Is egotism a metaphysical variety of this malady? The man runs round a ring formed by his own talent, falls into an admiration of it, and loses relation to the world. It is a tendency in all minds. One of its annoying forms is a craving for sympathy. The sufferers parade their miseries, tear the lint from their bruises, reveal their indictable crimes, that you may pity them. They like sickness, because physical pain will extort some show of interest from the bystanders, as we have seen children who finding themselves of no account when grown people come in, will cough till they choke, to draw attention.

This distemper is the scourge of talent—of artists, inventors and philosophers. Eminent spiritualists shall have an incapacity of putting their act or word aloof from them and seeing it bravely for the nothing it is. Beware of the man who says, "I am on the eve of a revelation." It is speedily punished, inasmuch as this habit invites men to humor it, and, by treating the patient tenderly, to shut him up in a narrower selfism and exclude him from the great world of God's cheerful fallible men and women. Let us rather be insulted, whilst we are insultable. Religious literature has eminent examples, and if we run over our private list of poets, critics, philanthropists and philosophers, we shall find them infected with this dropsy and elephantiasis, which we ought to have tapped.

This goitre of egotism is so frequent among notable persons that we must infer some strong necessity in nature which it subserves; such as we see in the sexual attraction. The preservation of the species was a point of such necessity that nature has secured it at all hazards by immensely overloading the passion, at the risk of perpetual crime and disorder. So egotism has its root in the cardinal necessity by which each individual persists to be what he is.

This individuality is not only not inconsistent with culture, but is the basis of it. Every valuable nature is there in its own right, and the student we speak to must have a mother-wit invincible by his culture—which uses all books, arts, facilities, and elegancies of intercourse, but is never subdued and lost in them. He only is a well-made man who has a good determination. And the end of culture is not to destroy this, God forbid! but to train away all impediment and mixture and leave nothing but pure power. Our student must have a style and determination, and be a master in his own specialty. But having this, he must put it behind him. He must have a catholicity, a power to see with a free and disengaged look every object. Yet is this private interest and self so overcharged that if a man seeks a companion who can look at objects for their own sake and without affection or self-reference, he will find the fewest who will give him that satisfaction; whilst most men are afflicted with a coldness, an incuriosity, as soon as any object does not connect with their self-love. Though they talk of the object before them, they are thinking of themselves, and their vanity is laying little traps for your admiration.

But after a man has discovered that there are limits to the interest which his private history has for mankind, he still converses with his family, or a few companions—perhaps with half a dozen personalities that are famous in his neighborhood. In Boston the question of life is the names of some eight or ten men. Have you seen Mr. Allston, Doctor Channing, Mr. Adams, Mr. Webster, Mr. Greenough? Have you heard Everett, Garrison, Father Taylor, Theodore Parker? Have you talked with Messieurs Turbinewheel, Summitlevel, and Lacofrupees? Then you may as well die. In New York the question is of some other eight, or ten, or twenty. Have you seen a few lawyers, merchants and brokers—two or three scholars, two or three capitalists, two or three editors of newspapers? New York is a sucked orange. All conversation is at an end when we have discharged ourselves of a dozen personalities, domestic or imported, which make up our American existence. Nor do we expect anybody to be other than a faint copy of these heroes.

Life is very narrow. Bring any club or company of intelligent men together again after ten years, and if the presence of some penetrating and calming genius could dispose them to frankness, what a confession

. . . .

of insanities would come up! The "causes" to which we have sacrificed, Tariff or Democracy, Whigism or Abolition, Temperance or Socialism would show like roots of bitterness and dragons of wrath; and our talents are as mischievous as if each had been seized upon by some bird of prey which had whisked him away from fortune, from truth, from the dear society of the poets—some zeal, some bias, and only when he was now gray and nerveless was it relaxing its claws and he awaking to sober perceptions.

Culture is the suggestion, from certain best thoughts, that a man has a range of affinities through which he can modulate the violence of any master-tones that have a droning preponderance in his scale, and succor him against himself. Culture redresses his balance, puts him among his equals and superiors, revives the delicious sense of sympathy and warns him of the dangers of solitude and repulsion.

It is not a compliment but a disparagement to consult a man only on horses, or on steam, or on theatres, or on eating, or on books, and, whenever he appears, considerately to turn the conversation to the bantling he is known to fondle. In the Norse heaven of our forefathers, Thor's house had five hundred and forty floors; and man's house has five hundred and forty floors. His excellence is facility of adaptation and of transition, through many related points, to wide contrasts and extremes. Culture kills his exaggeration, his conceit of his village or his city. We must leave our pets at home when we go into the street, and meet men on broad grounds of good meaning and good sense. No performance is worth loss of geniality. 'T is a cruel price we pay for certain fancy goods called fine arts and philosophy. In the Norse legend, All-fadir did not get a drink of Mimir's spring (the fountain of wisdom) until he left his eyes in pledge. And here is a pedant that cannot unfold his wrinkles, nor conceal his wrath at interruption by the best, if their conversation do not fit his impertinency—here is he to afflict us with his personalities. 'T is incident to scholars that each of them fancies he is pointedly odious in his community. Draw him out of this limbo of irritability. Cleanse with healthy blood his parchment skin. You restore to him his eyes which he left in pledge at Mimir's spring. If you are the victim of your doing, who cares what you do? We can spare your opera, your gazetteer, your chemic analysis, your history, your syllogisms. Your man of genius pays dear for his distinction. His head runs up into a spire, and, instead of a healthy man, merry and wise, he is some mad dominie. Nature is reckless of the individual. When she has points to carry, she carries them. To wade in marshes and sea-margins is the destiny of certain birds, and they are so accurately made for this that they are imprisoned in those places. Each animal out of its *habitat* would starve. To the physician, each man, each woman, is an amplification of one organ. A soldier, a locksmith, a bank-clerk and a dancer could not exchange functions. And thus we are victims of adaptation.

The antidotes against this organic egotism are the range and variety of attractions, as gained by acquaintance with the world, with men of merit, with classes of society, with travel, with eminent persons, and with the high resources of philosophy, art and religion; books, travel, society, solitude.

The hardiest skeptic who has seen a horse broken, a pointer trained, or who has visited a menagerie or the exhibition of the Industrious Fleas, will not deny the validity of education. "A boy," says Plato, "is the most vicious of all wild beasts"; and in the same spirit the old English poet Gascoigne says, "A boy is better unborn than untaught." The city breeds one kind of speech and manners; the back country a different style; the sea another; the army a fourth. We know that an army which can be confided in may be formed by discipline; that by systematic discipline all men may be made heroes: Marshal Lannes said to a French officer, "Know, Colonel, that none but a poltroon will boast that he never was afraid." A great part of courage is the courage of having done the thing before. And in all human action those faculties will be strong which are used. Robert Owen said, "Give me a tiger, and I will educate him." 'T is inhuman to want faith in the power of education, since to meliorate is the law of nature; and men are valued precisely as they exert onward or meliorating force. On the other hand, poltroonery is the acknowledging an inferiority to be incurable.

Incapacity of melioration is the only mortal distemper. There are people who can never understand a trope or any second or expanded sense given to your words, or any humor; but remain literalists, after hearing the music and poetry and rhetoric and wit of seventy or eighty years. They are past the help of surgeon or clergy. But even these can understand pitchforks and the cry of Fire! and I have noticed in some of this class a marked dislike of earthquakes.

Let us make our education brave and preventive. Politics is an

. . . .

after-work, a poor patching. We are always a little late. The evil is done, the law is passed, and we begin the uphill agitation for repeal of that of which we ought to have prevented the enacting. We shall one day learn to supersede politics by education. What we call our root-and-branch reforms, of slavery, war, gambling, intemperance, is only medicating the symptoms. We must begin higher up, namely in Education.

Our arts and tools give to him who can handle them much the same advantage over the novice as if you extended his life, ten, fifty, or a hundred years. And I think it the part of good sense to provide every fine soul with such culture that it shall not, at thirty or forty years, have to say, 'This which I might do is made hopeless through my want of weapons.'

But it is conceded that much of our training fails of effect; that all success is hazardous and rare; that a large part of our cost and pains is thrown away. Nature takes the matter into her own hands, and though we must not omit any jot of our system, we can seldom be sure that it has availed much, or that as much good would not have accrued from a different system.

Books, as containing the finest records of human wit, must always enter into our notion of culture. The best heads that ever existed, Pericles, Plato, Julius Cæsar, Shakspeare, Goethe, Milton, were well-read, universally educated men, and quite too wise to undervalue letters. Their opinion has weight, because they had means of knowing the opposite opinion. We look that a great man should be a good reader, or in proportion to the spontaneous power should be the assimilating power. Good criticism is very rare and always precious. I am always happy to meet persons who perceive the transcendent superiority of Shakspeare over all other writers. I like people who like Plato. Because this love does not consist with self-conceit.

But books are good only as far as a boy is ready for them. He sometimes gets ready very slowly. You send your child to the schoolmaster, but 't is the schoolboys who educate him. You send him to the Latin class, but much of his tuition comes, on his way to school, from the shop-windows. You like the strict rules and the long terms; and he finds his best leading in a by-way of his own, and refuses any companions but of his own choosing. He hates the grammar and *Gradus,* and loves guns, fishing-rods, horses and boats. Well, the boy is right, and you are not fit to direct his bringing-up if your theory leaves out his gymnastic training. Archery, cricket, gun and fishing-rod, horse and boat, are all educators, liberalizers; and so are dancing, dress and the street talk; and provided only the boy has resources, and is of a noble and ingenuous strain, these will not serve him less than the books. He learns chess, whist, dancing and theatricals. The father observes that another boy has learned algebra and geometry in the same time. But the first boy has acquired much more than these poor games along with them. He is infatuated for weeks with whist and chess: but presently will find out, as you did, that when he rises from the game too long played, he is vacant and forlorn and despises himself. Thenceforward it takes place with other things, and has its due weight in his experience. These minor skills and accomplishments, for example, dancing, are tickets of admission to the dress-circle of mankind, and the being master of them enables the youth to judge intelligently of much on which otherwise he would give a pedantic squint. Landor said, "I have suffered more from my bad dancing than from all the misfortunes and miseries of my life put together." Provided always the boy is teachable (for we are not proposing to make a statue out of punk), football, cricket, archery, swimming, skating, climbing, fencing, riding, are lessons in the art of power, which it is his main business to learn—riding, specially, of which Lord Herbert of Cherbury said, "A good rider on a good horse is as much above himself and others as the world can make him." Besides, the gun, fishing-rod, boat and horse, constitute, among all who use them, secret freemasonries. They are as if they belong to one club.

There is also a negative value in these arts. Their chief use to the youth is not amusement, but to be known for what they are, and not to remain to him occasions of heart-burn. We are full of superstitions. Each class fixes its eyes on the advantages it has not; the refined, on rude strength; the democrat, on birth and breeding. One of the benefits of a college education is to show the boy its little avail. I knew a leading man in a leading city who, having set his heart on an education at the university and missed it, could never quite feel himself the equal of his own brothers who had gone thither. His easy superiority to multitudes of professional men could never quite countervail to him this imaginary defect. Balls, riding, wine-parties and billiards pass to a poor boy for something fine and romantic, which they are not; and a free admission to them on an equal footing, if it were possible, only once or twice, would be worth ten times its cost, by undeceiving him.

I am not much an advocate for travelling, and I observe that men run away to other countries because they are not good in their own, and run back to their own because they pass for nothing in the new places. For the most part, only the light characters travel. Who are you that have no task to keep you at home? I have been quoted as saying captious things about travel; but I mean to do justice. I think there is a restlessness in our people which argues want of character. All educated Americans, first or last, go to Europe; perhaps because it is their mental home, as the invalid habits of this country might suggest. An eminent teacher of girls said, "the idea of a girl's education is, whatever qualifies her for going to Europe." Can we never extract this tape-worm of Europe from the brain of our countrymen? One sees very well what their fate must be. He that does not fill a place at home, cannot abroad. He only goes there to hide his insignificance in a larger crowd. You do not think you will find anything there which you have not seen at home? The stuff of all countries is just the same. Do you suppose there is any country where they do not scald milk-pans, and swaddle the infants, and burn the brushwood, and broil the fish? What is true anywhere is true everywhere. And let him go where he will, he can only find so much beauty or worth as he carries.

Of course, for some men, travel may be useful. Naturalists, discoverers and sailors are born. Some men are made for couriers, exchangers, envoys, missionaries, bearers of despatches, as others are for farmers and workingmen. And if the man is of a light and social turn, and nature has aimed to make a legged and winged creature, framed for locomotion, we must follow her hint and furnish him with that breeding which gives currency, as sedulously as with that which gives worth. But let us not be pedantic, but allow to travel its full effect. The boy grown up on a farm, which he has never left, is said in the country to have had *no chance*, and boys and men of that condition look upon work on a railroad, or drudgery in a city, as opportunity. Poor country boys of Vermont and Connecticut formerly owed what knowledge they had to their peddling trips to the Southern States. California and the Pacific Coast is now the university of this class, as Virginia was in old times. 'To have *some chance*' is their word. And the phrase 'to know the world,' or to travel, is synonymous with all men's ideas of advantage and superiority. No doubt, to a man of sense, travel offers advantages. As many languages as he has, as many friends, as many arts and trades, so many times is he a man. A foreign country is a point of comparison wherefrom to judge his own. One use of travel is to recommend the books and works of home—we go to Europe to be Americanized; and another, to find men. For as nature has put fruits apart in latitudes, a new fruit in every degree, so knowledge and fine moral quality she lodges in distant men. And thus, of the six or seven teachers whom each man wants among his contemporaries, it often happens that one or two of them live on the other side of the world.

Moreover, there is in every constitution a certain solstice when the stars stand still in our inward firmament, and when there is required some foreign force, some diversion or alterative to prevent stagnation. And, as a medical remedy, travel seems one of the best. Just as a man witnessing the admirable effect of ether to lull pain, and meditating on the contingencies of wounds, cancers, lockjaws, rejoices in Dr. Jackson's benign discovery, so a man who looks at Paris, at Naples, or at London, says, 'If I should be driven from my own home, here at least my thoughts can be consoled by the most prodigal amusement and occupation which the human race in ages could contrive and accumulate.'

Akin to the benefit of foreign travel, the æsthetic value of railroads is to unite the advantages of town and country life, neither of which we can spare. A man should live in or near a large town, because, let his own genius be what it may, it will repel quite as much of agreeable and valuable talent as it draws, and, in a city, the total attraction of all the citizens is sure to conquer, first or last, every repulsion, and drag the most improbable hermit within its walls some day in the year. In town he can find the swimming-school, the gymnasium, the dancing-master, the shooting-gallery, opera, theatre and panorama; the chemist's shop, the museum of natural history; the gallery of fine arts; the national orators, in their turn; foreign travellers, the libraries and his club. In the country he can find solitude and reading, manly labor, cheap living and his old shoes; moors for game, hills for geology and groves for devotion. Aubrey writes, "I have heard Thomas Hobbes say, that, in the Earl of Devon's house, in Derbyshire, there was a good library and books enough for him, and his lordship stored the library with what books he thought fit to be bought. But the want of good conversation was a very great inconvenience, and, though he conceived he could order his thinking as well as another, yet he found a great defect. In the country, in long time, for want of good conversation, one's understanding and invention contract a moss on them, like an old paling in an orchard."

Cities give us collision. It is said, London and New York take the nonsense out of a man. A great part of our education is sympathetic and social. Boys and girls who have been brought up with well-informed and superior people show in their manners an inestimable grace. Fuller says that "William, Earl of Nassau, won a subject from the King of Spain, every time he put off his hat." You cannot have one well-bred man without a whole society of such. They keep each other up to any high point. Especially women; it requires a great many cultivated women—saloons of bright, elegant, reading women, accustomed to ease and refinement, to spectacles, pictures, sculpture, poetry, and to elegant society—in order that you should have one Madame de Staël. The head of a commercial house or a leading lawyer or politician is brought into daily contact with troops of men from all parts of the country, and those too the driving-wheels, the business men of each section, and one can hardly suggest for an apprehensive man a more searching culture. Besides, we must remember the high social possibilities of a million of men. The best bribe which London offers to-day to the imagination is that in such a vast variety of people and conditions one can believe there is room for persons of romantic character to exist, and that the poet, the mystic and the hero may hope to confront their counterparts.

I wish cities could teach their best lesson—of quiet manners. It is the foible especially of American youth—pretension. The mark of the man of the world is absence of pretension. He does not make a speech, he takes a low business-tone, avoids all brag, is nobody, dresses plainly, promises not at all, performs much, speaks in monosyllables, hugs his fact. He calls his employment by its lowest name, and so takes from evil tongues their sharpest weapon. His conversation clings to the weather and the news, yet he allows himself to be surprised into thought and the unlocking of his learning and philosophy. How the imagination is piqued by anecdotes of some great man passing incognito, as a king in gray clothes; of Napoleon affecting a plain suit at his glittering levee; of Burns or Scott or Beethoven or Wellington or

Goethe, or any container of transcendent power, passing for nobody; of Epaminondas, "who never says anything, but will listen eternally"; of Goethe, who preferred trifling subjects and common expressions in intercourse with strangers, worse rather than better clothes, and to appear a little more capricious than he was. There are advantages in the old hat and box-coat. I have heard that throughout this country a certain respect is paid to good broadcloth; but dress makes a little restraint; men will not commit themselves. But the box-coat is like wine, it unlocks the tongue, and men say what they think. An old poet says—

> "Go far and go sparing,
> For you'll find it certain,
> The poorer and the baser you appear,
> The more you'll look through still."

Not much otherwise Milnes writes in the "Lay of the Humble"—

> "To me men are for what they are,
> They wear no masks with me."

It is odd that our people should have—not water on the brain, but a little gas there. A shrewd foreigner said of the Americans that "whatever they say has a little the air of a speech." Yet one of the traits down in the books as distinguishing the Anglo-Saxon is a trick of self-disparagement. To be sure, in old, dense countries, among a million of good coats a fine coat comes to be no distinction, and you find humorists. In an English party a man with no marked manners or features, with a face like red dough, unexpectedly discloses wit, learning, a wide range of topics and personal familiarity with good men in all parts of the world, until you think you have fallen upon some illustrious personage. Can it be that the American forest has refreshed some weeds of old Pictish barbarism just ready to die out—the love of the scarlet feather, of beads and tinsel? The Italians are fond of red clothes, peacock plumes and embroidery; and I remember one rainy morning in the city of Palermo the street was in a blaze with scarlet umbrellas. The English have a plain taste. The equipages of the grandees are plain. A gorgeous livery indicates new and awkward city wealth. Mr. Pitt, like Mr. Pym, thought

. . . .

the title of *Mister* good against any king in Europe. They have piqued themselves on governing the whole world in the poor, plain, dark Committee-room which the House of Commons sat in, before the fire.

Whilst we want cities as the centres where the best things are found, cities degrade us by magnifying trifles. The countryman finds the town a chop-house, a barber's shop. He has lost the lines of grandeur of the horizon, hills and plains, and with them sobriety and elevation. He has come among: a supple, glib-tongued tribe, who live for show, servile to public opinion. Life is dragged down to a fracas of pitiful cares and disasters. You say the gods ought to respect a life whose objects are their own; but in cities they have betrayed you to a cloud of insignificant annoyances—

> "Mirmidons, race féconde,
> Mirmidons,
> Enfin nous commandons:
> Jupiter livre le monde
> Aux mirmidons, aux mirmidons."

> 'T is heavy odds
> Against the gods,
> When they will match with myrmidons.
> We spawning, spawning myrmidons,
> Our turn to-day! we take command,
> Jove gives the globe into the hand
> Of myrmidons, of myrmidons.

What is odious but noise, and people who scream and bewail? people whose vane points always east, who live to dine, who send for the doctor, who coddle themselves, who toast their feet on the register, who intrigue to secure a padded chair and a corner out of the draught. Suffer them once to begin the enumeration of their infirmities and the sun will go down on the unfinished tale. Let these triflers put us out of conceit with petty comforts. To a man at work, the frost is but a color; the rain, the wind, he forgot them when he came in. Let us learn to live coarsely, dress plainly, and lie hard. The least habit of dominion over the palate has certain good effects not easily estimated. Neither will we be driven into a quiddling abstemiousness. 'T is a superstition to insist on a special diet. All is made at last of the same chemical atoms.

A man in pursuit of greatness feels no little wants. How can you mind diet, bed, dress, or salutes or compliments, or the figure you make in company, or wealth, or even the bringing things to pass—when you think how paltry are the machinery and the workers? Wordsworth was praised to me in Westmoreland for having afforded to his country neighbors an example of a modest household where comfort and culture were secured without display. And a tender boy who wears his rusty cap and outgrown coat, that he may secure the coveted place in college and the right in the library, is educated to some purpose. There is a great deal of self-denial and manliness in poor and middle-class houses in town and country, that has not got into literature and never will, but that keeps the earth sweet; that saves on superfluities, and spends on essentials; that goes rusty and educates the boy; that sells the horse but builds the school; works early and late, takes two looms in the factory, three looms, six looms, but pays off the mortgage on the paternal farm, and then goes back cheerfully to work again.

We can ill spare the commanding social benefits of cities; they must be used, yet cautiously and haughtily—and will yield their best values to him who best can do without them. Keep the town for occasions, but the habits should be formed to retirement. Solitude, the safeguard of mediocrity, is, to genius, the stern friend, the cold, obscure shelter where moult the wings which will bear it farther than suns and stars. He who should inspire and lead his race must be defended from travelling with the souls of other men, from living, breathing, reading and writing in the daily, time-worn yoke of their opinions. "In the morning—solitude"; said Pythagoras; that nature may speak to the imagination, as she does never in company, and that her favorite may make acquaintance with those divine strengths which disclose themselves to serious and abstracted thought. 'T is very certain that Plato, Plotinus, Archimedes, Hermes Newton, Milton, Wordsworth, did not live in a crowd, but descended into it from time to time as benefactors; and the wise instructor will press this point of securing to the young soul in the disposition of time and the arrangements of living periods and habits of solitude. The high advantage of university life is often the mere mechanical one, I may call it, of a separate chamber and fire—which parents will allow the boy without hesitation at Cambridge, but do not think needful at home. We say solitude, to mark the character of the tone of thought, but if it can be shared between two or more than two, it is happier and not less noble. "We four," wrote Neander to his sacred friends, "will enjoy at Halle the inward blessedness of a *civitas Dei*, whose foundations are forever friendship. The more I know you, the more I dissatisfy and must dissatisfy all my wonted companions. Their very presence stupefies me. The common understanding withdraws itself from the one centre of all existence."

Solitude takes off the pressure of present importunities, that more catholic and humane relations may appear. The saint and poet seek privacy to ends the most public and universal, and it is the secret of culture to interest the man more in his public than in his private quality. Here is a new poem, which elicits a good many comments in the journals and in conversation. From these it is easy at last to gather the verdict which readers passed upon it; and that is, in the main, unfavorable. The poet, as a craftsman, is only interested in the praise accorded to him, and not in the censure, though it be just. And the poor little poet hearkens only to that, and rejects the censure as proving incapacity in the critic. But the poet *cultivated* becomes a stockholder in both companies—say Mr. Curfew in the Curfew stock, and in the *humanity* stock—and, in the last, exults as much in the demonstration of the unsoundness of Curfew, as his interest in the former gives him pleasure in the currency of Curfew. For the depreciation of his Curfew stock only shows the immense values of the humanity stock. As soon as he sides with his critic against himself, with joy, he is a cultivated man.

We must have an intellectual quality in all property and in all action, or they are naught. I must have children, I must have events, I must have a social state and history, or my thinking and speaking want body or basis. But to give these accessories any value, I must know them as contingent and rather showy possessions, which pass for more to the people than to me. We see this abstraction in scholars, as a matter of course; but what a charm it adds when observed in practical men. Bonaparte, like Cæsar, was intellectual, and could look at every object for itself, without affection. Though an egotist *à outrance*, he could criticise a play, a building, a character, on universal grounds, and give a just opinion. A man known to us only as a celebrity in politics or in trade gains largely in our esteem if we discover that he has some intellectual taste or skill; as when we learn of Lord Fairfax, the Long Parliament's general, his passion for antiquarian studies; or of the French regicide Carnot, his sublime genius in mathematics; or of a living banker, his success in poetry; or of a partisan journalist, his devotion to ornithology. So, if in travelling in the dreary wilderness of Arkansas or Texas we should observe on the next seat a man reading Horace, or Martial, or Calderon, we should wish to hug him.

We only vary the phrase, not the doctrine, when we say that culture opens the sense of beauty. A man is a beggar who only lives to the useful, and however he may serve as a pin or rivet in the social machine, cannot be said to have arrived at self-possession. I suffer every day from the want of perception of beauty in people. They do not know the charm with which all moments and objects can be embellished, the charm of manners, of self-command, of benevolence. Repose and cheerfulness are the badge of the gentleman—repose in energy. The Greek battle-pieces are calm; the heroes, in whatever violent actions engaged, retain a serene aspect; as we say of Niagara that it falls without speed. A cheerful intelligent face is the end of culture, and success enough. For it indicates the purpose of nature and wisdom attained.

When our higher faculties are in activity we are domesticated, and awkwardness and discomfort give place to natural and agreeable movements. It is noticed that the consideration of the great periods and spaces of astronomy induces a dignity of mind and an indifference to death. The influence of fine scenery, the presence of mountains, appeases our irritations and elevates our friendships. Even a high dome, and the expansive interior of a cathedral, have a sensible effect on manners. I have heard that stiff people lose something of their awkwardness under high ceilings and in spacious halls. I think sculpture and painting have an effect to teach us manners and abolish hurry.

But, over all, culture must reinforce from higher influx the empirical skills of eloquence, or of politics, or of trade and the useful arts. There is a certain loftiness of thought and power to marshal and adjust particulars, which can only come from an insight of their whole connection. The orator who has once seen things in their divine order will never quite lose sight of this, and will come to affairs as from a higher ground, and though he will say nothing of philosophy, he will have a certain mastery in dealing with them, and an incapableness of being dazzled or frighted, which will distinguish his handling from that of attorneys and factors. A man who stands on a good footing with the heads of parties at Washington, reads the rumors of the newspapers and the guesses of provincial politicians with a key to the right and wrong in each statement, and sees well enough where all this will end. Archimedes will look through your Connecticut machine at a glance, and judge of its fitness. And much more a wise man who knows not only what Plato, but what Saint John can show him, can easily raise the affair he deals with to a certain majesty. Plato says Pericles owed this elevation to the lessons of Anaxagoras. Burke descended from a higher sphere when he would influence human affairs. Franklin, Adams, Jefferson, Washington, stood on a fine humanity, before which the brawls of modern senates are but pot-house politics.

But there are higher secrets of culture, which are not for the apprentices but for proficients. These are lessons only for the brave. We must know our friends under ugly masks. The calamities are our friends. Ben Jonson specifies in his address to the Muse:—

> "Get him the time's long grudge, the court's ill-will,
> And, reconciled, keep him suspected still,
> Make him lose all his friends, and what is worse,
> Almost all ways to any better course;
> With me thou leav'st a better Muse than thee,
> And which thou brought'st me, blessed Poverty."

We wish to learn philosophy by rote, and play at heroism. But the wiser God says, Take the shame, the poverty and the penal solitude that belong to truth-speaking. Try the rough water as well as the smooth. Rough water can teach lessons worth knowing. When the state is unquiet, personal qualities are more than ever decisive. Fear not a revolution which will constrain you to live five years in one. Don't be so tender at making an enemy now and then. Be willing to go to Coventry sometimes, and let the populace bestow on you their coldest contempts. The finished man of the world must eat of every apple once. He must hold his hatreds also at arm's length, and not remember spite. He has neither friends nor enemies, but values men only as channels of power.

He who aims high must dread an easy home and popular manners. Heaven sometimes hedges a rare character about with ungainliness and odium, as the burr that protects the fruit. If there is any great and good thing in store for you, it will not come at the first or the second call, nor in the shape of fashion, ease, and city drawing-rooms. Popularity is for dolls. "Steep and craggy," said Porphyry, "is the path of the gods." Open your Marcus Antoninus. In the opinion of the ancients he was the great man who scorned to shine, and who contested the frowns of fortune. They preferred the noble vessel too late for the tide, contending with winds and waves, dismantled and unrigged, to her companion borne into harbor with colors flying and guns firing. There is none of the social goods that may not be purchased too dear, and mere amiableness must not take rank with high aims and self-subsistency.

Bettine replies to Goethe's mother, who chides her disregard of dress—"If I cannot do as I have a mind in our poor Frankfort, I shall not carry things far." And the youth must rate at its true mark the inconceivable levity of local opinion. The longer we live the more we must endure the elementary existence of men and women; and every brave heart must treat society as a child, and never allow it to dictate.

"All that class of the severe and restrictive virtues," said Burke, "are almost too costly for humanity." Who wishes to be severe? Who wishes to resist the eminent and polite, in behalf of the poor, and low, and impolite? And who that dares do it can keep his temper sweet, his frolic spirits? The high virtues are not debonair, but have their redress in being illustrious at last. What forests of laurel we bring, and the tears of mankind, to those who stood firm against the opinion of their contemporaries! The measure of a master is his success in bringing all men round to his opinion twenty years later.

Let me say here that culture cannot begin too early. In talking with scholars, I observe that they lost on ruder companions those years of boyhood which alone could give imaginative literature a religious and infinite quality in their esteem. I find too that the chance for appreciation is much increased by being the son of an appreciator, and that these boys who now grow up are caught not only years too late, but two or three births too late, to make the best scholars of. And I think it a presentable motive to a scholar, that, as in an old community a well-born proprietor is usually found, after the first heats of youth, to be a careful husband, and to feel a habitual desire that the estate shall suffer no harm by his administration, but shall be delivered down to the next heir in as good condition as he received it—so a considerate man will reckon himself a subject of that secular melioration by which mankind is mollified, cured and refined; and will shun every expenditure of his forces on pleasure or gain which will jeopardize this social and secular accumulation.

The fossil strata show us that Nature began with rudimental forms and rose to the more complex as fast as the earth was fit for their dwelling-place; and that the lower perish as the higher appear. Very few of our race can be said to be yet finished men. We still carry sticking to us some remains of the preceding inferior quadruped organization. We call these millions men; but they are not yet men. Half engaged in the soil, pawing to get free, man needs all the music that can be brought to disengage him. If Love, red Love, with tears and joy; if Want with his scourge; if War with his cannonade, if Christianity with its charity; if Trade with its money; if Art with its portfolios; if Science with her telegraphs through the deeps of space and time can set his dull nerves throbbing, and by loud taps on the tough chrysalis can break its walls and let the new creature emerge erect and free—make way and sing pæan! The age of the quadruped is to go out, the age of the brain and of the heart is to come in. The time will come when the evil forms we have known can no more be organized. Man's culture can spare nothing, wants all the material. He is to convert all impediments into instruments, all enemies into power. The formidable mischief will only make the more useful slave. And if one shall read the future of the race hinted in the organic effort of nature to mount and meliorate, and the corresponding impulse to the Better in the human being, we shall dare affirm that there is nothing he will not overcome and convert, until at last culture shall absorb the chaos and gehenna. He will convert the Furies into Muses, and the hells into benefit.

SOCIETY AND
SOLITUDE

[Society and Solitude *is the title of a book Emerson published in 1870. Most of the chapters were already in existence as lectures in 1858 and 1859.*]

Seyd melted the days like cups of
    pearl,
Served high and low, the lord and
    churl
Loved harebells nodding on a rock,
A cabin hung with curling smoke,
Ring of axe or hum of wheel
Or gleam which use can paint on
    steel,
And huts and tents; nor loved he
    less
Stately lords in palaces,
Princely women hard to please,
Fenced by form and ceremony,
Decked by courtly rites and dress
And etiquette of gentilesse.
But when the mate of the snow and
    wind,

He left each civil scale behind:
Him wood-gods fed with honey
    wild
And of his memory beguiled.
In caves and hollow trees he crept
And near the wolf and panther slept.
He stood before the tumbling main
With joy too tense for sober brain;
He shared the life of the element,
The tie of blood and home was
    rent:
As if in him the welkin walked,
The winds took flesh, the mountains
    talked
And he the bard, a crystal soul,
Sphered and concentric with the
    whole.

That each should in his house abide,
Therefore was the world so wide.

SOCIETY AND SOLITUDE

I FELL IN with a humorist on my travels, who had in his chamber a cast of the Rondanini Medusa, and who assured me that the name which that fine work of art bore in the catalogues was a misnomer, as he was convinced that the sculptor who carved it intended it for Memory, the mother of the Muses. In the conversation that followed, my new friend made some extraordinary confessions. "Do you not see," he said, "the penalty of learning, and that each of these scholars whom you have met at S——, though he were to be the last man, would, like the executioner in Hood's poem, guillotine the last but one?" He added many lively remarks, but his evident earnestness engaged my attention, and in the weeks that followed we became better acquainted. He had good abilities, a genial temper and no vices; but he had one defect—he could not speak in the tone of the people. There was some paralysis on his will, such that when he met men on common terms he spoke weakly and from the point, like a flighty girl. His consciousness of the fault made it worse. He envied every drover and lumberman in the tavern their manly speech. He coveted Mirabeau's *don terrible de la familiarité*, believing that he whose sympathy goes lowest is the man from whom kings have the most to fear. For himself he declared that he could not get enough alone to write a letter to a friend. He left the city; he hid himself in pastures. The solitary river was not solitary enough; the sun and moon put him out. When he bought a house, the first thing he did was to plant trees. He could not enough conceal himself. Set a hedge here; set oaks there—trees behind trees; above all, set evergreens, for they will keep a secret all the year round. The most agreeable compliment you could pay him was to imply that you had not observed him in a house or a street where you had met him. Whilst he suffered at being seen where he was, he consoled himself with the delicious thought of the inconceivable number of places where he was not. All he wished of his tailor was to provide that sober mean of color and cut which would never detain the eye for a moment. He went to Vienna, to Smyrna, to London. In all the variety of costumes, a carnival, a

663

kaleidoscope of clothes, to his horror he could never discover a man in the street who wore anything like his own dress. He would have given his soul for the ring of Gyges. His dismay at his visibility had blunted the fears of mortality. "Do you think," he said, "I am in such great terror of being shot—I, who am only waiting to shuffle off my corporeal jacket to slip away into the back stars, and put diameters of the solar system and sidereal orbits between me and all souls—there to wear out ages in solitude, and forget memory itself, if it be possible?" He had a remorse running to despair of his social *gaucheries*, and walked miles and miles to get the twitchings out of his face, the starts and shrugs out of his arms and shoulders. God may forgive sins, he said, but awkwardness has no forgiveness in heaven or earth. He admired in Newton not so much his theory of the moon as his letter to Collins, in which he forbade him to insert his name with the solution of the problem in the Philosophical Transactions: "It would perhaps increase my acquaintance, the thing which I chiefly study to decline."

These conversations led me somewhat later to the knowledge of similar cases, and to the discovery that they are not of very infrequent occurrence. Few substances are found pure in nature. Those constitutions which can bear in open day the rough dealing of the world must be of that mean and average structure such as iron and salt, atmospheric air and water. But there are metals, like potassium and sodium, which, to be kept pure, must be kept under naphtha. Such are the talents determined on some specialty, which a culminating civilization fosters in the heart of great cities and in royal chambers. Nature protects her own work. To the culture of the world an Archimedes, a Newton is indispensable; so she guards them by a certain aridity. If these had been good fellows, fond of dancing, port and clubs, we should have had no Theory of the Sphere and no Principia. They had that necessity of isolation which genius feels. Each must stand on his glass tripod if he would keep his electricity. Even Swedenborg, whose theory of the universe is based on affection, and who reprobates to weariness the danger and vice of pure intellect, is constrained to make an extraordinary exception: "There are also angels who do not live consociated, but separate, house and house; these dwell in the midst of heaven, because they are the best of angels."

We have known many fine geniuses with that imperfection that they cannot do anything useful, not so much as write one clean sentence. 'T is worse, and tragic, that no man is fit for society who has fine traits. At a distance he is admired, but bring him hand to hand, he is a cripple. One protects himself by solitude, and one by courtesy, and one by an acid, worldly manner—each concealing how he can the thinness of his skin and his incapacity for strict association. But there is no remedy that can reach the heart of the disease but either habits of self-reliance that should go in practice to making the man independent of the human race, or else a religion of love. Now he hardly seems entitled to marry; for how can he protect a woman, who cannot protect himself?

We pray to be conventional. But the wary Heaven takes care you shall not be, if there is anything good in you. Dante was very bad company, and was never invited to dinner. Michael Angelo had a sad, sour time of it. The ministers of beauty are rarely beautiful in coaches and saloons. Columbus discovered no isle or key so lonely as himself. Yet each of these potentates saw well the reason of his exclusion. Solitary was he? Why, yes; but his society was limited only by the amount of brain nature appropriated in that age to carry on the government of the world. "If I stay," said Dante, when there was question of going to Rome, "who will go? and if I go, who will stay?"

But the necessity of solitude is deeper than we have said, and is organic. I have seen many a philosopher whose world is large enough for only one person. He affects to be a good companion; but we are still surprising his secret, that he means and needs to impose his system on all the rest. The determination of each is *from* all the others, like that of each tree up into free space. 'T is no wonder, when each has his whole head, our societies should be so small. Like President Tyler, our party falls from us every day, and we must ride in a sulky at last. Dear heart! take it sadly home to thee—there is no cooperation. We begin with friendships, and all our youth is a reconnoitring and recruiting of the holy fraternity they shall combine for the salvation of men. But so the remoter stars seem a nebula of united light, yet there is no group which a telescope will not resolve; and the dearest friends are separated by impassable gulfs. The cooperation is involuntary, and is put upon us by the Genius of Life, who reserves this as a part of his prerogative. 'T is fine for us to talk; we sit and muse and are serene and complete; but the moment we meet with anybody, each becomes a fraction.

Though the stuff of tragedy and of romances is in a moral union of two superior persons whose confidence in each other for long years, out of sight and in sight, and against all appearances, is at last justified by victorious proof of probity to gods and men, causing joyful emotions, tears and glory—though there be for heroes this *moral union*, yet they too are as far off as ever from an intellectual union, and the moral union is for comparatively low and external purposes, like the cooperation of a ship's company or of a fire-club. But how insular and pathetically solitary are all the people we know! Nor dare they tell what they think of each other when they meet in the street. We have a fine right, to be sure, to taunt men of the world with superficial and treacherous courtesies!

Such is the tragic necessity which strict science finds underneath our domestic and neighborly life, irresistibly driving each adult soul as with whips into the desert, and making our warm covenants sentimental and momentary. We must infer that the ends of thought were peremptory, if they were to be secured at such ruinous cost. They are deeper than can be told, and belong to the immensities and eternities. They reach down to that depth where society itself originates and disappears; where the question is, Which is first, man or men? where the individual is lost in his source.

But this banishment to the rocks and echoes no metaphysics can make right or tolerable. This result is so against nature, such a half-view, that it must be corrected by a common sense and experience. "A man is born by the side of his father, and there he remains." A man must be clothed with society, or we shall feel a certain bareness and poverty, as of a displaced and unfurnished member. He is to be dressed in arts and institutions, as well as in body garments. Now and then a man exquisitely made can live alone, and must; but coop up most men and you undo them. "The king lived and ate in his hall with men, and understood men," said Selden. When a young barrister said to the late Mr. Mason, "I keep my chamber to read law"—"Read law!" replied the veteran, "'t is in the court-room you must read law." Nor is the rule otherwise for literature. If you would learn to write, 't is in the street you must learn it. Both for the vehicle and for the aims of fine arts you must frequent the public square. The people, and not the college, is the writer's home. A scholar is a candle which the love and desire of all men will light. Never his lands or his rents, but the power to charm the disguised soul that sits veiled under this bearded and that rosy visage is his rent and ration. His products are as needful as those of the baker or the weaver. Society cannot do without cultivated men. As soon as the first wants are satisfied, the higher wants become imperative.

'T is hard to mesmerize ourselves, to whip our own top; but through sympathy we are capable of energy and endurance. Concert fires people to a certain fury of performance they can rarely reach alone. Here is the use of society: it is so easy with the great to be great; so easy to come up to an existing standard; as easy as it is to the lover to swim to his maiden through waves so grim before. The benefits of affection are immense; and the one event which never loses its romance is the encounter with superior persons on terms allowing the happiest intercourse.

It by no means follows that we are not fit for society, because *soirées* are tedious and because the *soirée* finds us tedious. A backwoodsman, who had been sent to the university, told me that when he heard the best-bred young men at the law-school talk together, he reckoned himself a boor; but whenever he caught them apart, and had one to himself alone, then they were the boors and he the better man. And if we recall the rare hours when we encountered the best persons, we then found ourselves, and then first society seemed to exist. That was society, though in the transom of a brig or on the Florida Keys.

A cold sluggish blood thinks it has not facts enough to the purpose, and must decline its turn in the conversation. But they who speak have no more—have less. 'T is not new facts that avail, but the heat to dissolve everybody's facts. Heat puts you in right relation with magazines of facts. The capital defect of cold, arid natures is the want of animal spirits. They seem a power incredible, as if God should raise the dead. The recluse witnesses what others perform by their aid, with a kind of fear. It is as much out of his possibility as the prowess of Cœur-de-Lion, or an Irishman's day's work on the railroad. 'T is said the present and the future are always rivals. Animal spirits constitute the power of the present, and their feats are like the structure of a pyramid. Their result is a lord, a general, or a boon companion. Before these what a base mendicant is Memory with his leathern badge! But this genial heat is latent in all constitutions, and is disengaged only by the friction of society. As Bacon said of manners, "To obtain them, it only needs not to despise them," so we say of animal spirits that they

. . . .

are the spontaneous product of health and of a social habit. "For behavior, men learn it, as they take diseases, one of another."

But the people are to be taken in very small doses. If solitude is proud, so is society vulgar. In society, high advantages are set down to the individual as disqualifications. We sink as easily as we rise, through sympathy. So many men whom I know are degraded by their sympathies; their native aims being high enough, but their relation all too tender to the gross people about them. Men cannot afford to live together on their merits, and they adjust themselves by their demerits—by their love of gossip, or by sheer tolerance and animal good nature. They untune and dissipate the brave aspirant.

The remedy is to reinforce each of these moods from the other. Conversation will not corrupt us if we come to the assembly in our own garb and speech and with the energy of health to select what is ours and reject what is not. Society we must have; but let it be society, and not exchanging news or eating from the same dish. Is it society to sit in one of your chairs? I cannot go to the houses of my nearest relatives, because I do not wish to be alone. Society exists by chemical affinity, and not otherwise.

Put any company of people together with freedom for conversation, and a rapid self-distribution takes place into sets and pairs. The best are accused of exclusiveness. It would be more true to say they separate as oil from water, as children from old people, without love or hatred in the matter, each seeking his like; and any interference with the affinities would produce constraint and suffocation. All conversation is a magnetic experiment. I know that my friend can talk eloquently; you know that he cannot articulate a sentence: we have seen him in different company. Assort your party, or invite none. Put Stubbs and Coleridge, Quintilian and Aunt Miriam, into pairs, and you make them all wretched. 'T is an extempore Sing-Sing built in a parlor. Leave them to seek their own mates, and they will be as merry as sparrows.

A higher civility will reëstablish in our customs a certain reverence which we have lost. What to do with these brisk young men who break through all fences, and make themselves at home in every house? I find out in an instant if my companion does not want me, and ropes cannot hold me when my welcome is gone. One would think that the affinities would pronounce themselves with a surer reciprocity.

Here again, as so often, nature delights to put us between extreme antagonisms, and our safety is in the skill with which we keep the diagonal line. Solitude is impracticable, and society fatal. We must keep our head in the one and our hands in the other. The conditions are met, if we keep our independence, yet do not lose our sympathy. These wonderful horses need to be driven by fine hands. We require such a solitude as shall hold us to its revelations when we are in the street and in palaces; for most men are cowed in society, and say good things to you in private, but will not stand to them in public. But let us not be the victims of words. Society and solitude are deceptive names. It is not the circumstance of seeing more or fewer people, but the readiness of sympathy, that imports; and a sound mind will derive its principles from insight, with ever a purer ascent to the sufficient and absolute right, and will accept society as the natural element in which they are to be applied.

FARMING

[*This essay was first published as one chapter of* Society and Solitude. *It was originally entitled* The Man with the Hoe *and was delivered at the Middlesex "Cattleshow" on September 29, 1858. Concord was mainly a farming country in Emerson's time. His own property consisted of a house and a ten-acre farm which was worked for him by hired labor. Although Emerson was not a handy man with tools and implements, he enjoyed gardening and took especial pride in his fruit trees and grapes and occasionally took prizes for good fruit at the annual agricultural fairs.*]

To these men
The landscape is an armory of
   powers,
Which, one by one, they know to
   draw and use.
They harness beast, bird, insect, to
   their work;
They prove the virtues of each bed
   of rock,
And, like the chemist mid his loaded
   jars,
Draw from each stratum its adapted
   use
To drug their crops or weapon their
   arts withal.
They turn the frost upon their
   chemic heap,
They set the wind to winnow pulse
   and grain,
They thank the spring-flood for its
   fertile slime,
And on cheap summit-levels of the
   snow

Slide with the sledge to inaccessible
   woods
O'er meadows bottomless. So, year
   by year,
They fight the elements with ele-
   ments,
And by the order in the field dis-
   close
The order regnant in the yeoman's
   brain.
What these strong masters wrote at
   large in miles,
I followed in small copy in my
   acre;
For there's no rood has not a star
   above it;
The cordial quality of pear or plum
Ascends as gladly in a single
   tree
As in broad orchards resonant with
   bees;
And every atom poises for itself,
And for the whole.

He planted where the deluge ploughed,
His hired hands were wind and cloud;
His eyes detect the Gods concealed
In the hummock of the field.

FARMING

THE GLORY of the farmer is that, in the division of labors, it is his part to create. All trade rests at last on his primitive activity. He stands close to Nature; he obtains from the earth the bread and the meat. The food which was not, he causes to be. The first farmer was the first man, and all historic nobility rests on possession and use of land. Men do not like hard work, but every man has an exceptional respect for tillage, and a feeling that this is the original calling of his race, that he himself is only excused from it by some circumstance which made him delegate it for a time to other hands. If he have not some skill which recommends him to the farmer, some product for which the farmer will give him corn, he must himself return into his due place among the planters. And the profession has in all eyes its ancient charm, as standing nearest to God, the first cause.

Then the beauty of Nature, the tranquillity and innocence of the countryman, his independence and his pleasing arts—the care of bees, of poultry, of sheep, of cows, the dairy, the care of hay, of fruits, of orchards and forests, and the reaction of these on the workman, in giving him a strength and plain dignity like the face and manners of Nature—all men acknowledge. All men keep the farm in reserve as an asylum where, in case of mischance, to hide their poverty—or a solitude, if they do not succeed in society. And who knows how many glances of remorse are turned this way from the bankrupts of trade, from mortified pleaders in courts and senates, or from the victims of idleness and pleasure? Poisoned by town life and town vices, the sufferer resolves: 'Well, my children, whom I have injured, shall go back to the land, to be recruited and cured by that which should have been my nursery, and now shall be their hospital.'

The farmer's office is precise and important, but you must not try to paint him in rose-color; you cannot make pretty compliments to fate and gravitation, whose minister he is. He represents the necessities. It is the beauty of the great economy of the world that makes his comeliness. He bends to the order of the seasons, the weather, the soils and crops, as the sails of a ship bend to the wind. He represents continuous hard labor, year in, year out, and small gains. He is a slow person, timed to Nature, and not to city watches. He takes the pace of seasons, plants and chemistry. Nature never hurries: atom by atom, little by little, she achieves her work. The lesson one learns in fishing, yachting, hunting or planting is the manners of Nature; patience with the delays of wind and sun, delays of the seasons, bad weather, excess or lack of water—patience with the slowness of our feet, with the parsimony of our strength, with the largeness of sea and land we must traverse, etc. The farmer times himself to Nature, and acquires that livelong patience which belongs to her. Slow, narrow man, his rule is that the earth shall feed and clothe him; and he must wait for his crop to grow. His entertainments, his liberties and his spending must be on a farmer's scale, and not on a merchant's. It were as false for farmers to use a wholesale and massy expense, as for states to use a minute economy. But if thus pinched on one side, he has compensatory advantages. He is permanent, clings to his land as the rocks do. In the town where I live, farms remain in the same families for seven and eight generations; and most of the first settlers (in 1635), should they reappear on the farms to-day, would find their own blood and names still in possession. And the like fact holds in the surrounding towns.

This hard work will always be done by one kind of man; not by scheming speculators, nor by soldiers, nor professors, nor readers of Tennyson; but by men of endurance—deep-chested, long-winded, tough, slow and sure, and timely. The farmer has a great health, and the appetite of health, and means to his end; he has broad lands for his home, wood to burn great fires, plenty of plain food; his milk at least is unwatered; and for sleep, he has cheaper and better and more of it than citizens.

He has grave trusts confided to him. In the great household of Nature, the farmer stands at the door of the bread-room, and weighs to each his loaf. It is for him to say whether men shall marry or not. Early marriages and the number of births are indissolubly connected with abundance of food; or, as Burke said, "Man breeds at the mouth." Then he is the Board of Quarantine. The farmer is a hoarded capital of health, as the farm is the capital of wealth; and it is from him that the health and power moral and intellectual, of the cities came. The city is always recruited from the country. The men in cities who are the centres of energy, the driving-wheels of trade, politics or practical arts, and the women of beauty and genius, are the children or grandchildren of farmers, and are spending the energies which their fathers' hardy, silent life accumulated in frosty furrows, in poverty, necessity and darkness.

He is the continuous benefactor. He who digs a well, constructs a stone fountain, plants a grove of trees by the roadside, plants an orchard, builds a durable house, reclaims a swamp, or so much as puts a stone seat by the wayside, makes the land so far lovely and desirable, makes a fortune which he cannot carry away with him, but which is useful to his country long afterwards. The man that works at home helps society at large with somewhat more of certainty than he who devotes himself to charities. If it be true that, not by votes of political parties but by the eternal laws of political economy, slaves are driven out of a slave state as fast as it is surrounded by free states, then the true abolitionist is the farmer, who, heedless of laws and constitutions, stands all day in the field, investing his labor in the land, and making a product with which no forced labor can compete.

We commonly say that the rich man can speak the truth, can afford honesty, can afford independence of opinion and action—and that is the theory of nobility. But it is the rich man in a true sense, that is to say, not the man of large income and large expenditure, but solely the man whose outlay is less than his income and is steadily kept so.

In English factories, the boy that watches the loom, to tie the thread when the wheel stops to indicate that a thread is broken, is called a *minder*. And in this great factory of our Copernican globe, shifting its slides, rotating its constellations, times and tides, bringing now the day of planting, then of watering, then of weeding, then of reaping, then of curing and storing—the farmer is the *minder*. His machine is of colossal proportions; the diameter of the water-wheel, the arms of the levers, the power of the battery, are out of all mechanic measure; and it takes him long to understand its parts and its working. This pump never "sucks;" these screws are never loose; this machine is never out of gear; the vat and piston, wheels and tires, never wear out, but are self-repairing.

Who are the farmer's servants? Not the Irish, nor the coolies, but Geology and Chemistry, the quarry of the air, the water of the brook, the lightning of the cloud, the castings of the worm, the plough of the frost. Long before he was born, the sun of ages decomposed the rocks, mellowed his land, soaked it with light and heat, covered it with vegetable film, then with forests, and accumulated the sphagnum whose decays made the peat of his meadow.

Science has shown the great circles in which Nature works; the manner in which marine plants balance the marine animals, as the land plants supply the oxygen which the animals consume, and the animals the carbon which the plants absorb. These activities are incessant. Nature works on a method of *all for each and each for all*. The strain that is made on one point bears on every arch and foundation of the structure. There is a perfect solidarity. You cannot detach an atom from its holdings, or strip off from it the electricity, gravitation, chemic affinity or the relation to light and heat and leave the atom bare. No, it brings with it its universal ties.

Nature, like a cautious testator, ties up her estate so as not to bestow it all on one generation, but has a forelooking tenderness and equal regard to the next and the next, and the fourth and the fortieth age. There lie the inexhaustible magazines. The eternal rocks, as we call them, have held their oxygen or lime undiminished, entire, as it was. No particle of oxygen can rust or wear, but has the same energy as on the first morning. The good rocks, those patient waiters, say to him: 'We have the sacred power as we received it. We have not failed of our trust, and now—when in our immense day the hour is at last struck—take the gas we have hoarded, mingle it with water, and let it be free to grow in plants and animals and obey the thought of man.'

The earth works for him; the earth is a machine which yields almost gratuitous service to every application of intellect. Every plant is a manufacturer of soil. In the stomach of the plant development begins. The tree can draw on the whole air, the whole earth, on all the rolling main. The plant is all suction-pipe—imbibing from the ground by its root, from the air by its leaves, with all its might.

The air works for him. The atmosphere, a sharp solvent, drinks the essence and spirit of every solid on the globe—a menstruum which melts the mountains into it. Air is matter subdued by heat. As the sea is the grand receptacle of all rivers, so the air is the receptacle from which all things spring, and into which they all return. The invisible and creeping air takes form and solid mass. Our senses are skeptics, and believe only the impression of the moment, and do not believe the

chemical fact that these huge mountain chains are made up of gases and
rolling wind. But Nature is as subtle as she is strong. She turns her capital day by day; deals never with dead, but ever with quick subjects.
All things are flowing, even those that seem immovable. The adamant
is always passing into smoke. The plants imbibe the materials which
they want from the air and the ground. They burn, that is, exhale and
decompose their own bodies into the air and earth again. The animal
burns, or undergoes the like perpetual consumption. The earth burns,
the mountains burn and decompose, slower, but incessantly. It is
almost inevitable to push the generalization up into higher parts of
Nature, rank over rank into sentient beings. Nations burn with internal fire of thought and affection, which wastes while it works. We shall
find finer combustion and finer fuel. Intellect is a fire: rash and pitiless it melts this wonderful bone-house which is called man. Genius
even, as it is the greatest good, is the greatest harm. Whilst all thus
burns—the universe in a blaze kindled from the torch of the sun—it
needs a perpetual tempering, a phlegm, a sleep, atmospheres of azote,
deluges of water, to check the fury of the conflagration; a hoarding to
check the spending, a centrifugence equal to the centrifugence; and this
is invariably supplied.

The railroad dirt-cars are good excavators, but there is no porter
like Gravitation, who will bring down any weights which man cannot
carry, and if he wants aid, knows where to find his fellow laborers.
Water works in masses, and sets its irresistible shoulder to your mills or
your ships, or transports vast boulders of rock in its iceberg a thousand
miles. But its far greater power depends on its talent of becoming little, and entering the smallest holes and pores. By this agency, carrying
in solution elements needful to every plant, the vegetable world exists.

But as I said, we must not paint the farmer in rose-color. Whilst
these grand energies have wrought for him and made his task possible,
he is habitually engaged in small economies, and is taught the power
that lurks in petty things. Great is the force of a few simple arrangements; for instance, the powers of a fence. On the prairie you wander
a hundred miles and hardly find a stick or a stone. At rare intervals a
thin oak-opening has been spared, and every such section has been long
occupied. But the farmer manages to procure wood from far, puts up a
rail-fence, and at once the seeds sprout and the oaks rise. It was only
browsing and fire which had kept them down. Plant fruit-trees by the

roadside, and their fruit will never be allowed to ripen. Draw a pine fence about them, and for fifty years they mature for the owner their delicate fruit. There is a great deal of enchantment in a chestnut rail or picketed pine boards.

Nature suggests every economical expedient somewhere on a great scale. Set out a pine-tree, and it dies in the first year, or lives a poor spindle. But Nature drops a pine-cone in Mariposa, and it lives fifteen centuries, grows three or four hundred feet high, and thirty in diameter—grows in a grove of giants, like a colonnade of Thebes. Ask the tree how it was done. It did not grow on a ridge, but in a basin, where it found deep soil, cold enough and dry enough for the pine; defended itself from the sun by growing in groves, and from the wind by the walls of the mountain. The roots that shot deepest, and the stems of happiest exposure, drew the nourishment from the rest, until the less thrifty perished and manured the soil for the stronger, and the mammoth Sequoias rose to their enormous proportions. The traveller who saw them remembered his orchard at home, where every year, in the destroying wind, his forlorn trees pined like suffering virtue. In September, when the pears hang heaviest and are taking from the sun their gay colors, comes usually a gusty day which shakes the whole garden and throws down the heaviest fruit in bruised heaps. The planter took the hint of the Sequoias, built a high wall, or—better—surrounded the orchard with a nursery of birches and evergreens. Thus he had the mountain basin in miniature; and his pears grew to the size of melons, and the vines beneath them ran an eighth of a mile. But this shelter creates a new climate. The wall that keeps off the strong wind keeps off the cold wind. The high wall reflecting the heat back on the soil gives that acre a quadruple share of sunshine—

> "Enclosing in the garden square
> A dead and standing pool of air,"

and makes a little Cuba within it, whilst all without is Labrador.

The chemist comes to his aid every year by following out some new hint drawn from Nature, and now affirms that this dreary space occupied by the farmer is needless; he will concentrate his kitchen-garden into a box of one or two rods square, will take the roots into his laboratory; the vines and stalks and stems may go sprawling about in the fields outside, he will attend to the roots in his tub, gorge them with food that is good for them. The smaller his garden, the better he can feed it, and the larger the crop. As he nursed his Thanksgiving turkeys on bread and milk, so he will pamper his peaches and grapes on the viands they like best. If they have an appetite for potash, or salt, or iron, or ground bones, or even now and then for a dead hog, he will indulge them. They keep the secret well, and never tell on your table whence they drew their sunset complexion or their delicate flavors.

See what the farmer accomplishes by a cart-load of tiles: he alters the climate by letting off water which kept the land cold through constant evaporation, and allows the warm rain to bring down into the roots the temperature of the air and of the surface soil; and he deepens the soil, since the discharge of this standing water allows the roots of his plants to penetrate below the surface to the subsoil, and accelerates the ripening of the crop. The town of Concord is one of the oldest towns in this country, far on now in its third century. The selectmen have once in every five years perambulated the boundaries, and yet, in this very year, a large quantity of land has been discovered and added to the town without a murmur of complaint from any quarter. By drainage we went down to a subsoil we did not know, and have found there is a Concord under old Concord, which we are now getting the best crops from; a Middlesex under Middlesex; and, in fine, that Massachusetts has a basement story more valuable and that promises to pay a better rent than all the superstructure. But these tiles have acquired by association a new interest. These tiles are political economists, confuters of Malthus and Ricardo; they are so many Young Americans announcing a better era—more bread. They drain the land, make it sweet and friable; have made English Chat Moss a garden, and will now do as much for the Dismal Swamp. But beyond this benefit they are the text of better opinions and better auguries for mankind.

There has been a nightmare bred in England of indigestion and spleen among landlords and loom-lords, namely, the dogma that men breed too fast for the powers of the soil; that men multiply in a geometrical ratio, whilst corn multiplies only in an arithmetical; and hence that, the more prosperous we are, the faster we approach these frightful limits nay, the plight of every new generation is worse than of the foregoing, because the first comers take up the best lands; the next, the second best; and each succeeding wave of population is driven to poorer, so that the land is ever yielding less returns to enlarging hosts of eaters. Henry Carey of Philadelphia replied: "Not so, Mr. Malthus, but just the opposite of so is the fact."

The first planter, the savage, without helpers, without tools, looking chiefly to safety from his enemy—man or beast—takes poor land. The better lands are loaded with timber, which he cannot clear; they need drainage, which he cannot attempt. He cannot plough, or fell trees, or drain the rich swamp. He is a poor creature; he scratches with a sharp stick, lives in a cave or a hutch, has no road but the trail of the moose or bear; he lives on their flesh when he can kill one, on roots and fruits when he cannot. He falls, and is lame; he coughs, he has a stitch in his side, he has a fever and chills; when he is hungry, he cannot always kill and eat a bear—chances of war—sometimes the bear eats him. 'T is long before he digs or plants at all, and then only a patch. Later he learns that his planting is better than hunting; that the earth works faster for him than he can work for himself—works for him when he is asleep, when it rains, when heat overcomes him. The sunstroke which knocks him down brings his corn up. As his family thrive, and other planters come up around him, he begins to fell trees and clear good land; and when, by and by, there is more skill, and tools and roads, the new generations are strong enough to open the lowlands, where the wash of mountains has accumulated the best soil, which yield a hundred-fold the former crops. The last lands are the best lands. It needs science and great numbers to cultivate the best lands, and in the best manner. Thus true political economy is not mean, but liberal, and on the pattern of the sun and sky. Population increases in the ratio of morality; credit exists in the ratio of morality.

Meantime we cannot enumerate the incidents and agents of the farm without reverting to their influence on the farmer. He carries out this cumulative preparation of means to their last effect. This crust of soil which ages have refined he refines again for the feeding of a civil and instructed people. The great elements with which he deals cannot leave him unaffected, or unconscious of his ministry; but their influence somewhat resembles that which the same Nature has on the child—of subduing and silencing him. We see the farmer with pleasure and respect when we think what powers and utilities are so meekly worn. He knows every secret of labor; he changes the face of the landscape. Put him on a new planet and he would know where to begin; yet there is no arrogance in his bearing, but a perfect gentleness. The farmer stands well on the world. Plain in manners as in dress, he would not shine in palaces; he is absolutely unknown and inadmissible therein; living or dying, he never shall be heard of in them; yet the drawing-room heroes put down beside him would shrivel in his presence; he solid and unexpressive, they expressed to gold-leaf. But he stands well on the world—as Adam did, as an Indian does, as Homer's heroes, Agamemnon or Achilles, do. He is a person whom a poet of any clime—Milton, Firdusi, or Cervantes—would appreciate as being really a piece of the old Nature, comparable to sun and moon, rainbow and flood; because he is, as all natural persons are, representative of Nature as much as these.

That uncorrupted behavior which we admire in animals and in young children belongs to him, to the hunter, the sailor—the man who lives in the presence of Nature. Cities force growth and make men talkative and entertaining, but they make them artificial. What possesses interest for us is the *naturel* of each, his constitutional excellence. This is forever a surprise, engaging and lovely; we cannot be satiated with knowing it, and about it; and it is this which the conversation with Nature cherishes and guards.

POEMS

[*The poetical strain is everywhere apparent in Emerson's philosophy. He was also a writer of verses all his life. Many of them appeared in* The Dial, *of which he, Margaret Fuller and Henry Thoreau served at various times as editor. He wrote many poems to serve as mottos for his lectures. The two principal volumes of poetry published during his lifetime were* May-Day *in 1867 and* Selected Poems *in 1876. The following poems have been selected from his complete works.*]

GOOD-BYE

GOOD-BYE, proud world! I'm going home:
Thou art not my friend, and I'm not thine.
Long through thy weary crowds I roam;
A river-ark on the ocean brine,
Long I've been tossed like the driven foam;
But now, proud world! I'm going home.

Good-bye to Flattery's fawning face;
To Grandeur with his wise grimace;
To upstart Wealth's averted eye;
To supple Office, low and high;
To crowded halls, to court and street;
To frozen hearts and hasting feet;
To those who go, and those who come;
Good-bye, proud world! I'm going home.

I am going to my own hearth-stone,
Bosomed in yon green hills alone—
A secret nook in a pleasant land,
Whose groves the frolic fairies planned;
Where arches green, the livelong day,
Echo the blackbird's roundelay,
And vulgar feet have never trod
A spot that is sacred to thought and God.

O, when I am safe in my sylvan home,
I tread on the pride of Greece and Rome;
And when I am stretched beneath the pines,
Where the evening star so holy shines,
I laugh at the lore and the pride of man,
At the sophist schools and the learned clan;
For what are they all, in their high conceit,
When man in the bush with God may meet?

THE PROBLEM

I LIKE a church; I like a cowl;
I love a prophet of the soul;
And on my heart monastic aisles
Fall like sweet strains, or pensive smiles;
Yet not for all his faith can see
Would I that cowlèd churchman be.

Why should the vest on him allure,
Which I could not on me endure?

Not from a vain or shallow thought
His awful Jove young Phidias brought;
Never from lips of cunning fell
The thrilling Delphic oracle;
Out from the heart of nature rolled
The burdens of the Bible old;
The litanies of nations came,
Like the volcano's tongue of flame,
Up from the burning core below—
The canticles of love and woe:
The hand that rounded Peter's dome
And groined the aisles of Christian Rome
Wrought in a sad sincerity;
Himself from God he could not free;
He builded better than he knew;—
The conscious stone to beauty grew.

Know'st thou what wove yon woodbird's nest
Of leaves, and feathers from her breast?
Or how the fish outbuilt her shell,
Painting with morn each annual cell?
Or how the sacred pine-tree adds
To her old leaves new myriads?
Such and so grew these holy piles,
Whilst love and terror laid the tiles.
Earth proudly wears the Parthenon,

As the best gem upon her zone,
And Morning opes with haste her lids
To gaze upon the Pyramids;
O'er England's abbeys bends the sky,
As on its friends, with kindred eye;
For out of Thought's interior sphere
These wonders rose to upper air;
And Nature gladly gave them place,
Adopted them into her race,
And granted them an equal date
With Andes and with Ararat.

These temples grew as grows the grass;
Art might obey, but not surpass.
The passive Master lent his hand
To the vast soul that o'er him planned;
And the same power that reared the shrine
Bestrode the tribes that knelt within.
Ever the fiery Pentecost
Girds with one flame the countless host,
Trances the heart through chanting choirs,
And through the priest the mind inspires.
The word unto the prophet spoken
Was writ on tables yet unbroken;
The word by seers or sibyls told,
In groves of oak, or fanes of gold,
Still floats upon the morning wind,
Still whispers to the willing mind.
One accent of the Holy Ghost
The heedless world hath never lost.
I know what say the fathers wise—
The Book itself before me lies,
Old *Chrysostom*, best Augustine,
And he who blent both in his line,
The younger *Golden Lips* or mines,
Taylor, the Shakspeare of divines.
His words are music in my ear,
I see his cowlèd portrait dear;

. . . .

And yet, for all his faith could see,
I would not the good bishop be.

URIEL

IT fell in the ancient periods
    Which the brooding soul surveys,
Or ever the wild Time coined itself
    Into calendar months and days.

This was the lapse of Uriel,
Which in Paradise befell.
Once, among the Pleiads walking,
Seyd overheard the yougods talking;
And the treason, too long pent,
To his ears was evident.
The young deities discussed
Laws of form, and metre just,
Orb, quintessence, and sunbeams,
What subsisteth, and what seems.
One, with low tones that decide,
And doubt and reverend use defied,
With a look that solved the sphere,
And stirred the devils everywhere,
Gave his sentiment divine
Against the being of a line.
'Line in nature is not found;
Unit and universe are round;
In vain produced, all rays return;
Evil will bless, and ice will burn.'
As Uriel spoke with piercing eye,
A shudder ran around the sky;
The stern old war-gods shook their heads,
The seraphs frowned from myrtle-beds;
Seemed to the holy festival
The rash word boded ill to all;
The balance-beam of Fate was bent;

The bounds of good and ill were rent;
Strong Hades could not keep his own,
But all slid to confusion.

A sad self-knowledge, withering, fell
On the beauty of Uriel;
In heaven once eminent, the god
Withdrew, that hour, into his cloud;
Whether doomed to long gyration,
In the sea of generation,
Or by knowledge grown too bright
To hit the nerve of feebler sight.
Straightway, a forgetting wind
Stole over the celestial kind,
And their lips the secret kept,
If in ashes the fire-seed slept.
But now and then, truth-speaking things
Shamed the angels' veiling wings;
And, shrilling from the solar course,
Or from fruit of chemic force,
Procession of a soul in matter,
Or the speeding change of water,
Or out of the good of evil born,
Came Uriel's voice of cherub scorn,
And a blush tinged the upper sky,
And the gods shook, they knew not why.

THE RHODORA:
ON BEING ASKED, WHENCE IS THE FLOWER?

IN May, when sea-winds pierced our solitudes,
I found the fresh Rhodora in the woods,
Spreading its leafless blooms in a damp nook,
To please the desert and the sluggish brook.
The purple petals, fallen in the pool,
Made the black water with their beauty gay;
Here might the red-bird come his plumes to cool,

And court the flower that cheapens his array.
Rhodora! if the sages ask thee why
This charm is wasted on the earth and sky,
Tell them, dear, that if eyes were made for seeing,
Then Beauty is its own excuse for being:
Why thou wert there, O rival of the rose!
I never thought to ask, I never knew:
But, in my simple ignorance, suppose
The self-same Power that brought me there brought you.

THE HUMBLE-BEE

BURLY, dozing humble-bee,
Where thou art is clime for me.
Let them sail for Porto Rique,
Far-off heats through seas to seek;
I will follow thee alone,
Thou animated torrid-zone!
Zigzag steerer, desert cheerer,
Let me chase thy waving lines;
Keep me nearer, me thy hearer,
Singing over shrubs and vines.

Insect lover of the sun,
Joy of thy dominion!
Sailor of the atmosphere;
Swimmer through the waves of air;
Voyager of light and noon;
Epicurean of June;
Wait, I prithee,till I come
Within earshot of thy hum—
All without is martyrdom.

When the south wind, in May days,
With a net of shining haze
Silvers the horizon wall,
And with softness touching all,

Tints the human countenance
With a color of romance,
And infusing subtle heats,
Turns the sod to violets,
Thou, in sunny solitudes,
Rover of the underwoods,
The green silence dost displace
With thy mellow, breezy bass.

Hot midsummer's petted crone,
Sweet to me thy drowsy tone
Tells of countless sunny hours,
Long days, and solid banks of flowers;
Of gulfs of sweetness without bound
In Indian wildernesses found;
Of Syrian peace, immortal leisure,
Firmest cheer, and bird-like pleasure.

Aught unsavory or unclean
Hath my insect never seen;
But violets and bilberry bells,
Maple-sap and daffodels,
Grass with green flag half-mast high,
Succory to match the sky,
Columbine with horn of honey,
Scented fern, and agrimony,
Clover, catchfly, adder's-tongue
And brier-roses, dwelt among;
All beside was unknown waste,
All was picture as he passed.

Wiser far than human seer,
Yellow-breeched philosopher!
Seeing only what is fair,
Sipping only what is sweet,
Thou dost mock at fate and care,
Leave the chaff, and take the wheat.
When the fierce northwestern blast

Cools sea and land so far and fast,
Thou already slumberest deep;
Woe and want thou canst outsleep;
Want and woe, which torture us,
Thy sleep makes ridiculous.

THE SNOW-STORM

ANNOUNCED by all the trumpets of the sky,
Arrives the snow, and, driving o'er the fields,
Seems nowhere to alight: the whited air
Hides hills and woods, the river, and the heaven,
And veils the farm-house at the garden's end.
The sled and traveller stopped, the courier's feet
Delayed, all friends shut out, the housemates sit
Around the radiant fireplace, enclosed
In a tumultuous privacy of storm.

    Come see the north wind's masonry.
Out of an unseen quarry evermore
Furnished with tile, the fierce artificer
Curves his white bastions with projected roof
Round every windward stake, or tree, or door.
Speeding, the myriad-handed, his wild work
So fanciful, so savage, nought cares he
For number or proportion. Mockingly,
On coop or kennel he hangs Parian wreaths;
A swan-like form invests the hidden thorn;
Fills up the farmer's lane from wall to wall,
Maugre the farmer's sighs; and at the gate
A tapering turret overtops the work.
And when his hours are numbered, and the world
Is all his own, retiring, as he were not,
Leaves, when the sun appears, astonished Art
To mimic in slow structures, stone by stone,
Built in an age, the mad wind's night-work,
The frolic architecture of the snow.

ODE

INSCRIBED TO W. H. CHANNING

THOUGH loath to grieve
The evil time's sole patriot,
I cannot leave
My honied thought
For the priest's cant,
Or statesman's rant.

If I refuse
My study for their politique,
Which at the best is trick,
The angry Muse
Puts confusion in my brain.

But who is he that prates
Of the culture of mankind,
Of better arts and life?
Go, blindworm, go,
Behold the famous States
Harrying Mexico
With rifle and with knife!

Or who, with accent bolder,
Dare praise the freedom-loving mountaineer?
I found by thee, O rushing Contoocook!
And in thy valleys, Agiochook!
The jackals of the negro-holder.

The God who made New Hampshire
Taunted the lofty land
With little men;
Small bat and wren
House in the oak:
If earth-fire cleave
The upheaved land, and bury the folk,

The southern crocodile would grieve.
Virtue palters; Right is hence;
Freedom praised, but hid;
Funeral eloquence
Rattles the coffin-lid.

What boots thy zeal,
O glowing friend,
That would indignant rend
The northland from the south?
Wherefore? to what good end?
Boston Bay and Bunker Hill
Would serve things still;
Things are of the snake.

The horseman serves the horse,
The neatherd serves the neat,
The merchant serves the purse,
The eater serves his meat;
'T is the day of the chattel,
Web to weave, and corn to grind;
Things are in the saddle,
And ride mankind.

There are two laws discrete,
Not reconciled—
Law for man, and law for thing;
The last builds town and fleet,
But it runs wild,
And doth the man unking.
'T is fit the forest fall,
The steep be graded,
The mountain tunnelled,
The sand shaded,
The orchard planted,
The glebe tilled,
The prairie granted,
The steamer built.

Let man serve law for man;
Live for friendship, live for love,
For truth's and harmony's behoof;
The state may follow how it can,
As Olympus follows Jove.

Yet do not I implore
The wrinkled shopman to my sounding woods,
Nor bid the unwilling senator
Ask votes of thrushes in the solitudes.
Every one to his chosen work;
Foolish hands may mix and mar;
Wise and sure the issues are.
Round they roll till dark is light,
Sex to sex, and even to odd;
The over-god
Who marries Right to Might,
Who peoples, unpeoples,
He who exterminates
Races by stronger races,
Black by white faces,
Knows to bring honey
Out of the lion;
Grafts gentlest scion
On pirate and Turk.

The Cossack eats Poland,
Like stolen fruit;
Her last noble is ruined,
Her last poet mute:
Straight, into double band
The victors divide;
Half for freedom strike and stand;
The astonished Muse finds thousands at her side.

FORBEARANCE

HAST thou named all the birds without a gun?
Loved the wood-rose, and left it on its stalk?
At rich men's tables eaten bread and pulse?
Unarmed, faced danger with a heart of trust?
And loved so well a high behavior,
In man or maid, that thou from speech refrained,
Nobility more nobly to repay?
O, be my friend, and teach me to be thine!

FORERUNNERS

LONG I followed happy guides,
I could never reach their sides;
Their step is forth, and, ere the day
Breaks up their leaguer, and away.
Keen my sense, my heart was young,
Right good-will my sinews strung,
But no speed of mine avails
To hunt upon their shining trails.
On and away, their hasting feet
Make the morning proud and sweet;
Flowers they strew—I catch the scent;
Or tone of silver instrument
Leaves on the wind melodious trace;
Yet I could never see their face.
On eastern hills I see their smokes,
Mixed with mist by distant lochs.
I met many travellers
Who the road had surely kept;
They saw not my fine revellers,
These had crossed them while they slept.
Some had heard their fair report,
In the country or the court.
Fleetest couriers alive

Never yet could once arrive,
As they went or they returned,
At the house where these sojourned.
Sometimes their strong speed they slacken,
Though they are not overtaken;
In sleep their jubilant troop is near,
I tuneful voices overhear;
It may be in wood or waste,
At unawares 't is come and past.
Their near camp my spirit knows
By signs gracious as rainbows.
I thenceforward and long after
Listen for their harp-like laughter,
And carry in my heart, for days,
Peace that hallows rudest ways.

GIVE ALL TO LOVE

GIVE all to love;
Obey thy heart;
Friends, kindred, days,
Estate, good-fame,
Plans, credit and the Muse,
Nothing refuse.

'T is a brave master;
Let it have scope:
Follow it utterly,
Hope beyond hope:
High and more high
It dives into noon,
With wing unspent,
Untold intent;
But it is a god,
Knows its own path
And the outlets of the sky.

It was never for the mean;
It requireth courage stout.
Souls above doubt,
Valor unbending,
It will reward,
They shall return
More than they were,
And every ascending.

Leave all for love;
Yet, hear me, yet,
One word more thy heart behoved,
One pulse more of firm endeavor,
Keep thee to-day,
To-morrow, forever,
Free as an Arab
Of thy beloved.

Cling with life to the maid;
But when the surprise,
First vague shadow of surmise
Flits across her bosom young,
Of a joy apart from thee,
Free be she, fancy-free;
Nor thou detain her vesture's hem,
Nor the palest rose she flung
From her summer diadem.

Though thou loved her as thyself,
As a self of purer clay,
Though her parting dims the day,
Stealing grace from all alive;
Heartily know,
When half-gods go,
The gods arrive.

THRENODY

THE South-wind brings
Life, sunshine and desire,
And on every mount and meadow
Breathes aromatic fire;
But over the dead he has no power,
The lost, the lost, he cannot restore;
But over the dead he has no power,
And, looking over the hills, I mourn
The darling who shall not return.

I see my empty house,
I see my trees repair their boughs;
And he, the wondrous child,
Whose silver warble wild
Outvalued every pulsing sound
Within the air's cerulean round,
The hyacinthine boy, for whom
Morn well might break and April bloom,
The gracious boy, who did adorn
The world whereinto he was born,
And by his countenance repay
The favor of the loving Day,
Has disappeared from the Day's eye;
Far and wide she cannot find him;
My hopes pursue, they cannot bind him.
Returned this day, the South-wind searches,
And finds young pines and budding birches;
But finds not the budding man;
Nature, who lost, cannot remake him;
Fate let him fall, Fate can't retake him;
Nature, Fate, men, him seek in vain.

And whither now, my truant wise and sweet,
O, whither tend thy feet?
I had the right, few days ago,

Thy steps to watch, thy place to know:
How have I forfeited the right?
Hast thou forgot me in a new delight?
I hearken for thy household cheer,
O eloquent child!
Whose voice, an equal messenger,
Conveyed thy meaning mild.
What though the pains and joys
Whereof it spoke were toys
Fitting his age and ken,
Yet fairest dames and bearded men,
Who heard the sweet request,
So gentle, wise and grave,
Bended with joy to his behest
And let the world's affairs go by,
A while to share his cordial game,
Or mend his wicker wagon-frame,
Still plotting how their hungry ear
That winsome voice again might hear;
For his lips could well pronounce
Words that were persuasions.

Gentlest guardians marked serene
His early hope, his liberal mien;
Took counsel from his guiding eyes
To make this wisdom earthly wise.
Ah, vainly do these eyes recall
The school-march, each day's festival,
When every morn my bosom glowed
To watch the convoy on the road;
The babe in willow wagon closed,
With rolling eyes and face composed;
With children forward and behind,
Like Cupids studiously inclined;
And he the chieftain paced beside,
The centre of the troop allied,
With sunny face of sweet repose,
To guard the babe from fancied foes.

The little captain innocent
Took the eye with him as he went;
Each village senior paused to scan
And speak the lovely caravan.
From the window I look out
To mark thy beautiful parade,
Stately marching in cap and coat
To some tune by fairies played;
A music heard by thee alone
To works as noble led thee on.

Now Love and Pride, alas! in vain,
Up and down their glances strain.
The painted sled stands where it stood;
The kennel by the corded wood;
His gathered sticks to stanch the wall
Of the snow-tower, when snow should fall;
The ominous hole he dug in the sand,
And childhood's castles built or planned;
His daily haunts I well discern,
The poultry-yard, the shed, the barn,
And every inch of garden ground
Paced by the blessed feet around,
From the roadside to the brook
Whereinto he loved to look.
Step the meek fowls where erst they ranged;
The wintry garden lies unchanged;
The brook into the stream runs on;
But the deep-eyed boy is gone.

On that shaded day,
Dark with more clouds than tempests are,
When thou didst yield thy innocent breath
In birdlike heavings unto death,
Night came, and Nature had not thee;
I said, 'We are mates in misery.'
The morrow dawned with needless glow;
Each snowbird chirped, each fowl must crow;

Each tramper started; but the feet
Of the most beautiful and sweet
Of human youth had left the hill
And garden—they were bound and still.
There's not a sparrow or a wren,
There's not a blade of autumn grain,
Which the four seasons do not tend
And tides of life and increase lend;
And every chick of every bird,
And weed and rock-moss is preferred.
O ostrich-like forgetfulness!
O loss of larger in the less!
Was there no star that could be sent,
No watcher in the firmament,
No angel from the countless host
That loiters round the crystal coast,
Could stoop to heal that only child,
Nature's sweet marvel undefiled,
And keep the blossom of the earth,
Which all her harvests were not worth?
Not mine—I never called thee mine,
But Nature's heir—if I repine,
And seeing rashly torn and moved
Not what I made, but what I loved,
Grow early old with grief that thou
Must to the wastes of Nature go—
'T is because a general hope
Was quenched, and all must doubt and grope.
For flattering planets seemed to say
This child should ills of ages stay,
By wondrous tongue, and guided pen,
Bring the flown Muses back to men.
Perchance not he but Nature ailed,
The world and not the infant failed.
It was not ripe yet to sustain
A genius of so fine a strain,
Who gazed upon the sun and moon
As if he came unto his own,

And, pregnant with his grander thought,
Brought the old order into doubt.
His beauty once their beauty tried;
They could not feed him, and he died,
And wandered backward as in scorn,
To wait an æon to be born.
Ill day which made this beauty waste,
Plight broken, this high face defaced!
Some went and came about the dead;
And some in books of solace read;
Some to their friends the tidings say;
Some went to write, some went to pray;
One tarried here, there hurried one;
But their heart abode with none.
Covetous death bereaved us all,
To aggrandize one funeral.
The eager fate which carried thee
Took the largest part of me:
For this losing is true dying;
This is lordly man's down-lying,
This his slow but sure reclining,
Star by star his world resigning.
O child of paradise,
Boy who made dear his father's home,
In whose deep eyes
Men read the welfare of the times to come,
I am too much bereft.
The world dishonored thou hast left.
O truth's and Nature's costly lie!
O trusted broken prophecy!
O richest fortune sourly crossed!
Born for the future, to the future lost!

The deep Heart answered, 'Weepest thou?
Worthier cause for passion wild
If I had not taken the child.
And deemest thou as those who pore,
With aged eyes, short way before—

Think'st Beauty vanished from the coast
Of matter, and thy darling lost?
Taught he not thee—the man of eld,
Whose eyes within his eyes beheld
Heaven's numerous hierarchy span
The mystic gulf from God to man?
To be alone wilt thou begin
When worlds of lovers hem thee in?
To-morrow, when the masks shall fall
That dizen Nature's carnival,
The pure shall see by their own will,
Which overflowing Love shall fill,
'T is not within the force of fate
The fate-conjoined to separate.
But thou, my votary, weepest thou?
I gave thee sight—where is it now?
I taught thy heart beyond the reach
Of ritual, bible, or of speech;
Wrote in thy mind's transparent table,
As far as the incommunicable;
Taught thee each private sign to raise
Lit by the supersolar blaze.
Past utterance, and past belief,
And past the blasphemy of grief,
The mysteries of Nature's heart;
And though no Muse can these impart,
Throb thine with Nature's throbbing breast,
And all is clear from east to west.

'I came to thee as to a friend;
Dearest, to thee I did not send
Tutors, but a joyful eye,
Innocence that matched the sky,
Lovely locks, a form of wonder,
Laughter rich as woodland thunder,
That thou might'st entertain apart
The richest flowering of all art:

And, as the great all-loving Day
Through smallest chambers takes its way,
That thou might'st break thy daily bread
With prophet, savior and head;
That thou might'st cherish for thine own
The riches of sweet Mary's Son,
Boy-Rabbi, Israel's paragon.
And thoughtest thou such guest
Would in thy hall take up his rest?
Would rushing life forget her laws,
Fate's glowing revolution pause?
High omens ask diviner guess;
Not to be conned to tediousness
And know my higher gifts unbind
The zone that girds the incarnate mind.
When the scanty shores are full
With Thought's perilous, whirling pool;
When frail Nature can no more,
Then the Spirit strikes the hour:
My servant Death, with solving rite,
Pours finite into infinite.
Wilt thou freeze love's tidal flow,
Whose streams through Nature circling go?
Nail the wild star to its track
On the half-climbed zodiac?
Light is light which radiates,
Blood is blood which circulates,
Life is life which generates,
And many-seeming life is one—
Wilt thou transfix and make it none?
Its onward force too starkly pent
In figure, bone and lineament?
Wilt thou, uncalled, interrogate,
Talker! the unreplying Fate?
Nor see the genius of the whole
Ascendant in the private soul,
Beckon it when to go and come,

Self-announced its hour of doom?
Fair the soul's recess and shrine,
Magic-built to last a season;
Masterpiece of love benign,
Fairer that expansive reason
Whose omen 't is, and sign.
Wilt thou not ope thy heart to know
What rainbows teach, and sunsets show?
Verdict which accumulates
From lengthening scroll of human fates,
Voice of earth to earth returned,
Prayers of saints that inly burned—
Saying, *What is excellent,*
As God lives, is permanent;
Hearts are dust, hearts' loves remain;
Heart's love will meet thee again.
Revere the Maker; fetch thine eye
Up to his style, and manners of the sky.
Not of adamant and gold
Built he heaven stark and cold;
No, but a nest of bending reeds,
Flowering grass and scented weeds;
Or like a traveller's fleeing tent,
Or bow above the tempest bent;
Built of tears and sacred flames,
And virtue reaching to its aims;
Built of furtherance and pursuing,
Not of spent deeds, but of doing.
Silent rushes the swift Lord
Through ruined systems still restored,
Broadsowing, bleak and void to bless,
Plants with worlds the wilderness;
Waters with tears of ancient sorrow
Apples of Eden ripe to-morrow.
House and tenant go to ground,
Lost in God, in Godhead found.'

CONCORD HYMN

SUNG AT THE COMPLETION OF THE BATTLE
MONUMENT, JULY 4, 1847

BY the rude bridge that arched the flood,
   Their flag to April's breeze unfurled,
Here once the embattled farmers stood
   And fired the shot heard round the world.

The foe long since in silence slept;
   Alike the conqueror silent sleeps;
And Time the ruined bridge has swept
   Down the dark stream which seaward creeps.

On this green bank, by this soft stream,
   We set to-day a votive stone;
That memory may their deed redeem,
   When, like our sires, our sons are gone.

Spirit, that made those heroes dare
   To die, and leave their children free,
Bid Time and Nature gently spare
   The shaft we raise to them and thee.

MAY-DAY

DAUGHTER of Heaven and Earth, coy Spring,
With sudden passion languishing,
Teaching barren moors to smile,
Painting pictures mile on mile,
Holds a cup with cowslip-wreaths,
Whence a smokeless incense breathes.
The air is full of whistlings bland;
What was that I heard
Out of the hazy land?
Harp of the wind, or song of bird,
Or vagrant booming of the air,

Voice of a meteor lost in day?
Such tidings of the starry sphere
Can this elastic air convey.
Or haply 't was the cannonade
Of the pent and darkened lake,
Cooled by the pendent mountain's shade,
Whose deeps, till beams of noonday break,
Afflicted moan, and latest hold
Even into May the iceberg cold.
Was it a squirrel's pettish bark,
Or clarionet of jay? or hark
Where yon wedged line the Nestor leads,
Steering north with raucous cry
Through tracts and provinces of sky,
Every night alighting down
In new landscapes of romance,
Where darkling feed the clamorous clans
By lonely lakes to men unknown.
Come the tumult whence it will,
Voice of sport, or rush of wings,
It is a sound, it is a token
That the marble sleep is broken,
And a change has passed on things.

When late I walked, in earlier days,
All was stiff and stark;
Knee-deep snows choked all the ways,
In the sky no spark;
Firm-braced I sought my ancient woods,
Struggling through the drifted roads;
The whited desert knew me not,
Snow-ridges masked each darling spot;
The summer dells, by genius haunted,
One arctic moon had disenchanted.
All the sweet secrets therein hid
By Fancy, ghastly spells undid.
Eldest mason, Frost, had piled

Swift cathedrals in the wild;
The piny hosts were sheeted ghosts
In the star-lit minster aisled.
I found no joy: the icy wind
Might rule the forest to his mind.
Who would freeze on frozen lakes?
Back to books and sheltered home,
And wood-fire flickering on the walls,
To hear, when, 'mid our talk and games,
Without the baffled North-wind calls.
But soft! a sultry morning breaks;
The ground-pines wash their rusty green,
The maple-tops their crimson tint,
On the soft path each track is seen,
The girl's foot leaves its neater print.
The pebble loosened from the frost
Asks of the urchin to be tost.
In flint and marble beats a heart,
The kind Earth takes her children's part,
The green lane is the school-boy's friend,
Low leaves his quarrel apprehend,
The fresh ground loves his top and ball,
The air rings jocund to his call,
The brimming brook invites a leap,
He dives the hollow, climbs the steep.
The youth sees omens where he goes,
And speaks all languages the rose,
The wood-fly mocks with tiny voice
The far halloo of human voice;
The perfumed berry on the spray
Smacks of faint memories far away.
A subtle chain of countless rings
The next into the farthest brings,
And, striving to be man, the worm
Mounts through all the spires of form.

The cagèd linnet in the Spring
Hearkens for the choral glee,
When his fellows on the wing
Migrate from the Southern Sea;
When trellised grapes their flowers unmask,
And the new-born tendrils twine,
The old wine darkling in the cask
Feels the bloom on the living vine,
And bursts the hoops at hint of Spring:
And so, perchance, in Adam's race,
Of Eden's bower some dream-like trace
Survived the Flight and swam the Flood,
And wakes the wish in youngest blood
To tread the forfeit Paradise,
And feed once more the exile's eyes;
And ever when the happy child
In May beholds the blooming wild,
And hears in heaven the bluebird sing,
'Onward,' he cries, 'your baskets bring,
In the next field is air more mild,
And o'er yon hazy crest is Eden's balmier spring.'

Not for a regiment's parade,
Nor evil laws or rulers made,
Blue Walden rolls its cannonade,
But for a lofty sign
Which the Zodiac threw,
That the bondage-days are told,
And waters free as winds shall flow.
Lo! how all the tribes combine
To rout the flying foe.
See, every patriot oak-leaf throws
His elfin length upon the snows,
Not idle, since the leaf all day
Draws to the spot the solar ray,
Ere sunset quarrying inches down,
And halfway to the mosses brown;
While the grass beneath the rime

Has hints of the propitious time,
And upward pries and perforates
Through the cold slab a thousand gates,
Till green lances peering through
Bend happy in the welkin blue.

    As we thaw frozen flesh with snow,
So Spring will not her time forerun,
Mix polar night with tropic glow,
Nor cloy us with unshaded sun,
Nor wanton skip with bacchic dance,
But she has the temperance
Of the gods, whereof she is one,
Masks her treasury of heat
Under east winds crossed with sleet.
Plants and birds and humble creatures
Well accept her rule austere;
Titan-born, to hardy natures
Cold is genial and dear.
As Southern wrath to Northern right
Is but straw to anthracite;
As in the day of sacrifice,
When heroes piled the pyre,
The dismal Massachusetts ice
Burned more than others' fire,
So Spring guards with surface cold
The garnered heat of ages old.
Hers to sow the seed of bread,
That man and all the kinds be fed;
And, when the sunlight fills the hours,
Dissolves the crust, displays the flowers.

    Beneath the calm, within the light,
A hid unruly appetite
Of swifter life, a surer hope,
Strains every sense to larger scope,
Impatient to anticipate
The halting steps of aged Fate.

Slow grows the palm, too slow the pearl:
When Nature falters, fain would zeal
Grasp the felloes of her wheel,
And grasping give the orbs another whirl.
Turn swiftlier round, O tardy ball!
And sun this frozen side.
Bring hither back the robin's call,
Bring back the tulip's pride.

Why chidest thou the tardy Spring?
The hardy bunting does not chide;
The blackbirds make the maples ring
With social cheer and jubilee;
The redwing flutes his o-ka-lee,
The robins know the melting snow;
The sparrow meek, prophetic-eyed,
Her nest beside the snow-drift weaves,
Secure the osier yet will hide
Her callow brood in mantling leaves—
And thou, by science all undone,
Why only must thy reason fail
To see the southing of the sun?

The world rolls round—mistrust it not—
Befalls again what once befell;
All things return, both sphere and mote,
And I shall hear my bluebird's note,
And dream the dream of Auburn dell.

April cold with dropping rain
Willows and lilacs brings again,
The whistle of returning birds,
And trumpet-lowing of the herds.
The scarlet maple-keys betray
What potent blood hath modest May,
What fiery force the earth renews,
The wealth of forms, the flush of hues;
What joy in rosy waves outpoured
Flows from the heart of Love, the Lord.

Hither rolls the storm of heat;
I feel its finer billows beat
Like a sea which me infolds;
Heat with viewless fingers moulds,
Swells, and mellows, and matures,
Paints, and flavors, and allures,
Bird and brier inly warms,
Still enriches and transforms,
Gives the reed and lily length,
Adds to oak and oxen strength,
Transforming what it doth infold,
Life out of death, new out of old,
Painting fawns' and leopards' fells,
Seethes the gulf-encrimsoning shells,
Fires gardens with a joyful blaze
Of tulips, in the morning's rays.
The dead log touched bursts into leaf,
The wheat-blade whispers of the sheaf.
What god is this imperial Heat,
Earth's prime secret, sculpture's seat?
Doth it bear hidden in its heart
Water-line patterns of all art?
Is it Dædalus? is it Love?
Or walks in mask almighty Jove,
And drops from Power's redundant horn
All seeds of beauty to be born?

Where shall we keep the holiday,
And duly greet the entering May?
Too strait and low our cottage doors,
And all unmeet our carpet floors;
Nor spacious court, nor monarch's hall,
Suffice to hold the festival.
Up and away! where haughty woods
Front the liberated floods:
We will climb the broad-backed hills,
Hear the uproar of their joy;

We will mark the leaps and gleams
Of the new-delivered streams,
And the murmuring rivers of sap
Mount in the pipes of the trees,
Giddy with day, to the topmost spire,
Which for a spike of tender green
Bartered its powdery cap;
And the colors of joy in the bird,
And the love in its carol heard,
Frog and lizard in holiday coats,
And turtle brave in his golden spots;
While cheerful cries of crag and plain
Reply to the thunder of river and main.

    As poured the flood of the ancient sea
Spilling over mountain chains,
Bending forests as bends the sedge,
Faster flowing o'er the plains—
A world-wide wave with a foaming edge
That rims the running silver sheet—
So pours the deluge of the heat
Broad northward o'er the land,
Painting artless paradises,
Drugging herbs with Syrian spices,
Fanning secret fires which glow
In columbine and clover-blow,
Climbing the northern zones,
Where a thousand pallid towns
Lie like cockles by the main,
Or tented armies on a plain.
The million-handed sculptor moulds
Quaintest bud and blossom folds,
The million-handed painter pours
Opal hues and purple dye;
Azaleas flush the island floors,
And the tints of heaven reply.

Wreaths for the May! for happy Spring
To-day shall all her dowry bring,
The love of kind, the joy, the grace,
Hymen of element and race,
Knowing well to celebrate
With song and hue and star and state,
With tender light and youthful cheer,
The spousals of the new-born year.

Spring is strong and virtuous,
Broad-sowing, cheerful, plenteous,
Quickening underneath the mould
Grains beyond the price of gold.
So deep and large her bounties are,
That one broad, long midsummer day
Shall to the planet overpay
The ravage of a year of war.

Drug the cup, thou butler sweet,
And send the nectar round;
The feet that slid so long on sleet
Are glad to feel the ground.
Fill and saturate each kind
With good according to its mind,
Fill each kind and saturate
With good agreeing with its fate,
And soft perfection of its plan—
Willow and violet, maiden and man.

The bitter-sweet, the haunting air
Creepeth, bloweth everywhere;
It preys on all, all prey on it,
Blooms in beauty, thinks in wit,
Stings the strong with enterprise,
Makes travellers long for Indian skies,
And where it comes this courier fleet
Fans in all hearts expectance sweet,

As if to-morrow should redeem
The vanished rose of evening's dream.
By houses lies a fresher green,
On men and maids a ruddier mien,
As if Time brought a new relay
Of shining virgins every May,
And Summer came to ripen maids
To a beauty that not fades.

I saw the bud-crowned Spring go forth,
Stepping daily onward north
To greet staid ancient cavaliers
Filing single in stately train.
And who, and who are the travellers?
They were Night and Day, and Day and Night,
Pilgrims wight with step forthright.
I saw the Days deformed and low,
Short and bent by cold and snow;
The merry Spring threw wreaths on them,
Flower-wreaths gay with bud and bell;
Many a flower and many a gem,
They were refreshed by the smell,
They shook the snow from hats and shoon,
They put their April raiment on;
And those eternal forms,
Unhurt by a thousand storms,
Shot up to the height of the sky again,
And danced as merrily as young men.
I saw them mask their awful glance
Sidewise meek in gossamer lids;
And to speak my thought if none forbids
It was as if the eternal gods,
Tired of their starry periods,
Hid their majesty in cloth
Woven of tulips and painted moth.
On carpets green the maskers march
Below May's well-appointed arch.

Each star, each god, each grace amain,
Every joy and virtue speed,
Marching duly in her train,
And fainting Nature at her need
Is made whole again.

'T was the vintage-day of field and wood,
When magic wine for bards is brewed;
Every tree and stem and chink
Gushed with syrup to the brink.
The air stole into the streets of towns,
Refreshed the wise, reformed the clowns,
And betrayed the fund of joy
To the high-school and medalled boy:
On from hall to chamber ran,
From youth to maid, from boy to man,
To babes, and to old eyes as well.
'Once more,' the old man cried, 'ye clouds,
Airy turrets purple-piled,
Which once my infancy beguiled,
Beguile me with the wonted spell.
I know ye skilful to convoy
The total freight of hope and joy
Into rude and homely nooks,
Shed mocking lustres on shelf of books,
On farmer's byre, on pasture rude,
And stony pathway to the wood.
I care not if the pomps you show
Be what they soothfast appear,
Or if yon realms in sunset glow
Be bubbles of the atmosphere.
And if it be to you allowed
To fool me with a shining cloud,
So only new griefs are consoled
By new delights, as old by old,
Frankly I will be your guest,
Count your change and cheer the best.

The world hath overmuch of pain—
If Nature give me joy again,
Of such deceit I'll not complain.'

Ah! well I mind the calendar,
Faithful through a thousand years,
Of the painted race of flowers,
Exact to days, exact to hours,
Counted on the spacious dial
Yon broidered zodiac girds.
I know the trusty almanac
Of the punctual coming-back,
On their due days, of the birds.
I marked them yestermorn,
A flock of finches darting
Beneath the crystal arch,
Piping, as they flew, a march—
Belike the one they used in parting
Last year from yon oak or larch;
Dusky sparrows in a crowd,
Diving, darting northward free,
Suddenly betook them all,
Every one to his hole in the wall,
Or to his niche in the apple-tree.
I greet with joy the choral trains
Fresh from palms and Cuba's canes.
Best gems of Nature's cabinet,
With dews of tropic morning wet,
Beloved of children, bards and Spring,
O birds, your perfect virtues bring,
Your song, your forms, your rhythmic flight,
Your manners for the heart's delight,
Nestle in hedge, or barn, or roof,
Here weave your chamber weather-proof,
Forgive our harms, and condescend
To man, as to a lubber friend,
And, generous, teach his awkward race
Courage and probity and grace!

Poets praise that hidden wine
Hid in milk we drew
At the barrier of Time,
When our life was new.
We had eaten fairy fruit,
We were quick from head to foot,
All the forms we looked on shone
As with diamond dews thereon.
What cared we for costly joys,
The Museum's far-fetched toys?
Gleam of sunshine on the wall
Poured a deeper cheer than all
The revels of the Carnival.
We a pine-grove did prefer
To a marble theatre,
Could with gods on mallows dine,
Nor cared for spices or for wine.
Wreaths of mist and rainbow spanned,
Arch on arch, the grimmest land;
Whistle of a woodland bird
Made the pulses dance,
Note of horn in valleys heard
Filled the region with romance.

None can tell how sweet,
How virtuous, the morning air;
Every accent vibrates well;
Not alone the wood-bird's call,
Or shouting boys that chase their ball,
Pass the height of minstrel skill,
But the ploughman's thoughtless cry,
Lowing oxen, sheep that bleat,
And the joiner's hammer-beat,
Softened are above their will,
Take tones from groves they wandered through
Or flutes which passing angels blew.
All grating discords melt,
No dissonant note is dealt,

And though thy voice be shrill
Like rasping file on steel,
Such is the temper of the air,
Echo waits with art and care,
And will the faults of song repair.

So by remote Superior Lake,
And by resounding Mackinac,
When northern storms the forest shake,
And billows on the long beach break,
The artful Air will separate
Note by note all sounds that grate,
Smothering in her ample breast
All but godlike words,
Reporting to the happy ear
Only purified accords.
Strangely wrought from barking waves,
Soft music daunts the Indian braves—
Convent-chanting which the child
Hears pealing from the panther's cave
And the impenetrable wild.

Soft on the South-wind sleeps the haze:
So on thy broad mystic van
Lie the opal-colored days,
And waft the miracle to man.
Soothsayer of the eldest gods,
Repairer of what harms betide,
Revealer of the inmost powers
Prometheus proffered, Jove denied;
Disclosing treasures more than true,
Or in what far to-morrow due;
Speaking by the tongues of flowers,
By the ten-tongued laurel speaking;
Singing by the oriole songs,
Heart of bird the man's heart seeking;
Whispering hints of treasure hid
Under Morn's unlifted lid,

Islands looming just beyond
The dim horizon's utmost bound;
Who can, like thee, our rags upbraid,
Or taunt us with our hope decayed?
Or who like thee persuade,
Making the splendor of the air,
The morn and sparkling dew, a snare?
Or who resent
Thy genius, wiles and blandishment?

There is no orator prevails
To beckon or persuade
Like thee the youth or maid:
Thy birds, thy songs, thy brooks, thy gales,
Thy blooms, thy kinds,
Thy echoes in the wilderness,
Soothe pain, and age, and love's distress,
Fire fainting will, and build heroic minds.

For thou, O Spring! canst renovate
All that high God did first create.
Be still his arm and architect,
Rebuild the ruin, mend defect;
Chemist to vamp old worlds with new,
Coat sea and sky with heavenlier blue,
New tint the plumage of the birds,
And slough decay from grazing herds,
Sweep ruins from the scarped mountain,
Cleanse the torrent at the fountain,
Purge alpine air by towns defiled,
Bring to fair mother fairer child,
Not less renew the heart and brain,
Scatter the sloth, wash out the stain,
Make the aged eye sun-clear,
To parting soul bring grandeur near.
Under gentle types, my Spring
Masks the might of Nature's king,
An energy that searches thorough

From Chaos to the dawning morrow;
Into all our human plight,
The soul's pilgrimage and flight;
In city or in solitude,
Step by step, lifts bad to good,
Without halting, without rest,
Lifting Better up to Best;
Planting seeds of knowledge pure,
Through earth to ripen, through heaven endure.

THE ADIRONDACS

A JOURNAL

DEDICATED TO MY FELLOW TRAVELLERS IN AUGUST, 1858

Wise and polite,—and if I drew
Their several portraits, you would own
Chaucer had no such worthy crew,
Nor Boccace in Decameron.

WE crossed Champlain to Keeseville with our friends,
Thence, in strong country carts, rode up the forks
Of the Ausable stream, intent to reach
The Adirondac lakes. At Martin's Beach
We chose our boats; each man a boat and guide—
Ten men, ten guides, our company all told.

Next morn, we swept with oars the Saranac,
With skies of benediction, to Round Lake,
Where all the sacred mountains drew around us,
Taháwus, Seaward, MacIntyre, Baldhead,
And other Titans without muse or name.
Pleased with these grand companions, we glide on,
Instead of flowers, crowned with a wreath of hills.
We made our distance wider, boat from boat,
As each would hear the oracle alone.
By the bright morn the gay flotilla slid
Through files of flags that gleamed like bayonets,

Through gold-moth-haunted beds of pickerel flower,
Through scented banks of lilies white and gold,
Where the deer feeds at night, the teal by day,
On through the Upper Saranac, and up
Père Raquette stream, to a small tortuous pass
Winding through grassy shallows in and out,
Two creeping miles of rushes, pads and sponge,
To Follansbee Water and the Lake of Loons.

   Northward the length of Follansbee we rowed,
Under low mountains, whose unbroken ridge
Ponderous with beechen forest sloped the shore.
A pause and council: then, where near the head
Due east a bay makes inward to the land
Between two rocky arms, we climb the bank,
And in the twilight of the forest noon
Wield the first axe these echoes ever heard.
We cut young trees to make our poles and thwarts,
Barked the white spruce to weatherfend the roof,
Then struck a light and kindled the camp-fire.

   The wood was sovran with centennial trees—
Oak, cedar, maple, poplar, beech and fir,
Linden and spruce. In strict society
Three conifers, white, pitch and Norway pine,
Five-leaved, three-leaved and two-leaved, grew thereby,
Our patron pine was fifteen feet in girth,
The maple eight, beneath its shapely tower.

   'Welcome!' the wood-god murmured through the leaves,
'Welcome, though late, unknowing, yet known to me.'
Evening drew on; stars peeped through maple-boughs,
Which o'erhung, like a cloud, our camping fire.
Decayed millennial trunks, like moonlight flecks,
Lit with phosphoric crumbs the forest floor.

   Ten scholars, wonted to lie warm and soft
In well-hung chambers daintily bestowed,

Lie here on hemlock-boughs, like Sacs and Sioux,
And greet unanimous the joyful change.
So fast will Nature acclimate her sons,
Though late returning to her pristine ways.
Off soundings, seamen do not suffer cold;
And, in the forest, delicate clerks, unbrowned,
Sleep on the fragrant brush, as on down-beds.
Up with the dawn, they fancied the light air
That circled freshly in their forest dress
Made them to boys again. Happier that they
Slipped off their pack of duties, leagues behind,
At the first mounting of the giant stairs.
No placard on these rocks warned to the polls,
No door-bell heralded a visitor,
No courier waits, no letter came or went,
Nothing was ploughed, or reaped, or bought, or sold;
The frost might glitter, it would blight no crop,
The falling rain will spoil no holiday.
We were made freemen of the forest laws,
All dressed, like Nature, fit for her own ends,
Adirondac lakes,
Essaying nothing she cannot perform.

　　　　　　　　　　　In Adirondac lakes,
At morn or noon, the guide rows bareheaded:
Shoes, flannel shirt, and kersey trousers make
His brief toilette: at night, or in the rain,
He dons a surcoat which he doffs at morn:
A paddle in the right hand, or an oar,
And in the left, a gun, his needful arms.
By turns we praised the stature of our guides,
Their rival strength and suppleness, their skill
To row, to swim, to shoot, to build a camp,
To climb a lofty stem, clean without boughs
Full fifty feet, and bring the eaglet down:
Temper to face wolf, bear, or catamount,
And wit to trap or take him in his lair.

Sound, ruddy men, frolic and innocent,
In winter, lumberers; in summer, guides;
Their sinewy arms pull at the oar untired
Three times ten thousand strokes, from morn to eve.

Look to yourselves, ye polished gentlemen!
No city airs or arts pass current here.
Your rank is all reversed; let men of cloth
Bow to the stalwart churls in overalls:
They are the doctors of the wilderness,
And we the low-prized laymen.
In sooth, red flannel is a saucy test
Which few can put on with impunity.
What make you, master, fumbling at the oar?
Will you catch crabs? Truth tries pretension here.
The sallow knows the basket-maker's thumb;
The oar, the guide's. Dare you accept the tasks
He shall impose, to find a spring, trap foxes,
Tell the sun's time, determine the true north,
Or stumbling on through vast self-similar woods
To thread by night the nearest way to camp?

Ask you, how went the hours?
All day we swept the lake, searched every cove,
North from Camp Maple, south to Osprey Bay,
Watching when the loud dogs should drive in deer,
Or whipping its rough surface for a trout;
Or, bathers, diving from the rock at noon;
Challenging Echo by our guns and cries;
Or listening to the laughter of the loon;
Or, in the evening twilight's latest red,
Beholding the procession of the pines;
Or, later yet, beneath a lighted jack,
In the boat's bows, a silent night-hunter
Stealing with paddle to the feeding-grounds
Of the red deer, to aim at a square mist.
Hark to that muffled roar! a tree in the woods

Is fallen: but hush! it has not scared the buck
Who stands astonished at the meteor light,
Then turns to bound away—is it too late?

Our heroes tried their rifles at a mark,
Six rods, sixteen, twenty, or forty-five;
Sometimes their wits at sally and retort,
With laughter sudden as the crack of rifle;
Or parties scaled the near acclivities
Competing seekers of a rumored lake,
Whose unauthenticated waves we named
Lake Probability—our carbuncle,
Long sought, not found.

                        Two Doctors in the camp
Dissected the slain deer, weighed the trout's brain,
Captured the lizard, salamander, shrew,
Crab, mice, snail, dragon-fly, minnow and moth;
Insatiate skill in water or in air
Waved the scoop-net, and nothing came amiss;
The while, one leaden pot of alcohol
Gave an impartial tomb to all the kinds.
Not less the ambitious botanist sought plants,
Orchis and gentian, fern and long whip-scirpus,
Rosy polygonum, lake-margin's pride,
Hypnum and hydnum, mushroom, sponge and moss,
Or harebell nodding in the gorge of falls.
Above, the eagle flew, the osprey screamed,
The raven croaked, owls hooted, the woodpecker
Loud hammered, and the heron rose in the swamp.
As water poured through hollows of the hills
To feed this wealth of lakes and rivulets,
So Nature shed all beauty lavishly
From her redundant horn.

                        Lords of this realm,
Bounded by dawn and sunset, and the day
Rounded by hours where each outdid the last

In miracles of pomp, we must be proud,
As if associates of the sylvan gods.
We seemed the dwellers of the zodiac,
So pure the Alpine element we breathed,
So light, so lofty pictures came and went.
We trode on air, contemned the distant town,
Its timorous ways, big trifles, and we planned
That we should build, hard-by, a spacious lodge
And how we should come hither with our sons,
Hereafter—willing they, and more adroit.

Hard fare, hard bed and comic misery—
The midge, the blue-fly and the mosquito
Painted our necks, hands, ankles, with red bands:
But, on the second day, we heed them not,
Nay, we saluted them Auxiliaries,
Whom earlier we had chid with spiteful names.
For who defends our leafy tabernacle
From bold intrusion of the travelling crowd—
Who but the midge, mosquito and the fly,
Which past endurance sting the tender cit,
But which we learn to scatter with a smudge,
Or baffle by a veil, or slight by scorn?

Our foaming ale we drank from hunters' pans,
Ale, and a sup of wine. Our steward gave
Venison and trout, potatoes, beans, wheat-bread;
All ate like abbots, and, if any missed
Their wonted convenance, cheerly hid the loss
With hunters' appetite and peals of mirth.
And Stillman, our guides' guide, and Commodore,
Crusoe, Crusader, Pius Aeneas, said aloud,
"Chronic dyspepsia never came from eating
Food indigestible"—then murmured some,
Others applauded him who spoke the truth.

Nor doubt but visitings of graver thought
Checked in these souls the turbulent heyday

'Mid all the hints and glories of the home.
For who can tell what sudden privacies
Were sought and found, amid the hue and cry
Of scholars furloughed from their tasks and let
Into this Oreads' fended Paradise,
As chapels in the city's thoroughfares,
Whither gaunt Labor slips to wipe his brow
And meditate a moment on Heaven's rest.
Judge with what sweet surprises Nature spoke
To each apart, lifting her lovely shows
To spiritual lessons pointed home,
And as through dreams in watches of the night,
So through all creatures in their form and ways
Some mystic hint accosts the vigilant,
Not clearly voiced, but waking a new sense
Inviting to new knowledge, one with old.
Hark to that petulant chirp! what ails the warbler?
Mark his capricious ways to draw the eye.
Now soar again. What wilt thou, restless bird,
Seeking in that chaste blue a bluer light,
Thirsting in that pure for a purer sky?

And presently the sky is changed; O world!
What pictures and what harmonies are thine!
The clouds are rich and dark, the air serene,
So like the soul of me, what if 't were me?
A melancholy better than all mirth.
Comes the sweet sadness at the retrospect,
Or at the foresight of obscurer years?
Like yon slow-sailing cloudy promontory
Whereon the purple iris dwells in beauty
Superior to all its gaudy skirts.
And, that no day of life may lack romance,
The spiritual stars rise nightly, shedding down
A private beam into each several heart.
Daily the bending skies solicit man,
The seasons chariot him from this exile,

The rainbow hours bedeck his glowing chair,
The storm-winds urge the heavy weeks along,
Suns haste to set, that so remoter lights
Beckon the wanderer to his vaster home.

With a vermilion pencil mark the day
When of our little fleet three cruising skiffs
Entering Big Tupper, bound for the foaming Falls
Of loud Bog River, suddenly confront
Two of our mates returning with swift oars.
One held a printed journal waving high
Caught from a late-arriving traveller,
Big with great news, and shouted the report
For which the world had waited, now firm fact,
Of the wire-cable laid beneath the sea,
And landed on our coast, and pulsating
With ductile fire. Loud, exulting cries
From boat to boat, and to the echoes round,
Greet the glad miracle. Thought's new-found path
Shall supplement henceforth all trodden ways,
Match God's equator with a zone of art,
And lift man's public action to a height
Worthy the enormous cloud of witnesses,
When linked hemispheres attest his deed.
We have few moments in the longest life
Of such delight and wonder as there grew—
Nor yet unsuited to that solitude:
A burst of joy, as if we told the fact
To ears intelligent; as if gray rock
And cedar grove and cliff and lake should know
This feat of wit, this triumph of mankind;
As if we men were talking in a vein
Of sympathy so large, that ours was theirs,
And a prime end of the most subtle element
Were fairly reached at last. Wake, echoing caves!
Bend nearer, faint day-moon! Yon thundertops,
Let them hear well! 't is theirs as much as ours.

A spasm throbbing through the pedestals
Of Alp and Andes, isle and continent,
Urging astonished Chaos with a thrill
To be a brain, or serve the brain of man.
The lightning has run masterless too long;
He must to school and learn his verb and noun
And teach his nimbleness to earn his wage,
Spelling with guided tongue man's messages
Shot through the weltering pit of the salt sea.
And yet I marked, even in the manly joy
Of our great-hearted Doctor in his boat
(Perchance I erred), a shade of discontent;
Or was it for mankind a generous shame,
As of a luck not quite legitimate,
Since fortune snatched from wit the lion's part?
Was it a college pique of town and gown,
As one within whose memory it burned
That not academicians, but some lout,
Found ten years since the Californian gold?
And now, again, a hungry company
Of traders, led by corporate sons of trade,
Perversely borrowing from the shop the tools
Of science, not from the philosophers,
Had won the brightest laurel of all time.
'T was always thus, and will be; hand and head
Are ever rivals: but, though this be swift,
The other slow—this the Prometheus,
And that the Jove—yet, howsoever hid,
It was from Jove the other stole his fire,
And, without Jove, the good had never been.
It is not Iroquois or cannibals,
But ever the free race with front sublime,
And these instructed by their wisest too,
Who do the feat, and lift humanity.
Let not him mourn who best entitled was,
Nay, mourn not one: let him exult,
Yea, plant the tree that bears best apples, plant,
And water it with wine, nor watch askance

Whether thy sons or strangers eat the fruit:
Enough that mankind eat and are refreshed.

We flee away from cities, but we bring
The best of cities with us, these learned classifiers,
Men knowing what they seek, armed eyes of experts.
We praise the guide, we praise the forest life:
But will we sacrifice our dear-bought lore
Of books and arts and trained experiment,
Or count the Sioux a match for Agassiz?
O no, not we! Witness the shout that shook
Wild Tupper Lake; witness the mute all-hail
The joyful traveller gives, when on the verge
Of craggy Indian wilderness he hears
From a log cabin stream Beethoven's notes
On the piano, played with master's hand.
'Well done!' he cries; 'the bear is kept at bay,
The lynx, the rattlesnake, the flood, the fire;
All the fierce enemies, ague, hunger, cold,
This thin spruce roof, this clayed log-wall,
This wild plantation will suffice to chase.
Now speed the gay celerities of art,
What in the desert was impossible
Within four walls is possible again—
Culture and libraries, mysteries of skill,
Traditioned fame of masters, eager strife
Of keen competing youths, joined or alone
To outdo each other and extort applause.
Mind wakes a new-born giant from her sleep.
Twirl the old wheels! Time takes fresh start again,
On for a thousand years of genius more.'

The holidays were fruitful, but must end;
One August evening had a cooler breath;
Into each mind intruding duties crept;
Under the cinders burned the fires of home;
Nay, letters found us in our paradise:
So in the gladness of the new event
We struck our camp and left the happy hills.

The fortunate star that rose on us sank not;
The prodigal sunshine rested on the land,
The rivers gambolled onward to the sea,
And Nature, the inscrutable and mute,
Permitted on her infinite repose
Almost a smile to steal to cheer her sons,
As if one riddle of the Sphinx were guessed.

BRAHMA

If the red slayer think he slays,
   Or if the slain think he is slain,
They know not well the subtle ways
   I keep, and pass, and turn again.

Far or forgot to me is near;
   Shadow and sunlight are the same;
The vanished gods to me appear
   And one to me are shame and fame.

They reckon ill who leave me out;
   When me they fly, I am the wings;
I am the doubter and the doubt,
   And I the hymn the Brahmin sings.

The strong gods pine for my abode.
   And pine in vain the sacred Seven;
But thou, meek lover of the good!
   Find me, and turn thy back on heaven.

MERLIN'S SONG

I

OF Merlin wise I learned a song,—
Sing it low or sing it loud,
It is mightier than the strong,
And punishes the proud.
I sing it to the surging crowd,—

Good men it will calm and cheer,
Bad men it will chain and cage—
In the heart of the music peals a strain
Which only angels hear;
Whether it waken joy or rage
Hushed myriads hark in vain,
Yet they who hear it shed their age,
And take their youth again.

II

Hear what British Merlin sung,
Of keenest eye and truest tongue.
Say not, the chiefs who first arrive
Usurp the seats for which all strive;
The forefathers this land who found
Failed to plant the vantage-ground;
Ever from one who comes to-morrow
Men wait their good and truth to borrow.
But wilt thou measure all thy road,
See thou lift the lightest load.
Who has little, to him who has less, can spare,
And thou, Cyndyllan's son! beware
Ponderous gold and stuffs to bear,
To falter ere thou thy task fulfil,—
Only the light-armed climb the hill.
The richest of all lords is Use,
And ruddy Health the loftiest Muse.
Live in the sunshine, swim the sea,
Drink the wild air's salubrity:
When the star Canope shines in May,
Shepherds are thankful and nations gay.
The music that can deepest reach,
And cure all ill, is cordial speech:
Mask thy wisdom with delight,
Toy with the bow, yet hit the white.
Of all wit's uses, the main one
Is to live well with who has none.

HYMN

SUNG AT THE SECOND CHURCH, AT THE ORDINATION
OF REV. CHANDLER ROBBINS

WE love the venerable house
    Our fathers built to God;—
In heaven are kept their grateful vows,
    Their dust endears the sod.

Here holy thoughts a light have shed
    From many a radiant face,
And prayers of humble virtue made
    The perfume of the place.

And anxious hearts have pondered here
    The mystery of life,
And prayed the eternal Light to clear
    Their doubts, and aid their strife.

From humble tenements around
    Came up the pensive train,
And in the church a blessing found
    That filled their homes again;

For faith and peace and mighty love
    That from the Godhead flow,
Showed them the life of Heaven above
    Springs from the life below.

They live with God; their homes are dust;
    Yet here their children pray,
And in this fleeting lifetime trust
    To find the narrow way.

On him who by the altar stands,
    On him thy blessing fall,
Speak through his lips thy pure commands,
    Thou heart that lovest all.

DAYS

DAUGHTERS of Time, the hypocritic Days,
Muffled and dumb like barefoot dervishes,
And marching single in an endless file,
Bring diadems and fagots in their hands.
To each they offer gifts after his will,
Bread, kingdoms, stars, and sky that holds them all.
I, in my pleached garden, watched the pomp,
Forgot my morning wishes, hastily
Took a few herbs and apples, and the Day
Turned and departed silent. I, too late,
Under her solemn fillet saw the scorn.

CHARACTER

THE sun set, but set not his hope:
Stars rose; his faith was earlier up:
Fixed on the enormous galaxy,
Deeper and older seemed his eye;
And matched his sufferance sublime
The taciturnity of time.
He spoke, and words more soft than rain
Brought the Age of Gold again:
His action won such reverence sweet
As hid all measure of the feat.

WALDEN

IN my garden three ways meet,
    Thrice the spot is blest;
Hermit-thrush comes there to build,
    Carrier-doves to nest.

There broad-armed oaks, the copses' maze,
    The cold sea-wind detain;
Here sultry Summer overstays
    When Autumn chills the plain.

Self-sown my stately garden grows;
    The winds and wind-blown seed,
Cold April rain and colder snows
    My hedges plant and feed.

From mountains far and valleys near
    The harvests sown to-day
Thrive in all weathers without fear,—
    Wild planters, plant away!

In cities high the careful crowds
    Of woe-worn mortals darkling go,
But in these sunny solitudes
    My quiet roses blow.

Methought the sky looked scornful down
    On all was base in man,
And airy tongues did taunt the town,
    'Achieve our peace who can!'

What need I holier dew
    Than Walden's haunted wave,
Distilled from heaven's alembic blue,
    Steeped in each forest cave?

[If Thought unlock her mysteries,
   If Friendship on me smile,
I walk in marble galleries,
   I talk with kings the while.]

How drearily in College hall
   The Doctor stretched the hours,
But in each pause we heard the call
   Of robins out of doors.

The air is wise, the wind thinks well,
   And all through which it blows,
If plants or brain, if egg or shell,
   Or bird or biped knows;

And oft at home 'mid tasks I heed,
   I heed how wears the day;
We must not halt while fiercely speed
   The spans of life away.

What boots it here of Thebes or Rome
   Or lands of Eastern day?
In forests I am still at home
   And there I cannot stray.

LINES TO ELLEN

TELL me, maiden, dost thou use
Thyself thro' Nature to diffuse?
All the angles of the coast
Were tenanted by thy sweet ghost,
Bore thy colors every flower,
Thine each leaf and berry bore;
All wore thy badges and thy favors
In their scent or in their savors,
Every moth with painted wing,
Every bird in carolling,

The wood-boughs with thy manners, waved,
The rocks uphold thy name engraved,
The sod throbbed friendly to my feet,
And the sweet air with thee was sweet.
The saffron cloud that floated warm
Studied thy motion, took thy form,
And in his airy road benign
Recalled thy skill in bold design.
Or seemed to use his privilege
To gaze o'er the horizon's edge,
To search where now thy beauty glowed,
Or made what other purlieus proud.

SELF-RELIANCE

HENCEFORTH, please God, forever I forego
The yoke of men's opinions. I will be
Light-hearted as a bird, and live with God.
I find him in the bottom of my heart,
I hear continually his voice therein.
. . . .
The little needle always knows the North,
The little bird remembereth his note,
And this wise Seer within me never errs.
I never taught it what it teaches me;
I only follow, when I act aright.
      October 9, 1832.

AND when I am entombèd in my place,
Be it remembered of a single man,
He never, though he dearly loved his race,
For fear of human eyes swerved from his plan.

OH what is Heaven but the fellowship
Of minds that each can stand against the world
By its own meek and incorruptible will?

THE days pass over me
And I am still the same;
The aroma of my life is gone
With the flower with which it came.
   1833.

WEBSTER
1831

LET Webster's lofty face
Ever on thousands shine,
A beacon set that Freedom's race
Might gather omens from that radiant sign.

From the Phi Beta Kappa Poem
1834

ILL fits the abstemious Muse a crown to weave
For living brows; ill fits them to receive:
And yet, if virtue abrogate the law,
One portrait—fact or fancy—we may draw;
A form which Nature cast in the heroic mould
Of them who rescued liberty of old;
He, when the rising storm of party roared,
Brought his great forehead to the council board,
There, while hot heads perplexed with fears the state,
Calm as the morn the manly patriot sate;
Seemed, when at last his clarion accents broke,
As if the conscience of the country spoke.
Not on its base Monadnoc surer stood,
Than he to common sense and common good:
No mimic; from his breast his counsel drew,
Believed the eloquent was aye the true;
He bridged the gulf from th' alway good and wise
To that within the vision of small eyes.
Self-centred; when he launched the genuine word

It shook or captivated all who heard,
Ran from his mouth to mountains and the sea,
And burned in noble hearts proverb and prophecy.

1854

WHY did all manly gifts in Webster fail?
He wrote on Nature's grandest brow, *For Sale.*

EZRA RIPLEY, D.D.

[*Dr. Ripley was Emerson's step-grandfather. He
lived in Concord in the Old Manse. Emerson visited
there frequently as a boy and again when as a young
man he had just returned from his first trip to
Europe. This sketch was prepared by Emerson for the
Social Circle of Concord, a group of twenty-five people who met in each other's homes in rotation during
the winter season from October to April. The chairs
were arranged in the form of a circle to promote general conversation.*]

We love the venerable house
    Our fathers built to God:
In Heaven are kept their grateful vows,
    Their dust endears the sod.

From humble tenements around
    Came up the pensive train,
And in the church a blessing found
    That filled their homes again.

EZRA RIPLEY, D.D.

EZRA RIPLEY was born May 1, 1751 (O. S.), at Woodstock, Connecticut. He was the fifth of the nineteen children of Noah and Lydia (Kent)
Ripley. Seventeen of these nineteen children married, and it is stated
that the mother died leaving nineteen children, one hundred and two
grandchildren and ninety-six great-grandchildren. The father was born
at Hingham, on the farm purchased by his ancestor, William Ripley, of
England, at the first settlement of the town; which farm has been occupied by seven or eight generations. Ezra Ripley followed the business of
farming till sixteen years of age, when his father wished him to be qualified to teach a grammar school, not thinking himself able to send one
son to college without injury to his other children. With this view, the
father agreed with the late Rev. Dr. Forbes of Gloucester, then minister of North Brookfield, to fit Ezra for college by the time he should
be twenty-one years of age, and to have him labor during the time sufficiently to pay for his instruction, clothing and books.

But, when fitted for college, the son could not be contented with
teaching, which he had tried the preceding winter. He had early manifested a desire for learning, and could not be satisfied without a public
education. Always inclined to notice ministers, and frequently attempting, when only five or six years old, to imitate them by preaching, now
that he had become a professor of religion he had an ardent desire to be
a preacher of the gospel. He had to encounter great difficulties, but,
through a kind providence and the patronage of Dr. Forbes, he entered
Harvard University, July, 1772. The commencement of the Revolutionary War greatly interrupted his education at college. In 1775, in
his senior year, the college was removed from Cambridge to this town.
The studies were much broken up. Many of the students entered the
army, and the class never returned to Cambridge. There were an
unusually large number of distinguished men in this class of 1776:
Christopher Gore, Governor of Massachusetts and Senator in Congress;
Samuel Sewall, Chief Justice of Massachusetts; George Thacher, Judge

743

of the Supreme Court; Royall Tyler, Chief Justice of Vermont; and the late learned Dr. Prince, of Salem.

Mr. Ripley was ordained minister of Concord November 7, 1778. He married, November 16, 1780, Mrs. Phebe (Bliss) Emerson, then a widow of thirty-nine, with five children. They had three children: Sarah, born August 18, 1781; Samuel, born May 11, 1783; Daniel Bliss, born August 1, 1784. He died September 21, 1841.

To these facts, gathered chiefly from his own diary, and stated nearly in his own words, I can only add a few traits from memory.

He was identified with the ideas and forms of the New England Church, which expired about the same time with him, so that he and his coevals seemed the rear guard of the great camp and army of the Puritans, which, however in its last days declining into formalism, in the heyday of its strength had planted and liberated America. It was a pity that his old meeting-house should have been modernized in his time. I am sure all who remember both will associate his form with whatever was grave and droll in the old, cold, unpainted, uncarpeted, square-pewed meeting-house, with its four iron-gray deacons in their little box under the pulpit—with Watts's hymns, with long prayers, rich with the diction of ages; and not less with the report like musketry from the movable seats. He and his contemporaries, the old New England clergy, were believers in what is called a particular providence—certainly, as they held it, a very particular providence—following the narrowness of King David and the Jews, who thought the universe existed only or mainly for their church and congregation. Perhaps I cannot better illustrate this tendency than by citing a record from the diary of the father of his predecessor, the minister of Malden, written in the blank leaves of the almanac for the year 1735. The minister writes against January 31st: "Bought a shay for 27 pounds, 10 shillings. The Lord grant it may be a comfort and blessing to my family." In March following he notes: "Had a safe and comfortable journey to York." But April 24th, we find: "Shay overturned, with my wife and I in it, yet neither of us much hurt. Blessed be our gracious Preserver. Part of the shay, as it lay upon one side, went over my wife, and yet she was scarcely anything hurt. How wonderful the preservation." Then again, May 5th: "Went to the beach with three of the children. The beast, being frightened when we were all out of the shay, overturned and broke it. I desire (I hope I desire it) that the Lord would teach me suitably to resent this Providence, to make suitable remarks on it, and to be suitably affected with it. Have I done well to get me a shay? Have I not been proud or too fond of this convenience? Do I exercise the faith in the Divine care and protection which I ought to do? Should I not be more in my study and less fond of diversion? Do I not withhold more than is meet from pious and charitable uses?" Well, on 15th May we have this: "Shay brought home; mending cost thirty shillings. Favored in this respect beyond expectation." 16th May: "My wife and I rode together to Rumney Marsh. The beast frighted several times." And at last we have this record, June 4th: "Disposed of my shay to Rev. Mr. White."

The same faith made what was strong and what was weak in Dr. Ripley and his associates. He was a perfectly sincere man, punctual, severe, but just and charitable, and if he made his forms a straitjacket to others, he wore the same himself all his years. Trained in this church, and very well qualified by his natural talent to work in it, it was never out of his mind. He looked at every person and thing from the parochial point of view. I remember, when a boy, driving about Concord with him, and in passing each house he told the story of the family that lived in it, and especially he gave me anecdotes of the nine church members who had made a division in the church in the time of his predecessor, and showed me how every one of the nine had come to bad fortune or to a bad end. His prayers for rain and against the lightning, "that it may not lick up our spirits," and for good weather; and against sickness and insanity; "that we have not been tossed to and fro until the dawning of the day; that we have not been a terror to ourselves and others"—are well remembered, and his own entire faith that these petitions were not to be overlooked, and were entitled to a favorable answer. Some of those around me will remember one occasion of severe drought in this vicinity, when the late Rev. Mr. Goodwin offered to relieve the Doctor of the duty of leading in prayer; but the Doctor suddenly remembering the season, rejected his offer with some humor, as with an air that said to all the congregation, "This is no time for you young Cambridge men; the affair, sir, is getting serious. I will pray myself." One August afternoon, when I was in his hayfield helping him with his man to rake up his hay, I well remember his pleading, almost reproachful looks at the sky, when the thunder-gust was coming up to spoil his hay. He raked very fast, then looked at the cloud, and said,

. . . .

"We are in the Lord's hand;" and seemed to say, "You know me; this field is mine—Dr. Ripley's—thine own servant!"

He used to tell the story of one of his old friends, the minister of Sudbury, who, being at the Thursday lecture in Boston, heard the officiating clergyman praying for rain. As soon as the service was over, he went to the petitioner, and said, "You Boston ministers, as soon as a tulip wilts under your windows, go to church and pray for rain, until all Concord and Sudbury are under water." I once rode with him to a house at Nine Acre Corner to attend the funeral of the father of a family. He mentioned to me on the way his fears that the oldest son, who was now to succeed to the farm, was becoming intemperate. We presently arrived, and the Doctor addressed each of the mourners separately: "Sir, I condole with you." "Madam, I condole with you." "Sir, I knew your great-grandfather. When I came to this town, your great-grandfather was a substantial farmer in this very place, a member of the church, and an excellent citizen. Your grandfather followed him, and was a virtuous man. Now your father is to be carried to his grave, full of labors and virtues. There is none of that large family left but you, and it rests with you to bear up the good name and usefulness of your ancestors. If you fail—'Ichabod, the glory is departed.' Let us pray." Right manly he was, and the manly thing he could always say. I can remember a little speech he made to me, when the last tie of blood which held me and my brothers to his house was broken by the death of his daughter. He said, on parting, "I wish you and your brothers to come to this house as you have always done. You will not like to be excluded; I shall not like to be neglected."

When "Put" Merriam, after his release from the state prison, had the effrontery to call on the Doctor as an old acquaintance, in the midst of general conversation Mr. Frost came in, and the Doctor presently said, "Mr. Merriam, my brother and colleague, Mr. Frost, has come to take tea with me. I regret very much the causes (which you know very well) which make it impossible for me to ask you to stay and break bread with us." With the Doctor's views it was a matter of religion to say thus much. He had a reverence and love of society, and the patient, continuing courtesy, carrying out every respectful attention to the end, which marks what is called the manners of the old school. His hospitality obeyed Charles Lamb's rule, and "ran fine to the last." His partiality for ladies was always strong, and was by no means abated by time. He claimed privilege of years, was much addicted to kissing; spared neither maid, wife nor widow, and, as a lady thus favored remarked to me, "seemed as if he was going to make a meal of you."

He was very credulous, and as he was no reader of books or journals, he knew nothing beyond the columns of his weekly religious newspaper, the tracts of his sect, and perhaps the Middlesex Yeoman. He was the easy dupe of any tonguey agent, whether colonizationist or anti-papist, or charlatan of iron combs, or tractors, or phrenology, or magnetism, who went by. At the time when Jack Downing's letters were in every paper, he repeated to me at table some of the particulars of that gentleman's intimacy with General Jackson, in a manner that betrayed to me at once that he took the whole for fact. To undeceive him, I hastened to recall some particulars to show the absurdity of the thing, as the Major and the President going out skating on the Potomac, etc. "Why," said the Doctor with perfect faith, "it was a bright moonlight night;" and I am not sure that he did not die in the belief in the reality of Major Downing. Like other credulous men, he was opinionative, and, as I well remember, a great browbeater of the poor old fathers who still survived from the 19th of April, to the end that they should testify to his history as he had written it.

He was a man so kind and sympathetic, his character was so transparent, and his merits so intelligible to all observers, that he was very justly appreciated in this community. He was a natural gentleman, no dandy, but courtly, hospitable, manly and public-spirited; his nature social, his house open to all men. We remember the remark made by the old farmer who used to travel hither from Maine, that no horse from the Eastern country would go by the Doctor's gate. Travellers from the West and North and South bear the like testimony. His brow was serene and open to his visitor, for he loved men, and he had no studies, no occupations, which company could interrupt. His friends were his study, and to see them loosened his talents and his tongue. In his house dwelt order and prudence and plenty. There was no waste and no stint. He was open-handed and just and generous. Ingratitude and meanness in his beneficiaries did not wear out his compassion; he bore the insult, and the next day his basket for the beggar, his horse and chaise for the cripple, were at their door. Though he knew the value of a dollar as well as another man, yet he loved to buy dearer and sell cheaper than others. He subscribed to all charities, and it is no reflection on others to say that he was the most public-spirited man in the town. The late Dr. Gardiner, in a funeral sermon on some parishioner whose virtues did not readily come to mind, honestly said, "He was good at fires." Dr. Ripley had many virtues, and yet all will remember that even in his old age, if the firebell was rung, he was instantly on horseback with his buckets, and bag.

He showed even in his fireside discourse traits of that pertinency and judgment, softening ever and anon into elegancy, which make the distinction of the scholar, and which, under better discipline, might have ripened into a Bentley or a Porson. He had a foresight, when he opened his mouth, of all that he would say, and he marched straight to the conclusion. In debate, in the vestry of the Lyceum, the structure of his sentences was admirable; so neat, so natural, so terse, his words fell like stones; and often, though quite unconscious of it, his speech was a satire on the loose, voluminous, draggle-tail periods of other speakers. He sat down when he had done. A man of anecdote, his talk in the parlor was chiefly narrative. We remember the remark of a gentleman who listened with much delight to his conversation at the time when the Doctor was preparing to go to Baltimore and Washington, that "a man who could tell a story so well was company for kings and John Quincy Adams."

Sage and savage strove harder in him than in any of my acquaintances, each getting the mastery by turns, and pretty sudden turns: "Save us from the extremity of cold and these violent sudden changes." "The society will meet after the Lyceum, as it is difficult to bring people together in the evening—and no moon." "Mr. N. F. is dead, and I expect to hear of the death of Mr. B. It is cruel to separate old people from their wives in this cold weather."

With a very limited acquaintance with books, his knowledge was an external experience, an Indian wisdom, the observation of such facts as country life for nearly a century could supply. He watched with interest the garden, the field, the orchard, the house and the barn, horse, cow, sheep and dog, and all the common objects that engage the thought of the farmer. He kept his eye on the horizon, and knew the weather like a sea-captain. The usual experiences of men, birth, marriage, sickness, death, burial; the common temptations; the common ambitions—he studied them all, and sympathized so well in these that

he was excellent company and counsel to all, even the most humble and
ignorant. With extraordinary states of mind, with states of enthusiasm
or enlarged speculation, he had no sympathy, and pretended to none.
He was sincere, and kept to his point, and his mark was never remote.
His conversation was strictly personal and apt to the party and the
occasion. An eminent skill he had in saying difficult and unspeakable
things; in delivering to a man or a woman that which all their other
friends had abstained from saying, in uncovering the bandage from a
sore place, and applying the surgeon's knife with a truly surgical spirit.
Was a man a sot, or a spendthrift, or too long time a bachelor, or suspected of some hidden crime, or had he quarrelled with his wife, or
collared his father, or was there any cloud or suspicious circumstances
in his behavior, the good pastor knew his way straight to that point,
believing himself entitled to a full explanation, and whatever relief to
the conscience of both parties plain speech could effect was sure to be
procured. In all such passages he justified himself to the conscience,
and commonly to the love, of the persons concerned. He was the more
competent to these searching discourses from his knowledge of family
history. He knew everybody's grandfather, and seemed to address each
person rather as the representative of his house and name, than as an
individual. In him have perished more local and personal anecdotes of
this village and vicinity than are possessed by any survivor. This intimate knowledge of families, and this skill of speech, and still more, his
sympathy, made him incomparable in his parochial visits, and in his
exhortations and prayers. He gave himself up to his feelings, and said
on the instant the best things in the world. Many and many a felicity
he had in his prayer, now forever lost, which defied all the rules of all
the rhetoricians. He did not know when he was good in prayer or sermon, for he had no literature and no art; but he believed, and therefore
spoke. He was eminently loyal in his nature, and not fond of adventure or innovation. By education, and still more by temperament, he
was engaged to the old forms of the New England Church. Not speculative, but affectionate; devout, but with an extreme love of order, he
adopted heartily, though in its mildest form, the creed and catechism of
the fathers, and appeared a modern Israelite in his attachment to the
Hebrew history and faith. He was a man very easy to read, for his
whole life and conversation were consistent. All his opinions and

actions might be securely predicted by a good observer on short acquaintance. My classmate at Cambridge, Frederick King, told me from Governor Gore, who was the Doctor's classmate, that in college he was called Holy Ripley.

And now, in his old age, when all the antique Hebraism and its customs are passing away, it is fit that he too should depart—most fit that in the fall of laws a loyal man should die.

EMANCIPATION IN THE BRITISH WEST INDIES

[Emerson delivered this address in the Court House in Concord on August 1, 1844. Many people in Concord were reluctant to have such a controversial subject discussed at a public meeting. It is said that Thoreau arranged the meeting at which Emerson spoke and rang the bell to summon the audience to the Court House.]

There a captive sat in chains,
Crooning ditties treasured well
From his Afric's torrid plains.
Sole estate his sire bequeathed,—
Hapless sire to hapless son,—
Was the wailing song he breathed,
And his chain when life was done.

ADDRESS
EMANCIPATION IN THE BRITISH WEST INDIES

FRIENDS AND FELLOW CITIZENS: We are met to exchange congratulations on the anniversary of an event singular in the history of civilization; a day of reason; of the clear light; of that which makes us better than a flock of birds and beasts; a day which gave the immense fortification of a fact, of gross history, to ethical abstractions. It was the settlement, as far as a great Empire was concerned, of a question on which almost every leading citizen in it had taken care to record his vote; one which for many years absorbed the attention of the best and most eminent of mankind. I might well hesitate, coming from other studies, and without the smallest claim to be a special laborer in this work of humanity, to undertake to set this matter before you; which ought rather to be done by a strict cooperation of many well-advised persons; but I shall not apologize for my weakness. In this cause, no man's weakness is any prejudice: it has a thousand sons; if one man cannot speak, ten others can; and, whether by the wisdom of its friends, or by the folly of the adversaries; by speech and by silence; by doing and by omitting to do, it goes forward. Therefore I will speak—or, not I, but the might of liberty in my weakness. The subject is said to have the property of making dull men eloquent.

It has been in all men's experience a marked effect of the enterprise in behalf of the African, to generate an overbearing and defying spirit. The institution of slavery seems to its opponent to have but one side, and he feels that none but a stupid or a malignant person can hesitate on a view of the facts. Under such an impulse, I was about to say, If any cannot speak, or cannot hear the words of freedom, let him go hence—I had almost said, Creep into your grave, the universe has no need of you! But I have thought better: let him not go. When we consider what remains to be done for this interest in this country, the dictates of humanity make us tender of such as are not yet persuaded. The hardest selfishness is to be borne with. Let us withhold every reproachful, and, if we can, every indignant remark. In this cause, we must renounce our temper, and the risings of pride. If there be any man who thinks the ruin of a race of men a small matter, compared with the last decoration and completions of his own comfort—who would not so much as part with his ice-cream, to save them from rapine and manacles, I think I must not hesitate to satisfy that man that also his cream and vanilla are safer and cheaper by placing the negro nation on a fair footing than by robbing them. If the Virginian piques himself on the picturesque luxury of his vassalage, on the heavy Ethiopian manners of his house-servants, their silent obedience, their hue of bronze, their turbaned heads, and would not exchange them for the more intelligent but precarious hired service of whites, I shall not refuse to show him that when their free-papers are made out, it will still be their interest to remain on his estate, and that the oldest planters of Jamaica are convinced that it is cheaper to pay wages than to own the slave.

The history of mankind interests us only as it exhibits a steady gain of truth and right, in the incessant conflict which it records between the material and the moral nature. From the earliest monuments it appears that one race was victim and served the other races. In the oldest temples of Egypt, negro captives are painted on the tombs of kings, in such attitudes as to show that they are on the point of being executed; and Herodotus, our oldest historian, relates that the Troglodytes hunted the Ethiopians in four-horse chariots. From the earliest time, the negro has been an article of luxury to the commercial nations. So has it been, down to the day that has just dawned on the world. Language must be raked, the secrets of slaughter-houses and infamous holes that cannot front the day, must be ransacked, to tell what negro slavery has been. These men, our benefactors, as they are producers of corn and wine, of coffee, of tobacco, of cotton, of sugar, of rum and brandy; gentle and joyous themselves, and producers of comfort and luxury for the civilized world—there seated in the finest climates of the globe, children of the sun—I am heart-sick when I read how they came there, and how they are kept there. Their case was left out of the mind and out of the heart of their brothers. The prizes of society, the trumpet of fame, the privileges of learning, of culture, of religion, the decencies and joys of marriage, honor, obedience, personal authority and a perpetual melioration into a finer civility—these were for all, but not for them. For the negro, was the slave-ship to begin with, in whose filthy hold he sat in irons, unable to lie down; bad food, and insufficiency of that; disfranchisement; no property in the rags that covered him; no marriage, no right in the poor black woman that cherished him in her bosom, no right to the children of his body; no security from the humors, none from the crimes, none from the appetites of his master: toil, famine, insult and flogging; and, when he sank in the furrow, no wind of good fame blew over him, no priest of salvation visited him with glad tidings: but he went down to death with dusky dreams of African shadow-catchers and Obeahs hunting him. Very sad was the negro tradition, that the Great Spirit, in the beginning offered the black man, whom he loved better than the buckra, or white, his choice of two boxes, a big and a little one. The black man was greedy, and chose the largest. "The buckra box was full up with pen, paper and whip, and the negro box with hoe and bill; and hoe and bill for negro to this day."

But the crude element of good in human affairs must work and ripen, spite of whips and plantation laws and West Indian interest. Conscience rolled on its pillow, and could not sleep. We sympathize very tenderly here with the poor aggrieved planter, of whom so many unpleasant things are said; but if we saw the whip applied to old men, to tender women; and, undeniably, though I shrink to say so, pregnant women set in the treadmill for refusing to work; when, not they, but the eternal law of animal nature refused to work; if we saw men's backs flayed with cowhides, and "hot rum poured on, superinduced with brine or pickle, rubbed in with a cornhusk, in the scorching heat of the sun;" if we saw the runaways hunted with bloodhounds into swamps and hills; and, in cases of passion, a planter throwing his negro into a copper of boiling cane-juice—if we saw these things with eyes, we too should wince. They are not pleasant sights. The blood is moral: the blood is anti-slavery: it runs cold in the veins: the stomach rises with disgust, and curses slavery. Well, so it happened; a good man or woman, a country boy or girl, it would so fall out, once in a while saw these injuries and had the indiscretion to tell of them. The horrid story ran and flew; the winds blew it all over the world. They who heard it asked their rich and great friends if it was true, or only missionary lies. The richest and greatest, the prime minister of England, the king's privy council were obliged to say that it was too true. It became plain to all men, the more this business was looked into, that the crimes and cruelties of the slave-traders and slave-owners could not be overstated. The more it was searched, the more shocking anecdotes came up— things not to be spoken. Humane persons who were informed of the reports insisted on proving them. Granville Sharpe was accidentally made acquainted with the sufferings of a slave, whom a West Indian planter had brought with him to London and had beaten with a pistol on his head, so badly that his whole body became diseased, and the man useless to his master, who left him to go whither he pleased. The man applied to Mr. William Sharpe, a charitable surgeon, who attended the diseases of the poor. In process of time, he was healed. Granville Sharpe found him at his brother's and procured a place for him in an apothecary's shop. The master accidentally met his recovered slave, and instantly endeavored to get possession of him. Sharpe protected the slave. In consulting with the lawyers, they told Sharpe the laws were against him. Sharpe would not believe it; no prescription on earth could ever render such iniquities legal. 'But the decisions are against you, and Lord Mansfield, now Chief Justice of England, leans to the decisions.' Sharpe instantly sat down and gave himself to the study of English law for more than two years, until he had proved that the opinions relied on, of Talbot and Yorke, were incompatible with the former English decisions and with the whole spirit of English law. He published his book in 1769, and he so filled the heads and hearts of his advocates that when he brought the case of George Somerset, another slave, before Lord Mansfield, the slavish decisions were set aside, and equity affirmed. There is a sparkle of God's righteousness in Lord Mansfield's judgment, which does the heart good. Very unwilling had that great lawyer been to reverse the late decisions; he suggested twice from the bench, in the course of the trial, how the question might be got rid of: but the hint was not taken; the case was adjourned again and again, and judgment delayed. At last judgment was demanded, and on the 22d June, 1772, Lord Mansfield is reported to have decided in these words:

"Immemorial usage preserves the memory of *positive law*, long after all traces of the occasion, reason, authority and time of its introduction, are lost; and in a case so odious as the condition of slaves, must be taken strictly (tracing the subject to *natural principles*, the claim of slavery never can be supported). The power claimed by this return never was in use here. We cannot say the cause set forth by this

return is allowed or approved by the laws of this kingdom; and therefore the man must be discharged."

This decision established the principle that the "air of England is
too pure for any slave to breathe," but the wrongs in the islands were
not thereby touched. Public attention, however, was drawn that way,
and the methods of the stealing and the transportation from Africa
became noised abroad. The Quakers got the story. In their plain meeting-houses and prim dwellings this dismal agitation got entrance. They
were rich: they owned, for debt or by inheritance, island property; they
were religious, tender-hearted men and women; and they had to hear
the news and digest it as they could. Six Quakers met in London on
the 6th of July, 1783—William Dillwyn, Samuel Hoar, George Harri-
son, Thomas Knowles, John Lloyd, Joseph Woods, "to consider what
step they should take for the relief and liberation of the negro slaves in
the West Indies, and for the discouragement of the slave-trade on the
coast of Africa." They made friends and raised money for the slave;
they interested their Yearly Meeting; and all English and all American
Quakers. John Woolman of New Jersey, whilst yet an apprentice, was
uneasy in his mind when he was set to write a bill of sale of a negro, for
his master. He gave his testimony against the traffic, in Maryland and
Virginia. Thomas Clarkson was a youth at Cambridge, England, when
the subject given out for a Latin prize dissertation was, "Is it right to
make slaves of others against their will?" He wrote an essay, and won
the prize; but he wrote too well for his own peace; he began to ask himself if these things could be true; and if they were, he could no longer
rest. He left Cambridge; he fell in with the six Quakers. They engaged
him to act for them. He himself interested Mr. Wilberforce in the matter. The shipmasters in that trade were the greatest miscreants, and
guilty of every barbarity to their own crews. Clarkson went to Bristol,
made himself acquainted with the interior of the slave-ships and the
details of the trade. The facts confirmed his sentiment, "that Providence had never made that to be wise which was immoral, and that the
slave-trade was as impolitic as it was unjust;" that it was found pecu-
liarly fatal to those employed in it. More seamen died in that trade in
one year than in the whole remaining trade of the country in two. Mr.
Pitt and Mr. Fox were drawn into the generous enterprise. In 1788, the
House of Commons voted Parliamentary inquiry. In 1791, a bill to
abolish the trade was brought in by Wilberforce, and supported by him

. . . .

and by Fox and Burke and Pitt, with the utmost ability and faithful-ness; resisted by the planters and the whole West Indian interest, and lost. During the next sixteen years, ten times, year after year, the attempt was renewed by Mr. Wilberforce, and ten times defeated by the planters. The king, and all the royal family but one, were against it. These debates are instructive, as they show on what grounds the trade was assailed and defended. Everything generous, wise and sprightly is sure to come to the attack. On the other part are found cold prudence, barefaced selfishness and silent votes. But the nation was aroused to enthusiasm. Every horrid fact became known. In 1791, three hundred thousand persons in Britain pledged themselves to abstain from all arti-cles of island produce. The planters were obliged to give way; and in 1807, on the 25th March, the bill passed, and the slave-trade was abol-ished.

The assailants of slavery had early agreed to limit their political action on this subject to the abolition of the trade, but Granville Sharpe, as a matter of conscience, whilst he acted as chairman of the London Committee, felt constrained to record his protest against the limitation, declaring that slavery was as much a crime against the Divine law as the slave-trade. The trade, under false flags, went on as before. In 1821, according to official documents presented to the Amer-ican government by the Colonization Society, 200,000 slaves were deported from Africa. Nearly 30,000 were landed in the port of Havana alone. In consequence of the dangers of the trade growing out of the act of abolition, ships were built sharp for swiftness, and with a fright-ful disregard of the comfort of the victims they were destined to transport. They carried five, six, even seven hundred stowed in a ship built so narrow as to be unsafe, being made just broad enough on the beam to keep the sea. In attempting to make its escape from the pursuit of a man-of-war, one ship flung five hundred slaves alive into the sea. These facts went into Parliament. In the islands was an ominous state of cruel and licentious society; every house had a dungeon attached to it; every slave was worked by the whip. There is no end to the tragic anecdotes in the municipal records of the colonies. The boy was set to strip and flog his own mother to blood, for a small offence. Looking in the face of his master by the negro was held to be violence by the island courts. He was worked sixteen hours, and his ration by law, in some islands, was a pint of flour and one salt herring a day. He suffered insult, stripes, mutilation at the humor of the master: iron collars were riveted on their necks with iron prongs ten inches long; capsicum pepper was rubbed in the eyes of the females; and they were done to death with the most shocking levity between the master and manager, without fine or inquiry. And when, at last, some Quakers, Moravians, and Wesleyan and Baptist missionaries, following in the steps of Carey and Ward in the East Indies, had been moved to come and cheer the poor victim with the hope of some reparation, in a future world, of the wrongs he suffered in this, these missionaries were persecuted by the planters, their lives threatened, their chapels burned, and the negroes furiously forbidden to go near them. These outrages rekindled the flame of British indignation. Petitions poured into Parliament: a million persons signed their names to these; and in 1833, on the 14th May, Lord Stanley, Minister of the Colonies, introduced into the House of Commons his bill for the Emancipation.

The scheme of the Minister, with such modification as it received in the legislature, proposed gradual emancipation; that on 1st August, 1834, all persons now slaves should be entitled to be registered as apprenticed laborers, and to acquire thereby all the rights and privileges of freemen, subject to the restriction of laboring under certain conditions. These conditions were, that the prædials should owe three fourths of the profits of their labor to their masters for six years, and the non-prædials for four years. The other fourth of the apprentice's time was to be his own, which he might sell to his master, or to other persons; and at the end of the term of years fixed, he should be free.

With these provisions and conditions, the bill proceeds, in the twelfth section, in the following terms: "Be it enacted, that all and every person who, on the first August, 1834, shall be holden in slavery within any such British colony as aforesaid, shall upon and from and after the said first August, become and be to all intents and purposes free, and discharged of and from all manner of slavery, and shall be absolutely and forever manumitted; and that the children thereafter born to any such persons, and the offspring of such children, shall, in like manner, be free, from their birth; and that from and after the first August, 1834, slavery shall be and is hereby utterly and forever abolished and declared unlawful throughout the British colonies, plantations, and possessions abroad."

The Ministers, having estimated the slave products of the colonies in annual exports of sugar, rum and coffee, at £1,500,000 per annum, estimated the total value of the slave property at 30,000,000 pounds sterling, and proposed to give the planters, as a compensation for so much of the slaves' time as the act took from them, 20,000,000 pounds sterling, to be divided into nineteen shares for the nineteen colonies, and to be distributed to the owners of slaves by commissioners, whose appointment and duties were regulated by the Act. After much debate, the bill passed by large majorities. The apprenticeship system is understood to have proceeded from Lord Brougham, and was by him urged on his colleagues, who, it is said, were inclined to the policy of immediate emancipation.

The colonial legislatures received the act of Parliament with various degrees of displeasure, and, of course, every provision of the bill was criticised with severity. The new relation between the master and the apprentice, it was feared, would be mischievous; for the bill required the appointment of magistrates who should hear every complaint of the apprentice and see that justice was done him. It was feared that the interest of the master and servant would now produce perpetual discord between them. In the island of Antigua, containing 37,000 people, 30,000 being negroes, these objections had such weight that the legislature rejected the apprenticeship system, and adopted absolute emancipation. In the other islands the system of the Ministry was accepted.

The reception of it by the negro population was equal in nobleness to the deed. The negroes were called together by the missionaries and by the planters, and the news explained to them. On the night of the 31st July, they met everywhere at their churches and chapels, and at midnight, when the clock struck twelve, on their knees, the silent, weeping assembly became men; they rose and embraced each other; they cried, they sung, they prayed, they were wild with joy, but there was no riot, no feasting. I have never read anything in history more touching than the moderation of the negroes. Some American captains left the shore and put to sea, anticipating insurrection and general murder. With far different thoughts, the negroes spent the hour in their huts and chapels. I will not repeat to you the well-known paragraph, in which Messrs. Thome and Kimball, the commissioners sent out in the year 1837 by the American Anti-Slavery Society, describe the occurrences of that night in the island of Antigua. It has been quoted in every newspaper, and Dr. Channing has given it additional fame. But I must be indulged in quoting a few sentences from the pages that follow it, narrating the behavior of the emancipated people on the next day.

"The first of August came on Friday, and a release was proclaimed from all work until the next Monday. The day was chiefly spent by the great mass of the negroes in the churches and chapels. The clergy and missionaries throughout the island were actively engaged, seizing the opportunity to enlighten the people on all the duties and responsibilities of their new relation, and urging them to the attainment of that higher liberty with which Christ maketh his children free. In every quarter, we were assured, the day was like a Sabbath. Work had ceased. The hum of business was still: tranquillity pervaded the towns and country. The planters informed us that they went to the chapels where their own people were assembled, greeted them, shook hands with them, and exchanged the most hearty good wishes. At Grace Hill, there were at least a thousand persons around the Moravian Chapel who could not get in. For once the house of God suffered violence, and the violent took it by force. At Grace Bay, the people, all dressed in white, formed a procession, and walked arm in arm into the chapel. We were told that the dress of the negroes on that occasion was uncommonly simple and modest. There was not the least disposition to gayety. Throughout the island, there was not a single dance known of, either day or night, nor so much as a fiddle played."

On the next Monday morning, with very few exceptions, every negro on every plantation was in the field at his work. In some places, they waited to see their master, to know what bargain he would make; but for the most part, throughout the islands, nothing painful occurred. In June, 1835, the Ministers, Lord Aberdeen and Sir George Grey, declared to the Parliament that the system worked well; that now for ten months, from 1st August, 1834, no injury or violence had been offered to any white, and only one black had been hurt in 800,000 negroes: and, contrary to many sinister predictions, that the new crop of island produce would not fall short of that of the last year.

But the habit of oppression was not destroyed by a law and a day of jubilee. It soon appeared in all the islands that the planters were disposed to use their old privileges, and overwork the apprentices; to take from them, under various pretences, their fourth part of their time; and to exert the same licentious despotism as before. The negroes complained to the magistrates and to the governor. In the island of Jamaica, this ill blood continually grew worse. The governors, Lord Belmore, the Earl of Sligo, and afterwards Sir Lionel Smith (a governor of their own class, who had been sent out to gratify the planters), threw themselves on the side of the oppressed, and were at constant quarrel with the angry and bilious island legislature. Nothing can exceed the ill humor and sulkiness of the addresses of this assembly.

I may here express a general remark, which the history of slavery seems to justify, that it is not founded solely on the avarice of the planter. We sometimes say, the planter does not want slaves, he only wants the immunities and the luxuries which the slaves yield him; give him money, give him a machine that will yield him as much money as the slaves, and he will thankfully let them go. He has no love of slavery, he wants luxury, and he will pay even this price of crime and danger for it. But I think experience does not warrant this favorable distinction, but shows the existence, beside the covetousness, of a bitter element, the love of power, the voluptuousness of holding a human being in his absolute control. We sometimes observe that spoiled children contract a habit of annoying quite wantonly those who have charge of them, and seem to measure their own sense of well-being, not by what they do, but by the degree of reaction they can cause. It is vain to get rid of them by not minding them: if purring and humming is not noticed, they squeal and screech; then if you chide and console them, they find the experiment succeeds, and they begin again. The child will sit in your arms contented, provided you do nothing. If you take a book and read, he commences hostile operations. The planter is the spoiled child of his unnatural habits, and has contracted in his indolent and luxurious climate the need of excitement by irritating and tormenting his slave.

Sir Lionel Smith defended the poor negro girls, prey to the licentiousness of the planters; they shall not be whipped with tamarind rods if they do not comply with their master's will; he defended the negro women; they should not be made to dig the cane-holes (which is the very hardest of the field work); he defended the Baptist preachers and the stipendiary magistrates, who are the negroes' friends, from the power of the planter. The power of the planters, however, to oppress, was greater than the power of the apprentice and of his guardians to withstand. Lord Brougham and Mr. Buxton declared that the planter had not fulfilled his part in the contract, whilst the apprentices had fulfilled theirs; and demanded that the emancipation should be hastened, and the apprenticeship abolished. Parliament was compelled to pass additional laws for the defence and security of the negro, and in ill humor at these acts, the great island of Jamaica, with a population of half a million, and 300,000 negroes, early in 1838, resolved to throw up the two remaining years of apprenticeship, and to emancipate absolutely on the 1st August, 1838. In British Guiana, in Dominica, the same resolution had been earlier taken with more good will; and the other islands fell into the measure; so that on the 1st August, 1838, the shackles dropped from every British slave. The accounts which we have from all parties, both from the planters (and those too who were originally most opposed to the measure), and from the new freemen, are of the most satisfactory kind. The manner in which the new festival was celebrated, brings tears to the eyes. The First of August, 1838, was observed in Jamaica as a day of thanksgiving and prayer. Sir Lionel Smith, the governor, writes to the British Ministry, "It is impossible for me to do justice to the good order, decorum and gratitude which the whole laboring population manifested on that happy occasion. Though joy beamed on every countenance, it was throughout tempered with solemn thankfulness to God, and the churches and chapels were everywhere filled with these happy people in humble offering of praise."

The Queen, in her speech to the Lords and Commons, praised the conduct of the emancipated population: and in 1840 Sir Charles Metcalfe, the new governor of Jamaica, in his address to the Assembly expressed himself to that late exasperated body in these terms: "All those who are acquainted with the state of the island know that our emancipated population are as free, as independent in their conduct, as well conditioned, as much in the enjoyment of abundance, and as strongly sensible of the blessings of liberty, as any that we know of in any country. All disqualifications and distinctions of color have ceased; men of all colors have equal rights in law, and an equal footing in society, and every man's position is settled by the same circumstances which regulate that point in other free countries, where no difference of color exists. It may be asserted, without fear of denial, that the former slaves of Jamaica are now as secure in all social rights, as freeborn

Britons." He further describes the erection of numerous churches, chapels and schools which the new population required, and adds that more are still demanded. The legislature, in their reply, echo the governor's statement, and say, "The peaceful demeanor of the emancipated population redounds to their own credit, and affords a proof of their continued comfort and prosperity."

I said, this event is signal in the history of civilization. There are many styles of civilization, and not one only. Ours is full of barbarities. There are many faculties in man, each of which takes its turn of activity, and that faculty which is paramount in any period and exerts itself through the strongest nation, determines the civility of that age: and each age thinks its own the perfection of reason. Our culture is very cheap and intelligible. Unroof any house, and you shall find it. The well-being consists in having a sufficiency of coffee and toast, with a daily newspaper; a well glazed parlor, with marbles, mirrors and centre-table and the excitement of a few parties and a few rides in a year. Such is one house, such are all. The owner of a New York manor imitates the mansion and equipage of the London nobleman; the Boston merchant rivals his brother of New York; and the villages copy Boston. There have been nations elevated by great sentiments. Such was the civility of Sparta and the Dorian race, whilst it was defective in some of the chief elements of ours. That of Athens, again, lay in an intellect dedicated to beauty. That of Asia Minor in poetry, music and arts; that of Palestine in piety; that of Rome in military arts and virtues, exalted by a prodigious magnanimity; that of China and Japan in the last exaggeration of decorum and etiquette. Our civility, England determines the style of, inasmuch as England is the strongest of the family of existing nations, and as we are the expansion of that people. It is that of a trading nation; it is a shopkeeping civility. The English lord is a retired shopkeeper, and has the prejudices and timidities of that profession. And we are shopkeepers, and have acquired the vices and virtues that belong to trade. We peddle, we truck, we sail, we row, we ride in cars, we creep in teams, we go in canals—to market, and for the sale of goods. The national aim and employment streams into our ways of thinking, our laws, our habits and our manners. The customer is the immediate jewel of our souls. Him we flatter, him we feast, compliment, vote for, and will not contradict. It was, or it seemed the dictate of trade, to keep the negro down. We had found a race who were less warlike, and less energetic shopkeepers than we; who had very little skill in trade. We found it very convenient to keep them at work, since, by the aid of a little whipping, we could get their work for nothing but their board and the cost of whips. What if it cost a few unpleasant scenes on the coast of Africa? That was a great way off; and the scenes could be endured by some sturdy, unscrupulous fellows, who could go, for high wages, and bring us the men, and need not trouble our ears with the disagreeable particulars. If any mention was made of homicide, madness, adultery, and intolerable tortures, we would let the church-bells ring louder, the church-organ swell its peal and drown the hideous sound. The sugar they raised was excellent: nobody tasted blood in it. The coffee was fragrant; the tobacco was incense; the brandy made nations happy; the cotton clothed the world. What! all raised by these men, and no wages? Excellent! What a convenience! They seemed created by Providence to bear the heat and the whippings, and make these fine articles.

But unhappily, most unhappily, gentlemen, man is born with intellect, as well as with a love of sugar; and with a sense of justice, as well as a taste for strong drink. These ripened, as well as those. You could not educate him, you could not get any poetry, any wisdom, any beauty in woman, any strong and commanding character in man, but these absurdities would still come flashing out—these absurdities of a demand for justice, a generosity for the weak and oppressed. Unhappily, too, for the planter, the laws of nature are in harmony with each other: that which the head and the heart demand is found to be, in the long run, for what the grossest calculator calls his advantage. The moral sense is always supported by the permanent interest of the parties. Else, I know not how, in our world, any good would ever get done. It was shown to the planters that they, as well as the negroes, were slaves; that though they paid no wages, they got very poor work; that their estates were ruining them, under the finest climate; and that they needed the severest monopoly laws at home to keep them from bankruptcy. The oppression of the slave recoiled on them. They were full of vices; their children were lumps of pride, sloth, sensuality and rottenness. The position of woman was nearly as bad as it could be; and, like other robbers, they could not sleep in security. Many planters have said, since the emancipation, that, before that day, they were the greatest slaves on the estates. Slavery is no scholar, no improver; it does not love the whistle of the railroad; it does not love the newspaper; the mail-bag, a college, a book or a preacher who has the absurd whim of saying what he thinks; it does not increase the white population; it does not improve the soil; everything goes to decay. For these reasons the islands proved bad customers to England. It was very easy for manufacturers less shrewd than those of Birmingham and Manchester to see that if the state of things in the islands was altered, if the slaves had wages, the slaves would be clothed, would build houses, would fill them with tools, with pottery, with crockery, with hardware; and negro women love fine clothes as well as white women. In every naked negro of those thousands, they saw a future customer. Meantime, they saw further that the slave-trade, by keeping in barbarism the whole coast of eastern Africa, deprives them of countries and nations of customers, if once freedom and civility and European manners could get a foothold there. But the trade could not be abolished whilst this hungry West Indian market, with an appetite like the grave, cried, 'More, more, bring me a hundred a day;' they could not expect any mitigation in the madness of the poor African war-chiefs. These considerations opened the eyes of the dullest in Britain. More than this, the West Indian estate was owned or mortgaged in England, and the owner and the mortgagee had very plain intimations that the feeling of English liberty was gaining every hour new mass and velocity, and the hostility to such as resisted it would be fatal. The House of Commons would destroy the protection of island produce, and interfere in English politics in the island legislation: so they hastened to make the best of their position, and accepted the bill.

These considerations, I doubt not, had their weight; the interest of trade, the interest of the revenue, and, moreover, the good fame of the action. It was inevitable that men should feel these motives. But they do not appear to have had an excessive or unreasonable weight. On reviewing this history, I think the whole transaction reflects infinite honor on the people and parliament of England. It was a stately spectacle, to see the cause of human rights argued with so much patience and generosity and with such a mass of evidence before that powerful people. It is a creditable incident in the history that when, in 1789, the first privy council report of evidence on the trade (a bulky folio embodying all the facts which the London Committee had been engaged for years in collecting, and all the examinations before the council) was presented to the House of Commons, a late day being named for the discussion, in order to give members time—Mr. Wilberforce, Mr. Pitt, the Prime Minister, and other gentlemen, took advantage of the postponement to retire into the country to read the report. For months and years the bill was debated, with some consciousness of the extent of its relations, by the first citizens of England, the foremost men of the earth; every argument was weighed, every particle of evidence was sifted and laid in the scale; and, at last, the right triumphed, the poor man was vindicated, and the oppressor was flung out. I know that England has the advantage of trying the question at a wide distance from the spot where the nuisance exists; the planters are not, excepting in rare examples, members of the legislature. The extent of the empire, and the magnitude and number of other questions crowding into court, keep this one in balance, and prevent it from obtaining that ascendency, and being urged with that intemperance which a question of property tends to acquire. There are causes in the composition of the British legislature, and the relation of its leaders to the country and to Europe, which exclude much that is pitiful and injurious in other legislative assemblies. From these reasons, the question was discussed with a rare independence and magnanimity. It was not narrowed down to a paltry electioneering trap; and, I must say, a delight in justice, an honest tenderness for the poor negro, for man suffering these wrongs, combined with the national pride, which refused to give the support of English soil or the protection of the English flag to these disgusting violations of nature.

Forgive me, fellow citizens, if I own to you, that in the last few days that my attention has been occupied with this history, I have not been able to read a page of it without the most painful comparisons. Whilst I have read of England, I have thought of New England. Whilst I have meditated in my solitary walks on the magnanimity of the English Bench and Senate, reaching out the benefit of the law to the most helpless citizen in her world-wide realm, I have found myself oppressed by other thoughts. As I have walked in the pastures and along the edge of woods, I could not keep my imagination on those agreeable figures, for other images that intruded on me. I could not see the great vision of the patriots and senators who have adopted the slave's cause—they turned their backs on me. No: I see other pictures—of mean men; I see very poor, very ill-clothed, very ignorant men, not surrounded by happy friends—to be plain—poor black men of obscure employment as mariners, cooks or stewards, in ships, yet citizens of this our Commonwealth of Massachusetts—freeborn as we—whom the slave-laws of the States of South Carolina, Georgia and Louisiana have arrested in the vessels in which they visited those ports, and shut up in jails so long as the vessel remained in port, with the stringent addition, that if the shipmaster fails to pay the costs of this official arrest and the board in jail, these citizens are to be sold for slaves, to pay that expense. This man, these men, I see, and no law to save them. Fellow citizens, this crime will not be hushed up any longer. I have learned that a citizen of Nantucket, walking in New Orleans, found a freeborn citizen of Nantucket, a man, too, of great personal worth, and, as it happened, very dear to him, as having saved his own life, working chained in the streets of that city, kidnapped by such a process as this. In the sleep of the laws, the private interference of two excellent citizens of Boston has, I have ascertained, rescued several natives of this State from these Southern prisons. Gentlemen, I thought the deck of a Massachusetts ship was as much the territory of Massachusetts as the floor on which we stand. It should be as sacred as the temple of God. The poorest fishing-smack that floats under the shadow of an iceberg in the Northern seas, or hunts whale in the Southern ocean, should be encompassed by her laws with comfort and protection, as much as within the arms of Cape Ann or Cape Cod. And this kidnapping is suffered within our own land and federation, whilst the fourth article of the Constitution of the United States ordains in terms, that, "The citizens of each State shall be entitled to all privileges and immunities of citizens in the several States." If such a damnable outrage can be committed on the person of a citizen with impunity, let the Governor break the broad seal of the State; he bears the sword in vain. The Governor of Massachusetts is a trifler; the State-House in Boston is a play-house; the General Court is a dishonored body, if they make laws which they cannot execute. The great hearted Puritans have left no posterity. The rich men may walk in State Street, but they walk without honor; and the farmers may brag their democracy in the country, but they are disgraced men. If the State has no power to defend its own people in its own shipping, because it has delegated that power to the Federal Government, has it no representation in the Federal Government? Are those men dumb? I am no lawyer, and cannot indicate the forms applicable to the case, but here is something which transcends all forms. Let the senators and representatives of the State, containing a population of a million freemen, go in a body before the Congress and say that they have a demand to make on them, so imperative that all functions of government must stop until it is satisfied. If ordinary legislation cannot reach it, then extraordinary must be applied. The Congress should instruct the President to send to those ports of Charleston, Savannah and New Orleans such orders and such force as should release, forthwith, all such citizens of Massachusetts as were holden in prison without the allegation of any crime, and should set on foot the strictest inquisition to discover where such persons, brought into slavery by these local laws at any time heretofore, may now be. That first; and then, let order be taken to indemnify all such as have been incarcerated. As for dangers to the Union, from such demands!—the Union already is at an end when the first citizen of Massachusetts is thus outraged. Is it an union and covenant in which the State of Massachusetts agrees to be imprisoned, and the State of Carolina to imprison? Gentlemen, I am loath to say harsh things, and perhaps I know too little of politics for the smallest weight to attach to any censure of mine—but I am at a loss how to characterize the tameness and silence of the two senators and the ten representatives of the State at Washington. To what purpose have we clothed each of those representatives with the power of seventy thousand persons, and each senator with near half a million, if they are to sit dumb at their desks and see their constituents captured and sold—perhaps to gentlemen sitting by them in the hall? There is a scandalous rumor that has been swelling louder of late years—perhaps wholly false—that members are bullied into silence by Southern gentlemen. It is so easy to omit to speak, or even to be absent when delicate things are to be handled. I may as well say, what all men feel, that whilst our very amiable and very innocent representatives and senators at Washington are accomplished lawyers and merchants, and very eloquent at dinners and at caucuses, there is a disastrous want of *men* from New England. I would gladly make exceptions, and you will not suffer me to forget one eloquent old man, in whose veins the blood of Massachusetts rolls, and who singly has defended the freedom of speech, and the rights of the free, against the usurpation of the slave-holder. But the reader of Congressional debates, in New England, is perplexed to see with what admirable sweetness and patience the majority of the free States are schooled and ridden by the minority of slave-holders. What if we should send thither representatives who were a particle less amiable and less innocent? I entreat you, sirs, let not this stain attach, let not this misery accumulate any longer. If the managers of our political parties are too prudent and too cold; if, most unhappily, the ambitious class of young men and political men have found out that these neglected victims are poor and without weight; that they have no graceful hospitalities to offer; no valuable business to throw into any man's hands, no strong vote to cast at the elections; and therefore may with impunity be left in their chains or to the chance of chains—then let the citizens in their primary capacity take up their cause on this very ground, and say to the government of the State, and of the Union, that government exists to defend the weak and the poor and the injured party; the rich and the strong can better take care of themselves. And as an omen and assurance of success, I point you to the bright example which England set you, on this day, ten years ago.

There are other comparisons and other imperative duties which come sadly to mind—but I do not wish to darken the hours of this day by crimination; I turn gladly to the rightful theme, to the bright aspects of the occasion.

This event was a moral revolution. The history of it is before you. Here was no prodigy, no fabulous hero, no Trojan horse, no bloody war, but all was achieved by plain means of plain men, working not under a leader, but under a sentiment. Other revolutions have been the insurrection of the oppressed; this was the repentance of the tyrant. It was the masters revolting from their mastery. The slave-holder said, 'I will not hold slaves.' The end was noble and the means were pure. Hence the elevation and pathos of this chapter of history. The lives of the advocates are pages of greatness, and the connection of the eminent senators with this question constitutes the immortalizing moments of those men's lives. The bare enunciation of the theses at which the lawyers and legislators arrived, gives a glow to the heart of the reader. Lord Chancellor Northington is the author of the famous sentence, "As soon as any man puts his foot on English ground, he becomes free." "I was a slave," said the counsel of Somerset, speaking for his client, "for I was in America: I am now in a country where the common rights of mankind are known and regarded." Granville Sharpe filled the ear of the judges with the sound principles that had from time to time been affirmed by the legal authorities: "Derived power cannot be superior to the power from which it is derived:" "The reasonableness of the law is the soul of the law:" "It is better to suffer every evil, than to consent to any." Out it would come, the God's truth, out it came, like a bolt from a cloud, for all the mumbling of the lawyers. One feels very sensibly in all this history that a great heart and soul are behind there, superior to any man, and making use of each, in turn, and infinitely attractive to every person according to the degree of reason in his own mind, so that this cause has had the power to draw to it every particle of talent and of worth in England, from the beginning. All the great geniuses of the British senate, Fox, Pitt, Burke, Grenville, Sheridan, Grey, Canning, ranged themselves on its side; the poet Cowper wrote for it: Franklin, Jefferson, Washington, in this country, all recorded their votes. All men remember the subtlety and the fire of indignation which the "Edinburgh Review" contributed to the cause; and every liberal mind, poet, preacher, moralist, statesman, has had the fortune to appear somewhere for this cause. On the other part, appeared the reign of pounds and shillings, and all manner of rage and stupidity; a resistance which drew from Mr. Huddlestone in Parliament the observation, "That a curse attended this trade even in the mode of defending it. By a certain fatality, none but the vilest arguments were brought forward, which corrupted the very persons who used them. Every one of these was built on the narrow ground of interest, of pecuniary profit, of sordid gain, in opposition to every motive that had reference to humanity, justice, and religion, or to that great principle which comprehended them all." This moral force perpetually reinforces and dignifies the friends of this cause. It gave that tenacity to their point which has insured ultimate triumph; and it gave that superiority in reason, in imagery, in eloquence, which makes in all countries anti-slavery meetings so attractive to the people, and has made it a proverb in Massachusetts, that "eloquence is dog-cheap at the anti-slavery chapel."

I will say further that we are indebted mainly to this movement and to the continuers of it, for the popular discussion of every point of practical ethics, and a reference of every question to the absolute standard. It is notorious that the political, religious and social schemes, with which the minds of men are now most occupied, have been matured, or at least broached, in the free and daring discussions of these assemblies.

Men have become aware, through the emancipation and kindred events, of the presence of powers which, in their days of darkness, they had overlooked. Virtuous men will not again rely on political agents They have found out the deleterious effect of political association. Up to this day we have allowed to statesmen a paramount social standing, and we bow low to them as to the great. We cannot extend this deference to them any longer. The secret cannot be kept, that the seats of power are filled by underlings, ignorant, timid and selfish to a degree to destroy all claim, excepting that on compassion, to the society of the just and generous. What happened notoriously to an American ambassador in England, that he found himself compelled to palter and to disguise the fact that he was a slave-breeder, happens to men of state. Their vocation is a presumption against them among well-meaning people. The superstition respecting power and office is going to the ground. The stream of human affairs flows its own way, and is very little affected by the activity of legislators. What great masses of men wish done, will be done; and they do not wish it for a freak, but because it is their state and natural end. There are now other energies than force, other than political, which no man in future can allow himself to disregard. There is direct conversation and influence. A man is to make himself felt by his proper force. The tendency of things runs steadily to this point, namely, to put every man on his merits, and to give him so much power as he naturally exerts—no more, no less. Of course, the timid and base persons, all who are conscious of no worth in themselves, and who owe all their place to the opportunities which the older order of things allowed them, to deceive and defraud men, shudder at the change, and would fain silence every honest voice, and lock up every house where liberty and innovation can be pleaded for. They would raise mobs, for fear is very cruel. But the strong and healthy yeomen and husbands of the land, the self-sustaining class of inventive and industrious men, fear no competition or superiority. Come what will, their faculty cannot be spared.

The First of August marks the entrance of a new element into modern politics, namely, the civilization of the negro. A man is added to the human family. Not the least affecting part of this history of abolition is the annihilation of the old indecent nonsense about the nature of the negro. In the case of the ship Zong, in 1781, whose master had thrown one hundred and thirty-two slaves alive into the sea, to cheat the underwriters, the first jury gave a verdict in favor of the master and owners: they had a right to do what they had done. Lord Mansfield is reported to have said on the bench, "The matter left to the jury is—Was it from necessity? For they had no doubt—though it shocks one very much—that the case of slaves was the same as if horses had been thrown overboard. It is a very shocking case." But a more enlightened and humane opinion began to prevail. Mr. Clarkson, early in his career, made a collection of African productions and manufactures, as specimens of the arts and culture of the negro; comprising cloths and loom, weapons, polished stones and woods, leather, glass, dyes, ornaments, soap, pipe-bowls and trinkets. These he showed to Mr. Pitt, who saw and handled them with extreme interest. "On sight of these," says Clarkson, "many sublime thoughts seemed to rush at once into his mind, some of which he expressed"; and hence appeared to arise a project which was always dear to him, of the civilization of Africa—a dream which forever elevates his fame. In 1791, Mr. Wilberforce announced to the House of Commons, "We have already gained one victory: we have obtained for these poor creatures the recognition of their human nature, which for a time was most shamefully denied them." It was the sarcasm of Montesquieu, "it would not do to suppose that negroes were men, lest it should turn out that whites were not"; for the white has, for ages, done what he could to keep the negro in that hoggish state. His laws have been furies. It now appears that the negro race is, more than any other, susceptible of rapid civilization. The emancipation is observed, in the islands, to have wrought for the negro a benefit as sudden as when a thermometer is brought out of the shade into the sun. It has given him eyes and ears. If, before, he was taxed with such stupidity, or such defective vision, that he could not set a table square to the walls of an apartment, he is now the principal if not the only mechanic in the West Indies; and is, besides, an architect, a physician, a lawyer, a magistrate, an editor, and a valued and increasing political power. The recent testimonies of Sturge, of Thome and Kimball, of Gurney, of Philippo, are very explicit on this point, the capacity and the success of the colored and the black population in employment of skill, of profit and of trust; and best of all is the testimony to their moderation. They receive hints and advances from the whites that they will be gladly received as subscribers to the Exchange, as members of this or that committee of trust. They hold back, and say to each other that "social position is not to be gained by pushing."

I have said that this event interests us because it came mainly from the concession of the whites; I add, that in part it is the earning of the blacks. They won the pity and respect which they have received, by their powers and native endowments. I think this a circumstance of the highest import. Their whole future is in it. Our planet, before the age of written history, had its races of savages, like the generations of sour paste, or the animalcules that wiggle and bite in a drop of putrid water. Who cares for these or for their wars? We do not wish a world of bugs or of birds; neither afterward of Scythians, Caraibs or Feejees. The grand style of Nature, her great periods, is all we observe in them. Who cares for oppressing whites, or oppressed blacks, twenty centuries ago, more than for bad dreams? Eaters and food are in the harmony of Nature; and there too is the germ forever protected, unfolding gigantic leaf after leaf, a newer flower, a richer fruit, in every period, yet its next product is never to be guessed. It will only save what is worth saving; and it saves not by compassion, but by power. It appoints no police to guard the lion but his teeth and claws; no fort or city for the bird but his wings; no rescue for flies and mites but their spawning numbers, which no ravages can overcome. It deals with men after the same manner. If they are rude and foolish, down they must go. When at last in a race a new principle appears, an idea—*that* conserves it; ideas only save races. If the black man is feeble and not important to the existing races, not on a parity with the best race, the black man must serve, and be exterminated. But if the black man carries in his bosom an indispensable element of a new and coming civilization; for the sake of that element, no wrong nor strength nor circumstance can hurt him: he will survive and play his part. So now, the arrival in the world of such men as Toussaint, and the Haytian heroes, or of the leaders of their race in Barbadoes and Jamaica, outweighs in good omen all the English and American humanity. The anti-slavery of the whole world is dust in the balance before this—is a poor squeamishness and nervousness: the might and the right are here: here is the anti-slave: here is man: and if you have man, black or white is an insignificance. The intellect—that is miraculous! Who has it, has the talisman: his skin and bones, though they were of the color of night, are transparent, and the everlasting stars shine through, with attractive beams. But a compassion for that which is not and cannot be useful or lovely, is degrading and futile. All the songs and newspapers and money subscriptions and vituperation of such as do not think with us, will avail nothing against a fact. I say to you, you must save yourself, black or white, man or woman; other help is none. I esteem the occasion of this jubilee to be the proud discovery that the black race can contend with the white: that in the great anthem which we call history, a piece of many parts and vast compass, after playing a long time a very low and subdued accompaniment, they perceive the time arrived when they can strike in with effect and take a master's part in the music. The civility of the world has reached that pitch that their more moral genius is becoming indispensable, and the quality of this race is to be honored for itself. For this, they have been preserved in sandy deserts, in rice-swamps, in kitchens and shoe-shops, so long: now let them emerge, clothed and in their own form.

There remains the very elevated consideration which the subject opens, but which belongs to more abstract views than we are now taking, this, namely, that the civility of no race can be perfect whilst another race is degraded. It is a doctrine alike of the oldest and of the newest philosophy, that man is one, and that you cannot injure any member, without a sympathetic injury to all the members. America is not civil, whilst Africa is barbarous.

These considerations seem to leave no choice for the action of the intellect and the conscience of the country. There have been moments in this, as well as in every piece of moral history, when there seemed room for the infusions of a skeptical philosophy; when it seemed doubtful whether brute force would not triumph in the eternal struggle. I doubt not that, sometimes, a despairing negro, when jumping over the ship's sides to escape from the white devils who surrounded him, has believed there was no vindication of right; it is horrible to think of, but it seemed so. I doubt not that sometimes the negro's friend, in the face of scornful and brutal hundreds of traders and drivers, has felt his heart sink. Especially, it seems to me, some degree of despondency is pardonable, when he observes the men of conscience and of intellect, his own natural allies and champions—those whose attention should be nailed to the grand objects of this cause, so hotly offended by whatever incidental petulances or infirmities of indiscreet defenders of the negro, as to permit themselves to be ranged with the enemies of the human race; and names which should be the alarums of liberty and the watchwords of truth, are mixed up with all the rotten rabble of selfishness and tyranny. I assure myself that this coldness and blindness will pass away. A single noble wind of sentiment will scatter them forever. I am sure that the good and wise elders, the ardent and generous youth, will not permit what is incidental and exceptional to withdraw their devotion from the essential and permanent characters of the question. There have been moments, I said, when men might be forgiven who doubted. Those moments are past. Seen in masses, it cannot be disputed, there is progress in human society. There is a blessed necessity by which the interest of men is always driving them to the right; and, again, making all crime mean and ugly. The genius of the Saxon race, friendly to liberty; the enterprise, the very muscular vigor of this nation, are inconsistent with slavery. The Intellect, with blazing eye, looking through history from the beginning onward, gazes on this blot and it disappears. The sentiment of Right, once very low and indistinct, but ever more articulate, because it is the voice of the universe, pronounces Freedom. The Power that built this fabric of things affirms it in the heart; and in the history of the First of August, has made a sign to the ages, of his will.

THE FUGITIVE SLAVE
LAW

[*This is one of two addresses on the same subject by
Emerson. He gave the first in Concord on May 3,
1851. Fugitive slaves were constantly passing through
Concord in those days and were helped on their way
by various individuals. The second address, which
follows, he delivered at the Tabernacle in New York
City on March 4, 1854.*]

"Of all we loved and honored, naught
    Save power remains,—
A fallen angel's pride of thought,
    Still strong in chains.

All else is gone; from those great eyes
    The soul has fled:
When faith is lost, when honor dies,
    The man is dead!"

                Whittier, *Ichabod!*

"We that had loved him so, followed him, honoured him,
    Lived in his mild and magnificent eye,
Learned his great language, caught his clear accents,
    Made him our pattern to live and to die!
Shakspeare was of us, Milton was for us,
    Burns, Shelley, were with us,—they watch from their graves!
He alone breaks from the van and the freemen,
    —He alone sinks to the rear and the slaves !"

              Browning, *The Lost Leader*

THE FUGITIVE SLAVE LAW

I DO NOT often speak to public questions—they are odious and hurtful, and it seems like meddling or leaving your work. I have my own spirits in prison—spirits in deeper prisons, whom no man visits if I do not. And then I see what havoc it makes with any good mind, a dissipated philanthropy. The one thing not to be forgiven to intellectual persons is, not to know their own task, or to take their ideas from others. From this want of manly rest in their own and rash acceptance of other people's watchwords come the imbecility and fatigue of their conversation. For they cannot affirm these from any original experience, and of course not with the natural movement and total strength of their nature and talent, but only from their memory, only from their cramped position of standing for their teacher. They say what they would have you believe, but what they do not quite know.

My own habitual view is to the well-being of students or scholars. And it is only when the public event affects them, that it very seriously touches me. And what I have to say is to them. For every man speaks mainly to a class whom he works with and more or less fully represents. It is to these I am beforehand related and engaged, in this audience or out of it—to them and not to others. And yet, when I say the class of scholars or students—that is a class which comprises in some sort all mankind, comprises every man in the best hours of his life; and in these days not only virtually but actually. For who are the readers and thinkers of 1854? Owing to the silent revolution which the newspaper has wrought, this class has come in this country to take in all classes. Look into the morning trains which, from every suburb, carry the business men into the city to their shops, counting-rooms, work-yards and warehouses. With them enters the car—the newsboy, that humble priest of politics, finance, philosophy, and religion. He unfolds his magical sheets—twopence a head his bread of knowledge costs—and instantly the entire rectangular assembly, fresh from their breakfast, are bending as one man to their second breakfast. There is, no doubt, chaff enough in what he brings; but there is fact, thought, and wisdom in the crude mass, from all regions of the world.

I have lived all my life without suffering any known inconvenience from American Slavery. I never saw it; I never heard the whip; I never felt the check on my free speech and action, until, the other day, when Mr. Webster, by his personal influence, brought the Fugitive Slave Law on the country. I say Mr. Webster, for though the Bill was not his, it is yet notorious that he was the life and soul of it, that he gave it all he had: it cost him his life, and under the shadow of his great name inferior men sheltered themselves, threw their ballots for it and made the law. I say inferior men. There were all sorts of what are called brilliant men, accomplished men, men of high station, a President of the United States, Senators, men of eloquent speech, but men without self-respect, without character, and it was strange to see that office, age, fame, talent, even a repute for honesty, all count for nothing. They had no opinions, they had no memory for what they had been saying like the Lord's Prayer all their lifetime: they were only looking to what their great Captain did: if he jumped, they jumped, if he stood on his head, they did. In ordinary, the supposed sense of their district and State is their guide, and that holds them to the part of liberty and justice. But it is always a little difficult to decipher what this public sense is; and when a great man comes who knots up into himself the opinions and wishes of the people, it is so much easier to follow him as an exponent of this. He too is responsible; they will not be. It will always suffice to say—"I followed him."

I saw plainly that the great show their legitimate power in nothing more than in their power to misguide us. I saw that a great man, deservedly admired for his powers and their general right direction, was able—fault of the total want of stamina in public men—when he failed, to break them all with him, to carry parties with him.

In what I have to say of Mr. Webster I do not confound him with vulgar politicians before or since. There is always base ambition enough, men who calculate on the immense ignorance of the masses; that is their quarry and farm: they use the constituencies at home only for their shoes. And, of course, they can drive out from the contest any honorable man. The low can best win the low, and all men like to be made much of. There are those too who have power and inspiration only to do ill. Their talent or their faculty deserts them when they undertake anything right. Mr. Webster had a natural ascendancy of aspect and carriage which distinguished him over all his contemporaries. His countenance, his figure, and his manners were all in so grand a style, that he was, without effort, as superior to his most eminent rivals as they were to the humblest; so that his arrival in any place was an event which drew crowds of people, who went to satisfy their eyes, and could not see him enough. I think they looked at him as the representative of the American Continent. He was there in his Adamitic capacity, as if he alone of all men did not disappoint the eye and the ear, but was a fit figure in the landscape.

I remember his appearance at Bunker's Hill. There was the Monument, and here was Webster. He knew well that a little more or less of rhetoric signified nothing: he was only to say plain and equal things—grand things if he had them, and, if he had them not, only to abstain from saying unfit things—and the whole occasion was answered by his presence. It was a place for behavior more than for speech, and Mr. Webster walked through his part with entire success. His excellent organization, the perfection of his elocution and all that thereto belongs—voice, accent, intonation, attitude, manner—we shall not soon find again. Then he was so thoroughly simple and wise in his rhetoric; he saw through his matter, hugged his fact so close, went to the principle or essential, and never indulged in a weak flourish, though he knew perfectly well how to make such exordiums, episodes and perorations as might give perspective to his harangues without in the least embarrassing his march or confounding his transitions. In his statement things lay in daylight; we saw them in order as they were. Though he knew very well how to present his own personal claims, yet in his argument he was intellectual—stated his fact pure of all personality, so that his splendid wrath, when his eyes became lamps, was the wrath of the fact and the cause he stood for.

His power, like that of all great masters, was not in excellent parts, but was total. He had a great and everywhere equal propriety. He worked with that closeness of adhesion to the matter in hand which a joiner or a chemist uses, and the same quiet and sure feeling of right to his place that an oak or a mountain have to theirs. After all his talents have been described, there remains that perfect propriety which animated all the details of the action or speech with the character of the whole, so that his beauties of detail are endless. He seemed born for the bar, born for the senate, and took very naturally a leading part in large private and in public affairs; for his head distributed things in their right places, and what he saw so well he compelled other people to see also. Great is the privilege of eloquence. What gratitude does every man feel to him who speaks well for the right—who translates truth into language entirely plain and clear!

The history of this country has given a disastrous importance to the defects of this great man's mind. Whether evil influences and the corruption of politics, or whether original infirmity, it was the misfortune of his country that with this large understanding he had not what is better than intellect, and the source of its health. It is a law of our nature that great thoughts come from the heart. If his moral sensibility had been proportioned to the force of his understanding, what limits could have been set to his genius and beneficent power? But he wanted that deep source of inspiration. Hence a sterility of thought, the want of generalization in his speeches, and the curious fact that, with a general ability which impresses all the world, there is not a single general remark, not an observation on life and manners, not an aphorism that can pass into literature from his writings.

Four years ago to-night, on one of those high critical moments in history when great issues are determined, when the powers of right and wrong are mustered for conflict, and it lies with one man to give a casting vote—Mr. Webster, most unexpectedly, threw his whole weight on the side of Slavery, and caused by his personal and official authority the passage of the Fugitive Slave Bill.

It is remarked of the Americans that they value dexterity too much, and honor too little; that they think they praise a man more by saying that he is "smart" than by saying that he is right. Whether the defect be national or not, it is the defect and calamity of Mr. Webster; and it is so far true of his countrymen, namely, that the appeal is sure to be made to his physical and mental ability when his character is assailed. His speeches on the seventh of March, and at Albany, at Buffalo, at Syracuse and Boston are cited in justification. And Mr. Webster's literary editor believes that it was his wish to rest his fame on the speech of the seventh of March. Now, though I have my own opinions on this seventh of March discourse and those others, and think them very transparent and very open to criticism—yet the secondary merits of a speech, namely, its logic, its illustrations, its points, etc., are not here in question. Nobody doubts that Daniel Webster could make a good speech. Nobody doubts that there were good and plausible things to be said on the part of the South. But this is not a question of ingenuity, not a question of syllogisms, but of sides. *How came he there?*

There are always texts and thoughts and arguments. But it is the genius and temper of the man which decides whether he will stand for right or for might. Who doubts the power of any fluent debater to defend either of our political parties, or any client in our courts? There was the same law in England for Jeffries and Talbot and Yorke to read slavery out of, and for Lord Mansfield to read freedom. And in this country one sees that there is always margin enough in the statute for a liberal judge to read one way and a servile judge another.

But the question which History will ask is broader. In the final hour, when he was forced by the peremptory necessity of the closing armies to take a side—did he take the part of great principles, the side of humanity and justice, or the side of abuse and oppression and chaos?

Mr. Webster decided for Slavery, and that, when the aspect of the institution was no longer doubtful, no longer feeble and apologetic and proposing soon to end itself, but when it was strong, aggressive, and threatening an illimitable increase. He listened to State reasons and hopes, and left, with much complacency we are told, the testament of his speech to the astonished State of Massachusetts, *vera pro gratis*; a ghastly result of all those years of experience in affairs, this, that there was nothing better for the foremost American man to tell his countrymen than that Slavery was now at that strength that they must beat down their conscience and become kidnappers for it.

This was like the doleful speech falsely ascribed to the patriot Brutus: "Virtue, I have followed thee through life, and I find thee but a shadow." Here was a question of an immoral law; a question agitated for ages, and settled always in the same way by every great jurist, that an immoral law cannot be valid. Cicero, Grotius, Coke, Blackstone, Burlamaqui, Vattel, Burke, Jefferson, do all affirm this, and I cite them, not that they can give evidence to what is indisputable, but because, though lawyers and practical statesmen, the habit of their profession did not hide from them that this truth was the foundation of States.

Here was the question, Are you for man and for the good of man; or are you for the hurt and harm of man? It was the question whether man shall be treated as leather? Whether the negro shall be, as the

Indians were in Spanish America, a piece of money? Whether this system, which is a kind of mill or factory for converting men into monkeys, shall be upheld and enlarged? And Mr. Webster and the country went for the application to these poor men of quadruped law.

People were expecting a totally different course from Mr. Webster. If any man had in that hour possessed the weight with the country which he had acquired, he could have brought the whole country to its senses. But not a moment's pause was allowed. Angry parties went from bad to worse, and the decision of Webster was accompanied with everything offensive to freedom and good morals. There was something like an attempt to debauch the moral sentiment of the clergy and of the youth. Burke said he "would pardon something to the spirit of liberty." But by Mr. Webster the opposition to the law was sharply called treason, and prosecuted so. He told the people at Boston "they must conquer their prejudices"; that "agitation of the subject of Slavery must be suppressed." He did as immoral men usually do, made very low bows to the Christian Church, and went through all the Sunday decorums; but when allusion was made to the question of duty and the sanctions of morality, he very frankly said, at Albany, "Some higher law, something existing somewhere between here and the third heaven—I do not know where." And if the reporters say true, this wretched atheism found some laughter in the company.

I said I had never in my life up to this time suffered from the Slave Institution. Slavery in Virginia or Carolina was like Slavery in Africa or the Feejees, for me. There was an old fugitive law, but it had become, or was fast becoming, a dead letter, and, by the genius and laws of Massachusetts, inoperative. The new Bill made it operative, required me to hunt slaves, and it found citizens in Massachusetts willing to act as judges and captors. Moreover, it discloses the secret of the new times, that Slavery was no longer mendicant, but was become aggressive and dangerous.

The way in which the country was dragged to consent to this, and the disastrous defection (on the miserable cry of Union) of the men of letters, of the colleges, of educated men, nay, of some preachers of religion—was the darkest passage in the history. It showed that our prosperity had hurt us, and that we could not be shocked by crime. It showed that the old religion and the sense of the right had faded and gone out; that while we reckoned ourselves a highly cultivated nation, our bellies had run away with our brains, and the principles of culture and progress did not exist.

For I suppose that liberty is an accurate index, in men and nations, of general progress. The theory of personal liberty must always appeal to the most refined communities and to the men of the rarest perception and of delicate moral sense. For there are rights which rest on the finest sense of justice, and, with every degree of civility, it will be more truly felt and defined. A barbarous tribe of good stock will, by means of their best heads, secure substantial liberty. But where there is any weakness in a race, and it becomes in a degree matter of concession and protection from their stronger neighbors, the incompatibility and offensiveness of the wrong will of course be most evident to the most cultivated. For it is—is it not?—the essence of courtesy, of politeness, of religion, of love, to prefer another, to postpone oneself, to protect another from oneself. That is the distinction of the gentleman, to defend the weak and redress the injured, as it is of the savage and the brutal to usurp and use others.

In Massachusetts, as we all know, there has always existed a predominant conservative spirit. We have more money and value of every kind than other people, and wish to keep them. The plea on which freedom was resisted was Union. I went to certain serious men, who had a little more reason than the rest, and inquired why they took this part? They answered that they had no confidence in their strength to resist the Democratic party; that they saw plainly that all was going to the utmost verge of licence; each was vying with his neighbor to lead the party, by proposing the worst measure, and they threw themselves on the extreme conservatism, as a drag on the wheel: that they knew Cuba would be had, and Mexico would be had, and they stood stiffly on conservatism, and as near to monarchy as they could, only to moderate the velocity with which the car was running down the precipice. In short, their theory was despair; the Whig wisdom was only reprieve, a waiting to be last devoured. They side with Carolina, or with Arkansas, only to make a show of Whig strength, wherewith to resist a little longer this general ruin.

I have a respect for conservatism. I know how deeply founded it is in our nature, and how idle are all attempts to shake ourselves free from it. We are all conservatives, half Whig, half Democrat, in our essences: and might as well try to jump out of our skins as to escape from our Whiggery. There are two forces in Nature, by whose antagonism we exist; the power of Fate, Fortune, the laws of the world, the order of things, or however else we choose to phrase it, the material necessities, on the one hand—and Will or Duty or Freedom on the other.

May and Must, and the sense of right and duty, on the one hand, and the material necessities on the other: May and Must. In vulgar politics the Whig goes for what has been, for the old necessities—the Musts. The reformer goes for the Better, for the ideal good, for the Mays. But each of these parties must of necessity take in, in some measure, the principles of the other. Each wishes to cover the whole ground; to hold fast *and* to advance. Only, one lays the emphasis on keeping, and the other on advancing. I too think the *musts* are a safe company to follow, and even agreeable. But if we are Whigs, let us be Whigs of nature and science, and so for all the necessities. Let us know that, over and above all the *musts* of poverty and appetite, is the instinct of man to rise, and the instinct to love and help his brother.

Now, Gentlemen, I think we have in this hour instruction again in the simplest lesson. Events roll, millions of men are engaged, and the result is the enforcing of some of those first commandments which we heard in the nursery. We never get beyond our first lesson, for, really, the world exists, as I understand it, to teach the science of liberty, which begins with liberty from fear.

The events of this month are teaching one thing plain and clear, the worthlessness of good tools to bad workmen; that official papers are of no use; resolutions of public meetings, platforms of conventions, no, nor laws, nor constitutions, any more. These are all declaratory of the will of the moment, and are passed with more levity and on grounds far less honorable than ordinary business transactions of the street.

You relied on the constitution. It has not the word slave in it; and very good argument has shown that it would not warrant the crimes that are done under it; that, with provisions so vague for an object not named, and which could not be availed of to claim a barrel of sugar or a barrel of corn, the robbing of a man and of all his posterity is effected. You relied on the Supreme Court. The law was right, excellent law for the lambs. But what if unhappily the judges were chosen from the wolves, and give to all the law a wolfish interpretation? You relied on the Missouri Compromise. That is ridden over. You relied on State sovereignty in the Free States to protect their citizens. They are driven with contempt out of the courts and out of the territory of the Slave States—if they are so happy as to get out with their lives—and now you relied on these dismal guaranties infamously made in 1850; and, before the body of Webster is yet crumbled, it is found that they have crumbled. This eternal monument of his fame and of the Union is rotten in four years. They are no guaranty to the free states. They are a guaranty to the slave states that, as they have hitherto met with no repulse, they shall meet with none.

I fear there is no reliance to be put on any kind or form of covenant, no, not on sacred forms, none on churches, none on bibles. For one would have said that a Christian would not keep slaves: but the Christians keep slaves. Of course they will not dare to read the Bible? Won't they? They quote the Bible, quote Paul, quote Christ, to justify slavery. If slavery is good, then is lying, theft, arson, homicide, each and all good, and to be maintained by Union societies.

These things show that no forms, neither constitutions, nor laws, nor covenants, nor churches, nor bibles, are of any use in themselves. The Devil nestles comfortably into them all. There is no help but in the head and heart and hamstrings of a man. Covenants are of no use without honest men to keep them; laws of none but with loyal citizens to obey them. To interpret Christ it needs Christ in the heart. The teachings of the Spirit can be apprehended only by the same spirit that gave them forth. To make good the cause of Freedom, you must draw off from all foolish trust in others. You must be citadels and warriors yourselves, declarations of Independence, the charter, the battle and the victory. Cromwell said, "We can only resist the superior training of the King's soldiers, by enlisting godly men." And no man has a right to hope that the laws of New York will defend him from the contamination of slaves another day until he has made up his mind that he will not owe his protection to the laws of New York, but to his own sense and spirit. Then he protects New York. He only who is able to stand alone is qualified for society. And that I understand to be the end for which a soul exists in this world—to be himself the counterbalance of all falsehood and all wrong. "The army of unright is encamped from pole to pole, but the road of victory is known to the just." Everything may be taken away; he may be poor, he may be houseless, yet he will know out of his arms to make a pillow, and out of his breast a bolster. Why have the minority no influence? Because they have not a real minority of one.

I conceive that thus to detach a man and make him feel that he is to owe all to himself, is the way to make him strong and rich; and here the optimist must find, if anywhere, the benefit of Slavery. We have many teachers; we are in this world for culture, to be instructed in realities, in the laws of moral and intelligent nature; and our education is not conducted by toys and luxuries, but by austere and rugged masters, by poverty, solitude, passions, War, Slavery; to know that Paradise is under the shadow of swords; that divine sentiments which are always soliciting us are breathed into us from on high, and are an offset to a Universe of suffering and crime; that self-reliance, the height and perfection of man, is reliance on God. The insight of the religious sentiment will disclose to him unexpected aids in the nature of things. The Persian Saadi said, "Beware of hurting the orphan. When the orphan sets a-crying, the throne of the Almighty is rocked from side to side."

Whenever a man has come to this mind, that there is no Church for him but his believing prayer; no Constitution but his dealing well and justly with his neighbor; no liberty but his invincible will to do right—then certain aids and allies will promptly appear: for the constitution of the Universe is on his side. It is of no use to vote down gravitation of morals. What is useful will last, whilst that which is hurtful to the world will sink beneath all the opposing forces which it must exasperate. The terror which the Marseillaise struck into oppression, it thunders again to-day—

"Tout est soldat pour vous combattre."

Everything turns soldier to fight you down. The end for which man was made is not crime in any form, and a man cannot steal without incurring the penalties of the thief, though all the legislatures vote that it is virtuous, and though there be a general conspiracy among scholars and official persons to hold him up, and to say, *"Nothing is good but stealing."* A man who commits a crime defeats the end of his existence. He was created for benefit, and he exists for harm; and as well-doing makes power and wisdom, ill-doing takes them away. A man who steals another man's labor steals away his own faculties; his integrity, his humanity is flowing away from him. The habit of oppression cuts out the moral eyes, and, though the intellect goes on simulating the moral as before, its sanity is gradually destroyed. It takes away the presentiments.

I suppose in general this is allowed, that if you have a nice question of right and wrong, you would not go with it to Louis Napoleon, or to a political hack, or to a slave-driver. The habit of mind of traders in power would not be esteemed favorable to delicate moral perception. American slavery affords no exception to this rule. No excess of good nature or of tenderness in individuals has been able to give a new character to the system, to tear down the whipping-house. The plea in the mouth of a slaveholder that the negro is an inferior race sounds very oddly in my ear. "The masters of slaves seem generally anxious to prove that they are not of a race superior in any noble quality to the meanest of their bondmen." And indeed when the Southerner points to the anatomy of the negro, and talks of chimpanzee—I recall Montesquieu's remark, "It will not do to say that negroes are men, lest it should turn out that whites are not."

Slavery is disheartening; but Nature is not so helpless but it can rid itself at last of every wrong. But the spasms of Nature are centuries and ages, and will tax the faith of short-lived men. Slowly, slowly the Avenger comes, but comes surely. The proverbs of the nations afffirm these delays, but affirm the arrival. They say, "God may consent, but not forever." The delay of the Divine Justice—this was the meaning and soul of the Greek Tragedy; this the soul of their religion. "There has come, too, one to whom lurking warfare is dear, Retribution, with a soul full of wiles; a violator of hospitality; guileful without the guilt of guile; limping, late in her arrival." They said of the happiness of the unjust, that "at its close it begets itself an offspring and does not die childless, and instead of good fortune, there sprouts forth for posterity ever-ravening calamity"—

> "For evil word shall evil word be said,
> For murder-stroke a murder-stroke be paid.
> Who smites must smart."

These delays, you see them now in the temper of the times. The national spirit in this country is so drowsy, preoccupied with interest, deaf to principle. The Anglo-Saxon race is proud and strong and selfish. They believe only in Anglo-Saxons. In 1825 Greece found America deaf, Poland found America deaf, Italy and Hungary found her deaf. England maintains trade, not liberty; stands against Greece; against Hungary; against Schleswig-Holstein; against the French Republic whilst it was a republic.

To faint hearts the times offer no invitation, and torpor exists here throughout the active classes on the subject of domestic slavery and its appalling aggressions. Yes, that is the stern edict of Providence, that liberty shall be no hasty fruit, but that event on event, population on population, age on age, shall cast itself into the opposite scale, and not until liberty has slowly accumulated weight enough to countervail and preponderate against all this, can the sufficient recoil come. All the great cities, all the refined circles, all the statesmen, Guizot, Palmerston, Webster, Calhoun, are sure to be found befriending liberty with their words, and crushing it with their votes. Liberty is never cheap. It is made difficult, because freedom is the accomplishment and perfectness of man. He is a finished man; earning and bestowing good; equal to the world; at home in Nature and dignifying that; the sun does not see anything nobler, and has nothing to teach him. Therefore mountains of difficulty must be surmounted, stern trials met, wiles of seduction, dangers, healed by a quarantine of calamities to measure his strength before he dare say, I am free.

Whilst the inconsistency of slavery with the principles on which the world is built guarantees its downfall, I own that the patience it requires is almost too sublime for mortals, and seems to demand of us more than mere hoping. And when one sees how fast the rot spreads—it is growing serious—I think we demand of superior men that they be superior in this—that the mind and the virtue shall give their verdict in their day, and accelerate so far the progress of civilization. Possession is sure to throw its stupid strength for existing power, and appetite and ambition will go for that. Let the aid of virtue, intelligence and education be cast where they rightfully belong. They are organically ours. Let them be loyal to their own. I wish to see the instructed class here know their own flag, and not fire on their comrades. We should not forgive the clergy for taking on every issue the immoral side; nor the Bench, if it put itself on the side of the culprit; nor the Government, if it sustain the mob against the law.

It is a potent support and ally to a brave man standing single, or with a few, for the right, and out-voted and ostracized, to know that better men in other parts of the country appreciate the service and will rightly report him to his own and the next age. Without this assurance, he will sooner sink. He may well say, 'If my countrymen do not care to be defended, I too will decline the controversy, from which I only reap invectives and hatred.' Yet the lovers of liberty may with reason tax the coldness and indifferentism of scholars and literary men. They are lovers of liberty in Greece and Rome and in the English Commonwealth, but they are lukewarm lovers of the liberty of America in 1854. The universities are not, as in Hobbes's time, "the core of rebellion," no, but the seat of inertness. They have forgotten their allegiance to the Muse, and grown worldly and political. I listened, lately, on one of those occasions when the university chooses one of its distinguished sons returning from the political arena, believing that senators and statesmen would be glad to throw off the harness and to dip again in the Castalian pools. But if audiences forget themselves, statesmen do not. The low bows to all the crockery gods of the day were duly made—only in one part of the discourse the orator allowed to transpire, rather against his will, a little sober sense. It was this 'I am, as you see, a man virtuously inclined, and only corrupted by my profession of politics. I should prefer the right side. You, gentlemen of these literary and scientific schools, and the important class you represent, have the power to make your verdict clear and prevailing. Had you done so, you would have found me its glad organ and champion. Abstractly, I should have preferred that side. But you have not done it. You have not spoken out. You have failed to arm me. I can only deal with masses as I find them. Abstractions are not for me. I go then for such parties and opinions as have provided me with a working apparatus. I give you my word, not without regret, that I was first for you; and though I am now to deny and condemn you, you see it is not my will but the party necessity.' Having made this manifesto and professed his adoration for liberty in the time of his grandfathers, he proceeded with his work of denouncing freedom and freemen at the present day, much in the tone and spirit in which Lord Bacon prosecuted his benefactor Essex. He denounced every name and aspect under which liberty and progress dare show themselves in this age and country, but with a lingering conscience which qualified each sentence with a recommendation to mercy.

But I put it to every noble and generous spirit, to every poetic, every heroic, every religious heart, that not so is our learning, our education, our poetry, our worship to be declared. Liberty is aggressive, Liberty is the Crusade of all brave and conscientious men, the Epic Poetry, the new religion, the chivalry of all gentlemen. This is the oppressed Lady whom true knights on their oath and honor must rescue and save.

Now at last we are disenchanted and shall have no more false hopes. I respect the Anti-Slavery Society. It is the Cassandra that has foretold all that has befallen, fact for fact, years ago; foretold all, and no man laid it to heart. It seemed, as the Turks say, "Fate makes that a man should not believe his own eyes." But the Fugitive Law did much to unglue the eyes of men, and now the Nebraska Bill leaves us staring. The Anti-Slavery Society will add many members this year. The Whig Party will join it; the Democrats will join it. The population of the free states will join it. I doubt not, at last, the slave states will join it. But be that sooner or later, and whoever comes or stays away, I hope we have reached the end of our unbelief, have come to a belief that there is a divine Providence in the world, which will not save us but through our own cooperation.

JOHN BROWN

[*When Emerson delivered this speech in Boston on
November 18, 1858, John Brown was under sentence
of death for his raid at Harper's Ferry. He was executed two weeks later. Emerson had known Brown
personally and had entertained him at his home in
Concord when Brown came to address a public meeting. Emerson made another address on John Brown
at Salem on the day when Brown was executed in
Charlestown, Va.*]

"John Brown in Kansas settled, like a steadfast Yankee farmer,
Brave and godly, with four sons—all stalwart men of might.
There he spoke aloud for Freedom, and the Border strife grew warmer
Till the Rangers fired his dwelling, in his absence, in the night;
                    And Old Brown,
                    Osawatomie Brown,
Came homeward in the morning to find his house burned down.

Then he grasped his trusty rifle, and boldly fought for Freedom;
Smote from border unto border the fierce invading band:
And he and his brave boys vowed—so might Heaven help and speed 'em—
They would save those grand old prairies from the curse that blights the
        land;
                    And Old Brown,
                    Osawatomie Brown,
Said, 'Boys, the Lord will aid us !' and he shoved his ram rod down."

                    Edmund Clarence Stedman, *John Brown.*

JOHN BROWN

MR. CHAIRMAN, AND FELLOW CITIZENS: I share the sympathy and sorrow which brought us together. Gentlemen who have preceded me have well said that no wall of separation could here exist. This commanding event which has brought us together, eclipses all others which have occurred for a long time in our history, and I am very glad to see that this sudden interest in the hero of Harper's Ferry has provoked an extreme curiosity in all parts of the Republic, in regard to the details of his history. Every anecdote is eagerly sought, and I do not wonder that gentlemen find traits of relation readily between him and themselves. One finds a relation in the church, another in the profession, another in the place of his birth. He was happily a representative of the American Republic. Captain John Brown is a farmer, the fifth in descent from Peter Brown, who came to Plymouth in the Mayflower, in 1620. All the six have been farmers. His grandfather, of Simsbury, in Connecticut, was a captain in the Revolution. His father, largely interested as a raiser of stock, became a contractor to supply the army with beef, in the war of 1812, and our Captain John Brown, then a boy, with his father was present and witnessed the surrender of General Hull. He cherishes a great respect for his father, as a man of strong character, and his respect is probably just. For himself, he is so transparent that all men see him through. He is a man to make friends wherever on earth courage and integrity are esteemed, the rarest of heroes, a pure idealist, with no by-ends of his own. Many of you have seen him, and every one who has heard him speak has been impressed alike by his simple, artless goodness, joined with his sublime courage. He joins that perfect Puritan faith which brought his fifth ancestor to Plymouth Rock with his grandfather's ardor in the Revolution. He believes in two articles—two instruments, shall I say?—the Golden Rule and the Declaration of Independence; and he used this expression in conversation here concerning them, "Better that a whole generation of men, women and children should pass away by a violent death than that one word of either should be violated in this country." There is a Union-ist—there is a strict constructionist for you. He believes in the Union of the States, and he conceives that the only obstruction to the Union is Slavery, and for that reason, as a patriot, he works for its abolition. The governor of Virginia has pronounced his eulogy in a manner that discredits the moderation of our timid parties. His own speeches to the court have interested the nation in him. What magnanimity, and what innocent pleading, as of childhood! You remember his words: "If I had interfered in behalf of the rich, the powerful, the intelligent, the so-called great, or any of their friends, parents, wives or children, it would all have been right. But I believe that to have interfered as I have done, for the despised poor, was not wrong, but right."

It is easy to see what a favorite he will be with history, which plays such pranks with temporary reputations. Nothing can resist the sympathy which all elevated minds must feel with Brown, and through them the whole civilized world; and if he must suffer, he must drag official gentlemen into an immortality most undesirable, of which they have already some disagreeable forebodings. Indeed, it is the *reductio ad absurdum* of Slavery, when the governor of Virginia is forced to hang a man whom he declares to be a man of the most integrity, truthfulness and courage he has ever met. Is that the kind of man the gallows is built for? It were bold to affirm that there is within that broad commonwealth, at this moment, another citizen as worthy to live, and as deserving of all public and private honor, as this poor prisoner.

But we are here to think of relief for the family of John Brown. To my eyes, that family looks very large and very needy of relief. It comprises his brave fellow sufferers in the Charlestown Jail; the fugitives still hunted in the mountains of Virginia and Pennsylvania; the sympathizers with him in all the states; and, I may say, almost every man who loves the Golden Rule and the Declaration of Independence, like him, and who sees what a tiger's thirst threatens him in the malignity of public sentiment in the slave states. It seems to me that a common feeling joins the people of Massachusetts with him.

I said John Brown was an idealist. He believed in his ideas to that extent that he existed to put them all into action; he said 'he did not believe in moral suasion, he believed in putting the thing through.' He saw how deceptive the forms are. We fancy, in Massachusetts, that we are free; yet it seems the government is quite unreliable. Great wealth, great population, men of talent in the executive, on the bench—all the forms right—and yet, life and freedom are not safe. Why? Because the judges rely on the forms, and do not, like John Brown, use their eyes to see the fact behind the forms. They assume that the United States can protect its witness or its prisoner. And in Massachusetts that is true, but the moment he is carried out of the bounds of Massachusetts, the United States, it is notorious, afford no protection at all; the government, the judges, are an envenomed party, and give such protection as they give in Utah to honest citizens, or in Kansas; such protection as they gave to their own Commodore Paulding, when he was simple enough to mistake the formal instructions of his government for their real meaning. The state judges fear collision between their two allegiances; but there are worse evils than collision; namely, the doing substantial injustice. A good man will see that the use of a judge is to secure good government, and where the citizen's weal is imperilled by abuse of the federal power, to use that arm which can secure it, viz., the local government. Had that been done on certain calamitous occasions, we should not have seen the honor of Massachusetts trailed in the dust, stained to all ages, once and again, by the ill-timed formalism of a venerable bench. If judges cannot find law enough to maintain the sovereignty of the state, and to protect the life and freedom of every inhabitant not a criminal, it is idle to compliment them as learned and venerable. What avails their learning or veneration? At a pinch, they are no more use than idiots. After the mischance they wring their hands, but they had better never have been born. A Vermont judge, Hutchinson, who has the Declaration of Independence in his heart; a Wisconsin judge, who knows that laws are for the protection of citizens against kidnappers, is worth a court-house full of lawyers so idolatrous of forms as to let go the substance. Is any man in Massachusetts so simple as to believe that when a United States Court in Virginia, now, in its present reign of terror, sends to Connecticut, or New York, or Massachusetts, for a witness, it wants him for a witness? No; it wants him for a party; it wants him for meat to slaughter and eat. And your *habeas corpus* is, in any way in which it has been, or, I fear, is likely to be used, a nuisance, and not a protection; for it takes away his right reliance on himself, and the natural assistance of his friends and fellow citizens, by offering him a form which is a piece of paper.

But I am detaining the meeting on matters which others understand better. I hope, then, that, in administering relief to John Brown's family, we shall remember all those whom his fate concerns, all who are in sympathy with him, and not forget to aid him in the best way, by securing freedom and independence in Massachusetts.

THE EMANCIPATION PROCLAMATION

[*Emerson spoke with others at a meeting held in Boston in September, 1862, to celebrate the significance of the Emancipation Proclamation which Lincoln had issued on September 22. This address was published in the* Atlantic Monthly *for November, 1862.*]

To-day unbind the captive,
So only are ye unbound;
Lift up a people from the dust,
Trump of their rescue, sound !

Pay ransom to the owner
And fill the bag to the brim.
Who is the owner? The slave is owner
And ever was. Pay him.

O North! give him beauty for rags,
And honor, O South! for his shame;
Nevada! coin thy golden crags
With freedom's image and name.

Up! and the dusky race
That sat in darkness long—
Be swift their feet as antelopes,
And as behemoth strong.

Come, East and West and North,
By races, as snow-flakes,
And carry my purpose forth,
Which neither halts nor shakes.

My will fulfilled shall be,
For in daylight or in dark,
My thunderbolt has eyes to see
His way home to the mark.

THE EMANCIPATION PROCLAMATION

IN SO MANY ARID FORMS which states encrust themselves with, once in a century, if so often, a poetic act and record occur. These are the jets of thought into affairs, when, roused by danger or inspired by genius, the political leaders of the day break the else insurmountable routine of class and local legislation, and take a step forward in the direction of catholic and universal interests. Every step in the history of political liberty is a sally of the human mind into the untried Future, and has the interest of genius, and is fruitful in heroic anecdotes. Liberty is a slow fruit. It comes, like religion, for short periods, and in rare conditions, as if awaiting a culture of the race which shall make it organic and permanent. Such moments of expansion in modern history were the Confession of Augsburg, the plantation of America, the English Commonwealth of 1648, the Declaration of American Independence in 1776, the British emancipation of slaves in the West Indies, the passage of the Reform Bill, the repeal of the Corn-Laws, the Magnetic Ocean Telegraph, though yet imperfect, the passage of the Homestead Bill in the last Congress, and now, eminently, President Lincoln's Proclamation on the twenty-second of September. These are acts of great scope, working on a long future and on permanent interests, and honoring alike those who initiate and those who receive them. These measures provoke no noisy joy, but are received into a sympathy so deep as to apprise us that mankind are greater and better than we know. At such times it appears as if a new public were created to greet the new event. It is as when an orator, having ended the compliments and pleasantries with which he conciliated attention, and having run over the superficial fitness and commodities of the measure he urges, suddenly, lending himself to some happy inspiration, announces with vibrating voice the grand human principles involved—the bravos and wits who greeted him loudly thus far are surprised and overawed; a new audience is found in the heart of the assembly—an audience hitherto passive and unconcerned, now at last so searched and kindled that they come forward, every one a representative of mankind, standing for all nationalities.

The extreme moderation with which the President advanced to his design—his long-avowed expectant policy, as if he chose to be strictly the executive of the best public sentiment of the country, waiting only till it should be unmistakably pronounced—so fair a mind that none ever listened so patiently to such extreme varieties of opinion—so reticent that his decision has taken all parties by surprise, whilst yet it is just the sequel of his prior acts—the firm tone in which he announces it, without inflation or surplusage—all these have bespoken such favor to the act that, great as the popularity of the President has been, we are beginning to think that we have underestimated the capacity and virtue which the Divine Providence has made an instrument of benefit so vast. He has been permitted to do more for America than any other American man. He is well entitled to the most indulgent construction. Forget all that we thought shortcomings, every mistake, every delay. In the extreme embarrassments of his part, call these endurance, wisdom, magnanimity; illuminated, as they now are, by this dazzling success.

When we consider the immense opposition that has been neutralized or converted by the progress of the war (for it is not long since the President anticipated the resignation of a large number of officers in the army, and the secession of three states, on the promulgation of this policy)—when we see how the great stake which foreign nations hold in our affairs has recently brought every European power as a client into this court, and it became every day more apparent what gigantic and what remote interests were to be affected by the decision of the President—one can hardly say the deliberation was too long. Against all timorous counsels he had the courage to seize the moment; and such was his position, and such the felicity attending the action, that he has replaced government in the good graces of mankind. "Better is virtue in the sovereign than plenty in the season," say the Chinese. 'T is wonderful what power is, and how ill it is used, and how its ill use makes life mean, and the sunshine dark. Life in America had lost much of its attraction in the later years. The virtues of a good magistrate undo a world of mischief, and, because Nature works with rectitude, seem vastly more potent than the acts of bad governors, which are ever tempered by the good nature in the people, and the incessant resistance which fraud and violence encounter. The acts of good governors work a geometrical ratio, as one midsummer day seems to repair the damage of a year of war.

A day which most of us dared not hope to see, an event worth the dreadful war, worth its costs and uncertainties, seems now to be close before us. October, November, December will have passed over beating hearts and plotting brains: then the hour will strike, and all men of African descent who have faculty enough to find their way to our lines are assured of the protection of American law.

It is by no means necessary that this measure should be suddenly marked by any signal results on the negroes or on the rebel masters. The force of the act is that it commits the country to this justice—that it compels the innumerable officers, civil, military, naval, of the Republic to range themselves on the line of this equity. It draws the fashion to this side. It is not a measure that admits of being taken back. Done, it cannot be undone by a new administration. For slavery overpowers the disgust of the moral sentiment only through immemorial usage. It cannot be introduced as an improvement of the nineteenth century. This act makes that the lives of our heroes have not been sacrificed in vain. It makes a victory of our defeats. Our hurts are healed; the health of the nation is repaired. With a victory like this, we can stand many disasters. It does not promise the redemption of the black race; that lies not with us: but it relieves it of our opposition. The President by this act has paroled all the slaves in America; they will no more fight against us: and it relieves our race once for all of its crime and false position. The first condition of success is secured in putting ourselves right. We have recovered ourselves from our false position, and planted ourselves on a law of Nature:—

"If that fail,
The pillared firmament is rottenness,
And earth's base built on stubble."

The government has assured itself of the best constituency in the world: every spark of intellect, every virtuous feeling, every religious heart, every man of honor, every poet, every philosopher, the generosity of the cities, the health of the country, the strong arms of the mechanic, the endurance of farmers, the passionate conscience of women, the sympathy of distant nations—all rally to its support.

Of course, we are assuming the firmness of the policy thus declared. It must not be a paper proclamation. We confide that Mr. Lincoln is in earnest, and as he has been slow in making up his mind, has resisted the importunacy of parties and of events to the latest moment, he will be as absolute in his adhesion. Not only will he repeat and follow up his stroke, but the nation will add its irresistible strength. If the ruler has duties, so has the citizen. In times like these, when the nation is imperilled, what man can, without shame, receive good news from day to day without giving good news of himself? What right has any one to read in the journals tidings of victories, if he has not bought them by his own valor, treasure, personal sacrifice, or by service as good in his own department? With this blot removed from our national honor, this heavy load lifted off the national heart, we shall not fear henceforward to show our faces among mankind. We shall cease to be hypocrites and pretenders, but what we have styled our free institutions will be such.

In the light of this event the public distress begins to be removed. What if the brokers' quotations show our stocks discredited, and the gold dollar costs one hundred and twenty-seven cents? These tables are fallacious. Every acre in the free states gained substantial value on the twenty-second of September. The cause of disunion and war has been reached and begun to be removed. Every man's house-lot and garden are relieved of the malaria which the purest winds and strongest sunshine could not penetrate and purge. The territory of the Union shines to-day with a lustre which every European emigrant can discern from far; a sign of inmost security and permanence. Is it feared that taxes will check immigration? That depends on what the taxes are spent for. If they go to fill up this yawning Dismal Swamp, which engulfed armies and populations, and created plague, and neutralized hitherto all the vast capabilities of this continent—then this taxation, which makes the land wholesome and habitable, and will draw all men unto it, is the best investment in which property-holder ever lodged his earnings.

Whilst we have pointed out the opportuneness of the Proclamation, it remains to be said that the President had no choice. He might look wistfully for what variety of courses lay open to him; every line but one was closed up with fire. This one, too, bristled with danger, but through it was the sole safety. The measure he has adopted was imperative. It is wonderful to see the unseasonable senility of what is called the Peace Party, through all its masks, blinding their eyes to the main feature of the war, namely, its inevitableness. The war existed long before the cannonade of Sumter, and could not be postponed. It might have begun otherwise or elsewhere, but war was in the minds and bones of the combatants, it was written on the iron leaf, and you might as easily dodge gravitation. If we had consented to a peaceable secession of the rebels, the divided sentiment of the border states made peaceable secession impossible, the insatiable temper of the South made it impossible, and the slaves on the border, wherever the border might be, were an incessant fuel to rekindle the fire. Give the Confederacy New Orleans, Charleston, and Richmond, and they would have demanded St. Louis and Baltimore. Give them these, and they would have insisted on Washington. Give them Washington, and they would have assumed the army and navy, and, through these, Philadelphia, New York, and Boston. It looks as if the battlefield would have been at least as large in that event as it is now. The war was formidable, but could not be avoided. The war was and is an immense mischief, but brought with it the immense benefit of drawing a line and rallying the free states to fix it impassably—preventing the whole force of Southern connection and influence throughout the North from distracting every city with endless confusion, detaching that force and reducing it to handfuls, and, in the progress of hostilities, disinfecting us of our habitual proclivity, through the affection of trade and the traditions of the Democratic party, to follow Southern leading.

These necessities which have dictated the conduct of the federal government are overlooked especially by our foreign critics. The popular statement of the opponents of the war abroad is the impossibility of our success. "If you could add," say they, "to your strength the whole army of England, of France and of Austria, you could not coerce eight millions of people to come under this government against their will." This is an odd thing for an Englishman, a Frenchman or an Austrian to say, who remembers Europe of the last seventy years—the condition of Italy, until 1859—of Poland, since 1793—of France, of French Algiers—of British Ireland, and British India. But granting the truth, rightly read, of the historical aphorism, that "the people always conquer," it is to be noted that, in the Southern States, the tenure of land and the local laws, with slavery, give the social system not a democratic but an aristocratic complexion; and those states have shown every year a more hostile and aggressive temper, until the instinct of self-preservation forced us into the war. And the aim of the war on our part is indicated by the aim of the President's Proclamation, namely, to break up the false combination of Southern society, to destroy the piratic feature in it which makes it our enemy only as it is the enemy of the human race, and so allow its reconstruction on a just and healthful basis. Then new affinities will act, the old repulsion will cease, and, the cause of war being removed, Nature and trade may be trusted to establish a lasting peace.

We think we cannot overstate the wisdom and benefit of this act of the government. The malignant cry of the Secession press within the free states, and the recent action of the Confederate Congress, are decisive as to its efficiency and correctness of aim. Not less so is the silent joy which has greeted it in all generous hearts, and the new hope it has breathed into the world. It was well to delay the steamers at the wharves until this edict could be put on board. It will be an insurance to the ship as it goes plunging through the sea with glad tidings to all people. Happy are the young, who find the pestilence cleansed out of the earth, leaving open to them an honest career. Happy the old, who see Nature purified before they depart. Do not let the dying die: hold them back to this world, until you have charged their ear and heart with this message to other spiritual societies, announcing the melioration of our planet:—

> "Incertainties now crown themselves assured,
> And Peace proclaims olives of endless age."

Meantime that ill-fated, much-injured race which the Proclamation respects will lose somewhat of the dejection sculptured for ages in their bronzed countenance, uttered in the wailing of their plaintive music—a race naturally benevolent, docile, industrious, and whose very miseries sprang from their great talent for usefulness, which, in a more moral age, will not only defend their independence, but will give them a rank among nations.

THOREAU

[*Thoreau and Emerson were neighbors and friends during most of Thoreau's mature years. Thoreau was fourteen years Emerson's junior. In 1841 Thoreau lived in Emerson's home as a member of the family, freeing Emerson from many practical duties for which he was unfitted; and he lived there again in 1847-48 when Emerson was in England. Thoreau built his renowned hut at Walden Pond on land that belonged to Emerson. There were marked differences in temperament that made friendship harsh and difficult at times, and apparently there were also periods of estrangement. But Thoreau believed in Emerson's philosophy; and being of passionate disposition carried the philosophy to its logical conclusion of personal rebellion. Thoreau died from tuberculosis on May 6, 1862. Emerson made the address at the funeral services. In August it was printed with some changes in the* Atlantic Monthly. *This is the printed version of the memorial address.*]

A queen rejoices in her peers,
And wary Nature knows her own,
By court and city, dale and down,
And like a lover volunteers,
And to her son will treasures more,
And more to purpose, freely pour
In one wood walk, than learned men
Will find with glass in ten times ten.

It seemed as if the breezes brought him,
It seemed as if the sparrows taught him,
As if by secret sign he knew
Where in far fields the orchis grew.

THOREAU

HENRY DAVID THOREAU was the last male descendant of a French ancestor who came to this country from the Isle of Guernsey. His character exhibited occasional traits drawn from this blood, in singular combination with a very strong Saxon genius.

He was born in Concord, Massachusetts, on the 12th of July, 1817. He was graduated at Harvard College in 1837, but without any literary distinction. An iconoclast in literature, he seldom thanked colleges for their service to him, holding them in small esteem, whilst yet his debt to them was important. After leaving the University, he joined his brother in teaching a private school, which he soon renounced. His father was a manufacturer of lead-pencils, and Henry applied himself for a time to this craft, believing he could make a better pencil than was then in use. After completing his experiments, he exhibited his work to chemists and artists in Boston, and having obtained their certificates to its excellence and to its equality with the best London manufacture, he returned home contented. His friends congratulated him that he had now opened his way to fortune. But he replied that he should never make another pencil. "Why should I? I would not do again what I have done once." He resumed his endless walks and miscellaneous studies, making every day some new acquaintance with Nature, though as yet never speaking of zoology or botany, since, though very studious of natural facts, he was incurious of technical and textual science.

At this time, a strong, healthy youth, fresh from college, whilst all his companions were choosing their profession, or eager to begin some lucrative employment, it was inevitable that his thoughts should be exercised on the same question, and it required rare decision to refuse all the accustomed paths and keep his solitary freedom at the cost of disappointing the natural expectations of his family and friends: all the more difficult that he had a perfect probity, was exact in securing his own independence, and in holding every man to the like duty. But Thoreau never faltered. He was a born protestant. He declined to give up his large ambition of knowledge and action for any narrow craft or profession, aiming at a much more comprehensive calling, the art of living well. If he slighted and defied the opinions of others, it was only that he was more intent to reconcile his practice with his own belief. Never idle or self-indulgent, he preferred, when he wanted money, earning it by some piece of manual labor agreeable to him, as building a boat or a fence, planting, grafting, surveying or other short work, to any long engagements. With his hardy habits and few wants, his skill in wood-craft, and his powerful arithmetic, he was very competent to live in any part of the world. It would cost him less time to supply his wants than another. He was therefore secure of his leisure.

A natural skill for mensuration, growing out of his mathematical knowledge and his habit of ascertaining the measures and distances of objects which interested him, the size of trees, the depth and extent of ponds and rivers, the height of mountains and the air-line distance of his favorite summits—this, and his intimate knowledge of the territory about Concord, made him drift into the profession of land-surveyor. It had the advantage for him that it led him continually into new and secluded grounds, and helped his studies of Nature. His accuracy and skill in this work were readily appreciated, and he found all the employment he wanted.

He could easily solve the problems of the surveyor, but he was daily beset with graver questions, which he manfully confronted. He interrogated every custom, and wished to settle all his practice on an ideal foundation. He was a protestant à outrance, and few lives contain so many renunciations. He was bred to no profession, he never married; he lived alone; he never went to church; he never voted; he refused to pay a tax to the State; he ate no flesh, he drank no wine, he never knew the use of tobacco; and, though a naturalist, he used neither trap nor gun. He chose, wisely no doubt for himself, to be the bachelor of thought and Nature. He had no talent for wealth, and knew how to be poor without the least hint of squalor or inelegance. Perhaps he fell into his way of living without forecasting it much, but approved it with later wisdom. "I am often reminded," he wrote in his journal, "that if I had bestowed on me the wealth of Crœsus, my aims must be still the same, and my means essentially the same." He had no temptations to fight against—no appetites, no passions, no taste for elegant trifles. A fine house, dress, the manners and talk of highly cultivated people were all thrown away on him. He much preferred a good Indian, and considered these refinements as impediments to conversation, wishing to meet his companion on the simplest terms. He declined invitations to dinner-parties, because there each was in every one's way, and he could not meet the individuals to any purpose. "They make their pride," he said, "in making their dinner cost much; I make my pride in making my dinner cost little." When asked at table what dish he preferred, he answered, "The nearest." He did not like the taste of wine, and never had a vice in his life. He said—"I have a faint recollection of pleasure derived from smoking dried lily-stems, before I was a man. I had commonly a supply of these. I have never smoked anything more noxious."

He chose to be rich by making his wants few, and supplying them himself. In his travels, he used the railroad only to get over so much country as was unimportant to the present purpose, walking hundreds of miles, avoiding taverns, buying a lodging in farmers' and fishermen's houses, as cheaper, and more agreeable to him, and because there he could better find the men and the information he wanted.

There was somewhat military in his nature, not to be subdued, always manly and able, but rarely tender, as if he did not feel himself except in opposition. He wanted a fallacy to expose, a blunder to pillory, I may say required a little sense of victory, a roll of the drum, to call his powers into full exercise. It cost him nothing to say No; indeed he found it much easier than to say Yes. It seemed as if his first instinct on hearing a proposition was to controvert it, so impatient was he of the limitations of our daily thought. This habit, of course, is a little chilling to the social affections; and though the companion would in the end acquit him of any malice or untruth, yet it mars conversation. Hence, no equal companion stood in affectionate relations with one so pure and guileless. "I love Henry," said one of his friends, "but I cannot like him; and as for taking his arm, I should as soon think of taking the arm of an elm-tree."

Yet, hermit and stoic as he was, he was really fond of sympathy, and threw himself heartily and childlike into the company of young people whom he loved, and whom he delighted to entertain, as he only could, with the varied and endless anecdotes of his experiences by field and river: and he was always ready to lead a huckleberry-party or a search for chestnuts or grapes. Talking, one day, of a public discourse, Henry remarked that whatever succeeded with the audience was bad. I said, "Who would not like to write something which all can read, like Robinson Crusoe? and who does not see with regret that his page is not solid with a right materialistic treatment, which delights everybody?" Henry objected, of course, and vaunted the better lectures which reached only a few persons. But, at supper, a young girl, understanding that he was to lecture at the Lyceum, sharply asked him, "Whether his lecture would be a nice, interesting story, such as she wished to hear, or whether it was one of those old philosophical things that she did not care about." Henry turned to her, and bethought himself, and, I saw, was trying to believe that he had matter that might fit her and her brother, who were to sit up and go to the lecture, if it was a good one for them.

He was a speaker and actor of the truth, born such, and was ever running into dramatic situations from this cause. In any circumstance it interested all bystanders to know what part Henry would take, and what he would say; and he did not disappoint expectation, but used an original judgment on each emergency. In 1845 he built himself a small framed house on the shores of Walden Pond, and lived there two years alone, a life of labor and study. This action was quite native and fit for him. No one who knew him would tax him with affectation. He was more unlike his neighbors in his thought than in his action. As soon as he had exhausted the advantages of that solitude, he abandoned it. In 1847, not approving some uses to which the public expenditure was applied, he refused to pay his town tax, and was put in jail. A friend paid the tax for him, and he was released. The like annoyance was threatened the next year. But as his friends paid the tax, notwithstanding his protest, I believe he ceased to resist. No opposition or ridicule had any weight with him. He coldly and fully stated his opinion without affecting to believe that it was the opinion of the company. It was of no consequence if every one present held the opposite opinion. On one occasion he went to the University Library to procure some books. The librarian refused to lend them. Mr. Thoreau repaired to the President, who stated to him the rules and usages, which permitted the loan of books to resident graduates, to clergymen who were alumni, and to some others resident within a circle of ten miles' radius from the College. Mr. Thoreau explained to the President that the railroad had destroyed the old scale of distances—that the library was useless, yes, and President and College useless, on the terms of his rules—that the

. . . .

one benefit he owed to the College was its library—that, at this moment, not only his want of books was imperative, but he wanted a large number of books, and assured him that he, Thoreau, and not the librarian, was the proper custodian of these. In short, the President found the petitioner so formidable, and the rules getting to look so ridiculous, that he ended by giving him a privilege which in his hands proved unlimited thereafter.

No truer American existed than Thoreau. His preference of his country and condition was genuine, and his aversation from English and European manners and tastes almost reached contempt. He listened impatiently to news or *bonmots* gleaned from London circles; and though he tried to be civil, these anecdotes fatigued him. The men were all imitating each other, and on a small mould. Why can they not live as far apart as possible, and each be a man by himself? What he sought was the most energetic nature; and he wished to go to Oregon, not to London. "In every part of Great Britain," he wrote in his diary, "are discovered traces of the Romans, their funereal urns, their camps, their roads, their dwellings. But New England, at least, is not based on any Roman ruins. We have not to lay the foundations of our houses on the ashes of a former civilization."

But idealist as he was, standing for abolition of slavery, abolition of tariffs, almost for abolition of government, it is needless to say he found himself not only unrepresented in actual politics, but almost equally opposed to every class of reformers. Yet he paid the tribute of his uniform respect to the Anti-Slavery party. One man, whose personal acquaintance he had formed, he honored with exceptional regard. Before the first friendly word had been spoken for Captain John Brown, he sent notices to most houses in Concord that he would speak in a public hall on the condition and character of John Brown, on Sunday evening, and invited all people to come. The Republican Committee, the Abolitionist Committee, sent him word that it was premature and not advisable. He replied—"I did not send to you for advice, but to announce that I am to speak." The hall was filled at an early hour by people of all parties, and his earnest eulogy of the hero was heard by all respectfully, by many with a sympathy that surprised themselves.

It was said of Plotinus that he was ashamed of his body, and 't is very likely he had good reason for it—that his body was a bad servant, and he had not skill in dealing with the material world, as happens often to men of abstract intellect. But Mr. Thoreau was equipped with a most adapted and serviceable body. He was of short stature, firmly built, of light complexion, with strong, serious blue eyes, and a grave aspect—his face covered in the late years with a becoming beard. His senses were acute, his frame well-knit and hardy, his hands strong and skilful in the use of tools. And there was a wonderful fitness of body and mind. He could pace sixteen rods more accurately than another man could measure them with rod and chain. He could find his path in the woods at night, he said, better by his feet than his eyes. He could estimate the measure of a tree very well by his eye; he could estimate the weight of a calf or a pig, like a dealer. From a box containing a bushel or more of loose pencils, he could take up with his hands fast enough just a dozen pencils at every grasp. He was a good swimmer, runner, skater, boatman, and would probably outwalk most countrymen in a day's journey. And the relation of body to mind was still finer than we have indicated. He said he wanted every stride his legs made. The length of his walk uniformly made the length of his writing. If shut up in the house he did not write at all.

He had a strong common sense, like that which Rose Flammock, the weaver's daughter in Scott's romance, commends in her father, as resembling a yardstick, which, whilst it measures dowlas and diaper, can equally well measure tapestry and cloth of gold. He had always a new resource. When I was planting forest trees, and had procured half a peck of acorns, he said that only a small portion of them would be sound, and proceeded to examine them and select the sound ones. But finding this took time, he said, "I think if you put them all into water the good ones will sink;" which experiment we tried with success. He could plan a garden or a house or a barn; would have been competent to lead a "Pacific Exploring Expedition;" could give judicious counsel in the gravest private or public affairs.

He lived for the day, not cumbered and mortified by his memory. If he brought you yesterday a new proposition, he would bring you to-day another not less revolutionary. A very industrious man, and setting, like all highly organized men, a high value on his time, he seemed the only man of leisure in town, always ready for any excursion that promised well, or for conversation prolonged into late hours. His trenchant sense was never stopped by his rules of daily prudence, but was always up to the new occasion. He liked and used the simplest food, yet, when some one urged a vegetable diet, Thoreau thought all diets a very small matter, saying that "the man who shoots the buffalo lives better than the man who boards at the Graham House." He said— "You can sleep near the railroad, and never be disturbed: Nature knows very well what sounds are worth attending to, and has made up her mind not to hear the railroad-whistle. But things respect the devout mind, and a mental ecstasy was never interrupted." He noted what repeatedly befell him, that, after receiving from a distance a rare plant, he would presently find the same in his own haunts. And those pieces of luck which happen only to good players happened to him. One day, walking with a stranger, who inquired where Indian arrowheads could be found, he replied, "Everywhere," and, stooping forward, picked one on the instant from the ground. At Mount Washington, in Tuckerman's Ravine, Thoreau had a bad fall, and sprained his foot. As he was in the act of getting up from his fall, he saw for the first time the leaves of the *Arnica mollis*.

His robust common sense, armed with stout hands, keen perceptions and strong will, cannot yet account for the superiority which shone in his simple and hidden life. I must add the cardinal fact, that there was an excellent wisdom in him, proper to a rare class of men, which showed him the material world as a means and symbol. This discovery, which sometimes yields to poets a certain casual and interrupted light, serving for the ornament of their writing, was in him an unsleeping insight; and whatever faults or obstructions of temperament might cloud it, he was not disobedient to the heavenly vision. In his youth, he said, one day, "The other world is all my art; my pencils will draw no other; my jack-knife will cut nothing else; I do not use it as a means." This was the muse and genius that ruled his opinions, conversation, studies, work and course of life. This made him a searching judge of men. At first glance he measured his companion, and, though insensible to some fine traits of culture, could very well report his weight and calibre. And this made the impression of genius which his conversation sometimes gave.

He understood the matter in hand at a glance, and saw the limitations and poverty of those he talked with, so that nothing seemed concealed from such terrible eyes. I have repeatedly known young men of sensibility converted in a moment to the belief that this was the man they were in search of, the man of men, who could tell them all they should do. His own dealing with them was never affectionate, but superior, didactic, scorning their petty ways—very slowly conceding, or not conceding at all, the promise of his society at their houses, or even at his own. "Would he not walk with them?" "He did not know. There was nothing-so important to him as his walk; he had no walks to throw away on company." Visits were offered him from respectful parties, but he declined them. Admiring friends offered to carry him at their own cost to the Yellowstone River—to the West Indies—to South America. But though nothing could be more grave or considered than his refusals, they remind one, in quite new relations, of that fop Brummel's reply to the gentleman who offered him his carriage in a shower, "But where will *you* ride, then?"—and what accusing silences, and what searching and irresistible speeches, battering down all defences, his companions can remember!

Mr. Thoreau dedicated his genius with such entire love to the fields, hills and waters of his native town, that he made them known and interesting to all reading Americans, and to people over the sea. The river on whose banks he was born and died he knew from its springs to its confluence with the Merrimack. He had made summer and winter observations on it for many years, and at every hour of the day and night. The result of the recent survey of the Water Commissioners appointed by the State of Massachusetts he had reached by his private experiments, several years earlier. Every fact which occurs in the bed, on the banks or in the air over it; the fishes, and their spawning and nests, their manners, their food; the shad-flies which fill the air on a certain evening once a year, and which are snapped at by the fishes so ravenously that many of these die of repletion; the conical heaps of small stones on the river-shallows, the huge nests of small fishes, one of which will sometimes overfill a cart; the birds which frequent the stream, heron, duck, sheldrake, loon, osprey; the snake, muskrat, otter, woodchuck and fox, on the banks; the turtle, frog, hyla and cricket, which make the banks vocal—were all known to him, and, as it were, townsmen and fellow creatures; so that he felt an absurdity or violence in any narrative of one of these by itself apart, and still more of its dimensions on an inch-rule, or in the exhibition of its skeleton, or the specimen of a squirrel or a bird in brandy. He liked to speak of the manners of the river, as itself a lawful creature, yet with exactness, and always to an observed fact. As he knew the river, so the ponds in this region.

. . . .

One of the weapons he used, more important to him than micro-scope, or alcohol-receiver to other investigators, was a whim which grew on him by indulgence, yet appeared in gravest statement, namely, of extolling his own town and neighborhood as the most favored cen-tre for natural observation. He remarked that the Flora of Massachusetts embraced almost all the important plants of America—most of the oaks, most of the willows, the best pines, the ash, the maple, the beech, the nuts. He returned Kane's Arctic Voyage to a friend of whom he had borrowed it, with the remark, that "Most of the phenomena noted might be observed in Concord." He seemed a little envious of the Pole, for the coincident sunrise and sunset, or five min-utes' day after six months: a splendid fact, which Annursnuc had never afforded him. He found red snow in one of his walks, and told me that he expected to find yet the *Victoria regia* in Concord. He was the attor-ney of the indigenous plants, and owned to a preference of the weeds to the imported plants, as of the Indian to the civilized man, and noticed, with pleasure, that the willow bean-poles of his neighbor had grown more than his beans. "See these weeds," he said, "which have been hoed at by a million farmers all spring and summer, and yet have pre-vailed, and just now come out triumphant over all lanes, pastures, fields and gardens, such is their vigor. We have insulted them with low names, too—as Pigweed, Wormwood, Chickweed, Shad-blossom." He says, "They have brave names, too—Ambrosia, Stellaria, Amelanchier, Amaranth, etc."

I think his fancy for referring everything to the meridian of Con-cord did not grow out of any ignorance or depreciation of other longitudes or latitudes, but was rather a playful expression of his con-viction of the indifferency of all places, and that the best place for each is where he stands. He expressed it once in this wise: "I think nothing is to be hoped from you, if this bit of mould under your feet is not sweeter to you to eat than any other in this world, or in any world."

The other weapon with which he conquered all obstacles in science was patience. He knew how to sit immovable, a part of the rock he rested on, until the bird, the reptile, the fish, which had retired from him, should come back and resume its habits, nay, moved by curios-ity, should come to him and watch him.

It was a pleasure and a privilege to walk with him. He knew the country like a fox or a bird, and passed through it as freely by paths of his own. He knew every track in the snow or on the ground, and what creature had taken this path before him. One must submit abjectly to such a guide, and the reward was great. Under his arm he carried an old music-book to press plants; in his pocket, his diary and pencil, a spy-glass for birds, microscope, jack-knife and twine. He wore a straw hat, stout shoes, strong gray trousers, to brave scrub-oaks and smilax, and to climb a tree for a hawk's or a squirrel's nest. He waded into the pool for the water-plants, and his strong legs were no insignificant part of his armor. On the day I speak of he looked for the Menyanthes, detected it across the wide pool, and, on examination of the florets, decided that it had been in flower five days. He drew out of his breast-pocket his diary, and read the names of all the plants that should bloom on this day, whereof he kept account as a banker when his notes fall due. The Cypripedium not due till to-morrow. He thought that, if waked up from a trance, in this swamp, he could tell by the plants what time of the year it was within two days. The redstart was flying about, and presently the fine grosbeaks, whose brilliant scarlet "makes the rash gazer wipe his eye," and whose fine clear note Thoreau compared to that of a tanager which has got rid of its hoarseness. Presently he heard a note which he called that of the night-warbler, a bird he had never identified, had been in search of twelve years, which always, when he saw it, was in the act of diving down into a tree or bush, and which it was vain to seek; the only bird which sings indifferently by night and by day. I told him he must beware of finding and booking it, lest life should have nothing more to show him. He said, "What you seek in vain for, half your life, one day you come full upon, all the family at dinner. You seek it like a dream, and as soon as you find it you become its prey."

His interest in the flower or the bird lay very deep in his mind, was connected with Nature—and the meaning of Nature was never attempted to be defined by him. He would not offer a memoir of his observations to the Natural History Society. "Why should I? To detach the description from its connections in my mind would make it no longer true or valuable to me: and they do not wish what belongs to it." His power of observation seemed to indicate additional senses. He saw as with microscope, heard as with ear-trumpet, and his memory was a photographic register of all he saw and heard. And yet none knew better than he that it is not the fact that imports, but the impression

. . . .

or effect of the fact on your mind. Every fact lay in glory in his mind, a type of the order and beauty of the whole.

His determination on Natural History was organic. He confessed that he sometimes felt like a hound or a panther, and, if born among Indians, would have been a fell hunter. But, restrained by his Massachusetts culture, he played out the game in this mild form of botany and ichthyology. His intimacy with animals suggested what Thomas Fuller records of Butler the apiologist, that "either he had told the bees things or the bees had told him." Snakes coiled round his legs; the fishes swam into his hand, and he took them out of the water; he pulled the woodchuck out of its hole by the tail, and took the foxes under his protection from the hunters. Our naturalist had perfect magnanimity; he had no secrets: he would carry you to the heron's haunt, or even to his most prized botanical swamp—possibly knowing that you could never find it again, yet willing to take his risks.

No college ever offered him a diploma, or a professor's chair; no academy made him its corresponding secretary, its discoverer or even its member. Perhaps these learned bodies feared the satire of his presence. Yet so much knowledge of Nature's secret and genius few others possessed; none in a more large and religious synthesis. For not a particle of respect had he to the opinions of any man or body of men, but homage solely to the truth itself; and as he discovered everywhere among doctors some leaning of courtesy, it discredited them. He grew to be revered and admired by his townsmen, who had at first known him only as an oddity. The farmers who employed him as a surveyor soon discovered his rare accuracy and skill, his knowledge of their lands, of trees, of birds, of Indian remains and the like, which enabled him to tell every farmer more than he knew before of his own farm; so that he began to feel a little as if Mr. Thoreau had better rights in his land than he. They felt, too, the superiority of character which addressed all men with a native authority.

Indian relics abound in Concord—arrow-heads, stone chisels, pestles and fragments of pottery; and on the river-bank, large heaps of clam-shells and ashes mark spots which the savages frequented. These, and every circumstance touching the Indian, were important in his eyes. His visits to Maine were chiefly for love of the Indian. He had the satisfaction of seeing the manufacture of the bark canoe, as well as of trying his hand in its management on the rapids. He was inquisitive about the making of the stone arrow-head, and in his last days charged youth setting out for the Rocky Mountains to find an Indian who could tell him that: "It was well worth a visit to California to learn it." Occasionally, a small party of Penobscot Indians would visit Concord, and pitch their tents for a few weeks in summer on the river-bank. He failed not to make acquaintance with the best of them; though he well knew that asking questions of Indians is like catechizing beavers and rabbits. In his last visit to Maine he had great satisfaction from Joseph Polis, an intelligent Indian of Oldtown, who was his guide for some weeks.

He was equally interested in every natural fact. The depth of his perception found likeness of law throughout Nature, and I know not any genius who so swiftly inferred universal law from the single fact. He was no pedant of a department. His eye was open to beauty, and his ear to music. He found these, not in rare conditions, but wheresoever he went. He thought the best of music was in single strains; and he found poetic suggestion in the humming of the telegraph-wire.

His poetry might be bad or good; he no doubt wanted a lyric facility and technical skill, but he had the source of poetry in his spiritual perception. He was a good reader and critic, and his judgment on poetry was to the ground of it. He could not be deceived as to the presence or absence of the poetic element in any composition, and his thirst for this made him negligent and perhaps scornful of superficial graces. He would pass by many delicate rhythms, but he would have detected every live stanza or line in a volume and knew very well where to find an equal poetic charm in prose. He was so enamoured of the spiritual beauty that he held all actual written poems in very light esteem in the comparison. He admired Aeschylus and Pindar; but when some one was commending them, he said that Aeschylus and the Greeks, in describing Apollo and Orpheus, had given no song, or no good one. "They ought not to have moved trees, but to have chanted to the gods such a hymn as would have sung all their old ideas out of their heads, and new ones in." His own verses are often rude and defective. The gold does not yet run pure, is drossy and crude. The thyme and marjoram are not yet honey. But if he want lyric fineness and technical merits, if he have not the poetic temperament, he never lacks the causal thought, showing that his genius was better than his talent. He knew the worth of the Imagination for the uplifting and consolation of human life, and liked to throw every thought into a symbol. The fact you tell is of no value, but only the impression. For this reason his presence was poetic, always piqued the curiosity to know more deeply the secrets of his mind. He had many reserves, an unwillingness to exhibit to profane eyes what was still sacred in his own, and knew well how to throw a poetic veil over his experience. All readers of Walden will remember his mythical record of his disappointments:—

"I long ago lost a hound, a bay horse and a turtle-dove, and am still on their trail. Many are the travellers I have spoken concerning them, describing their tracks, and what calls they answered to. I have met one or two who have heard the hound, and the tramp of the horse, and even seen the dove disappear behind a cloud; and they seemed as anxious to recover them as if they had lost them themselves."

His riddles were worth the reading, and I confide that if at any time I do not understand the expression, it is yet just. Such was the wealth of his truth that it was not worth his while to use words in vain. His poem entitled "Sympathy" reveals the tenderness under that triple steel of stoicism, and the intellectual subtility it could animate. His classic poem on "Smoke" suggests Simonides, but is better than any poem of Simonides. His biography is in his verses. His habitual thought makes all his poetry a hymn to the Cause of causes, the Spirit which vivifies and controls his own:—

> "I hearing get, who had but ears,
> And sight, who had but eyes before;
> I moments live, who lived but years,
> And truth discern, who knew but learning's lore."

And still more in these religious lines:—

> "Now chiefly is my natal hour,
> And only now my prime of life;
> I will not doubt the love untold,
> Which not my worth nor want have bought,
> Which wooed me young, and woos me old,
> And to this evening hath me brought."

Whilst he used in his writings a certain petulance of remark in reference to churches or churchmen, he was a person of a rare, tender and absolute religion, a person incapable of any profanation, by act or by thought. Of course, the same isolation which belonged to his original thinking and living detached him from the social religious forms. This is neither to be censured nor regretted. Aristotle long ago explained it, when he said, "One who surpasses his fellow citizens in virtue is no longer a part of the city. Their law is not for him, since he is a law to himself."

Thoreau was sincerity itself, and might fortify the convictions of prophets in the ethical laws by his holy living. It was an affirmative experience which refused to be set aside. A truth-speaker he, capable of the most deep and strict conversation; a physician to the wounds of any soul; a friend, knowing not only the secret of friendship, but almost worshipped by those few persons who resorted to him as their confessor and prophet, and knew the deep value of his mind and great heart. He thought that without religion or devotion of some kind nothing great was ever accomplished: and he thought that the bigoted sectarian had better bear this in mind.

His virtues, of course, sometimes ran into extremes. It was easy to trace to the inexorable demand on all for exact truth that austerity which made this willing hermit more solitary even than he wished. Himself of a perfect probity, he required not less of others. He had a disgust at crime, and no worldly success would cover it. He detected paltering as readily in dignified and prosperous persons as in beggars, and with equal scorn. Such dangerous frankness was in his dealing that his admirers called him "that terrible Thoreau," as if he spoke when silent, and was still present when he had departed. I think the severity of his ideal interfered to deprive him of a healthy sufficiency of human society.

The habit of a realist to find things the reverse of their appearance inclined him to put every statement in a paradox. A certain habit of antagonism defaced his earlier writings—a trick of rhetoric not quite outgrown in his later, of substituting for the obvious word and thought its diametrical opposite. He praised wild mountains and winter forests for their domestic air, in snow and ice he would find sultriness, and commended the wilderness for resembling Rome and Paris. "It was so dry, that you might call it wet."

The tendency to magnify the moment, to read all the laws of Nature in the one object or one combination under your eye, is of course comic to those who do not share the philosopher's perception of identity. To him there was no such thing as size. The pond was a small ocean; the Atlantic, a large Walden Pond. He referred every minute fact to cosmical laws. Though he meant to be just, he seemed haunted by a certain chronic assumption that the science of the day pretended completeness, and he had just found out that the *savants* had neglected to discriminate a particular botanical variety, had failed to describe the seeds or count the sepals. "That is to say," we replied, "the blockheads were not born in Concord; but who said they were? It was their unspeakable misfortune to be born in London, or Paris, or Rome; but, poor fellows, they did what they could, considering that they never saw Bateman's Pond, or Nine-Acre Corner, or Becky Stow's Swamp; besides, what were you sent into the world for, but to add this observation?"

Had his genius been only contemplative, he had been fitted to his life, but with his energy and practical ability he seemed born for great enterprise and for command; and I so much regret the loss of his rare powers of action, that I cannot help counting it a fault in him that he had no ambition. Wanting this, instead of engineering for all America, he was the captain of a huckleberry-party. Pounding beans is good to the end of pounding empires one of these days; but if, at the end of years, it is still only beans!

But these foibles, real or apparent, were fast vanishing in the incessant growth of a spirit so robust and wise, and which effaced its defeats with new triumphs. His study of Nature was a perpetual ornament to him, and inspired his friends with curiosity to see the world through his eyes, and to hear his adventures. They possessed every kind of interest.

He had many elegancies of his own, whilst he scoffed at conventional elegance. Thus, he could not bear to hear the sound of his own steps, the grit of gravel; and therefore never willingly walked in the road, but in the grass, on mountains and in woods. His senses were acute, and he remarked that by night every dwelling-house gives out bad air, like a slaughter-house. He liked the pure fragrance of melilot. He honored certain plants with special regard, and, over all, the pond-lily—then, the gentian, and the *Mikania scandens*, and "life-everlasting," and a bass-tree which he visited every year when it bloomed, in the middle of July. He thought the scent a more oracular inquisition than the sight—more oracular and trustworthy. The scent, of course, reveals what is concealed from the other senses. By it he detected earthiness. He delighted in echoes, and said they were almost the only kind of kindred voices that he heard. He loved Nature so well, was so happy in her solitude, that he became very jealous of cities and the sad work which their refinements and artifices made with man and his dwelling. The axe was always destroying his forest. "Thank God," he said, "they cannot cut down the clouds!" "All kinds of figures are drawn on the blue ground with this fibrous white paint."

I subjoin a few sentences taken from his unpublished manuscripts, not only as records of his thought and feeling, but for their power of description and literary excellence:—

"Some circumstantial evidence is very strong, as when you find a trout in the milk."

"The chub is a soft fish, and tastes like boiled brown paper salted."

"The youth gets together his materials to build a bridge to the moon, or, perchance, a palace or temple on the earth, and, at length the middle-aged man concludes to build a wood-shed with them."

"The locust z-ing."

"Devil's-needles zigzagging along the Nut-Meadow brook."

"Sugar is not so sweet to the palate as sound to the healthy ear."

"I put on some hemlock-boughs, and the rich salt crackling of their leaves was like mustard to the ear, the crackling of uncountable regiments. Dead trees love the fire."

"The bluebird carries the sky on his back."

"The tanager flies through the green foliage as if it would ignite the leaves."

"If I wish for a horse-hair for my compass-sight I must go to the stable; but the hair-bird, with her sharp eyes, goes to the road."

"Immortal water, alive even to the superficies."

"Fire is the most tolerable third party."

"Nature made ferns for pure leaves, to show what she could do in that line."

"No tree has so fair a bole and so handsome an instep as the beech."

"How did these beautiful rainbow-tints get into the shell of the fresh-water clam, buried in the mud at the bottom of our dark river?"

"Hard are the times when the infant's shoes are second-foot."

"We are strictly confined to our men to whom we give liberty."

"Nothing is so much to be feared as fear. Atheism may comparatively be popular with God himself."

"Of what significance the things you can forget? A little thought is sexton to all the world."

"How can we expect a harvest of thought who have not had a seed-time of character?"

"Only he can be trusted with gifts who can present a face of bronze to expectations."

"I ask to be melted. You can only ask of the metals that they be tender to the fire that melts them. To nought else can they be tender."

There is a flower known to botanists, one of the same genus with our summer plant called "Life-Everlasting," a *Gnaphalium* like that, which grows on the most inaccessible cliffs of the Tyrolese mountains, where the chamois dare hardly venture, and which the hunter, tempted by its beauty, and by his love (for it is immensely valued by the Swiss maidens), climbs the cliffs to gather, and is sometimes found dead at the foot, with the flower in his hand. It is called by botanists the *Gnaphalium leontopodium*, but by the Swiss *Edelweisse*, which signifies *Noble Purity*. Thoreau seemed to me living in the hope to gather this plant, which belonged to him of right. The scale on which his studies proceeded was so large as to require longevity, and we were the less prepared for his sudden disappearance. The country knows not yet, or in the least part, how great a son it has lost. It seems an injury that he should leave in the midst his broken task which none else can finish, a kind of indignity to so noble a soul that he should depart out of Nature before yet he has been really shown to his peers for what he is. But he, at least, is content. His soul was made for the noblest society; he had in a short life exhausted the capabilities of this world; wherever there is knowledge, wherever there is virtue, wherever there is beauty, he will find a home.

ABRAHAM LINCOLN

[*The nineteenth of April was the anniversary of the battle of Concord and Lexington. In 1865, however, it was the day when funeral services were held in Concord for the martyred President. Emerson was one of the speakers in the old meeting house that day. In 1862 Emerson had been taken to the White House to meet Lincoln who recalled having attended one of Emerson's lectures.*]

"Nature, they say, doth dote,
And cannot make a man
Save on some worn-out plan,
Repeating us by rote:
For him her Old-World moulds aside she threw,
And, choosing sweet clay from the breast
Of the unexhausted West,
With stuff untainted shaped a hero new,
Wise, steadfast in the strength of God, and true.
How beautiful to see
Once more a shepherd of mankind indeed,
Who loved his charge, but never loved to lead;
One whose meek flock the people joyed to be,
Not lured by any cheat of birth,
But by his clear-grained human worth,
And brave old wisdom of sincerity!
They knew that outward grace is dust;
They could not choose but trust
In that sure-footed mind's unfaltering skill,
And supple-tempered will
That bent, like perfect steel, to spring again and thrust
. . . .

Nothing of Europe here,
Or, then, of Europe fronting mornward still,
Ere any names of Serf and Peer
Could Nature's equal scheme deface; . . .
Here was a type of the true elder race,
And one of Plutarch's men talked with us face to face."
Lowell, Commemoration Ode.

ABRAHAM LINCOLN

WE MEET under the gloom of a calamity which darkens down over the minds of good men in all civil society, as the fearful tidings travel over sea, over land, from country to country, like the shadow of an uncalculated eclipse over the planet. Old as history is, and manifold as are its tragedies, I doubt if any death has caused so much pain to mankind as this has caused, or will cause, on its announcement; and this, not so much because nations are by modern arts brought so closely together, as because of the mysterious hopes and fears which, in the present day, are connected with the name and institutions of America.

In this country, on Saturday, every one was struck dumb, and saw at first only deep below deep, as he meditated on the ghastly blow. And perhaps, at this hour, when the coffin which contains the dust of the President sets forward on its long march through mourning states, on its way to his home in Illinois, we might well be silent, and suffer the awful voices of the time to thunder to us. Yes, but that first despair was brief: the man was not so to be mourned. He was the most active and hopeful of men; and his work had not perished: but acclamations of praise for the task he had accomplished burst out into a song of triumph, which even tears for his death cannot keep down.

The President stood before us as a man of the people. He was thoroughly American, had never crossed the sea, had never been spoiled by English insularity or French dissipation; a quite native, aboriginal man, as an acorn from the oak; no aping of foreigners, no frivolous accomplishments, Kentuckian born, working on a farm, a flatboatman, a captain in the Black Hawk War, a country lawyer, a representative in the rural legislature of Illinois—on such modest foundations the broad structure of his fame was laid. How slowly, and yet by happily prepared steps, he came to his place. All of us remember—it is only a history of five or six years—the surprise and the disappointment of the country at his first nomination by the convention at Chicago. Mr. Seward, then in the culmination of his good fame, was the favorite of the Eastern States. And when the new and comparatively unknown name of Lincoln was announced (notwithstanding the report of the acclamations of that convention), we heard the result coldly and sadly. It seemed too rash, on a purely local reputation, to build so grave a trust in such anxious times; and men naturally talked of the chances in politics as incalculable. But it turned out not to be chance. The profound good opinion which the people of Illinois and of the West had conceived of him, and which they had imparted to their colleagues, that they also might justify themselves to their constituents at home, was not rash, though they did not begin to know the riches of his worth.

A plain man of the people, an extraordinary fortune attended him. He offered no shining qualities at the first encounter; he did not offend by superiority. He had a face and manner which disarmed suspicion, which inspired confidence, which confirmed good will. He was a man without vices. He had a strong sense of duty, which it was very easy for him to obey. Then, he had what farmers call a long head; was excellent in working out the sum for himself; in arguing his case and convincing you fairly and firmly. Then, it turned out that he was a great worker; had prodigious faculty of performance; worked easily. A good worker is so rare; everybody has some disabling quality. In a host of young men that start together and promise so many brilliant leaders for the next age, each fails on trial; one by bad health, one by conceit, or by love of pleasure, or lethargy, or an ugly temper—each has some disqualifying fault that throws him out of the career. But this man was sound to the core, cheerful, persistent, all right for labor, and liked nothing so well.

Then, he had a vast good nature, which made him tolerant and accessible to all; fair-minded, leaning to the claim of the petitioner; affable, and not sensible to the affliction which the innumerable visits paid to him when President would have brought to any one else. And how this good nature became a noble humanity, in many a tragic case which the events of the war brought to him, every one will remember; and with what increasing tenderness he dealt when a whole race was thrown on his compassion. The poor negro said of him, on an impressive occasion, "Massa Linkum am eberywhere."

Then his broad good humor, running easily into jocular talk, in which he delighted and in which he excelled, was a rich gift to this wise man. It enabled him to keep his secret; to meet every kind of man and every rank in society; to take off the edge of the severest decisions, to mask his own purpose and sound his companion; and to catch with true instinct the temper of every company he addressed. And, more than all, it is to a man of severe labor, in anxious and exhausting crises, the natural restorative, good as sleep, and is the protection of the over-driven brain against rancor and insanity.

He is the author of a multitude of good sayings, so disguised as pleasantries that it is certain they had no reputation at first but as jests; and only later, by the very acceptance and adoption they find in the mouths of millions, turn out to be the wisdom of the hour. I am sure if this man had ruled in a period of less facility of printing, he would have become mythological in a very few years, like Aesop or Pilpay, or one of the Seven Wise Masters, by his fables and proverbs. But the weight and penetration of many passages in his letters, messages and speeches, hidden now by the very closeness of their application to the moment, are destined hereafter to wide fame. What pregnant definitions; what unerring common sense; what foresight; and, on great occasion, what lofty, and more than national, what humane tone! His brief speech at Gettysburg will not easily be surpassed by words on any recorded occasion. This, and one other American speech, that of John Brown to the court that tried him, and a part of Kossuth's speech at Birmingham, can only be compared with each other, and with no fourth.

His occupying the chair of state was a triumph of the good sense of mankind, and of the public conscience. This middle-class country had got a middle-class president, at last. Yes, in manners and sympathies, but not in powers, for his powers were superior. This man grew according to the need. His mind mastered the problem of the day; and as the problem grew, so did his comprehension of it. Rarely was man so fitted to the event. In the midst of fears and jealousies, in the Babel of counsels and parties, this man wrought incessantly with all his might and all his honesty, laboring to find what the people wanted, and how to obtain that. It cannot be said there is any exaggeration of his worth. If ever a man was fairly tested, he was. There was no lack of resistance, nor of slander, nor of ridicule. The times have allowed no state secrets; the nation has been in such ferment, such multitudes had to be trusted, that no secret could be kept. Every door was ajar, and we know all that befell.

Then, what an occasion was the whirlwind of the war. Here was place for no holiday magistrate, no fair-weather sailor; the new pilot was hurried to the helm in a tornado. In four years—four years of battle-days—his endurance, his fertility of resources, his magnanimity, were sorely tried and never found wanting. There, by his courage, his justice, his even temper, his fertile counsel, his humanity, he stood a heroic figure in the centre of a heroic epoch. He is the true history of the American people in his time. Step by step he walked before them; slow with their slowness, quickening his march by theirs, the true representative of this continent; an entirely public man; father of his country, the pulse of twenty millions throbbing in his heart, the thought of their minds articulated by his tongue.

Adam Smith remarks that the axe, which in Houbraken's portraits of British kings and worthies is engraved under those who have suffered at the block, adds a certain lofty charm to the picture. And who does not see, even in this tragedy so recent, how fast the terror and ruin of the massacre are already burning into glory around the victim? Far happier this fate than to have lived to be wished away; to have watched the decay of his own faculties; to have seen—perhaps even he—the proverbial ingratitude of statesmen; to have seen mean men preferred. Had he not lived long enough to keep the greatest promise that ever man made to his fellow men—the practical abolition of slavery? He had seen Tennessee, Missouri and Maryland emancipate their slaves. He had seen Savannah, Charleston and Richmond surrendered; had seen the main army of the rebellion lay down its arms. He had conquered the public opinion of Canada, England and France. Only Washington can compare with him in fortune.

And what if it should turn out, in the unfolding of the web, that he had reached the term; that this heroic deliverer could no longer serve us; that the rebellion had touched its natural conclusion, and what remained to be done required new and uncommitted hands—a new spirit born out of the ashes of the war; and that Heaven, wishing to show the world a completed benefactor, shall make him serve his country even more by his death than by his life? Nations, like things, are not good by facility and complaisance. "The kindness of kings consists in justice and strength." Easy good nature has been the dangerous foible of the Republic, and it was necessary that its enemies should outrage it, and drive us to unwonted firmness, to secure the salvation of this country in the next ages.

The ancients believed in a serene and beautiful Genius which ruled in the affairs of nations; which, with a slow but stern justice, carried forward the fortunes of certain chosen houses, weeding out single offenders or offending families, and securing at last the firm prosperity of the favorites of Heaven. It was too narrow a view of the Eternal Nemesis. There is a serene Providence which rules the fate of nations, which makes little account of time, little of one generation or race, makes no account of disasters, conquers alike by what is called defeat or by what is called victory, thrusts aside enemy and obstruction, crushes everything immoral as inhuman, and obtains the ultimate triumph of the best race by the sacrifice of everything which resists the moral laws of the world. It makes its own instruments, creates the man for the time, trains him in poverty, inspires his genius, and arms him for his task. It has given every race its own talent, and ordains that only that race which combines perfectly with the virtues of all shall endure.

CARLYLE

[*Emerson and Carlyle first met in 1833 when neither of them was well known. In spite of grave differences in temperament they were strongly attached to each other; out of mutual esteem each served as spokesman for the other in England or America, respectively. They corresponded frequently all their lives. They met for the second time in 1847 and 1848 when Emerson was lecturing in England. After Carlyle's death the Massachusetts Historical Society invited Emerson to speak at a meeting in Boston in February, 1881. At this time, well on in years and failing mentally, Emerson was unable to prepare an address. But he did read this brief paper, most of which he took from a letter written in 1848 after his second visit with Carlyle.*]

Hold with the Maker, not the Made.
Sit with the Cause, or grim or glad.

CARLYLE

Thomas Carlyle is an immense talker, as extraordinary in his conversation as in his writing—I think even more so.

He is not mainly a scholar, like the most of my acquaintances, but a practical Scotchman, such as you would find in any saddler's or iron-dealer's shop, and then only accidentally and by a surprising addition, the admirable scholar and writer he is. If you would know precisely how he talks, just suppose Hugh Whelan (the gardener) had found leisure enough in addition to all his daily work to read Plato and Shakspeare, Augustine and Calvin, and, remaining Hugh Whelan all the time, should talk scornfully of all this nonsense of books that he had been bothered with, and you shall have just the tone and talk and laughter of Carlyle. I called him a trip-hammer with "an Aeolian attachment." He has, too, the strong religious tinge you sometimes find in burly people. That, and all his qualities, have a certain virulence, coupled though it be in his case with the utmost impatience of Christendom and Jewdom and all existing presentments of the good old story. He talks like a very unhappy man—profoundly solitary, displeased and hindered by all men and things about him, and, biding his time, meditating how to undermine and explode the whole world of nonsense which torments him. He is obviously greatly respected by all sorts of people, understands his own value quite as well as Webster, of whom his behavior sometimes reminds me, and can see society on his own terms.

And, though no mortal in America could pretend to talk with Carlyle, who is also as remarkable in England as the Tower of London, yet neither would he in any manner satisfy us (Americans), or begin to answer the questions which we ask. He is a very national figure, and would by no means bear transplantation. They keep Carlyle as a sort of portable cathedral-bell, which they like to produce in companies where he is unknown, and set a-swinging, to the surprise and consternation of all persons—bishops, courtiers, scholars, writers—and, as in companies here (in England) no man is named or introduced, great is the

effect and great the inquiry. Forster of Rawdon described to me a dinner at the *table d'hôte* of some provincial hotel where he carried Carlyle,
and where an Irish canon had uttered something. Carlyle began to talk,
first to the waiters, and then to the walls, and then, lastly, unmistakably
to the priest, in a manner that frightened the whole company.

Young men, especially those holding liberal opinions, press to see
him, but it strikes me like being hot to see the mathematical or Greek
professor before they have got their lesson. It needs something more
than a clean shirt and reading German to visit him. He treats them
with contempt; they profess freedom and he stands for slavery; they
praise republics and he likes the Russian Czar; they admire Cobden
and free trade and he is a protectionist in political economy; they will
eat vegetables and drink water, and he is a Scotchman who thinks
English national character has a pure enthusiasm for beef and mutton—
describes with gusto the crowds of people who gaze at the sirloins in
the dealer's shop-window, and even likes the Scotch nightcap; they
praise moral suasion, he goes for murder, money, capital punishment
and other pretty abominations of English law. They wish freedom of
the press, and he thinks the first thing he would do, if he got into Parliament, would be to turn out the reporters, and stop all manner of
mischievous speaking to Buncombe, and wind-bags. "In the Long Parliament," he says, "the only great Parliament, they sat secret and silent,
grave as an ecumenical council, and I know not what they would have
done to anybody that had got in there and attempted to tell out of
doors what they did." They go for free institutions, for letting things
alone, and only giving opportunity and motive to every man; he for a
stringent government, that shows people what they must do, and makes
them do it. "Here," he says, "the Parliament gathers up six millions of
pounds every year to give to the poor, and yet the people starve. I think
if they would give it to me, to provide the poor with labor, and with
authority to make them work or shoot them—and I to be hanged if I
did not do it—I could find them in plenty of Indian meal."

He throws himself readily on the other side. If you urge free trade,
he remembers that every laborer is a monopolist. The navigation laws
of England made its commerce. "St. John was insulted by the Dutch;
he came home, got the law passed that foreign vessels should pay high
fees, and it cut the throat of the Dutch, and made the English trade." If
you boast of the growth of the country, and show him the wonderful

results of the census, he finds nothing so depressing as the sight of a great mob. He saw once, as he told me, three or four miles of human beings, and fancied that "the airth was some great cheese, and these were mites." If a tory takes heart at his hatred of stump-oratory and model republics, he replies, "Yes, the idea of a pigheaded soldier who will obey orders, and fire on his own father at the command of his officer, is a great comfort to the aristocratic mind." It is not so much that Carlyle cares for this or that dogma, as that he likes genuineness (the source of all strength) in his companions.

If a scholar goes into a camp of lumbermen or a gang of riggers, those men will quickly detect any fault of character. Nothing will pass with them but what is real and sound. So this man is a hammer that crushes mediocrity and pretension. He detects weakness on the instant, and touches it. He has a vivacious, aggressive temperament, and unimpressionable. The literary, the fashionable, the political man, each fresh from triumphs in his own sphere, comes eagerly to see this man, whose fun they have heartily enjoyed, sure of a welcome, and are struck with despair at the first onset. His firm, victorious, scoffing vituperation strikes them with chill and hesitation. His talk often reminds you of what was said of Johnson: "If his pistol missed fire, he would knock you down with the butt-end."

Mere intellectual partisanship wearies him; he detects in an instant if a man stands for any cause to which he is not born and organically committed. A natural defender of anything, a lover who will live and die for that which he speaks for, and who does not care for him or for anything but his own business, he respects; and the nobler this object, of course, the better. He hates a literary trifler, and if, after Guizot had been a tool of Louis Philippe for years, he is now to come and write essays on the character of Washington, on "The Beautiful" and on "Philosophy of History," he thinks that nothing.

Great is his reverence for realities—for all such traits as spring from the intrinsic nature of the actor. He humors this into the idolatry of strength. A strong nature has a charm for him, previous, it would seem, to all inquiry whether the force be divine or diabolic. He preaches, as by cannonade, the doctrine that every noble nature was made by God, and contains, if savage passions, also fit checks and grand impulses, and, however extravagant, will keep its orbit and return from far.

Nor can that decorum which is the idol of the Englishman, and in attaining which the Englishman exceeds all nations, win from him any obeisance. He is eaten up with indignation against such as desire to make a fair show in the flesh.

Combined with this warfare on respectabilities, and, indeed, pointing all his satire, is the severity of his moral sentiment. In proportion to the peals of laughter amid which he strips the plumes of a pretender and shows the lean hypocrisy to every vantage of ridicule, does he worship whatever enthusiasm, fortitude, love or other sign of a good nature is in a man.

There is nothing deeper in his constitution than his humor, than the considerate, condescending good nature with which he looks at every object in existence, as a man might look at a mouse. He feels that the perfection of health is sportiveness, and will not look grave even at dulness or tragedy.

His guiding genius is his moral sense, his perception of the sole importance of truth and justice; but that is a truth of character, not of catechisms. He says, "There is properly no religion in England. These idle nobles at Tattersall's—there is no work or word of serious purpose in them; they have this great lying Church; and life is a humbug." He prefers Cambridge to Oxford, but he thinks Oxford and Cambridge education indurates the young men, as the Styx hardened Achilles, so that when they come forth of them, they say, "Now we are proof; we have gone through all the degrees, and are case-hardened against the veracities of the Universe; nor man nor God can penetrate us."

Wellington he respects as real and honest, and as having made up his mind, once for all, that he will not have to do with any kind of a lie. Edwin Chadwick is one of his heroes—who proposes to provide every house in London with pure water, sixty gallons to every head, at a penny a week; and in the decay and downfall of all religions, Carlyle thinks that the only religious act which a man nowadays can securely perform is to wash himself well.

Of course the new French revolution of 1848 was the best thing he had seen, and the teaching this great swindler, Louis Philippe, that there is a God's justice in the Universe, after all, was a great satisfaction. Czar Nicholas was his hero; for in the ignominy of Europe, when all thrones fell like card-houses, and no man was found with conscience enough to fire a gun for his crown, but every one ran away in a *coucou*, with his head shaved, through the Barrière de Passy, one man remained who believed he was put there by God Almighty to govern his empire, and, by the help of God, had resolved to stand there.

He was very serious about the bad times; he had seen this evil coming, but thought it would not come in his time. But now 't is coming, and the only good he sees in it is the visible appearance of the gods. He thinks it the only question for wise men, instead of art and fine fancies and poetry and such things, to address themselves to the problem of society. This confusion is the inevitable end of such falsehoods and nonsense as they have been embroiled with.

Carlyle has, best of all men in England, kept the manly attitude in his time. He has stood for scholars, asking no scholar what he should say. Holding an honored place in the best society, he has stood for the people, for the Chartist, for the pauper, intrepidly and scornfully, teaching the nobles their peremptory duties.

His errors of opinion are as nothing in comparison with this merit, in my judgment. This *aplomb* cannot be mimicked; it is the speaking to the heart of the thing. And in England, where the *morgue* of aristocracy has very slowly admitted scholars into society—a very few houses only in the high circles being ever opened to them—he has carried himself erect, made himself a power confessed by all men, and taught scholars their lofty duty. He never feared the face of man.

A NOTE ON THE TYPE

The principal text of this Modern Library edition
was composed in a digitized version of
Horley Old Style, a typeface issued by
the English type foundry Monotype in 1925.
It has such distinctive features
as lightly cupped serifs and an oblique horizontal bar
on the lowercase "e."